WHO
WHO

in Greater Manchester

Manchester Literary and
Philosophical Publications Ltd

Colonel John Bradford Timmins OBE TD JP

Greater Manchester Lieutenancy Office

Byrom House

Quay Street

Manchester

M3 3JD

Tel. No. 0161-834 0490

I am delighted that the Manchester Literary and Philosophical Society have undertaken the considerable task of producing a fourth edition of "Who's Who in Greater Manchester".

The success of the first three editions has established the need for this excellent work of reference and I know that for some time the expectation of a new edition has existed, not least amongst those involved with the many organisations across our County and City to whom it is a constant source of information.

The "Lit. & Phil." has played a major role in the intellectual activities of the City of Manchester for more than 200 years. Now, sitting astride the largest University Campus in Europe, and in a thriving business community, it has the opportunity to go forward in an environment that could not be more appropriate for future success. I am sure the Society will retain its unique position.

John Timmins

"THERE IS NO DOUBT

OUR researchers were constantly told 'our such-and-such team is as good as Addleshaw Sons & Latham's', but

THAT ADDLESHAW SONS & LATHAM

Addleshaw Sons & Latham did not feel the need to tell us its teams were comparable with anyone's.

IS *the* FIRM IN THE REGION"

The Legal 500 - The Client's Guide to UK Law Firms, 1995.

To find out how we can be *the* firm to help your business, please contact Paul Lee, Managing Partner, on 0161-832 5594.

INVESTOR IN PEOPLE

ADDLESHAW SONS & LATHAM
SOLICITORS

DENNIS HOUSE · MARSDEN STREET · MANCHESTER M2 1JD TELEPHONE: 0161 832 5594 · FAX: 0161 832 2250

About the Society

The Manchester Literary & Philosophical Society is, apart from the Royal Society of London, one of the oldest learned societies in Britain. Always an outward-looking organisation, it retains a special interest in science, but today particularly promotes the arts and an awareness of current social issues. It was formally instituted on 28 February 1781, and in 1799 it acquired 36 George Street, which remained its home until 1980.

Most of the original members were physicians, surgeons or apothecaries, By 1861 membership was over 200, and also included merchants, engineers and manufacturers. Today the membership of over 450 includes scholars and professional people from many walks of life, as well as interested members of the general public.

John Dalton, 'father of modern chemistry' and justly famed, among other things, for his atomic theory, joined the Lit & Phil in 1794, became Secretary in 1800, Vice-President in 1808 and President in 1816, an office he held until his death in 1844. He and his gifted pupil, James Prescott Joule, were both scientists of international repute. Other important past members include William Fairbairn the engineer, Henry Roscoe the chemist, Ernest Rutherford the nuclear physicist and Joseph Whitworth the precision engineer.

Today the Society has an excellent programme of lectures and is involved in many aspects of Manchester life. Entry to all lectures is free. There is a small charge for the optional refreshments which follow. The Society issues a newsletter three or four times a year, and its annual journal, the *Manchester Memoirs*, was first published in 1785. The Lit & Phil is a registered charity.

Details concerning membership are available from The Administrative Secretary, Manchester Literary and Philosophical Society, Tel: 0161 228 3638 Fax: 0161 228 3571.

Sponsors' Foreword

Manchester is the commercial, financial, educational and cultural capital of the UK's largest economic region outside London. From a past steeped in stories of the industrial revolution to a present where Manchester's commitment to progress is evident in the development of the NYNEX Arena, Bridgewater Hall and the facilities which will allow it to play host to the 2002 Commonwealth Games, Manchester is one of Europe's leading cities.

The city has welcomed more than 600 overseas-owned companies and is home to a multicultural population which has brought great strength to the region in business and living experience.

There is a quality of life in Manchester which permeates the business, intellectual and social spirit of the region, and is reflected in an attitude to commerce which is international in approach yet personal in style. This *Who's Who in Greater Manchester* contains details of just some of those individuals who are shaping the city's future. It is designed to be personal, to emphasise the achievements of our senior people in their chosen discipline, and to provide a signpost for further linkages which will benefit our city and the wider region.

Many of us who live and work in Manchester tend to take for granted its regular achievements and accolades. We all have our part to play in making Manchester one of the world's most important cities. With three new international sporting stadia, a large bustling Chinatown adjacent to its thriving financial quarter, one of Europe's largest student communities and an unrivalled reputation for being the centre for pop music and youth fashion, Manchester in 1996 has a vitality and confidence that is clearly evident.

Add to this the well documented successes of Manchester United coupled with Manchester's recent hosting of the Euro '96 Football championship, and the introduction of the UK's first light rapid transport system, the Metrolink, and you have a city which is worthy to take its place amongst those the rest of the world holds in high regard.

It is impossible in a short foreword to do justice to all of the conurbation's attractions, but a focus on two key areas serves as a vivid reminder of our city's strength. With 80% of the 'Financial Times Top 100' UK companies represented in Manchester, the great commercial names associated with the city's present illustrate how its major role in international trade has grown since the city, as the crucible of the industrial revolution, established the foundation of Britain's wealth.

That's not all, with around half of the 1,200 foreign-owned companies in the North West located within Greater Manchester it is easy to see the diversity of industry and commerce within the city and, as you would

expect, to support such investment Manchester is home to one of Europe's major business services communities, employing around 80,000 people.

Not only is Manchester one of the UK's leading regional, financial and professional services centres, it is also rated as one of the leading European business centres. The city is home to the largest regional branch of the Bank of England and is the pre-eminent insurance centre outside London, both in terms of premiums written and employment. The business services community, whether it be accountants, lawyers, bankers, stockbrokers or venture capitalists, has the skills to provide all the necessary support for business without resorting to London. Indeed, there are an increasing number of cases where Manchester-based advisers are sought in preference to their London counterparts because of their attitude and skills.

No matter how much emphasis is placed on the size and quality of our infrastructure, the plain and undisputed fact is that people make it happen - people who live and work in Manchester. People whose imagination, commercial flair and business acumen have maintained the city's position and will continue to assist it to be even better. Those people are represented in this book and are the reason why we feel it worthy of our sponsorship.

Acknowledgements

In the six years since the last edition there have been profound social and economic changes which have left their mark on Greater Manchester.

Despite the tragic setback resulting from the IRA bombing there is a confidence about the region reflected in the new buildings rising about us, typified by the Bridgewater Hall, and also a determination that destruction will not halt progress.

The changes have brought to the forefront a new generation of people who influence and contribute to life in Greater Manchester. One of the recurring problems for a new editorial team compiling a book of this kind is to identify potential entrants.

We have tried as before to include and extend throughout Greater Manchester, the traditional sources of industry, commerce, administration, education, the professions and public service with increased emphasis on sport, the arts and media which had been under-represented.

In this context it has been gratifying to receive a number of entries from arts 'expatriates' who have left us to seek their fortune elsewhere but return regularly for professional engagements and/or to support their favourite football team.

We are very grateful to everyone who has suggested names for inclusion and to all who responded to our invitation. Inevitably there are many who, for a variety of reasons, prefer not to do so and whilst respecting their reluctance we regret their absence.

The last edition was the first to be sponsored thanks to Siemens plc

Energy and Automation. Sponsorship makes a major contribution to the potential success of the publication by underwriting the critical costs of compilation and production.

We are most grateful to our five co-sponsors, Michael Evans, Paul Lee, Jim Leonard, Jonathan Diggines and Michael Seal, their companies and colleagues, all of whom have worked together with us to ensure success.

The production of this fourth edition has been in every way a team effort and I should also like to acknowledge the contributions made by Colonel J.B. Timmins, Lord Lieutenant of Greater Manchester, for his introduction and for his encouragement: Philip Livesey for his persuasive diplomacy in seeking sponsorship: John Timperley who wrote and co-ordinated the Sponsors' Foreword: Brian Rarity and the staff of Rarity and Company for computer and typesetting services: Janet Allan for consultancy on the book design and David Bowden of Artimus Design for the cover design. Andrew Caesar and John Liggett our printers. My co-directors Alison Lever, Eddie Cass and Angus Yeaman for their support. Leslie Smyth for much wise advice. Maureen Kennedy, Heather Bradshaw and Mary Urell for their invaluable secretarial, and administrative help. And finally but by no means least Stella Lowe, who edited the book and by her skill brought order and balance to a very difficult task.
Thank you all

NORMAN LEECE
Chairman, Manchester Literary and Philosophical Publications Ltd

ABBREVIATIONS

Details of the abbreviations used in the text will be found
at the end of the book, from page 310 onwards.

First published in 1996
by Manchester Literary and Philosophical Publications Ltd
Churchgate House, 56 Oxford Street
Manchester M60 7HJ

© 1996 Manchester Literary and Philosophical Publications Ltd

A CIP catalogue record for this book
is available from the British Library

ISBN 0-902428-18-7

Prelim design by Janet Allan
Cover design by Artimus
Front cover photographs from Apollo Leisure (UK) Ltd
Marketing Manchester and UMIST
Compiled and typeset by Rarity & Co Ltd
Printed in Great Britain by MFP Design and Print,
Stretford, Manchester M32 OJT

ABBOTT, John Noel, TD (1975),First Bar (1981) Second Bar (1993), Queen's Silver Jubilee Medal (1977),DL(1993),FCIT (1982)

Financial Adviser, GAN Financial Services Ltd; Logistics Consultant, Abbott Associates; Chairman, Marlboro' Properties (St Albans) Ltd. *b.* 10 March 1939; Sandiway, Chester. *m.* 1965 Janet Vivien Robarts; one *s.* one *d. Education:* Beech Hall Preparatory School; Bradfield College, Berks; Manchester College of Commerce. *Military Service:* Major; National Service, RASC (1958-60); Royal Corps of Transport (TA); Royal Logistics Corps (TA); Engineer & Transport Staff Corps RE (TA). *Career Profile:* Chairman, FJA (Holdings) Ltd; Managing Director, Duncan Transrail Ltd; Fredk J. Abbott plc, Bennett & Taylor Ltd; Chairman, Marlboro' Motors (St Albans) Group Ltd and ex-officio director of Manchester Chamber of Commerce & Industry (1972-86). Junior Chamber International Senator (1973); Past President, Manchester Junior Chamber of Commerce (1972-73). Past Chairman, NW Section, The Chartered Institute of Transport (1982-83); Chairman, East Cheshire Branch, Army Benevolent Fund (1983-86);President, Manchester Royal Army Service Corps/Royal Corps of Transport Association (1992-); Past President, Manchester Luncheon Club (1992-93). *Prizes:* Student Medal (Chartered Institute of Transport) (1965). *Societies:* St James's Club, Manchester; NW of England and IOM TAVR Association; Army Benevolent Fund; Movement Control Officers Club; Manchester Luncheon Club; Rotary Club of Manchester; Commanderie de Bordeaux a Manchester. *Recreations, Interests:* Travel, beagling, rambling and watching sport. *Address:* GAN Financial Services Ltd, 3rd Floor, King's Court, Exchange Street, Manchester M2 7HA (*tel:-* 0161 832 0494; *fax:* 0161 839 0913); Gilgo Cottage, Gore Lane, Alderley Edge, Cheshire SK9 7SP (01625-582720).

ADAMS, Jack, FCIB

Regional Director, NW England, Barclays Bank Plc. *b.* 16 January 1943 Manchester. *m.* 1969 Barbara; two *d. Public Offices:* CBI NW Regional Council. *Education:* Stand Grammar School, Whitefield. *Career Profile:* Joined Martins Bank (1969); Local Director for East London (1981); Corporate Director, Yorks and Humberside (1987); Regional Director, Manchester Region (1992). *Societies:* Prestbury Badminton Club. *Recreations, Interests:* Walking, theatre, public speaking. *Address:* Barclays Bank Plc, 51 Mosley Street, Manchester, M60 2AU (*tel:* 0161 200 5110); Prestbury.

ADAMS, John, BSc (Hons) Leicester,ACT,FCA

Financial Controller, Commercial Aerospace Sector, British Aerospace plc. *b.* 21 September 1948; Farnham, Surrey. *m.* 1971 (divorced 1995); one *s.* one *d. Education:* Farnham Grammar School; University of Leicester. *Career Profile:* Company Chief Accountant, British Aircraft Corp Ltd; Assistant Treasurer, Chief Internal Auditor, Finance Director, Manchester Division, British Aerospace plc. *Recreations, Interests:* Tennis and most sports. *Address:* British Aerospace plc, Woodford, Stockport, Cheshire (*tel:* 0161-955 3240); 14 Lisson Grove, Hale, Altrincham, Cheshire (*tel:* 0161 941 2917).

ADLER, Jacqueline (Jacqui) (*née* Vanderstock), BA(Hons)

Councillor, Bury MBC; Secretary, Labour Group (10 yrs); Chairman, School Sub-Committee, Deputy Chairman, Personnel Committee; Chairman, Ribble Drive County Primary School. *b.* Oldham. *m.* 1967 Emmanuel Wolfe Adler (Monty); two *d.* (Remarried Emmanuel Wolfe Adler in 1981 after conversion to Judaism.) *Public Offices:* Mayor, Bury MB (1987-88), Deputy Mayor (1988-89), Mayoress (1990-91). *Education:* Bolton Business Institute (1994-95), University of Manchester (1991-94). *Career Profile:* Chairman, Middleton, Prestwich & Whitefield Constituency (1978-80); Chairman of Twinning (1986-87); Chairman, Community Drugs Team (1986-87); County Council Agent; Local Election Agent; Member of Oldham Rep. *Prizes:* Hon Member, Royal Marines Assoc (Bury), Sub-mariners Assoc (Bury). *Publications:* (co-author) 'Poverty in the NW'; 'Who We Are' (Bolton TH Publication). *Societies:* Radcliffe & Whitefield Lion's Club (Secretary, 1994). *Recreations, Interests:* Classical music, Egyptology, jazz, reading, East Lancs Steam Railway (given the honour of opening it 1987). *Address:* 20 Douglas Close, Whitefield, Manchester M45 8LT (*tel:* 0161-766 8206).

AGARWAL, Raj Nath, MCom Agra (1954), BCom Agra (1952)

General Manager/Financial Controller, Rajan Imports Ltd, Manchester (1993-). *b.* 1 September 1933; Moradabad (UP), India. *m.* 1957 Rajeshwari Agarwal; one *s.* two *d.* *Education:* Agra University, India. *Career Profile:* General Manager, Prosperous Finance Ltd, Manchester (1986-92); Regional Manager, Oriental Credit Ltd, Manchester (1984-86); Zonal Manager (controlling 59 Branches) Norther Indian Zone Bank of India, New Delhi (1983); Senior Manager, Bank of India, (controlling Manchester, Leeds, Huddersfield and Preston Branches) (1978-83); banking career spanned 32 years. *Publications:* Wrote several articles for 'Mancunian India' editorial board (1990-91). *Societies:* Hon Treasurer (1986), Hon President (1987-88), Executive Committee Member (1989-92), Indian Association, Manchester; Founder Trustee of Hindu Religious Society (1986-92); Founder Member, Indian Studies Committee of Manchester Polytechnic (1989). *Recreations, Interests:* Keen interest in meeting people, organising and conducting social functions, walking, reading, badminton, etc. *Address:* 83 Oakdale Drive, Heald Green, Cheshire SK8 3SN (*tel:* 0161-437 8460). *Additional Information:* Widely travelled in India, Western Europe, Egypt and America. Lived in India, Germany, Kenya and now UK.

AHMED, Kabir

Director, Hilal Restaurants Ltd. *b.* 31 August 1940 Sylhet, Bangladesh. *m.* 1978 Nazia Ahmed; two *d.* *Public Offices:* JP (1985); Hon Secretary, (1980-84), Vice-Chairman (1984-93), Chairman (1993-96) Manchester Council for Community Relations; Founder Member, Chairman, Greater Manchester Bangladeshi Association and Community Centre; Member, Home Office's Working Party on Crime Prevention (1990-91); Member of former Race Relations Advisory Group, Manchester City Council now appointed as Director of City Progress Group, Manchester City Council; Member, Strangeways Prison Board of Visitors and Local Review Committee for the Parole Board. *Education:* Stretford College of Technology; Salford College of Technology; St John's College, Manchester. *Recreations, Interests:* Sports, theatre, voluntary work. *Address:* Hilal Restaurant Ltd, 90 Wilmslow Road, Handforth, Cheshire, SK9 3ES (*tel:* 01625 524942).

AIKMAN, William Henry, ERD (1957),TD (1964); MA (Oxon, 1947),BA (Manchester, 1993)

Past President, Rotary Club (Didsbury & District). *b.* 2 August 1919; Germiston. *m.* 1950 Jean Kirkwood; three *d. Public Offices:* City Councillor, Manchester (1976-95); Governor, Chetham's School of Music (1984-93). *Education:* Bradford Grammar School (1928-38); Queen's College, Oxford (1938, 1946-47); Royal Military College of Science (1943). *War Service:* Royal Artillery (1938-67). *Career Profile:* Director, Tootal Ltd; Managing Consultant 3i. *Societies:* Didsbury and District Rotary; Oxford Society; Manchester Literary & Philosophical Society. *Address:* Rose Hey, 21A Millgate Lane, Didsbury, Manchester M20 2SW (*tel:* 0161-445 5488).

AINSWORTH, Marjorie Ellen (*née* Lolley), DipEd Psych,MEd Manchester

Retired. *b.* 7 January 1922; Manchester. *m.* 1942 Herbert Thomas Ainsworth. *Education:* Manchester Central High School for Girls; Manchester Training College; University of Manchester. *Previous Positions:* Assistant Teacher, Newall Green County Secondary School, Wythenshawe (1954-58), Sharston County Secondary School, Wythenshawe (1959-64); Teacher Therapist, Schools Psychological Service, Manchester (1964-66); Research Associate, University of Manchester (1966-72); Senior Lecturer, Manchester Polytechnic (1972-76). *Publications:* 'The Effects of Social and Environmental Factors on Secondary Educational Attainment in Manchester' - Ainsworth and Batten (McMillan 1974); and contributions to educational journals. *Societies:* Manchester Literary & Philosophical Society (1955-); Portico Library; Manchester and Salford Film Society. *Recreations, Interests:* Reading, film, knitting. *Address:* 64 Egerton Road, Fallowfield, Manchester M14 6RA (*tel:* 0161-224 1243).

ALA-UD-DIN, Syed, BCom,MCom Dhaka,MSc St Andrews,MEd Manchester,LLB Blackstone School of Law Chicago,Dr Juris,LLM,Dr JurSc Thomas Jefferson,PhD TIU Kansas, PPIL Harvard Law School,PPLIL (The Hague Academy of International Law), English Legal Methods (Cambridge), Postgraduate Research Scholar (Oxford),FBIM,FRSA, FIMA

Adjunct Professor of Law & Business, Thomas Jefferson College of Law, Florida; Adjunct Professor of Economics, TIU, Kansas; Director & Secretary General, Institute of Community Development; Incorporated Association of Managers and Administrators; General Secretary, Institute of Certified Public Accountants; International Management & Law Consultant; Policy Adviser to various governments and authorities. *b.* 18 April 1933; Murshidabad, India. *m.* 1971 Khondekar Tahmina; one *s.* one *d. Public Offices:* Member, Local Valuation Court (1976-86); Supplementary Benefit Appeal Tribunal; Transport Users' Consultative Committee; Central District Health Authority; Education Committee Manchester Council for Community Relations, Greater Manchester Council for Voluntary Service; Member, Central District Health Council; Member, Court of the University of Salford; Member, Post Office Advisory Committee, Manchester; Member, Telecommunications Advisory Committee, Manchester; Manchester Area Committee, Electricity Consultative Council, North West; Member, Executive Committee, Manchester Council for Voluntary Service; Elected member, Convocation Committee, University of Manchester (1995-98); Environment Councillor, appointed by the Environment Council (1995-96);

Founder Member, Minority Arts Advisory Service; Victoria Park Housing Co-op, Manchester; Governor, Open College Federation,Manchester (1991); Life Member, Oxford University Union Society; Hon Secretary, North Manchester Law Centre (1991-94); Ex-Member, Passenger Transport Executive Central & North Advisory Committees (1982-86); Vice-Chairman, Rusholme Ward, The Labour Party (1995-97). *Education:* University of Dhaka, Bangladesh; University of St Andrews, Scotland; Blackstone School of Law, Chicago; Thomas Jefferson College of Law; University of Manchester; International University, Independence, Kansas; University of Oxford; University of Cambridge; Harvard Law School; Hague Academy of International Law. *Career Profile:* International Management & Law Consultant; numerous positions as Company Secretary/Director in many companies; freelance lecturer in economics, law and business studies. *Creative Works:* Founder President, The Syed Ala-ud-din Foundation for Third World; Travellers Aid Centre; Foundation for Promoting Islamic Knowledge. *Publications:* 'The Commercial Use of Computers in Britain'; 'The Bangladeshis in Britain'; 'An economic sociology of the ethnic minorities from the New Commonwealth in Great Britain'; 'Policy issues: an ethnic view'; numerous articles published in the USA, UK, India and Bangladesh. *Societies:* Hansard Society for Parliamentary Government; Didsbury, Life Member Rusholme, and Fallowfield Civic Societies. *Recreations, Interests:* Travel, badminton, football, charity and voluntary work. *Address:* 25 Sunnybank Road, Longsight, Manchester M13 0XF *(tel:* 0161-248 6844); 32 Veronica Road, Didsbury, Manchester M20 0SU. *Additional Information:* President, Afro-Asian Society, Manchester (1969-); President, NSPCC, Longsight Area; Hon Secretary, Manchester Council for Voluntary Service; Parliamentary Candidate - Central Constituency, Manchester (1979) Stretford (1983). President, Federation of Afro-Asian Associations (UK). Rector's Candidate, University of St Andrew's (1985, 1988); Chancellor's Candidate, University of Manchester (1995). Fought in the liberation movements of British India and Bangladesh.

ALBUTT, Kenneth John, BSc Aston (1962),PhD Birmingham (1967),FIM,CEng

Chief Executive, ATR Group Ltd; Chairman and Managing Director, PI Castings Ltd; Chairman, AMTAC Laboratories Ltd, AMTAC Certification Services Ltd, Turbotech Precision Products Ltd, Metal Injection Mouldings Ltd. *b.* 8 March 1939; Birmingham. *m.* 1963 Jane Andree Blick; one *s.* one *d. Education:* University of Aston (1958-62); University of Birmingham (1964-67). *Career Profile:* Senior Research Metallurgist, BSA Group Research Centre; Managing Director, Altrincham Laboratories Ltd; Technical Director, P I Castings Ltd. *Publications:* Various technical papers. *Societies:* Past President, Union Internationale des Laboratoires Independents; Past President, British Investment Casters Association; Council of Association of Consulting Scientists. *Recreations, Interests:* 41 Club, country sports, sailing, music, gardening. *Address:* ATR Group Ltd, Davenport Lane, Broadheath, Altrincham, Cheshire, WA14 5DS *(tel:* 0161-928 5811).

ALEXANDER, Professor Martin Swinburn, MA(Oxon),DPhil(Oxon)

Professor of Contemporary History & Politics, University of Salford. *b.* 6 January 1955 West Hartlepool. *m.* 1980 Rosalie Hughes. *Education:* Royal Grammar School, Lancaster (1968-73); Exeter College, Oxford (1973-76); St Antony's College, Oxford (1976-80); Université de Paris IV, Sorbonne (1977-78). *Career Profile:* Franco-British Council Fellow (1980-82); Lecturer in History, University of Southampton (1982-93); Visiting Fellow, Yale

University (1988-89); Assoc. Professor of Strategy, US Naval War College (1991-92); Professor of Contemporary History, University of Salford (1993-). *Publications/Creative Work:* Co-editor 'The French and Spanish Popular Fronts' (CUP, 1989); Author 'The Republic in Danger: General Maurice Gamelin and the Politics of French Defence (CUP, 1992). *Societies:* Royal United Services Institute for Defence Studies; American Historical Association; Society for French Historical Studies; Yorkshire County Cricket Club; Old Lancastrian Club. *Recreations, Interests:* Yorkshire cricket, rugby football, jazz and big band music, good beer, classic Rover motor cars. *Address:* Department of Politics & Contemporary History, University of Salford, Crescent House, Salford, M5 4WT (*tel:* 0161 745 5166; *fax:* 0161 745 5077; *e-mail:* m.s.alexander@pch.salford.ac.uk); 4 Blyborough Close, Chaseley Gardens, Salford, M6 7DD (*tel:* 0161 736 8768).

ALEXANDER, Sonia Dorothy (*née* Shibko)

Chairman, Salford and Trafford Health Authority; JP. *b.* 11 February 1931; Swansea. *m.* 1955 Benjamin Leslie; three *s.* (*widowed 1989*) *Public Offices:* Manchester City Councillor (1962-74) (1974-79); Member, Valuation Panel. *Education:* Wales, France, Switzerland. *Career Profile:* Chairman, Children's Committee (1968-72). *Recreations, Interests:* Music, sport, my grandchildren, the garden. *Address:* Salford and Trafford Health Authority, Peel House, Albert Street, Eccles, Manchester M30 0NJ (0161-787 0078); 1 Plowley Close, Didsbury, Manchester M20 2DB.

ALLAN, Janet Rosemary (*née* Hampden)

Book Production Consultant. *b.* 18 October 1934. *m.* 1965 Robin; one *s.* two *d.* *Public Offices:* Trustee, Buxton Opera House. *Education:* St Christopher's School, Letchworth; Central School of Arts & Crafts, London. *Career Profile:* Production Manager, Associated Book Publishers, London (1956-65); Librarian, The Portico Library (1982-91); Marketing Manager then Production Manager, Carcanet Press (1992-94). *Societies:* Gaskell Society; Manchester Bibliographical Society. *Recreations, Interests:* Books, theatre, family and friends. *Address:* 10 Dale Road, New Mills, Stockport, SK12 4NW (*tel:* 01663 744233; *fax:* 01633 744233).

ALLAN, John Hamilton Birkett, MA,FCA

Group Finance Director, Renold plc. *b.* 26 July 1940 Newcastle upon Tyne. *Education:* Rossall School; St John's College, Cambridge. *Career Profile:* Group Finance Director, Renold plc (1987-); Mardon Packaging International Ltd (1969-87) (various financial positions; Group Finance Director 1980-87). *Recreations, Interests:* Cricket, postal history. *Address:* Renold plc, Renold House, Styal Road, Wythenshawe, Manchester, M22 5WL (*tel:* 0161 437 5221; *fax:* 0161 437 7782).

ALLAN, Robin, MA (Hons) Cantab (1957) PhD (Exeter)

Artistic Director, InterTheatre; Part-time Lecturer, University of Manchester Drama & Extra Mural Departments. *b.* 21 April 1934; Zomba, Nyasaland. *m.* 1965 Janet; one *s.* two *d.* *Education:* Park Town School, Johannesburg; Dumpton House School, Wimborne; Haileybury College, Hertford; Cambridge University (MA); Exeter University (PhD); University of London (PGCE); British Theatre Association (ADB); Central School of Speech

5

& Drama (ACSD). *Military Service:* National Service with the Royal Artillery and Royal Army Education Corps (Sergeant). *Career Profile:* Typographical Designer, Eyre & Spottiswoode, London; Lecturer & Television Officer with The British Council, Kuwait, Malta, Iran and London; Lecturer in Drama, English & Film, College of Adult Education, Manchester. *Publications:* 'Come Into My Castle' (Macmillan 1964); 'Beyond the Blue Mountains' (Macmillan 1979); articles on animation in specialist magazines. *Societies:* Portico Library. *Recreations, Interests:* Cycling. *Address:* 10 Dale Road, New Mills, Stockport SK12 4NW (*tel:* 01663-742809).

ALLEN, Charles Lamb, FCMA,FHCIMA,FRSA

Chief Executive, Granada Group plc; Chairman: Granada Television, London Weekend Television, Forte Hotels, GMTV. *b.* 4 January 1957 Lanark, Scotland. *Public Offices:* Governor, Royal Northern College of Music. *Education:* Bellshill Academy, Strathclyde; Bell College, Strathclyde. *Career Profile:* Deputy Chairman, GMTV (1994-96); Chief Executive, London Weekend Television (1994-96); Chairman, Granada Leisure, Services to Business Division (1994-); Chief Executive, Granada Television (1992-96); Chief Executive, Granda Group plc, Leisure Division (1991-92); Managing Director, Compass Group plc (1988-91); Managing Director, GIS Middle East Ltd (1987-88); Group Managing Director, Compass Vending and Grand Metropolitan Innovations Ltd (1986-87); Director, Management Services, Grandmet International Services Ltd (1982-85); Deputy Audit Manager, Gallaghers plc, TM Group (1979-82); Accountant, British Steel (1974-79). *Recreations, Interests:* Boating, theatre, travel, charity, business in the community. *Address:* Stornoway House, 13 Cleveland Row, London, SW1A 1GG (*tel:* 0171 451 6402).

ALLEN, William Frederick

Group Editor, Bury Times Newspapers (1990-). *b.* 20 January 1947 Radcliffe, Manchester. *m.* 1969 Lynne; two *s.* one *d. Education:* Canon Slade Grammar School, Bolton. *Career Profile:* Trainee Journalist, Bury Times Group; Journalist (briefly in Australia, TV and newspapers); Deputy Editor, Farnworth & Worsley Journal (1974-79); Editor, Manchester Journal Series (1979-88); Assistant Editor (1988-90), Group Editor (1990-) Bury Times Group. *Recreations, Interests:* All sports, politics, Second World War. *Address:* Bury Times Newspaper Group, PO Box 1, Market Street, Bury, BL9 0PF (*tel:* 0161 764 9421; *fax:* 0161 763 1315); 91 Higher Ainsworth Road, Radcliffe, Greater Manchester, M26 4JJ (*tel:* 0161 764 1661).

ALLWEIS, His Honour Judge Martin Peter, BA(Cantab, 1969)

Designated Family Judge for Greater Manchester (March 1996-). *b.* 22 December 1947 Prestwich, Manchester. *m.* 1984 Tracy Ruth (neé Barr); one *s.* one *d. Public Offices:* Circuit Judge (April 1994). *Education:* Manchester Grammar School; Sidney Sussex College, Cambridge. *Career Profile:* Call to the Bar, Inner Temple (1970); in practice as a Barrister, Northern Circuit (1971-94); A Recorder (1990-94). *Recreations, Interests:* Family interests, football (Manchester City FC), squash. *Address:* Manchester County Court, Courts of Justice, Crown Square, Manchester, M60 9DJ.

ALMOND, George Haylock, MBE (1993); FIFireE,FRSH,FIPD

County Fire Officer & Chief Executive, Greater Manchester Fire & Civil Defence Authority. *b.* 19 January 1944 Portsmouth. *m.* 1968 Elizabeth; one *s.* one *d. Education:* Technical High School, Portsmouth; Southampton Technical College. *Career Profile:* Fireman, Leading Fireman, Sub Officer, Hampshire Fire Service (1962-69); Station Officer, Assistant Divisional Officer, Divisional Officer III, Divisional Officer I, Cheshire Fire Brigade (1970-82); Assistant County Fire Officer, Deputy County Fire Officer, Greater Manchester County Fire Service (1982-95); County Fire Officer & Chief Executive (1995-). *Publications:* 'Accidents, Injuries and Illnesses to Firemen in Great Britain'; 'Students Handbook for Fire Engineers'. *Prizes:* Fire Engineering Scholarship (1972). *Societies:* Rotary Club of Manchester. *Recreations, Interests:* Music, reading, walking. *Address:* GMC Fire Service HQ, 146 Bolton Road, Swinton, Manchester, M27 8US (*tel:* 0161 736 5866; *fax:* 0161 743 1777). *Additional Information:* Professional Appointments: International President, Institution of Fire Engineers; Chairman, North West District, Chief & Assistant Fire Officers Association; Chairman, North West District, Fire Services National Benevolent Fund; AMA Adviser.

ALSBERG, Fred Richard, Deputy Lieutenant (Greater Manchester County) (1983)

Retired (formerly Dyestuff Technologist). *b.* 26 August 1920; Cologne, Germany. *m.* 1960 Reabie Hodgson Thomas. *Education:* Elementary and Grammar School (Cologne); Manchester College of Science and Technology (UMIST). *War Service:* Home Guard. *Previous Positions:* Assistant Works Chemist, Senior Technologist (Dye Using & Dye Making Industries). *Publications:* Scientific papers and patents in UK, Germany, Hungary, Switzerland relating to application of dyes to textiles by printing. *Societies:* Hallé Concerts Society; Manchester Council for Community Relations (Hon Sec); Manchester and Salford Family Service Unit (Hon Treasurer); Association of Friends of RNCM (Council Member); Lord Mayor of Manchester's Fund for Family Holidays Fund (Co-optative Trustee). *Recreations, Interests:* Music, opera, current affairs, travel, community relations. *Address:* Prestwich (*tel:* 0161-773 5712).

ALSOP, Geoffrey, BA(Hons),BArch,RIBA

Partner, Buttress Fuller Alsop Williams. *b.* 10 December 1949 Leicester. *m.* 1974 Maureen; one *s.* one *d. Education:* Forest Grammar School, Wokingham (1961-64); Colchester Royal Grammar School (1964-68); Manchester University, School of Architecture (1968-74). *Career Profile:* Hugh Wilson and Lewis Womersley, Manchester (1972-73); The Moxham Clark Partnership, Manchester (1974-76); The National Building Agency, Manchester (1976-82); Sole Proprietor, The Geoffrey Alsop Practice, Manchester (1982-88); Buttress Fuller Alsop Williams (1988-). *Societies:* Manchester Society of Architects (President 1996-97); Bramhall Park Golf Club. *Recreations, Interests:* Watching Manchester United, playing golf, walking Lakeland fells. *Address:* Buttress Fuller Alsop Williams, 31 Princess Street, Manchester, M2 4BF (*tel:* 0161 236 3303; *fax:* 0161 236 3603).

ANDERTON, Sir (Cyril) James, Kt (1991),QPM (1977),OStJ (1978),CStJ (1982),CBE (1982),KStJ (1989),DL (1989),Cross Pro Ecclesia et Pontifice (1982),Hon RNCM (1984), Hon FBCA (1976), CIMgt (1980)

Former Chief Constable, Greater Manchester Police; Member, Home Office Police Discipline Appeals Tribunal. *b.* 24 May 1932; Wigan, Lancashire. *m.* 1955 Joan Baron; one *d. Public Offices:* Chairman, Salvation Army Central North (Manchester) Advisory Board, The Malcolm Sargent Cancer Fund for Children - Hospital Carol Concerts Committee in Manchester; Member, Chapter-General of the Order of St John, The Salvation Army Territorial Advisory Board; President, Altrincham Town Centre Partnership, Bolton Outward Bound Association, Disabled Living - Manchester, Manchester & District RSPCA, Wythenshawe Hospital League of Friends; Vice-President, The Boys' Brigade, Adelphi Lads' Club (Salford), Birmingham University Visual Impairment Appeal; Greater Manchester Federation of Boys' Clubs, Greater Manchester West County Scout Council, Manchester & District RLSS, Manchester YMCA, NSPCC (Manchester, Salford & District), Sharp Street Ragged School (Manchester), Wigan Hospice; Patron, ACROSS Stockport Group, British College of Accordianists, Greater Manchester LUPUS Group, Greater Manchester Youth Field Gun Association, Henshaw's Society for the Blind, Hindley Community Association, Mottram & Hattersley Amateur Boxing Club, North Cheshire (Trafford) Branch of the Multiple Sclerosis Society, North Manchester Hospital Broadcasting Service, North West Campaign for Kidney Donors, Stockport Canal Trust; Wigan & District RSPCA. *Education:* St Matthew's Church School, Highfield, Wigan; Wigan Grammar School; Certificate in Criminology, Manchester University (1960); Police Staff College (1962 and 1967). *Military Service:* Corps of Royal Military Police (1950-53). *Career Profile:* Constable to Chief Inspector, Manchester City Police (1953-67); Chief Superintendent, Cheshire Constabulary (1967-68); Assistant Chief Constable, Leicester & Rutland (1968-72); Assistant to HM Chief Inspector of Constabulary, Home Office, London (1972-75); Deputy Chief Constable, Leicestershire (1975), Greater Manchester (1975-76); President, Association of Chief Police Officers (1986-87); Interpol Conference (Paris, 1973); Foreign & Commonwealth Office Lecture Tour of Far East & SE Asia (1973); UK Delegate, UN Congress on Prevention of Crime (Budapest, 1974); President, Christian Police Association (1979-81); County Director, St John Ambulance in Greater Manchester (1976-89), Commander (1989-96). *Prizes and Awards:* Mancunian of the Year (1980); Certificate of Merit, British Institute of Management (1990); Freeman of the City of London (1990). *Societies:* Association for the Propagation of the Faith; Association of Friends of the RNCM; The British Trust; Broughton Catholic Charitable Society; The Catholic Union of Great Britain; Chief Constables Club; Christian Police Association; Council of Christians & Jews; Friends of Buglawton Hall School; Friends of Israel Association; Institute of Management; Manchester Literary & Philosophical Society; National Trust; Portico Library; RLSS; Royal Military Police Association; Royal School of Church Music; RSPCA; RSPB; Royal Society of St George; St John House Club, London; Wigan Little Theatre. *Recreations, Interests:* Fell walking, music, Rugby League Football. *Address:* 9 The Avenue, Sale M33 4PB (*tel:* 0161 969 8140).

ANDI, Su see *SuAndi*

ANDREWS, Anthony John David, MA,BEd

Principal, Xaverian College, Manchester. *b.* 6 September 1946 Cheltenham. *m.* 1970 Barbara Marianne; one *s.* two *d. Education:* Stonyhurst College, Lancashire; Manchester University; Reading University. *Societies:* Catenian Association; Lymm Golf Club; Lymm

Tennis Club. *Recreations, Interests:* Travel, golf, tennis. *Address:* Xaverian College, Lower Park Road, Manchester, M14 5RB *(tel:* 0161 224 1781; *fax:* 0161 248 9039).

ANGEL, Doris *(née* Loewenstein),MBE(1995),JP(1963); MIPM,CertInstMan(City of Manchester Training College of Domestic Economy)

Company Secretary. *b.* 13 October 1924 Stuttgart, Germany. *m.* 1951 Arnold; two *d. Public Offices:* Chairman of Voluntary Board Members Forum Housing Associations North West; Past Chair and Member of Portico Housing Association; School Governor, Trafford; Past Chairman, Greater Manchester Probation Service; Past Deputy Chairman, Central Council of Probation Committees; Magistrate, Manchester City Bench (1963-94). *Education:* Manchester High School; College of Domestic Economy, Manchester; Personnel Management, UMIST. *War Service:* Assistant Catering Manager, Neath, Glamorgan and Wellington, Somerset. *Career Profile:* Catering Manager (1942-58); Company Personnel Manager (1966-90); Company Secretary. *Recreations, Interests:* Walking, travelling, reading and gardening. *Address:* Chenies, Park Road, Bowdon, Altrincham, WA14 3JJ *(tel:* 0161 928 4585) *(fax:* 0161 928 4585).

ANTON, Luis, Pro Ecclesia et Pontifice "Cross" from John Paul (1982),Title of Comendador by the Presidente of Portugal (1986); Commercial degree (Spanish Commercial School)

Consul for Portugal (North England); Company Director (Textiles). *b.* 24 February 1936; Lisbon. *m.* one *s.* one *d. (separated 1988) Education:* Primary School (Lisbon); Secondary School (Spain). *Prizes:* Decoration from Portugese Govt. (1984) for Service to Export. *Recreations, Interests:* Reading, light music, sailing. *Address:* 93A Princess Street, Manchester M1 4HT *(tel:* 0161-834 1821).

ANTROBUS, David Lowden

Managing Director, Northern Executive Aviation Ltd. *b.* 8 May 1940 Manchester. *m.* 1973 Christine Anne; one *d. Education:* Bradfield College, Berkshire (1953-58); London School of Flying (1961-62). *Career Profile:* First employee & small shareholder, Northern Executive Aviation (1963); Managing Director (1968). *Recreations, Interests:* Gardening, motor racing. *Address:* Northern Executive Aviation Ltd, Hangar 522, Manchester Airport, Wilmslow, SK9 4LP *(tel:* 0161 436 6666; *fax:* 0161 436 3450). *Additional Information:* Commercial Pilot since 1962; Founder Member of the Air Taxi Operators Association (Chairman, 1978-88); responsible for amalgamation with the General Aviation Manufacturers and Trades Association in 1988 (Founder Member); Chairman, GAMTA Air Transport Committee; Member, Civil Aviation Authority Operations Advisory Committee, Finance Advisory Committee & Flight Times Working Group; Member, Joint Aviation Authority FTL Working Group; Governor, European Business Aircraft Association (representing UK & GAMTA)(1990-).

ARDITTI, Samuel Jack Victor MBE(1984),DL(1987),Officer, Order of Civil Merit(1981), Knight of the Order of Isabel La Catolica (1975),Special Constabulary Long Service Medal (1965) 2 Bars (1975)(1985); MA(Hons)

Chairman, Trafford Healthcare NHS Trust. *b.* 13 December 1927 Manchester. *m.* 1962 Carol; one *s.* two *d. Public Offices:* Hon Treasurer, Tidy Britain Group; Director, Tidy Britain Enterprises; Honorary Consul for Mexico; Member, Executive Council, Broughton House Home for Disabled Ex-Servicemen; Member, Greater Manchester Police Policy Advisory Group on Racial Issues; Trustee, Greater Manchester Police Community Charity; Trustee, Greater Manchester Shrievalty Police Trust; General Commissioner for Income Tax; Member of Court, University of Manchester. *Education:* Rydal School; Jesus College, Cambridge. *Military Service:* Lieutenant, 7th Royal Tank Regiment (1947-48). *Career Profile:* Worked in the family business, Victor S Arditti & Son, subsequently William Baird plc; Non-Executive Director (1991-95). *Societies:* Rotary Club of Manchester; Manchester Literary & Philosophical Society; Commanderie de Bordeaux de Manchester; Manchester Naval Officers Association; St James's Club, Manchester. *Address:* Dunham Belfry, Charcoal Road, Bowdon, Altrincham, WA14 4RY *(tel:* 0161 928 4826) *(fax:* 0161 928 4826). *Additional Information:* Previous public offices include: High Sheriff of Greater Manchester (1992-93); Secretary, Manchester Consular Association (1979-91) (President 1990); Honorary Vice Consul for Spain (1973-86) Cheshire Special Constabulary (1956-91) appointed Chief Commandant (1976); Chairman, China Technology Link (1991-94); Chairman, Greater Manchester Regional Appeal, The Prince's Trust (1993-94); Director of the Manchester Chamber of Commerce & Industry (1987-94).

ARNOLD, Professor John André, MSc,MA(Econ),FCA

Director, Manchester Business School. *b.* 30 April 1944 Preston. *m.* 1975 Lynne; two *d. (marr. diss. 1995) Education:* Haberdashers Askes School; London School of Economics. *Career Profile:* Articled Clerk, D F Webster & Co, London (1962-67); Teaching Fellow (Management Studies), London School of Economics (1967-69); Lecturer in Accounting, University of Kent (1969-71); Lecturer in Accounting (1971-75), Senior Lecturer in Accounting (1975-77); KPMG Professor of Accounting, University of Manchester (1977-94); Visiting Professor of Accounting, University of Washington, USA (1981-82); Director of Manchester Business School (1994-). *Publications/Creative Work:* Books include: 'Pricing and Output Decisions' (1973); 'Financial Accounting' (1985, 2nd edition 1994); 'Accounting for Management Decisions' (1983, 2nd edition 1990, 3rd edition 1996); 'Goodwill and Other Intangibles' (1992); numerous journal articles and monographs. *Societies:* Marple Cricket and Squash Club. *Recreations, Interests:* Squash, tennis, opera, watching Stockport County FC. *Address:* Manchester Business School, Booth Street West, Manchester, M15 6PB *(tel:* 0161 275 6413; *fax:* 0161 275 6585).

ARTHAPRIYA, Dharmachari

Chairman, Senior Teacher, Manchester Buddhist Centre. *b.* 30 April 1955 Stoke-on-Trent. *Career Profile:* Government Service (1973-88); Ordained, Western Buddhist Order (1987); Teacher, Bristol Buddhist Centre (1987-89), Manchester Buddhist Centre (1989), Chairman (1992-). *Address:* Manchester Buddhist Centre, 16/20 Turner Street, Manchester, M4 1DZ *(tel:* 0161 834 9232; *fax:* 0161 839 4815; *e-mail:* mbc@c-vision.demon.co.uk). *Additional Information:* The Manchester Buddhist Centre is the largest urban Buddhist Centre in Europe and is a centre of the 'Friends of the Western Buhddist Order (FWBO)'.

ARUNDEL, Canon Michael, Hon Canon, Manchester Cathedral (1982),MA

Rector, St Ann's Church, Manchester. *b*. 7 November 1936 Wakefield, Yorkshire. *m*. 1965 Barbara; two *s*. *Education:* Queen Elizabeth Grammar School, Wakefield (1947-55); The Queen's College, Oxford (1957-60); Scholae Cancellarii Lincoln(1960-62). *Military Service:* Royal Air Force (1955-57). *Career Profile:* Asst. Curate, St Margaret, Hollinwood (1962-65); St Thomas, Leesfield (1965-69); Rector, All Saints, Newton Heath (1969-80); Area Dean, North Manchester (1975-80); Vicar of Eccles Parish Church (1980-91); Team Rector, Eccles. *Societies:* Manchester Literary & Philosophical Society; St James' Club. *Recreations, Interests:* Walking, ornithology, gardening, music. *Address:* St Ann's Church, St Ann's Street, Manchester, M2 7LF(*tel:* 0161 834 0239); St Ann's Rectory, 449 Wilbraham Road, Manchester, M21 0UZ (*tel:* 0161 881 1229).

ASHBOURNE, Lorraine

Actress. *b*. 10 April 1961 Manchester. *Education:* Wilbraham High School; Webber Douglas Academy. *Career Profile:* Played in many productions at the Royal Exchange, Manchester; Royal Court; drama documentary (Granada); Member of the Royal Shakespeare Company. *Prizes:* Best Actress Manchester Evening News Award ('She Stoops to Conquer', Royal Exchange); Best Actress Manchester Evening News Award ('Decadance', Bolton Octagon). *Recreations, Interests:* Ice climbing, Paragliding.

ASHWORTH, Professor Graham William, CBE (1980); BArch (1958),MCD (1959),FRSA

Director General, Tidy Britain Group;Chairman & Chief Executive, Going for Green; Research Professor, University of Salford; Chairman, Ravenhead Renaissance, St Helens. *b*. 14 July 1935; Plymouth. *m*. 1960 Gwyneth Mai Morgan Jones; three *d*. *Public Offices:* Member, Merseyside Development Corporation (1981-); Member, Countryside Commission (1966-69). *Education:* Devonport High School, Plymouth; University of Liverpool. *Career Profile:* Director of CAMPUS (Campaign to promote the University of Salford) (1981-87); Professor, Urban Environmental Studies, University of Salford (1973-87); Director, NW Civic Trust (1965-73). *Publications:* 'An Encyclopaedia of Planning' (Barrie & Jenkins); 'The Role of Local Government in Environmental Protection' (Longman). *Recreations, Interests:* Walking, swimming, church. *Address:* The Tidy Britain Group, The Pier, Wigan WN3 4EX (*tel:* 01942 824620); Going for Green Ltd, 56 Oxford Street, Manchester M60 7HJU (*tel:* 0161 237 4158); Manor Court Farm, Preston New Road, Samlesbury, Preston PR5 OUP (*tel:* 01254 812011).

ATHERTON, Michael Andrew, BA(Hons)(Cantab,1989)

Cricketer, Lancashire County Cricket Club; England Captain. *b*. 23 March 1968 Manchester. *Education:* Manchester Grammar School; Downing College, Cambridge. *Societies:* The Groucho Club, London. *Recreations, Interests:* Golf, fishing.

ATKINSON, Richard BA(Econ)(Manchester),DipCIM

Group Chief Executive, Eurocamp plc. *b*. Elstree, Herts. *m*. 1986 Catherine; one *s*. two *d*. *Education:* Barton Peveril GS, Eastleigh, Hants (1964-71); University of Manchester (1971-74). *Career Profile:* Eurocamp - Joined as temporary summer employee (1975); Full-time

Overseas Manager (1976); General Manager (1979); Managing Director (1983); Led MBO (1988); Flotation (1991); Group Chief Executive (1996-). *Prizes:* Medaille d'Or for services to French tourism. *Societies:* CIM; Tytherington Club; Prestbury Tennis Club; Prestbury Squash Club. *Recreations, Interests:* Family and various sports - especially tennis and golf, home computing. *Address:* Eurocamp plc, Canute Court, Toft Road, Knutsford, Cheshire, WA16 0NL(*tel:* 01565 625524; *fax:* 01565 625539).

AUGHTON, Frederic, HND (Mech & Prod Eng),FRAeS

Director & General Manager, British Aerospace Aerostructures Ltd, Chadderton. *b.* 20 September 1945 Lancaster. *m.* 1969 Mary; two *s.* *Education:* Technical School, Lancaster; Harris College, Preston; London Business School. *Career Profile:* Apprenticed, BAe, Preston (1962-67); Project Managment, BAe, Preston (1968-72); Manager, BAe, Preston & Samlesbury (1973-81); Purchasing Manager, Tornado Project, BAe (1981-84); Tornado Project Manager, BAe, Samlesbury (1984-88); Works Manager, BAe, Preston (1989-91); Programme Director, BAe, Brough (1991-94); Director & General Manager, BAe, Chadderton (1995-). *Recreations, Interests:* Golf. *Address:* British Aerospace, Greengate, Middleton, Manchester M24 1SA (*tel:* 0161 955 8605; *fax:* 0161 955 8552).

AXFORD, Colonel Arthur, DL (1977),MBE (1958),OBE (1964),TD (1964),ADC to HM Queen (1965-70)

Vice President and Fellow, Institute of Quality Assurance; Gtr Manchester County Vice-President, SSAFA. *b.* 10 August 1921; Ashton-under-Lyne. *m.* 1941 Flora Isobel Hampson; two *s.* one *d.* *Public Offices:* High Sheriff (1987-88). *Education:* Ashton-under Lyne Grammar School. *War Service:* The Manchester Regiment (1939-46); Royal Ulster Rifles (1950-52) Korean War; 9th Bn The Manchester Regt (TA) (1952-64); Deputy Commander 127 Brigade (TA) (1964-70); Commandant, East Lancs ACF (1970-74); Hon Colonel, East Lancs ACF (1980-85). *Societies:* Ashton-under-Lyne Golf Club; High Peak Golf Club; English Golf Union. *Recreations, Interests:* Golf. *Address:* Flat 18, Temple Court, Temple Road, Buxton, SK17 9BA (*tel:* 01298 73468)

BACON, Philip, InstHSM

Chief Executive, Bury Health Care NHS Trust. *b.* 20 March 1945 Sheffield. *m.* 1966 Mavis; one *s.* three *d.* *Education:* King Edward VII School, Sheffield. *Career Profile:* 33 years experience of NHS management. *Societies:* Bury Rotary Club; Greenlands, Henley on Thames. *Recreations, Interests:* Fell walking, gardening, reading. *Address:* Bury Health Care NHS Trust, Roch House, Fairfield General Hospital, Bury, BL9 7TD (*tel:* 0161 705 3827); 30 Gisburn Drive, Bury, BL8 3DH.

BAGLEY, Philip William, MA Oxon,CertEd Leeds

Retired barrister; lecturer. *b.* 1 April 1931; Darlington. *m.* 1958 Margaret Kathleen Tong; two *s.* *Public Offices:* Former Chairman of Social Security Appeal Tribunals (Part-time). *Education:* Repton School; Hertford College, Oxford. *Military Service:* National Service RAOC (Egypt) (1949-51) and TA (1951-56). *Career Profile:* Senior Lecturer in Law, Manchester Polytechnic (Retired 1988); Councillor (Liberal) Oldham MB (1973-76); Also formerly practising barrister on Northern Circuit; Clerk of Saddleworth Parish Council (1978-95). *Societies:* Manchester Literary & Philosophical Society; Saddleworth Historical Society. *Recreations, Interests:* Local affairs, gardening, travel. *Address:*2 Wharmton Rise, Grasscroft, Oldham OL4 4ET (*tel:* 01457-872778).

BAHL, Kamlesh, LLB(Hons)

Chairwoman, Equal Opportunities Commission. *b.* 28 May 1956 Nairobi, Kenya. *m.* 1986 Nitin Lakhani. *Public Offices:* Council Member, Law Society; Member, Diplomatic Service Appeals Board; Member, Council of Justice; Member, Ethnic Minorities Advisory Committee; Member, Parkside Health Authority; Member, National Association of Health Authorities and Trusts. *Education:* Minchenden School, Southgate; University of Birming ham. *Career Profile:* Solicitor, Greater London Council (1978-81); Legal Advisor, British Steel Corporation (1981-84); Solicitor, Texaco Ltd (1984-87); Datalogic Ltd: Company Secretary & Manager, Legal Services (1989-93). *Publications/Creative Work:* Managing Legal Practice in Business. *Societies:* The Law Society; RSA. *Recreations, Interests:* Walking, reading, dancing, travelling. *Address:* Equal Opportunities Commission, Overseas House, Quay Street, Manchester, M3 3HN (*tel:* 0161 838 8231; *fax:* 0161 835 1657).

BAILEY, Richard, BA(Hons),ACA

Managing Director, N M Rothschild & Sons Ltd. *b.* 26 December 1951 Wakefield, West Yorkshire. *m.* 1977 Hilary; two *s.* one *d.* *Education:* The King's School, Pontefract; Manchester University. *Career Profile:* Commercial Manager, Marks & Spencer plc; Chartered Accountant, Price Waterhouse; Senior Director, N M Rothschild & Sons Ltd; Managing Director, Rothschild Northern Division. *Prizes:* Silver and Bronze Prizes in Mobberley Garden Competition. *Societies:* Mere Golf & Country Club; Bowdon Lawn Tennis Club; Royal Yacht Club, Salcombe. *Recreations, Interests:* Rugby, tennis, skiing, swimming, running, music, drama, gardening, reading. *Address:* N M Rothschild & Sons

Ltd, Trinity Court, 16 John Dalton Street, Manchester, M2 6HY (*tel:* 0161 827 3800; *fax:* 0161 835 3789).

BAKER, Professor Christopher Thomas Hale, MA,DPhil(Oxon),FIMA

Professor of Mathematics, Head, Department of Pure and Applied Mathematics, University of Manchester. *b.* 14 January 1939 Cliftonville, Kent. *m.* 1963 Helen; one *s.* one *d.* *Education:* Colchester Royal Grammar School (1951-58); Jesus College, Oxford (1958-64). *Publications/Creative Work:* Technical books (3) and research papers in mathematics. *Societies:* Fellow, Institute of Mathematics and Its Applications; Member, London Mathematical Society; Member, Society for Industrial Applied Mathematics. *Recreations, Interests:* Family, ornithology, travel. *Address:* Department of Mathematics, The University, Oxford Road, Manchester, M139PL (*tel:* 0161 275 5800; *fax:* 0161 275 5819).

BAKER, David John

Director, Manchester Financial & Professional Forum. *b.* 25 October 1930 Bramley, Hants. *m.* 1956 Sylvia Mary Dearman; two *d.* *Public Offices:* Association of European Financial Centres (President 1996-98). *Education:* Maidstone Grammar School. *Military Service:* National Service (1949-50). *Career Profile:* Bank of England, Head Office & Branch Service (1950-90); Manchester Financial & Professional Forum (1990-); consultancy work mainly for Manchester Metropolitan University. *Societies:* Manchester Literary & Philosophical Society (Council); Manchester Statistical Society; Manchester Luncheon Club (President 1996-97); Royal Society of Arts; Franco British Business Club; St Williams' Foundation; St James's Club. *Recreations, Interests:* Ranges from woodworking to walking. *Address:* Manchester Financial & Professional Forum, 56 Oxford Street, Manchester, M60 7HJ (*tel:* 0161 228 3698; *fax:* 0161 236 4160).

BAKER, Huw, MA (Cantab),Solicitor

Head of Construction Law, Addleshaw Sons & Latham. *b.* 22 September 1962 Swanage, Dorset. *m.* 1989 Helen; one *d.* *Education:* Wymondham College, Norfolk; Troy State University, Alabama, USA; Downing College, Cambridge. *Career Profile:* Qualified, McKenna & Co (1987); Booth & Co, Leeds (1990); Addleshaw Sons & Latham (1993). *Publications/Creative Work:* Numerous articles on aspects of Construction Law. *Prizes:* Various Scholarships, including Governor's Scholarship, Troy State University, Alabama. *Societies:* Society of Construction Lawyers. *Address:* Addleshaw Sons & Latham, Dennis House, Marsden Street, Manchester, M2 1JD (*tel:* 0161 832 5994; *fax:* 0161 832 2250).

BAKER, Robert Stanley, BSc,PhD,CertEd,FIMgt

Principal, South Trafford College. *b.* 18 December 1946 Birmingham. *m.* 1972 Marian; *(marr. diss. 1984)*; *m.* 1984 Christine. *Education:* Moseley Grammar School (1958-65); University College Cardiff (1966-72). *Career Profile:* Research Assistant, Dunlop Research Centre, Birmingham (1965-66); Research Officer, University of Wales, Institute of Technology (1972-73); Lecturer, Harlow Technical College (1973-77); Calderdale College (1977-84); Head of Department, Accrington & Rossendale College (1984-87); Vice Principal, Tameside College of Technology (1987-94); Principal, South Trafford College

(1994-). *Publications/Creative Work:* Research papers in Atomic Physics in Journal of Physics (1972 and 1973). *Societies:* Institute of Management; National Trust. *Recreations, Interests:* Angling, wine, theatre. *Address:* South Trafford College, Manchester Road, West Timperley, Altrincham, WA14 5PQ (*tel:* 0161 952 4601; *fax:* 0161 952 4612; *e-mail:* robbaker@stcoll.ac.uk).

BAKER, Stephen Roy, BSc,FCA

National Head of Corporate Finance, Grant Thornton. *b.* 16 August 1955 Kent. *m.* 1980 Marité; one *s.* one *d.* *Education:* Erith Grammar School; Manchester University. *Career Profile:* Grant Thornton: Manchester (1976-83), San Francisco (1983-85), Manchester (1985-); (partner, 1987). *Address:* Grant Thornton, Heron House, Albert Square, Manchester, M60 8GT(*tel:* 0161 834 5414; *fax:* 0161 832 6042).

BANERJEE, Arup Kumar, OBE(1996), JP (1988); MB BS Calcutta (1958), MRCP London (1967), MRCP Edinburgh (1967), MRCP Glasgow (1965), FRCP London (1982), FRCP Edinburgh (1980), FRCP Glasgow (1979)

Consultant Physician & Medical Director, Bolton Hospital NHS Trust; Executive Member, Bolton Hospital NHS Trust Board. *b.* 28 November 1935; Calcutta, India. *m.* 1959 Dr Aleya Banerjee; three *s.* *Public Offices:* President, British Geriatrics Society (1996-); Member, Vice-Chair, North West Regional Health Authority; Member, Central Consultants and Specialists Committee, BMA; Member, Executive Council of British Geriatrics Society. *Education:* Primary Education in Calcutta India; Presidency College and Medical College, Calcutta; University of Calcutta, India. *Career Profile:* Various Junior Hospital appointments in India and in UK (1958-67); Senior Registrar in Medicine at Southend General Hospital (1967-68); Lecturer in Medicine, University of Malaya Medical School, Kuala Lumpur (1968-71); Senior Registrar in Medicine (Elderly), Portsmouth & Southampton University Hospitals (1971-73). *Publications:* Approximately 70 scientific papers and articles in various medical journals in United Kingdom and abroad; chapters in medical text books and monographs. *Societies:* Manchester Medical Society (President Elect, Medical Section); BMA; BGS; Magistrates' Association. *Recreations, Interests:* Travel, music, reading. *Address:* Department of Medicine for the Elderly, Bolton General Hospital, Minerva Road, Farnworth, Bolton BL4 0JR (*tel:* 01204-390685/6 & 390390; *fax:* 390933); 2 Pilling Field, Egerton, Bolton BL7 9UG (*tel:* 01204-305482).

BARBOUR, James Jack, OBE(1992); BA(Univ. of Strathclyde, 1977),MHSM(1986)

Chief Executive, Central Manchester NHS Trust (1994-). *b.* 16 January 1953 Perth, Scotland. *m.* Rosalind Marjorie Doig; one *s.* two *d.* *Public Offices:* Burgess of City of Aberdeen; Member of Court, University of Manchester; Honorary Senior Fellow, University of Manchester; Member of Board of Governance, Aberdeen College of Education. *Education:* Madras College, St Andrews (1964-70); University of Strathclyde; Alumnus, London Business School (1989). *Career Profile:* Graduate Management Trainee, NHS Scotland (1977-79); Administrator, GGHB (1979-83); Unit Administrator, Gt Ormond St Hospitals (1983-86); General Manager, Royal Manchester Childrens Hospital (1986-87); General Manager, Acute Services, Grampian Health Board (1987-92); Chief Executive, Aberdeen Royal Hospitals NHS Trust (1992-94). *Prizes:* EEC Exchange Scholarship, West

Germany (1981). *Societies:* Royal Society of Arts; Royal Northern Club, Aberdeen. *Recreations, Interests:* Sport, keeping fit, my children. *Address:* Central Manchester NHS Trust, Trust Headquarters, Cobbett House, Oxford Road, Manchester, M13 9WL *(tel:* 0161 276 4755; *fax:* 0161 272 6931).

BARKER, James Kenneth, TD (Cyprus) (1959)

Director and General Manager, Royal Mail North Wales & North West Division. *b.* 21 November 1938; Wigan. *m.* 1970 Elizabeth; three *s. Education:* Wigan Grammar School; Chorley Grammar School; Blackpool Grammar School. *Military Service:* National Service Royal Signals, Cyprus (1958-59); Royal Engineers (V) (1969-93); Colonel, Commander TA Postal and Courier Service (rebadged Royal Logistic Corps on formation). *Career Profile:* Director & General Manager, Royal Mail South Wales & South West Division; Head Postmaster, Manchester; Head Postmaster, Sheffield; Controller, RM Operations NE Postal Board and Eastern Postal Board. *Societies:* Prince's Trust Volunteers; Rochdale RUFC. *Recreations, Interests:* Rugby Union, yachting. *Address:* Royal Mail North Wales & North West Division, Royal Mail House, Clippers Quay, Salford, M5 2NW *(tel:* 0161-869 7000).

BARLOW, Kenneth Alexander, MSc Salford (1972),PhD Manchester (1978)

Consultant to Museums and Galleries (Conservation, Restoration, Display and Working of Exhibits). *b.* 16 October 1932; Whitefield, Manchester. *m.* 1953 Muriel Hughes; one *s. Education:* Junior Technical School (1944-47); Bolton Institute of Technology (1948-53) (1962-67); Technical Teacher Training (1959-60). *Military Service:* RAF (1953-56) Service in UK and Middle East. *Career Profile:* Engineering Apprenticeship (1947-53); Military Service (1953-56); Works Director (1956-59); Lecturer, Mechanical Engineering (1959-77); Keeper (Technology) later Deputy Director, Greater Manchester Museum of Science and Industry (1973-88). *Creative Works:* Responsible for the technical development of the Greater Manchester Museum of Science and Industry i.e. establishing extensive technical workshops to provide facilities for the restoration, erection and commissioning of exhibits now displayed daily in full working order. *Publications:* 'The Formative Years of the Gas Engine', Manchester Association of Engineers (1976); 'The Internal Combustion Engine Introduction into England' (Diesel Engineering 1978); 'N A Auto and the Four Stroke Engine' (Newcomen Society, 1995). *Societies:* Newcomen Society. *Recreations, Interests:* Music, industrial archaeology. *Address:* 102 Longsight Road, Ramsbottom, Bury BL0 9SZ *(tel:* 01204 884245). *Additional Information:* Curatorial Advisor to Bolton Steam Museum (formerly Northern Mill Engine Society).

BARNES, David Stewart, DipArch Manchester (1964),RIBA

Architect Partner, Building Design Partnership, Manchester. *b.* 6 September 1938; Salford, Lancashire. *m.* 1967 Gwendoline Edith Irene; one *d. Education:* Tootil Drive Primary School, Salford; Salford Grammar School, Salford. *Career Profile:* Architect, Cruickshank & Seward, Manchester; Principal, Barnes, Heap & Associates, Glossop. *Creative Works:* Architect Partner responsible for the following projects; Chloride Technical Limited, Swinton (RIBA Award 1978) (Structural Steel Design Award 1979); GMC County Fire Service, Swinton (Civic Trust Award 1981); Manchester Airport plc Main Concourse

Refurbishment Project; Museum of Science and Industry, Manchester: conversion of the Lower Byrom Street Warehouse to the new Science Museum (RIBA North West Regional Award 1989) (RICS/Times Conservation Awards 1989 Commendation), conversion of the 1830 Carriage Sheds to new museum uses (Civic Trust Commendation, 1989); City of Manchester Olympic Bids for 1996 and 2000 Games; British Gas/British Council HQ offices (BCO Design Award, 1995); refurbishment of the Christie Building, University of Manchester (Europa Nostra Diploma of Merit (1994), Manchester Society of Architects Design Award (1994)); restoration of Plas Mawr, Conway, Cadw Welsh Historic Monuments; refurbishment of the Halifax HQ offices, Halifax. *Societies:* Ex-President, Manchester University Soccer Club; Member of Manchester University XXI Club. *Recreations, Interests:* Golf, soccer. *Address:* Building Design Partnership, PO Box 85, Sunlight House, Quay Street, Manchester M60 3JA (*tel:* 0161-834 8441).

BARNES, John Kenneth, TD (1967); FCA

Director (Non-Exec), Ensol Holdings plc *b.* 4 July 1935; Rochdale. *m.* 1986 Mary; one *s.* one *d.* one *steps.* one *stepd.* *Public Offices:* Governor, North Cestrian Grammar School; Hon Treasurer, The Charity Service; Community Exchange. *Education:* Rossall School. *Military Service:* National Service, REME (1954-56); Territorial Army (1956-67). *Career Profile:* Partner, Robson Rhodes. *Recreations, Interests:* Golf, walking, gardening. *Address:* J K Barnes & Co, Mere Heyes House, Rowley Bank Lane, High Legh, Knutsford WA16 0QJ (*tel:* 01565-830617).

BARNETT, The Rt Hon Lord Joel, Privy Counsellor (1975), Peerage (1983); Hon Doctorate (Law) Strathclyde (1982),FCA

Chairman,Select Committee on the European Union (House of Lords). *b.* 14 October 1923; Manchester. *m.* 1949 Lilian Stella; one *d.* *Public Offices:* Former Chairman, Hansard Society for Parliamentary Government; President, Royal Institute Public Administration; Former Trustee, Victoria & Albert Museum; Former Trustee, Birkbeck College London University; Former Member of Council, Hallé Society. *Education:* Manchester Central High School; Accountancy Correspondence Course. *War Service:* Army (1939-45). *Career Profile:* MP, Heywood & Royton (1964-83); Chief Secretary to the Treasury (1974-79); Member of Cabinet (1977-79). *Publications:* 'Inside the Treasury' (1982). *Recreations, Interests:* Walking hills of Derbyshire, watching sport, the arts. *Address:* House of Lords, London SW1A 0PW (*tel:* 0171 219 5440; *fax:* 0171 219 5979); Bodycote International plc, 140 Kingsway, Manchester M19 1BB (*tel:* 0161 257 2345; *fax:* 0161 257 2353); 7 Hillingdon Road, Whitefield, Manchester M25 7QQ (*tel:* 0161 766 3634).

BARRATT, Peter William, FCA,Member of Securities and Futures Authority

Director, Greig Middleton Ltd. *b.* 7 May 1934 Monton, Eccles. *m.* 1960 Shirley; one *s.* two *d.* *(marr. diss. 1978)*; *m.* 1990 Pamela; one *steps.* one *stepd.* *Education:* De La Salle College, Salford (1942-46); Prior Park College, Bath (1946-52). *Career Profile:* Chartered Accountant and Stockbroker; Articled Clerk, E A Radford-Edwards, Manchester (1952-59); Ashworth Sons, Barratt, Manchester, Administrator (1959-62), Partner (1962-88); Director, FPG Securities Ltd (1988-90); Director, Allied Provincial Securities Ltd (1990-95); Director, Greig Middleton Ltd (1995-). *Societies:* Broughton Park RFC; Life Member,

Lancashire RFC; Sale RFC. *Recreations, Interests:* Sport particularly watching rugby, reading history and biographies, theatre, travel, antiques, the good things in life!!. *Address:* Greig Middleton Ltd, PO Box 419, 38/40 Kennedy Street, Manchester, M60 1PW (*tel:* 0161 237 7717; *fax:* 0161 237 7707).

BARRETT, Professor Peter Stephen, MSc,PhD,FRICS

Director, Research Centre for the Built and Human Environment, University of Salford. *b.* 16 November 1957 London. *m.* 1980 Lucinda; one *s.* three *d. Public Offices:* Chairman, Research Committee, Royal Institution of Chartered Surveyors; Deputy Chairman, Construction Industry Council Research and Innovation Committee; Member, Construction Research and Innovation Strategy Panel. *Education:* Royal Institution of Chartered Surveyors Direct Exams; Brunel University (MSc); South Bank University (part-time)(PhD). *Career Profile:* Chartered Building Surveyor, King and Chasemore, Oxford; Buckell and Ballard, Oxford; Hunter and Partners, London (1976-85); Lecturer, South Bank University (1985-88); Salford University (1988-91), Professor (1992), Chairman of Department of Surveying (1993-96). *Publications/Creative Work:* Books on practice management and facilities management; around 50 papers in the professional literature. *Prizes:* Guy Biscoe RICS Prize Paper (1986); Commended Young Chartered Surveyor of the Year (1992). *Societies:* Member, Conseil International du Batiment. *Recreations, Interests:* Badminton, calligraphy, walking. *Address:* Department of Surveying, University of Salford, Salford, M5 4WT (*tel:* 0161 745 5588; *fax:* 0161 745 5011; *e-mail*: P.S.Barrett @surveying.salford.ac.uk).

BARROWMAN, Douglas Alan, BAcc(Glasgow),CA

Senior Principal, Barrowman Associates, Corporate Finance Advisers. *b.* 1 March 1965 Glasgow. *m.* 1992 Christine; one *s.* one *d. Education:* Kings Park Secondary School (1977-82); Glasgow University (1982-85); ICAS (1985-88). *Career Profile:* Venture capital and corporate finance, joined 3i (1989) Investment Controller, Sheffield/Manchester; Principal, The McInnes Partnership (1992); set up Barrowman Associates (1994). *Publications:* 'Venture Capital Law & Practice' (with Daryl Cook)(FT Law & Practice). *Prizes:* Runner-up Young Scottish Business Accountant of the Year (1988). *Societies:* North West Society of ICAS. *Recreations, Interests:* Skiing, travel, sport in general, modern history, family, book writing. *Address:* Barrowman Associates, Waldorf House, 5 Cooper Street, Manchester M2 2FW (*tel:* 0161 236 0951; *fax:* 0161 236 0952); The Gables, Woodbrook Road, Alderley Edge, SK9 7BY.

BARTLETT, John Bramwell, BA(Hons)

Chief Superintendent, Greater Manchester Police. *b.* 16 May 1950 London. *m.* 1975 Thelma; two *s.* one *d. Education:* Trinity School of John Whitgift, Croydon; Durham University. *Career Profile:* Cadet to Chief Inspector, Metropolitan Police (1967-86); Greater Manchester Police (1986-). *Societies:* Member, Executive Committee of Manchester City Mission.

BATTERS, Royce, FICA

Director of Finance, Christie Hospital NHS Trust. *b.* 12 June 1938 Stockport. *m.* 1961 Jill H Allen; one *s.* one *d. (marr. diss.)*; *m.* 1994 Susan Dorney; one *steps. Public Offices:* Member of Court, Council, Chairman of Finance, University of Salford; Hon Treasurer (1989-91), Captain (1996) Heaton Moor Golf Club; President, Old Stoconians Associations (1989-90). *Education:* Stockport School. *Career Profile:* Partner, Ernst & Young (1975-93); Partner, Appleby Wood; Appleby English & Parnters (1967-75); Taxation Accountant, Turner & Newall plc (1963-67). *Societies:* Freeman of City of London; Member of Worshipful Company of Chartered Accountants; Freemason. *Recreations, Interests:* Golf. *Address:* Christie Hospital NHS Trust, Wilmslow Road, Withington, Manchester, M20 4BX(*tel:* 0161 446 3704; *fax:* 0161 446 3977); Maple Tree, 7 Sunny Bank Road, Bowdon, Cheshire, WA14 3PW (*tel:* 0161 928 0359).

BATTRICK, Peter John, BA(Hons)(1974),PGCE(1977)

Chief Executive Officer, Quarry Bank Mill. *b.* 16 March 1953 Blackburn. *m.* 1976 Karen Elizabeth Walsh; one *s. Education:* Queen Elizabeth's Grammar School, Blackburn (1960-70); Lancaster University (1971-74); St Martins College, Lancaster (1976-77). *Career Profile:* Teacher, King Edward VII School, Lytham (1977-86); National Trustel: Regional Information Officer (NW Region)(1986-89), Regional Public Affairs Manager (Kent & E Sussex)(1989-96), Quarry Bank Mill (1996-). *Publications/Creative Work:* Numerous articles on work of the National Trust published in NW, SE and nationally. *Prizes:* Queen's Scholar. *Societies:* Henry Doubleday Association. *Recreations, Interests:* Walking, cricket, conservation, gardening and managing an unruly acre of woodland. *Address:* Quarry Bank Mill, Styal, Wilmslow, Cheshire, SK9 4LA(*tel:* 01625 527468; *fax:* 01625 539267).

BATTYE, John Bernard, FIBS

Leader, Oldham Council. *b.* 4 June 1945 Oldham. *m.* 1969 one *s.* one *d. (marr. diss. 1975)*; *m.* 1976 Annette; two *s. Public Offices:* Chairman, Association of Greater Manchester Authorities; Alternate Member, Committee of The Regions; Board Member, Manchester Airport; Board Member, Marketing Manchester; Member, Policy Committee Association of Metropolitan Authorities. *Education:* Hulme Grammar School, Oldham; Medical School, Manchester University. *Career Profile:* Pathology Service, Royal Oldham Hospital (1962-96); Head of Blood Transfusion Department (1971-96); Co-Chairman, GMex Ltd; Leader, Oldham Council (1985-). *Recreations, Interests:* Football, cricket spectator, occasional (poor) golfer. *Address:* Leader Oldham Council, Room 346, Civic Centre, Oldham (*tel:* 0161 911 4023; *fax:* 0161 911 4026); 21 Hillside Avenue, Grotton, Oldham, OL4 5SG (*tel:* 0161 633 2802; *fax:* 0161 633 2802).

BEER, E Stuart, MA(Oxon)

Music Master, Chetham's School of Music; Part-time Teacher, Faculty of Music, Manchester University. *b.* 19 August 1952 Heston, Middlesex. *m.* 1975 Kathryn; four *s.* one *d. Education:* Exeter School, Exeter, Devon (1968-71); Magdalen College, Oxford (1971-74); Royal Academy of Music (1974-75); Bath College of Higher Education (1977-78). *Career Profile:* Director of Music, Manchester Cathedral (1980-96). *Address:* 28 Rathen Road, Withington, Manchester, M20 4GH.

BELCHAM, Amanda Anne

Administrative Director, The Octagon Theatre, Bolton. *b.* 24 August 1954; London. *m.* 1984 Les Smith; two *steps.* two *stepd. Education:* Notting Hill & Ealing High School; New College of Speech & Drama; City University. *Career Profile:* Administrator, Paines Plough - The Writer's Company; Administrator, Theatre Foundry. *Recreations, Interests:* Gardening, reading, food and wine. *Address:* The Octagon Theatre, Howell Croft South, Bolton BL1 1SB (*tel:* 01204 529407).

BELL, Christopher John, MA(Cantab),Barrister at Law,FCCA,FCT

Regional Director North West, Robson Rhodes. *b.* 24 January 1939 Didsbury, Manchester. *m.* 1960 Winny; four *d. Education:* Pownall Hall School, WIlmslow; Terra Nova School, Jodrell Bank; Sedbergh School, Cumbria. *Career Profile:* Management Accountancy, Dunlop Group, Ford of Britain; Director, United Dominions Trust, Christian Salvesen plc; Managing Director, Manchester Exchange & Investment Bank; Regional Director North West, Robson Rhodes. *Publications:* 'Treasury Management Case Study' (on cassette) Institute of Chartered Accountant 'Top Up' Series. *Prizes:* Foulkes Lynch Prize, Accountancy Finals. *Societies:* St James's Club, Manchester; Kirby Lonsdale Golf Club. *Recreations, Interests:* Bridge, golf, fell walking. *Address:* Robson Rhodes, Colwyn Chambers, 19 York Street, Manchester, M2 3BA (*tel:* 0161 236 3777; *fax:* 0161 455 3444); Bargh Cottage, Stainforth, Settle, North Yorkshire, BD24 9PF (*tel:* 01729 823184; *fax:* 01729 825123). *Additional Information:* Invited lecturer, Treasury Management Seminars, Institute of Chartered Accountants, Reuters and City University Business School.

BENZIE, Alan A E, FCA

Senior Partner, KPMG North West Region, based in Manchester. *b.* 5 May 1947; Aberdeen. *m.* 1971 Penny; two *s.* one *d. Public Offices:* Executive Committee, Christie Hospital Centenary Candlelight Appeal. *Education:* Lindisfarne College, North Wales. *Career Profile:* Managing Partner, KPMG, Manchester. *Societies:* Knutsford Golf Club; St James's Club; Alderley Edge Cricket Club. *Recreations, Interests:* Golf, shooting, fishing, gardening. *Address:* C/o KPMG, St James' Square, Manchester M2 6DS (*tel:* 0161-838 4000).

BERG, Alan, Solicitor

Stipendiary Magistrate, Manchester. *b.* 17 February 1943 Preston. *m.* 1967 Lorna; two *s. Education:* King George V Grammar School, Southport; Law College, Liverpool. *Career Profile:* Articled in Liverpool & Preston admitted as Solicitor (1967); Senior Partner, Liverpool firm of solicitors (1976-94); Deputy Stipendiary (1992-94); Full-time Stipendiary, Manchester (1994-). *Recreations, Interests:* Reading, gardening, swimming, worrying. *Address:* Manchester City Magistrates' Court, Crown Square, Manchester, M60 1PR.

BERG, Reuben Leonard, LLB(Hons),Solicitor

Senior Partner, Berg & Co, Solicitors. *b.* 7 January 1951 Liverpool. *m.* 1974 Fiona; one *s.* two *d. Education:* Hillfoot Hey Grammar School, Liverpool (1962-69); Manchester University (1969-72). *Career Profile:* Trained at Linder Myers; Assistant, Halliwell

Landau; Established own practice as Berg & Co (1980). *Societies:* Mere Golf Club; Dunham Forrest Golf Club; Manchester Law Society. *Recreations, Interests:* Skiing, walking, cycling, aerobics, food, travel, historical biographies, family, motor racing. *Address:* Berg & Co, Byrom Court, 7 Byrom Street, Manchester, M3 4PF *(tel:* 0161 833 9211; *fax:* 0161 834 5566; *e-mail:* help@berg.co.uk).

BERRY, Paul Karfoot, MA Oxford (1966),FIA (1973)

Principal Assistant Actuary, CIS Ltd; Honorary Secretary, Manchester Statistical Society. *b.* 31 May 1943; Birmingham. *Education:* Calday Grange Grammar School; St Peter's College, Oxford. *Societies:* Manchester Statistical Society (Hon Sec); Manchester Mid-Day Concerts Society (Committee); Manchester Literary & Philosophical Society; Manchester Actuarial Society; Lancashire County Cricket Club; Talyllyn Railway Preservation Society; Havergal Brian Society; Lancashire & Cheshire Cricket Society. *Recreations, Interests:* Opera, music, theatre, cricket, railway preservation, fell-walking. *Address:* CIS Ltd, Miller Street, Manchester M60 0AL *(tel:* 0161 837 4167).

BESTERMAN, Tristram Paul, BA(Hons)(Cantab,1971), MA(1979), FGS(1978), FMus Assoc (1986)

Director, The Manchester Museum. *b.* 19 September 1949 Taplow. *m.* 1977 Perry; two *s.* one *d.* *Public Offices:* Convenor, Museums Association Ethics Committee. *Education:* Stowe School; Cambridge University. *Career Profile:* City Curator, Plymouth Museums and Art Gallery (1985-93); Deputy Curator & Keeper of Geology, Warwickshire Museums Service (1978-85); Asst Keeper, Extension Services, Sheffield City Museum (1974-78); Research Assistant, Geological & Mining Museum, Sydney, Australia. *Publications:* Many articles on museum matters. *Recreations, Interests:* Amateur musician, tennis, gardening. *Address:* The Manchester Museum, The University of Manchester, Oxford Road, Manchester, M13 9PL *(tel:* 0161 275 2650; *fax:* 0161 275 2676; *e-mail:* T.Besterman @man.ac.uk).

BETHELL, John E, DMus (Hon) Scicluna International University Foundation

Music Librarian, BBC Manchester (1961-90); Director, Northern Chamber Orchestra (1987-95); Conductor, BBC Philharmonic Club Choir (1989-). *Career Profile:* Conductor, Oldham Symphony Chorus; Musical Director/Conductor, Oldham Choral Society (1971-) & Manx Festival Chorus (1968-); Member, Isle of Man Arts Council; has conducted many Local Operatic Societies, Orchestras and Brass Bands; Founder, Director, Mannanan International Festival of Music and Arts (1975-); Founder, Director, Latour de France Festival of Music and Arts (1993-); Director, Lionel Tertis International Viola Competition and Workshop (1980-). *Creative Works:* Recording of Manx Folk Songs. *Prizes:* Albert Einstein Academy Bronze Medal (1989); Catenian Assoc. Gold Medal. *Societies:* Sir Arthur Sullivan Society; Vice-President, Rushen Silver Band; Royal Society of Musicians; Patron, Stanley Lewis Society. *Recreations, Interests:* Walking, swimming, gardening, good food. *Address:* B House, Darrag, Port Erin, Isle of Man IM9 6JB *(tel:* 01624 832870).

BHATT, Kanak, BCom,MCT

Finance Director, British Vita plc. *b.* 30 March 1939 Nairobi, Kenya. *m.* 1968 Christine; two *d. Societies:* FRSA. *Recreations, Interests:* Sailing. *Address:* British Vita plc, Middleton, Manchester, M24 2DB *(tel:* 0161 643 1133; *fax:* 0161 653 5411); Whiteoaks, Chester Road, Mere, Cheshire, WA16 6LG *(tel:* 01565 830173).

BIGLEY, Roger Graham, FRNCM, ARAM, MMus(hc)(Keele), NMus(hc)(Sheffield), LRAM

Assistant Head of Strings, Royal Northern College of Music. *b.* 30 October 1943 Gloucester. *m.* 1967 Hilary Hart; two *d. (marr. diss. 1995); m.* 1996 Sandra Maggs. *Public Offices:* Artistic Director, Manchester Chamber Concerts Society; Associate Artistic Director, Lake District Summer Music. *Education:* Crypt Grammar School, Gloucester; Royal Academy of Music, London. *Career Profile:* Lindsay String Quartet (1967-86); BBC Philharmonic Orchestra (1986-89); Royal Northern College of Music (1989-). *Publications/Creative Work:* Recordings of complete Beethoven and Bartok String Quartets; Schubert String Quintet; 3 Quartets by Tippett; Brahms Clarinet Quintet. *Prizes:* Chamber Music of the Year Award (1984) Gramaphone. *Address:* Royal Northern College of Music, 124 Oxford Road, Manchester, M13 9RD *(tel:* 0161 273 6283).

BINDLESS, Richard, TCert(1970),BA(OU,1976),DipManEd(1980)

Chief Executive, Bolton Bury Training & Enterprise Council. *b.* 11 May 1949 Ambleside. *m.* 1970 Susan; one *s.* one *d. Education:* Morecambe Grammar School (1960-67); Didsbury College of Education (1967-70); Open University (1972-76); Sheffield University (1995-). *Career Profile:* Teacher in Secondary Schools (1970-85); Lecturer/Manager in Tertiary College, Bury (1985-92); seconded to BBTEC (1992-93); Deputy Chief Executive, BBTEC (1993-95); Acting Chief Executive, (1995-96); Chief Executive (1996-). *Recreations, Interests:* Sport, rugby of both codes, jogging (slowly), travel, walking. *Address:* Bolton Bury TEC, Clive House, Clive Street, Bolton, BL1 1ET *(tel:* 01204 397350).

BIRCHALL, Stephen Jeremy, MA(Cantab)

Partner, Commercial Property, Vaudreys. *b.* 10 May 1958 Preston, Lancashire. *m.* 1983 Judith; one *s.* two *d. Public Offices:* Deacon, Altrincham Baptist Church; Trustee, City Light Trust. *Education:* Mostyn House School, Wirral; Harrow; Gonville & Caius College, Cambridge; Chester College of Law. *Career Profile:* Trainee, Frere Cholmeley Bischoff, London; Solicitor, Addleshaw Sons & Latham, Manchester; Partner, Vaudreys, Manchester. *Publications/Creative Work:* Various articles and numerous lectures on commercial property. *Prizes:* Sir Winston Churchill Essay Prize. *Societies:* Law Society; Manchester Law Society. *Recreations, Interests:* Piano and keyboards in band, croquet, song writing, inner-city work. *Address:* Vaudreys, 13 Police Street, Manchester, M2 7WA *(tel:* 0161 834 6877; *fax:* 0161 834 2440; *e-mail:* 10071,3605@compuserve.com).

BIRD, Nicholas Charlton Penrhys, OStJ (1991); FCA

Partner, Finlay Robertson, Chartered Accountants, Manchester & Liverpool; Financial Adviser to numerous private companies. *b.* 28 September 1952; Bramhall. *Public Offices:* Honorary Treasurer, Member of Council, Order of St John, Greater Manchester; Financial Adviser, St John Ambulance County Commander's Fund. *Education:* Tre Arddur House School; Malvern College. *Publications:* Several papers on 'The Role of Accountants in Matrimonial Breakdowns & Disputes' and the taxation consequences of divorce and separation. *Societies:* St James's Club. *Address:* Finlay Robertson, Brook House, 77 Fountain Street, Manchester M2 2EE (0161-228 3924); The Mews, The Cedars, Woodbrook Road, Alderley Edge, Cheshire SK9 7DB *(tel:* 01625-585169).

BIRKETT, Ursula Marion *(née* Croome), BA,Diploma in Librarianship

Retired. *b.* 21 July 1936 Claygate, Surrey. *m.* 1958 Peter Lloyd Birkett; two *s.* one *d.* *Education:* Cranborne Chase School; Newnham College, Cambridge; Manchester Polytechnic. *Career Profile:* Chatto & Windus, London; Unilever, London; Northampton Public Library; Portico Library, Manchester; Salford City Libraries. *Publications/Creative Work:* (ed.)'Mildred Minturn' by Leslie Minturn Allison (Shoreline Press, 1995). *Societies:* Portico Library; Buxton Musical Society. *Recreations, Interests:* Books, music, friends, gardening, walking, volunteer work for National Trust. *(tel:* 01663 765561).

BISHOP, Professor Raymond Francis, MA,PhD,CPhys,FInstP,CMath,FIMA

Professor of Theoretical Physics; Head of Department of Physics, UMIST. *b.* 27 August 1945 Berkhamsted. *m.* 1968 Elaine (née Gilbert); two *s. Education:* Haberdashers Aske's Hatcham Boys Grammar School (1956-63); The Queen's College, Oxford University (1963-66); Stanford University, California (1966-71). *Career Profile:* Department of Physics, Manchester University: SRC Research Fellow (1972-73), Research Associate (1973-74), Lecturer in Theoretical Physics (1974-78); Consultant to the Theory Group, Science Research Council Daresbury Laboratory (1974-78); Lawrence Berkeley Laboratory, Staff Scientist (1978-79); Department of Physics, University of California at Berkeley, Lecturer (1978-79); Department of Mathematics, UMISTEL: Lecturer (1979-83), Senior Lecturer (1983-86), Reader (1986-88), Professor of Theoretical Physics (1988-95), Head of Department (1991-94); Department of Physics, UMISTEL: Professor of Theoretical Physics (1995-), Head of Department (1996-). *Publications/Creative Work:* Over 125 publications in professional journals; (co-Editor): 'Condensed Matter Theories' Vols. 2 and 3, 'Recent Progress in Many-Body Theories', Vol.1. *Prizes:* State Scholarship to Oxford University (1963-66); Open Scholarship, The Queen's College, Oxford (1963-66); SRC/NATO Postgraduate Scholarship at Stanford University (1966-69); Fulbright Fellowship (1966-72); SRC Postdoctoral Fellowship (1972-73). *Societies:* Member, The American Physical Society (1978-); International Association of Mathematical Physics (1991-); Chairman, Rusholme and Fallowfield Civic Society (1992-). *Recreations, Interests:* Food, wine, travel, music, conversation and intellectual argument, all aspects of physics and the physical sciences, local affairs. *Address:* Department of Physics, UMIST, PO Box 88, Manchester, M60 1QD *(tel:* 0161 200 3674; *fax:* 0161 200 3669; *e-mail:* R.F.Bishop@umist.ac.uk). *Additional Information:* Chairman, International Selection Cttee for the Eugene Feenberg Memorial Medal in Many-Body Physics (1985-87); Chairman, International Advisory Committee for Recent Progress in Many-Body Theories (1991-); Member, Series Editorial Board of "Condensed Matter Theories"; Member, EPSRC

Physics Programme College (1995-); Member, SERC Nuclear Structure Cttee (1986-89) and Nuclear Physics Subcommittee (1985-90).

BLAIN, Carolyn (*née* Berg), JP(1982)

Chairman, Manchester Civic Society; Director, Cygnet Historic Buildings Trust. *b.* 12 July 1939 Manchester. *m.* 1962 Raymond; two *s. Education:* Stand Grammar School, Whitefield. *Career Profile:* Shoe model, Sheelagh Wilson Model Agency; own secretarial agency (1960-76); involvement with various family businesses (1976-). *Publications:* Article on construction of some historic stables. *Societies:* Manchester Civic Society; Victorian Society; Friends of Stalybridge Station; British Horse Society; Magistrates Association; British Dressage Supporters Club; Medlock & Thame Valley Conservation Society; Manchester Luncheon Club. *Recreations, Interests:* Conservation, tourism, dressage.

BLANK, Stephen Martin, MSc,MA(Oxon),FCA

Director, Lawson Alexander Blank Ltd. *b.* 14 November 1951 Sale, Cheshire. *m.* 1973 Marilyn; one *s.* three *d. Education:* Manchester Grammar School; St John's College, Oxford. *Career Profile:* Partner, BDO Binder Hamlyn (1981-89); Group Planning & Finance Director, Swinton Holdings Ltd (1989-90); Group Chief Executive, Mynshul Group plc (1991); Lawson Alexander Blank Ltd (1992-). *Societies:* Vincents Club, Oxford; St James's Club, Manchester; Institute of Fiscal Studies, North West Branch Committee; Friends of Templeton College, Oxford; Dunham Forest Golf & Country Club. *Recreations, Interests:* Golf, charitable work, family, bridge. *Address:* Lawson Alexander Blank Ltd, Pembroke House, Hawthorn Street, Wilmslow, SK9 5EH (*tel:* 01625 549059; *fax:* 01625 549039; *e-mail:* 100612.3034@compuserve.com); 26 Grey Road, Altrincham, Cheshire, WA14 4BU (*tel:* 0161 928 0324; *fax:* 0161 929 0406; *e-mail:* 100102.1477@compuserve .com).

BLANKS, David Alfred, BA Open,FCII

General Manager, Methodist Insurance plc, Manchester. *b.* 7 January 1937; Clapton, London. *m.* 1959 Doreen Elizabeth; one *d. Education:* Sir George Monoux Grammar School, Walthamstow, London. *Military Service:* National Service RAOC. *Career Profile:* City Fire Manager, Vehicle & General Insurance Co; Fire Superintendent, Bishopgate Insurance Co. *Recreations, Interests:* Local Preacher, Methodist Church and member of several Methodist bodies, DIY, walking. *Address:* Methodist Insurance plc, Brazennose House West, Brazennose Street, Manchester M2 5AS (0161-833 9696); 23 Hollingford Place, Knutsford, Cheshire WA16 9DP (*tel:* 01565-651387).

BLOOM, Charles, QC; LLB (Hons) Manchester (1962)

Barrister; Queen's Counsel. *b.* 6 November 1940; Manchester. *m.* 1967 Janice Rachelle; one *s.* one *d. Public Offices:* Crown Court Recorder; Chairman, Medical Appeal Tribunals. *Education:* Manchester Central Grammar School; Manchester University; College of Law, London. *Societies:* Friedland Postmusaf Tennis. *Recreations, Interests:* Gardening, travel, tennis. *Address:* 28 St John Street, Manchester M2 4DJ (*tel:* 0161-834 8418)

BODMER, Sir Walter Fred, FRS;BA(Cambridge,1956),PhD(Cambridge,1959),FRCPath

Principal, Hertford College, Oxford (1996-); Chancellor, University of Salford (1995-). *b.* 10 January 1936 Frankfurt Am Main, Germany. *m.* 1956 Julia Gwynaeth; two *s.* one *d.* *Public Offices:* Vice-President, The Royal Institution (1981-82); Chairman, BBC Science Consultative Group (1981-87); Trustee of Sir John Soane's Museum (1982-); Trustee, Natural History Museum (1983-93), President (1988-93); President, Royal Statistical Society (1984-85); President, The British Association for the Advancement of Science (1987-88); Trustee, Greater Manchester Museum of Science & Industry (1989-90); President, HUGO (the Human Genome Organisation) (1990-92); First President, IFAAST (International Federation of Assocs for the Advancement of Science & Technology (1992-94); Chancellor, University of Salford (1995-). *Education:* Manchester Grammar School; University of Cambridge. *Career Profile:* Research Fellow (1958-60), Official Fellow (1961) Clare College, Cambridge; Demonstrator, Department of Genetics, University of Cambridge (1960-61); Fellow and Visiting Assistant Professor, Dept of Genetics, Stanford University School of Medicine (1961-62); Assistant Professor (1962-66), Associate Professor (1966-68), Professor (1968-70), Stanford University; Professor of Genetics, University of Oxford (1970-79); Director of Research (1979-91), Director-General (1991-96) Imperial Cancer Research Campaign. *Publications/Creative Work:* 'Genetics of Human Populations'; co-author 'Our Future Inheritance Choice or Chance' (1971); co-author 'Genetics, Evolution and Man' (1974); co-author 'The Book of Man' (1994); over 500 papers. *Prizes:* Numerous awards and honours including; Foreign Honorary Member, American Academy of Arts and Sciences (1972); Fellow of the Royal Society (1974); Foreign Associate, National Academy of Sciences (1981); Hon Fellow, Keble College, Oxford (1981); Hon Fellow, Royal College of Physicians (1985); Hon Fellow, Royal College of Surgeons of England (1986); Hon DSc, University of Oxford (1988); Foreign Member of the American Philosophical Society (1989); Hon Fellow, Clare College, Cambridge (1989); Hon Fellow, Royal Society of Edinburgh (1992); Hon Fellow, Green College, Oxford (1993). *Recreations, Interests:* Piano, horse riding, swimming. *Address:* Hertford College, Oxford, OX1 3BW (*tel:* 01865 279407; *fax:* 01865 279437; *e-mail*: walter.bodmer@hertford.ox.ac).

BOLTON, George Vincent Richard, CEng,FIEE

Retired. *b.* 4 January 1928 Birkenhead. *m.* 1950 Dorothy; two *d.* *Public Offices:* Hon Secretary, Institution of Electrical Engineers, North Western Centre. *Education:* Birkenhead School; Bradford Technical College. *Military Service:* Captain, REME (1947-53). *Career Profile:* Decca Radar Ltd (1953-58); AEI Military Radar Division (1958-68); ICL, West Gorton (1968-91). *Societies:* Bowdon 60 Club. *Recreations, Interests:* Gardening, computing, travel. *Address:* IEE Regional Office, North Gate Office Block, PO Box 137, Trafford Park, Manchester, M60 1AW (*tel:* 0161 872 3024; *fax:* 0161 877 6021); Tanglewood, 12 Churchfields, Bowdon, Altrincham, WA14 3PJ (*tel:* 0161 928 4929).

BONSER, The Rt. Rev. David, MA Manchester (1975),AKC London (1962)

Bishop of Bolton. *b.* 1 February 1934; Huddersfield. *m.* 1960 Shirley; one *s.* two *d.* *Public Offices:* Canon of Manchester Cathedral (1980-82); Area Dean of Hulme (1981-82). *Education:* Hillhouse Secondary School, Huddersfield; Huddersfield Technical College;

King's College, London University; Manchester University. *Career Profile:* Chaplain, Sheffield University; Rector, St Clement's, Chorlton-cum-Hardy; Area Dean, Hulme; Vicar of Rochdale. Archdeacon of Rochdale (1982-91). *Societies:* Royal Commonwealth, London. *Recreations, Interests:* Walking, antiques, reading, music, theatre, golf, skiing. *Address:* 4 Sandfield Drive, Lostock, Bolton (*tel:* 01204 843400).

BOOTH, Arthur Thomas, CBE; FCA

Chairman, Refuge Group plc, J N Nichols (Vimto) plc, Henry Cooke Group plc; Member, Board of Management Cheadle Royal Hospital, Manchester Metropolitan University. *b.* 22 September 1935; Glossop. *m.* 1963 Patricia Alys Julian; one *s.* one *d.* *Education:* St Peter's School, York (1948-53). *Military Service:* Royal Artillery (1959-61). *Career Profile:* Chairman, NW Region Confederation of British Industry (1986-88). *Prizes:* Appointed Accountant Laureate by Founding Societies of Chartered Accountants (1989). *Societies:* St James's Club; Manchester Luncheon Club. *Recreations, Interests:* Golf, gardening, walking. *Address:* Refuge House, Alderley Road, Wilmslow SK9 1PF (*tel:* 01625-535959).

BOOTHMAN, Derek Arnold, FCA

Non-Executive Director, David Glass Associates plc, L Gardner Group plc, Northumbrian Residential Properties plc and others. *b.* 5 June 1932; Manchester. *m.* 1958 Brenda Margaret; one *s.* one *d.* *Public Offices:* Non-Executive Director, Remploy Ltd. *Education:* William Hulme's Grammar School. *Military Service:* National Service, Royal Air Force. *Career Profile:* Senior Partner, Binder Hamlyn Chartered Accountants, North West Region; President, Institute of Chartered Accountants in England and Wales; President, Manchester Society of Chartered Accountants. *Publications:* Many Accountancy publications and articles. *Societies:* St James's Club, Manchester; Withington Golf Club. *Recreations, Interests:* Cricket, football, gardening. *Address:* Ashworth Dene, Wilmslow Road, Mottram St Andrew, Cheshire SK10 4QH (*tel:* 01625-829101).

BOUCHER, Professor Robert Francis, PhD,FEng,FIMechE,MASME,MIEEE,FRSA

Principal and Vice-Chancellor, UMIST. *b.* 25 April 1940 London. *m.* 1966 Rosemary; two *s.* one *d.* *Public Offices:* Director, Higher Education Quality Council; Director, Universities and Colleges Staff Development Agency. *Education:* St Ignatius College, London; Northampton College, London; Borough Polytechnic, London; Nottingham University. *Career Profile:* Graduate Trainee, Central Electricity Generating Board; Research Fellow, Lecturer, Queen's University, Belfast; Lecturer, Senior Lecturer, Professor, Pro-Vice-Chancellor, University of Sheffield. *Publications/Creative Work:* More than 100 scientific publications in learned journals/conference proceedings in the area of Fluid Mechanics. *Societies:* Athaenaeum. *Recreations, Interests:* Hill walking, music, classical and modern novels. *Address:* UMIST, PO Box 88, Sackville Street, Manchester, M60 1QD (*tel:* 0161 200 4010; *fax:* 0161 236 7219; *e-mail:* r.boucher@umist.ac.uk).

BOULTON, Professor Andrew James Michael MB BS(Hons)(Newcastle-upon-Tyne, 1976),MD(Newcastle-upon-Tyne,1985),FRCP(London,1992), MRCP(UK)(1979)

Professor of Medicine, University of Manchester; Consultant Physician (Diabetes),

Manchester Royal Infirmary. *b.* 21 February 1953 Nottingham. *m.* 1976 Helen Frances Robson; one *s.* two *d.* *(separated 1995) Education:* Nottingham High School (1961-71); Newcastle-upon-Tyne University (1971-76). *Career Profile:* Research Fellow, Senior Registrar, Sheffield University Hospitals (1980-86); Visiting Assistant Professsor of Diabetes, University of Miami, USA (1983-84); Senior Lecturer (1986), Reader (1991), Professor of Medicine (1995), Manchester University. *Publications/Creative Work:* Author of over 200 papers and 5 books on diabetes and its complications. *Prizes:* RD Lawrence Lecturer, British Diabetic Association (1990); Shri Prakesh Diabetes Prize, University of Madras, India (1990); R Pecoraro Memorial Lecturer, American Diabetes Association (1996). *Societies:* Member, British European, American and International Diabetes Associations; Chairman of Postgraduate Education, European Diabetes Association. *Recreations, Interests:* Church bellringing, classical music. *Address:* Department of Medicine, Manchester Royal Infirmary, Oxford Road, Manchester, M13 9WL *(tel:* 0161 276 4452; *fax:* 0161 274 4740).

BOULTON, (Frances) Ann *(née* Gwillim)

North West Fundraising Co-ordinator, Turning Point. *b.* 11 October 1938; Aldershot, Surrey. *m.* 1960 Roger Boulton; one *s.* one *d.* *(marr. diss. 1971) Public Offices:* Parish Councillor; Chairman, Hayfield Parish Council (1989, 1990, 1995); Hon Secretary, Manchester Luncheon Club (1984-96). *Education:* Maude Allan School, Littlehampton, Sussex; Preston Technical College, Brighton. *Military Service:* WRNS (1956-60); PO Wren, Senior Stenographer; AOF Earl Mountbatten of Burma. *Career Profile:* Sales Manager, Carcanet Press; Admin Secretary, Manchester Literary & Philosophical Society; Medical Secretary, National Guard, King Khalid Hospital, Jeddah; Daily Mail; own guest house; Personal Assistant, Lord Bowden, UMIST; Personal Assistant, Lord Selkirk, UK Commissioner for Singapore and UK Commissioner-General for South East Asia. *Publications:* Editor, 'Bushwhackers' and Landtrekkers' Guide to Eastern Saudi Arabia'. *Societies:* Manchester Luncheon Club; Manchester Statistical Society; Manchester Literary & Philosophical Society; Hon Life Patron, Hayfield Sheepdog Trials. *Recreations, Interests:* Gardening, people and living life to the full. *Address:* 157 Kinder Road, Hayfield, High Peak, Derbyshire SK12 5LE.

BOYD, Professor Robert David Hugh, MA,MB,BChir (Cantab),FRCP,MSc (hc)(Univ. of Manchester)

Principal, St George's Hospital Medical School, London. *b.* 14 May 1938 Cambridge. *m.* 1966 Meriel Cornelia; one *s.* two *d. Education:* Clare College, Cambridge; University College Hospital Medical School, London. *Career Profile:* Senior Lecturer, University College London; Visiting Professor, Oregon Health Sciences University; Assistant Registrar, Royal College of Physicians (1979-80); Professor of Paediatrics, University of Manchester (1981-96); Dean of Medicine, University of Manchester (1989-93); Chair, Manchester Health Authority (1994-96); Chair, National Primary Care Research and Development Centre (1994-96); Chair, Academic Board, British Paediatric Association (88-90). *Publications/Creative Work:* Editor *Placenta* (1989-96); 'Placental Transport' (co-editor, 1981); 'Perinatal Medicine' (co-editor, 1983); 'Paediatric Problems in General Practice' (co-author, 3rd ed, 1996). *Prizes:* Goldschmidt Travelling Fellowship (MRC)(1970-71); Entrance Scholarship, University College Hospital (1959). *Societies:*

Scientific and medical societies. *Address:* St George's Hospital Medical School, Cranmer Terrace, London, SW17 0RE(*tel:* 0181 725 5008; *fax:* 0181 672 6940); The Stone House, Adlington, Macclesfield, SK10 4NU (*tel:* 01625 872400).

BRACEGIRDLE, Cyril

Author. *b.* 23 December 1920; Moston, Manchester. *m.* 1977 Lili Dyfyr Roberts. *Education:* Private. *War Service:* Home Guard. *Career Profile:* Engineering Buyer (1950-80). *Publications:* Books: 'A First Book of Antiques'; 'Zoos are News'; 'The Dark River'; 'Collecting Railway Antiques'; magazine and newspaper articles; short stories; one-act plays. *Societies:* Society of Authors. *Recreations, Interests:* Walking, live theatre, antiques. *Address:* 7 Langdale Road, off Eastway, Sale, Cheshire M33 4EN (*tel:* 0161-973 6215).

BRADLEY, Keith John Charles, BA(Hons)(MMU),MPhil(York University),Diploma in Accountancy

Member of Parliament, Manchester Withington. *b.* 17 May 1950 Warwickshire. *m.* 1987 Rhona; two *s.* one *d.* *Public Offices:* Councillor, Manchester City Council (1983-88). *Education:* Bishop Vesey's Grammar School, Sutton Coldfield (1961-69); Aston University (1969-70); Manchester Metropolitan University (1973-76); York University (1976-78). *Career Profile:* Accountant (1969-73); Research Officer, Manchester City Council (1978-81); Chief Officer, Stockport Community Health Council (1981-87); Member of Parliament, Manchester Withington (1987-). *Publications/Creative Work:* Various articles in newspapers and journals. *Societies:* Labour Party; Cooperative Party and a number of voluntary organisations. *Recreations, Interests:* Sport, food and drink, theatre, cinema. *Address:* 509 Wilmslow Road, Withington, Manchester, M20 3BA (*tel:* 0161 446 2047; *fax:* 0161 445 5543).

BRADY, Mark David, LLB (Hons),ACA,AMSI

Director, Wise Speke Ltd. *b.* 23 September 1961. *m.* 1990 Susan Jayne; one *s.* one *d.* *Education:* Chislehurst & Sidcup Grammar School; University of Leeds. *Career Profile:* KPMG (1983-88); Thomas Coombs/Stoy Hayward (1988); Charlton Seal Schaverien/Wise Speke Ltd (1988-90); Manchester Exchange & Investment Bank Ltd (1990-91); Wise Speke Ltd (1991-). *Societies:* St James's Club, Manchester. *Address:* Wise Speke Ltd, PO Box 512, 8 King Street, Manchester, M60 2EP (*tel:* 0161 953 9700; *fax:* 0161 832 1672).

BRANDON, Professor Peter Samuel, DSc,MSC,FRICS

Pro-Vice-Chancellor, Research & Graduate Studies, Professor of Quantity & Building Surveying, University of Salford. *b.* 4 June 1943 *m.* 1968 Mary Ann Elizabeth Canham; one *s.* two *d.* *Public Offices:* Member of the Council, University Parliamentary Group; Member, EPSRC IMI Programme Sector Target Advisory Group for Construction. *Education:* Bournemouth Grammar School; Bristol University. *Career Profile:* Private practice and local government (1963-69); Lecturer, Portsmouth Polytechnic (1969-73); Principal Lecturer, Bristol Polytechnic (1973-81); Head of Department, Portsmouth Polytechnic (1981-85); Chairman, Surveying Department, University of Salford (1985-93) Pro-Vice-Chancellor (1993-). *Publications/Creative Work:* 'Cost Planning of Buildings'

(6th edn 1990); (ed.) 'Building Cost Techniques' (1982); 'Microcomputers in Building Appraisal' (1983); (ed.) 'Quality and Profit in Building Design' (1984); 'Computer programs for Building Cost Appraisal' (1985); 'Building Costs Modelling and Computers' (1987); 'Expert Systems: the strategic planning of constructions projects' (1988); (ed.) 'Investment, Procurement & Performance in Construction' (1991); (ed.) 'Management Quality and Economics in Building' (1991). *Societies:* Royal Institution of Chartered Surveyors, Chairman of various committees. *Recreations, Interests:* Horse riding, walkng, travel, modern art, swimming, caravanning. *Address:* Department of Surveying, University of Salford, Salford, M5 4WT *(tel:* 0161 745 5839; *fax:* 0161 745 5164; *e-mail:* P.S. Brandon@surveying.salford.ac.uk).

BREAKELL, John Cunliffe, FRICS

Managing Director, Raab Karcher Properties. *b.* 16 May 1936; Timperley, Altrincham, Cheshire. *m.* 1962 Margaret; two *d. Education:* New College School, Oxford (1946-49); Shrewsbury School (1949-54). *Military Service:* National Service, Royal Artillery (1954-56). *Career Profile:* Articled Pupil, W H Robinson & Co (1956-59); Assistant, WH Robinson & Co (1959-62); Assistant, G F Singleton & Co (1962-67); Partner, G F Singleton & Co (1967-89). *Societies:* Past Chairman, Greater Manchester Branch, Royal Institution of Chartered Surveyors, General Practice Division; Manchester Society of Land Agents and Surveyors; St James's Club; 1925 Club; Manchester Luncheon Club. *Recreations, Interests:* Music, bowls. *Address:* Raab Karcher (UK) plc, South Langworthy Road, Salford M5 2PX *(tel:* 0161-737 0932); 8 Manor Road, Wilmslow, Cheshire SK9 5PU.

BRENNAN, Charles Anthony Beresford

Chairman, Walkden Warehousing Ltd; Chairman, Manchester City Magistrates Court (1994-96). *b.* 26 May 1934 Didsbury, Manchester. *m.* 1958 Mary Louise Hendrick; three *d. Education:* Avisford School, Arundel; Ampleforth College, York. *Military Service:* National Service Commission, Grenadier Guards. *Career Profile:* Trainee Manager, family textile concern; various sales managerships, directorships; subsequently into clothing industry, became Public Warehouse Keeper (1978-). *Societies:* First Guards Club; Grenadier Guards Old Comrades; South Caernarvonshire Yacht Club; Wallasey Yacht Club; Wyresdale Anglers. *Recreations, Interests:* Fishing, sailing, shooting. *Address:* Walkden Warehousing Ltd, Unit 3, Orion Trade Centre, Tenax Road, Trafford Park, Manchester, M17 1JT*(tel:* 0161 848 7684; *fax:* 0161 877 5373); North Wing, Hoghton Tower, Preston, PR5 0SH *(tel:* 01254 852301).

BRIERLEY, Ronald, OBE (1984),MM (1945),Croix de Guerre (1944),Mentioned in Despatches 3 times; Hon LLD (Manchester)

Chairman, Insurance Brokers Registration Council (1987-91); Member of Court, University of Manchester. *b.* 31 July 1921; Oldham. *m.* 1950 Mary Barlow; one *s. Public Offices:* JP, Manchester (1961); Treasurer, University of Manchester (1983-88); St Ann's Hospice Council; Industrial Adviser, Design Council; Past Hon Treasurer, Manchester Chamber of Commerce; Past President, Manchester Junior Chamber; Lay Member, Chartered Accountants' Disciplinary Committee. *Education:* Oldham High School. *War Service:* Army (1940-46) The Border Regt, RTR, SOE. Parachuted twice into occupied

France and similarly in Burma. *Career Profile:* Various Appointments in Insurance from 1938; Deputy Chairman, Sedgwick UK Ltd (1977-81); Insurance Brokers Registration Council (1981-93); Corporation of Insurance Brokers NW, Secretary (1950-58) Chairman (1962-64). *Societies:* Founder Chairman, GM Outward Bound Assoc.; Past President, Manchester Luncheon Club; Chairman, Trustee and Past President, The Manchester Club. *Address:* 52 Trafford Road, Alderley Edge, Cheshire SK9 7DN (*tel:* 01625 585273).

BRIGGS, Patrick David, MA Cantab.

Head Master, William Hulme's Grammar School. *b.* 24 August 1940; Timperley, Cheshire. *m.* 1968 Alicia Dorothy Mary O'Donnell; two *s.* one *d.* *Education:* Pocklington School (1951-59); Christ's College, Cambridge (1960-64). *Career Profile:* Assistant Master, (1965-87), Senior Housemaster, Bedford School (1983-87). *Publications:* 'The Parents' Guide to Independent Schools'. *Societies:* Headmasters' Conference; Cheshire and Lancashire CCC's; Manchester FC; Chorlton-cum-Hardy and Anglesey Golf Club. *Recreations, Interests:* Cricket, rugby, golf, poetry, theatre, cinema. *Address:* William Hulme's Grammar School, Spring Bridge Road, Manchester M16 8PR (*tel:* 0161-226 2054); "Dunoon", 254 Wilbraham Road, Manchester M16 8GN.

BRILL, Barbara Gladys (*née* Lamb)

Housewife and Free-Lance Writer. *b.* 28 November 1910; Acton, London. *m.* 1933 Eric William Brill *decd* 1980; two *s.* one *d.* *Education:* Haberdashers' Aske's Girls School, Acton. *War Service:* Caring for billeted Airmen from Maintenance Unit Handforth. *Previous Positions:* Poultry Farm Assistant (1930-33); Teacher of Creative Writing at Adult Education Centres - WEA, Cheadle Hulme and Wilmslow Guild; Free Lance Journalist writing regularly (1955-80) for 'Stockport Advertiser' and 'Cheshire Life' on Local History and Countryside. *Creative Works:* Play 'Valiant in Velvetel: A Stage Study of R L Stevenson'; writer of lunchtime entertainment scripts for National Portrait Gallery; many radio scripts for BBC. *Publications:* 'Life of R L Stevenson' and 'Life of Mrs Gaskell' (Ladybird Books); 'Walks from the Car in East Cheshire' (Dalesman); 'Remembering in Rhyme' (Stockport Historical Society); 'Centenary of Macclesfield Public Library' (Cheshire Museums & Libraries); 'William Gaskell: A Portrait' (Manchester Lit & Phil Soc). *Prizes:* 1st Prize in Stockport Writers' Circle Annual Literary Competition (1971, 1984, 1986). *Societies:* Stockport Writers' Circle; Gaskell Society, Founder Member and Member of the Journal's Editorial Board; Portico Library. *Recreations, Interests:* Reading, writing, local history, walking, gardening, the theatre, knitting. *Address:* 12 Thorn Road, Bramhall, Stockport, Cheshire SK7 1HQ (*tel:* 0161-439 2486).

BROADBENT, Herbert Henry, OBE (1955),TD (1945),DL (1974)

Consultant. *b.* 26 April 1914; Slough. *m.* 1938 Mary; one *d.* *Education:* Ashton-under-Lyne Grammar School. *War Service:* Commissioned 9BN Manchester Regt TA (1933); Served in Europe, Sudan, Eritrea and Burma; Mentioned in Despatches (1946); Promoted Colonel (1957). *Career Profile:* Chairman, Steel Castings Research & Trade Association (1975). *Societies:* Liveryman; Worshipful Company of Founders; Vice President, Prestbury Branch, Royal British Legion. *Address:* Glebe House, Prestbury Village, Macclesfield, Cheshire SK10 4DG (*tel:* 01625-827734).

BROCKLEHURST, Alastair Robin, FRICS,IRRV

Regional Managing Partner, Grimley. *b.* 29 June 1944 Oldham. *m.* 1974 Jane Kathleen; two *s.* *Public Offices:* Past Chairman, Royal Institution of Chartered Surveyors (Greater Manchester Branch); Chairman, Professional Firms Group, Business in the Community; Member, Corporation City College, Manchester; Chairman, Policing & Safety Group, City Centre Steering Committee. *Education:* Hulme Grammar School, Oldham. *Career Profile:* Railton & Knowles, Manchester (1964-69); Grimley, Birmingham (1970-79), Manchester (1979-); Chairman, RICS Business Support Panel; Member, RICS Education & Membership Committee. *Societies:* Royal Institution of Chartered Surveyors; St James Club; Institute of Rating & Revenue Valuers; Lymm Golf Club; Lymm 41 Club. *Recreations, Interests:* Golf, rugby. *Address:* Grimley, 81 Fountain Street, Manchester, M2 2EE (*tel:* 0161 956 4300; *fax:* 0161 956 4008).

BROOK, Clive Matthew, FCA

Director, Corporate Finance, Pannell Kerr Forster, Manchester. *b.* 9 May 1950 Taplow, Bucks. *m.* Marjorie. *Education:* Farnham Grammar School. *Career Profile:* Pannell Kerr Forster (1994-); Independent Corporate Financier (1992-94); 3i plc, latterly as Director responsible for regional operation (1981-92); various commercial positions (1973-81); Clarm Whitehill, Chartered Accountants (1968-73). *Recreations, Interests:* Music, sport. *Address:* Pannell Kerr Forster, Sovereign House, Queen Street, Manchester, M2 5HR (*tel:* 0161 832 5481; *fax:* 0161 832 3849).

BROWN, Dr Alan Geoffrey, MB,ChB(Manchester,1960),DRCOG(1963), MRCGP(1971)

Retired General Medical Practitioner. *b.* 7 November 1935 Manchester. *m.* 1968 Meriel; two *s.* one *d.* *Education:* George Heriots School, Edinburgh; Leigh Grammar School; Manchester University. *Career Profile:* House Surgeon, House Physician, Trafford General Hospital (1961-62); General Practitioner, NHS (1963-95); Past Member, Salford Local Medical Committee (Chairman 1983-86). *Societies:* Swinton & Pendlebury Rotary Club; Swinton Park Golf Club; Manchester Jazz Society; Club Doctor, Salford RLFC. *Recreations, Interests:* Golf, jazz, rugby league. *Address:* 2 Woodstock Drive, Worsley, Manchester, M28 2WW (*tel:* 0161 728 2769) (*e-mail:* agb@worsley.u-net.com).

BROWN, Stewart Martin, Sloan Fellow, London Business School

Chief Executive, BWI plc. *b.* 23 March 1944 London. *m.* Christine; two *d.* *Education:* Rugby School; The Polytechnic, Regent Street, London; London Business School. *Career Profile:* Various management positions, Stone Platt Industries (1963-78); Managing Director, Barry Wehmiller Ltd (1978-87); Director, Barry Wehmiller Co, St Louis, USA (1984-87); Chief Executive, BWI plc (1987-). *Recreations, Interests:* Walking, sailing, skiing, fishing, music. *Address:* BWI plc, PO Box 95, Atlantic Street, Altrincham, WA14 5EW (*tel:* 0161 925 5000; *fax:* 0161 926 8654).

BRUMHEAD, Derek Derwent, BA (Southampton, 1955), MEd (Manchester, 1981), MA (Manchester Polytechnic, 1986)

Part-time Administrator, New Mills Heritage & Information Centre; Part-time Tutor,

CDCE, Manchester University; WEA. *b.* 19 April 1930 Woolwich. *m.* 1966 Ann Smith; one *s.* one *d. (marr. diss. 1976)*; *m.* 1977 Alice Sik Yin Wu; one *s. Public Offices:* Secretary, Manchester Geological Association (1974-96); Chairman, New Mills Local History Society (1989-92). *Education:* Dartford Grammar School (1941-49); Southampton University (1951-56); Manchester University (part-time, 1978-81, 1989-96); Manchester Polytechnic (part-time 1983-86). *Career Profile:* Head of Department of Geography, Gosport Grammar School (1956-63); Assistant Warden, Orielton Field Centre (1963-65); Tutor, College of Adult Education, Manchester (1965-77); Head, North Hulme Community Education Centre (1977-83). *Publications/Creative Work:* 'Geology Explained in the Yorkshire Dales and on the Yorkshire Coast' (David and Charles)(1979); 'A Walk Round All Saints' (with Terry Wyke)(Manchester Polytechnic)(1987); 'A Walk Round Castlefield' (with Terry Wyke)(Manchester Polytechnic)(1989); 'A Walk Round Manchester Statues' (with Terry Wyke)(Walkround Books)(1990); 'Cumbrian Industrial Archaeology' (with David George)(1989); Various booklets and articles on Local History in and around New Mills including 'New Mills, 1894-1994' (Editor). *Societies:* Hon Member, Manchester Geological Association; Manchester Region Industrial Archaeology Society; Association of Industrial Archaeology; Geologists' Association; Yorkshire Geological Society; New Mills Local History Society; New Mills Natural History Society. *Recreations, Interests:* Geology, local history, industrial archaeology, collecting Penguin Books and Haydn Quartets, visiting Cumbria and Las Vegas. *Address:* New Mills Heritage & Information Centre, Rock Mill Lane, New Mills, via Stockport, SK12 3BN(*tel:* 01663 746904); Gayton, Laneside Road, New Mills, via Stockport, SK12 4LU (*tel:* 01663 744863).

BUCKLEY, Group Captain Jack

Retired. *b.* 19 January 1922; Leicester. *m.* 1942 Penny Simpson; one *s.* one *d. Public Offices:* Deputy Lieutenant, Greater Manchester (1987); Member, Executive Council, Broughton House; Director, Greater Manchester Community Trust, SSAFA. *Education:* Loughborough Junior College. *War Service:* RAF (1938-1975), overseas service in Iceland, Malaya, Singapore, Cyprus and Belgium. *Career Profile:* Bursar, Royal Northern College of Music (1975-78); Secretary, St Ann's Hospice (1978-1986). *Societies:* Rotary International; SHAPE Officers' Association; Bollin Club; Manchester Naval Officers' Association. *Recreations, Interests:* Travel, theatre, music. *Address:* 10 Summerfield Place, Wilmslow, Cheshire SK9 1NE (*tel:* 01625-531227).

BUCKLEY, John Spencer

Managing Director, PDA Partnership Ltd. *b.* 28 June 1943; Southport, Lancs. *m.* 1977 Susan Janet Maslin; one *d.* one *stepd. Public Offices:* Chairman, Executive Committee, East Manchester Partnership; Chairman, Heywood District Scout Council; Director, Manchester Chamber of Commerce & Industry; Advisor to the Board, Greater Manchester Visitor & Convention Bureau. *Education:* Heywood Grammar School; Wigan and District Mining and Technical College; Liverpool College of Building. *Previous Positions:* Architectural appointments with Eric Levy and Partners, Oldham and Rochdale Borough Councils, Ardin and Brookes and Partners. *Societies:* The St James's Club; Lancashire County Cricket Club; Bury Football Club; Heywood Civic Society. *Recreations, Interests:* Football, cricket, reading, theatre, walking. *Address:* PDA Partnership Ltd, St Andrews

House, 62 Bridge Street, Manchester M3 3BW (*tel:* 0161-832 2393); "Greenbank", 7 Newhouse Road, Heywood, Lancs OL10 2NR (*tel:* 01706-365677).

BUIST, Jack Mitchell, BSc(Hons) St Andrews (1940),DTech(hc) Loughborough (1982), CPhys, FInstP, HonFIM

Proprietor, Abelard Management Consultancy; Editor, Cellular Polymers. *b.* 16 June 1918; Leven, Fife. *m.* 1944 Eloise Joyce Mercer Millar; one *s.* two *d. Public Offices:* Board of Visitors Strangeways Prison (1978-88), Chairman (1983-86); Member, NEDO Chemicals EDC Study Group Thermosetting Plastics (1969-72); Chairman, Advisory Board Institute Polymer Technology and Mechanical Engineering (1976-93); Member Visiting Committee, Cranfield Institute of Technology (1977-1983). *Education:* Buckhaven High School; St Andrews University. *War Service:* Home Guard. *Career Profile:* ICI Dyestuffs Division (1940-76) Head Application Research and Technical Service Department, Business Area Manager for Rubber Chemicals and Polyurethanes; Director, Anchor Chemical Co (1976-79); Chairman, ISOTC/45 (1957-64); Chairman, Institution Rubber Industry Council (1969-70) and (1972-75); Plastics and Rubber Institute Chairman of Council (1975-76), President (1977-79). *Publications:* Monograph 'Ageing and Weathering' (1956); Editor, 7 books; published many technical papers, 20 Patents. *Prizes:* 12th Foundation Lecture Inst. Rubber Industry (1957); 10 medals from Internation Organisations. Hon President, Internation Rubber Conference Organisation; 3rd man to be inducted to Polyurethane Hall of Fame, USA. *Societies:* The Caledonian Club; Lancashire County Cricket Club. *Recreations, Interests:* Music, theatre, photography, history of polymer industry. *Address:* Abelard Management Consultancy, Bank House, 266/8 Chapel Street, Salford M3 3JZ (*tel:* 01625-529990); Kingslea, Cliff Side, Wilmslow, Cheshire SK9 4AF (*tel:* 01625-522954).

BULLAS, John Laurence

Education Correspondent, Manchester Evening News. *b.* 31 August 1935; Cannock, Staffs. *m.* 1958 Sylvia Joan; four *d. Public Offices:* Leader, Bury MBC (1986-88); Councillor, Bury CB (1971-74); Councillor, Bury MB (1973-94). *Education:* Rugeley Grammar School, Staffs. *Military Service:* National Service RAF (1953-55). *Societies:* Royal Society for Protection of Birds; National Trust. *Recreations, Interests:* non-stipendiary Methodist Minister,walking, music, school governor, Bury FC Supporter.

BURDEKIN, Professor Frederick Michael, MA(Cantab),MSc(Manchester),PhD(Cantab), FEng, FRS,FICE,FIMechE, FInstNDT,FIStructE,FWeldI

Professor of Civil and Structural Engineering, UMIST. *b.* 5 February 1938; Hawarden, Clwyd, N Wales. *m.* 1965 Jennifer Meadley; two *s. Education:* The King's School, Chester; Trinity Hall, Cambridge - 1st Class Hons. Mech. Sciences Tripos. *Career Profile:* The Welding Institute (1961-68); Messrs Sandberg (1968-77); Vice Principal, UMIST (1983-85); Deputy Principal, UMIST (1984). *Publications:* Various research publications, particularly on fracture and fatigue in welded structures; I.Mech.E. John Player Lecture (1981). *Prizes:* Ludwig Mond (1971); I.Mech.E. James Clayton (1981); ICE James Alfred Ewing Medal (1995). *Societies:* Macclesfield Cricket Club. *Recreations, Interests:* Research into structural behaviour, music, sport and problem solving. *Address:* UMIST,

Department of Civil and Structural Engineering, PO Box 88, Manchester M60 1QD (*tel:* 0161-200 4600); 27 Springbank, Bollington, Macclesfield, Cheshire SK10 5LQ.

BURDEN, Arthur James

Chairman, W T Burden Ltd; Senior Partner, Beever and Struthers. *b.* 26 January 1926 Birmingham. *m.* 1959 Sheila Sixsmith; three *s.* one *d. Public Offices:* Chairman, National Library for the Blind (1996-); Chairman of Governors, Royce County Primary School; Deputy Chairman, Manchester Prison Visitors Centre; Hon Treasurer, Manchester Citizens Advice Bureaux; Hon Treasurer, Manchester & Salford Methodist Mission; Past President, Manchester Society of Chartered Accountants. *Education:* Colwyn Bay Grammar School; Chorlton-cum-Hardy High School. *Military Service:* Royal Air Force (1951-53). *Societies:* Whalley Range Methodist Church. *Recreations, Interests:* Gardening, caravaning, table-tennis, cycling, church organist. *Address:* St George's House, 215-219 Chester Road, Manchester, M15 4JE (*tel:* 0161 832 4901).

BURGESS, Derek, BA(Hons)

Head of Northern Corporate Banking, Svenska Handelsbanken. *b.* 10 February 1951 Johannesburg, South Africa. *Education:* University of Natal, Durban, South Africa. *Career Profile:* Various banking positions (1975-90); Svenska Handelsbanken (1990-). *Address:* Svenska Handelsbanken, St John's Court, 66 Quay Street, Manchester, M3 3EJ (*tel:* 0161 839 0568; *fax:* 0161 839 0570).

BURKE, John Kenneth, QC, Called to Bar (Middle Temple) (1965); Circuit Judge (1995)

Queen's Counsel (1985); Recorder of the Crown Court (1980). *b.* 4 August 1939; Stockport. *m.* 1962 Margaret Anne Scattergood; three *d. Education:* Stockport Grammar School. *Military Service:* Cheshire Regt (1958-60); Parachute Regt (TA) (1963-67). *Recreations, Interests:* Drawing and painting, skiing. *Address:* Courts of Justice, Crown Square, Manchester M3 3FL.

BURNIE, Professor James Peter, MA,MSc,MD,PhD,MRCP,MRCPath

Professor of Medical Microbiology, Head of Department of Pathological Sciences, Manchester University; Clinical Director of Departments of Clinical Bacteriology & Virology, Central Manchester Healthcare Trust. *b.* 17 August 1956 Rotherham, Yorkshire. *m.* 1981 Ruth Matthews; two *s. Education:* Epsom College (1970-74); Selwyn College, Cambridge (1974-77); St Thomas' Hospital, London (1977-80). *Career Profile:* Senior Lectureship, St Bartholomew's Hospital; Lister Fellow. *Publications/Creative Work:* Published over 100 papers; filed patents on the Fungal Heat Shock Proteins Pack Antigen of Streptococci & Helicobacter Pylori Urease. *Societies:* Member of the American Society of Microbiology. *Address:* 2nd Floor, Clinical Sciences Building, Manchester Royal Infirmary, Oxford Road, Manchester, M12 9WL(*tel:* 0161 276 4280; *fax:* 0161 276 8826); 1 Greystoke Drive, Alderley Edge, Cheshire (*tel:* 01625 590386). *Additional Information:* Research interests are in epidemiology, early diagnosis and treatment of systematic fungal infections (sytematic candidiasis and invasive aspergillosis). The diagnosis and management

of cases of culture negative and culture positive endocarditis. The immunodominant antigens of streptococci.

BURNS, Anthony

Chair, Highways & Cleansing, Manchester City Council. *b.* 19 December 1940 Sunderland, Co Durham. *m.* Sheila. *Education:* St Joseph's RC School, Sunderland; Newcastle College of Further Education; Plater College, Oxford; Manchester Polytechnic. *Career Profile:* Gas Board (Northern); Trade Union (GMB); Union Solicitors. *Societies:* RAFA; KSC. *Recreations, Interests:* Canal boating, flying. *Address:* 39 Paulden Avenue, Baguley, Manchester, M23 1PH (*tel:* 0161 998 5784) (*fax:* 0161 945 8739).

BURNS, Joan, MBE (1994)

Part-time Lecturer, Manchester University CDCE Dept; Visiting Lecturer at Alston Hall, Preston, Pendrell Hall, Staffs, Higham Hall, Cumbria, 'The Hill', Abergavenny; Founder & Director of the Manchester Music Lovers; Pianist - giving recitals here and in USA. *b.* Manchester. *Education:* Manchester Central Grammar School for Girls; Manchester University; Piano Study with Louis Kentner. *Societies:* Incorporated Society of Musicians; Hallé Concerts Society; Manchester Chamber Concerts Society. *Recreations, Interests:* Literature & drama, theatre & film going, foreign travel, Siamese cats. *Address:* 24 Howard Road, Northenden, Manchester M22 4EG (*tel:* 0161-998 3715).

BURNS, Julian Delisle

Joint Managing Director, Granada Television; Managing Director, Divisional Operations, Granada Media Group. *m.* 1975 Cheryl; one *s.* one *d. Education:* Haberdashers Askes' School, Elstree. *Career Profile:* Manager, EL Mendel Ltd (1968-72); Professional Musician (1972-76); Granada Television Ltd (1976-). *Societies:* Royal Television Society. *Recreations, Interests:* Reading, music, walking, the Lake District. *Address:* Granada Television, Quay Street, Manchester, M60 9EA (*tel:* 0161 827 2090; *fax:* 0161 953 0282).

BURROWS, Robert (Bob), BA(Hons)

Deputy Agent, Bank of England, Manchester. *b.* 13 February 1953 Iver Heath, Bucks. *m.* 1975 Pauline Anne; two *s. Education:* Castleford Grammar School (1964-71); Lanchester Polytechnic (1971-74). *Career Profile:* Joined Bank of England, London (1974-); Accountants Department (1974-75); Overseas Department (1975-78); Exchange Control Department (1978-79); Banking Department (1980-91); Seconded to Berkshire & Southern Bucks Local Enterprise Agency (1991-93); Manchester Branch (1994-95); Deputy Agent, Industrial Liaison Group, Manchester Branch (1995-). *Recreations, Interests:* All types of music, reading, walking, swimming, tennis, cycling. *Address:* Bank of England, PO Box 301, Manchester, M60 2HP (*tel:* 0161 237 5609; *fax:* 0161 228 0088).

BURSLEM, Alexandra Vivien (*née* Thornley), OBE(1993); BA(Hons)(Manchester, 1971), DipBA,MBS(1986),FRSA(1989)

Deputy Vice-Chancellor, Manchester Metropolitan University. *b.* 6 May 1940 Shanghai, China. *m.* 1960 two *s.* (*marr. diss. 1971*); *m.* 1977 Richard Waywell Burslem; one *d.* one

35

steps. Public Offices: JP, Inner Manchester Bench (1981-); Board Member, Anchor Trust (1995-), Chairman, Manchester & Cheshire Anchor Trust (1995-); Member, Board of Governors, Eccles College (1996-); Former Chairman, BBC Regional Advisory Council (1983-92); Former Member, Vice-Chairman, Manchester FPC (1974-89). *Education:* Arnold High School for Girls, Blackpool (1951-58); University of Manchester (1968-73); Manchester Business School (1984-87). *Career Profile:* Lecturer (1973-82); Head of Department (1982-86); Dean of Faculty (1986-88); Academic Director (1988-92), Manchester Polytechnic; Deputy Vice-Chancellor (1992-), Manchester Metropolitan University. *Societies:* Manchester Literary & Philosophical Society; Royal Society of Arts. *Recreations, Interests:* Opera, theatre. *Address:* The Manchester Metropolitan University, All Saints, Manchester, M15 6BH (*tel:* 0161 247 1020; *fax:* 0161 247 6311; *e-mail:* a.v.burslem@mmu.ac.uk); Lone Oak, Mereside Road, Mere, Knutsford, WA16 6QR (*tel:* 01565 830100; *fax:* 01565 830790).

BURT, Alistair James Hendrie, BA Oxford (1977)

MP Bury North (1983-); Parliamentary Private Secretary to The Rt Hon Kenneth Baker MP. *b.* 25 May 1955; Manchester. *m.* 1983 Eve Alexandra; one *s.* one *d. Public Offices:* Councillor, Haringey (1982-84). *Education:* Bury Grammar School; St John's College, Oxford; Chester College of Law. *Career Profile:* Articled Clerk, Slater Heelis & Co, Manchester (1977-80); Secretary, Conservative NW MPs Group (1983-88). *Societies:* Friend of the Royal Academy; Friend of the Tate Gallery; Vice President, Lancashire Federation of Conservative Clubs. *Recreations, Interests:* Modern art, football, Christianity and church affairs, family life. *Address:* House of Commons, London SW1A 0AA (0171-219 3527).

BURTON, David John, BA Oxon (1966),Solicitor (admitted 1969)

Chief Executive, Metropolitan Borough of Bury. *b.* 31 December 1944; Oldham, Lancs. *m.* 1971 two *s. Education:* Manchester Grammar School (1956-63); The Queen's College, Oxford (1963-66); The College of Law, Guildford (1968-69). *Career Profile:* Assistant Solicitor, Manchester Corporation (1969-73); Principal Solicitor then Acting County Legal Officer, Greater Manchester Council (1973-86); Deputy Chief Executive, Metropolitan Borough of Bury (1986-88). *Address:* Town Hall, Bury BL9 0SW (0161-253 5000).

BURTON, Gordon William, QPM(1995)

Divisional Police Commander, Greater Manchester Police, Wigan Division. *b.* 30 July 1939 Kearsley. *m.* 1970 Angela Hill; two *d. (marr. diss. 1989)*; *m.* 1993 Lauretta Dwire; two *steps. Education:* Bolton School. *Career Profile:* Lancashire Constabulary (1956-74); Police Constable to Detective Inspector; Greater Manchester Police Detective Superintendent, North Manchester, Rochdale; Chief Superintendent, Administration (1985), Specialist Operations (1986-89); Divisional Commander, Wigan (1989-). *Recreations, Interests:* Canal and narrow boats, walking, rugby league, brass bands.

BURTON, Sidney Charles Richard, TD (1964) MA (Cantab, 1956),MIMC (1968)

Chairman, Portico Library & Gallery (1992-). *b.* 9 March 1930 Aldershot. *m.* 1961 Julia

Brockbank; *(widowed 1965)*; *m.* 1976 Khumi Tonsing. *Public Offices:* Senior Trustee, Armoury Trust; Trustee, Portico Libary. *Education:* Various schools; Exhibitioner, Queens' College, Cambridge (1947). *Military Service:* Short Service Officer, Duke of Wellington's Regiment (1948); ERE Adriatic (Trieste), Vienna (1949-51); TA, 7th Bn, The 22nd (Cheshire) Regiment - Major, Company Commander (1952-72). *Career Profile:* PA Management Consultants (1960-72) - Resident, Supervisor, Survey Consultant, latterly Head of Marketing (NW); Chairman,DSE Marketing (1972-92); now retired but with continuing business interests in India and the Far East. *Publications/Creative Work:* Various articles on aspects of military history for journals and magazines. *Societies:* Army & Navy Club, London; Royal Asiatic Society; Army Historical Research Society; Military History Society; Orders & Medals Research Society. *Recreations, Interests:* Globe trotting, book collecting, wines, fine carpets and rugs. *Address:* Cliff Cottage, Lacey Green, Wilmslow, SK9 4BA *(tel:* 01625 548664) *(fax:* 01625 532002).

BUSH, Professor Stephen Frederick, MA (Cantab), Msc (Man), PhD (Cantab), CEng, FIMechE,FIChemE,FPRI,FIM

Professor of Polymer Engineering, UMIST; Managing Director, Prosyma Research Ltd; Chairman, North of England Plastics Processing Consortium (NEPPCO); Director, Process Manufacturing Centre. *b.* 6 May 1939 Bath. *m.* 1963 Gillian Mary; one *s.* one *d.* *Public Offices:* Formerly: Chairman Science & Engineering Research Council (SERC) Applied Mechanics Committee; Member, Schools Examination & Assessment Council (SEAC) Technology Committee. *Education:* City of Bath School; Isleworth Grammar School; Trinity College, Cambridge; Massachusetts Institute of Technology (MIT). *Career Profile:* ICI Corporate Laboratory (Bozedown, Oxfordshire): successively Technical Officer; Section Manager; Process Technology Group Manager (1963-71); ICI Europa Ltd (Holland and Belgium) Systems Technology Department Manager (1971-79); Professor of Polymer Engineering, UMIST (1979-); Chairman, Dept of Mechanical Engineering, UMIST (1982-83) and (1985-87); Advisor to Board of Synterials plc (1984-86); Managing Director, Prosyma Research Ltd (1987-); Chairman, North of England Plastics Processors' Consortium (1990-); Director, Process Manufacturing Centre (1996-). *Publications:* Over 70 scientific papers and more than 115 conference presentations on various aspects of polymer engineering, mathematical modelling, design and control of manufacturing processes; 27 granted patents on polymer composites and chemical processes; 'Britain's Future: No Middle Way' (1989); 'More Matter Less Artel: How to Improve British Education' (1990); 'The Meaning of The Maastricht Treaty (with G M Bush)(1992); numerous letters and articles in the national press on educational, political and industrial matters. *Prizes:* Sir George Nelson Prize for Applied Mechanics, Cambridge; NATO Research Scholarship, Massachusetts Insitute of Technology; Senior Moulton Medal of the Institution of Chemical Engineers; Sir George Beilby Medal and Prize (Joint award of the Royal Society of Chemistry, Institute of Metals and Society of Chemical Industry). *Societies:* National Vice Chairman, Campaign for an Independent Britain, London; Member, Royal Overseas League, London. *Recreations, Interests:* Mountain climbing, hill walking, British imperial history, economics, music, tennis. *Address:* Polymer Engineering, UMIST, PO Box 88, Manchester, M60 1QD *(tel:* 0161 200 3760; *fax:* 0161 200 3767; *e-mail*: s.f.bush@umist.ac.uk); Genval, Millstone Close, Poynton, SK12 1XS *(tel:* 01625 878142; *fax:* 01625 878142).

BUTLER, Stella Vera Frances, BSc(Hons)(Manchester,1977),PhD(UMIST,1982),PGCE (Manchester, 1983)

Heritage Consultant. *b.* 8 May 1956 Bath, Somerset. *m.* 1988 Andrew J Taylor; one *s.* one *d. Public Offices:* JP. *Education:* Lenzie Academy, Dunbartonshire (1969-72); Roundhay School, Leeds (1972-74); Manchester University (1974-77)(1982-83); UMIST (1977-80). *Career Profile:* Research Fellow, UMIST (1980-81); Science Teacher (1981-83); Head of Curatorial Services, Museum of Science & Industry Manchester (1984-90); Science Tutor, Open University (1983-91). *Publications/Creative Work:* Articles on museums and the history of science and medicine in the North West; 'Science and Technology Museums' (Leicester University Press, 1992); 'Scientific Activity Guide' (Catalyst, 1993). *Prizes:* International Visitor to the United States of America (1985). *Societies:* Pankhurst Trust; British Society of History of Science. *Recreations, Interests:* Alice and Harry. *Address:* 3 Brooklyn Crescent, Cheadle, Cheshire, SK8 1DX (*tel:* 0161 491 1452; *fax:* 0161 282 9476; *e-mail:* butler@zetnet.co.uk).

BUTTERWORTH, Joseph Roger, BA(Hons)(Dunelm),IHSM,Dip Soc Admin (Manc)

Chief Executive, Tameside & Glossop Acute NHS Trust (1994-). *b.* 6 October 1942 Blackpool. *m.* 1970 Patricia. *Education:* Kirkham Grammar School; Durham University; Manchester University. *Career Profile:* 32 years in hospital administration/management; Deputy Hospital Secretary, Chapel Allerton Hospital, Leeds; Hospital Secretary, Rotherham, Moorgate General and Badsley Moor Hospitals; Sector Administrator, Operational Services Manager, Unit Administrator, Tameside General Hospital (1975-84); General Manager, Tameside Hospital (1984-94). *Recreations, Interests:* History, travel, all forms of sport. *Address:* 65 Stalyhill Drive, Stalybridge, Cheshire (*tel:* 01457 764229).

BYERS-BROWN, Professor William, BSc(Hons. Chemistry) Manchester (1950),MSc (Manchester, 1953),DSc (Manchester, 1967),FRSC

Emeritus Professor of Theoretical Chemistry, University of Manchester (1989-); Professorial Fellow, University of Manchester (1989-); Director, Mass Action Research Consultancy (1992-); Retained Consultant to ICI plc (1982-); Member of Hulme Hall Trust Foundation (1987-). *b.* 6 November 1929; Glasgow, Scotland. *m.* 1956 Pauline Ellen Knight; one *s.* two *d.* *(marr. diss. 1964)*; *m.* 1982 Josephine Alice Langham; two *stepd.* *Education:* Harrogate Grammar School (1941-47); University of Manchester (1947-53). *Military Service:* RAF (1953-55). *Career Profile:* Governor of Giggleswick School (1982-89); Professor of Theoretical Chemistry, University of Manchester (1967-89); Dean of Music, University of Manchester (1981-84); Professor of Theoretical Chemistry Institute, University of Wisconsin, Madison, USA (1963-67); Lecturer in Chemistry, University of Edinburgh (1960-62); Lecturer in Theoretical Chemistry, University of Manchester (1955-60). *Publications:* Numerous papers in scientific journals; Editor, 'Advances in Theoretical Chemistry', Vol 1 (Medical and Technical Press, London, 1972). *Prizes:* Mercer Prize (1950); Flintoff Research Medal (1951). *Societies:* Manchester Literary & Philosophical Society; National Trust; Save British Science; Amnesty International; Scientific & Medical Network; Society for Psychical Research; John Muir Trust. *Recreations, Interests:* Music,

mountains, psychology, reading. *Address:* Department of Chemistry, University of Manchester, Manchester M13 9PL *(tel:* 0161-275 4686).

BYRNE, Martin Patrick Joseph, MA (Chemistry) TCD (1963)

International Trade Consultant (high tech industries, transfer of technology). *b.* 24 October 1939; London. *m.* 1981 Ann Lesley; two *s. Public Offices:* Member of Council, Manchester Chamber of Commerce & Industry; Past President, Manchester Junior Chamber of Commerce (1976-77). *Education:* The John Fisher School, Purley, Surrey; The University of Dublin Trinity College. *Career Profile:* International Sales Management and Marketing, ICI (1964-95); two year secondment, Dept of Trade & Industry, UK Export Promoter for Turkey. *Societies:* TCD Association; Institute of Directors; Bombay Gymkhana; Manchester Luncheon Club; Catenian Association. *Recreations, Interests:* Family activities, philosophy, literature, technical innovations, Oriental & African Art, anthropology, travel. *Address:* 10 Gorse Bank Road, Hale Barns, Altrincham WA15 0AL *(tel:* 0161 980 8049).

BYROM, Richard John, BA,MPhil,ARIBA,FSVA,FCIArb

Director, Byrom Clark Roberts Ltd. *b.* 12 October 1939 Bury, Lancs. *m.* two *s.* one *d. Public Offices:* JP (1972). *Education:* Denstone College; Manchester University School of Architecture. *Career Profile:* Partner, latterly Director, Byrom Clark Roberts Ltd (formerly Byrom Hill)(1962-); Practising architect and construction arbitrator. *Societies:* Manchester Society of Architects; Chairman, Manchester & District Branch, Incorporated Society of Valuers & Auctioneers (1995); St James's' Club; Chartered Institute of Arbitrators NW Branch; Society of Construction Law; Chairman, Manchester Diocesan Redundant Churches Uses Committee (1995-). *Recreations, Interests:* Industrial archaeology, antiquarian books. *Address:* Byrom Clark Roberts Ltd, 117 Portland Street, Manchester, M1 6EH *(tel:* 0161 236 9601; *fax:* 0161 236 8675).

C

CADMAN, James Rodney, TD (1969),JP (1983)

Chairman, James Cadman & Sons Ltd; Chairman, James Cadman & Co Ltd. *b.* 21 April 1933; Eccles, Manchester. *m.* 1958 Birgit; one *s.* one *d. Public Offices:* President, Manchester, Salford & District Building Trades Employers Federation (1972); President, National Federation of Plastering Contractors (1974); Justice of the Peace, Salford Bench (1983). *Education:* Manchester Grammar School (1943-49); Manchester College of Technology (1949-54). *Military Service:* National Service, Royal Engineers (1954-56); Territorial Army, Royal Engineers (1956-70)(retired with rank of Major). *Societies:* Fellow of the Institute of Building (1973); Worshipful Company of Plaisterers, London; Swinton & Pendlebury Rotary Club (Past President 1978-79); Army and Navy Club, Pall Mall, London. *Recreations, Interests:* Rugby football, fell walking, boating, gardening, travelling. *Address:* James Cadman & Sons Ltd, 89 Chorley Road, Swinton, Manchester M27 2AA (0161-794 1804); Rostellan, Broadoak Park, Worsley, Manchester M28 2NT (*tel:* 0161-794 3730).

CANNON, Professor Thomas BSc(Hons),CIM,FRSA,FInstEx,FCIM

Chief Executive, Manchester Charter Initiative. *b.* 20 November 1945 Liverpool. *m.* 1971 Fran; one *s.* one *d. Public Offices:* Director, Clothing & Allied Products Industry Training Board Trust. *Education:* St Francis Xavier's Grammar School, Liverpool. *Career Profile:* Research Executive, ASKE Research; Research Associate, Warwick University; Lecturer, Middlesex University; Mercer's Memorial Chair of Commerce at Gresham College; Visiting Professor of Business at Kingston University; Product Manager, Imperial Group; Lecturer, Durham University; Professor, Stirling University; Director, Manchester Business School; Chief Executive, MDE Services. *Publications/Creative Work:* 'Guinness Book of Business Records' (1996); 'A Textbook on Business Ethics, Governance and the Environment' (1994); 'How to Get Ahead in Business' (1994); 'Corporate Responsibility' (1992); 'Basic Marketing' 5th Edition (1996); 'Women as Entrepreneurs' (1991); 'Enterprise: Creation, Development and Growth' 1991; 'The World of Business' (1991); 'The Role and Contribution of Small Firms Research' (1989); 'Small Business Development' (1988); 'How to Buy and Sell Overseas' (1985); 'How to Win Profitable Business' (1984); 'The Marketing Workbook' (1981); 'Advertising: The Economic Implications' (1977); 'Distribution Research' (1976); 'Advertising Research' (1975). *Societies:* Royal Society of Arts; Institute of Management; Chartered Institute of Marketing; Institute of Export. *Recreations, Interests:* Walking, modern history, computing and supporting Everton FC. *Address:* Management Charter Initiative, 10-12 Russell Square, London, WC1B 5BZ (*tel:* 0171 872 6918; *fax:* 0171 872 9099; *e-mail:* 100536,665@com puserve.com); 13 Old Broadway, Manchester, M20 3DH.

CARDWELL, Professor Donald Stephen Lowell, BSc, PhD(Physics), DSc (London), MSc (hc)(Manchester)

Retired; Emeritus Professor, Honorary Research Fellow, Dept of Physics, UMIST. *b.* 4 August 1919; Gibraltar. *m.* 1953 Olive Grace Pumphrey; two *s.* one *d. Public Offices:*

Vice-President, Trustees Greater Manchester Museum of Science & Industry. *Education:* Plymouth College (1929-36); London University (1936-40, 1946-49). *War Service:* ASRE (1940-46). *Career Profile:* Lecturer, History & Philosophy of Science, Leeds University(to 1962); Reader, History of Science and Technology, UMIST (1963-73), Professor (1974-84). *Publications:* 'Organisation of Science in England' (Heinemann, London, 1957, 1972 reprint 1981); 'Steam Power in the Eighteenth Century' (1963); 'John Dalton and the Progress of Science' (ed), (MUP, 1968); 'Watt to Clausius' (Heinemann, 1973, University of Iowa Press, 1989); 'Technology, Science and History' (Heinemann, 1972); 'Artisan to Graduate' (ed), (MUP, 1974); 'James Joule: a Biography' (MUP, 1989); 'The Fontana History of Technology' (Fontana, 1994). *Prizes:* Dexter Prize, Society for the History of Technology (USA, 1973); Dickinson Medal, Newcomen Society (UK, 1978); Leonardo da Vinci Medal, SHOT (1981). *Societies:* Honorary Member, Manchester Literary & Philosophical Society; Newcomen Society (Chairman, North Western Branch). *Recreations, Interests:* Keeping on working. *Address:* C/o Department of Pure & Applied Physics, UMIST, Manchester M60 1QD; 7 Tabley Close, Knutsford, Cheshire WA16 0NP (*tel:* 01565 651421).

CAREY, Kathleen (*née* Andries)

Company Secretary, Marketing Director, Carey Electrical Engineering. *b.* 9 January 1941 Audenshaw, Manchester. *m.* 1961 Barry; two *d.* *Public Offices:* Member, Greater Manchester Industrial Mission Council; Christians in Public Life; General Commissioner for Taxation (Manchester & Salford); Governor, Tameside College of Technology; Member, Magistrates Advisory Council; Chairman, Edward House Ltd (reg. charity for the housing & support of single persons with mental health problems). *Education:* Tameside College of Technology. *Career Profile:* NHS; Local Authorities; 22 years progression with present company. *Prizes:* Tameside Mayor's Award for Outstanding Services to the Community. *Societies:* MIoD; MIM. *Recreations, Interests:* Motor cruising, keep fit, employment issues. *Address:* Carey Electrical Engineering, Caroline House, Audenshaw, Manchester, M34 5HQ (*tel:* 0161 370 9202; *fax:* 0161 370 4106); Woodside Farm, Matley, Hyde, SK14 4DX (*tel:* 0161 368 6913).

CAREY, Terence, BA (Hons) London (1956),AMCST,MBA Manchester Business School (1965),FID,FBIM,MIEx

Managing Director (retired 1994), Constantine International Services Ltd, Constantine Wingate Ltd, Constantine Air Freight Services Ltd, Evan Cook Ltd, Wingate & Johnston Ltd, Neale & Wilkinson Ltd, Edward Needham Ltd. *b.* 8 April 1934; Liverpool. *m.* 1959 Margaret Elizabeth Whiston (decd); one *s.* one *d.* *Education:* St Mary's College, Crosby, Liverpool (1945-52); University of Hull (1952-56). *Military Service:* RASC (1956-58). *Career Profile:* Industrial Engineer, Metropolitan Vickers; Asst Traffic Manager, AEI Ltd; Works Director/MD, Lloyds Machinery Packing Co Ltd; Managing Director, Constantine-Lloyd Ltd, Howitt Bros Ltd. *Societies:* Member, Catenian Association. *Recreations, Interests:* Golf, snooker, football, photography, travel. *Address:* 27 Marlfield Road, Hale Barns, Altrincham, Cheshire WA15 0SB (*tel:* 0161-980 5592).

CARLEBACH, Rabbi Felix, MA(Manchester); Rabbinical Diploma, Diaspora Talmudical College, Jerusalem

Rabbi, South Manchester Synagogue (1946-86) (now Emeritus Minister). *b.* 15 April 1911; Lubeck, Western Germany. *m.* 1936 Babette; three *d. Public Offices:* Hon Chaplain to 5 Lord Mayors of Manchester, Chairman, Greater Manchester Council, High Sheriff in Manchester, Christie Cancer Hospital, Blind Society. *Education:* Katharineum Grammar School, Lubeck; Cologne University (Theology and Music). *Career Profile:* Deputy Headmaster, Jewish Day School, Leipzig; Minister, Palmers Green, Southgate United Synagogue, London. *Prizes:* The Annual Rabbi Felix Carlebach Concert of the Halle Society (1982-). *Societies:* Hon Freeman of the Hanseatic City of Lubeck (together with Willy Brandt and Thomas Mann). *Recreations, Interests:* Music theory and practice. *Additional Information:* In 1989 conducted a symphony orchestra in Lubeck, by invitation. *Tel:* 0161-445 5716.

CARLISLE OF BUCKLOW, Lord Mark, Baron,(Life Peer)(1987),PC(1979),QC (1971), DL Cheshire (1983); LLB Manchester (1954)

Chairman, Criminal Injuries Compensation Board; Recorder. *b.* 7 July 1929; Montevideo. *m.* 1959 Sandra Joyce des Voeux; one *d. Public Offices:* MP (C) Runcorn (1964-83), Warrington South (1983-87); Minister of State, Home Office (1972-74); Secretary of State for Education (1979-81); Chairman, Parole Review Committee (1988). *Education:* Radley College; Manchester University (1952). *Career Profile:* Called to the Bar, Gray's Inn (1953); QC (1971); Bencher (1980); Judge of the Court of Appeal of Jersey & Guernsey (1990-). *Societies:* Wilmslow Golf Club; St James's Club, Manchester; Garrick Club, London. *Recreations, Interests:* Golf. *Address:* 18 St John Street, Manchester (0161-834 9843).

CARROLL, Raymund Noel Patrick, MB BCh BAO (1962) BSc (1964) National University of Ireland,FRCS(Ed) (1967),FRCS(Eng) (1970)

Consultant Urological Surgeon, Manchester Royal Infirmary, St Mary's Hospital Manchester; Clinical Lecturer in Urology, University of Manchester; Medical Director, Lithotripter Unit, Manchester Clinic. *b.* 25 November 1938; Dublin City. *m.* 1967 Elizabeth Delphine Barraclough; two *s.* one *d. Education:* Belvedere College, Dublin; University College, Dublin. *Career Profile:* Lecturer in Anatomy, University College Dublin (1963); Registrar in Surgery and Urology, Hammersmith Hospital, London (1967-69); Registrar in Urology, St Peters Hospital, London and Institute of Urology (1969); Rotating Senior Registrar in Urology, Manchester (1970-74). *Publications:* Co-author of book on Surgery; contributor of chapters to major surgical textbooks; publications in national and international medical journals on urological topics; production of videos for teaching purposes as part of MEDIVISION Series. *Prizes:* Gold Medal for Surgery, University College Dublin (1962). *Societies:* Carlton Club, St James's Club, Manchester; British Medical Association; British Associations of Urological Surgeons; Charriere Association of Urologists; Manchester Medical Society; The Royal Society of Medicine; Sale Medical & Dental Society;European Urology Association; International Urology Society; Manchester & District Medico-Legal Society; Immediate Past President of the Urostomy Association. *Recreations, Interests:* Rugby Union, collecting books and glass, travel,cricket. *Address:* The Beeches, Mill Lane, Cheadle, Cheshire (*tel:* 0161-491 2698;

fax: 0161 428 1692); Cranford, 8 Parkfield Road South, Didsbury, Manchester M20 0DB (*tel:* 0161 434 2266; *fax:* 0161 445 2623).

CARTER, His Honour Judge Frederick Brian, LLB(1954),QC(1980)

Circuit Judge. *b.* 11 May 1933 Stretford. *m.* 1960 Elizabeth; one *s.* three *d. Education:* Stretford Grammar School; King's College, London University. *Military Service:* National Service, Royal Air Force (1955-57). *Career Profile:* Practised Northern Circuit (1957-85); Prosecuting Counsel for Inland Revenue, Northern Circuit (1973-80); Queen's Counsel (1980); Recorder (1978-85); Circuit Judge (1985-). *Societies:* Big Four, Manchester; Chorlton-cum-Hardy Golf Club; Circuit Judges Golfing Society. *Recreations, Interests:* Golf, travel.

CARTER, June Audrey (*née* Greenwood), ATD,NDD,DA (Manchester)

College Lecturer (Art & Design)(retd); full time painter. *b.* 26 May 1929 Manchester. *m.* 1952 Gerard; one *s.* *(widowed 1966) Education:* Prestwich High School; Bury Junior Art School; Manchester Regional College of Art. *Career Profile:* Teaching and painting; Head of Art Department, Rochdale Girls' Technical High School, College of Nursery Nursing; Fielden Park College; lecturer for the Educational Development Association. *Publications/Creative Work:* Lancashire Today (cover design & article,1987). *Prizes:* Manchester Evening News (North West Artists Exhibition); T H Saunders & Bockingford - Artists in Watercolours. *Societies:* Prestwich 'Wednesday Association' (President). *Recreations, Interests:* Reading, travel, theatre, exhibitions, music, exploring the British Isles. *Address:* Tanglewood, 11 Hamilton Road, Prestwich, Manchester, M25 9GG (*tel:* 0161 773 3277). *Additional Information:* Exhibited regularly in one man shows in public and private galleries.

CASKEN, Professor John, BMus,MA(Birmingham),DMus(Dunelm)

Professor of Music, University of Manchester (1992-). *b.* 15 July 1949 Barnsley, Yorkshire. *Education:* University of Birmingham (1967-71); Academy of Music, Warsaw, Poland (1971-72). *Career Profile:* Lecturer in Music, University of Birmingham (1973-79); Research Fellow in Musical Composition, Huddersfield Polytechnic (1980-81); Lecturer in Music, University of Durham (1981-92); Professor of Music, University of Manchester (1992-). *Publications/Creative Work:* Recent compositions include 'Golem' (Chamber Opera)(1989); Cello Concerto (1991); 'Still Mine' (orchestral song-cycle)(1992); Violin Concerto (1995); 'Sortilege' (for full orchestra)(1996). *Prizes:* First Britten Award (1990); Gramophone Award (1990) for best contemporary recording - 'Golem'; Musical Prize of the Fondation Prince Pierre de Monaco (1993) for 'Still Mine'. *Recreations, Interests:* Painting, visual arts, gardening, cooking. *Address:* Department of Music, University of Manchester, Denmark Road, Manchester, M15 6HY (*tel:* 0161 275 4987; *fax:* 0161 275 4994; *e-mail*: John.Casken@man.ac.uk).

CASS, Edward Fletcher, MA,ACIB

Retired. *b.* 12 February 1937 Manchester. *m.* 1961 Catherine Sheila Curtis; three *s. Public Offices:* Immediate Past President, Manchester Literary & Philosophical Society; Secretary, Trustees of the National Museum of Labour History; Vice-Chairman, Friends of the

Museum of Science & Industry in Manchester. *Publications/Creative Work:* Papers in learned journals. *Prizes:* Haddo-Drummond Fraser Prize (1962); Murray-Drummond Fraser Prize (1963). *Societies:* Manchester Literary & Philosophical Society; Manchester Bibliographical Society; Portico Library. *Recreations, Interests:* Labour history, museums, the arts.

CASTREE, Alan James

Assistant Chief Constable, Greater Manchester Police. *b.* 25 April 1942 Corbridge, Northumberland. *m.* 1963 Catherine; two *d. Education:* Royal Grammar School, Newcastle-upon-Tyne; Edinburgh University. *Career Profile:* Police service in different parts of the country and abroad; currently Secretary to Chief Police Officers' Standing Committee on 'Drugs'; National Police Spokesman on Drugs. *Societies:* Sale Rugby Football Club (former Chairman); Portico Library, Manchester; National Art Collections Fund; National Trust. *Recreations, Interests:* Rugby football, cycling, study of modern languages. *Address:* Greater Manchester Police, Chester House, Boyer Street, Manchester, M16 0RE (*tel:* 0161 856 2016; *fax:* 0161 856 2036). *Additional Information:* Member of Board of Manchester Prince's Youth Business Trust. Fluent in French (used as interpreter on many occasions). Speaks German and Italian.

CATER, Iain Charles Douglas, Bsc(Liverpool,1974),FCMA

Chief Executive, Seton Healthcare Group plc, Oldham. *b.* 29 January 1952; Cheltenham, Gloucestershire. *m.* 1983 Joanne; three *s.* one *d. Education:* Eastbourne College; Liverpool University (1971-74). *Societies:* Mere Golf & Country Club. *Recreations, Interests:* Business, golf, theatre. *Address:* Seton Healthcare Group plc, Tubiton House, Oldham OL1 3HS (*tel:* 0161-652 2222); Gainsborough, Park Drive, Hale, Cheshire WA15 9DH (*tel:* 0161-903 9093)

CATLOW, Richard BSc(Hons)

Group Editor, Rochdale Observer Series of Newspapers (1995-). *b.* 13 October 1949 Brierfield near Burnley. *m.* 1974 Helen; four *d. Public Offices:* Director, Rochdale Town Centre Trust (1995-); Chairman, Queen Street Mill Working Museum (1984-87). *Education:* Bacup & Rawtenstall Grammar School; Salford University. *Career Profile:* Editor, Nelson Leader Series (1986-88); Editor, Burnley Express (1988-92); Editor, West Lancashire Evening Gazette (1992-94); Head of Catlow Communications (1994-95); Group Editor, Rochdale Observer Series (1995-); Voluntary: Founder Editor Pennine Magazine (1978-88). *Publications/Creative Work:* 'The Pendle Witches'; 'Burnley - a Town Trail'; 'A Lakeland Looking Glass'; 'Over the Setts'; 'Exploring Historic Lancashire'; 'Ribble Valley Rendezvous'; 'Burnley in Old Postcards'; 'A Closer Look at Lakeland'; co-author 'Images of Rochdale'. *Societies:* Bacup Natural History Society; Kimberley Club, Stacksteads nr Bacup; National Trust; RSPB,; Woodland Trust; John Muir Trust; Mountain Bothies Association. *Recreations, Interests:* Fell walking, local history, running. *Address:* Rochdale Observer Group, Drake Street, Rochdale, OL16 1PH (*tel:* 01706 354321; *fax:* 01706 341595); 12 Bonfire Hill Close, Crawshawbooth, Rossendale, Lancashire, BB4 8PP (*tel:* 01706 220765).

CATLOW, Ronald Eric, BEd,MA,PhD,DipManEd,FRGS

Educational Consultant; Lecturer & Researcher; Teacher. *b.* 3 June 1941 Hyde. *Public Offices:* BBC Regional Advisory Council for the North West of England; OFWAT North West Customer Service Committee. *Education:* Greenfield County Secondary School, Hyde (1952-56); Ashton College of FE (1957-61); Derby Training College (1961-64); North East Wales Institute of Higher Education (p-t)(1973-76); Manchester Polytechnic (p-t)(1975-77); University of York (p-t)(1977-79); University of Hull (part time)(1982-91). *Career Profile:* Assistant Teacher, Head of Geography, Humanities, Fifth Year, Upper School; Director of Studies, Deputy Headteacher and Acting Headteacher (1964-94). *Societies:* Manchester Literary and Philosophical Society, Council Member; Royal Geographical Society; Society for Cooperative Studies; National Association of Headteachers. *Recreations, Interests:* Theatre, walking in the Peak District, seasoned traveller, supporter of Manchester United, Hallé. *Address:* 2 Lychwood, Station Road, Marple, Stockport, SK6 6AL (*tel:* 0161 427 5771). *Additional Information:* Research on option curriculum choice, curriculum development and effective schools.

CEBERTOWICZ, Janina Dorota, BA(Hons)(Bath Academy of Art),PGCE(Manchester Polytechnic)

Artist; Head of Art and Design, Bury Grammar School for Girls; Resident Artist, Royal Northern College of Music. *b.* 30 April 1953 Manchester. *Education:* Werneth Convent, Oldham; Loreto Grammar School for Girls, Manchester; Manchester Polytechnic (1971-72); Bath Academy of Art (1972-75); Manchester Polytechnic (1977-78). *Career Profile:* Exhibiting Artist (1980-); Head of Art & Design, Bury Grammar School for Girls (1989-). *Publications/Creative Work:* Numerous one person exhibitions; Visiting Artist: Manchester Childrens' Hospital; Royal Liverpool Hospital; Women in Arts Festival; St Andrew's University. *Societies:* Manchester Academy of Fine Arts; Manchester Literary & Philosophical Society; Artists' General Benevolent Institution; Salford Choral Society; Friend ofax: Royal Northern College of Music; Manchester City Art Gallery; Opera North; Welsh National Opera; Ass Member of Friends of Musicians' Benevolent Fund; National Trust; Manchester Greek Circle. *Recreations, Interests:* Vocal and piano studies, modern Greek language and culture, travel, educational visits abroad, gardening. *Address:* Bury Grammar School (Girls), Bridge Road, Bury, Lancs, BL9 0HH.

CHAPLIN, David Lawton, MA,FCA

Chairman, Hulme Trust; Chairman, Wilmslow Opera. *b.* 14 December 1928; Eccles, Lancs. *m.* 1954 Hilary Anne; one *s.* three *d. Education:* Oriel House, St Asaph; Manchester Grammar School; Balliol College, Oxford. *Military Service:* National Service (1948-50). *Career Profile:* Partner, Spicer & Oppenheim (retired 1986); Chairman, Manchester Midday Concerts Society (retired 1987). *Publications:* 'Private Client Investment Advice and Management' (Henley Distance Learning Ltd, 1987). *Prizes and Awards:* Domus Scholarship in Mathematics, Balliol College, Oxford (1944). *Societies:* Wilmslow Golf Club. *Recreations, Interests:* Opera, golf. *Address:* The Meadows, Ryleys Lane, Alderley Edge, Cheshire SK9 7UU (*tel:* 01625-582046).

CHAPMAN, J K (Ben), FIM

Director: On the Waterfront (Manchester) Ltd; Wirral Chamber of Commerce; Heswall Society; Trans China Consultants; Ben Chapman Associates; Chairman: Rural Challenge

Cumbria; Advisory Committee China; Gateway, North West; Advisory Board, China Technology Link; Honorary Position: Ambassador for Cumbria; Member of Council of Management, Lake District Summer Music Ltd. *b.* 8 July 1940 Kirkby Stephen, Westmorland. *m.* 1967 Jane Deirdre Roffe; three *d.* '*(marr. diss. 1984) Education:* Appleby Grammar School. *Military Service:* Pilot Officer, RAFVR(T) (1959-61). *Career Profile:* Ministry of Pensions & National Insurance (1958-61); British Airports Authority (1961-67); Assistant Secretary, Rochdale Committee (1967-71); DTI (1971-74); First Secretary, British High Commission, Tanzania (1974-78); First Secretary, British High Commission, Ghana (1978-81); DTI (1981-86); Commercial Counsellor, British Embassy (1986-90); Director, Merseyside DTI (1990-93); Regional Director, DTI North West (1993-94); Director, Trade & Industry Government Office, North West (1994-95). *Publications:* Many published articles and abstracts. *Societies:* Portico Library. *Recreations, Interests:* Opera, football, (*tel:* 0151 342 7293, *fax:* 0151 342 7293).

CHAPMAN, Reginald James, MA, DipArch Sheffield (1970),RIBA

Architect Partner, R James Chapman Architects. *b.* 6 November 1945; Bingley, West Yorkshire. *m.* 1970 Joan Mary Eagling. *Public Offices:* Vice President, RIBA; Past President, Manchester Society of Architects. *Education:* Bradford Grammar School; Sheffield University (1965-70). *Creative Works:* University projects for UMIST & Salford; Granada Television: Bonded Warehouse (Civic Trust Award), Stage 1 - Studios (Civic Trust Commendation), Dock Traffic Office, Liverpool News Studio (Civic Trust Award, Europa Nostra Award), Granada Studios Tour (RICS Inner City Award Commendation, English Tourist Board Award for Excellence); Refuge Assurance, Wilmslow RIBA Regional Award (Office of the Year Award); Stafford District General Hospital; The Manchester Olympic & Commonwealth Games Bid Concept & technical bid. *Prizes:* Civic Trust Awards, Granada (1985) & (1987); Europa Nostra Award (1987); Office of the Year (1989) Refuge; RICS Commendation for Granada Studios Tour (1989). *Societies:* Manchester Society of Architects; Friends of Royal Exchange; Sale Rugby Football Club. *Recreations, Interests:* Design, theatre, music, rugby football, golf and squash. *Address:* Commercial Wharf, 6 Commercial Street, Manchester M15 4PZ (*tel:* 0161 832 9460);19 Burlington Road, Altrincham, Cheshire WA14 1HR (*tel:* 0161-941 5389).

CHATTERJEE, Petula Christine, MB ChB Manchester (1976),BSc St Andrews (1973)

Principal in General Practice; Medical Officer in Occupational Health. *b.* 6 January 1951; Manchester. *m.* 1978 Peter Woodbyrne; one *s.* *Public Offices:* Member of the Council to the Order of St John. *Education:* Withington Girls' School, Manchester; University of St Andrews; University of Manchester. *Recreations, Interests:* Cooking, gardening. *Address:* The Orchard, 18A Chapel Lane, Wilmslow, Cheshire (01625-525731). *Additional Information:* Serving Sister to Order of St John.

CHATTERJEE, Satya Saran, OBE(1971),JP(1971); MB,BS (1944),FRCP (1973),FRCPE (1974),FCCP (USA) (1974)
Consultant Chest Physician; Chairman, Overseas Doctors Association News Review. *b.* 16 July 1922; Calcutta, India. *m.* 1948 Enid May; one *s.* two *d.* *Public Offices:* Magistrate, Manchester City; Trustee, Telethon Trust; Member, Advisory Council, BBC North West. *Education:* Patna University, India; United Kingdom, Sweden and USA. *War Service:*

Captain MO, Indian Army (1944-47). *Career Profile:* Member, General Medical Council (1979-92); Member, North West Regional Health Authority (1976-86); Consultant in Charge, Respiratory Physiology Unit, Wythenshawe Hospital (1959-88). *Publications:* Respiratory Physiology and Thoracic Medicine and allied subjects. *Prizes:* Fulbright Fellowship (USA 1954); Travelling Fellow (Sweden 1958-59). *Societies:* Rotary Club, Wythenshawe; Bramhall Bridge Club; Cheadle Hulme Bridge Club. *Recreations, Interests:* Community work, gardening, bridge. *Address:* 41 The Downs, Altrincham, Cheshire (*tel:* 0161-928 0611); "March", 20 Macclesfield Road, Wilmslow, Cheshire SK9 2AF (*tel:* 01625-522559). *Additional Information:* Past President, Overseas Doctors Association, Indian Association (Manchester), Wythenshawe Rotary Club (1975-76,1988-89).

CHATTERTON, Mark, BA(Hons)(RBC,1986)

Freelance Theatre Practitioner; Actor/Writer/Director. *b.* 22 July 1963 Stockport. *Education:* Bramhall Comprehensive School; Salford College of Technology; Rose Bruford College of Speech and Drama. *Career Profile:* 12 years in the theatre. *Creative Work:* Directed numerous plays including: 'An Evening with Gary Lineker'; 'Just Between Ourselves'; 'Man of Mode'; 'Cinderella'; Writer of 'Ham'. *Societies:* Amnesty International; Greenpeace; Equity. *Recreations, Interests:* Photography, walking, music, history. *Additional Information:* Continual work with students. Recently directed shows for The Derby Playhouse, The Cheltenham Everyman and The Oldham Coliseum. Written for Derby Playhouse and Oldham Coliseum. Writing, directing and performing in '96 Pantomime, 'Cinderella' for the Coliseum.

CHESHIRE, Christopher Michael, BSc,MBChB,FRCP,DCH

Consultant Physician in Geriatric & General Medicine, Manchester Royal Infirmary; Medical Director, Central Manchester Healthcare Trust. *b.* 18 July 1946 West Bromwich. *m.* 1970 Jane Mary; one *s.* one *d.* *Education:* West Bromwich Grammar School; Manchester University. *Career Profile:* Pharmacist (1969-71); Graduate in Medicine (1976); Lecturer in Geriatric Medicine, Withington Hospital (1970-83); Consultant Physician (1983-); Dean of Clinical Studies, Manchester Medical School (1991-93). *Publications/Creative Work:* Various articles on Geriatric Medicine and Medical Management. *Prizes:* British Geriatrics Society Dhole Bursary (1981). *Societies:* British Geriatrics Society; British Association of Medical Managers. *Recreations, Interests:* Hill running, gardening, reading, family. *Address:* Manchester Royal Infirmary, Oxford Road, Manchester.

CHISHOLM, Professor Alexander William John, BSc(London,1943),CEng, FIMechE, FIProdE

Emeritus Professor, University of Salford; Self-employed Consultant in Engineering. *b.* 18 April 1922; Sheffield. *m.* 1945 Aline Mary Eastwood (*decd* 1995); one *s.* one *d.* *Public Offices:* Governor and Engineering Board Vice-Chairman, National Council for Technological Awards (1959-65); Technology Sub-Cttee University Grants Cttee (1969-74); Engineering Process Committee, Science and Engineering Research Council (1980-83); Chairman, Engineering Professors' Conference (1976-80); Court, Cranfield Institute of Technology (1974-92); Chairman, Salford City-Salford University Joint Cttee on Science

Parks (1979-81). *Education:* Quarry Bank High School, Liverpool; Brentwood School, Essex; Northampton Polytechnic, London; Manchester College of Science and Technology; Royal Technical College, Salford; engineering apprenticeship with Metropolitan Vickers Electrical Co Ltd, Manchester; graduated University of London, First Class Hons. *War Service:* National Fire Service, part-time (1941-45). *Career Profile:* Research Section Leader, Metropolitan Vickers Elec Co Ltd (1944-49); Research Group Head, Mech Eng Res Laboratory, East Kilbride (1949-57); Eng Liaison Officer, British Embassy, USA (1952-54); Head of Dept then Professor of Mechanical Engineering, Royal College of Advanced Technology (1957-67); Professor of Mechanical Engineering, Research Professor, Professorial Fellow, University of Salford (1967-93); Visiting Fellow, Wolfson Coll, Cambridge (1973-74); Chairman, Salford University Industrial Centre & Chairman of Board (1969-82); Director, Programme for the Improvement for the Quality of Engineering Education (1990-96). *Creative Works:* Major influence on the development of eng teaching & research of the University of Salford; promoted formation of an internationally recognized research school in manufacturing engineering as well as innovations in engineering teaching and technology transfer; established the University's Campus consulting company; helped to create and pioneer the national Teaching Company Scheme for engineering; established the Engineering Professors' Conference as a national force. *Publications:* Numerous publications on production and manufacturing engineering research, on engineering education and training, technology transfer, engineering design, human factors in manufacturing, including international comparisons. *Prizes:* Institution of Mechanical Engrs' Whitworth ⁻Prize (1965), Honorary Life Member of CIRP (The International Institution for Production Eng Res). *Societies:* Member, CIRP (1964-) President (1983-84). *Recreations, Interests:* Hill walking, sailing, local environment and conservation. *Address:* University of Salford, Salford M5 4WT (*tel:* 0161-745 5000); 12 Legh Road, Prestbury, Macclesfield, Cheshire SK10 4HX (*tel:* 01625-829412). *Additional Information:* Club: The Athenaeum, London.

CHISWICK, Professor Malcolm Leon, MB,BS(Newcastle-upon-Tyne,1965),DCH (London,1967),MRCP(London,1969),MD(Newcastle-upon-Tyne,1974),FRCP(London,1980)

Professor of Child Health & Paediatrics, University of Manchester; Consultant Paediatrician, St Mary's Hospital, Manchester; Editor, Archives of Disease in Childhood. *b.* 26 July 1940 Hampton, Middlesex. *m.* 1964 Claire Dodds; one *s.* one *d. Education:* Preston Manor Grammar School, Middlesex (1951-59); Medical School, University of Newcastle-upon-Tyne (1960-65). *Career Profile:* Registrar in Paediatrics, St Georges Hospital, London; Research Fellow, Department of Child Health, University of Manchester; Honorary Secretary, British Association of Perinatal Medicine; Chairman, Liaison Commitee of British Paediatric Association and Royal College of Obstetricians & Gynaecologists. *Publications/Creative Work:* 'Neonatal Medicine' (1978); 'The Complete Book of Baby Care' (1988); 'Recent Advances in Perinatal Medicine' (1983, 1985); 'Contemporary Issues in Fetal and Neonatal Medicine' (1985-89); author of various research papers on paediatrics. *Societies:* European Association of Science Editors; British Association of Perinatal Medicine; British Paediatric Association; British Medical Association. *Recreations, Interests:* Coronation Street, writing. *Address:* St Mary's Hospital, Whitworth Park, Manchester, M13 0JH (*tel:* 0161 276 6331; *fax:* 0161 276 6536;

e-mail: mchiswick@fs1.mci.man.ac.uk); Highclere, Parkfield Road, Altrincham, WA14 2BT (*tel:* 0161 928 8579; *fax:* 0161 929 5564).

CHOWN, Mark John Hardwick, BA (Econ) Manchester (1979), ACA (1982), DipManSci UMIST(1991)

David M Brown, Consultants. *b.* 4 February 1958; Durban, S Africa. *m.* 1983 Sharon Ann; one *s.* one *d. Education:* Christchurch Grammar; Brockenhurst College; University of Manchester. *Previous Positions:* Deloitte Haskins & Sells (1979-84); 3i plc (1984-89); North of England Ventures (1990-92); The Space Group (1992-95). *Recreations, Interests:* Golf, squash, skiing, food and wine. *Address:* Aspinall House, Walker Business Park, Walker Road, Guide, Blackburn BB1 2QE (*tel:* 01254 689269; *fax:* 01254 689217); 6 Mayfield Road, Mobberley, Cheshire WA16 7PX (*tel:* 01565-873592).

CHRISTOPHER, Richard, CBE (1979); BA (London), MA (Manc), MEd (Manc)

Retired (formerly Secretary, Joint Matriculation Board). *b.* 29 October 1915; Wheatley Hill, Co Durham. *m.* 1940 Muriel Baron Knowles; two *s.* one *d. Public Offices:* Member of Court, Manchester University; Member of Court, UMIST; Governor, Manchester High School for Girls; President, Cheadle Civic Society. *Education:* Henry Smith School, Hartlepool; University College, Hull; University of Manchester. *War Service:* Major, Duke of Wellington's Regiment (1940-46); Mentioned in Dispatches (1945). *Societies:* Manchester Literary & Philosophical Society; Manchester Luncheon Club. *Address:* 113 Styal Road, Heald Green, Cheadle, Cheshire SK8 3TG (0161-428 7258).

CHUI, Peter Chee Keung, JP; BA(Econ)(Manchester,1962),FCA,ATII,MIMgt, FHKSA, MILPA

Practitioner; Travel Agent. *b.* 8 February 1936; Hong Kong. *m.* 1971 Rosalie; two *s.* one *d. Public Offices:* JP (Manchester City Bench, 1985-); Founder member, EU Migrant Forum (1991-); Judge, CRE Race in the Media awards (1994-); Founder and Chair, Tung Sing (Orient) Housing Association; Board Member, Northern Counties Housing Association; Trustee and Board Member, Manchester Care; Trustee and Treasurer, Central Manchester Victims' Support Scheme; Member, Manchester Action Committee on Health Care for Ethnic Minorities; Member, Manchester TEC; Founder and member, Steering Group of Chinese Health Information Centre; Founder and Chair, Chinese Information Centre; Chair, Chinese Professional Association (NW); Co-opted Member, Manchester Council for Community Relations. *Education:* Pui Ching Middle School, Hong Kong; Manchester College of Commerce; Manchester University (1959-62). *Career Profile:* Chair, Chinese Arch; Chair, fund raising for the Queen's Scholarship to China (1986); Member, Civic Party to Wu Han, China (1986)(twin city); Member, GMR Manchester Advisory Committee; elected Chinese representative, Manchester City Council Race subcommittee; Chair, Council of Chinese Organisations (NW); First Vice-Chair, Manchester and District Chinese Chamber of Commerce; Member, Manchester Family Practitioner Committee; Chair, informal Dental & Opthalmic Complaints Committee; Deputy Chair, Dental & Pharmaceutical Service Committee; Chair, Manchester Chinatown Neighbour Association; Chair, Sunset Radio. *Societies:* Manchester Society of Chartered Accountants; Manchester Luncheon Club; Manchester Literary & Philosophical Society.

Recreations, Interests: Reading, photography. *Address:* 2 Waterloo Street, Manchester M1 6HY.

CHURCHILL, Winston S, Hon Fellow, Churchill College, Cambridge (1969),Hon DL, Westminster College, Fulton, Mo (1972); MA Oxford

MP(C) Davyhulme; Journalist and Author; Member, House of Commons Defence Select Committee. *b.* 10 October 1940. *m.* 1964 *sep.* 1995; two *s.* two *d. Education:* Eton; Christchurch, Oxford. *Career Profile:* War Correspondent for 'The Times' in Yemen, The Congo, Angola, Borneo, Vietnam and the Middle East; Current Affairs Presenter, BBC Radio; MP for Stretford (1970) (following boundary changes, MP Davyhulme); Front Bench Spokesman on Defence (1976-78); Party Spokesman on Defence (1982-84); numerous speaking tours of USA and Canada. *Publications:* 'First Journey' (1964); 'The Six Day War' (1967); 'Defending the West' (1981); 'Memories and Adventures' (1989); 'His Father's Son' (1996). *Recreations, Interests:* Flying (qualified commercial pilot), skiing, tennis and sailing. *Address:* House of Commons, London SW1A 0AA (*tel:* 0171-219 3405).

CIALIS, Russell

Public Affairs Adviser, Department of the Environment; Consultant to several NW companies. *b.* 11 October 1938 Blackburn. *m.* 1963 Elizabeth; one *d. Public Offices:* Director of Public Affairs, Manchester Business School (1984-89). *Education:* Cheadle Hulme School, Cheshire. *Military Service:* Commissioned, Royal Army Service Corps, Germany (1959-61). *Career Profile:* Journalist and Public Relations Consultant in UK and Africa (1956-59); News Editor, Rhodesian TV (1961-62); Station Editor, Zambian TV (1963-65); Director, Anglo American Film Unit (1966-69); Deputy PR Consultant, Anglo American, Zambia (1969-71); Independent PR Consultant (1972-). *Publications/Creative Work:* Director of more than 30 TV documentaries; Editor, Book of collected stories by parents of children with epilepsy; Producer of more than 20 theatre productions. *Prizes:* Silver Medal, Royal Society of Arts (Central & Local Government); Bronze Medal, Royal Society of Arts (English Literature). *Societies:* Old Waconians' Association. *Recreations, Interests:* Theatre, golf. *Address:* Russell Cialis & Associates, Indaba House, Grangeway, Handforth, Wilmslow, SK9 3HZ (*tel:* 01625 529383; *fax:* 01625 529383).

CLARK, Professor Mark John, MSc(Univ. of Aston),PhD(CNAA)

Director of Academic Information Services, University of Salford. *b.* 12 April 1951 Portsmouth. *m.* Denise Christine; two *s.* one *d. Education:* Aston University. *Career Profile:* Essex University: Lecturer, Senior Lecturer, Director of Computing Service; Director of Academic Information Service, Salford University. *Publications/Creative Work:* Numerous articles in learned journals. *Recreations, Interests:* Reading, sailing, squash. *Address:* Director of Academic Information Services, University of Salford, M5 4WT (*tel:* 0161 745 5028; *fax:* 0161 745 5666; *e-mail:* m.j.clark@salford.ac.uk).

CLAYTON, Dorothy Joan BA(Hons)(Liverpool),MA(London), PhD (Liverpool), ALA, FRHistSoc

Editor, Bulletin of the John Rylands University Library of Manchester. *b.* 11 December 1951 Liverpool. *m.* 1981 Ray Roberts; one *s.* one *d. Education:* Huyton College, (1960-69); Liverpool University (1970-73)(1975-77); London University (1974-75). *Career Profile:* Manchester University: John Rylands Library, History Librarian (1979-90), Editor of the Bulletin (1990-). *Publications/Creative Work:* 'The Administration of the County Palatine of Chester, 1442-85' (Chetham Society, 1991); Texts and several articles in the fields of medieval history and archives. *Societies:* Record Society of Lancashire and Cheshire (Secretary to Council); Manchester Medieval Society (Secretary); Chetham Society, Lancashire and Cheshire Antiquarian Society (Member of Council). *Recreations, Interests:* History, theatre, travel, family. *Address:* John Rylands University Library of Manchester, Oxford Road, Manchester, M13 9PP (*tel:* 0161 275 3757; *fax:* 0161 273 7488; *e-mail:* dclayton@fs1.li.man.ac.uk).

CLUCKIE, Professor Ian David, BSc(Hons),MSc,PhD,CEng,FRSA,FICE,FCIWEM

Chairman, Department of Civil & Environmental Engineering; Director of Telford Institute of Environmental Systems, University of Salford. *b.* 20 July 1949 Edinburgh. *m.* 1972; one *s.* one *d. Public Offices:* Chairman, Aquatic, Atomospheric & Physical Sciences Research Grants Committee, NERC (1991-94); Hydrological Adviser, DOE Reservoir Safety Committe (1987-). *Education:* University of Surrey; University of Birmingham. *Career Profile:* Central Water Planning Unit (1974-76); Lecturer, Dept of Civil Engineering, University of Birmingham (1976-88); Professor, Water Resources, Dept of Civil & Environmental Engineering, University of Salford (1988-). *Publications/Creative Work:* Over 100 articles in professional journals and conference proceedings. *Societies:* British Hydrological Society; International Association of Hydraulic Research; International Association of Water Quality. *Recreations, Interests:* Sailing, reading, mountain walking. *Address:* Dept of Civil & Environmental Engineering, University of Salford, Manchester, M5 4WT (*tel:* 0161 745 5036; *fax:* 0161 745 5060).

COCKSHAW, Sir Alan, Knight Bachelor (1992); BSc,FEng,FICE,FIHT

Chairman, AMEC plc. *b.* 14 July 1937 Worsley, Greater Manchester. *m.* 1960 Brenda; one *s.* three *d. Public Offices:* Vice President, Institution of Civil Engineers; Chairman of the Oils and Gas Projects and Supplies Office, DTI; Deputy Chairman, North West Business Leadership Team. *Education:* Farnworth Grammar School; Leeds University. *Career Profile:* Early career: engineering design and construction in both public and private sector; joined Fairclough Civil Engineering (1973), Chief Executive (1978); Board Member, Fairclough Construction Group (1981); Group Chief Executive, AMEC plc (1984); Chairman, AMEC plc (1988). *Recreations, Interests:* Rugby (both codes), cricket, walking. *Address:* AMEC plc, Sandiway House, Hartford, Northwich, CW8 2YA (*tel:* 01606 883885; *fax:* 01606 888104).

COE, Albert Henry, FCA,ATII

Deputy Chief Executive & Group Financial Director, Airtours plc. *b.* 28 May 1944 Manchester. *m.* Beryl Margaret; two *d. Career Profile:* Chartered Accountant, Hesketh Hardy Hirshfield (1962-67); Coopers & Lybrand (1967-70); Group Financial Controller, Aerialite Ltd (1970-72); Group Financial Director, London Scottish Bank plc (1972-75); Finance Director, Smurfit Flexibile Packaging (1975-81); Finance Director, Granada

Television (1981-88). *Societies:* Alderley Edge Cricket Club; Wilmslow Golf Club; Styal Golf Club; Manchester Ski Club. *Recreations, Interests:* Golf, tennis, skiing. *Address:* Airtours plc, Parkway Business Centre, 300 Princess Road, Manchester, M14 7QU.

COFFEY, Ann (*née* Brown), BSc,MSc

MP Stockport. *b.* 31 August 1946 Inverness. *Public Offices:* Councillor, Stockport MBC, Leader (1988-92). *Education:* Navin Academy, Bodrum; Bushey Grammar School; Polytechnic of the South Bank; Manchester University. *Career Profile:* Social worker for a number of local authorities (1971-92); Last position Team Leader, Fostering and Adoption Team, Oldham. *Recreations, Interests:* Reading, drawing, photography, riding. *Address:* House of Commons, London, SW1A 0AA (*tel:* 0171 219 2342; *fax:* 0171 219 2442).

COLEMAN, (Elisabeth) Kay (*née* Wild), OBE(1994)

Chief Executive, Harveys & Co (Clothing) Ltd. *b.* 28 December 1945 Shaw, Lancashire. *m.* 1971 one *s.* one *d.* (*marr. diss. 1985*); *m.* 1993 Rodney Graves; one *steps.* *Public Offices:* Member, Advisory Group on Women's Issues, Secretary of State for Education & Employment; Member, North West Industrial Council; Chairman, Fair Play North West; Member, Armed Forces Pay Review Body. *Education:* Brentwood Girls' School. *Career Profile:* Director, Galerie Unique Ltd (1973-85); BOAC (British Airways) (1968-73). *Societies:* Carlton Club; Forum UK; Royal Society of Arts. *Recreations, Interests:* Bridge, opera, horseracing. *Address:* Harveys & Co (Clothing) Ltd, Glodwick Road, Oldham, OL4 1YU (*tel:* 0161 624 9535; *fax:* 0161 627 2028); Tudor Lodge, Hale, Cheshire.

COLEMAN, Patricia Mary (*née* Dalziel), BA(Hons)(Univ. of East Anglia)

Deputy Chief Executive, Manchester City Council. *b.* 27 April 1949 Derby. *m.* 1972 Joseph Coleman; (*marr. diss. 1980*); *m.* 1989 David Skinner. *Education:* Parkfield Cedars Grammar School, Derby (1960-67); University of East Anglia (1967-70); Manchester Polytechnic (1972). *Career Profile:* Graduate Trainee (1970), Branch Librarian (1972), Area Librarian (1974), Manchester City Libraries; Principal Assistant County Librarian, Derbyshire CountryLibriaries (1981-83); Director of Libraries & Information, Sheffield City Council (1983-89); Director of Library Services (1989-93), Director of Social Services (1993-94), Birmingham City Council; Deputy Chief Executive, Manchester City Council (1994-). *Societies:* Fellow of the Royal Society of Arts. *Recreations, Interests:* Theatre and the arts generally, gardening. *Address:* The Town Hall, Albert Square, Manchester, M60 2LA (*tel:* 0161 234 3229; *fax:* 0161 234 3122).

COLLINGE, Brian, CPFA,DipIntManAcc

Chief Executive, Bolton Metropolitan Borough Council. *b.* 13 August 1938 Manchester. *m.* 1963 Barbara; two *s.* one *d.* *Education:* Self-educated. *Career Profile:* Service with six local authorities and the former Electricity Generating Board; Former Director of Finance, Bolton; Chief Finance Officer, Bradford; Senior Assistant County Treasurer, Staffordshire. *Publications/Creative Work:* Several financial and accountancy articles. *Prizes:* 1st place CIPFA-inter (1961). *Recreations, Interests:* Family, open space, caravanning, personal computers. *Address:* Bolton MBC, Town Hall, Bolton.

COLLINSON, Leonard, FIPD,FIMC,CMC,CIMgt,FRSA

Chair, Grosvenor Career Services; Director, Newsco Publications; Director, Universities' Superannuation Scheme. *b.* 30 March 1934 Healing, Lincolnshire. *m.* 1955 Shirley Grace; two *s. Public Offices:* Member, National Council of CBI; Trustee, National Museum of Labour History; Member, Court and Finance Committee, University of Manchester; Chair, Manchester Diocesan Council for Industrial and Economic Affairs; Director, Salford Compact Partnership. *Education:* Humberstone Foundation School, Cleethorpes; University of Nottingham. *Military Service:* National Service, Royal Air Force (1952-54). *Career Profile:* Founded Collinson Grant, Management Consultants (1971); National Provincial Bank; Education Officer of Trades Union Congress; Personnel Officer, Bristol Co-operative Society; Deputy National Manager, Baking Group of Co-operative Wholesale Society; Director of Manpower, Plessey Telecommunications and Office Systems. *Publications/Creative Work:* (with C M Hodkinson) 'Employment Law Keynotes' (1985); 'The Line Manager's Employment Law' (1995, 16th edition). *Prizes:* Anniversary Cup, Institute of Training & Development (for significant contribution to human resource management)(1992); Service award, Institute of Personnel and Development (1994). *Societies:* Royal Automobile Club; The Portico Library. *Recreations, Interests:* Wales, collecting picture postcards, restoring 'Esther' oldest fishing trawler in the world. *Address:* Colgran House, 20 Worsley Road, Swinton, Manchester, M27 5WW (*tel:* 0161 793 9028; *fax:* 0161 794 0012). *Additional Information:* Chair, European Consortium of Management Consortium of Management Consultants; Chair, Network for Professionals; Director, Forum of Private Business.

COMMON, David J, MHSM,DipHSM

Chief Executive, West Pennine Health Authority. *b.* 13 June 1953 Altrincham. *m.* 1988 Jayne; one *s. Education:* North Cestrian Grammar School; University College of Salford. *Career Profile:* Chief Executive, West Pennine Health Authority (1994-); Chief Executive (concurrently), Oldham & Tameside Family Health Services (1994-96); Chief Executive, West Pennine Health Purchasing Consortium (1993-94); Chief Executive, Oldham Health Authority (1993); Joint Chief Executive, Oldham HA and Oldham FHSA (1992-93); Chief Executive, Oldham FPC/FHSA (1989-92); General Manager, Community Services Unit, Oldham HA (1988-89); Deputy General Manager, West Lancs HA & Ormskirk & District General Hospital (1987-88); Administration/General Management appointments, Stockport Health Authority (1975-87); National Administrative Trainee, North Western Regional Health Authority (1971-75). *Publications/Creative Work:* Contributor - "Value for Money" study, Partners in Primary Care (NHSE); several articles in the professional literature.. *Societies:* Old Cestrian's Association; Commanderie de Bordeaux; 1820 Club. *Recreations, Interests:* Sailing, skiing, running, theatre, reading. *Address:* West Pennine Health Authority Headquarters, Westhulme Avenue, Oldham, OL1 2PL (*tel:* 0161 455 5702; *fax:* 0161 455 5709).

COMPSTON, David Gerald, CEng,FICE,MASCE,MConsE

Chairman, Allott & Lomax (Holdings) Ltd, Allott & Lomax , Allott & Lomax (International) Ltd, Allott & Lomax (Hong Kong) Ltd, Fairbairn Services Ltd, Allott Projects Ltd, Ceramic Industrial Projects Ltd, Manchester TEC Ltd, Supervisory Boards of

INKOPLAN GmbH and Allott & Lomax (Deutschland) GmbH; Director: Trafford Park Manufacturing Institute, Marketing Manchester; Member, Training & Enterprise National Council. *b.* 21 October 1938; Rosthwaite, Cumbria. *m.* 1962 Helga Anne Compston Postlethwaite; one *s. Education:* Mill Hill School, London; Manchester College of Science & Technology. *Career Profile:* C S Allott & Son/Allott & Lomax (1961-89) (Director 1975); Manchester Ship Canal Company (1956-61). *Publications:* 'Rihand Power Station Civil Works - An Indo-British Solution' (Institution of Civil Engineers M W Association, 1986); 'Design and Construction of Buried Thin Walled Pipes' (Construction Industry Research and Information Association 1978). *Societies:* Royal Overseas League; St James's Club. *Recreations, Interests:* Fishing. *Address:* Allott & Lomax, Fairbairn House, Ashton Lane, Sale, Manchester M33 1WP *(tel:* 0161-962 1214).

CONNOLLY, Edward Thomas, LLB Liverpool (1957)

Regional Chairman of Industrial Tribunals, Manchester Region. *b.* 5 September 1935; Liverpool. *m.* 1962 Pamela Marie Hagan; one *s.* one *d. Public Offices:* Chairman of Industrial Tribunals Manchester (1976-77); Chairman of Industrial Tribunals Liverpool (1977-Aug 1988). *Education:* St Mary's College, Crosby, Merseyside; Prior Park College, Bath; Liverpool University. *Career Profile:* Assistant Solicitor, Lancashire County Council (1960-63); Assistant Prosecuting Solicitor, Liverpool City Council (1963-65); Deputy Chief Legal Officer, Skelmersdale Development Corporation (1965-68); Assistant Clerk of the Peace, Lancashire County Council (1968-71); Deputy Circuit Administrator, Northern Circuit, Lord Chancellors Department (1971-76). *Societies:* RAC London. *Recreations, Interests:* Reading and walking. *Address:* Regional Office of Industrial Tribunals, Alexandra House, The Parsonage, Manchester *(tel:* 0161-833 0581; *fax:* 0161 832 0249).

CONNOR, John Francis, JP (1978),PhD World University (1989); BSc Hull (1962),FCP

Proprietor and Head of Hale Prep School; Independent Educational Consultant. *b.* 31 July 1940; Coventry. *m.* 1964 Ann; two *s.* two *d. Public Offices:* JP Trafford Division. *Education:* Xaverian College, Manchester; Hull University. *Career Profile:* Headmaster, Hillcrest Grammar School, Bramhall; Senior Teacher, Xaverian College, Manchester; Lecturer, Rochdale College; Lecturer, Worker Educational Centre; Chief Examiner for a number of GCE, CSE and professional bodies. *Creative Works:* Child Educational profile 7+-12+. *Publications:* 'Rules of Maths' (in conjunction with P Soper); 'Data Response in Economics'; 'Study Guide to Economics'; 'Rules of Spelling'; series of articles in the 'Times Educational Supplement', 'Political Journal', (with P Soper) 'Modular Maths' and 'Study Pack: Intelligence Testing'. *Prizes:* Rhodes' Scholarship (1959). *Societies:* Regional Executive, Independent Schools Association Incorporated; Magistrates' Association. *Recreations, Interests:* Theatre, travel, sport. *Address:* Hale Preparatory School, Broomfield Lane, Hale, Cheshire *(tel:* 0161-928 2386); 6 Acacia Drive, Hale, Altrincham, Cheshire *(tel:* 0161-928 0030).

COOKE, Darryl John, LLB,LLM

Partner, Addleshaw Sons & Latham (Head of Venture Capital Unit). *b.* 1 January 1959 Oldham. *m.* 1985 Pamela; two *s. Education:* Hulme Grammar School, Oldham; Leeds University. *Career Profile:* Practising Barrister; In-house legal advisor, Hoechst UK Ltd;

SJ Berwin & Co; Halliwell Landau; Addleshaw Sons & Latham. *Publications/Creative Work:* 'Management Buy-outs' (FT Law & Tax); 'Venture Capital: Law & Practice' (FT Law & Tax). *Societies:* Tytherington Golf Club; Prestbury Squash Club. *Recreations, Interests:* Golf, squash, jogging. *Address:* Addleshaw Sons & Latham, Dennis House, Marsden Street, Manchester, M2 1JD(*tel:* 0161 832 5994; *fax:* 0161 832 2250).

COOPER, Professor Cary Lynn, FBPsS,FRSM,FRSA,FBAM,BSc UCLA (1964),MBA UCLA (1966),PhD Leeds (1968),MSc (Hon) Manchester (1979)

Professor of Organizational Psychology & Pro-Vice-Chancellor, UMIST. *b.* 28 April 1940; Los Angeles, California. *m.* Edna June Taylor Bromley; one *s.* one *d.*; *m.* 1985 Rachel Faith; two *d.* *Public Offices:* President, British Academy of Management (1986-90); Editor-in-Chief, Journal of Organizational Behavior (1980-); Co-editor, Stress Medicine; Chairman, MED Division, American Academy of Management (1979-80); Trustee, American Institute of Stress (1985-). *Education:* Fairfax High School, Los Angeles. *Military Service:* US Naval Air Force (Reserve). *Career Profile:* Lecturer in Psychology, University of Southampton. *Creative Works:* Presenter and co-writer Channel Four TV series 'How to Survive the Nine to Five'. *Publications:* Over 80 books eg 'Living with Stress' (Penguin Books) (1988); 'Career Couples' (Unwin Hyman) (1989); 'Change Makers' (Harper & Row) (1986), 'Workplace Revolution' (1993), 'Handbook of Streess, Medicine & Health' (1996) etc; over 250 scholarly articles in journals; frequent contributor to newspapers (eg Sunday Times, The Guardian, etc). *Prizes:* Recipient of the Myers Lecture, British Psychological Society (1986). *Societies:* St James's Club. *Recreations, Interests:* Russian literature (19th century), swimming, television documentaries and political commentaries, living in hope with Manchester City FC. *Address:* Manchester School of Management, UMIST, PO Box 88, Manchester M60 1QD (*tel:* 0161-200 3440); Poynton, Cheshire.

COPLEY, Rev David H, BSocSc(Birmingham,1966),BA(Cantab,1970), MA(Liverpool, 1986)

Superintendent Methodist Minister, Manchester and Salford Mission. *b.* 20 July 1944 Manchester. *m.* 1970 Margaret; two *s.* one *d.* *Public Offices:* Board Member, Christian Aid; Vice-Chair, Merseyside Improved Houses (-1996); Board Member, Manchester Methodist Housing Association. *Career Profile:* Child Care Officer, Leeds (1966-68); Methodist Minister: Isle of Man (1971-73); Birkenhead (1973-78); Liverpool (Toxteth) (1978-86); Superintendent, Widnes (1986-96). *Societies:* Amnesty International; RSPB. *Recreations, Interests:* Cooking, walking, photography, cricket, Manchester United. *Address:* Manchester & Salford Mission, Central Hall, Oldham Street, Manchester, M1 1JT (*tel:* 0161 236 5141; *fax:* 0161 237 1585).

CORLETT, William Irving, LLB,Solicitor

Retired. *b.* 5 July 1925; Southport. *m.* 1953 Norah Valmai Hooper; one *s.* one *d.* *Public Offices:* Hon Treasurer, The Manchester Law Society (1978-83); Member of Governing Body and Board of Governors, Manchester Polytechnic (1983-91); Chairman, The Garden History Society (1989-92). *Education:* Stockport Grammar School; Manchester University. *Career Profile:* Solicitor, Co-operative Insurance Society Ltd (1984-90). *Societies:* St

James's Club, Manchester; The Rucksack Club; Manchester Pedestrian Club. *Recreations, Interests:* Cartophily, gardening, hill walking, music, wine, food.

CORRIE, Wallace Rodney, CBE(1977); MA Cantab (1944)

Retired (1980). *b.* 25 November 1919; Swinton, Lancashire. *m.* 1952 Helen Margaret Morice; one *s.* one *d. Education:* Leigh Grammar School, Lancashire; Christ's College, Cambridge; University of Nancy, France. *War Service:* Royal Signals, Mentioned in Despatches. *Career Profile:* Entered Civil Service 1947, served in Ministry of Town & Country Planning, Ministry of Housing & Local Government, Department of Economic Affairs; Chairman, NW Economic Planning Board; Regional Director (NW) of the Departments of the Environment and of Transport (until 1980). *Recreations, Interests:* Exploring byways, catching up on things, family history, voluntary service with housing associations working in inner cities. *Address:* "Brambledown", Chapel Lane, Hale Barns.

COVER, Michael David, LLB(Southampton,1972),Barrister (1973),Solicitor (1988)

Managing Partner, Davies Arnold Cooper, Manchester. *b.* 29 November 1950 Bognor Regis, West Sussex. *m.* 1990 Allyson; two *s. Education:* Portsmouth Grammar School; University of Southampton. *Military Service:* Southampton University Air Squadron (1969-72). *Career Profile:* The Distillers Company Ltd (1972-74); Allied-Lyons plc (1974-87); Davies Arnold Cooper (1987-). *Societies:* Royal Thames Yacht Club; Itchenor Sailing Club; Lancashire Aero Club. *Recreations, Interests:* Sailing, flying, railways. *Address:* Davies Arnold Cooper, 60 Fountain Street, Manchester, M2 2FE (*tel:* 0161 839 8396; *fax:* 0161 839 8309).

COWAN, Peter Lawrence, FBCO

Chief Executive, United Optical Industries Ltd. *b.* 22 February 1944 Salford. *m.* three *s.* one *d. (marr. diss.) Education:* Salford Grammar School; UMIST. *Career Profile:* Chairman, Henlys Optical Group Ltd (1981-84); Deputy Non-Executive Chairman, Prestwich Holdings plc (1984-89); Executive Chairman and Chief Executive, The Intercare Group plc (1989-95); Non-Executive Director, Eaglet Investment Trust plc (1993-). *Societies:* Mere Golf Club. *Address:* United Optical Industries Ltd, Pennine House, Manchester Road, Heaton Norris, Stockport, SK4 1TX (*tel:* 0161 477 7077; *fax:* 0161 476 0528).

CRAIG, Ian Alexander, BA(Law)(Sheffield, 1982),Solicitor (1985)

Partner and Head of Corporate Department, Halliwell Landau, Manchester; Non-Executive Director of various public and private companies. *b.* 28 September 1957 Glasgow. *m.* 1991 Sally; three *s. Education:* Wellfield High School, Leyland; Sheffield University; College of Law, London. *Career Profile:* Articled in Sheffield; Joined Halliwell Landau, Manchester (1985), Partner (1989), Head of Corporate Dept (1995). *Societies:* RAC Club, London; St James' Club, Manchester; Law Society; Alderley Edge Cricket Club; Member, Securities Institute. *Recreations, Interests:* Soccer, golf, family. *Address:* Halliwell Landau, St James's Court, Brown Street, Manchester (*tel:* 0161 835 3003; *fax:* 0161 831 2641);

Greencote, Warford Hall Drive, Alderley Edge, SK9 7TR (*tel:* 01565 872852; *fax:* 01565 872153).

CRAIG, Robert Dominic Peter, MB,CHB(Manchester, 1954),FRCS(Eng)(1958), MD (Manchester, 1972)

Consultant Plastic Surgeon, Alexandra Hospital. *b.* 4 August 1927 Salford. *m.* 1962 Veronica Ann; two *d.* *Public Offices:* President, Manchester Medico Ethical Society (1982); President, Surgical Section Manchester Medical Society (1988); Member of Council, British Association of Plastic Surgery (1981-83). *Education:* De La Salle College, Salford; Medical School, University of Manchester. *Military Service:* Army (1945-48). *Career Profile:* Junior Resident Appointments, Manchester Royal Infirmary; Demonstrator in Physiology, Manchester University; Senior Registrar, Plastic Surgery, Manchester; Associate Lecturer, Plastic Surgery, Manchester University. *Publications/Creative Work:* Over 30 publications on general and plastic surgery including a history of the unit in Manchester. *Societies:* Royal Yachting Association; Hale and North Wales Golf Clubs. *Recreations, Interests:* Golf, cookery. *Address:* Alexandra Hospital, Mill Lane, Cheadle, Cheshire, SK8 2PX (*tel:* 0161 428 3656; *fax:* 0161 491 3867); Hiverley, Twemlow Green, Cheshire, CW4 8BP.

CRASTON, Revd Canon Richard Colin,BA(Hons)(Bristol,1949),BD(Hons)(London, 1951) DD(Lambeth, 1992)

Retired. *b.* 31 December 1922 Preston. *m.* 1948 Ruth; one *s.* one *d.* *(widowed 1992)*; *m.* 1993 Brenda. *Public Offices:* Chaplain to HM The Queen (1985-92); Vice-Chairman (1986-90), Chairman (1990-96), Anglican Consultative Council; Chairman, Business Sub-Committee, General Synod (1991-95). *Education:* Preston Grammar School (1934-41); University of Bristol (1946-49); University of London (external)(1949-51); Tyndale Hall, Bristol (1946-51). *War Service:* Royal Navy (1941-46). *Career Profile:* Curate, St Nicholas, Durham (1951-54); Team Rector, St Paul with Emmanuel, Bolton (1954-93); Area Dean, Bolton (1972-92). *Publications/Creative Work:* 'Biblical Headship and the Ordination of Women' (1986); 'Authority and the Anglican Communion' (contributor)(1987); 'Open to the Spirit' (editor)(1987); 'Anglicanism and the Universal Church' (joint author)(1990); 'By Word and Deed' (editor)(1992). *Societies:* Union Jack Club, London. *Recreations, Interests:* Football, cricket. *Address:* 12 Lever Park Avenue, Horwich, Bolton, BL6 7LE (*tel:* 01204 699972; *fax:* 01204 690813).

CRAVEN, Diana Margaret, LLB (Nottingham)

Solicitor; Partner, Addleshaw, Sons & Latham. *b.* Halifax, West Yorkshire. *m.* 1977 Howard M Colquhoun. *Public Offices:* Governor, Withington Girls' School. *Education:* Ackworth School, Pontefract; Nottingham University. *Societies:* The Association of Women Solicitors; Network North. *Recreations, Interests:* Professional and managerial level womens groups, gardening, travelling in France. *Address:* Addleshaw, Sons & Latham, Dennis House, Marsden Street, Manchester M2 1JD (0161-832 5994).

CREED, Professor Francis Hunter, MA,BChir,MD,FRCP,FRCPsych

Professor of Community Psychiatry, University of Manchester. *b.* 22 February 1947

Truro, Cornwall. *m.* Ruth Alison; two *s.* two *d.* *Education:* Kingsworth School, Bath; Cambridge University & St Thomas' Hospital; Postgraduate: Maudsley Hospital and the London Hospital. *Career Profile:* Training post in Medicine and Psychiatry; Academic posts in Psychiatry, with emphasis on community treatments and psychiatry in the General Hospital. *Publications/Creative Work:* Numerous research articles concerning the treatment of psychiatric disorder in the community; the interface between medicine and psychiatry - "Psychosomatic Mechanisms". *Prizes:* Pilley Scholarship, Downing College, University of Cambridge. *Societies:* Fellow of Royal Colleges of Physicians and Psychiatrists; Fellow of Royal Society of Medicine. *Recreations, Interests:* Hill walking. *Address:* Department of Psychiatry, Rawnsley Building, Manchester Royal Infirmary, Oxford Road, Manchester, M13 9PL (*tel:* 0161 276 5331; *fax:* 0161 273 2135).

CRESSEY, Vernon Edward, Cross Pro Ecclesia Et Pontifice from John Paul (1982),DMA (1970), FCIS(1983)

Director of Administration, Greater Manchester Police (1994-). *b.* 22 November 1945 Oldham. *m.* 1968 Carole Lesley Clarke; one *s.* *Public Offices:* Associate Member of Association of Chief Police Officers (ACPO); Member, ACPO Finance Committee; Member, Saddleworth Deanery Synod; Secretary, Dobcross Church PCC; Vice Chairman, Ferney Field Special School Governors; Governor, South Chadderton Secondary School; Trustee, Friends of St Ann's Church, Manchester; Director and Secretary, Global Forum '94. *Education:* Counthill Grammar School, Oldham. *Career Profile:* Oldham Metropolitan Borough (1963-79); Manchester City Council (1979-94) becoming Assistant Town Clerk (1982), City Administrator (1988). *Societies:* Chairman, Greater Manchester Police Sports & Social Club; Dovestones Sailing Club; Oldham Athletic Football Club; Saddleworth Peace Movement; Manchester Luncheon Club. *Address:* PO Box (S West PDO), Chester House, Boyer Street, Manchester, M16 0RE; 63 Nudger Green, Dobcross, Saddleworth, Oldham, OL3 5AW.

CRILLY, Samuel, OBE (1990),JP; BSc (Econ) London (1953)

Retired. *b.* 20 July 1920; Darkley, County Armagh. *m.* 1945 Josephine Benah Brand; one *s.* one *d.* *Public Offices:* JP, Manchester City Bench (1965-90); General Commissioner of Taxes (1978-95); Deputy Chairman, Manchester City Bench (1980-81); Chairman, Manchester City Bench (1982-84); Hon Secretary, Cross Street Chapel Trustees (1972-94). *Education:* Wallace High School, Lisburn, Co Antrim; College of Commerce, Leeds. *War Service:* Royal Air Force (1942-46). *Career Profile:* Principal, Personnel & Administration Directorate, British Nuclear Fuels Ltd. *Societies:* Manchester Literary & Philosophical Society (formerly Vice-President); Manchester Luncheon Club (President 1988); Portico Library; Friends of Greater Manchester Museum of Science & Industry. *Recreations, Interests:* Walking, silversmithing, reading. *Address:* "Whitecroft", 7 Brooklands Road, Sale, Cheshire M33 3QH (0161-962 4362). *Additional Information:* Parliamentary Liberal Candidate Middleton & Prestwich constituency General Elections 1964, 1966 and 1970.

CROLL, Michael John

Director, Greater Manchester Employment Association, St Mark's Enterprises Ltd. *b.* 16 September 1929; Lincoln. *m.* 1956 Rita; one *d.* *Education:* Worksop College (1942-47).

Military Service: The Gordon Highlanders (1948-50). *Career Profile:* Partner, Heywood Shepherd, Chartered Accountants (1963-89); Member, Manchester Diocesan Board of Finance (1980-94); Director, Mancheser Diocesan Church House Ltd (1986-94); Council of Manchester Junior Chamber of Commerce (1967-69); Founder Member, Didsbury & District Rotary Club (1970-72). *Societies:* The Manchester Luncheon Club. *Recreations, Interests:* Travel and reading. *Address:* 625 Wilmslow Road, Didsbury, Manchester M20 6DF (*tel:* 0161-434 3685).

CROSBY, John Charles, MSc Manchester (1984),BSc(Tech) Manchester (1948), CEng, MICE

Retired Chartered Engineer. *b.* 19 September 1927; Blackpool. *m.* 1954 Jeanne Dorothy Malcouronne; one *s.* two *d. Education:* St Josephs College, Blackpool; Manchester University, Faculty of Technology (1945-48). *Career Profile:* Civil Engineer, London County Council (1948-54) (Festival of Britain 1951); Civil Engineer, Air Ministry (1954-57); Building Officer, UMIST (1957-72); Director, Department of Building Services, University of Manchester (1972-83). *Societies:* Trustee, Henshaws Society for the Blind; Trustee, International Society; Bowdon Bowling & Lawn Tennis Club; Lancashire CCC; Cheshire Wildlife; National Trust. *Recreations, Interests:* Sport, music, gardening. *Address:* 10 Highgate Road, Altrincham, Cheshire WA14 4QZ (*tel:* 0161-928 3849).

CROWTHER, Professor Derek, BA(Cantab, 1959),MA(Cantab, 1963),MBBChir(Cantab, 1963),MRCP(London,1966),PhD(London,1969), MSc (Manchester,1974), FRCP (London, 1976),FRCR(London,1994)

Professor of Medical Oncology; Director, Department of Medical Oncology, Christie Hospital, Manchester University. *b.* 1 July 1937 London. *m.* 1959 Margaret Frances Dickinson; one *s. decd* two *d. Public Offices:* Chairman, Cancer Research Campaign (Phase I Biological Agents Committee); Member, Medical Research Council (Molecular and Cellular Medicine Board); Member, Government Gene Therapy Advisory Committee. *Education:* City of London School; Cambridge University; Baylor University, Texas; S Bartholomew's Hospital, London; Royal Marsden Hospital, Institute of Cancer Research; Hammersmith Postgraduate Medical School. *Career Profile:* Deputy Director, Imperial Cancer Research Fund; Department of Medical Oncology. *Publications/Creative Work:* 300 publications in the field of cancer medicine; textbooks of haematology, oncology, lymphoma, leukemia, ovarian cancer. *Prizes:* in Paediatrics Pathology/General Medicine and Gold Medal Obstetrics & Gynaecology (St Bartholomew's Hospital); Foundation Scholar, Clare College Cambridge, Fulbright Scholar (1959-60); Wellcome Fellowship (1966-69). *Societies:* European Organisation for Research in Treatment of Cancer; British Association for Cancer Research; European Association for Haematology; American Society of Cancer Research; American Society of Clinical Oncology. *Recreations, Interests:* Art, cosmology, physical sciences. *Address:* Department of Medical Oncology, Christie Hospital, Wilmslow Road, Manchester, M20 4BX (*tel:* 0161 446 3209; *fax:* 0161 446 3109); 52 Barlow Moor Road, Didsbury, Manchester, M20 2TR (*tel:* 0161 434 6685).

CRUICKSHANK, Durward William John, FRS; BSc(Eng),MA,PhD,ScD,CChem,FRSC

Scientist, active in macromolecular crystallography; Emeritus Professor of Chemistry. *b.* 7

March 1924; London. *m.* 1953 Marjorie Alice Travis; one *s.* one *d. (widowed 1983) Education:* St Lawrence College, Ramsgate; Loughborough College (now Loughborough University of Technology); St John's College, Cambridge (Wrangler, Mathematical Tripos, 1949). *War Service:* Engineering Assistant, Inter-Services Research Bureau. *Career Profile:* Lecturer, then Reader in Mathematical Chemistry, Leeds University (1950-62); Fellow of St John's College, Cambridge (1953-56); Joseph Black Professor of Chemistry (Theoretical Chemistry), Glasgow University (1962-67); Professor of Chemistry, UMIST (1967-83); Honorary Visiting Professor of Physics, York University (1985-88); Companion, UMIST (1992). *Publications:* Scientific papers on Crystallography, Molecular Structure Determination and Theoretical Chemistry. *Prizes:* Chemical Society Award for Structural Chemistry (1977); Dorothy Hodgkin Prize, British Crystallographic Association (1991). *Societies:* Treasurer (1966-72), General Secretary (1970-72), International Union of Crystallography. *Recreations, Interests:* Science, genealogy, golf. *Address:* Chemistry Department, UMIST, Manchester M60 1QD.

CUDDY, Philip Adrian, BA(1977),Solicitor(1980)

Clerk to the Justices, Stockport; Justices' Chief Executive, Stockport; Secretary to the Advisory Committee, Stockport. *b.* 20 July 1952 Stockport. *m.* 1977 Mary Cecilia; one *s.* one *d. Education:* Marple Hall Grammar School for Boys; Manchester Polytechnic. *Career Profile:* Court Clerk, Tameside (1970-81); Deputy Justices' Clerk, Cheshire (1981-82), Tameside (1982-86); Justices' Clerk, Derwentside (1986-88), Middleton & Heywood (1988-90), Rochdale (1990-92), Stockport (1992-). *Societies:* Justices' Clerks' Society; Law Society; Institute of Management; Institute of Personnel and Development. *Address:* Magistrates' Court, PO Box 155, Edward Street, Stockport, SK1 3NF (*tel:* 0161 477 2020; *fax:* 0161 474 1115).

CULLEN, Raymond, MA Cantab

Retired. *b.* 27 May 1913. *m.* 1940 Doris Paskin; two *d. Public Offices:* Member, Textile Council (1967-69); Council, Institute of Directors (1967-69); NW Economic Planning Council (1968-69); Governor, Manchester Grammar School (1968-83); Local Board Director, Barclays Bank Ltd (1965-69). *Education:* King's School, Macclesfield; St Catharines College, Cambridge. *Career Profile:* Chairman, The Calico Printers Association Ltd and Subsidiaries (1964-68), joined Association (1934), overseas service, India and China (1938); Director, W A Beardsell & Co Ltd, Madras (1946) (Chairman and Managing Director (1949-55); Chairman and Managing Director, Mettur Industries Ltd (1949-55); Chairman and Managing Director, Marshall Fabrics Ltd (1955-62); Director, Calico Printers Association (1962-68). *Societies:* President, Cheshire Union of Golf Clubs (1977-78). *Recreations, Interests:* Fishing, golf. *Address:* Cranford, Ladybrook Road, Bramhall, Cheshire SK7 3NB.

CUTTLE, Malcolm Barry

Senior Partner, M B Cuttle & Co, Solicitors. *b.* 13 July 1939 Ashton-under-Lyne. *m.* 1965 Shena Marshall; one *s.* two *d. Education:* Worksop college. *Military Service:* Formerly commissioned with 7th Battalian, The Cheshire Regiment (TA). *Career Profile:* Qualified as Solicitor (1963); short period in private practice followed by entry into Crown

Prosecution Service, Manchester; appointed Chief Prosecuting Solicitor for Bolton Borough Police Authority; entered private practice, forming M B Cuttle & Co 22 years ago. *Societies:* Member of the Law Society. *Recreations, Interests:* Sport particularly rugby and swimming. *Address:* M B Cuttle & Co, Bridge Street Chambers, 72 Bridge Street, Manchester, M3 2RJ (*tel:* 0161 835 2050; *fax:* 0161 831 7986). *Additional Information:* Appointed as Negotiator Solicitor within the Strangeways Prison Riot 1990 by Authorities.

D

DA-COCODIA, Louise Adassa (*née* Wright), BEM(1992), MA(hc)(Manchester,1989) SRN,RGN,SCM,QN,NDN,H/V Certs

Project Consultant; former Nurse Manager. *b.* 9 November 1934 St Catherine, Jamaica. *m.* 1964 Edward (*decd*); one *s.* one *d.* (*widowed 1994*) *Public Offices:* Non-Executive Member, Manchester Health Authority; Assessor, Manchester County Courts; JP, Manchester Bench; Manchester Advisory Committee Member, City Magistrates Court; Cariocca Enterprises Workspace Complex; Positive Action Cariocca Training; Arawak Walton Housing Association; Agency for Economic Development (Moss Side); served as Deputy Chair, Voluntary Action Manchester; a number of directorships and committee positions in the voluntary organisation sector. *Education:* Formal education in Jamaica. *Career Profile:* District Nurse, Midwife, Health Visitor, Berkshire County Council (1960-66); Assistant Superintendent, District Nurses, Manchester Corporation (1968-71); Health Visitor/Fieldwork Instructor, Cheshire County Council (1971-75); Nursing Officer, Senior Nursing Officer, District Night Superintendent, Deputy Director, Acting Senior Director (Acute Services), Tameside Area Health Auhthority (1975-88); Counsellor/Advisor, Haemoglobinopathies, Sickle Cell & Thalassaemia Central Health Authority (1990); Associate Consultant, (Training Dept), North West Regional Health Authority (1991); Project Consultant/Advisor, The Government Moss Side & Hulme Task Force, DoE (1991-95). *Prizes:* Manchester National Anti-Racist Day Award (1995) for promoting good race relations. *Societies:* Royal College of Nursing; General Synod of Church of England Rep (1995-2000). *Recreations, Interests:* Music, reading, dancing, travel, voluntary community activities. *Address:* 9 Arliss Avenue, Levenshulme, Manchester, M19 2PD (*tel:* 0161 224 0209).

DALBY, Ven John Mark Meredith, MA Oxford (1965),PhD Nottingham (1977)

Archdeacon of Rochdale; Examining Chaplain to the Bishop of Manchester. *b.* 3 January 1938; Southport. *Education:* King George V School, Southport; Exeter College, Oxford; Ripon Hall, Oxford; University of Nottingham. *Military Service:* RAF (1956-58). *Career Profile:* Curate, Hambleden Valley, Buckinghamshire; Chaplain, RAF, Medmenham; Vicar, St Peter, Birmingham; Rural Dean of Birmingham City; Secretary, Committee for Theological Education, Advisory Council for Church's Ministry; Team Rector of Worsley; Area Dean of Eccles. *Publications:* 'Open Communion in the Church of England'; 'The Gospel and the Priest'; 'The Cocker Connection'; 'Open Baptism'. *Societies:* Royal Commonwealth Society. *Recreations, Interests:* Travel, family history, philately, liturgy, detective novels. *Address:* 21 Belmont Way, Rochdale, OL12 6HF. (tel/fax: 01706 48640).

DALEY, Peter C W, BA(Hons),MA,PGCE

Principal, Pendleton College, Salford. *b.* 22 January 1955 Bristol. *m.* 1977 Nicola C; two *s.* (*marr. diss. 1992*); *m.* 1993 Susan R. *Education:* Llanrumney High School, Cardiff (1966-68); Cardiff High School (1968-73); University of Birmingham (1973-78). *Career Profile:* Teacher in two Coventry High Schools; Head of Drama, King Edward VI College, Nuneaton; Head of English, St Philip's College, Birmingham; Vice-Principal, Wilberforce College, Hull. *Societies:* Director, Centra (Chorley); Chair, Sixth Form Colleges' Staff

Development Committee. *Recreations, Interests:* Old houses, furniture, cars, gardening, writing. *Address:* Pendleton College, Dronfield Road, Salford, M6 7FR (*tel:* 0161 736 5074; *fax:* 0161 737 4103; *e-mail:* pencoll@rmplc.co.uk).

DARROCH, Lieutenant Colonel Peter Lyle Keith

Army Careers Officer, Grade 1; Commanding, Greater Manchester Army Careers Information Group. *b.* 27 June 1937 Glasgow. *m.* 1959 Anita Robinson; one *s. Public Offices:* Member, Greater Manchester Army Benevolent Fund Committee; President, Tameside (1st UK) Branch 8th Army Veterans Association; Member, Executive Council Broughton House Home for Disabled Ex-Servicemen; Council Member, Order of St John in Greater Manchester. *Education:* Gordons School, Woking; Army Apprentices College, Chepstow; Royal Army Medical College, London. *Military Service:* Enlisted RAMC (1952), Commissioned (1972); Service in Kenya (1959-62), Malaya (1966), Hong Kong (1966-68); Germany (1971 and 1977-80), Australia (1982-84), USA (1988); Retired (1991); Re-employed Army Careers Service (1991-). *Career Profile:* Commander Medical HQ Eastern District (1989-91); Technical Training Officer RAMC (1985-89); Staff Officer Grade 1, Surgeon Generals Department, MOD (1984-85); British Defence Liaison Staff Australia (1982-84). *Publications/Creative Work:* History of the Royal Chapel, Royal Victoria Hospital, Netley; Report on All Arms Medical Training; Analysis of the Requirements for Medical Training for Non RAMC Personnel in the British Army. *Societies:* Member of Conseil, Commanderie de Bordeaux, Manchester; Chevalier of 3 French Wine Orders; British Americal Association, Manchester; RAMC Association; RAMC Non-Medical Officers Dinner Club, London; Movement Control Officers Club, London. *Recreations, Interests:* Good food and wine, travel, countryside pursuits, golf, cricket, ex-servicements organisations. *Address:* Army Careers Information Office, Barnett House, 53 Fountain Street, Manchester, M2 2AJ (*tel:* 0161 228 3300; *fax:* 0161 228 2750).

DASH, John Raymond

Programme Director, KEY103/Piccadillly 1152 Radio. *b.* 6 April 1959 Cwmbran, Gwent. *Education:* West Monmouth Grammar School, Pontypool; University of Bradford. *Career Profile:* Presenter, Pennine Radio, Bradford (1980-83); Sports Editor, Gwent Broadcasting (1983-85); Head of Music, 2CR, Bournemouth (1985-87); Presenter, Red Dragon Radio (1987-91), Programme Director (1991-94); Programme Director, Piccadilly Radio (1995-96). *Societies:* Barker, Variety Club of Great Britain. *Address:* Piccadilly Radio, 127/131 The Piazza, Piccadilly Plaza, Manchester, M1 4AW (*tel:* 0161 236 9913; *fax:* 0161 228 1503).

DAVENPORT, Colin, FCIB

Managing Director, Davenham Group plc. *b.* 4 April 1943 Wigan. *m.* 1970 Constance; two *s. Public Offices:* Current Member, Deposit Protection Board. *Education:* Wigan Grammar School. *Career Profile:* Williams & Glyns Bank (1959-85), last appointment Manager, International Division; Regional Manager, ABN Bank (1985-89); Managing Director, Burns Anderson Trust (1989-91). *Societies:* Wigan Golf Club; Houghwood Golf Club. *Recreations, Interests:* Cycling, golf, running, biography and history. *Address:* Davenham Group plc, 8 St John Street, Manchester, M3 4DU (*tel:* 0161 832 8484; *fax:* 0161 832

9164). *Additional Information:* Visiting Lecturer on banking topics, Manchester Business School Chairman, Manchester Merchant and International Bankers Association (1993-95).

DAVID, Ann Rosalie (*née* David), BA (Hons) London (1967),PhD Liverpool (1971)

Keeper of Egyptology, Manchester Musuem, University of Manchester (with status of Senior Lecturer); Honorary Lecturer, Dept of Comparative Religion, University of Manchester; Director, Centre for Biomedical Egyptology, University of Manchester. *b.* 30 May 1946; Cardiff, S Wales. *m.* 1970 Antony Edward David. *Education:* Howell's Scholar, Howell's School, Llandaff, Cardiff (1957-64); University College, London (1964-67); University of Liverpool (1967-71). *Career Profile:* Assistant Keeper of Archaeology, Manchester Museum (1972-88). *Publications:* Various articles to learned journals and eighteen books, including: 'A Guide to Religious Ritual at Abydos' (1973); 'The Manchester Mummy Project' (ed), (1979); 'Science in Egyptology' (ed), (1986); 'The Ancient Egyptians: Their Religious Beliefs and Practices' (1982); 'Discovering Ancient Egypt' (1995). *Prizes:* Leverhulme Travelling Scholarship (1969); British Academy (Personal Award) (1987); Wellcome Trust Research Grant (1989); Leverhulme Trust Award (1996). *Societies:* Egypt Exploration Society (Hon Secretary of Society's Northern Branch); International Association of Egyptologists; British Association for the History of Religions. *Recreations, Interests:* Photography, travel. *Address:* The Manchester Museum, University of Manchester, Manchester M13 9PL (*tel:* 0161-275 2647). *Additional Information:* Director of Mummy Research Project since 1973, Consultant to BBC TV on several films, guest lecturer in Egypt, Germany, USA, Canada and Australia

DAVID, Professor T J, MB,ChB,PhD,MD,FRCP,DCH

Professor of Child Health & Paediatrics, University of Manchester. *b.* 13 January 1948 London. *m.* two *s.* *Education:* Clifton College, Bristol; Bristol University. *Career Profile:* Professor of Paediatrics & Child Health, Head of Department, University of Manchester; Consultant Paediatrician: Booth Hall Children's Hospital; Royal Manchester Children's Hospital; St Mary's Hospital. *Publications/Creative Work:* 250 publications including 12 books. *Societies:* President, Section of Paediatrics, Royal Society of Medicine (1996-97). *Recreations, Interests:* Gardening, music, skiing, baseball. *Address:* Booth Hall Children's Hospital, Charlestown Road, Blackley, Manchester, M9 7AA.

DAVIES, Bryan, BA(Univ College, London),BSc (LSE),PGCE(Univ. of London)

Member of Parliament, Oldham Central and Royton. *b.* 9 November 1939 Tredegar, Gwent. *m.* 1963 Monica; two *s.* one *d.* *Public Offices:* Member of Parliament, Enfield North (1974-79); Secretary of Parliamentary Labour Party and of the Shadow Cabinet (1979-92); Member, Medical Research Council (1977-79). *Education:* Redditch High School, Worcestershire (1953-58); University of London (1958-62). *Prizes:* Honorary Doctorate, Middlesex University. *Recreations, Interests:* Sport and literature. *Address:* House of Commons, London, SW1A 0AA (*tel:* 0171 219 4064); 9 Lydgate Fold, Oldham, OL4 4DL.

DAVIES, Chris, MA(Cantab)

MP for Littleborough and Saddleworth. *b.* 7 July 1954 Lytham, Lancashire. *m.* 1979

Carol; one *d*. *Education:* Cheadle Hulme School (1965-72); Gonville & Caius College, Cambridge (1972-75). *Career Profile:* Prior to election in 1995 Communications and Marketing Consultant. *Recreations, Interests:* Fell running. *Address:* Constituency Office, 51 High Street, Lees, Oldham, OL4 3BN(*tel:* 0161 628 4778; *fax:* 0161 628 5180); 4 Higher Kinders, Greenfield, Oldham, OL3 7BH (*tel:* 01457 870236; *fax:* 01457 877034).

DAVIES, David Garfield, CBE (1996)

General Secretary, Union of Shop, Distributive & Allied Workers (USDAW); President, EURO-FIET Executive. *b.* 24 June 1935; Glamorgan. *m.* 1960 Marian; four *d*. *Public Offices:* JP (1972-79); Rural District Councillor (1966-69); Parish Councillor (1963-69); Employment Appeal Tribunal (1991-); Corporation Member, Birmingham College of food, Tourism & Creative Studies. *Education:* Secondary education; Part-time technical. *Military Service:* National Service, RAF (1956-58). *Career Profile:* National Officer, USDAW; Deputy Divisional Officer, USDAW; Area Organiser, USDAW; Electrician, British Steel Corporation. *Societies:* Lancashire County Cricket Club; Reform Club. *Recreations, Interests:* Spectator sport - soccer, rugby, cricket; participating - golf; reading. *Address:* USDAW, 188 Wilmslow Road, Fallowfield, Manchester M14 6LJ (*tel:* 0161-224 2804).

DAVIES, Hyman, MB,ChB,FRCGP

Retired General Practitioner. *b.* 30 December 1918; Manchester. *m.* 1944 Rose Babsky; one *d*. *Education:* Jews' School, Derby Street (1923-29); Manchester Central High School for Boys, Whitworth Street (1930-37); Manchester University (1937-43). *War Service:* RAMC (1944-47). Served in India, W Africa. *Career Profile:* Part-time Lecturer in General Practice, Manchester University; Course Organiser, Salford GP Trainees Day Release Course (Manchester University Department of Post Graduate Medical Studies); Medical Adviser, Personnel Department, Salford University; President, Section of General Practice, Manchester Medical Society (1978-79); Member, Salford Local Medical Committee (1968-82). *Societies:* Life Fellow, Manchester Medical Society; Friends of the Camerata; Friends of the Whitworth; Friends of the BBC Philharmonic; Friends of the Jewish Museum; Friends of the Working Class Movement Library. *Recreations, Interests:* Music, World safety, human progress. *Address:* 19 Danesway, Prestwich, Manchester M25 0ET (*tel:* 0161-740 6571).

DAVIES, James Christopher Meredith, Solicitor

Chief Executive, Davies Wallis Foyster, Solicitors. *b.* 23 October 1946 London. *m.* 1972 Shirley; two *d*. *Public Offices:* Chairman, Merseyside Artists Exhibition (1988, 1989, 1990); Co-Founder Trustee, Merseyside Bone Marrow Transplant Trust; Committee of Barnardos Centenary Appeal for Merseyside; Committee of Merseyside Youth Association. *Education:* Liverpool College; Liverpool Polytechnic (now John Moores University). *Career Profile:* Articled Layton & Co (1965-70); admitted Solicitor (1971); Assistant Solicitor and Partner, Bullivant & Co (1972-77); Co-founder with Guy Wallis of Davies Wallis & Co (1977); merged with Dodds Ashcroft (Liverpool)(1988) and with Foysters (Manchester)(1989); Chief Executive (1991-). *Prizes:* The David Lobley Debating Prize. *Societies:* The Law Society, Manchester and Liverpool; The Artists Club, Liverpool; Caldy Golf Club; British Society of Field Sports; Game Conservancy; The Racquets Club,

Manchester. *Recreations, Interests:* Fishing, shooting, golf, the Arts. *Address:* Davies Wallis Foyster, Harvester House, 37 Peter Street, Manchester, M2 5GB (*tel:* 0161 228 3702; *fax:* 0161 835 2407; *e-mail:* gbdwajcd@ibmmail.com).

DAVIES, His Honour Judge Rhys, QC

Honorary Recorder of Manchester. *b.* 13 January 1941 Hengoed, Glamorgan. *m.* 1963 Katharine Anne; one *s.* one *d.* *Public Offices:* Chairman, Greater Manchester Area Criminal Justice Liaison Committee; Member, Court and Council, The University of Manchester (LLB). *Education:* Cowbridge and Neath Grammar Schools; University of Manchester. *Career Profile:* Called to the Bar (1964); Practised Northern Circuit; QC (1981); Honorary Recorder and Resident Judge, Manchester (1990); Former Head of Chambers,18 St John Street, Manchester; Bencher of Gray's Inn. *Recreations, Interests:* Music, walking, travel. *Address:* Manchester Crown Court, Crown Square, Manchester, M3 3FL (*tel:* 0161 954 1800).

DAVIES, Professor Rodney Deane, CBE (1995);FRS(1992),MSc (1953),PhD (1956), DSc (1971),FRAS (1956),FInstP (1972),CPhys (1986)

Professor of Radioastronomy; Director, Nuffield Radio Astronomy Laboratories, Jodrell Bank. *b.* 8 January 1930; Mallala, South Australia. *m.* 1953 Valda Beth Treasure; two *s.* two *d.* *Education:* Adelaide High School; Adelaide University; Manchester University. *Career Profile:* Research Officer, CSIRO, Sydney. *Publications:* 'Radio Studies of the Universe' (RKP 1959); 'Radio Astronomy Today' (MUP 1963); contributions to scientific journals. *Societies:* Royal Astronomical Society (Secretary 1978-86) (President 1987-89). *Recreations, Interests:* Cricket, gardening, fell walking. *Address:* Nuffield Radio Astronomy Laboratories, Jodrell Bank, Macclesfield, Cheshire SK11 9DL (*tel:* 01477-71321); Parkgate House, Fulshaw Park, Wilmslow, Cheshire SK9 1QG (*tel:* 01625-523592).

DAVIS, Michael Ian, CA(1969),MSI,FRSA

Office Managing Partner, Ernst & Young, Liverpool; Project Finance Partner Northern Region. *b.* 11 December 1945; Ealing, West London. *m.* 1970 Dinah Mary; three *s.* one *d.* *Public Offices:* Governor, Manchester Grammar School; Member, Parish Management Team, St Vincent's Church, Altrincham. *Education:* St Benedict's School, Ealing, West London (-1964); Edinburgh University (1966-67). *Career Profile:* Corporate Finance Partner, Ernst & Young, Manchester (1988-95); Business Services Partner, Arthur Young, Manchester (1980-88); National Director, Business Services, Arthur Young (1987-88); Principal, Industrial Development Unit, Dept of Trade & Industry (1976-78). *Creative Works:* Regular Judge on Granada TV's 'Flying Start' Programme (1986-). *Publications:* 'Financial Incentives and Assistance for Industry' (3 editions published by Arthur Young). *Societies:* Freeman of City of London; Liveryman of Worshipful Company of Painter-Stainers; Bowdon Lawn Tennis Club (Trustee). *Recreations, Interests:* Family, tennis, music, enterprise. *Address:* Ernst & Young, Silkhouse Court, Tithebarn Street, Liverpool L2 2LE (*tel:* 0151 236 8214);Ernst & Young, Commercial Union House, Albert Square, Manchester M2 6LP (*tel:* 0161-953 9000); Hurlstone House, 8 Bentinck Road, Altrincham WA14 2BP (*tel:* 0161-941 3899).

DAWSON, Peter, Called to the Bar, Grays Inn (1971)

Clerk to the Justices, Bolton; Chairman of the Family Law Committee of the Justices' Clerks Society (1988-94). *b.* 20 August 1939; Huddersfield. *m.* 1966 Marie Teresa; two *d.*; widowed 1992 *Public Offices:* Member of the Council of the Justices' Clerks Society (1986-96); Chairman of the Standing Conference of Clerks to Magistrates' Courts Committees (1989-91); Member of the Executive Committee of Standing Conference of Training Officers for Magistrates (1982-92); President, Justices' Clerks Society (1994-95). *Education:* Wentworth Private School, Huddersfield (1944-45); St Patricks Primary School (1945-50); St Bedes Grammar School (1950-55); Grays Inn (1966-71). *Military Service:* National Service RAPC (1960-62). *Career Profile:* Worked in Magistrates' Courts in Huddersfield, Bradford; Deputy Clerk to the Justices, Derby (1973-78). *Publications:* Co-author A Handbook on the Children Act 1989 and the Rules for Practitioners and Others; Secure Accommodation - A Labyrinthine Law. *Societies:* Justices' Clerks Society; Bury Golf Club. *Recreations, Interests:* Family law, marriage guidance counselling, golf. *Address:* The Courts, Civic Centre, Le Mans Crescent, Bolton BL1 1QX *(tel:* 01204-522244).

DAY, Michael Philip, BSc(Wales),MSc(Sheffield)

Librarian & Director of Library Information Services, UMIST. *b.* 14 April 1947 Barnet, Herts. *m.* 1969 Lesley Diane Jones; two *s. Education:* Queen Elizabeth's Grammar School for Boys, Barnet; University College, Cardiff; University of Sheffield. *Career Profile:* Information Officer, Hatfield Polytechnic Library (1968-74); Sub-Librarian, Preston Polytechnic (1975-78); Deputy Librarian, Preston Polytechnic (1979); Deputy Librarian, UMIST (1980-81); Acting Librarian/Librarian, UMIST (1981-). *Recreations, Interests:* Walking, cycling, music, travel. *Address:* UMIST Library & Information Service, PO Box 88, Manchester, M60 1QD.

DAY, Stephen Richard, MIEx

Member of Parliament, Cheadle. *b.* 30 October 1948 Leeds. *m.* 1982 Frances Booth. *Public Offices:* Vice-President, Stockport Chamber of Commerce (1987-); Stockport and District Heart Foundation (1985-); Chairman, Yorks Area cons. Political Centre (1983-86); Vice-Chairman, NW Leeds Constituency (1983-86); Town Councillor, Otley (1975-76) (1979-83); City Councillor, Leeds (1975-80); Member, Select Committee on Social Security (1990-); Co-Chairman, Parliamentary Advisory Council for Transport Safety (1989-); Vice-Chairman, All-Party Non-Profit Making Clubs Group; Co-Chairman, West Coast Main Line Group; Vice-Chairman, Commonwealth Parliamentary Association UK Branch (1996-); Vice-Chairman, Association of Conservative Clubs (1995-). *Education:* Otley Secondary Modern; Leeds Polytechnic. *Career Profile:* Sales Clerk, William Sinclair & Sons (1965-70); Assistant Sales Manager (1970-77), Sales Represenative, Larkfield Printing Co Ltd (1977-80); A H Leach & Co (1980-84); Sales Executive, PPL Chromacopy (1984-86); Chromogene (1986-87). *Publications/Creative Work:* Pamphlets on Otley and Rates Reform. *Societies:* Bramhall & Woodford Rotary Club (Hon Member); Royal Wharfedale, Otley; Cheadle Hulme Conservatives. *Recreations, Interests:* Movies, music, history (particularly Roman). *Address:* The House of Commons, London, SW1A 0AA.

DEAN, Alan Martin, MA(Oxon)

Chief Executive, Hallé Concerts Society. *b.* 28 March 1949 Prestbury, Cheshire. *m.* 1972 Rayna; two *s.* *(marr. diss. 1991)*; *m.* 1993 Janet; two *stepd.* *Education:* Manchester Grammar School (1960-67); Brasenose College, Oxford University (1967-70). *Career Profile:* NM Rothschild & Sons Ltd (1970-85)(Director from 1981); Chief Executive, N Brown Group plc (1985-90); Group Business Development Director, North West Water Group plc (1990-94); Hallé Concerts Society (1995-). *Societies:* Institute of Directors; Manchester Statistical Society. *Recreations, Interests:* Music, theatre, opera, travel. *Address:* Hallé Concerts Society, The Bridgewater Hall, Manchester, M2 3WS *(tel:* 0161 237 7000; *fax:* 0161 237 7029). *Additional Information:* Treasurer, Manchester Grammar School Non-Executive Director, ISA International plc.

DEAN, Rayna (*née* Rothblatt), MA,FCA,MSI

Director, Rickitt Mitchell & Partners Ltd. *b.* 3 July 1952 Manchester. *m.* 1972 Alan; two *s.* *(marr. diss. 1992)*; *m.* 1995 Peter Jackson; two *stepd.* *Public Offices:* Non-Executive Director, Christie Hospital NHS Trust; Treasurer, Withington Girls' School; Member, Horserace Betting Levy Appeal Tribunal. *Education:* Withington Girls' School; St Hilda's College, Oxford. *Career Profile:* Former Partner, Price Waterhouse, Manchester. *Societies:* Manchester Statistical Society; Royal Society of Arts. *Recreations, Interests:* Theatre, opera. *Address:* Rickitt Mitchell & Partners Ltd, Clarence House, Clarence Street, Manchester, M2 4DW *(tel:* 0161 834 0600; *fax:* 0161 834 0452); Moss Farm, Moss Lane, Over Tabley, Knutsford, WA16 0PH *(tel:* 01565 651648; *fax:* 01565 651648).

de COVERLEY-WILKINS, John A, ERD (1966),DL (1989); DipRADA (1953), Order of Arts & Letters (France,1990)

Public Relations Consultant, Special Events; retired as PRO for Granada Television, retained by Granada as Consultant. *b.* 28 June 1931; Southsea, Hants. *m.* 1959 Patricia Cox; one *d.* *Public Offices:* DL, Manchester (1989); Chairman, Greater Manchester Army Benevolent Fund (1988); Honorary Colonel, 75 Engineer Regt (V) (1990-96); Maitre, Commanderie de Bordeaux a Manchester (1987); Member, Grand Conseil of Bordeaux. *Education:* Purbrook, Hants (1939-45); Portsmouth S Grammar (1945-49); Royal Academy of Dramatic Art (1953). *Military Service:* National Service, Royal Engineers/RCT Movement Control TA (Retired 1970). *Career Profile:* Senior Floor Manager, Alpha TV, Birmingham (1958-68); Facilities Manager, Yorkshire TV (1968-70); Senior Floor Manager, Granada TV (1970-79); Public Relations Officer, Granada Television (1979-89). *Societies:* Royal Commonwealth Society, London; Franco-British Club, Manchester; Movement Control Officers Club, London; Chevalier of 9 French Wine Orders. *Recreations, Interests:* Motoring abroad, theatre, television, wines of Bordeaux and Burgundy. *Address:* "Flaundon", 114 Altrincham Road, Wilmslow, Cheshire SK9 5NQ *(tel:* 01625-526606). *Additional Information:* My wife has a place in ITV history as the first woman newscaster for ATV in Midlands.

de FERRANTI, Naomi Angela Ziani (*née* Pattinson), DL(1996)

b. 8 March 1928 Bolton. *m.* 1951 J E K Rae; one *s.* three *d.* *(marr. diss. 1978)*; *m.* 1982 S Z de Ferranti; one *steps.* two *stepd.* *Public Offices:* Trustee, Quarry Bank Mill; Trustee,

Drug Watch; President, The Hallé Friends; Chairman, Turning Point North West; Member, Greater Manchester Police Policy Avisory Group on Drugs Misuse, South Cheshire Drugs Action Team; Chairman, Cheshire Hunt. *Education:* Privately; St Mary's Wantage; Eastbourne College. *Recreations, Interests:* Gardening, travelling, music, outdoor sports. *Address:* Macclesfield, Cheshire

de FERRANTI, Sebastian Basil Joseph Ziani, Hon DSc Salford (1967),Hon Fellow UMIST (1970),Hon DSc Cranfield Inst of Technology (1973),DL (Cheshire)

Director, GEC plc; Chairman, Hallé Concerts Society. *b.* 5 October 1927; Alderley Edge, Cheshire. *m.* 1953 Mona Helen Cunningham; one *s.* two *d.* *(marr. diss. 1983);* *m.* 1983 Naomi Angela Rae DL(Greater Manchester). *Public Offices:* President, Electrical Research Assocation (1968-69); Centre for Education in Science, Education and Technology, Manchester & Region (1972-82); Chairman, International Electrical Association (1970-72); Member, National Defence Industries Council (1969-77); Council, IEEE (1970-73); Trustee, Tate Gallery (1971-78); Chairman, Civic Trust for the North West (1978-83); Commissioner, Royal Commission for Exhibition of 1851 (1984-); Vice President, RSA (1980-84); Governor, RNCM (1988-); Chairman of Assessors, architect for Manchester City Art Gallery Extension (1995-); Freeman of the City of London; Liveryman of The Worshipful Company of Wheelwrights. *Education:* Ampleforth. *Military Service:* 4th/7th Dragoon Guards (1947-49). *Career Profile:* Chairman (1963-82), Managing Director, Ferranti plc (1958-75); Director, British Airways Helicopters (1982-84), National Nuclear Corporation (1984-88); High Sheriff of Cheshire (1988-89). *Creative Works:* Granada Guildhall Lecture (1966); Royal Institution Lecture (1969); Louis Bleriot Lecture, Paris (1970); Faraday Lecture (1970-71). *Clubs:* Cavalry & Guards; Pratt's. *Address:* Henbury Hall, Macclesfield, Cheshire SK11 9PJ.

DELAMORE, Irvine William, MB ChB (1954),PhD (1962),FRCPE (1968),FRCP Lond (1978), FRCPath (1973)

Honorary Consultant Physician, Manchester Royal Infirmary. *b.* 16 July 1930; Sutton Bridge. *m.* 1955 Hilda Rosemary Thomas; two *d.* *Public Offices:* Chairman of Governors, Rivington Primary School; Rivington Parish Councillor. *Education:* Spalding Grammar School (1941-48); Edinburgh University (1948-54); Yale University, USA (1960-66). *Military Service:* National Service, Medical Officer, RNVR (1955-57). *Career Profile:* Consultant Physician, Royal Infirmary Blackburn (1966-70); Senior Lecturer, Dept of Medicine, Manchester Royal Infirmary (1970-71). *Publications:* Books: 'Myeloma and Other Paraproteinaemias' (1986); 'Leukeamia' (1986); 'Haematological Aspects of Systemic Disease' (1976). *Prizes:* Obstetrics & Gynaecology Prize, Edinburgh University (1954); Damon Runyon Memorial Fellowship, USA (1960). *Societies:* British Society of Haematology; Medical Research Society. *Recreations, Interests:* Reading, gardening, golf. *Address:* Fisher House, Rivington, Bolton BL6 7SL *(tel:* 01204-696437).

DEMETRIADES, Alexander Theodore Aristide, BA Manchester (1942),MA Manchester (1950)

b. 2 October 1925; Manchester. *m.* 1960 Brigid; two *d.* *(marr. diss. 1977);* *m.* 1977 Shelagh Mary. *Public Offices:* JP, Manchester City Bench (1968-), Deputy Chairman

(1988-90), Chairman (1991-93); General Commissioner of Taxes, Central and South Manchester Division (1980-); Member of Greater Manchester Police Authority (1989-93). *Education:* Manchester Grammar School (1936-42); Manchester University (1942-44) (1950). *War Service:* (1944-47). *Address:* C P Demetriades & Son, Churchgate House, 56 Oxford Street, Manchester M1 6EU (*tel:* 0161-236 7925).

DEMPSEY, Anthony Thomas, LLB(Hons)

Partner, Wacks Caller Solicitors. *b.* 9 May 1961 Sale, Cheshire. *m.* 1987 Ann; one *s.* one *d. Education:* Xaverian College, Manchester (1973-78); Manchester University (1979-82); Law College, Chester (1983). *Career Profile:* Articled Clerk and Solicitor, Linder Myers, Manchester (1983-88); Assistant (1988), Partner (1989-), Wacks Caller, Manchester. *Prizes:* John Mackrell Prize (1983). *Societies:* Member, Law Society; Employment Lawyers Association. *Recreations, Interests:* Manchester United FC, food, wine. *Address:* Wacks Caller, Steam Packet House, 76 Cross Street, Manchester, M2 4JU (*tel:* 0161 957 8888; *fax:* 0161 957 8899).

DERBYSHIRE, Michael Joseph Christian, BSc (London, 1969),MBA (Manchester, 1976)

Group Chief Executive, Whitecroft plc. *b.* 20 September 1947 Sutton Coldfield, Warwickshire. *m.* 1976 Sandra Catherine; two *d. Public Offices:* Member of National Manufacturing Council, CBI. *Education:* Oundle School (1960-66); Imperial College, London. *Career Profile:* Graduate Trainee & various Marketing posts, Esso Petroleum (1969-74); Manchester Business School (1974-76); Various General Management roles, Divisional Chief Executive (Print & Packaging), Divisional Chief Executive (International Ceramics), Norcros plc (1976-91); Group Managing Director (1992), Group Chief Executive (1993-), Whitecroft plc. *Societies:* Trentham Golf Club; Stone Tennis Club. *Recreations, Interests:* Keen tennis player, golf, skiing, theatre, concerts, reading. *Address:* Whitecroft plc, Water Lane, Wilmslow, SK9 5BX (*tel:* 01625 524677; *fax:* 01625 535821).

DEVITT, Paul, LLB(Hons)(Bristol, 1985),Solicitor (1988)

Partner, Addleshaw Sons & Latham. *b.* 19 August 1964 Barrow-in-Furness, Cumbria. *m.* 1993 Catherine Lucy; one *d. Education:* Barrow-in-Furness Grammar School for Boys; University of Bristol; College of Law, Guildford. *Career Profile:* Assistant Solicitor, Turner Kenneth Brown, London (1988-91), Freshfields, London (1991-93), Addleshaw Sons & Latham, Manchester (1993-95); Partner, Addleshaw Sons & Latham (1993-). *Address:* Addleshaw Sons & Latham, Dennis House, Marsden Street, Manchester, M2 1JD (*tel:* 0161 832 5994; *fax:* 0161 832 2250).

DEWHIRST, Paul, MusBac(Univ. of Manchester),MTC (Univ. of London)

Retired (though open to offers!!). *b.* 8 February 1941 Leeds. *Education:* Roundhay School, Leeds (1952-59); Manchester University (1959-62); London University (1962-63). *Career Profile:* Music Master (subsequently Head of Music), Notre Dame High School, Manchester (1963-77); Music Critic, Daily Telegraph (1968-95). *Publications/Creative Work:* Reviews for The Guardian, Daily Telegraph, Music and Musicians, Opera. *Societies:* Amnesty International; Greenpeace; Campaign Against the Arms Trade; CND;

Friends of the Western Buddhist Order; Buddhist Society; Tibet Society; Tibet Foundation; Tibet Support Group; Friends of the Earth; Green Party; Wagner Society; Schubert Institute UK; Vegetarian Society. *Recreations, Interests:* Buddhism, classical music, walking, Tibet. *Additional Information:* Sponsors Tibetan Refugees - children & monks - in India & Nepal.

DEWSBURY, Sheila Mary (*née* Navesey)

Artist. *b.* 23 March 1939 Oldham. *m.* two *d.* (*marr. diss. 1972*) *Public Offices:* Archivist, Manchester Academy of Fine Arts. *Education:* Notre Dame Grammar School, Manchester; Sedgeley Park Teacher Training College, Manchester. *Career Profile:* Teacher in Comprehensive & Further Education for 25 years. *Publications/Creative Work:* Illustrations for 'Northern Lass' (a compilation of traditional music); scenic designer for amateur theatrical productions. *Prizes:* Edward Oldham Travelling Bursary (Manchester Academy of Fine Arts)(1996). *Societies:* Manchester Academy of Fine Arts. *Recreations, Interests:* Music, walking, riding, swimming, social history.

DIGGINES, Jonathan Brett, BA (Oxon, 1974),MA (Oxon, 1977),Solicitor (1977)

Director, Murray Johnstone Ltd; various other directorships. *b.* 16 February 1953 Manchester. *m.* 1979 Susan Catherine; two *s. Public Offices:* Governor, Manchester Grammar School. *Education:* Manchester Grammar School (1964-71); Lincoln College (1971-74); College of Law, Christleton (1975). *Career Profile:* GMC: Articled Clerk/Solicitor (1975-80), Policy Co-ordination Officer (1980-82); J B Diggines & Co, Solicitors (1982-89); Murray Johnstone Private Equity Ltd: Investment Manager (1989), Director (1990). *Societies:* Manchester Financial & Professional Forum; Manchester Merchant & International Bankers Association. *Address:* Riversdale, 297 Ashley Road, Hale, WA14 3NH (*tel:* 0161 941 7239).

DIGGINES, Susan Catherine (*née* Lawlor), Solicitor (1984)

Partner, Addleshaw Sons & Latham. *b.* 14 October 1956. *m.* 1979 Jonathan; two *s. Career Profile:* Formed Hall Brydon Diggines (1985); merged with Lace Mawer (1989); joined Addleshaw Sons & Latham (1994). *Societies:* Manchester Literary & Philosophical Society. *Recreations, Interests:* Greatest interest and (often) the best recreation is looking after two sons, then (time permitting) reading, walking, theatre, antique furniture. *Address:* Addleshaw Sons & Latham, Dennis House, Marsden Street, Manchester, M2 1JD.

DIGGORY, Elizabeth Mary, BA(Univ. of London, 1967),PGCE(Cantab, 1968)

Head Mistress, Manchester High School for Girls (1994-). *b.* 22 December 1945 Ealing, London. *Education:* Shrewsbury High School for Girls (1950-55)(1957-64); Notting Hill & Ealing High School for Girls (1955-57); Westfield College, University of London (1964-67); Hughes Hall, Cambridge (1967-68). *Career Profile:* Assistant Teacher (1968-73), Head of History Dept (1973-82) King Edward VI High School for Girls, Birmingham; Head Mistress, St Albans High School for Girls (1983-94); President, Girls' Schools Association (1991-92). *Societies:* Historical Association; Girls' School Association; Fellow, Royal Society of Arts. *Recreations, Interests:* Theatre, concerts, walking, gardening,

travel, school/industry links. *Address:* Manchester High School for Girls, Grangethorpe Road, Manchester, M14 6HS (*tel:* 0161 224 0447; *fax:* 0161 224 6192). *Additional Information:* Director, General Teaching Council for England & Wales (1995-) Member, Bloxham Project Committee (1993-).

DOBELL, Anthony Russell, FCA (1971)

A R Dobell & Co (1988-). *b.* 15 September 1948; Altrincham. *m.* 1983 Hilary; two *s.* *Public Offices:* Hon Sec, Manchester Society of Chartered Accountants (1986-90); Hon Sec, Friends of Manchester Northern Hospital (1975-94); Member and Chairman, Peover Superior Parish Council (1985-). *Education:* Rugby School. *Career Profile:* Partner, Ashworth Mosley & Co (1978-80), Robson Rhodes (1980-88). *Societies:* St James's Club; Knutsford Golf Club; Alderley Edge Tennis & Squash Club. *Recreations, Interests:* Family, walking, most sports. *Address:* A R Dobell & Co, 13 Hyde Road, Denton, Manchester M34 3AF (*tel:* 0161-320 4111); Pear Tree Farm, Peover Heath, Knutsford WA16 8UN.

DOCHERTY, William (Bill) Thomas, BA(Hons),CA

Tax Partner, Arthur Andersen - Head of Tax Investigation Practice. *b.* 10 July 1951 Lanark, Scotland. *m.* 1995 Carol O'Hare. *Public Offices:* Commissioner for the General Purposes of the Income Tax (General Commissioner). *Education:* Our Lady's High School (Boys), Motherwell (1963-69); Strathclyde University (1969-73). *Career Profile:* Inspector of Taxes, District Inspector of Taxes, Member of Enquiry Branch, Inland Revenue (1973-83); Qualified as Scottish Chartered Accountant, Arthur Andersen, Senior Tax Manager (1983-89); Managing Tax Consultant, Price Waterhouse (1989-91); Joint Head of Tax, Robson Rhodes, Manchester, Partner in Charge, National Tax Investigation Unit (1991-96); Partner in Charge Tax Investigations Practice, Arthur Andersen (1996-). *Publications/Creative Work:* Columnist, Tax Journal; Contributor, Tollys Tax Investigation Manual. *Societies:* Secretary, Portico Library; Director, Manchester YMCA; Manchester Literary & Philosophical Society. *Recreations, Interests:* Adventure, reading, music, playing the violin, ballet, keep fit, dieting. *Address:* Arthur Andersen, Bank House, 9 Charlotte Street, Manchester, M1 4EU (*tel:* 0161 200 0473; *fax:* 0161 236 0248); 1 Linden Road, Didsbury, Manchester, M20 2QJ (*tel:* 0161 434 6292).

DONNACHIE, Professor Alexander, BSc,PhD (Glasgow),FInstP

Professor of Theoretical Physics, Dean of Faculty of Science & Engineering, University of Manchester. *b.* 25 May 1936; Kilmarnock. *m.* 1960 Dorothy Paterson; two *d.* *Public Offices:* SRC: Member, Theory Sub-Committee (1975-77), Particle Physics Committee, Nuclear Physics Board (1977-81), Postgraduate Training Committee, (1978-81); SERC: Chairman, Nuclear Physics Board (1989-93), Vice-Chairman, Particle Space and Astronomy Board (1993-94); Member of SERC Council (1989-94); Chairman, Standing Committee of Physics Professors (1993-); Member, Commission on Particles and Fields, IUPAP (1984-90), Secretary (1987-90); Chairman, SPSL Programme Committee, CERN (1988-82), Member, Scientific Policy Committee, CERN (1988-92), Research Board, CERN (1988-94); UK Scientific Delegate to CERN Council (1988-94); Chairman of Scientific Advisory Committee to NIKHEF-H, The Netherlands (1992-); Member of the Dutch Universities Review Committee for Physics (1996). *Education:* Kilmarnock

Academy (1948-54); BSc(Hons) (1958), PhD (1961) Glasgow University. *Career Profile:* DSIR Research Fellow, University College, London (1961-63); Lecturer, UCL (1963-65); Res Associate, CERN, Geneva (1965-67); Senior Lecturer, University of Glasgow (1967-69); Professor of Physics (1969-). *Publications:* 160 publications in scientific journals. *Societies:* Manchester Literary & Philosophical Society, Budworth Sailing Club, Knutsford Golf Club. *Recreations, Interests:* Golf, sailing, walking, history. *Address:* Department of Physics & Astronomy, University of Manchester, Manchester M13 9PL (*tel:* 0161-275 4210, *fax:* 0161 275 4218, *e-mail:* ad@a3.ph.man.ac.uk).

DONNAN, Professor Stuart Paul Briot, MA(Manchester),MSc (London),MPhil (Southampton), MD (Sydney),FRCP,FRCS,FFPHM

Professor of Epidemiology & Public Health, University of Manchester. *b.* 2 September 1940 Sydney, Australia. *m.* 1964 Beryl; one *s.* one *d. Public Offices:* Member, North Manchester Health Authority (1992-94). *Education:* Shore School, Sydney; Universities of Sydney and London. *Career Profile:* Surgical Posts, Sydney & London (1963-69); Lecturer in Surgery, University of London (1970-73); Senior Lecturer in Clinical Epidemiology, University of Southampton (1975-81); Foundation Professor of Community Medicine, The Chinese University of Hong Kong (1981-90); Present position (1990-). *Publications:* In medical education, epidemiology and public health. *Societies:* Manchester Medical Society; Manchester Tennis & Racquets Club. *Recreations, Interests:* Real tennis, choral singing. *Address:* The Medical School, University of Manchester, Oxford Road, Manchester, M13 9PL (*tel:* 0161 275 5195; *fax:* 0161 275 5219; *e-mail:* stuart.donnan@man.ac.uk); 1 Ford Lodge, Ford Lane, Didsbury, Manchester M20 2RU (*tel:* 0161 445 6155; *fax:* 0161 448 8199).

DONOHOE, Peter Howard, FRNCM (1983); GRNCM (1976),BA BMus Leeds (1972)

Vice-President, Birmingham Conservatoire; Principal Conductor and Artistic Director, Orchestra of the Mill. *b.* 18 June 1953; Manchester. *m.* 1980 Elaine Burns; one *d. Education:* Chorlton Park Primary School; Chetham's School of Music; University of Leeds; Royal Manchester College of Music; Royal Northern College of Music; Paris Conservatoire. *Creative Works:* Concert Pianist, Debut Manchester Free Trade Hall (1966), London Debut (1979), US Debut (1983); Winner 7th International Tchaikovsky Competition, Moscow (1982); performances throughout the World, including several tours of USA, USSR, Japan, Australia, continental Europe, Canada and Scandinavia; appearances at many international festivals, including every year at Henry Wood Promenade Concerts in London; Since 1979 - Edinburgh, Cheltenham, Bath, City of London, Cardiff, Wellington (New Zealand), Adelaide, Hong Kong, Hollywood Bowl; exclusive Recording Artist with EMI/Angel since 1989; several internationally released since 1982, including complete works for piano and orchestra - Tchaikovsky, Concerto No 1 Brahms, Rhapsody in Blue, Gershwin. *Prizes:* Gramophone Concerto Record of the Year Award (1988). *Address:* C/o IMG Artists, Media House, 3 Burlington Lane, London W4 2TH (*tel &fax:* 0181 233 5800).

DOWD, Raymond Anthony, BA,MSc,DipEdMgt,CertEd,MIMgt

Chief Executive/Principal, Hopwood Hall College. *b.* 17 December 1951 Stretford. *m.* Claire; three *d. Education:* Barlow Hall Secondary Modern; Huddersfield University/

Polytechnic; Manchester College of Building; Polytechnic of Wales; Open University. *Career Profile:* Worked in construction industry until aged 24; entered further education in 1977; taught in Lewisham, Blackpool and Fylde, Cardiff; Deputy Principal, Sandwell College of F and HE (1991); Chief Executive, Cardiff Group Training Consortium (1984-91); Chief Executive/Principal, Hopwood Hall (1994-). *Publications/Creative Work:* 'Number in Construction' (Longman Press); ILEA Learning Materials Service: Number in Construction. *Societies:* Association for College Management (President Elect); Association of College Principals; Rochdale Rotary 86 Club. *Recreations, Interests:* Opera follower, wine sampling. *Address:* Hopwood Hall College, Rochdale Road, Middleton, Manchester, M24 6XH (*tel:* 0161 643 7560; *fax:* 0161 643 0899; *e-mail:* dwodra@rmplc.co.uk).

DOWNS, Barry, FCA (1957)

Principal, B Downs & Co, Chartered Accountants, Stockport. *b.* 6 September 1931; Stockport. *m.* 1957 Kay Etchells; one *s.* one *d.* *Public Offices:* Councillor, GMC (1975-86); Councillor, Stockport MBC (1986-90). *Education:* Heaton Moor College (1945-48). *Career Profile:* Secretary, S Casket Ltd (1960-63); Lecturer, Textile Council Productivity Centre (1964-69). *Publications:* '5815 The First 50 Years'. *Societies:* Mellor Cricket Club; Bramhall Golf Club. *Recreations, Interests:* Cricket umpiring, golf, politics. *Address:* 5 Egerton Road, Davenport, Stockport (*tel:* 0161-483 4615).

DOWNS, John Stuart

Managing Director, Cosmo Leisure Group of Companies. *b.* 9 January 1944 Bradford, Yorkshire. *m.* 1972 Linda; two *s.* one *d.* *Public Offices:* Chairman, West Pennine Health Auhority. *Education:* Hulme Grammar School Prep., Oldham; Ryleys Preparatory School, Alderley Edge; Denstone College, Uttoxeter; Manchester College of Commerce. *Career Profile:* Oldham Health Authority - Non-Executive Member (1990), Chairman (1991), Chairman OHA (Purchasing)(1992); West Pennine Health Authority, Lead Chairman, WPHA Purchasing Consortium (1993), Chairman (1994-); Vice President, Cinema Exhibitors' Association, London; Delegate to General Council, CEA, London; Former Chairman, Northern Branch, CEA; Regional Representative, North West England & North Wales, London National Executive Bingo Association of Great Britain. *Societies:* Hallé Concerts Society; Grahams 1820 Club; Cinema and Theatre Association; North West Cinema Preservation Society; Manchester Lunch and Laughter Club; Commanderie de Bordeaux; Associate Member, British Academy of Film and Television Arts; Membership of NSPCC; Christian Childrens Fund. *Recreations, Interests:* Cinema, music, theatre, reading, gardening, keep-fit. *Address:* Cosmo Leisure Group, 62-64 Market Street, Stalybridge, Cheshire, SK15 2AB. *Additional Information:* Town Councillor, former Mossley Borough Council (1971-73); Lifetime's association in cinema exhibition and involved in the Bingo industry since 1971.

DOWNWARD, Sir William Atkinson, Kt(1977),KStJ(1974),JP (1973), DL,FRSA (1978); Hon LLD Manchester,Hon RNCM

Hon Alderman, City of Manchester (1975); President, Broughton House, Greater Manchester Fed Boys' Clubs, Norbrook Boys' Club, Manchester Opera Society, Manchester & Salford Family Service Unit; Vice President, United Nations Ass (NW); President, West

Indian Sport & Social Club, Sharp Street Ragged School; Chairman, Pat Seed Appeal; President, SSAFA (Manchester County); Vice President, St Ann's Hospice; President, Wallness Children's Kidney Project, Greater Manchester NSPCC, Northenden Civic Society. *b.* 5 December 1912; Manchester. *m.* 1946 Enid Wood. *Public Offices:* JP (1974); DL (Greater Manchester) (1987). *Education:* Heald Place Elementary; Manchester Central High School; Manchester College of Technology. *Career Profile:* Lord Lieutenant, Greater Manchester (1974-87); Deputy Lieutenant, Lancashire (1971-74); Chairman, Manchester Overseas Welfare Conference (1972-86); Councillor, Manchester City Council (1946-75); Alderman (1971-74); Chairman, Manchester City Labour Party (1970-73); Chairman, Greater Manchester Labour Party (1972-74); President, United Nations Ass (NW); President, Gorton Philharmonic. *Societies:* Manchester Literary & Philosophical Society. *Address:* 23 Kenmore Road, Northenden, Manchester M22 4AE (*tel:* 0161-998 4742).

DOYLE, Leslie, MB,BCh (Dublin),FRCPI,DCH

Retired Consultant Chest Physician. *b.* 23 July 1919; Greystones, Co Wicklow, Ireland. *m.* 1950 Joan Beaumont; two *s.* two *d.* *Education:* Wesley College Dublin; Trinity College, University of Dublin. *Military Service:* RAMC (1948-50). *Career Profile:* Consultant Chest Physician, Wythenshawe Hospital, Altrincham General Hospital and Manchester Chest Clinic. *Publications:* Papers in several medical journals. *Prizes:* Sizarship (Science), Trinity College, Dublin. *Societies:* Life Member, Honorary Librarian and former Council Member, Manchester Medical Society; Past-President, Section of Medicine, Manchester Medical Society; Chairman (1988-95), North Western Regional Association of Physicians; Past President and Secretary, North West Thoracic Society; Member, British Thoracic Society; Member, UMIST Association; President (1991-94), Trustee and Council Member, Lancashire and Cheshire Antiquarian Society. *Recreations, Interests:* History, rugby football. *Address:* "Cheviot", Clay Lane, Manchester M23 9LG (*tel:* 0161-945 1414). *Additional Information:* Co-founder and Life Member, Greystones Rugby Football Club.

DUCKWORTH, His Honour Judge Brian Roy, DL(1995) MA(Hons)(Oxon),Barrister

HM Circuit Judge. *b.* 26 July 1934 Blackburn. *m.* 1964 Nancy Carolyn; three *s.* one *d.* *Education:* Sedbergh School; Worcester College, Oxford; Lincoln's Inn. *Career Profile:* Barrister, Northern Circuit in Manchester (1957-83); Recorder of Crown Court (1972-83); HM Circuit Judge (1983-). *Societies:* Pleasington Golf Club. *Recreations, Interests:* Golf, gardening, fell walking, sailing, classical music, literature, theatre. *Address:* The Law Courts, Ringway, Preston, PR1 2LL (*tel:* 01772 832300; *fax:* 01772 832376).

DUNSTAN, Thomas Anthony, FCIT,MInstTA

Principal, Deva Management & Transport Consultancy, Stockport; Chairman, Bluebird Coaches Ltd, Bluebird Bus & Coach, Middleton, Manchester; Director, Stockport Chamber of Commerce & Industry. *b.* 6 April 1936; Wigan. *m.* 1962 Barbara (decd); one *s.* two *d.* *Public Offices:* Member, North West Social Security Appeals Tribunal, Disability Living Appeals Tribunal, Child Support Tribunal. *Education:* Wigan Grammar School; Thornleigh College, Bolton. *Career Profile:* Managing Director, Greater Manchester Buses South Ltd (1986), General Manager (1982-86) and other managerial positions in passenger transport including, Manager, Hebble Motor Services, Halifax; Traffic Manager, North

Western Road Car Co, Stockport; Director/General Manager, Selnec Cheshire Bus Co. *Prizes:* Grade VIII (Final) Associated Boards, Royal Schools of Music. *Societies:* Lancashire County Cricket Club; Ormskirk RUFC; Davenport RUFC; Transport Golfing Society. *Recreations, Interests:* Politics, rugby, cricket, walking. *Address:* Deva House, Deva Close, Hazel Grove, Stockport SK7 6HH (*tel:* 0161-483 7065).

DWEK, Joe C, BSc,BA,FTI,AMCT

Chairman, Bodycote International plc, Penmarric Securities Ltd. Director of various companies *b.* 1 May 1940; Brussels. *m.* Linda; one *s.* one *d.* *Public Offices:* Chairman, CBI NW Regional Council and Member of various CBI committees; Chairman, Dwek Family Charitable Trust; Member of Court, Manchester University; Court of Governors, UMIST. *Education:* Carmel College (1949-57); Manchester University (1958-63); Nottingham University (1980-86). *Career Profile:* IFS National Council; CBI National Council; NSACC Regional Deputy Chairman; Director, Manchester Chamber of Commerce. *Societies:* Dunham Forest Golf & Country Club; Textile Institute; Manchester Literary & Philosophical Society; Society of Business Economists; Manchester Statistical Society. *Recreations, Interests:* Golf, music, reading. *Address:* Bodycote International plc, 140 Kingsway, Manchester M19 1BA (0161-257 2345); The Coppins, Hill Top, Hale, Nr Altrincham WA15 0NJ (*tel:* 0161-980 2522).

DYKSTRA, Ronald Gerrit Malcolm, FCIArb

Retired; Director, Vernon Building Society. *b.* 4 March 1934 Edinburgh. *m.* 1960 Jennifer Mary Cramer; three *s.* (*marr. diss. 1985*); *m.* 1986 Sonia Hoole; three *steps.* *Public Offices:* Trustee, Henshaw's Society for the Blind. *Education:* The Edinburgh Academy (1943-51). *Career Profile:* Addleshaw Sons & Latham: Assistant Solicitor (1957-61), Partner (1961-87), Senior Partner (1987-94). *Societies:* Law Society; Society of Construction Arbitrators; Wilmslow Green Room Society. *Recreations, Interests:* Amateur dramatics, swimming, walking. *Address:* 7 Racecourse Road, Wilmslow, Cheshire, SK9 5LF (*tel:* 01625 525856).

DYSON, Richard George, MA(Cantab),FCA

Head of Corporate Finance, Ernst & Young, Manchester. *b.* 6 April 1949 Huddersfield. *m.* 1986 Valerie; two *d.* (*separated 1996*) *Public Offices:* President, Manchester Society of Chartered Accountants (1995-96). *Education:* Clifton College; Queens' College, Cambridge. *Career Profile:* Articled with Whinney Murray & Co, London, Qualified (1974), transferred to Manchester (1982); Partner, Ernst & Whinney (1983) (now Ernst & Young). *Societies:* Hawks Club, Cambridge; St James' Club, Manchester; Stockport Golf Club; Denham Golf Club. *Recreations, Interests:* Golf, music. *Address:* Ernst & Young, Commercial Union House, Albert Square, Manchester, M2 6LP (*tel:* 0161 953 9000; *fax:* 0161 832 0761).

EADIE, Paul James McGregor, AIL

Export Promoter; General Manager, Mesdan GB Ltd (1991-). *b.* 18 February 1943; Cairo, Egypt. *m.* 1965 Victoria; two *s.* two *d. Public Offices:* Councillor for Dean Row Wilmslow (1976-79), (Lacey Green) (1979-82) at Macclesfield UDC; Director and Member of Council, MCCI; Chairman Intl Committee, MCCI. *Education:* Ramillies Hall, Cheadle Hulme (1948-56); Oundle School (1956-61); Geneva, Munich, Madrid, Perugia Universities. *Career Profile:* Chairman & Chief Executive Eadie Bros & Co Ltd (1964-91); Director, BRT Ltd (1978-94); BTMA Executive Member (Vice-Chairman 1990-94); Member, Latin American Trade Advisory Group Exec (1986-94); Director & Secretary, Eadie International (1987-91); DTI Export Promoter for Brazil (1994-) Sales Director, Plastex, Bologna (1991-94); Director, Carl Hofmann, Chemitz (1992-93). *Recreations, Interests:* Reading, theatre and cinema, Latin American affairs. *Address:* Mesdan GB Ltd, Globe House, Chadderton (*tel:* 0161 627 0336; The Pole Mews, Pole Lane, Antrobus, Cheshire, CW9 6NN (*tel:* 01606 891522; *fax:* 01606 892234).

EARNSHAW, Peter Joseph, BA(Hons)(Liverpool)

Governor, HM Prison, Manchester. *b.* 18 September 1946 Nelson, Lancs. *m.* 1972 Christine; three *s.* one *d. Education:* St Joseph's, Blackpool; St Mary's, Toddington; Liverpool University. *Recreations, Interests:* Walking, cycling, music. *Address:* HM Prison Manchester, Southall Street, Manchester, M60 9AH (*tel:* 0161 834 8626).

EASSON, Professor Angus, BA Nottingham (1962),DPhil Oxford (1968)

Professor of English and Chairman, Department of English, Salford University. *b.* 18 July 1940; England. *Education:* William Ellis School, London (1951-59); Nottingham University (1959-62); Oxford University (1963-65). *Career Profile:* Lecturer, Newcastle University (1965-71); Lecturer, Royal Holloway College (London University) (1971-77). *Publications:* 'Elizabeth Gaskell' (1979); editions of works by Dickens and Gaskell; articles on nineteenth and twentieth century literature. *Recreations, Interests:* Opera. *Address:* English Department, The University, Salford M5 4WT (*tel:* 0161-745 5029).

EAST, John

Chairman Elect, Hallé Concerts Society; Non-Executive Director, Hallé Concerts Society; Non-Executive Director, Hallogen Ltd. *b.* 2 April 1935; Chelsea, London. *m.* 1965 Vivian; three *s. Education:* Sloane Grammar School, Chelsea; University College, London. *Military Service:* National Service, Royal Artillery (1954-56). *Career Profile:* Deputy Managing Director, BASF plc; Director, Fritzsche, Dodge & Olcott (UK) Ltd; Cheadle Colour & Chemicals Ltd; Chairman, British Chemical Distributors' & Traders' Association. *Societies:* Manchester Lit & Phil; Hallé Concerts Society. *Recreations, Interests:* Music, literature, walking. *Address:* Hallé Concerts Society, The Bridgewater Hall, Manchester, M2 3WS.

EDMUNDSON, David M R, DASE, MEd(Manchester)

Cricket Secretary, LCCC; Secretary, Lancashire Cricket Board. *b.* 19 September 1951 Blackburn. *m.* 1978 Anne; two *s. Education:* Accrington Grammar School; St John's College, York; Manchester University. *Career Profile:* Director of PE, Queen Elizabeth's Grammar School, Blackburn (1980-96); Head of PE, The Derby School, Bury (1979-80); Assistant (1973-79). *Publications/Creative Work:* 'See the Conquering Hero - The Official History of the Lancashire League'; regular broadcaster for BBC Radio; cricket writer for the Daily Telegraph and the Cricketer. *Societies:* Cricket Writers Club; XL Club. *Recreations, Interests:* Cricket, most sports. *Address:* Lancashire CCC, Old Trafford, Manchester, M16 0PX(*tel:* 0161 282 4000; *fax:* 0161 282 4100).

EFRON, Professor Nathan, BSc(Optom), PhD(Melbourne), DSc(UMIST), FAAO, FVCO, MCOptom

Professor of Clinical Optometry; Head of Department & Director, European Centre for Contact Lens Research, UMIST. *b.* 3 September 1954 Melbourne, Australia. *m.* 1991 Suzanne Elizabeth; one *s.* one *d. Education:* University of Melbourne, Australia (1973-76, 1977-83). *Career Profile:* Research Fellow: University of Melbourne (1981); University of California, Berkeley (1982); University of New South Wales (1983); Lecturer (1983-86), Senior Lecturer (1987-90), Department of Optometry, University of Melbourne; Honorary Senior Visiting Fellow, The City University, London (1987-88). *Publications/Creative Work:* Published 110 papers in peer-reviewed scientific journals; 3 yearbooks; 5 textbooks chapters; 150 non-refereed papers, and co-produced an educational compact disc set. *Prizes:* Numerous prizes and awards. *Societies:* Numerous professional societies and associations relating to Optometry. *Recreations, Interests:* Physical fitness, spectating sport, aviation. *Address:* Department of Optometry & Vision Sciences, UMIST, PO Box 88, Manchester, M60 1QD (*tel:* 0161 200 3886; *fax:* 0161 200 3887; *e-mail:* n.efron @umist.ac.uk).

EGERTON, William

Vice Chairman, St Gregory's RC High School, Openshaw; Vice Chairman, St Willibrords RC Primary School, Clayton; Chairman, Barrington Club, Clayton. *b.* 12 December 1944; Manchester. *m.* Maureen Helen; one *s. Public Offices:* Non-Executive Director and Vice-Chairman, North Manchester Healthcare Trust;Justice of the Peace (inner Manchester); Member: Relief in Need, Lord Mayor's Family Holiday Fund, Myshalls Education Trust, Mayes Trust Youth & Community Trust, Manchester. *Education:* St Willibrord's School, Clayton, Manchester. *Career Profile:* Leader Manchester City Council (1982-84); Lord Mayor of Manchester (1992-93); Manchester City Councillor for 24 years. *Societies:* Fabian. *Address:* 333 North Road, Clayton, Manchester M11 4NY (*tel:* 0161 223 0062). *Additional Information:* OFSTED Lay Inspector.

ELDER, William Marriott, CStJ (1994),OStJ (1978),TD (1969),3 Clasps (1975) (1981) (1987),DL (1987); MB ChB Glasgow (1956),MFOMRCP (1978),MInstRP (1983)

Formerly Area Medical Officer (North), Nuclear Electric plc. *b.* 12 August 1932; Glasgow. *m.* 1958 Agnes Ann Macdonald; one *s.* two *d. Public Offices:* High Sheriff GMC

(1989-90); Royal Appointments: QHP (TA) (1981-83), ADC (TA) (1986-88); GM CELT Chairman; ABF Appeal Warrington District (1986). *Education:* Kelvinside Academy, Glasgow (1944-50); Glasgow University (1950-56). *Military Service:* TA (1951-58); RAMC (SSC) (1958-61); TA (1961-88). *Career Profile:* Senior Medical Officer, UKAEA, Risley; CO 207 (Manchester) General Hospital (V) (1979-82); RMO DLOY (1983-84); TA Col NW District (1984-88); County Surgeon, St John Ambulance Brigade (1983-88); Commander, St John Ambulance, Cheshire (1991-96). *Publications:* 'Some Manchester Doctors' (jointly) (1984); 'Sodium Burns' (treatment of radiation casulaties) (1976). *Prizes:* McKail Prize in Psychiatry (Univ of Glasgow) (1955); Ure Prize in Surgery (Univ of Glasgow) (1954). *Societies:* Society of Occupational Medicine; Caravan Club; Manchester Literary & Philosophical Society. *Recreations, Interests:* Caravanning, fishing.

ELLERAY, Anthony John, MA(Cantab),Barrister (1977),QC (1993)

b. 19 August 1954 Northampton. *m.* 1982 Alison Elizabeth Potter; one *s.* one *d.* *Public Offices:* Assistant Recorder. *Education:* Bishop's Stortford College (1967-72); Trinity College, Cambridge (1973-76); Bar Finals (1976-77). *Career Profile:* Practice as Barrister, QC in 1993; Area of work: Chancery (always had principal chambers in Manchester). *Prizes:* Inner Temple Major Award (1976). *Societies:* Manchester Tennis & Racquets Club. *Recreations, Interests:* Paintings, garden, garden tennis, wine. *Address:* St James's Chambers, 68 Quay Street, Manchester, M3 3EJ(*tel:* 0161 834 7000; *fax:* 0161 834 2341).

ELLIOTT, Grahame Nicholas, FCA

Former Senior Partner, Elliott Templeton Sankey, Manchester, and Stoy Hayward, Manchester. *b.* 23 December 1938; Hale, Altrincham, Cheshire. *m.* 1968 Zita; two *s.* one *d.* *Education:* Mill Hill School. *Career Profile:* Non Executive Director, Thomas French & Sons plc, Airlines of Britain Holding plc, ELMBI; East Lancs Masonic Hall Co Ltd; Elprem Ltd; Booth Group Ltd; Chairman, Astral Finishes Ltd and various other private companies. *Societies:* St James's Club; President, Sale and Altrincham Spastic Society (Stockdales); Governor, Pictor School; Governor, Pownall Hall School; The Turf Club; Manchester Tennis & Racquet Club; *Address:* Peter House, St Peter's Square, Manchester M1 5BH (*tel:* 0161-228 6791); "Highbury", Harrop Road, Hale, Altrincham, Cheshire WA15 9DQ (*tel:* 0161-980 4857).

ELTON, Peter J, MB,ChB,MSc,FFPHM

Director of Public Health, Wigan & Bolton Health Authority. *b.* 2 March 1952 Croydon. *m.* 1977 Mavis; two *s.* *Public Offices:* Chairman, Outreach Community & Residential Services. *Education:* Manchester University (1970-75)(1977-79). *Career Profile:* Director of Community Services, North Manchester (1986-92); Consultant in Public Health Medicine, North Manchester (1983-92); Tameside to West Pennines (after merger with Oldham)(1992-95). *Publications/Creative Work:* 20 papers published in peer-reviewed journals. *Societies:* Manchester Medical Society, President, Public Health Section (1995-96). *Recreations, Interests:* Trying to learn the piano, Council Member, NW ASH. *Address:* Wigan & Bolton HA, 43 Churchgate, Bolton, BL1 1JF (*tel:* 01204 390067; *fax:* 01204 390194); 172 Bury Old Road, Manchester, M7 4QY (*tel:* 0161 720 7169).

EMMOTT, Susan

Mayor, Rochdale MBC. *b.* 1 December 1950 Nottingham. *Public Offices:* Deputy Mayor, Rochdale MBC (1991-92)(1995-96). *Career Profile:* Served on Education, Environment and Employment and Community Leisure Committees; Past Member of Greater Manchester Fire Authority. *Recreations, Interests:* Ice-skating, football, cricket, reading. *Address:* Rochdale MBC, PO Box 15, Town Hall, Rochdale, OL16 1AB (*tel:* 01706 47474; *fax:* 01706 59475).

ENSOR, His Honour Judge George Anthony, LLB

Circuit Judge, Manchester Crown Court. *b.* 4 December 1936 Portmadoc. *m.* 1968 Jennifer Caile; two *d.* *Public Offices:* HM Deputy Coroner, Liverpool (1965-95); Part-time Chairman, Industrial Tribunals (1975-95); Deputy Circuit Judge (1978-83); Recorder of the Crown Court (1983-95). *Education:* Malvern College (1950-55); Liverpool University (1955-58). *Career Profile:* Partner, Rutherfords (solicitors)(later Weightman Rutherfords)(1962-95); senior partner (1992-95); Director, Liverpool FC (1985-93)(resigned); Trustee, Empire Theatre Liverpool Trust (1986-); Governor, Malvern College (1993-). *Prizes:* Law Society: Atkinson Conveyancing Medal (1961); Timpron Martin Medal (1961). *Societies:* Artists Club, Liverpool (President 1976); Liverpool Law Society (President, 1982); Formby Golf Club; Waterloo Football Club (Rugby Union). *Recreations, Interests:* Golf, music, theatre.

ESTRIDGE, Christopher Robert Ivan, MA Cantab (1949),FCII,FPMI

Managing Director, Estridge & Powell Ltd. *b.* 10 July 1926; Minehead. *m.* 1952 Patricia Archibald; one *s.* one *d.*; *m.* 1986 Ann Davies; two *steps.* *Public Offices:* JP; Past Chairman, Alderley Edge Parish Council, Styal Prison Board of Visitors, St James's Club. *Education:* St Pauls; Cambridge University. *Military Service:* Royal Navy. *Career Profile:* Director, Leslie & Godwin Ltd. *Publications:* 'Punch'. *Societies:* MCC; Alderley Edge Cricket Club; Wilmslow Golf Club; St James's. *Recreations, Interests:* Golf, cricket, theatre, reading. *Address:* Whins Brow, Macclesfield Road, Alderley Edge, Cheshire SK9 7BL (*tel:* 01625-583091).

EVANS, Michael Norman Gwynne, BSc Bristol (1963)

Senior Partner (Manchester), Coopers & Lybrand *b.* 12 December 1939; Southport, Lancashire. *m.* 1963 Janet Elizabeth; three *s.* *Education:* Kings School, Macclesfield; Bristol University. *Prizes:* Deloitte Plender Prize for Accounting. *Societies:* The St James's Club; The Royal Over-seas League; Manchester Football Club & Cheadle Hulme Cricket Club; Treasurer, Hallé Concerts Society; Chairman, Manchester Airport Support Group. *Recreations, Interests:* Gardening and other outdoor pursuits. *Address:* Coopers & Lybrand, Abacus Court, 6 Minshull Street, Manchester M1 3ED (*tel:* 0161-236 9191); 144 Grove Lane, Cheadle Hulme, Cheshire SK8 7NH (*tel:* 0161-439 2088).

EVANS, Richard George, BSc(Hons),MEd,PhD,PGCE,FInstP

Principal, Stockport College of Further & Higher Education. *b.* 1 September 1942 Shirley, Warwickshire. *Public Offices:* Chair, GNVQ Science Advisory Committee; Chair,

80

Association for Science Post-16 Committee. *Education:* Hilsea Secondary Modern School, Portsmouth; Portsmouth College of Technology; Essex University; London University; Manchester University. *Career Profile:* Supply Teacher in London Schools; Great Yarmouth College; Blackpool College; Peterborough College; Cornwall College. *Publications/Creative Work:* Numerous publications on educational issues. *Societies:* Fellow of the Institute of Physics; Fellow of the Royal Society of Arts; Member of Association for Science. *Recreations, Interests:* Cinema - horror films (pre-1960), film noir, Philosophy - existential phenomenology, Surrealist art. *Address:* Stockport College, Wellington Road South, Stockport, SK1 3UQ(*tel:* 0161 958 3400; *fax:* 0161 958 3428).

F

FAIRCLOUGH, William Derrick, LLB London,Barrister-at-Law

Stipendiary Magistrate of the County of Greater Manchester; Assistant Parliamentary Boundary Commissioner; Crown Court Recorder. *b.* 5 March 1929; Barton, Preston. *m.* 1957 Dr. Margaret Latham; two *s. Education:* Preston Grammar School; King's College, University of London; Council of Legal Education. *Military Service:* Flying Offcer, RAF. *Career Profile:* Head of Chambers, 1 Dean's Court, Manchester. *Societies:* Honourable Society of Gray's Inn; London House Fellowship. *Recreations, Interests:* Association football, travel, food and wine. *Address:* City Magistrates' Court, Crown Square, Manchester M60 1PR *(tel:* 0161-832 7272).

FAIRHURST, Harry Marshall, OBE (1993),Hon Fellow UMIST; MA Cambridge, DipARCH Northern Polytechnic,Hon MA Manchester

Architect in Private Practice; Commissioned Architect, English Heritage. *b.* 18 June 1925; Alderley Edge. *m.* 1959 Elizabeth Mary Thorp; one *s.* three *d. Public Offices:* Nominated Member, Mancheser City Museums & Galleries Committee; Member of Court, University of Manchester, Whitworth Art Gallery. *Education:* Terra Nova School; Clifton College; Clare College, Cambridge; Northern Polytechnic, London. *Career Profile:* Partner and Senior Partner, Harry S Fairhurst & Son (later Fairhursts Architects) (1950-80); Cathedral Architect, Manchester (1970-90). *Creative Works:* Buildings for commerce, industry, education, medicine and scientific research; Survey of English Cathedrals, English Heritage (1991). *Prizes:* Civic Trust Award (1960), (1975); Housing Medal (1954). *Societies:* Manchester Society of Architects (former President); Cathedral Architects Association (former Chairman); Ecclesiastical Architects & Surveyors Association; Ancient Monuments Society; St James's Club; Manchester Literary & Philosophical Society (former President); Portico Library. *Recreations, Interests:* Gardening and forestry, contemporary art, design and crafts. *Address:* 33 Macclesfield Road, Wilmslow, Cheshire SK9 2AF *(tel:* 01625-523784). *Additional Information:* Grandfather, Harry S Fairhurst practised architecture in Manchester from 1894, Father, P Garland Fairhurst from 1924.

FALDER, Stephen Brian, BSc (London)

Marketing Director, H Marcel Guest Ltd. *b.* 9 July 1960 Sale. *m.* 1983 Christine; one *s.* two *d. Public Offices:* Regional Councillor, CBI; Chair of Education & Training, Manchester Citypride Bid; Chair, CBI Business Growth Forum. *Education:* Sale Grammar School; Kings College, London. *Career Profile:* H Marcel Guest (1981); Bradite Paints (1982-83); H Marcel Guest (1984), director (1990). *Address:* H Marcel Guest Ltd, Riverside Works, Collyhurst Road Manchester M40 7RU *(tel:* 0161 205 7631; *fax:* 0161 205 8146: *e-mail:* stevef@popmail.dircon.co.uk).

FAVELL, Anthony Rowland, LLB (Univ. of Sheffield, 1960),Solicitor (1964)

Solicitor, Gorvin Kenyon (Stockport), Favell & Smith (Sheffield); Chairman, Tameside & Glossop Acute Services NHS Trust; Chairman (part-time), Mental Health Review Tribunals. *b.* 29 May 1939 Sheffield. *m.* 1966 Susan Rosemary; one *s.* one *d. Public*

Offices: President, Stockport MENCAP. *Education:* St Bees School, Cumbria; Sheffield University. *Career Profile:* Founder & Senior Partner, Favell & Smith (Sheffield), Favell Smith & Henson (Hathersage); Director and Chairman of several companies; Member, Conservative National Union Executive (1980-83); MP for Stockport (1983-92); Parliamentary Private Secretary to Rt Hon John Major (1986-90). *Publications/Creative Work:* Contributor to policy papers: 'The NHS: A Suitable Case for Treatment'; 'Choice and Responsibility - the Enabling State' and others; joint editor with Patrick Minford of 'EU Review'. *Societies:* St James Club, Manchester; Lansdowne Club, London. *Recreations, Interests:* Music, tennis, gardening, golf, hill walking, drystone walling. *Address:* Gorvin Kenyon, 12/14 Millgate, Stockport, SK1 2NN *(tel:* 0161 480 3632; *fax:* 0161 477 0789); Skinners Hall, Edale, S30 2ZE *(tel:* 01433 670281; *fax:* 01433 670481).

FAWCUS, Judge Simon James David, MA Cantab (1961)

Circuit Judge. *b.* 12 July 1938; Lee-on-Solent, Hampshire. *m.* 1966 Joan Mary Oliphant; one *s.* four *d. Education:* Aldenham School; Trinity Hall, Cambridge. *Career Profile:* Junior of Northern Circuit (1965); Crown Court Recorder (1980-85); President, Council of Circuit Judges (1996). *Societies:* MCC; Manchester Tennis & Racquet. *Recreations, Interests:* Real tennis, golf, bridge, music (listening), travel. *Address:* c/o The Courts of Justice, Crown Square, Manchester.

FERGUSON, Alexander Chapman, CBE(1995),OBE(1984); BMA(hc) MA(hc) (Salford)

Manager, Manchester United Football Club. *b.* 31 December 1941 Govan, Glasgow. *m.* 1966 Catherine Russell; three *s. Education:* Govan High School, Glasgow. *Career Profile:* Footballer: Queens Park (1958-60); St Johnstone (1960-64); Dunfermline Athletic (1964-67); Glasgow Rangers (1967-69; Falkirk (1969-73); Ayr United (1973-74); Manager: St Mirren (1974-78); Aberdeen (1978-86); Manchester United Football Club: Premier League Champions (1993); Premier League & FA Cup (1994); Premier League & FA Cup (1996); FA Cup (1990); European Cup Winners (1991); Super Cup (1991); League Cup (1992); Charity Shield (1990, 1993, 1994). *Publications/Creative Work:* 'A Light in the North' (1984); 'Six Years at United' (1992); 'Just Champion' (1993); 'A Year in the Life' (1995). *Recreations, Interests:* Golf, snooker. *Address:* Manchester United Football Club, Sir Matt Busby Way,, Old Trafford, Manchester, M16 0RA *(tel:* 0161 872 1661; *fax:* 0161 872 5502).

FERGUSON, Professor Mark William James, Winston Churchill Fellow (1978); BSc (Hons)(1976), BDS (Hons) (1978),PhD (1982) Belfast, FFD Royal College of Surgeons, Ireland (1990)

Professor of Basic Dental Sciences; Dean of the School of Biological Sciences, University of Manchester. *b.* 11 October 1955; Belfast, Northern Ireland. *Public Offices:* Chairman, UK Government Technology Foresight Panel on Health and Life Sciences including Pharmaceuticals; Higher Education Funding Council Panel on Basic Medical & Dental Sciences; Vice Chairman for Science, International Union for the Conservation of Nature, Species Survival Commission Crocodile Specialist Group, Geneva, Switzerland; Governor, 'Research Into Ageing'; Councillor, European Research Group of Oral Biology; Secretary & Treasurer, European Tissue Repair Society. *Education:* Coleraine Academical Institut-

ion; The Queen's University of Belfast. *Career Profile:* Lecturer in Anatomy, The Queen's University of Belfast (1978-84); Wellcome Trust Visiting Research Fellow, University of Southern California, USA. *Creative Works:* Television documentaries mostly on alligators/crocodiles/sex determination/birth defects, wound healing; Numerous radio programmes. *Publications:* Over 200 scientific papers on: Palate Development and Cleft Palate, Sex Determination, Alligator and Crocodile Biology, Embryonic Development, Wound Healing and Egg Incubation; Books: 'The Structure, Development and Evolution of Reptiles' (Academic Press 1984); 'Cleft Lip and Palate: Long Term Results and Future Prospects' (with A Huddart) (MUP 1990); 'Egg Incubation: Its Effects on Embryonic Development in Birds & Reptiles' (with C Deeming) (CUP 1990); 'Crocodiles and Alligators' (Wheldon Australia): An Encyclopaedic Account By International Experts (1989); 38th Edition of 'Gray's Anatomy' (with 6 others) (Churchill-Livingstone, 1996). *Prizes:* Pindborg Prize (Copenhagen) for Internationally Outstanding Achievements in Oral Biology (1996), Sheldon Friel Medal & Lecture, European Orthodontic Society (1996),Broadhurst Lecture, Harvard Schepens Eye Institute (1996), 86th Lord Kelvin Lecture, IEE London (1995), Teale Lecture, Royal College of Physicians London (1994), Founders Day Lecture, University of Witwatersrand, South Africa (1994), Steeger Professor and Lecture, New York University Medical Centre (1992), Presidents Medal, British Association of Oral & Maxillofacial Surgeons (1990), John Tomes Medal & Prize for Dental Science Research, Royal College of Surgeons London (1989); Distinguished Scientist/Young Investigator Award, International Association for Dental Research, Washington (1988); Darwin Lecturer, British Association (1987); Conway Medal (Biological Sciences) Royal Academy of Medicine in Ireland (1985); American Dental Association Achievement Award (1981); Anatomical Society Prize (1979); Craniofacial Society Prize (1979); British Dental Association Prize (1979); Colyer Prize Royal Society of Medicine (1980). *Societies:* Anatomical Society of Great Britain and Ireland (Council, Editorial Board); British Society for Developmental Biology; British Society for Cell Biology; British Dental Association; Royal Academy of Medicine in Ireland (Fellow); American Society of Zoologists; Craniofacial Society of Great Britain & Ireland (President & Council); British Association for the Advancement of Science (President, Medical Section); Manchester Medical Society (President, Section of Odontology); Research Defence Society (Council). *Recreations, Interests:* Scientific research, Biology, wildlife, travel, reading, antiques particularly furniture, philately. *Address:* School of Biological Sciences, 3.239 Stopford Building, University of Manchester, Oxford Road, Manchester, M13 9PT *(tel:* 0161-275 6775; *fax:* 0161 275 5945).

FERRANTI, N A Z de see *de Ferranti, N A Z.*

FERRANTI, Sebastian Basil Joseph Ziani de see *de Ferranti, S B J Z.*

FIELDEN, John Anthony Haigh, MA(Oxon),Solicitor

Senior Partner, Cobbetts. *b.* 18 March 1937 Bury, Lancashire. *m.* 1962 Deryl Anne Collinson; one *s.* one *d.* *Public Offices:* Vice-Chairman, Manchester Financial & Professional Forum; Clerk to the Trustees, Manchester Guardian Society Charitable Trust; Trustee, Wood Street Mission. *Education:* Heronwater Preparatory School, North Wales (1945-50); Rossall School, Fleetwood (1950-55); Keble College, Oxford (1955-58). *Career*

Profile: Solicitor (1961); Partner, Emerson & Fielden (1962-68), Whitworths (1968-70), Leak Almond & Parkinson (1970-87); Senior Partner, Cobbett Leak Almond (now Cobbetts) (1985-). *Societies:* MCC; Manchester Tennis & Racquet Club; Bowdon Cricket, Hockey & Squash Club. *Recreations, Interests:* Cricket, real tennis, antiques, old houses. *Address:* Cobbetts, Ship Canal House, King Street, Manchester, M2 4WB *(tel:* 0161 833 3333; *fax:* 0161 833 3030); Rosehill, Rostherne, Knutsford, WA16 6RT *(tel:* 01565 830430).

FINCH, Alec, FCII

Chairman, Alec Finch & Co Ltd, Insurance Brokers. *b.* 14 August 1947 Salford. *m.* 1970 Joan; two *s.* one *d. Education:* Stand Grammar School, Whitefield; Manchester College of Commerce. *Career Profile:* Early career spent in Manchester with C T Bowring and Lowndes Lambert; moved to London as UK Director for Golding Collins Ltd Lloyds Brokers; negotiated MBO of Golding Collins provincial operations (1983) to form Alec Finch & Co Ltd. *Societies:* RSA; Tame Valley Tennis & Squash Club. *Recreations, Interests:* Family, sport (Manchester City FC), music, theatre. *Address:* Alec Finch & Co Ltd, Sussex House, 83-85 Mosley Street, Manchester, M2 3LG *(tel:* 0161 228 1466; *fax:* 0161 228 0979); 9 Higher Lydgate Park, Grasscroft, Oldham, OL4 4KF *(tel:* 01457 872580). *Additional Information:* Director, British Insurance and Investment Brokers Association; Past President, International Broker Network.

FINLAY, Ian, DipArch,DA(Manchester),RIBA

Principal, Ian Finlay Architects. *b.* 26 February 1951 Birmingham. *m.* 1982 Diane; one *d. (marr. diss. 1993) Public Offices:* Chair, RIBA Community Architecture Group, London & Founder, RIBA Community Projects Fund (1982-93); Founding Trustee, Ancoats Buildings Preservation Trust (1996-). *Education:* Bournville Technical Grammar School, Birmingham (1962); Manchester Polytechnic School of Architecture (1969). *Career Profile:* Project Architect, Rod Hackney Associates (1976-81); Founder Member, Design Co-operative (1981-85); Director, DC Architects (1985-91); Principal, Ian Finlay Architects (1991-); Partner, Paradise Wharf Partnership (1988-). *Publications/Creative Work:* Co-author: 'Community Architects Services' (RIBA); contributor to and co-designer, SRB2 Document for Miles Platting, Ancoats & the Northern Quarter; co-author: 'The Ancoats Urban Village Planning and Design Guide'. *Societies:* Vice Chair, Manchester Civic Society (founder member). *Recreations, Interests:* Improving the environment, saving historic buildings from destruction, watching Birmingham City FC, having fun with daughter Sophie. *Address:* Ian Finlay Architects, The Stables, Paradise Wharf, Ducie Street, Manchester, M1 2JN *(tel:* 0161 272 8475/6; *fax:* 0161 274 4140).

FIRTH, Mary Flora McKinnon (*née* Hunter), MBE(1993), DL(1991), JP(1971)

High Sheriff of Greater Manchester (1996-67); Chairman, Oldham NHS Trust (1992-). *b.* 13 October 1929; Oldham. *m.* 1949 Gilbert Hamilton Campbell; one *s.* two *d.*; *m.* 1985 Lees Firth; three *stepd. Public Offices:* President, Greater Manchester East Euro Conservative Constituency, Littleborough & Saddleworth Conservative Association. *Education:* Hulme Grammar School for Girls, Oldham. *Career Profile:* Chairman, Oldham Health Authority (1986-92); President, Greater Manchester Red Cross (1988-94);

Chairman of Licensing Bench; Member of the Board of Visitors, Buckley Hall Detention Centre; Member of the Probation Committee, Greater Manchester (1976-86). *Societies:* New Cavendish Club, London. *Recreations, Interests:* Bridge, swimming, golf and tennis. *Address:* Oldham NHS Trust, Trust Headquarters, Westhulme Avenue, Oldham *(tel:* 0161 627 8714); 'The Orchards', Westfield Drive, Grasscroft, Oldham OL4 4HT *(tel:* 01457 872186).

FISH, His Honour Judge Peter Stuart, MA(Cantab),Solicitor

Circuit Judge. *b.* 18 December 1938 Preston. *m.* 1963 Nolan Ann Worrall; two *s.* two *d.* (one deceased). *Education:* Rydal School, N Wales; Trinity Hall, Cambridge. *Career Profile:* Admitted Solicitor (1963); Partner, Brighouses, Southport (1964); District Judge (1987); Circuit Judge (1994). *Societies:* Royal Birkdale Golf Club; Formby Choral Society. *Recreations, Interests:* Golf, music, gardening.

FISHER, Nicholas, BA(Hons),MLitt,Diploma in Criminology

Sub-Divisional Police Commander, Stockport. *b.* 16 November 1948 Darlington, Co.Durham. *m.* 1975 Pamela; one *s.* two *d. Education:* Moseley Grammar School, Birmingham (1960-68); University of Newcastle upon Tyne (1968-71), University of Leeds (part-time, 1996-). *Career Profile:* Joined Birmingham Police Force; variety of operational and HQ posts, West Midlands Police; Greater Manchester Police (1995-). *Recreations, Interests:* Choral Music, 17th century English poetry, Church of England Lay Reader (1993-). *Address:* Greater Manchester Police HQ, Chester House, Boyer Street, Manchester.

FISHWICK, Avril (*née* Platt),DL; Solicitor (1948),LLB Liverpool (1946),LLM Liverpool (1947), MA(hc) Manchester (1994)

Vice Lord-Lieutenant of Greater Manchester *b.* 30 March 1924; Hindley. *m.* 1950 Thomas William Fishwick; two *d. Public Offices:*Chairman, ERCU Ltd (Tidy Britain); President, Wigan RSPCA, Friends of Drumcroon Arts Centre; Trustee, Friends of Rose, Skelton Bounty, Greater Manchester Police Community Charity; Vice-President, Greater Manchester West County Scout Council; Member of Court, University of Manchester. *Education:* Woodfield Private School; Wigan High School for Girls; Liverpool University. *War Service:* Foreign Office (Bletchley Park) (1942-45). *Career Profile:* Solicitor in private practice (1049-1994); Chairman, Billinge Ashton & Pemberton Hospitals (1968-73), Wigan Area Health Authority (1973-82), CT Scanner Appeal (1990-92); President (in Wigan), Civic Trust, Little Theatre, Gilbert & Sullivan Society, Law Society, Soroptomist International, RC Nursing, League of Hospital Friends; Director, Nat West Bank plc (Northern Board), Groundwork Trading Ltd. *Prizes:* Liverpool Law Society Prize for Conveyancing (1946); International Law Scholarship, Columbia University (1946); Paul Harris Fellow, Rotary Foundation (1995). *Societies:* World wild life; RSPB; RSPCA; Civic Trust; Royal Overseas Society *Recreations, Interests:* Family, natural history, heraldry, Rugby League (watching). *Address:* Haighlands, Haigh Country Park, Haigh WN2 1PB *(tel:* 01942-831291).

FLINT, George Norman Clayton, MA, LLM (Cantab,1937),MA (hc) Manchester (1988)

Retired Solicitor. *b.* 10 January 1914; Wisbech, Cambridgeshire. *m.* 1942 Ruth Ellin McLaurin Maddox; two *s. Education:* Greshams School, Holt; Clare College, Cambridge. *War Service:* Army (1940-46), India and Malaya (1945-46). *Career Profile:* Senior Partner, Addleshaw Sons & Latham Solicitors; Deputy Treasurer, University of Manchester; Governor, Manchester Grammar School; Chairman, Cheadle Royal Hospital; Chairman, Whitworth Art Gallery; Chairman, Museum of Science & Industry; various Directorships and Chairmanships. *Societies:* The Royal Society of Arts; Hawks Club, Cambridge. *Recreations, Interests:* Reading. *Address:* 19 Whalley Road, Hale, Altrincham WA15 9DF *(tel:* 0161-980 3104).

FLOWERS, Lord Brian Hilton, Knight(1969),Life Peer(1979); MA,DSc,ScD,LLD,FInstP FRS

Chancellor of the University of Manchester; Chairman, The Nuffield Foundation. *b.* 13 September 1924 Blackburn. *m.* 1951 Mary Frances Behrens; two *steps. Education:* Swansea Grammar School; Gonville & Caius College, Cambridge; University of Birmingham. *Career Profile:* Atomic Energy (1944-58); Professor of Physics, University of Manchester (1958-67); Chairman, Science Research Council (1967-73); Rector, Imperial College, London (1973-85); Vice-Chancellor, University of London (1985-90). *Publications/Creative Work:* 'Properties of Matter' (with E Mendoza) (1970); 'An Introduction to Numerical Methods in C + +'(1995); Numerous articles in learned journals on nuclear physics, science policy and environmental policy. *Prizes:* Rutherford Medal; Glazebrook Medal; Hon FIEE, Hon MRIA, Hon FInstP, Hon FRCP, etc. *Societies:* Institute of Physics; Insitute of Electrical Engineers (Hon); Royal College of Physicians (Hon). *Recreations, Interests:* Gardening, travelling, computing. *Address:* The House of Lords, London, SW1A 0PW.

FORD, James Glyn

Member of the European Parliament, Greater Manchester East. *b.* 28 January 1950 Gloucester. *m.* Hazel Nancy Mahey; one *d. (marr. diss. 1990)*; *m.* Daniela Zannelli; one *s. Public Offices:* Councillor for Tameside (1978-86). *Education:* Marling School; Reading University; University College, London; Manchester University. *Career Profile:* Apprentice, BAC (1967-68); academic posts at the Open University, UMIST, Sussex, Manchester & Tokyo Universities. *Publications/Creative Work:* 'Future of Ocean Technology' (1987); Fascist Europe (1992); 'The Evolution of a European' (1994); 'Changing States' (1996). *Address:* 46 Stamford Road, Mossley, Lancashire, OL5 0BE *(tel:* 01457 836276; *fax:* 01457 834927; *e-mail:* glynford.euromp@zen.co.uk). *Additional Information:* Chaired the European Parliament's first Committee of Enquiry into the growth of racism and fascism in Europe. Rapporteur for the 2nd Committee of Inquiry on Racism and Xenophobia (1989-90), Countertrade (1986), EUREKA & SDI and European Arms Trade (1987,91,93). Member of Civil Liberties, Research & Rules Committees; former vice chair of the Japan Delegation (1992-94). Leader of the European Parliamentary Labour Party (1989-93), member of the Labour Party NEC (1989-93); vice-chair of the Group of

the Party of European Socialists (1993-94); Deputy Leader of the PES (1989-93); National Treasurer, Anti-Nazi League; President, European Parliament Section, Inter-Parliamentary Council against Anti-Semitism; Member, Editorial Board, Tribune; Management Committee of Science & Technology Office of Assessment; columnist for Tribune, Searchlight and Research Fortnight.

FORDE-JOHNSTON, James, BA (1952),MA Liverpool (1954),FSA

Retired. *b.* 7 May 1927; Liverpool. *m.* 1962 Kathleen Mary Healy; three *s.* one *d.* *Education:* St Edward's College, Liverpool (1938-44); Liverpool University (1949-54). *Military Service:* 1946-48 (RASC and RAEC). *Career Profile:* Asst Keeper, Archaeology, Liverpool Museum (1954-56); Investigator, Royal Commission Historical Monuments (1956-58); Keeper (Senior Lecturer) Manchester Museum, Archaeology & Ethnology (1958-82). *Publications:* 8 books and about two dozen papers in learned journals. *Prizes:* Leverhulme Award (1958); Wenner-Gren (USA) (1966). *Societies:* Fellow, Society of Antiquaries; Member, Royal Archaeological Institute. *Recreations, Interests:* Walking, photography, medieval castles, monuments in general. *Address:* 6 Greystoke Avenue, Sale, Cheshire M33 3NT *(tel:* 0161-962 4218).

FORECAST, The Revd Christopher Keith, MA(Cantab)

Moderator, North Western Province, United Reformed Church. *b.* 8 June 1935 Letchworth, Herts. *m.* 1960 Frances Ann; two *s.* two *d.* *Education:* Perse School, Cambridge (1946-54); Downing College, Cambridge (1956-59); Western College, Bristol (1959-60). *Military Service:* Pilot Officer, Fighter Control RAF (1954-56). *Career Profile:* Minister, Arley Chapel, Bristol (1960-64); Derriford, Plymouth (1964-70); Roath Park, Cardiff (1970-76); Palmers Green, London (1981-92); Christian Education Secretary, United Reformed Church (1976-81); Moderator, General Assembly, United Reformed Church (1989-90). *Recreations, Interests:* Walking, travelling, DIY, model railways, sightseeing. *Address:* Provincial Office, Franklin Street, Patricroft, Eccles, Manchester, M30 0QZ*(tel:* 0161 789 5583; *fax:* 0161 707 9117); 4 Marlowe Drive, Didsbury, Manchester, M20 6DE *(tel:* 0161 445 9608).

FOSKETT, Eric William, OBE (1985); BSc (Econ) London (1957),DPA London (1951), FCIEH (1978),FRSH (1970)

President (1987-90), Institution of Environmental Health Officers; President (1991-94), International Federation of Environmental Health; Hon Vice-President, Hon Co-ordination Officer, Directory Editor, International Federation of Environmental Health. *b.* 14 May 1920; Woodville, Swadlincote, Derbyshire. *m.* 1945 Beryl Edge; two *s.* one *d.* *Education:* Hanley High School, Stoke on Trent; Matthew Boulton Technical College, Birmingham. *War Service:* Royal Army Medical Corps (1940-46). Service in the Middle East. *Career Profile:* Deputy Chief Public Health Inspector, City of Stoke on Trent (1961-67); Deputy Chief Environmental Health Officer, City of Manchester (1967-69); Chief Environmental Health Officer, City of Manchester (1969-74); Director of Environmental Health, City of Manchester (1974-85); Advisor in Environmental Health to the Association of Metropolitan Authorities (1974-85); Member Health and Safety Executive/Local Authority Liaison Committee (1975-85); Chairman LAMSAC Environmental Health Computer Application

Committee (1975-85). *Publications:* History of the International Federation of Environmental Health 1985-95); numerous papers on environmental health topics. *Recreations, Interests:* Reading, foreign travel. *Address:* 26 Grebe Close, Poynton, Stockport, Cheshire SK12 1HU *(tel:* 01625-876670).

FOSTER, Professor Peter William, BSc,PhD,CTex,FTI

Professor of Textiles, UMIST. *b.* 6 December 1930 Rotherham. *m.* 1952 Elizabeth; two *s.* two *d. Public Offices:* Director, Manchester Business Link (1992-94); Chairman, Management Board, Contact (1991-94); Director, Arkwright Trust. *Education:* Leeds Modern School (1941-48); University College, London (1948-54); University of Nebraska (1957-58). *Career Profile:* ICI (1954-57); EI du Pont de Nemours Inc (1958-66); Managing Director, Heathcoat Yarns & Fibres (1966-84); Director, John Heathcoat (1971-84); Development Director, Coats Patons plc (1978-85); Director, Axiom Electronics Ltd (1981-86); Managing Director, Universal Carbon Fibres (1982-85); Head of Department (1986-93), Vice-Principal (1991-93), Deputy Principal (1993-94), UMIST. *Publications/Creative Work:* Various articles in the professional journals and several patents. *Prizes:* Ramsay Memorial Medal (1950). *Societies:* Royal Chemical Society; Textile Institute; Royal Society of Arts; Manchester Literary & Philosophical Society. *Recreations, Interests:* Music, books, walking, cooking. *Address:* Dept of Textiles, UMIST, PO Box 88, Sackville Street, Manchester, M60 1QD *(tel:* 0161 200 4142; *fax:* 0161 200 4019; *e-mail:* peter.foster@umist.ac.uk); 6 Aldford Place, Alderley Edge, SK9 7RQ *(tel:* 01625 582832; *fax:* 01625 582832).

FOX, David, BSc London (1952),MA California (1958),FRGS

Hon. Fellow in Geography, University of Manchester; Consul for Chile; Secretary-General, International Congress of Americanists. *b.* 15 July 1931; London. *Public Offices:* Past Vice Chairman, Latin American Committee of Oxfam; Past Chairman, current Secretary, Manchester Consular Association; Past Chairman, current Treasurer, Society for Latin American Studies; Vice President, International Congress of Americanists; Past Secretary, Rusholme & Fallowfield Civic Society. *Education:* Chipping Camden Grammar School; Woking County School for Boys; University College (University of London); McGill University (Montreal); University of California (Berkeley). *Military Service:* RAF. *Career Profile:* Research Assistant, McGill University; Sub-Arctic Research Laboratory, Quebec; Visiting Professor, Southern Illinois University (USA); Warden, Woolton Hall, University of Manchester. *Publications:* numerous publications on Latin America. *Societies:* Institute of British Geographers; Society for Latin American Studies; Manchester Consular Association. *Recreations, Interests:* Writing, walking, exploring. *Address:* Chilean Consulate, 22 Bollin Hill, Wilmslow, Cheshire SK9 4AW *(tel:* 01625-528000).

FOX, Tina, CertPA,DipPA

Chief Executive, The Vegetarian Society. *b.* 10 November 1950 Germany (British Military Hospital). *Education:* La Sagesse High School, Liverpool; Liverpool University (p-t). *Career Profile:* Twenty years service in local government; Service Area Co-ordinator, Highways & Planning Departments, Liverpool City Council; Chief Executive, Vegetarian Society (1995-). *Publications/Creative Work:* Articles on vegetarian travel (various

publications); articles on animal folklore (mainly Prediction Magazine); Editor, 'The Vegetarian'. *Societies:* Patron, Wirral Green Alliance; Member many green and animal welfare groups. *Recreations, Interests:* Gardening, green issues, writing, circle dancing, antiques, travel. *Address:* The Vegetarian Society, Parkdale, Dunham Road, Altrincham, WA14 4QG *(tel:* 0161 928 0793; *fax:* 0161 926 9182). *Additional Information:* The Charity is a registered charity. *World Wide Web Page:* http://www.veg.org/veg/orgs/ vegsocuk/.

FRANCE, Elizabeth Irene (*née* Salem), BSc(Econ) (1971),DSc(hc) (1996)

Data Protection Registrar. *b.* 1 February 1950 Leicester. *m.* 1971 Dr Michael William France; two *s.* one *d. Education:* Oadby Beauchamp Grammar School; UCW, Aberystwyth. *Career Profile:* Home Office (1971-94). *Societies:* Fellow Royal Society of Arts. *Address:* Data Protection Registrar, Wycliffe House, Water Lane, Wilmslow, SK9 5AF *(tel:* 01625 545709; *fax:* 01625 524510; *e-mail:* data@wycliffe.demon.co.uk).

FREEMAN, M Anthony, FCA,MSPI

Senior Partner, Levy Gee, chartered accountants. *b.* 29 July 1953 Manchester. *m.* 1976 Sharon; one *s.* one *d. Recreations, Interests:* Theatre, music, reading.

FRENCH, Thomas Jeremy, FCA

Chairman, French plc. *b.* 3 April 1939; Altrincham. *m.* 1966 Gillian Lesley Edington; two *d. Education:* Trearddur House, Anglesey; Rugby School; Grenoble University. *Societies:* St James's Club, Manchester. *Address:* French plc, Sharston Road, Wythenshawe, Manchester M22 4TH *(tel:* 0161-998 1811).

FRIEDMAN, Ellis Harold Ian, MB ChB,MSc,MFCM,FFPHM

Director of Public Health, West Pennine Health Authority. *b.* 24 April 1954; London. *m.* 1980 Sandra Jean Klepper; two *s. Public Offices:* Board Member and ex-Chairman, Collingwood Housing Group. *Education:* Haberdashers Aske's School, Elstree; Manchester Medical School. *Career Profile:* Head of Community Medicine Dept, South Manchester Health Authority, Director for Public Health, Oldham Health Authority. *Publications:* 'Medicine: The Bare Bones' with R E Moshy (Wiley 1986); 'Medicine: The Bare Essentials' with R E Moshy (Wiley 1989), 'Medicine: A Guide to Study and Practice' (with R E Moshy) (Wiley 1992) and many papers in medical journals. *Societies:* British Medical Association. *Recreations, Interests:* Sport, travel, chess, theatre. *Address:* West Pennine Health Authority, Westhulme Avenue, Oldham OL1 2PL *(tel:* 0161 455 5735); 16 Hastings Close, Whitefield, Manchester.

FRISBY, Norman Sidney

Retired, Chief Press/PR Officer Granada Television, Manchester (1959-88). *b.* 9 January 1928; Tuxford, Notts. *m.* 1951 Iris; one *s.* two *d. Public Offices:* JP, Manchester City Bench (1973-); Deputy Lieutenant, Gtr Manchester (1992-). *Education:* Retford (Notts) Grammar School (1939-46); Sheffield University (1948-49). *Military Service:* Sixth Airborne Division, Palestine (1946-48). *Career Profile:* Journalist, Newspapers and

Magazines. *Societies:* Manchester Luncheon Club; Rochdale Probus Club. *Recreations, Interests:* Community work, Member of Council of St Ann's Hospice, Chairman (1991-94). *Address:* 6 Lowerfold Way, Healey, Rochdale, Lancs OL12 7HX *(tel:* 01706-44224).

FROST, Ronald, FRMCM (1971),Hon RSCM (1973); BMus (Durham),FRCO,ARMCM (Performers Diploma with Distinction)

Principal Lecturer, Royal Northern College of Music; Organist, Hallé Concerts Society; Organist and Choirmaster, St Ann's Church, Manchester. *b.* 30 March 1933; Bury, Lancashire. *m.* 1959 Barbara Hartley. *Education:* Bury Grammar School (1945-51); Royal Manchester College of Music (1951-54); Kirtland Organ Schol, RMCM (1951), Lancs County Major Schol (1953), Meadowcroft Organ Schol, RMCM (1953). *Career Profile:* Organist and Choirmaster, Stretford Parish Church (1958-69); Director of Studies, RMCM (1970-73); Chorus Master, Hallé Concerts Society (1972-92); Tutor, RMCM (1955-73). *Creative Works:* Organ and choral compositions; pen and ink drawings; watercolour paintings. *Prizes:* Limpus Prizes ARCO (1953) and FRCO (1955); Royal Manchester Institution Medal for Organ Playing (1954). *Societies:* Manchester Organists' Association (President, 1996-97); Rochdale, Oldham & Tameside Organists' Association (Hon President); Manchester Luncheon Club; Royal Society of Arts; Ramsbottom Music Festival (Hon President). *Recreations, Interests:* Crosswords, dog walking, watching football and cricket, painting and drawing. *Address:* 510 Holcombe Road, Greenmount, Bury, Lancs BL8 4EJ *(tel:* 01204-883338). *Additional Information:* Organ Recitalist, Examiner, Teacher and Adjudicator.

FROW, Ruth *(née* Engel), MA(hc) (Salford),Hon Fellow, University of the Midlands MEd (Manchester)

Retired. *b.* 28 July 1922 London. *Education:* Downhurst School, Hendon; Hampton Teaching Training Centre; Manchester University. *War Service:* WAAF (1940-45). *Career Profile:* Teacher; Deputy Head, Yew Tree High School; Manchester Teachers' Committee, NUT. *Publications/Creative Work:* (With E Frow): 9 books and 30 pamphlets. *Recreations, Interests:* Walking. *Address:* Working Class Movement Library, 51 Crescent, Salford, M5 4DY *(tel:* 0161 736 3601; *fax:* 0161 736 415).

FROW, Stephen Edmund, Hon Fellow, Manchester Polytechnic,MA(hc) (Salford),Hon Fellow, University of the Midlands

Retired. *b.* 5 June 1906 Harrington, Lincs. *Education:* Elementary. *Career Profile:* Tool maker; Shop Steward, Manchester District Secretary (1961-67), AEU; Co-founder, Working Class Movement Library. *Publications/Creative Work:* 9 books and 30 pamphlets. *Recreations, Interests:* Walking. *Address:* Working Class Movement Library, 51 Crescent, Salford, M5 4DY *(tel:* 0161 736 3601; *fax:* 0161 736 4115).

FRY, Mike, BA(Hons) (1979),MA(1980)

Chief Executive, Christie Hospital NHS Trust. *b.* 16 January 1958 Preston, Lancashire. *m.* 1986 Lindsay Herrington. *Education:* Lostock Hall County Secondary; WR Tuson College, Preston; University of Newcastle-upon-Tyne; University of Leeds. *Career Profile:* NHS

National Training Scheme (1980); various administrative posts in Bath and Newcastle-upon-Tyne; General Manager, Christie Hospital (1989). *Publications/Creative Work:* Various articles and book chapters. *Recreations, Interests:* Motorsport, tennis, opera. *Address:* Christie Hospital NHS Trust, Wilmslow Road, Withington, Manchester, M20 9BX *(tel:* 0161 446 3700; *fax:* 0161 446 3977). *Additional Information:* Honorary Fellow, University of Manchester.

FUTTER, Royston Geoffrey, DipLS Belfast (1971),DMS Sheffield Hallam (1981)

Arts & Leisure Manager, City of Salford. *b.* 6 August 1946; Salhouse, Norfolk. *m.* 1972 Joy McLements; *(marr. diss. 1989)*; one *d.*; *m.* 1989 Pamela Drury; one *steps.* one *stepd.* *Public Offices:* National Secretary, The Library Campaign (1989); Trustee Working Class Movement Library (1990). *Education:* Wymondham College, Norfolk; Queens University, Belfast; Sheffield Hallam. *Career Profile:* Divisional Leisure Services Officer, Humberside CC; Chief Assistant, Isle of Wight CC; Cataloguer, British Library. *Creative Works:* Director, Lowry Centenary Festival (1987); Commissioner, Ballet 'A Simple Man' (1987); co-author: 'Postcards for the Cause' (1994), 'Marching for the Cause' (1995). *Societies:* Library Association (Associate Member); Institute of Leisure & Amenity Management; The National Trust; The Marks Memorial Library; Patron of Salford Choral Society. *Recreations, Interests:* Painting of L S Lowry; history of Manchester, cycling,industrial archaeology, gardening, woodworking. *Address:* Vulcan House, Albion Place, Crescent, Salford M5 4NY *(tel:* 0161 736 9448; *fax:* 0161 745 7806); 8 Simpson Grove, Boothstown, Manchester M28 1LY.

G

GALASKO, Professor Charles Samuel Bernard, MB BCh Witwatersrand (1962),FRCS Edinburgh (1966),FRCS England (1966),ChM Witwatersrand (1970),Hon MSc Manchester (1980)

Professor of Orthopaedic Surgery, University of Manchester; Honorary Consultant Orthopaedic Surgeon, Salford Royal Hospitals NHS Trust, Manchester Children's Hospitals NHS Trust. *b.* 29 June 1939; Johannesburg, South Africa. *m.* 1967 Carol Freyda Lapinsky; one *s.* one *d.* *Public Offices:* Executive Committee, International Orthopaedic Research Society (1981-), President (1990-93); Treasurer, International Assoc of Olympic Medical Officers (1988-); Chairman, Association of Professors of Orthopaedic Surgery (1983-86); Joint Committee for Higher Surgical Training (1989-93,1993-); RCS England:- Member of Council (1991-), Chairman of Training Board (1995-), Panel of External Assessors for Consultant Appointments, Representative on Complaints Procedure (1988-); British Olympic Association Medical Sub-Committee (1988-); NW Health Authority, Chairman, Orthopaedic Speciality Training Group (1977-) Orthopaedic Advisory Sub-Committee (1976-); Chairman, Physiotherapy Training Cmtee, Salford College of Technology (1979-90); Medical Appeals Tribunal (1978-); Vaccine Damage Tribunal (1980-); GM Centre for Disabled Living Aids Council (1983-85); . *Education:* King Edward VII School, Johannesburg; University of Witwatersrand, Johannesburg. *Career Profile:* Johannesburg General Hospital (1963-66); University of Witwatersrand (1964, 1965-66); Hammersmith Hospital and Royal Postgraduate Medical School (1966-69); Director of Orthopaedic Surgery (1973-76); Nuffield Orthopaedic Centre, Oxford (1969-73). *Publications:* 200 articles in the medical press and the following books: (with Weber, D A) (eds) 'Radionucleide Scintigraphy in Orthopaedics' (Churchill Livingstone, 1984); (ed) 'Principles of Fracture Management' (Churchill Livingstone, 1984); 'Skeletal Metastases' (Butterworths, 1986); (ed) 'Neuromuscular Problems in Orthopaedics' (Blackwell, 1987); (with Noble, J) (eds) 'Recent Developments in Orthopaedic Surgery' (MUP, 1987); (with Noble, J) 'Current Trends in Orthopaedic Surgery' (MUP, 1988); (with Isherwood, I) (eds) 'Imaging Techniques in Orthopaedics' (Springer Verlag, 1989). *Prizes:* Moyniham Prize of the Association of Surgeons of GB & Ireland (1969); Hunterian Professor, RCS England (1971); AO Interntional Award, Society International de Chirurgie Orthopedique (1981); Australian Commonwealth Fellowship (1981-82); Annandale Lecturer RCS Edin (1979), Stanford Cade Memorial Lecturer, RCS Eng (1993) and other Lectureships in USA, Switzerland, Israel, India, Singapore, Japan and elsewhere. *Societies:* Fellow, British Orthopaedic Research Society; Founder Member, International Orthopaedic Research Society; Founder Member, Metastasis Research Association; Founder Member, British Association of Surgical Oncology; Fellow, Royal Society of Medicine; Past-President, Manchester and Salford Medical Engineering Club; Fellow, Manchester Medical Society; membership of many other UK and Overseas Medical Societies. *Recreations, Interests:* Sport - Member of British Olympic Association Medical Sub-Committee; Vice-President (1996-), Chairman (1989-96); British Amateur Wrestling Association, music, theatre. *Address:* Department of Orthopaedic Surgery, Clinical Sciences Building, Hope Hospital, Eccles Old Road, Salford M6 8HD (0161-787 4291).

GARNER, Alan

Writer. *b.* 17 October 1934; Congleton. *m.* 1956 Anne Cook; one *s.* two *d.* *(marr. diss. 1971)*; *m.* 1972 Griselda Greaves; one *s.* one *d.* *Education:* Alderley Edge Council School; Manchester Grammar School; Magdalen College, Oxford. *Military Service:* National Service, Royal Artillery. *Publications:* 'The Weirdstone of Brisingamen'; 'The Moon of Gomrath'; 'Elidor'; 'The Owl Service'; 'Red Shift'; 'The Stone Book'; 'Granny Reardun'; 'The Aimer Gate'; 'Tom Fobble's Day'; 'The Hamish Hamilton Book of Goblins'; 'The Guiser'; 'Once Upon a Time'; 'Strandloper'; 'Fairy Tales of Gold'; 'The Lad of the Gad'; 'The Breadhorse'; 'A Book of British Fairy Tales'; Films - 'Places and Things'; 'Images'; Libretti - 'The Belly Bag'; 'Potter Thompson'; Dance Drama - 'The Green Mist'; Television Plays - 'To Kill a King'; 'The Keeper'; 'Lamaload'. *Prizes:* The Guardian Award (1958); Library Association Carnegie Medal (1957); Gold Plaque, Chicago International Film Festival (1981); The Phoenix Award of America (1996). *Societies:* The Portico Library. *Recreations, Interests:* Work. *Address:* Blackden, Holmes Chapel, Crewe CW4 8BY.

GARSTON, Clive Richard, LLB (Hons) Leeds (1965)

Partner, Halliwell Landau Solicitors, Manchester; Non-Executive Director, The Intercare Group plc. *b.* 25 April 1945; Blackpool. *m.* 1973 Racheline Raymonde Sultan; one *s.* one *d.* *Education:* Manchester Grammar School (1955-62); University of Leeds (1962-65); College of Law (1965-66). *Career Profile:* Partner, Hall Brydon & Co, Solicitors (1971-78). *Societies:* The Royal Automobile Club; Mere Golf & Country Club. *Recreations, Interests:* Skiing and sport in general. *Address:* Halliwell Landau, St James's Court, Brown Street, Manchester M2 2JF (0161-835 3003); Sandy Ridge, Bollinway, Hale, Cheshire WA15 0NZ (0161-904 9822).

GARTSIDE, Edmund Travis ,TD(1968),DL(1990); MA(Cantab)

Chairman & Managing Director, Shiloh plc. *b.* 11 November 1933 Rochdale. *m.* 1959 Margaret Claire Nicholls; one *s.* one *d.* *(marr. diss. 1982)*; *m.* 1983 Valerie Cox (neé Vowels); one *steps.* two *stepd.* *Public Offices:* High Sheriff of Greater Manchester (1995-96); Deputy Lieutenant Greater Manchester (1990-); General Commissioner of Taxes, Rochdale Division (1966-); Governor, Manchester Grammar School (1984-); President/Representative on various National, European and International Textile Associations. *Education:* Winchester College (1947-52); Trinity College, Cambridge (1954-57). *Military Service:* National Service (1952-54) Royal Engineers; Lancashire Fusiliers; Territorial Army Service (1954-68) - 5th Bn XX The Lancashire Fusiliers (Major). *Career Profile:* Joined Shiloh plc (formerly Shiloh Spinners Ltd) (1957); Management Trainee, various Management Positions; Director (1960); Deputy Chairman (1963); Managing Director (1965); Chairman & Managing Director (1966); Chairman of six operating subsidiaries of Shiloh plc. *Societies:* Army & Navy Club, London; Hon Member, St James's Club, Manchester. *Recreations, Interests:* Travel, skiing, tennis, reading. *Address:* Shiloh plc, Holden Fold, Royton, Oldham, OL2 5ET *(tel:* 0161 624 8161; *fax:* 0161 627 3840).

GATENBY, John Keirl, MA, LLM (Cantab), FCIArb,MCIM, Solicitor, Barrister & Solicitor (New Zealand)

94

Partner, Addleshaw Sons & Latham; elder, Poynton Baptist Church; non-executive Director, Centre for Dispute Resolution (CEDR). *b.* 26 April 1950; Darlington, Co Durham. *m.* 1975 Thelma Eunice Holmes; two *d. Education:* Hartlepool Grammar School; Trinity Hall, Cambridge. *Previous Positions:* Head of Litigation Department, Withers (1983-84); Articled Clerk (1973-75) Solicitor (1975-82) Linklaters & Paines. *Publications:* 'Recovery of Money' (Longman, 8th edn 1993); 'Notes on Discovery and Inspection of Documents' (2nd edn). *Societies:* Hallé Concerts Society; National Trust; RSPB; Manchester Law Society; London Solicitors' Litigation Association; Solicitors European Group; International Bar Association. *Recreations, Interests:* Music (play piano, organ and clarinet), gardening, photography, computers and walking the dog. *Address:* Addleshaw Sons & Latham, Dennis House, Marsden Street, Manchester M2 1JD (tel: 0161-832 5994).

GAVAN, John Vincent, BA (Oxon),Solicitor of the Supreme Court

Solicitor, Managing Partner, Laytons, Manchester. *b.* 2 December 1955 England. *m.* 1979 Pauline; two *d. Education:* St Michael's College, Leeds; St Peter's College, Oxford. *Career Profile:* Qualified as solicitor (1980); partner, Laytons, London (1986); Managing Partner, Laytons, Manchester (1990); Member, Laytons Finance Committee, Remuneration Committee. *Prizes:* Open Scholarship in Law, St Peter's College, Oxford. *Societies:* St James's Club, Manchester; The Law Society. *Recreations, Interests:* Music, fell walking, fine wine, literature, theatre. *Address:* Laytons, 22 St John Street, Manchester, M3 4EB (*tel:* 0161 834 2100; *fax:* 0161 834 6862; *e-mail:* laytons@laytonsm.demon.co.uk).

GEAKE, His Honour Judge Jonathan Richard Barr, BA(Cantab,1968),Called to Bar (1969)

Crown Court Judge. *b.* 27 May 1946 Woking, Surrey. *m.* 1978 Sally; three *s. Education:* Sherborne School, Dorset; Fitzwilliam College, Cambridge. *Career Profile:* Practised at the Bar in Manchester (1970-94); Circuit Judge. *Recreations, Interests:* Sport and family. *Address:* Manchester Crown Court, Minshull Street, Manchester, M1 3FF.

GEE, Edward Charles, LLB (Univ. of Manchester, 1953)

Consultant, Lace Mawer, Solicitors; Member, Criminal Injuries Compensation Board; Part Time Chairman, Medical Appeals Board. *b.* 4 April 1931 Manchester. *m.* 1955 June; one *s.* one *d. Education:* Manchester Grammar School; Manchester University. *Career Profile:* Articled (1950-55), Assistant Solicitor (1955-57), A W Mawer & Co; Assistant & Acting Sectretary, Lancashire Steel Corporation (1957-61); Partner, A W Mawer & Co (1961-88); Partner, Lace Mawer & Co (1988-81). *Societies:* Manchester Law Society (Hon Member); Manchester Medical Legal Association; Wilmslow Golf Club. *Recreations, Interests:* Philately, golf, all types of sport, reading, gardening. *Address:* Lace Mawer, 42 King Street West, Manchester(*tel:* 0161 236 2002); 6 Lindisfarne Close, Sale, Cheshire (*tel:* 0161 962 1431).

GEE, Professor Kenneth Philip, BSc,PhD,DLitt

Head of Department, Department of Business Studies, University of Salford. *b.* 27 December 1946 Manchester. *m.* 1971 Hilary, one *d. Education:* Cheadle Hulme School (1955-65); University of Bristol (1965-68); UMIST (1968-71). *Career Profile:* Lecturer,

Department Management Sciences, UMIST (1972-74); Senior Lecturer, Department Accounting & Finance, University of Lancaster (1974-79); Professor of Accountancy, University of Salford (1979-). *Publications/Creative Work:* 'Management Control and Information' (Macmillan Press, 1973)(with R Beresford Dew); 'Management Planning and Control in Inflation' (Macmillan Press, 1977); 'Advanced Management Accounting Problems' (Macmillan Press, 1986). *Address:* Department of Business Studies, University of Salford, Salford, M5 4WT (*tel:* 0161 745 5581; *fax:* 0161 745 5556; *e-mail:* k.p.gee @business.salford.ac.uk); 50 Broad Road, Sale, M33 2BN (*tel:* 0161 973 4034).

GELDART, William

Freelance Illustrator/Artist; Gallery Owner. *b.* 21 March 1936; Marple, Cheshire. *m.* 1958 Anne Mary; one *s.* one *d. Education:* All Saints Church School, Marple, Cheshire; Hyde Grammar School; Regional College of Art, Manchester. *Military Service:* National Service as Cine Photographer with 14 Squadron RAF (Fighters) Germany (1953-55). *Career Profile:* Art Editor to the Whitethorn Press (the then Publishers of 'Cheshire Life', 'Lancashire Life' and their sister county publications). *Creative Works:* Many drawings and paintings of architectural subjects, animals, landscapes, trees, etc as well as such subjects as studies of the Hallé Orchestra, People at Functions, Festivals, etc. *Publications:* 'Geldart's Cheshire' (A Limited Edition of 1000 copies each signed and numbered); Books illustrated for Hodder & Stoughton, Dents, Viking Kestrel, Michael Joseph, Editions Gallimord, Michael O'Mara, Sphere, Puffin, Julia MacRae, Lion Publishing, Andre Deutsch. *Prizes:* Exhibited at the Royal Academy. *Recreations, Interests:* Music, walking, reading and drawing, listening to the radio, going to the theatre, some lecturing. *Address:* Geldart Gallery, Chelford Road, Henbury, Nr Macclesfield, Cheshire SK11 9PG (tel: 01625-425392); Spinks Farm, Chelford Road, Henbury, Nr Macclesfield, Cheshire SK11 9PG.

GEORGE, His Honour Judge William, LLB,LLM,Called to the Bar (1968)

Circuit Judge, Northern Circuit. *b.* 28 September 1944 Cromford. *m.* 1973 Susan Isabel Pennington; two *d. Public Offices:* Assistant Recorder (1990-93); Recorder of the Crown Court (1993-95). *Education:* Herbert Strutt Grammar School, Belper (1956-63); University of Manchester (1963-67). *Career Profile:* Practice at the Chancery Bar (1969-95); Head of Chambers in Liverpool (1985-95); Tutor (part-time), University of Manchester (1968-72); Standing Counsel to the Treasury in Charity Matters, Liverpool (1984-95); Chairman, Northern Circuit Chancery Bar Association (1992-94). *Prizes:* Mansfield Scholar (Lincoln's Inn,1968); Dauntsey Senior Legal Scholarship (University of Manchester, 1966). *Societies:* Athenaeum, Liverpool; The Kite Society; Institute of Conveyancers. *Recreations, Interests:* Arts (contemporary English artists), military history (the American Civil War), English history, kite flying, gardening. *Address:* c/o Northern Circuit Office, 15 Quay Street, Manchester.

GEORGHIOU, Professor Luke Gregory, BSc(Hon),PhD

Professor, Science & Technology Policy & Management; Director of PREST, University of Manchester. *b.* 13 July 1955 Beirut. *m.* 1977 Roberta Powell; two *d. (marr. diss. 1992);* *m.* 1993 Katharine Barker. *Education:* King Richards Army Childrens School, Dhekalia;

Selhurst Grammar School, Croydon; University of Manchester. *Career Profile:* University of Manchester: Research Associate (1976-84); Senior Fellow (1984-90); Executive Director, PREST (1990-95); Chairman, PREST (1995-). *Publications/Creative Work:* 'Post-Innovation Performance - Technological Development & Competition' (MacMillan, 1986); 'Evaluation of the Alvey Programme' (HMSO, London, 1991); 'United Kingdom Technology Foresight Programme Delphi Survey' (PREST/OST, 1996); over 100 other academic and popular publications. *Societies:* Council Member, Manchester Statistical Society. *Recreations, Interests:* English and Japanese gardens, theatre. *Address:* PREST, University of Manchester, Oxford Road, Manchester, M13 9PL *(tel:* 0161 275 5921; *fax:* 0161 273 1123; *e-mail:* L.Georghiou @man.ac.uk). *Additional Information:* Chairman, EU Innovation Policy Network (1993-) Chairman, Human Capital and Mobility Network on S&T Policy Evaluation (1993-96).

GIBBS, Colonel Donald Edwin, TD (1960),JP (1969),CBE (1970),ADC (1973),DL (1974)

Chief Executive, Broughton House Home for Disabled Ex-Servicemen. *b.* 13 March 1926; Manchester. *m.* 1950 Heather (decd 1993); one *s.* one *d. Education:* Queen Elizabeth Grammar School, Middleton. *War Service:* RAC & Indian Army (1943-47). *Military Service:* TA (1947-76); Hon Col 156 Regiment RCT (V) (1975-89). *Career Profile:* High Sheriff, Greater Manchester (1981-82); Executive Member, Manchester Regiment Trustees; Chairman, Juvenile Bench (1977-83); Chairman, Army Benevolent Fund, Gtr Manchester Committee (1969-88); Chairman, Broughton House (1976-77); Sales Executive, National Food Company (1953-77). *Publications:* 'Collects of the Services'. *Societies:* President, BLESMA Salford Branch; Army & Navy Club, London; Manchester Luncheon Club; Joint University Defence Dining Club. *Recreations, Interests:* Ex-Service Organisation, football, cricket. *Address:* Broughton House, Park Lane, Salford M7 4JD (tel: 0161-740 2737); 228 Manchester New Road, Alkrington, Middleton, Manchester M24 4BX (tel: 0161-643 2794).

GIL DE CARRASCO, Antonio Caballero Isabel La Catolica Oficial del Merito Civil (Spain,1991) BA,MA

Director of the Instituto Cervantes, Manchester and Leeds. *b.* 16 August 1954 Granada, Spain. *m.* 1977 Maria Angeles Ibanez Sanchez; one *d. Education:* Languages: Spanish, English, French, Italian, Arabic (limited knowledge). *Military Service:* Voluntary military service in Spain at age of 16. *Career Profile:* Primary and Secondary Teacher in Spain (1977-87); Director (1987-92); Coordinator, Leeds, Liverpool and Manchester (1992-93); Director, Leeds and Manchester (1993-96), Instituto Cervantes. *Publications/Creative Work:* Several publications about literary translation English-Spanish. *Societies:* Member of All, Ahila, Consular Association. *Recreations, Interests:* Sport, computers. *Address:* Instituto Cervantes, Brook House, 70 Spring Gardens, Manchester, M2 2BQ *(tel:* 0161 237 3376; *fax:* 0161 228 7467).

GILBERT, Anthony John, FRNCM(1981) MA,DMus(Leeds)

Director of Composition Studies, Royal Northern College of Music. *b.* 26 July 1934 London. *Career Profile:* Composer. *Publications/Creative Work:* 2 symphonies, 2 operas, 3 string quartets, 2 piano sonatas, 5 song-cycles; numerous works for chamber ensemble;

instrumental duo etc; also for chamber orchestra. *Recreations, Interests:* Reading, walking, cross-country running, wildlife photography, visual arts. *Address:* Royal Northern College of Music, 124 Oxford Road, Manchester, M13 9RD *(tel:* 0161 273 6283; *fax:* 0161 273 7611).

GILLESPIE, Professor Iain Erskine, MB ChB Glasgow (1953),MD (Hons) Glasgow (1963),MSc Manchester (1974),FRCS Edinburgh (1959),FRCS England (1963),FRCS Glasgow (1970)

Professor Emeritus, University of Manchester. *b.* 4 September 1931; Glasgow. *m.* 1957 Mary Muriel McIntyre; one *s.* one *d. Public Offices:* President, Royal Scottish Country Dance Society, Manchester Branch; Founder Chairman, Stockport Grammar School Parents Association; Governor, Stockport Grammar School. *Education:* Hillhead High School, Glasgow; University of Glasgow. *Military Service:* Royal Army Medical Corps (National Service) (1954-56). *Career Profile:* Professor of Surgery, University of Manchester; Honorary Consultant Surgeon, Manchester Royal Infirmary (1970-92); Presenter of Honorary Graduands, University of Manchester (1980-92); Series of progressive appointments, Universities of Glasgow, Sheffield, Glasgow again (1953-70); USPHS Post-Doctoral Research Fellow, Los Angeles (1961); Dean Medical School, Manchester University (1983-86); Member, University Grants Committee, Medical Sub-Committee (1975-86); Member University & Polytechnic Grants Committee, Hong Kong (1984-89). *Publications:* Joint Editor and Author of several books, chapters and articles, mainly on Gastroenterological topics in UK, Europe and USA. *Societies:* Surgical Research Society of GB & Ireland; Association of Surgeons of GB & Ireland; British Society of Gastroenterology; Manchester Medical Society (President 1993-94); Association of Professors of Surgery; 1942 Club of Clinical Professors; Hon Member of Gastroenterology Societies of Australia, Belgium, Argentina. *Recreations, Interests:* Golf - Bramhall Park Golf Club and New Club, St Andrews; music. *Address:*27 Athol Road, Bramhall, Cheshire SK7 1BR *(tel:* 0161-439 2811).

GILLILAND, His Honour Judge James Andrew David, QC(1984); LLB (Queens Univ. Belfast, 1960),Barrister-at-Law (Grays Inn, 1964)

Circuit Judge and Office Referee at Manchester. *b.* 29 December 1937 Belfast. *m.* 1961 Elsie; two *s. Education:* Campbell College (1951-56); Queens University, Belfast (1956-60). *Career Profile:* Lecturer, Manchester University (1960-72); Secretary to the Faculty of Law, Manchester University (1965-72); Barrister (1964); QC (1984); Circuit Judge (1992). *Prizes:* Arden, Atkin & Macaskie Scholar of Grays Inn. *Societies:* Athenaeum, Liverpool. *Recreations, Interests:* Skiing, music, stamp collecting. *Address:* Salford County Court, Prince William House, Peel Cross Road, Salford *(tel:* 0161 745 7511; *e-mail:* JGilliland@wx.compulink.co.uk).

GILLINGS, The Venerable Richard John, BA,DipBibStud

Archdeacon of Macclesfield & Vicar of Bramhall. *b.* 17 September 1945 Harrogate. *m.* 1972 Kathryn Mary; two *s.* one *d. Education:* Sale Grammar School; St Chad's College, University of Durham; Lincoln Theological College. *Career Profile:* Ordained Deacon (1970, Priest (1971), Chester Cathedral; Curate, St George's, Altrincham (1970-75); Priest

in charge then Rector, St Thomas, Stockport (1975-83); Priest in charge, St Peter's, Stockport (1978-83); Rector of Birkenhead (1983-93); Rural Dean of Birkenhead (1983-93); Honorary Canon, Chester Cathedral (1992-94); Member of the General Synod of the Church of England (1980-); Vicar of Bramhall (1993-); Archdeacon of Macclesfield (1994-pres.). *Societies:* Rotary Club (Hazel Grove). *Recreations, Interests:* Music, cinema, theatre, railways, football. *Address:* The Vicarage, 5 Robin's Lane, Bramhall, Stockport, SK7 2PE (*tel:* 0161 439 2254; *fax:* 0161 439 0878).

GLIDEWELL, Sir Iain, DL Knighted (1980),Privy Counsellor(1985); MA (Oxon),ARICS (hc)

Former Lord Justice of Appeal. *b.* 8 June 1924 Wigan, Lancs. *m.* 1950 Hilary Winant; one *s.* two *d.* *Education:* Bromsgrove School; Worcester College, Oxford. *War Service:* RAFVR (Pilot)(1942-46). *Career Profile:* QC (1969); Recorder of the Crown Court (1976-80); Judge of Appeal (Isle of Man)(1979-80); High Court Judge (1980-85); Lord Justice of Appeal (1985-95); Chairman, Judicial Studies Board (1989-92); Treasurer, Gray's Inn (1995). *Societies:* President (1967-68), the former Manchester (Reform) Club; The Garrick Club. *Recreations, Interests:* Fell & hill walking, theatre, travel. *Address:* c/o The Treasury Office, 8 South Square, Gray's Inn, London, WC1R 5EU. *Additional Information:* Practised at the Bar in Manchester (1949-70), London (1970-80).

GODDARD, Harold Keith, QC; MA,LLM

QC; Head of Chambers. *b.* 9 July 1936 Stockport. *m.* 1963 Susan Elizabeth; two *s.* *(marr. diss.)*; *m.* 1983 Maria Alicja; one *steps.* one *stepd.* *Public Offices:* Deputy High Court Judge; Recorder of the Crown Court; Member of the Criminal Injuries Compensation Board. *Education:* Manchester Grammar School; Corpus Christi College, Cambridge. *Career Profile:* Called to the Bar, Gray's Inn (1959); QC (1979); Member of the Northern Circuit. *Recreations, Interests:* Golf. *Address:* Keith Goddard QC, Deans Court Chambers, Cumberland House, Crown Square, Manchester, M3 3HA.

GODDARD, Paul Frederick, MVO (1990), Pro Ecclesia et Pontifice Cross (1982)

Clerk to the ,Greater Manchester Lieutenancy. *b.* 5 May 1942; Manchester. *m.* 1965 Frances Elizabeth Rocca; one *s.* one *d.* *Public Offices:* Member of Court, University of Manchester (1992-); Chairman of Governors, All Saints Primary School, Sale (1995-); Trustee, Manchester Guardian Society Charitable Trust (1994-). *Education:* Chetham's Hospital School, Manchester. *Career Profile:* Adminstrative posts, Greater Manchester Council, Manchester City Council, Salford City Council. *Societies:* Manchester Luncheon Club (President 1994-95). *Recreations, Interests:* Cycling, current affairs, cinema. *Address:* Greater Manchester Lieutenancy Office, Byrom House, Quay Street, Manchester M3 3JD (*tel:* 0161-834 0490); 7 Stretton Avenue, Sale M33 5EG (*tel:* 0161-973 2532).

GOLDBERG, Jack, Hon DLitt (Salford) (1981),DL (Greater Manchester) (1986); BA MA Oxford (1949),BCL (1950)

Chairman, Salford University Council; Pro-Chancellor, Salford University; Governor, Bolton IHE. *b.* 16 May 1924; Salford, Lancs. *m.* 1952 Maria Luise Wolff; three *d.*

Education: Manchester Grammar School; Magdalen College, Oxford. *War Service:* Hon Artillery Co (1943-46); Army Education Corps (1946-47). *Career Profile:* Formerly Senior Partner, Goldberg Blackburn & Howards (now Pannone & Partners); Salford City Labour Party; NW Regional Labour Party Executive; Council of European Municipalities; Labour Committee for Europe; NW Regional Economic Council; North West Arts Association; Manchester Royal Exchange Theatre; EAO Ltd (Partnership) Goldberg Ensemble Ltd; Manchester & Salford CSS; Greater Manchester CVS; Salford CVS; Salford FMSA; GM Community Trust; Action for Victims of Medical Accidents; Salford College of Technology. *Publications:* (with P Booth) 'The Role of National and Regional Bodies in Overseeing and Co-ordinating Cultural Decentralisation Policies' (1976). *Societies:* Fabian Society; Manchester Literary & Philosophical Society. *Recreations, Interests:* Walking, stamp collecting, music. *Address:* 1 Lullington Road, Salford M6 8GW (0161-736 1872). *Additional Information:* Personal Achievements: Twinning of Salford and Clermont-Ferrand, and the creation of Greater Manchester CVS.

GOLDSMITH, Professor Michael James Frederick, BA(Reading,1960),MA (Manchester, 1963)

Pro-Vice-Chancellor and Professor of Government and Politics, University of Salford. *b.* 20 June 1939 London. *m.* 1963 Anne Beatrice; one *s.* two *d. Education:* Trinity School, Croydon; Universities of Reading and Manchester. *Career Profile:* Lecturer, Senior Lecturer and Professor, University of Salford (1963-); Visiting Professor, Queen's University, Kingston, Ontario (1970-72); Research Coordinator, ESRC (1979-85). *Publications/Creative Work:* Author/Editor of several books including: 'Politics, Planning and the City' (Hutchinson,1980); 'New Directions in Central-Local Government Relations' (1986); co-author 'Urban Politics and Policy, A Comparative Analysis' (Blackwells, 1992). *Societies:* Political Studies Association UK (Currently President); American Political Science Assocation; International Political Science Association; Vice-Chair, European Constortium for Political Research; Chair, Retinet. *Recreations, Interests:* Jazz, cricket, walking, photography. *Address:* Maxwell 233, University of Salford, Salford, M5 4WT (*tel:* 0161 745 5282; *fax:* 0161 745 5545; *e-mail:* m.j.f.goldsmith@pch.salford.)

GOLDSTONE, Anthony Stewart, MBE (1984),DL (1990); BA (Com) Manchester, FCA, Honorary Fellowship UMIST (1984),FRSA

Chairman, Sterling McGregor Group. *b.* 6 October 1938; Salford. *m.* 1963 Marilyn Green; one *s.* three *d. Public Offices:* Chairman, North West Tourist Board, Northern Consortium of Tourist Boards, OFWAT North West; President & Director, Manchester Chamber of Commerce & Industry; Life Vice-President, Manchester Museum of Science & Industry (former Chairman); General Commissioner of Taxes; Vice-Chairman of North West Chambers, Board Member, of British Chamber of Commerce. *Education:* Manchester Grammar School; Manchester University. *Career Profile:* Part-time Director, North Western Electricity Board; Councillor, Manchester City Council (1970-74); Councillor, Greater Manchester Council (1973-86); Member, Design Council; Chairman, Greater Manchester Youth Association; Chairman, North West Region of Youth; Founder & Chairman of Prince's Trust Volunteers. *Recreations, Interests:* Watching Manchester City and playing golf. *Address:* Sterling McGregor Ltd, Ashton Road West, Failsworth,

Manchester M35 0FQ (*tel:* 0161-681 3161); "Savoia", 8 Gorsey Lane, Altrincham, Cheshire WA14 4BN.

GOLIGHTLY, William, BA Manchester (1957)

Former Headmaster, Hursthead Junior School, Cheadle Hulme (1967-96); Chairman Administrator, Hallé Choir; Member of the Board of the Halle Concerts Society. *b.* 2 June 1935; South Shields, Co Durham. *m.* 1962 Elizabeth Doidge; one *s.* one *d. Education:* Wellfield Grammar School, Wingate, Co Durham; University of Manchester. *Societies:* The Hallé Choir; Halle Concerts Society; National Trust; Heald Green Methodist Church; Sunderland Association Football Club; National Association of Head Teachers. *Recreations, Interests:* Singing, music, walking, motoring, sport, Sunderland AFC. *Address:* 92 Brown Lane, Heald Green, Cheadle, Cheshire SK8 3RA (*tel & fax:* 0161-437 5991).

GOODDIE, Howard Rowsley, MA Cambridge (1956),DipTP Manchester (1957);FRICS, Lord of the Manor of Bramhall

Proprietor, Longden & Cook Commercial, Chartered Surveyor and Auctioneer of Property; Director, Unilateral Property Co Ltd. *b.* 2 July 1932; Manchester. *m.* 1958 Sheila Mary; one *s.* one *d. (marr. diss. 1983); m.* 1988 Ruth Edwina Fingerhut. *Public Offices:* Board Member, Anchor Trust; NW Turning Point Development Board and Events Committee; Member of Court, University of Manchester. *Education:* William Hulme's School, Manchester; Cambridge and Manchester Universities. *Military Service:* National Service RAF. *Career Profile:* Founder Chairman, Manchester Heritage Trust Ltd; Public Relations Officer, Rotary District 1050 (1989-92); *Socieites:* Rotary Club of Manchester; Manchester Literary & Philosophical Society; Member of the Institute of Advanced Motorists. *Recreations, Interests:* Kite flying and ballooning, photography, classical music, tropical and reef fish keeping, good food and wine in convivial company, furniture restoration and tiling. *Address:* Longden and Cook Commercial, 43-45 Piccadilly, Manchester M1 2AP (*tel:* 0161-236 1114); Magnolia Cottage, Apsley Grove, Bowdon, Cheshire WA14 3AH.

GOODEY, Felicity Margaret Sue, BA(Hons)(Oxon),DLitt

BBC Presenter, Northwestminster, North West Tonight. *b.* 25 July 1949 Plymouth. *m.* 1973 John Marsh; two *s. Public Offices:* Chairman, The Lowry Centre Trust Ltd, The Landmark Millenium Project; Director, Manchester 2002 (Commonwealth Games) Ltd; Deputy Chairman, 'Excellence Northwest' to promote total quality management through the North West Quality Awards; Member, 'Going for Green'; Director, Sustainability North West'; Governor, The Manchester Grammar School; Chairman, Trafford Macmillan Day Care Centre Appeal; Hon. Vice President, Riding for the Disabled; Trustee, 'Friends of Rosie'. *Education:* Devonport High, Plymouth; Camborne Grammar School, Cornwall; St Austell Grammar School, Cornwall; St Hugh's College, Oxford University. *Career Profile:* Joined BBC (1971); first woman Industrial Correspondent in Broadcasting; National News; North of England; presented/reported many BBC TV and Radio news and current affairs programmes. Feelance (1980); independent production and communications company. *Prizes:* Blue Circle Award for Industrial Journalism. *Societies:* The Portico Library.

GOODMAN, Professor John Francis Bradshaw, CBE (1995); BSc(Econ),MSc,PhD, CIPD

Frank Thomas Professor of Industrial Relations (UMIST) and Head, Manchester School of Management (UMIST). *b.* 2 August 1940; Chesterfield. *m.* 1967 Elizabeth Mary Towns; one *s.* one *d. Public Offices:* Council Member, ACAS; Panel of Arbitrators, ACAS; Council Member, Economic & Social Science Research Council; Trustee, Withington Girls School; Deputy Chairman, Management Committee, Wood Street Mission; President, Manchester Industrial Relations Society. *Education:* Chesterfield Grammar School (1951-58); London School of Economics (1958-62). *Career Profile:* Personnel Officer, Ford Motor Co (1962-64); Lecturer, Industrial Economics, University of Nottingham (1964-69); Industrial Relations Adviser, Prices and Incomes Board (1969-70); Senior Lecturer, Industrial Relations, University of Manchester (1970-74); Vice Principal, UMIST (1979-81). *Publications:* 8 books and over 50 papers on a range of employment topics including collective bargaining, conflict resolution, labour markets, employment law and employee participation. *Prizes:* Lillian Knowles Prize (1960); Leverhulme Prize (1961). *Recreations, Interests:* Fell walking, squash, soccer. *Address:* Manchester School of Management, UMIST, PO Box 88, Manchester M60 1QD (*tel:* 0161-200 3418); Lundy Rise, Brookledge Lane, Adlington, Macclesfield, Cheshire SK10 4JX.

GOODSON, Paul Andrew, BA(Oxon)

Investment Director, 3i plc. *b.* 29 December 1963 Oxford. *m.* 1991 Lydia Mary; one *s. Education:* King Edward's School, Birmingham; Mansfield College, Oxford. *Career Profile:* IBM (UK) (1986-89); 3i (1989-). *Recreations, Interests:* Shooting, golf. *Address:* 3i plc, Carlton House, 18 Albert Square, Manchester, M2 5PE (*tel:* 0161 839 3131; *fax:* 0161 833 9182).

GOODWIN, Neil, MBA (1986),FIHSM

Chief Executive, Manchester Health Authority; Hon. Fellow, Health Services Management Unit, University of Manchester. *b.* 1 March 1951 Manchester. *m.* 1980 Sian Elizabeth Mary Holliday; two *s. (marr. diss. 1992) Education:* North Salford County Secondary School (1962-67); London Business School (1984-86). *Career Profile:* Chief Executive, St Mary's Hospital NHS Trust, London (1988-94); General Manager, Central Middlesex Hospital, London (1985-88); NHS Management posts, London, Manchester, Liverpool (1969-85). *Publications/Creative Work:* Articles in Health Services Management; 'Customer Care in Hospitals'; 'Management Needs of Chief Executives'; 'Role of New Health Authorities'. *Societies:* Royal Society of Arts; Richard III Society; Institute of Management. *Recreations, Interests:* Cycling, learning French, Coronation Street. *Address:* Manchester Health Authority, Gateway House, Piccadilly South, Manchester, M60 7LP(*tel:* 0161 237 2011; *fax:* 0161 237 2264). *Additional Information:* Member, King's Fund College Organisational Audit Council (1993-); Member, Investors in People Recognition Panel, Manchester TEC (1995-).

GOODWIN, Philip Walter, MA(Oxon)

Director, HSBC Private Equity Europe Ltd. *b.* 17 February 1961 Nottingham. *m.* 1984 Estelle; one *s.* two *d. Education:* Bemrose School, Derby; Keble College, Oxford. *Career*

Profile: Unilever plc (1982-83); 3i Group plc, Manchester (1983-95); HSBC, Manchester (1995-). *Recreations, Interests:* Cycling, travel, arts. *Address:* HSBC Private Equity, 56 Spring Gardens, Manchester, M60 2RX (*tel:* 0161 910 2229; *fax:* 0161 910 2238).

GORDON, Winston Victor, LLB(Hons)(Manchester, 1963),Solicitor (1967)

Justices' Chief Executive & Justices' Clerk, Tameside PSD. *b.* 23 June 1940 Manchester. *m.* 1963 Claire; two *d. Education:* Maritzburg College; Natal University (South Africa); Manchester University. *Career Profile:* Articles (1963) to Justices' Clerk, Ashton under Lyne; Prosecuting Solicitor, Manchester & Salford Police; Solicitor, Private Practice. *Publications/Creative Work:* Co-author 'The Sentence of the Courtel: A Handbook for Magistrates' (1995); Co-author 'Introduction to the Youth Court' (1996); Co-producer of National Training Packs (Magistrates). *Societies:* Justices' Clerks' Society; Tameside & Glossop Law Society; Leisure & Health Club and various sporting clubs. *Recreations, Interests:* Participating in competitive tennis and squash/gym/swimming, watching football/cricket, writing and arranging legal seminars for solicitors. *Address:* Tameside Magistrates' Court, Manchester Road, Ashton under Lyne, OL7 0BG(*tel:* 0161 330 2023; *fax:* 0161 343 1498).

GORODKIN, Leonard Malcolm, LLB Manchester (1953),Solicitor (1956)

HM Coroner for the GMC City District. *b.* 16 July 1933; Manchester. *m.* 1981 Anna Georgina; two *s.* one *d. Education:* Stand Grammar School, Whitefield (1943-50); Manchester University (1950-53). *Military Service:* National Service, Intelligence Corps, Linguist (1956-58). *Societies:* Coroners' Society of England & Wales (President 1988-89); N West & N Wales Coroners' Society (President 1986-88); Salford Rotary Club (President 1982-83); Cheshire Reform Congregation (President 1973-74); Dunham Forest Golf & Country Club; Manchester & District Medico-Legal Society. *Recreations, Interests:* Golf, bridge, photography, theatre. *Address:* Coroner's Court, London Road, Manchester M1 2PH (*tel:* 0161-236 4542)

GOUGH, Roger, LLB(Hons)(London)

Partner, Corporate Finance, Alsop Wilkinson. *b.* 5 October 1960 Manchester. *m.* Catherine; two *d. Education:* Kings College, London (1979-82); College of Law, Chester (1982-83). *Career Profile:* Jaques & Lewis, London (1983-88)(Solicitor, 1985); Addleshaw Sons & Latham, Manchester (1988-93); Alsop Wilkinson, Manchester (1993-) Partner (1995-). *Societies:* Law Society. *Recreations, Interests:* Squash, orienteering, travel, cinema and theatre. *Address:* Alsop Wilkinson, 11 St James's Square, Manchester, M2 6DR (*tel:* 0161 834 7760; *fax:* 0161 831 7515).

GOULD, John Roger Beresford, MA Oxon,FCA,CIMgt

Deputy Chairman, Seton Healthcare Group plc. *b.* 1 January 1940; Bolton, Lancs. *m.* 1968 Catherine Faulkner; one *s.* one *d. Public Offices:* Vice Chairman, Institute of Management; Vice-President Manchester Branch of IM; Council Member, Institute of Chartered Accountants; Governor, Manchester Metropolitan University; *Education:* Bolton School; Merton College, Oxford. *Career Profile:* North West Chairman, IM; Chairman,

Manchester Branch of IM; President, Manchester Society of Chartered Accountants. *Recreations, Interests:* Methodist Local Preacher,golf, theatre. *Address:* Seton Healthcare Group plc, Tubiton House, Oldham OL1 3HS (*tel*:0161-652 2222); 4 The Park, Grasscroft, Oldham OL4 4ES (*tel*: 01457-876422).

GOWENLOCK, Alan Hadfield, BSc(1944),MSc(1945),PhD(1947),MB,ChB(1953) Manchester, CChem,FRSC,FRCPath

Retired Consultant Chemical Pathologist. *b.* 4 March 1923; Oldham, Lancs. *m.* 1948 Mabel Joyce Naphtali; two *s.* one *d.* *(widowed 1982)*; *m.* 1983 Thelma Elizabeth Little. *Education:* Oldham High School; University of Manchester. *Career Profile:* Medical Research Council Clinical Research Fellow; Reader in Chemical Pathology, University of Manchester; Consultant Chemical Pathologist, Central Manchester Health Authority. *Publications:* Many scientific papers on biochemical aspects of medicine; 3 books, the most recent being 'Practical Clinical Biochemistry' 6th ed (1988, Heinemann). *Prizes:* Wellcome Prize, Association of Clinical Biochemists (1983); Emeritus Member (1987) Association of Clinical Biochemists. *Societies:* Member, Association of Clinical Biochemists; Manchester Medical Society - Fellow, Trustee and former President. *Recreations, Interests:* Gardening, photography and learning Greek. *Address:* 27 Park Lodge Close, Cheadle, Cheshire SK8 1HU (*tel*: 0161-491 0330).

GRAHAM-SMITH, Sir Francis, FRS (1970),Astronomer Royal (1982-90),Kt Bachelor (1986); PhD Cantab (1952)

Emeritus Professor, Manchester University. *b.* 25 April 1923; Roehampton, Surrey. *m.* 1945 Dorothy Elizabeth Palmer; three *s.* one *d.* *Public Offices:* 13th Astronomer Royal (1982-90), Royal Astronomical Society Secretary (1964-71), President (1975-77); Chair of Governors, Manchester Grammar School (1987-); Pro-Vice-Chancellor, University of Manchester (1988-90); Physical Secretary and Vice-President, The Royal Society (1988-94). *Education:* Epsom College; Rossall School; Downing College, Cambridge (Nat Sci Tripos 1941-43/1946-47). *War Service:* Telecommunications Research Establishment, Malvern (1943-46). *Career Profile:* Cavendish Laboratory (1946-64); Fellow, Downing College (1953-64); Professor of Radio Astronomy (1964-74)(1981-87), Langworthy Professor of Physics (1987-90) University of Manchester, Director, Jodrell Bank (1981-88), Director Royal Greenwich Observatory (1976-81). *Publications:* 'Radio Astronomy' (1960); (with J H Thomson) 'Optics' 2nd edition (1988); 'Pulsars' (1977); (with Sir A C B Lovell) 'Pathways to the Universe' (1988); (with A G Lyne) 'Pulsar Astronomy' (1989). *Prizes:* Royal Medal (Royal Society)(1987); Glazebrook Medal, Institute of Physics (1991); DSc Queens University Belfast (1986), Keele (1987), Birmingham (1989), Dublin (1990), Nottingham (1990), Manchester (1993) *Societies:* Athenaeum. *Recreations, Interests:* Building, walking, gardening, sailing, croquet. *Address:* Nuffield Radio Astronomy Laboratories, Jodrell Bank, Macclesfield, Cheshire (*tel*:01477-571321); Old School House, Henbury, Macclesfield, Cheshire SK11 9PH (*tel*: 01625 612657).

GRAINGER, Roy, MIOP,CEI (Tech),MIOB

Managing Director, Roy Grainger & Co Ltd, Heating Engineers; Chairman, NW Sanctuary

Housing Association. *b.* 8 September 1924; Ancoats, Manchester. *Education:* St Cuthbert's School, Withington; Manchester College of Building; College of Technology, Manchester. *War Service:* Fleet Air Arm (1942-46). *Career Profile:* Member of Governors, Salford Technical College; Chairman, Heating & Ventilation Contractors Association NW Region; Regional Manager, Haden Young Ltd, Building Services Engineers; Former County Councillor, Old Moat/Barlow Moor, Manchester Wards; Past Chairman, Mersey Valley Joint Committee; Past Chairman, Manchester "Impact" Committee; City Councillor, Barlow Moor (1971-74); City Councillor, Moss Side Ward (1975-79); Past President, Manchester Plumbing & Heating Contractors; Past Chairman, Manchester No 2 Lodge, Plumbers Union; Member, Joint Committee, Castlefield Conservation and Central Station Development Area. *Societies:* Manchester Press Club. *Recreations, Interests:* Cycling, politics (Labour Party), theatre. *Address:* 134 Barlow Moor Road, West Didsbury, Manchester M20 8PU (*tel:* 0161-445 4810).

GRAY, Professor John Oliver, MSc(Queens,Belfast),PhD, DSc(Univ. of Manchester)

Chairman, Department of Electronic & Electrical Engineering; Director, Telford Research Institute, University of Salford. *b.* 31 December 1937 Belfast. *m.* 1964 Margaret; two *s.* one *d. Education:* Queens University, Belfast (1959); University of Manchester (1961). *Career Profile:* Graduate Apprenticeship. Short Bros, Belfast; Senior Development Engineer (1964); Lecturer/Senior Lecturer, UMIST (1964-79); Professor of Control & Systems Engineering, University of Salford (1979-); Research Director, National Advanced Robotics Research Centre (1990-92); Director, Telford Research Institute, University of Salford (1994-96). *Publications/Creative Work:* Various research publications and edited books on control instrumentation and robotics. *Prizes:* Sir Harold Hartley Medal (1994), Institute of Measurement and Control; IEE Hartree Premium (1977). *Societies:* Institution of Electrical Engineers, Chairman, Computation & Control Board (1996-97); Editor, Transactions of the Institution of Measurement & Control; International Federation of Automatic Control (Chairman, International Technical Committee on Computer Aided Control System Design). *Address:* Department of Electrical & Electronic Engineering, University of Salford, Salford, M5 4WT (*tel:* 0161 7455952; *fax:* 0161 745 5975).

GREEN, Sir Kenneth, Kt (1988), CIMgt, Honorary Member of the Royal Northern College of Music (1987),FRSA (1987), Hon Member, Manchester Literary & Philosophical Society (1991) LLD(hc) Manchester; BA (Hons) Wales (1955),MA London (1967)

Vice Chancellor, The Manchester Metropolitan University (1992-); Director, Manchester Polytechnic (1981-92). *b.* 7 March 1934; Runcorn. *m.* 1961 Glenda Williams; one *d. Education:* Helsby Grammar School (1945-52); University of Wales at Bangor (1952-55); University of London (1966-67). *Public Offices:* Joint Chairman of Council, Rathbone Community Industry; Chairman of Governors, Victoria Road County Primary School, Runcorn. *Military Service:* National Service, South Wales Borderers (2nd Lieutenant), anti-terrorist operations in Malaya (1955-57). *Career Profile:* Short spell in industry; teacher; extensive experience in Colleges of Further and Higher Education; Dean, Faculty of Community Studies and Education, Manchester Polytechnic (1973-81). *Societies:* Manchester Literary & Philosophical Society. *Recreations, Interests:* Philosophy, political theory, Rugby football. *Address:* The Manchester Metropolitan University, All Saints,

Manchester M15 6BH (*tel*: 0161-228 6171); 40 Royden Avenue, Runcorn, Cheshire WA7 4SP (*tel*: 01928 575201).

GREEN, Lorna, BA(Hons)(Manchester Polytechnic, 1982),MPhil(Univ. of Leeds, 1991)

Sculptor/Lecturer. *b.* Manchester. *m.* David Rose FRCS Ed; two *d.* *Education:* Stand Grammar School for Girls; Stockport College of Technology; Manchester Polytechnic; University of Leeds. *Career Profile:* Sculptor in Public Art, Earthworks and Landscape Sculpture; visiting lecturer. *Publications/Creative Work:* Numerous solo exhibitions, group exhibitions and landscape projects in the UK and abroad. *Societies:* Royal Society of British Sculptors; Manchester Academy of Fine Art; Landscape and Art Network; International Sculpture Center, USA. *Address:* Mount Pleasant Farm, 105 Moss Lane, Bramhall, Cheshire, SK7 1EG (*tel:* 0161 439 7459). *Additional Information:* Has worked in a variety of materials in both urban and rural landscapes, indoors and outdoors, large and small scale, permanent and temporary. Sculpture is site specific relating totally to the site/project taking into consideration the architecture, the landscape, the history, the economy or mythology.

GREENE, John Patrick, OBE (1991), BSc (1969), PhD Leeds (1986), FMA, FSA

Director, Museum of Science & Industry, Manchester. *b.* 8 September 1946; Dorchester, Dorset. *Public Offices:* Chairman, Greater Manchester Visitor and Convention Bureau; Member of Board, Marketing Manchester; President, ICOM-CIMUSET (International Committee of Museums of Science & Industry). *Education:* King Edward VI Grammar School, Totnes, Devon; Leeds University. *Career Profile:* Directed excavation and created Norton Priory Museum, Runcorn (1971-82); Directed the development of the Museum of Science & Industry in Manchester from its inception. *Publications:* 'Norton Priory' (CUP, 1989); 'Medieval Monasteries' (Leicester University Press, 1992) (paper back 1994). *Prizes:* Mancunian of the Year; President's Award, Manchester Society of Architects. *Recreations, Interests:* Walking, cycling, theatre, music, travel, gardening and especially taking part in all of these with my wife Julia and children. *Address:* Museum of Science & Industry, Castlefield, Manchester M3 4FP (*tel:* 0161-832 2244, *fax:* 0161 833 2184, *e-mail:* greene@mussci.smart.co.uk).

GREENHALGH, Donald, CEng,MICE,MIHT

Chairman, Allen plc. *b.* 20 January 1933 Bolton. *m.* 1951 Doreen; two *s.* two *d.* *(separated) Education:* Bolton School (1944-50). *Military Service:* Two years in RAF. *Career Profile:* Worked in various local authorities in the North West (1950-64); Chief Engineer, Allen Brothers (1964-68); Managing Director, Allen Brothers (Lancashire) Ltd (now Allen plc)(1968-95); Executive Chairman, Allen plc (1981-). *Societies:* IoD; Bolton Golf Club. *Recreations, Interests:* Golf, snooker, walking. *Address:* Allen plc, Northern House, Chorley Road, Blackrod, Bolton, BL6 5JS (*tel:* 01204 699277; *fax:* 01204 698188).

GREENWOOD, Michael John, BSc,MSc,IPFA,MIMgt

Chief Executive, Tameside MBC. *b.* 8 September 1947 Fleetwood. *m.* 1973 Rita Clare; two *d.* *Education:* Fleetwood Grammar School; Leeds University; Bradford University

Management Centre. *Career Profile:* Cadbury Schweppes Foods; IBM UK Scientific Centre; Leeds City Council; Chief Executive & County Treasurer, Powys County Council. *Recreations, Interests:* Literature, cricket (passively), cooking, wine, gardening, countryside. *Address:* Council Offices, Wellington Road, Ashton-under-Lyne, OL6 6DL.

GREGORY, Victoria Jane (*née* Wilkins)

Chief Executive, Hallogen Ltd. *b.* 16 November 1945 Brighton. *m.* 1971 two *s.* *(marr. diss. 1984) Education:* Varndean Grammar School, Brighton (1957-64); Central School of Speech & Drama, London (1964-65). *Career Profile:* Journalism, IPC; Public Relations, J Walter Thompson; Marriage/child rearing; Manchester Theatres Ltd; Southport Arts Centre; Philharmonic Hall, Liverpool; Free Trade Hall, Manchester. *Recreations, Interests:* Staying alive - with passion. *Address:* Hallogen Ltd, Bridgewater Hall, Manchester, M2 3WS (*tel:* 0161 950 0001; *fax:* 0161 950 0000).

GREGSON, The Lord, Baron Gregson of Stockport, Life Peer (1975) for services to Government and Industry, Deputy Lieutenant Greater Manchester (1980); Hon Fellow Manchester Polytechnic, Hon DUniv Open University, Hon DSc Aston, Hon DTech Brunel, Hon FIProdE (1982), Hon FEng (1986), Hon FICE (1987), AMCT, CIMgt

Non-executive Director: Innvotech Corporate Ventures Ltd. *b.* 29 January 1924; Manchester. *Public Offices:* Member of Court, UMIST (1976-); Member of Court, University of Manchester; President, Finance and Industry Group, Labour Party (1978-); Member, Select Committee on Science and Technology, House of Lords (1980-); President, Defence Manufacturers Association (1984-); Member, House of Lords European Community Committee's Sub-Committee on Energy, Industry and Transport; Chairman, BNFL Expert Panel; Chairman, Advisory Council for RMCS Shrivenham; Chairman, Waste Management Industry Training and Advisory Board. *Education:* Birchfield Road School, Withington, Manchester; Stockport College of Technology; UMIST. *Career Profile:* Director of various Fairey Group Companies. *Recreations, Interests:* Mountaineering, skiing, sailing, gardening. *Address:* 12 Rosemont Road, Richmond, Surrey, TW10 6QL

GREGSON, Professor Edward, FRAM (1990) BMus(London),GRSM,LRAM

Principal, Royal Northern College of Music. *b.* 23 July 1945 Sunderland. *m.* 1967 Susan Carole Smith; two *s. Education:* Royal Academy of Music (1963-67); University of London (1975-77). *Career Profile:* Professional composer (1968-); conductor, broadcaster (radio & TV); Senior Lecturer (1976-89), Reader (1989-94), Professor of Music (1994-96), Goldsmiths College, London; Principal RNCM (1996-). *Publications/Creative Work:* Many commissions by orchestras and organisations since 1968; major works include: Music for Chamber Orchestra (1968); Tuba Concerto (1976); Connotations (1977); Metamorphoses (1979); Trumpet Concerto (1983); Piano Sonata (1983); Missa Brevis Pacem (1988); Of Men and Mountains (1991); Clarinet Concerto (1994). *Prizes:* Edward Hecht Prize (1965); Battison Haynes Prize (1965); Cuthbert Nunn Prize (1964); Frederick Corder Memorial Prize (1967); nominated for the Ivor Novello Award (1988). *Societies:* Royal Society of Arts. *Recreations, Interests:* Food, wine, watching sport, walking. *Address:* Royal

Northern College of Music, 124 Oxford Road, Manchester M13 9RD (*tel:* 0161 273 6283; *fax:* 0161 273 8188).

GRICE, Professor Roger, BA(Cantab, 1963),PhD(Harvard, 1967)

Professor of Physical Chemistry, University of Manchester. *b.* 27 July 1941 Ormskirk, Lancs. *m.* 1964 Patricia Margaret; three *d. Public Offices:* Member of Faraday Council, Royal Society of Chemistry. *Education:* Ormskirk Grammar School; Cambridge University; Harvard University. *Career Profile:* Frank Knox Fellow, Harvard University (1963-67); DFG Fellow, Bonn University (1967-68); Lecturer, Bristol University (1968-69); SAIR & ADR, Cambridge University (1969-76); Professor of Physical Chemistry, University of Manchester (1976-). *Publications/Creative Work:* Scientific papers on Chemical Reaction Dynamics in the learned journals. *Prizes:* Marlow Medal, Royal Society of Chemistry; Corday Morgan Medal, Royal Society of Chemistry; Tilden Lecturer, Royal Society of Chemistry; Kelvin Lecturer, British Association. *Societies:* The Royal Society of Chemistry. *Recreations, Interests:* Classical music, theatre, hill walking. *Address:* Department of Chemistry, University of Manchester, Oxford Road, Manchester, M13 9PL (*tel:* 0161 275 4667; *fax:* 0161 275 4598; *e-mail:* Roger.Grice @man.ac.uk).

GRIFFITH, Professor Thomas Gwynfor, MA Oxon. Dublin & Manchester,BLitt Oxon.

Emeritus Professor, University of Manchester. *b.* 29 March 1926; Cilffriw, Wales. *m.* 1953 Rhiannon Howell; three *d. (widowed 1980)*; *m.* 1984 Paola Seganti. *Public Offices:* Chairman, Society for Italian Studies of Great Britain and Ireland (1974-79); Chairman, Manchester Dante Society (1971-89); Hon President, Association of Teachers of Italian of GB (1988-89). *Education:* Neath County Grammar School for Boys; The Queen's College, Oxford. *War Service:* In mines, under Bevin Scheme (1944-45). *Career Profile:* Lecturer in Italian, Leeds University (1948-52); Head of Italian Department, Dublin University (1952-58); Fellow of Trinity College, Dublin (1955-58); University Lecturer in Italian, Oxford University (1958-66); Fellow of St Cross College, Oxford (1965-66); Professor of Italian, Hull University (1966-71); Professor of Italian Language and Literature, Manchester University (1971-88). *Publications:* 'Boccaccio: Detholion o'r Decameron' (Cardiff, 1951); 'Bandello's Fiction: an Examination of the Novelle' (Oxford, 1955); 'Avventure linguistiche del Cinquecento' (Florence, 1961); 'The Italian Language' (with Bruno Migliorini) (London & New York, 1966 - new edition 1984); 'Petrarch: Selected Poems' (ed with P R J Hainsworth) (Manchester 1971, repr 1979); 'Dau Ben y Daith' (Llandysul, 1995). *Recreations, Interests:* Sometime adjudicator, National Eisteddfod of Wales; Member, Gorsedd of Bards (1979-). *Address:* Department of Italian Studies, University of Manchester M13 9PL; Hendre, Davey Lane, Alderley Edge, Cheshire (*tel:* 01625-583705). *Additional Information:* One of the editors of 'Italian Studies' (1971-88).

GRIFFITHS, Captain Jacqui, CQSW,DipMS,AdvCounDip

Team Leader, Manchester City Team, The Salvation Army. *b.* 1 March 1946 Cheltenham. *Career Profile:* Minister of Religion; Senior positions in Local Government Social Services Departments; Head of Training, NSPCC (UK responsibility). *Recreations, Interests:* Reading, walking. *Address:* The Salvation Army, 71 Grosvenor Street, Chorlton-on-Medlock, Manchester, M13 9UB(*tel:* 0161 273 2081; *fax:* 0161 273 2081); 54 Arbory

Avenue, Moston, Manchester, M40 5HE (*tel:* 0161 688 0553). *Additional Information:* Considerable experience of working with children and young people in vulnerable situations; in working with the homeless and 'street people'; the objective is to improve the quality of life of everyone of all those with whom contact is made.

GUHATHAKURTA, Manoj Kumar, JP(1989); LRSC,MIMgt,MIQA

Industrial Chemist/Quality Assurance Consultant. *b.* 1 February 1936 Calcutta, India. *m.* 1966 Malaya; one *s.* one *d.* *Public Offices:* Magistrate, Manchester City Magistrates' Court; Director, New Start Charitable Trust; Governor, Stretford Grammar School; Member, Victims Support Central Management Council; Treasurer, Bengali Cultural Association of Lancashire; Council Member, Manchester Council for Community Relations. *Career Profile:* Analytical Services Manager, Rhone Poulnec Chemicals, Manchester (1961-92); Technical Consultant, Potter's Herbal Supplies, Wign; Quality Manager, A1 (Urmston) Ltd; Self Employed, Industrial Chemist/QA Consultant. *Prizes:* Scholarship, Indo-German Technical Co-operation Scheme (1958). *Societies:* Treasurer, Bengali Cultural Association of Lancashire; Life Member, RVM, Manchester; Indian Association, Manchester. *Recreations, Interests:* bridge, Indian cooking, victims support, interest in cultural activities of Bengali tradition. *Address:* 23 Hewlett Road, Chorlton-cum-Hardy, Manchester, M21 9WB (*tel:* 0161 861 8412). *Additional Information:* As Magistrate - Chairmanship Committee Member, Ex Vice-Chair, Probation Liaison Committee, Licensing Justices Committee Member.

GUILLEMAIN, Virginia, (*née* Sever), BA(Hons), DEA (Pantheon-Sorbonne, Paris), Certificat Science Politiques (Paris)

Honorary Consul, Czech Republic. *b.* 15 January 1952 Bratislava. *m.* 1975 Alain M J; two *s.* one *d.* *Societies:* Manchester Consular Association. *Address:* Honorary Consulate, Czech Republic, 26 Church Street, Altrincham, WA14 4DW(*tel:* 0161 928 9988; *fax:* 0161 926 8726).

H

HABBESHON, Paul, BA (Hons) (1972),MA Cantab (1976)

Head of Corporate Relations, BBC North. *b.* 18 June 1950; Hull. *m.* 1983 Jane; one *d.* *Education:* Hull Grammar School; Peterhouse, Cambridge. *Career Profile:* Film Officer, North West Arts; Funding and Development Officer, British Film Institute; Administrator, BAFTA North. *Address:* BBC North West, Oxford Road, Manchester M60 1SJ (*tel:* 0161-200 2020); 29 Bower Road, Hale, Altrincham, Cheshire WA15 9DR.

HADFIELD, Alan

Managing Director, Umbro UK Ltd. *b.* 9 November 1949 Ashton under Lyne. *m.* 1972 Jean Thomas; one *s.* one *d.* *Education:* Hyde Grammar School (1961-66). *Career Profile:* National Provincial Bank/Natwest Bank (1966-71); joined Umbro as Trainee Salesman (1971), progressed via PA, Salesman, Regional Manager, Sales Manager, Merchandising Manger, Sales Director to Managing Director. *Recreations, Interests:* All sport especially football, reading, travel, family. *Address:* Umbro UK Ltd, PO Box 33, Dallimore Road, Roundthorn Industrial Estate, Wythenshawe, Manchester M23 9GJ (*tel:* 0161 946 0966; *fax:* 0161 945 4121).

HADFIELD, John Peter Brookes, OBE(1994), JP (1969),DL (1986); CBIM,FRSA

b. 9 March 1926; Leeds. *m.* 1949 Iris Brailsford (decd 1995); two *d.* *Public Offices:* National Council Member, CBI (also NW Region), BIM (also Chairman, NW Region 1984 and President North Cheshire 1985); Trustee, The Hammond School, Chester; Patron, Henshaws Society for the Blind; Director, Greater Manchester Economic Development Council, MCCI; Chairman, Greater Manchester Residuary Body, Greater Manchester Property Trust. *Education:* Brighton Grammar School; RMA, Sandhurst. *War Service:* 2 RECCE Regt 25 Dragoons, RAC (1942-47) Served Far East. *Career Profile:* Joined Bass Ratcliffe and Gretton Ltd (1947) and Bass Mitchells and Butlers (Northern) Ltd (1966); Director, Mitchells and Butlers Ltd, Bass Marketing Ltd, Bass UK Ltd (1968) and Bass South West Ltd (1975); Chairman and MD, Bass North West Ltd (1976-86); Vice-Chairman, Bass North Ltd (ret 1986); Chairman (1976-86); Bass Mitchells and Butlers NW Ltd, Bents Brewery Co Ltd, Catterall and Swarbricks Brewery Ltd, Fred Anderton Ltd, Gartsides Brookside Brewery Ltd, Masseys Burnley Brewery Ltd, Park Hall Leisure; Chairman, Trafford Park Development Corporation; Director, Central Station Properties Ltd, Lloyds Bank plc (NW Region), Burtonwood Brewery plc, Petros Depts Ltd, Savoy Hotel (Blackpool) plc, Midland Hotel Crowne Plaza Manchester; Chairman, South Manchester University Hospitals NHS Trust. *Societies:* St James's, Manchester; The Athenaeum, Royal Lytham Golf; Prestbury Golf. *Recreations, Interests:* Golf, shooting, gardening.

HAGUE, Geoffrey Noel, CBE (1989),OBE (1980); FCIS (1954)

Retired *b.* 19 August 1920; Ashton-under-Lyne. *m.* 1942 Irene Phyllis; one *d.* *(widowed 1965)*; *m.* 1968 Maria Esther; one *s.* *Public Offices:* Member, Court of Governors and of various committees, University of Manchester. Trustee, Manchester Dental Education Trust. *Education:* Ashton-under-Lyne Grammar School; Manchester College of Commerce;

110

Salford Technical College. *War Service:* RAF (1939-45). *Career Profile:* Director, Robert Barclay & Co Ltd, Manchester & Argentina; Chairman/Managing Director, Welwyn [Garments] Ltd, Leigh; Member, Economic Development Cttee, Clothing Industry; Member, Clothing Industry Training Board; Chairman, North West Industrial Development Board (1982-90); Chairman, Wigan Health Authority (1986-94); President, Manchester Junior Chamber of Commerce (1954); President, Manchester Chamber of Commerce (1974-75); Chairman, Overall Manufacturers Association of Gt Britain (1980-81). *Recreations, Interests:* Golf, cricket, gardening. *Address:* 6 Edgehill Chase, Adlington Road, Wilmslow, Cheshire SK9 2DJ (*tel:* 01625-533631).

HALL, Daniel Charles Joseph, LLB(Hons)(Bristol),Solicitor of the Supreme Court

Partner, Eversheds. *b.* 29 August 1962 Ashton-under-Lyne. *m.* 1996 Melanie Jane. *Education:* Repton Preparatory School; Repton School; Bristol University; London College of Law. *Career Profile:* Articled Eversheds, Manchester (1985-87); Solicitor, Clifford Chance, London (1987-92); Partner, Eversheds, Manchester (1992-). *Prizes:* Sir John Port Prize (Repton). *Societies:* Prestbury Golf Club; The Law Society; Manchester Law Society; British American Business Group. *Recreations, Interests:* Golf, shooting. *Address:* Eversheds, 24 Mount Street, Manchester, M2 3DB (*tel:* 0161 832 6666; *fax:* 0161 832 5337); 3 Holly Cottages, Altrincham Road, Wilmslow, Cheshire, SK9 5NW (*tel:* 01625 526626) (*fax:* 01625 526626). *Additional Information:* Specialises in plc work, new and secondary issues and M&A.

HALL, Ian Murray, MSc,PhD,FIMA,FRAeS

Acting Head, Aerospace Division, Manchester School of Engineering, University of Manchester. *b.* 22 December 1931 Cannock, Staffs. *m.* 1960 Ann Heulwen; two *s.* two *d.* *Education:* Rugeley Grammar School; University of Manchester. *Career Profile:* Scientific Office, National Physical Laboratory (1955-57); Senior Scientific Officer (1958-59); Lecturer (1960-67), Senior Lecturer (1967-), University of Manchester. *Publications:* Numerous articles in various scientific journals. *Societies:* BATD. *Recreations, Interests:* Music, Scottish dancing. *Address:* Aerospace Division, Manchester School of Engineering, University of Manchester, Manchester, M13 9PL (*tel:* 0161 275 4328; *fax:* 0161 275 4261; *e-mail:* i.m.hall@man.ac.uk).

HALL, Nigel Richard, BSc(Econ),MEd

Dean of Faculty, Business, Management & Consumer Studies, University of Salford. *b.* 30 August 1945 Madras, India. *m.* 1968 Kathleen Hoye; three *s.* *Public Offices:* School Governor posts. *Education:* London School of Economics (1963-66); University of Manchester (1973-74). *Career Profile:* GKN, Birmingham; Lecturer, Preston/Lancashire Polytechnic; Head of Business & Industrial Centre, Lancashire Polytechnic; Head of Business & Management, Salford College of Technology. *Publications/Creative Work:* Cost Benefit Analysis in Industrial Training, Manchester Monographs (1975). *Societies:* British Institute of Management. *Recreations, Interests:* Walking, inland waterways, reading. *Address:* University of Salford, Allerton Building, Frederick Road, Salford, M6 6PU (*tel:* 0161 745 3282; *fax:* 0161 736 7538; *e-mail:* n.hall@ucsalf.ac.uk).

HAMBURGER, Sir Sidney Cyril, Kt (1981),CBE (1966),DL Greater Manchester (1981),JP (1957); MA Salford (1979),Hon Fellow Bar Ilan (1979),LLD Manchester (1983),Papal Honour Pro Ecclesia & Pontifice

National President, Trades Advisory Council (1984-); Life President, Manchester Jewish Homes for the Aged; Life President, Zionist Central Council; Vice-President, Anglo-Israel Friendship League; Chairman, North West ASH; Chairman, Age Concern, Salford. *b.* 14 July 1914; Salford. *m.* 1940 Gertrude Sterling; three *s. Public Offices:* Member, Manchester Regional Hospital Board (1965-74); Councillor and Alderman, Salford City Council (1946-71); Mayor, City of Salford (1967-68); Member, Supplementary Benefits Commission (1966-75); President, Peter Green Youth Centre; Member, Manchester University Court; Past President, Council of Manchester and Salford Jews; Chairman, NWRHA (1974-82); Vice President, King David High School (1991-); Joint Life President, JIA (1987); President, Citizens Advice Bureau for Greater Manchester (1990), Chairman (1985-90). *Education:* Salford Grammar School; Manchester Technical College. *War Service:* RAOC and RAPC (1940-46). *Publications:* Articles on Health Service, Zionism and Middle East. *Prizes:* Bnei Brith Award (1984). *Societies:* Royal Commonwealth Society, London. *Recreations, Interests:* Football, music. *Address:* C/o Searchlight Elec Ltd, Water Street, Manchester M3 4JU (*tel:* 0161-834 5452); 26 New Hall Road, Salford M7 4HQ.

HAMMOND, Donald W, BA Lancaster (1969),MBA Manchester Business School (1974)

Chairman, Halton General Hospital NHS Trust, William Hammond Ltd, Waterwise Technology Ltd. *b.* 5 March 1948; Cheshire. *m.* 1982 Carole. *Public Offices:* Councillor and Deputy Leader, London Borough of Ealing (1978-86); Gt Budworth Parish Council (1995-). *Education:* Kings School, Macclesfield; Lancaster University; Manchester Business School. *Career Profile:* Multicoast (NW) Ltd (1991-93); Henry Cooke Group plc, Edington plc (1986-90); Banco Hispano Americano Ltd (1976-86); Citibank (1974-76); Turner & Newall Ltd (1969-73). *Publications:* various. *Societies:* Treasurer, RNCM Association of Friends; Secretary, Commanderie de Bordeaux (Manchester); FInstD; Association of MBAs. *Recreations, Interests:* Riding, shooting, wine, business angel. *Address:* The Butts, Smithy Lane, Great Budworth, Cheshire CW9 6HL.

HAMMOND, His Honour Judge James Anthony, MA,Barrister

Circuit Judge. *b.* 25 July 1936 Manchester. *m.* 1993 Sheila Mary Stafford; three *d. Public Offices:* Counillor, Upholland UDC, Skelmersdale & Holland UDC; various School Governorships; Chairman, Ince CLP (1968-70, 1979-84), Society of Labour Lawyers North West (1971-86). *Education:* Wigan Grammar School; St Catherine's College, Oxford. *Military Service:* National Service (1959-61). *Career Profile:* Called to the Bar (1959); Barrister, Northern Circuit (Manchester)(1961-86); Deputy County Court/Circuit Judge (1971-80); Recorder (1980-86); Circuit Judge (1986-). *Societies:* Wigan Hockey Club (Vice-President); Orrell RUFC; Northern Circuit Rugby Club (Acting President). *Recreations, Interests:* Walking, theatre, gardening. *Address:* Courts of Justice, Crown Square, Manchester, M3 3PL (*tel:* 0161 954 1800; *fax:* 0161 832 5179).

HAMMOND, Robert Michael

Consultant to Hammond Raggett Jaworski & Partners Ltd; Director, Assured Asset Management plc (Macclesfield). *b.* 12 December 1932 Manchester. *m.* 1972 Sally Ann Gibson; two *steps*. *Public Offices:* JP (1963); Deputy Chairman, City of Manchester Bench (1996); Consul for Norway (1989); Lay Member, Institute of Chartered Accountants Disciplinary Committee (1995); Past Member, BBC NW Advisory Committee (1976-80), BBC Radio Manchester Ad Com (1977-79); Manchester & District Home for Lost Dogs, Manchester Housing (1926) Ltd. *Education:* Stockport Grammar School (1942-52). *Military Service:* National Service, Royal Air Force, RAFVR. *Career Profile:* Liberal Candidate, Manchester Blackley (1959, 1964), Macclesfield (1969, 1971). *Societies:* Past President, The Manchester Club (1977); St James's Club, Manchester; Country Gentleman's Association. *Recreations, Interests:* Reading, walking, theatre visits. *Address:* C/o Royal Norwegian Consulate, Lincoln House, 1 Brazennose Street, Manchester, M2 5BH *(tel:* 0161 832 8290; *fax:* 0161 834 2067); Merryman's Cottage, Merryman's Lane, Great Warford, Alderley Edge, SK9 7TP *(tel:* 01565 872002).

HAND, John Lester, LLB,Queen's Counsel

Head of Chambers, 9 St John Street Chambers. *b.* 16 June 1947 Huddersfield. *m.* 1972 Andrea McWatt; *(marr. diss. 1989)*; *m.* 1990 Lynda Ferrigno; one *d.* *Public Offices:* Recorder; Legal Assessor to General Medical and Dental Councils. *Education:* Huddersfield New College; University of Nottingham. *Career Profile:* Practised on Northern Circuit from 1972; QC(1988-). *Address:* 9 St John Street, Manchester, M3 4DN *(tel:* 0161 955 9000; *fax:* 0161 955 9001).

HANKINS, Professor Harold Charles Arthur CBE(1996),Hon Fellow (Manchester Polytechnic) (1984),DSc(hc)(Univ. of Manchester) (1995),DUniv(hc)(Open University) (1996),DEng(hc) (UMIST)(1996) BSc(Tech)(1955),PhD(1971),FIEE(1974),FEng(1993)

Former Principal & Vice Chancellor, UMIST (retired 1995). *b.* 18 October 1930 Crewe, Cheshire. *m.* 1955 Kathleen; three *s.* one *d.* *Public Offices:* Member of (at various times): Engineering Council; Board of Governors, Manchester Metropolitan University; Board of South Cheshire College; Board of INWARD; Board of Trafford Park Development Corporation; President of Cheadle Hulme School. *Education:* Crewe Grammar School (1943-46); Manchester College of Science & Technology (1948-52); UMIST (1952-55). *Career Profile:* Engineering Apprentice, British Rail; Assistant Chief Engineer, Metropolitan Vickers Elec. Co.; Professor of Communication Engineering, UMIST; Principal & Vice-Chancellor of UMIST; Non-Executive Director, Thorn EMI; Non-Executive Director, Bodycote International plc; Consultant to various engineering companies and educational organisations. *Publications/Creative Work:* 100 plus papers, patents, books on educational topics and on visual communication systems. *Prizes:* IEE Thorrowgood Scholar (1950, 1952); Reginald Mitchell Gold Medal (1989). *Societies:* Athenaeum Club, London; Hon Life Member, Manchester Literary & Philosophical Society. *Recreations, Interests:* History of the Great War, hill walking, music. *Address:* Rosebank, Kidd Road, Glossop, SK13 9PN *(tel:* 01457 853895).

HANNAH, Sophie, BA(Hons), MA

Writer-in-Residence, The Portico Library, Manchester. *b.* 28 June 1971 Manchester. *Public Offices:* Patron 1995 UK Year of Literature and Writing (reprsenting young writers). *Education:* Parrs Wood High School, Manchester; Xaverian College, Manchester; University of Manchester. *Career Profile:* Publicity Assistant, Manchester Theatres Ltd (1987-89); Admin Assistant (1994-), Writer-in-Residence (1996-), The Portico Library. *Publications/Creative Work:* Book: 'Carrot The Goldfish' (Hamish Hamilton, 1992); Poetry: 'Early Bird Blues' (Smith/Doorstop, 1993); 'Second Helping of Your Heart' (Frogmore Press, 1994); 'The Hero and the Girl Next Door' (Carcanet Press, 1995); 'Hotels Like Houses' (forthcoming)(Carcanet Press, 1996); Poems in magazines including The Spectator, The Times Literary Supplement and the Independent. *Prizes:* Eric Gregory Award (1995); North West Arts Writer's Award (1995); Arts Council Writer's Award (1996). *Recreations, Interests:* Cars and driving, crime fiction, pub quizzes, country music, cinema. *Address:* The Portico Library & Gallery, 57 Mosley Street, Manchester, M2 3HY (*tel:* 0161 236 6785); Rusholme, Manchester.

HANNAM, Stephen John, BSc(UMIST,1970)

Group Chief Executive, BTP plc. *b.* 26 April 1949 Skipton, Yorkshire. *m.* 1970 Jean; two *s. Education:* Pudsey Grammar School. *Address:* BTP plc, Hayes Road, Cadishead, Manchester, M44 5BX(*tel:* 0161 775 3945).

HARDIE, Reginald George, FCA,FCT

Chairman & Chief Executive, Harbury Group Ltd. *b.* 6 December 1938 Newcastle-upon-Tyne. *m.* 1968 Christine Mary; two *s.* one *d. Education:* Stockport Grammar School. *Career Profile:* Chartered Accountant, Walton Watts & Co (1964); Finance Director, Johnson & Firth Brown plc (1972); Group Managing Director (1989); led the MBO of 11 companies from Johnson & Firth Brown; formed Harbury Group Ltd (1994). *Recreations, Interests:* Music, sport - particularly golf and cricket, DIY. *Address:* Harbury Group Ltd, Oliver House, Priestley Road, Worsley, Manchester, M28 2LY (*tel:* 0161 794 9911; *fax:* 0161 794 8111).

HARDING, Neil Raymond

Local Director, Charlton Seal. *b.* 21 November 1955 Wakefield. *m.* 1976 Janet McLean Blair; one *s.* one *d. Education:* North Manchester Grammar School. *Career Profile:* Stockbroker: Cazenove & Co, London (-1978); Charlton Seal (1978-). *Societies:* Past Area Chairman of Round Tables in Manchester & South West Pennines. *Recreations, Interests:* Round Table, Manchester United, cricket, squash. *Address:* Charlton Seal, A Division of Wise Speke, 8 King Street, Manchester, M60 2EP (*tel:* 0161 953 9700; *fax:* 0161 832 9092); 105 Dean Lane, Hazel Grove, Stockport, SK7 6EJ (*tel:* 01625 871143).

HARKIN, Guy James, BA Oxford (1971),MA Oxford (1974),MSc London (1972),MBA Liverpool (1981),FBIM (1983)

Senior Lecturer in Public Sector Management, Lancashire Polytechnic; Deputy Leader, Bolton Council; Deputy Chairman, Greater Manchester Passenger Transport Authority. *b.*

114

17 February 1947; Bolton. *m.* 1979 Colette; one *s.* one *d. Education:* Thornleigh College, Bolton; Hertford College, Oxford; London School of Economics; Liverpool University. *Career Profile:* Research Officer, Nuffield College, Oxford (1972-74); WEA Tutor/Organiser, Manchester (1974-75); Research Fellow, Manchester Business School (1975-77). *Publications:* 'Government Control': Chapter in 'Control of Work', J Purcell & R Smith (McMillans 1983); plus sundry articles and papers. *Societies:* Rumworth Labour Club, Bolton; United Harriers. *Recreations, Interests:* Athletics, fishing during annual holiday. *Address:* GMPTE, Magnum House, Portland Street, Manchester *(tel:* 0161-228 6400); 2 Wade Bank, Westhoughton, Bolton *(tel:* 01942-811932).

HARNDEN, Professor David Gilbert, Hon MRCP (1987),FRSE (1982),FRCPath(1982), FIBiol (1969); BSc (Hons) (1954),PhD Edinburgh (1957)

Director, Paterson Institute for Cancer Research, Manchester; Professor of Experimental Oncology, University of Manchester. *b.* 22 June 1932; London. *m.* 1955 Thora Margaret Seatter; three *s. Public Offices:* Member, National Radiological Protection Board; Director, Christie Hospital NHS Trust; formerly Chairman, British Association for Cancer Research. *Education:* George Heriot's School, Edinburgh (1940-50); University of Edinburgh (1950-57). *Career Profile:* Lecturer, University of Edinburgh (1956-57); Scientific Member, Medical Research Council (1957-69); Research Fellow in Oncology, University of Wisconsin (1963-64); Professor of Cancer Studies, University of Birmingham and Hon Consulting Pathologist, Queen Elizabeth Hospital, Birmingham (1969-83). *Publications:* Many publications on Genetics and Cancer in learned journals; Chairman, Editorial Board, British Journal of Cancer. *Address:* Paterson Institute for Cancer Research, Christie Hospital NHS Trust, Manchester M20 9BX *(tel:* 0161-446 3101).

HARRIES, Andy, BA(Hons)(Hull)

Controller of Comedy & Entertainment, Granada Television. *b.* 7 April 1954 Inverness. *m.* 1992 Rebecca Frayn; two *s. Education:* Glebe House, Hunstanton (1963-67); Oakham School, Rutland (1967-71); Hull University (1972-75). *Career Profile:* Granada TV (1976-81) - presenter, researcher, writer; freelance Producer/Director (1981-91); Head of Comedy (1992), Controller of Entertainment & Comedy (1994-), Granada TV. *Recreations, Interests:* Skiing, tennis, swimming. *Address:* Granada TV, Upper Ground, London, SE1 9LT *(tel:* 0171 261 3908; *fax:* 0171 261 3093).

HARRIS, Professor Colin George Scott, BA Hull (1966),MA McMaster (1968),MLS Western Ontario (1970),BPhil Open (1984),PhD Hull (1989),FLA,FIInfSc

University Librarian, The Manchester Metropolitan University. *b.* 4 April 1944; Gravesend, Kent. *m.* 1974 Colleen Fairclough; two *s. Education:* Gravesend Grammar School for Boys; University of Hull; McMaster University; University of Western Ontario; Open University. *Career Profile:* Director of Academic Information Services & University Librarian, Salford University; Director, Centre for Research on User Studies, University of Sheffield. *Publications:* numerous on Librarianship. *Address:* All Saints Library, The Manchester Metropolitan University, Manchester M15 6BH *(tel:* 0161 247 6100; *fax:* 0161 247 6349; *e-mail:* c.harris@mmu.ac.uk); 36 Belfield Road, Didsbury, Manchester M20 6BH *(tel:* 0161-434 5257).

HARRIS, Jennifer, BA Manchester (1971),MA London (1973),PhD Manchester (1977), FRSA

Deputy Director & Curator (Textiles), Whitworth Art Gallery, University of Manchester. *b.* 22 September 1949; Preston, Lancs. *m.* 1977 Paul Howe; two *d. Education:* Queen Mary School, Lytham, Lancs. *Publications:* 'William Morris and the Middle Ages' (MUP, 1984) co-author; '1966 And All That! Design and the Consumer in Britain 1960-69' (Trefoil Books, 1986) co-author; '5000 Years of Textiles' (British Museum Press, 1993); 'Lucienne Day: A Career in Design' (Whitworth Art Gallery, 1993). *Recreations, Interests:* Travel, foreign languages, gardening, reading novels. *Address:* Whitworth Art Gallery, University of Manchester, Manchester M15 6ER (*tel:* 0161-275 7450; *fax:* 0161 275 7451; *e-mail:* jennifer.harris @man.ac.uk).

HARRIS, Professor Martin Best, CBE (1992); MA (Cantab),PhD (London)

Vice-Chancellor, University of Manchester. *b.* 28 June 1944 Ruabon, Wales. *m.* 1966 Barbara; two *s. Public Offices:* Member, University Grants Committee (1983-87); Chairman, National Curriculum Modern Languages Group (1990-92); Vice-chairman, Committee of Vice-Chancellors & Principals (1995-); Chairman, Clinical Standards Advisory Group (1996-); chairman of various groups dealing with higher education. *Education:* Devonport High School, Plymouth (1955-62); Queens' College, Cambridge (1962-65); University of London (1965-68). *Career Profile:* Lecturer, University of Leicester (1967-72); Senior Lecturer, Professor, Dean, Pro-Vice Chancellor, University of Salford (1972-87); Vice-Chancellor, University of Essex (1987-92); Vice-Chancellor, University of Manchester (1992-). *Publications/Creative Work:* Numerous articles and monographs on the Romance languages. *Prizes:* Honorary doctorates from the University of Salford, Essex and Belfast; Honorary Fellow, Queens' College Cambridge (1992), Bolton Institute (1995). *Recreations, Interests:* Gardening, walking. *Address:* Vice-Chancellor's Office, University of Manchester, Oxford Road, Manchester, M13 9PL (*tel:* 0161 275 2010; *fax:* 0161 272 6313; *e-mail*: admjf@ccg-acu.man.ac.uk).

HARRIS, Paul

Editor, Director, Jewish Telegraph. *b.* 2 June 1951; Salford. *m.* 1974 Lauren Lipshaw; two *s. Education:* Manchester Grammar School. *Career Profile:* Deputy Editor, Jewish Telegraph. *Publications:* 'Israel at 40: The Manchester Connection' (Archive Publications) (1988). *Recreations, Interests:* Photography, travel, theatre, wines, sport, dining out. *Address:* Telegraph House, 11 Park Hill, Bury Old Road, Prestwich, Manchester M25 0HH (*tel:* 0161-740 9321).

HARRIS, Peter, QPM(1996) LLB(Hons)(Manchester)

Chief Superintendent, Divisional Commander, A Division City Centre & North Manchester. *b.* 21 July 1943 Northwich. *m.* 1966 Christina Lynn; one *d. Education:* St John Deane's Grammar School, Northwich; University of Manchester. *Career Profile:* Police Cadet, Metropolitan Police (1962); Cheshire Constabulary (1962-74); Greater Manchester Police: Inspector (1974), Superintendent (1987), Chief Superintendent (1990-). *Prizes:* Several Chief Constable's Commendations. *Recreations, Interests:* Fell walking, conservation, collecting Doulton pottery. *Address:* Greater Manchester Police, Divisional

Police HQ, Bootle Street, Manchester, M2 5GU (*tel:* 0161 856 3005; *fax:* 0161 856 63039).

HARRIS, The Venerable Reginald Brian, MA Cantab

Archdeacon of Manchester; Residentiary Canon and Sub-Dean of Manchester Cathedral. *b.* 14 August 1934; Sidcup. *m.* 1959 Anne Patricia Hughes; one *s.* one *d. Education:* Eltham College, London; Christ's College, Cambridge; Ridley Hall, Cambridge. *Previous Positions:* Vicar, St Peter's, Bury (1964-70); Vicar of Walmsley (Bolton) (1970-80); Rural Dean of Walmsley (1970-80). *Recreations, Interests:* Walking, painting, music. *Address:* 4 Victoria Avenue, Eccles, Manchester M30 9HX (*tel:* 0161-707 6444).

HARRIS, Professor Rodney, CBE; BSc Liverpool (1954),MD Liverpool (1961),FRCP London (1964)

Professor of Medical Genetics, St Mary's Hospital, Manchester. *b.* 27 May 1932; Liverpool. *m.* 1959 Ruth Levy; one *s.* one *d. (widowed 1975); m.* 1976 Hilary Jean Melsher; one *stepd. Public Offices:* Director R&D, Central Manchester Health Care NHS Trust; Chairman, EU Concerted Action on Genetics Serivces in Europe; Chairman, Steering Committee of National Confidential Enquiry into Counselling for Genetic Disorder; President, Manchester Medical Society. *Education:* John Bright School, Llandudno; Quarry Bank School, Liverpool; Liverpool University. *Previous Positions:* Lecturer in Medicine, University of Liverpool. *Publications:* Many on Medical Genetics. *Societies:* Clinical Genetic Society; Charles O'Neil Club. *Recreations, Interests:* Travel, cycling, Modern European History. *Address:* Medical Genetics, St Mary's Hospital, Manchester (*tel:* 0161-276 6262).

HARRISON, Derek, FIPD (1968),FGCL (1981),FIMgt (1981),FIIM (1982),MIWM, Freedom of City of London (1979)

Inventor; Former Proprietor, Moorside Laundry. *b.* 5 January 1929; Oswaldtwistle. *m.* Joy; one *s.* one *d. Education:* St Stephen's, Astley (1936-39); Leigh Grammar School (1939-47); Regional College of Art, Department of Architecture (1947-52); Manchester University (1947-52). *Public Offices:* Deputy Master, College of Fellows, Guild of Cleaners & Launderers (1989-); Vice-Chairman (1994-96) and Chairman (1996), Manchester Branch of the Institute of Management; Chairman, Salford Branch of the British Diabetic Association (1995-). *Military Service:* National Service, Royal Engineers. *Career Profile:* Assistant Manager (1955-57), Manager (1957-71), Proprietor (1971-) Moorside Laundry; Senior Lecturer, Laundry Technology, Hollings College (1962); Member, Laundry Wages Council (1972-88); National Executive Council Association of British Laundry Cleaning and Rental Services Ltd (1984-87); Governor & Registrar; Bridgewater School, Worsley. *Prizes:* Drummond Cup (1947 and 1948). *Societies:* Life Member, Manchester University Motor Club (Vice-President 1969-70); Past President, Manchester Society of Architects Students Association (1953); Guild of Cleaners & Launderers (Hon Vice-President 1978, Deputy Master 1989). *Address:* 5 Woodlands Avenue, Swinton, Manchester M27 0DJ (*tel & fax:* 0161-794 1198). *Additional Information:* Liveryman of City of London and Worshipful Company of Launderers; Life Member, City Livery Club.

HARRISON, Jane Elinor (*née* Parry), DL(1994); BSc(Univ. of London)

b. Pwllheli, North Wales. *m*. George Anthony; two *s*. one *d*. *(widowed 1992) Public Offices:* Magistrate, Bolton; Member, Bolton Community Health Council; Chairman, Bolton Community Care Forum; Chairman, Mrs Lum Housing Association. *Education:* Pwllheli Grammar School; Howell's School, Denbigh; University of London. *Career Profile:* Social Worker, Wolverhampton MBC; Training Officer, Social Services Department, City of Salford; Student Supervisor, various voluntary agencies. *Societies:* Magistrates Association; Royal Horticultural Society; Bolton Ladies' Speakers Club. *Recreations, Interests:* Community work, gardening, photography, theatre, travel. *Address:* 20 Crompton Road, Lostock, Bolton, BL6 4LP.

HARRISON, Susan Rowledge (*née* Eaton), Cert Ed, MEd, Adv Dip for Dance in Education, Diploma in Professional Studies (Management)

Chief Executive, North West Arts Board. *b*. 2 September 1944 Walsall, England. *m*. 1967 William Harrison; one *s*. *Public Offices:* Governor, Bretton Hall College, West Bretton, Yorkshire; Trustee, Dance In Partnership; Chair, Regional Arts Board Directors Group; Examiner, Derby University (for Dance). *Education:* Queen Mary's High School, Walsall, West Midlands; I M Marsh College of Physical Education; Derby University; Keele University. *Career Profile:* In Education in England, Scotland, Canada (1966-84); Dance Officer (1985); Assistant Director (1989), Acting Director (1990), Yorkshire Arts; Deputy Director, Yorkshire & Humberside Arts (1991); Chief Executive, North West Arts Board (1995); Practising Choreographer. *Publications/Creative Work:* Dance in Education; Arts in Primary Health Care; Arts in Terminal Care; Arts for Health Care; African & Caribbean Dancing & Drumming; Research into Assessment in the Arts; Dance in Schools; South Asian Dance; Performance Indicators. *Societies:* Institute of Directors. *Recreations, Interests:* Sport, the Arts, contemporary literature. *Address:* North West Arts Board, Manchester House, 22 Bridge Street, Manchester (*tel:* 0161 834 6644; *fax:* 0161 834 6969).

HARTSHORNE, Susan Vipont (*née* Brown), JP LLB(Hons)(Univ. of Manchester,1958), Barrister (Gray's Inn,1988)

Appeal Tribunal Chairman (part-time), Social Security, Disability & Incapacity (1977-); Director, Manchester Crematorium (1982-). *b*. 20 December 1935 Manchester. *m*. 1957 John Norman; one *s*. two *d*. *(widowed 1992) Public Offices:* JP (Manchester City Bench, Family Panel Chair); Chair, St Mary's Hospital Infertility Unit, Ethical Committee; Council Member, Hulme Hall. *Education:* Withington Girls' School, Manchester; The Mount School, York; Manchester University; Manchester Polytechnic. *Career Profile:* Hon Sec., Manchester Students Day Nursery (1967-83); NHS: HMC, CHC, AHA (1971-82); Vice-Chairman, Manchester Central Health Authority (1982-85); Mosscare Housing Ltd (1971-85)(Chairman, 1978-85); IBA LRAC (1974-80)(Chairman, 1978-80); Magistrates Association: Local Executive (1976-91), National Council (1986-91); Committee Member, Motor Neurone Disease (1991-95). *Publications/Creative Work:* '100 years of Music Making in Manchester - The Beethoven Society 1888-1988'. *Societies:* The Beethoven Society Orchestra (Vice-President); Society of Quakers - Member of Manchester Meeting. *Recreations, Interests:* Singing (Manchester Philharmonic Choir), swimming, family.

Address: 22 Denison Road, Victoria Park, Manchester, M14 5SQ. *Additional Information:* British Representative on Friends World Committee for Consultation and other national and local Quaker committees.

HAWORTH, Donald Edwin

Freelance writer and film director. *b.* 18 January 1924; Bacup, Lancashire. *Education:* Burnley Grammar School. *War Service:* RAF. *Career Profile:* Journalist, News Chronicle, Manchester Guardian, Associated Press of America, Canadian Broadcasting Corporation, BBC Television News; Film director, Tonight; Producer, Panorama; Documentary film producer and director, based at BBC Manchester. *Creative Works:* Producer/director of more than 300 documentary films for BBC Television; Author of fifty plays, mostly for radio. *Publications:* 'We All Come to It in the End' (radio plays, 1972); 'Figures in a Bygone Landscape' (memoirs 1986); Contributor to 'Best Radio Plays' (1978) (1981) (1984); 'Bright Morning', (memoirs 1990). *Prizes:* For radio plays: Society of Authors' Award (1976); German Academy of Arts Award (1977); Giles Cooper Memorial Award (1979, 1982, 1985); Writers' Guild Award (1991); For films: John Grierson Memorial Award (1979); BAFTA Award for documentary (1980); For memoirs: Portico Literary Award (1986). *Address:* 43 Ogden Road, Bramhall, Stockport SK7 1HL (*tel:* 0161-439 4360).

HAYDOCK, James William, Called to the Bar (Inner Temple, 1984), Diploma in Magisterial Law, Manchester Polytechnic (1979)

Clerk to the Justices, Leigh and Wigan. *b.* 23 March 1955 Blackburn. *m.* 1982 Wendy. *Public Offices:* Clerk to the Wigan Magistrates Courts Committee; Secretary to the Wigan Advisory Committee. *Education:* St Andrews Primary School, Livesey, Blackburn; Billinge Grammar School, Blackburn; Blackburn Technical College; Manchester Polytechnic. *Career Profile:* Senior Court Clerk, Preston Magistrates Court; Deputy Clerk, Makerfield/Wigan Magistrates Court. *Prizes:* High Speed Trial Award, Cadwell Park (1987). *Societies:* Justices' Clerks Society; Pendle Ski Club; Ariel Owners Motor Cycle Club; East Lancashire Railway Preservation Society. *Recreations, Interests:* Motorcycling, inland waterways, steam railways, skiing, cycling, real ale. *Address:* Wigan Magistrates Court, Darlington Street, Wigan, WN1 1DW (*tel:* 01942 405405; *fax:* 01942 405444).

HAYES, Nicholas Francis

Chief Emergency Planning Officer. *b.* 27 January 1950 Salford. *m.* 1979 Meryl; one *s.* one *d. Education:* St Mary College, Blackburn; Middlesex Polytechnic. *Career Profile:* In industry prior to 1991. *Recreations, Interests:* Off-road driving, reading. *Address:* Emergency Planning Unit, Bury Fire Station, The Rock, Bury, BL9 5AH (*tel:* 0161 797 0700; *fax:* 0161 797 1235; *e-mail:* grman@epline.implex.co.uk); 1 Victoria Road, Chatburn, Clitheroe, Lancs, BB7 4AZ (*tel:* 01200 441178; *fax:* 01200 441178; *e-mail:* 100610.301.compuserve.com).

HAYES, Richard William, MA Cambridge,LLB Cambridge,Solicitor of the Supreme Court

Partner, Addleshaw Sons & Latham (corporate tax & employee share options) *b.* 31

October 1947; Walton-on-Thames. *m.* 1985 Laura Mary Yates. *Education:* Scholar of Winchester College; Open Scholarship to Trinity Hall, Cambridge. *Societies:* Manchester Lit & Phil; Talyllyn Railway Preservation Society; National Trust; Wildfowl & Wetlands Trust; Wexford Festival Opera Friends; Society of Share Option Practitioners; Treasurer, Manchester Incorporated Law Library; the Scotch Malt Whisky Society; Chairman, Manchester Midday Concerts Society. *Recreations, Interests:* Railways, opera, chamber music, sheep. *Address:* Addleshaw Sons & Latham, Dennis House, Marsden Street, Manchester M2 1JD (tel: 0161-832 5994).

HAYWARD, Jane Elizabeth, LLB(Wales),Barrister

Stipendiary Magistrate, Greater Manchester. *b.* 31 August 1946 Cardiff. *m.* 1967 one *s.* one *d.* *(marr. diss. 1981) Education:* Marlborough Grammar School; University College of Wales, Aberystwyth (1964-67). *Career Profile:* Called to the Bar, Gray's Inn (1968); Practice, Wales & Chester Circuit (1970-91); Stipendiary Magistrate (1991); Crown Court Recorder (1996). *Recreations, Interests:* Tennis, theatre, ballet, travel. *Address:* Manchester City Magistrates Court, Crown Square, Manchester, M60 1PR *(tel:* 0161 832 7272).

HAYWOOD, Christopher Warren, FCA,ATII

Senior Partner, Haywood & Co. *b.* 17 November 1945 Bolton. *m.* 1969 Lynda Anne; one *s.* one *d.* *(marr. diss. 1979); m.* 1980 Julie Anne; three *s.* *Public Offices:* Director & Treasurer, Bolton Lads & Girls Club (1973-); President, Bolton Chamber of Commerce & Industry (1989-90); President, Bolton Society of Chartered Accountants (1974-75); Chairman, The Bolton Club (1985-87); Joint Chairman, Bolton Economic Forum (1990-). *Education:* St Bees, Cumbria. *Career Profile:* Partner, Kevan Pilling & Co (1973-89), Spicer & Oppenheim (1989-90), Touche Ross & Co (1990-92), Haywood & Co (1992-). *Societies:* Bolton Golf Club; Markland Hill LTC; Windermere Motor Boat Racing Club; The Bolton Club. *Recreations, Interests:* Golf, family pursuits. *Address:* Elsinore House, 32 Albert Road, Bolton, BL1 5HF *(tel:* 01204 848817; *fax:* 01204 845958).

HEALEY, David Anthony, LLB(Hons),Solicitor and Notary Public

Senior Partner, Vaudreys. *b.* 14 March 1950 Littleborough, Lancs. *Public Offices:* Honorary Secretary, Manchester Law Society. *Education:* Oundle School; University of Manchester. *Career Profile:* Articled Clerk (1973-75), Solicitor (1975-79), Associate (1979-81) Addleshaw Sons & Latham; Partner (1981-), Managing Partner (1991-93), Senior Partner (1993-) Vaudreys. *Publications/Creative Work:* Various legal articles in legal journals. *Societies:* Lancashire County Cricket Club; St James's Club, Manchester. *Recreations, Interests:* Cricket, football, fell walking, travel, theatre. *Address:* Vaudreys, 13 Police Street, Manchester, M2 7WA *(tel:* 0161 834 6877; *fax:* 0161 834 2440).

HEALY, Professor Thomas Edward John, MB, BS, MD,Bsc, Msc, LRCP,MRCS,FRCA, DA

Professor of Anaesthesia, University of Manchester; Hon Consultant Anaesthetist, Manchester Royal Informary, Withington Hospital, Hope Hospital. *b.* 11 December 1935 Don-

caster. *m.* 1965 Lesley; one *s.* three *d.* *Public Offices:* Member, Parish Council, Stanton-on-the-Wolds (1979-81); Member, South Manchester Health Authority (1981-89). *Education:* St Brendan's College, Bristol; Guys Hospital Medical School. *Career Profile:* House Officer, Senior House Officer, Registrar, Guy's Hospital; Senior Registrar, Dept of Clinical Research & Investigation, Dudley Road Hospital, Queen Elizabeth Hospital, Children's Hospital, Maternity Hospital, Birmingham; Consultant Anaesthetist, Reader in Anaesthesia, University of Nottingham (1971-81); Editor-in-chief, European Journal of Anaesthesiology; Member, Editorial Board, Journal of Evaluation in Clinical Practice; Former member, Editorial Board, Postgraduate Medical Journal, Japanese Anaesthesiology Reviews, Journal of the Royal Society of Medicine. *Publications/Creative Work:* Over 150 publications in scientific journals; Books: 'Anaesthesia for Day Case Surgery'; 'Aids to Anaesthesia' (Books 1 & 2); 'A Practice of Anaesthesia' (6th ed). *Prizes:* Michael Harris Certificate in Anatomy; Honorary Membership, Romanian Society of Anaethesiology. *Societies:* Member of Council, Royal College of Anaesthetists (1989-); Chairman, Quality of Practice Committee; Royal Society of Medicine (1987), President, Section of Anaesthetics (1996-97); Member, Worshipful Society of Apothecaries (1978); Freeman, City of London (1979); Former Member of council, Association of Anaesthetists (1973-76); Member of Council, Anaesthetics Research Society (1978-80). *Recreations, Interests:* Walking, sleeping. *Address:* Department of Anaesthesia, Manchester Royal Infirmary, Oxford Road, Manchester, M13 9WL (*tel:* 0161 276 8650; *fax:* 0161 273 5685; *e-mail:* healy@fs3.mci.man.ac.uk).

HEARLE, Professor John William Stanley, MA Cantab (1950),PhD Manchester (1952), ScD Cantab (1973),Hon FTI (1985),FInstP

Emeritus Professor of Textile Technology, University of Manchester; Chairman Emeritus and Senior Consultant, Tension Technology International Ltd; Editor-in-Chief, Academic Publications, Textile Institute. *b.* 5 June 1925; Gloucester. *m.* 1954 Marjorie Joyce Pebody; three *s.* (*widowed* 1982); *m.* 1985 Ann Maureen Ashworth (née Aldous); one *steps.* one *stepd.* *Education:* Crypt School, Gloucester; St John's College, Cambridge University. *Career Profile:* Assistant Lecturer to Professor, UMIST (1949-85); Dean of Faculty of Technology, University of Manchester (1979-80); Visiting Professor, MIT (1963-64); Distinguished Visiting Professor of Mechanical Engineering, University of Delaware (1986-88); Visiting Professor of Chemical Engineering, Materials Science Program, University of Delaware (to May 1990). *Publications:* 'Physical Properties of Textile Fibres' (with W E Morton); 'Structural Mechanics of Fibers, Yarns and Fabrics' (with S Backer and P Grosberg); 'Polymers and their properties' ; and many research papers, articles and contributions. *Prizes:* Warner Medal of Textile Institute (1960). *Societies:* Textile Institute (Chairman of Council 1993-95); Institute of Physics; Fiber Society; Institute of Materials; Society of Rheology. *Recreations, Interests:* Walking, theatre, literature, art. *Address:* The Old Vicarage, Mellor, Stockport SK6 5LX (*tel:* 0161-427 1149).

HEATON, John, BA(Hons)(Wales, 1963)

Headteacher, Hayward School, Bolton. *b.* 5 August 1942 Bury. *m.* 1965 Eileen; one *s.* *Public Offices:* Justice of the Peace (Bury). *Education:* Stand Grammar School, Whitefield; University College of Wales, Aberystwyth. *Societies:* Hon. Sec., Lancashire Youth

Cricket; Hon. Sec., Lancashire Schools Cricket Association; Member, Lancashire Cricket Board. *Recreations, Interests:* Cricket, sport, computing, theatre. *Address:* Hayward School, Lever Edge Lane, Bolton, BL3 3HH(*tel:* 01204 62353; *fax:* 01204 653154; *e-mail:* hayward@dial.pipex.com); 59 Turks Road, Radcliffe, Manchester, M26 4GA (*tel:* 0161 723 3882).

HEELEY, Michael David, FCIB

Chairman, Lorien plc; Chairman, Williams Motor Co (Holdings) Ltd. *b.* 16 April 1938 Huddersfield. *m.* 1963 Ann; two *s.* *(marr. diss. 1975)*; *m.* 1984 Susie. *Education:* Queen Elizabeth Grammar School, Wakefield; King George V School, Southport. *Career Profile:* Merchant Banker to 1986; latterly, Main Board Director, British Linen Bank; Group Chief Executive, Vernons Organization (1986-88); Deputy Chairman, Gola Lamb plc (1988-91); various other appointments to quoted and unquoted companies since 1986. *Societies:* St James' Club, Manchester; Huddersfield Golf Club, Fixby; Royal Birkdale Golf Club. *Recreations, Interests:* Golf, Rugby, game shooting, music. *Address:* Lorien plc, 30 Brindley Road, City Park, Manchester M16 9HQ(*tel:* 0161 877 0545; *fax:* 0161 877 0515).

HEGINBOTHAM, Peter, LLB Leeds (1967)

Senior Partner, Davis Blank Furniss, Manchester; Director, Council Member & President (1995-96), Manchester Chamber of Commerce & Industry; Director, Manchester TEC Ltd, Marketing Manchester; Chairman, Glossop North End AFC Ltd; Vice-Chairman, North West Counties Football League. *b.* 25 February 1946; Oldham, Lancashire. *m.* 1972 Jean; two *s. Education:* Werneth Preparatory School, Oldham (1950-53); Oldham Hulme Preparatory School (1953-56); Oldham Hulme Grammar School for Boys (1956-64); Leeds University (1964-67). *Address:* Davis Blank Furniss, 90 Deansgate, Manchester M3 2QJ (*tel:* 0161-832 3304); 19 Grange Road, Bramhall, Stockport SK7 3BD (*tel:* 0161-439 3932).

HELLIWELL, Professor John Richard, FInstP,FRSC,Fellow of the Society of Crystallographers of Australia BA (York,1974),DPhil (Oxon, 1978),DSc (York, 1996)

Professor of Structural Chemistry, University of Manchester. *b.* 19 September 1953 Wickersley, South Yorkshire. *m.* 1978 Madeleine Berry; two *s.* one *d. Public Offices:* Chairman, Manchester & District Branch, Institute of Physics (1990-97); Chairman, International Union of Crystallography's; Commission on Synchrotron Radiation (1989-93); joint Main Editor, Journal of Synchrotron Radiation; Vice-President, British Crystallographic Association (1989-93). *Education:* Ossett School (1966-71); University of York (1971-74); Balliol College, Oxford (1974-78). *Career Profile:* Junior Research Fellow, MRC Post-doctoral Research Assistant, Linacre College, Oxford (1978); Lecturer in Biophysics, University of Keele (1979-83); SSO/PSO, Daresbury Laboratory (1983-85); Lecturer in Biophysics, University of York (1985-88); Professor of Structural Chemistry, University of Manchester (1989-); joint appointee at Daresbury Laboratory (1979-83) (1985-93). *Publications:* 'Macromolecular Crystallography with Synchrotron Radiation' (CUP,1992); (with others) 'Time Resolved Macromolecular Crystallography' (OUP & The Royal Society, 1992); (with others) 'Synchrotron Radiation in the Biosciences' (OUP, 1994); over 150 publications in the professional literature. *Prizes:* Hon. Fellow, Society of

Crystallographers of Australia. *Societies:* British Crystallographic Association; American Crystallographic Association; Biochemical Society; Manchester Literary & Philosophical Society. *Recreations, Interests:* Squash, swimming, walking the dog with the family. *Address:* Department of Chemistry, The University of Manchester, M13 9PL (*tel:* 0161 275 4694; *fax:* 0161 275 4734; *e-mail:* john.helliwell @man.ac.uk).

HENDLEY, Timothy Arthur, LLB(Hons)(London),FCIS

Secretary and Clerk to the Board of Governors, The Manchester Metropolitan University. *b.* 14 January 1947 Birmingham. *m.* 1968 Rosemary Heathcote; three *d.* *Public Offices:* Trustee/Hon Secretary, The North West Film Archive Charitable Trust; Director/Company Secretary, Dryden Street Nursery Limited. *Education:* George Dixon Grammar School, Birmingham; Redditch College of FE; Bristol Polytechnic. *Career Profile:* Various administrative posts: Birmingham City Council; South Bristol Technical College; West Midlands Advisory Council for FE; Manchester Polytechnic. *Recreations, Interests:* Badminton, gardening, watching rugby union. *Address:* The Manchester Metropolitan University, Bellhouse Building, Lower Ormond Street, Manchester, M15 6BX (*tel:* 0161 247 3400; *fax:* 0161 247 3424).

HENFIELD, Martin Owen, BSc(Econ)(London University, Ext)

Presenter 'North West Tonight', BBC TV North. *b.* 10 January 1944 Stourport-on-Severn, Worcestershire. *m.* 1970 Margaret Joy Bamford. *Education:* Queen Elizabeth's Grammar School; Hartlebury, Worcestershire; Oxford College of Technology. *Career Profile:* Newspaper Reporter, Worcester Evening News (1966-68); Birmingham Post & Mail (1968-70); News Editor, BBC Radio Birmingham (1970-75); Manchester Programme Organiser, BBC Radio Manchester (1975-79); Reporter, 'North West Tonight' (1979-88); Manager, BBC GMR (1988-93); Presenter, 'North West Tonight' (1994-). *Societies:* Rossendale Golf Club, Haslingden, Lancs. *Recreations, Interests:* Golf, cinema, theatre, watching TV, telling stories. *Address:* BBC TV, New Broadcasting House, Oxford Road, Manchester, M60 1SJ (*tel:* 0161 244 3140; *fax:* 0161 244 3122). *Additional Information:* News-a-holic.

HENRIQUES, His Honour Judge Richard Henry Quixano, BA(Oxon,1964),QC(1986)

Leader of the Northern Circuit; Recorder of the Crown Court. *b.* 27 October 1943 Lytham St Annes. *m.* 1979 Joan Hilary (Toni); one *s.* one *steps.* *Education:* Bradfield College; Worcester College, Oxford. *Career Profile:* Practised at Bar in Manchester, Preston and Liverpool (1967-). *Recreations, Interests:* Bridge, golf. *Address:* None (*tel:* 0161 834 4097).

HERSOV, Gregory Adam, BA(Oxford,1977)

Artistic Director, Royal Exchange Theatre Company. *b.* 4 May 1956 London. *Education:* Bryanston School, Dorset; Mansfield College, Oxford University. *Career Profile:* Thames Television Regional Director; Bursary, Farnham; Artistic Director, Stiletto Theatre, Bristol; Assistant Director, Royal Exchange Theatre. *Publications/Creative Work:* Productions at the Royal Exchange include: Shakespeare; Jonson; Ibsen; Feydean; Granville Barker; O'Casey; Osborne; Orton; Miller etc; The Marx Brothers World

Premiers; Jeff Noon, Woundings; Jonathan Moore, Behind Heaven; Alex Finlayson, Winding the Ball and Misfits. *Prizes:* The Martini Awards, Best Director, Romeo & Juliet and A View from the Bridge (1993). *Address:* Royal Exchange Theatre Co Ltd, St Ann's Square, Manchester, M2 7DH (*tel:* 0161 833 9333; *fax:* 0161 832 0881).

HEWITT, Peter James, BA (Hons) Cambridge (1964),DipAdvStud Manchester (1966)

Director of Social Services, City of Salford (1992-). *b.* 19 May 1943; Leeds. *Education:* Clare College, Cambridge (1961-64); Manchester University (1964-66). *Career Profile:* Director of Social Services, Bury MBC (1987-92); Assistant Director of Social Services, Stockport MBC (1977-87); District Officer for Social Services, Warrington District, Cheshire CC (1974-77). *Prizes and Awards:* Honorary Companion, Victoria University of Manchester (1995). *Recreations, Interests:* Steam trains. *Address:* Social Services Department, Crompton House, 100 Chorley Road, Swinton, Salford M27 6BP (*tel:* 0161-793 2200).

HICKS, Professor Peter John, BSc,PhD,CEng,MIEE,MInstP

Professor of Microelectronic Circuit Design; Vice-Principal (Information Systems Strategy), UMIST. *b.* 14 June 1948 Bristol. *m.* 1985 Ruth Helen; one *s.* two *d.* *Education:* Cotham Grammar School, Bristol; University of Manchester. *Career Profile:* Research Assistant, University of Manchester (1973-78); Lecturer (1978-84), Senior Lecturer (1984-88), UMIST; present position (1988-). *Publications/Creative Work:* Author/co-author of over 100 articles and papers in the scientific literature; (ed) 'Semi-custom IC Design and VLSI' (Peter Peregrinus, 1983). *Societies:* Institute of Electrical & Electronics Engineers (UK & USA); National Trust; RSPB; World Wildlife Fund; Friends of the Earth. *Recreations, Interests:* Walking, swimming, squash, travel, computers and multimedia, fine food and wine. *Address:* Dept of Electrical Engineering & Electronics, UMIST, PO Box 88, Manchester, M60 1QD (*tel:* 0161 200 4702; *fax:* 0161 200 4781; *e-mail:* p.j.hicks@umist.ac.uk). *Additional Information:* Director, Integrated Sensors Ltd, Edec Multimedia Ltd.

HIGGINS, Geoffrey Paul, BA(Hons),MA,MPhil,FRSA,PGCE,ACP

Principal, Ashton-under-Lyne Sixth Form College. *b.* 26 May 1947 Bristol. *m.* 1972 Jennifer Anne; one *s.* two *d.* *Public Offices:* JP, Tameside PSD. *Education:* St Brendan's College, Bristol (1958-65); University of Liverpool (1965-70); University of London (external)(1971-72). *Career Profile:* Teaching in Grammar & Comprehensive Schools in Cheshire and the Wirral (1970-82); Vice-Principal, Yale Sixth Form College, Wrexham (1982-85); Principal, Ashton Sixth Form College (1985-). *Publications/Creative Work:* Articles and reviews on local history. *Societies:* Chetham Society; Lancashire & Cheshire Historic Society; Lancashire & Cheshire Historical Record Society; Ashton-under-Lyne Rotary Club; Dukinfield Golf Club; Royal Society of Arts. *Recreations, Interests:* County history, all sport - especially golf and cricket, reading, theatre, opera, concert-going. *Address:* Ashton-under-Lyne VIth Form College, Darnton Road, Ashton-under-Lyne, OL6 9RL (*tel:* 0161 330 2330; *fax:* 0161 339 1772; *e-mail:* ashton.ol6.9rl.fu@campus.bt.); 17 Seymour Grove, Marple, SK6 6NR (*tel:* 0161 449 9801).

HILDITCH, Leoné, BA (Admin) (1957),DipEd (1961),MEd (1965) Manchester

Retired Headmistress. *b.* 10 January 1932; Manchester. *Public Offices:* Vice Chairman, North West Regional Examinations Board (1980-85); Headmistress, Bramhall High School (1971-85); Headmistress, The Lakes Secondary School, Dukinfield (1961-71); Deputy Head, Stalybridge Secondary School (1959-61); Member, Stockport Education Committee (1974-80). *Education:* Werneth Primary School, Oldham; Manchester High School for Girls; Lincoln Training College; Manchester University. *Career Profile:* President, NUT: Stalybridge and Dukinfield (1962), Cheshire County (1972), East Cheshire (1974), Stockport (1975); President, Oldham Soroptimist Club (1965); Chairman, Stockport Teachers' Panel (1976-81). *Recreations, Interests:* Sewing, painting, card games, reading. *Address:* 250 Yew Tree Lane, Dukinfield, Cheshire SK16 5DE (*tel*: 0161-338 5303).

HILLS, Revd Dr Richard Leslie, CIME, FMA (1983), BA Cambridge (1960),MA Cambridge (1963),DIC London (1965),PhD Manchester (1968)

Honorary Research Fellow, UMIST. *b.* 1 September 1936; Lee Green, London. *Education:* Charterhouse School, Godalming (1950-55); Queens' College, Cambridge (1957-62) with Certificate in Education; Imperial College, London (1963-64); UMIST, Research Assistant (1965-68); St Deiniol's Library, Hawarden, General Ministry Examination (1985-87). *Military Service:* National Service, Royal Artillery (1955-57). *Previous Positions:* Founder and Director, North Western Museum of Science and Industry, Manchester (1968-85). *Creative Works:* Films: 'Power Behind the Spindle'; 'The George Saxon Engine at Magnet Mill'; 'The Newcomen Engine'; 'Woven by Hand'; 'Hand Made Paper'; '1,000 Pounds per Square Inch: Manchester's Hydraulic Power Supply'. *Publications:* 'Machines, Mills and Uncountable Costly Necessities, A Short History of the Drainage of the Fens' (1967); 'Power in the Industrial Revolution' (1970); 'Richard Arkwright' (1973); 'Beyer Peacock, Locomotive Builders to the World' (1982); 'Paper Making in Britain, 1488-1988: a Short History' (1988); 'Power from Steam: a History of the Stationary Steam Engine' (1989); 'Power from Wind: A History of Windmill Technology' (1994). *Prizes:* Abbot Usher Payson Prize (1973). *Societies:* Newcomen; British, and also International Associations of Paper Historians; Vintage Sports Car Club; Climbers Club; Manchester Region Industrial Archaeology Society; Manchester Literary & Philosophical Society. *Recreations, Interests:* Gardening, vintage cars, mountain walking. *Address:* Stamford Cottage, 47 Old Road, Mottram, Hyde, Cheshire SK14 6LW (*tel*: 01457-63104).

HILTON, Rabbi Michael C, MA,DPhil,PGCE

Minister of Menorah Synagogue, Cheshire Reform Congregation. *b.* 27 February 1951 London. *m.* 1983 Claire; two *s. Education:* Merchant Taylors' School, Northwood (1964-69); The Queen's College, Oxford (1970-74); Wolfson College, Oxford (1974-80); London Institute of Education (1977-78); Leo Baeck College, London (1982-87). *Career Profile:* Housing Officer, London Borough of Hammersmith & Fulham (1980-82). *Publications/Creative Work:* (with Fr Gordian Marshall) 'The Gospels and Rabbinic Judaism' (SCM Press, 1988); 'The Christian Effect on Jewish Life' (SCM Press, 1994). *Societies:* Member, Council of Christians and Jews. *Recreations, Interests:* Country

walking, camping. *Address:* Cheshire Reform Congregation, 198 Altrincham Road, Manchester, M22 4RZ (*tel:* 0161 428 7746).

HINDS, Charles William Victor, MA(hc)(Univ. of Salford,1996)

Leader, Salford City Council. *b.* 6 May 1945 Davyhulme. *m.* 1967 Janet; one *s.* one *d.* *Education:* Welcacre Secondary School. *Career Profile:* Trade: Engineer (-1986); Member, Shop Steward and Convener, Amalgamated Engineering Electrical Union; Councillor, Leader, Salford City Council; Parliamentary candidate for Gloucester (1983) and Feltham & Heston (1987). *Recreations, Interests:* Sport, reading (especially historical), music, ballet, opera, theatre, bird watching, travelling, foreign affairs, political interests, economic affairs. *Address:* Salford City Council, Salford Civic Centre, Chorley Road, Swinton, M27 5DA (*tel:* 0161 793 3059; *fax:* 0161 793 3043).

HIRST, Philip, BA

Editor, Oldham Evening Chronicle; Director, Hirst, Kidd and Rennie Ltd. *b.* 7 May 1951 Oldham. *m.* 1974 Frances Kate; one *s.* one *d.* *Education:* Hulme Grammar School, Oldham; Oxford Polytechnic (now Brookes University, Oxford). *Career Profile:* Reporter (1973-76), Sub-editor (1976-79), Diary Editor/Leader Writer (1979-82), Deputy Editor (1982-91), Editor (1991-) Oldham Evening Chronicle. *Publications/Creative Work:* Since 1979, over 4000 leader articles, innumerable features and reports. *Societies:* Committee Member, Oldham Health Charity (Royal Oldham Hospital MR Scanner Appeal); Member, Oldham Beekeepers' Association. *Recreations, Interests:* Beekeeping, fishing, hiking, gardening. *Address:* Oldham Evening Chronicle, PO Box 47, 172 Union Street, Oldham, OL1 1EQ (*tel:* 0161 633 2121; *fax:* 0161 627 0905; *e-mail:* 100556.2032 @compuserve. com).

HODSON, Philip, MA(Oxon),Solicitor,FCIArb

Solicitor, Beardsells, Stockport. *b.* 2 October 1944 Peterborough. *Education:* Oundle School (1956-63); St Edmund Hall, Oxford (1963-66). *Career Profile:* Assistant Solicitor, Manchester Corporation (1969-73); Partner, Leak Almond & Parkinson (1974-87); Partner, Cobbett Leak Almond (1987-96). *Societies:* St James' Club; Stockport Squash Club. *Recreations, Interests:* Squash, golf, theatre. *Address:* Beardsells, Vienna House, 281 Wellington Road South, Stockport, SK2 6ND(*tel:* 0161 477 2288; *fax:* 0161 474 7268). *Additional Information:* Member, Solicitors Disciplinary Tribunal President, Manchester Law Society (1988-89) Chairman, Manchester Young Solicitors Association (1980).

HODSON, His Honour Judge Thomas David Tattersall, LLB(Hons)

Circuit Judge. *b.* 24 September 1942 Haslingden, Lancashire. *m.* 1969 Patricia Ann; two *s.* one *d.* *Public Offices:* Assistant Recorder (1981-83); Recorder (1983-87). *Education:* Sedbergh; Manchester University. *Career Profile:* Leader Writer, The Yorkshire Post (1964-65); Called to the Bar (1966); Practised Northern Circuit (1967-87); Junior of the Circuit (1968). *Publications/Creative Work:* 'One Week in August - The Kaiser at Lowther Castle 1895' (1995). *Societies:* Lancashire County Cricket Club. *Recreations, Interests:* Family history/genealogy, listening to music, fell-walking, watching cricket and soccer.

Address: c/o The Courts of Justice, Crown Square, Manchester *(tel:* 0161 954 1800).
Additional Information: Elected President, South Lancashire Branch, Magistrates' Association (1994) Liaison Judge, Bury PSD (1988-), Member, Parole Board (1996).

HOGAN, Terence John, BA,BSc,CEng,MIEE,CertEd

Principal, Bolton College. *b.* 22 July 1943 Castleford. *m.* 1966 Maureen; one *s.* one *d.*
Education: Whitwood Technical School (1956-58); Whitwood College (1958-65); Leeds College of Technology (1965-69); Huddersfield College of Education (1972-73); Open University (1972-76); Leeds Polytechnic (1981-84). *Career Profile:* Apprentice & electrician, NCB (1958-65); electrical fitter/trainee engineer, CEGB (1965-69); commissioning engineer, Thorn Automation (1969-70); electrical engineer, Kodak (1970-72); lecturer, Barnsley College (1973-77); Senior Lecturer, North East Derbyshire College (1977-80); Principal Lecturer, York College of Arts & Technology (1980-82); Head of Department, St Helens College (1982-88); Vice-Principal, North Lincolnshire College (1988-90); Bolton College (1990-). *Societies:* Dean Wood Golf Club; South Leeds Golf Club (Captain, 1981). *Recreations, Interests:* Golf, lifelong supporter of Castleford Rugby League, Yorkshire cricket. *Address:* Bolton College, Manchester Road, Bolton, BL2 1ER *(tel:* 01204 531411; *fax:* 01204 380774).

HOLDEN, Robin John, FCA

Retired; freelance writer; non-executive Director, the Open College; Partner, Coopers & Lybrand, Manchester (1974-95). *b.* 22 May 1942; Southport, Lancashire. *m.* 1964 Margaret Susan Rushton; two *s. Public Offices:* Council Member, Institute of Chartered Accountants in England & Wales (1989-95); Council Member, Manchester Chamber of Commerce and Industry (1983-95); Steering Committee Member, Manchester Financial and Professional Forum (1988-95); Asst Hon Treasurer, Family Welfare Assoc of Manchester; Hon Treasurer, Manchester Luncheon Club. *Education:* Trearddur House School; Oundle School. *Career Profile:* President, Manchester Society of Chartered Accountants (1984-85); Hon Treasurer, Manchester Chamber of Commerce and Industry (1983-86); Hon Secretary, Manchester Society of Chartered Accountants (1979-83). *Prizes:* Scholarship to Oundle School (1955). *Societies:* Royal Overseas League; Royal Birkdale and Hale Golf Clubs; Manchester Tennis & Racquets Club; Manchester Literary & Philosophical Society; Chartered Accountants Club. *Recreations, Interests:* Theatre, photography, golf, real tennis, collecting foreign bank notes and matchbooks. *Address:* Tall Trees, Barry Rise, Bowdon, Cheshire WA14 3JS *(tel:* 0161-928 8700).

HOLE, Lieutenant Colonel Haldon Edward, MBE, Order of St John,Deputy Lieutenant, Greater Manchester (1983)

Voluntary: Chairman, Committee and Appeals, Stockport Institute for the Blind, the Deaf and the Dumb; Chairman, Committee 'A Week to Help the Deaf' Appeal; Henesy House, Residential and Community Centre for the Deaf; Appeals Officer, St John Ambulance, Greater Manchester; Appeals Organiser, Royal National Institute for the Blind; Only surviving Senior Committee Member of 'Piles of Pennies Appeal for the Blind'. £1,400,000 donated to the Royal National Institute for the Blind in 25 years. *b.* 29 March 1906; Manchester. *m.* 1935 Fay Edwards; one *s. (widowed 1971) Education:* St Margarets

Church of England Central School, Manchester. *War Service:* Volunteered into Army as Private soldier (won Lightweight Battalion Boxing title); commissioned 2nd Lt 1940; after various postings (all with Armour) as OC as Captain or Major, posted from Belgium to India to assist in formation of No 3 Armoured Replacement Group; posted from India to Burma 1945 as Lt Col; Assistant Director Ordnance Services to the Group in SE Asia Command; after fall of Rangoon moved with Group to Ceylon to prepare Armoured forces for attack and occupation of Malaya; after Japanese surrender posted to Singapore to form and Command 221 Indian Veh Coy and Command Western Zone of island for defence and security (20,000 Japanese POWs ... armed one in ten and 700 Comfort Girls); appointment involved responsibilities in Java and Sumatra; after duties in ten countries in all - returned to UK August, 1946; final appointment - Commander, Royal Ordnance Corp, 42nd Lancashire Inf Division TA; retired 1955. *Career Profile:* Merchandise Controller, Lewis's Ltd, Manchester. Retired 1969; Organised and Chaired Committee 'The Matchstalk Appeal' to bring to the Manchester area for the first time 'Dr Barnardos'; The 'Matt Busby Close' was opened in Pendlebury in 1979; For over 25 years member of Drapery Trade Charities, Purley Schools, Cottage Homes, Porters Benevolent. *Societies:* The Royal Society of St George. *Recreations, Interests:* Entertaining, endeavouring to persuade those with much to think more kindly of those with little. *Address:* Stockport Institute for the Blind, the Deaf and the Dumb, 112 Shaw Heath, Stockport SK4 6QS (*tel:* 0161-480 2612); 69 Elmsfield Avenue, Norden, Rochdale OL11 5XW (*tel:* 01706-861848). *Additional Information:* Country Address: 'Bramblewood', Clarenden Road, Alderbury, Salisbury SP5 3AT (*tel:* 01722-710977).

HOLLIER, Professor Robert Henry, BSc(1956),MSc(1959),PhD(1966),MSc(hc) (1981), CEng

Professor of Operations Management, Deputy-Vice Chancellor, UMIST; Director, UMIST Ventures Ltd, Trafford Park Manufacturing Institute. *b.* 18 September 1934 Birmingham. *m.* 1960 Pauline; one *s.* one *d. Education:* Wrekin College (1947-52); University of Birmingham (1952-56). *Career Profile:* Tube Investments Research Fellow (1960-63), Lecturer (1963-70), Department of Engineering Production, University of Birmingham; Visiting Associate Professor, Department of Operations Research, Cornell University, USA (1967-68); Visiting Associate Professor, Krannert Graduate School of Industrial Administration, Purdue University, USA (1968-70); Senior Lecturer (1970-72), Green Shield Professor of Stock Control and Materials Handling (1972-77), Department of Engineering Production, University of Birmingham; Professor of Operations Management, Department of Management Sciences (from 1988 Manchester School of Management UMIST)(1977-); Vice-Principal for Finance and latterly Deputy Principal, UMIST (1981-83); Head of Department of Management Sciences (1983-85); Pro-Vice-Chancellor, UMIST (1994-). *Publications/Creative Work:* Numerous articles in the professional journals. *Prizes:* IMM Gold Medal Award (1992). *Societies:* Member, Institution of Mechanical Engineers; Member, Institution of Electrical Engineers; Fellow, Institute of Logistics; Hon Member, Japan Industrial Management Association (1977-). *Recreations, Interests:* Chairman, The Benchmarking Centre Ltd, sailing, photography, gardening. *Address:* Manchester School of Management, UMIST, PO Box 88, Manchester, M60 1QD (*tel:* 0161 200 3421; *fax:* 0161 200 8787; *e-mail:* bob.hollier@umist.ac.uk).

HOLT, Victor St George, Assoc MCT,ACII,MIMgt

Retired. *b.* 11 June 1922; Blackpool. *m.* 1955 Elsie Winifred Brown; one *s.* one *d.* *Education:* Manchester Grammar School. *War Service:* RAF (1942-46). *Career Profile:* Deputy General Manager, Refuge Assurance plc. *Societies:* UMIST Association; Manchester Literary & Philosophical Society (Honorary Curator 1977-80). *Recreations, Interests:* Music. *Address:* 23 Brayton Avenue, Didsbury, Manchester M20 5LP (*tel:* 0161-445 3353).

HONER, Christopher Douglas, BA(Hons)(Oxon,1969)

Artistic Director, Library Theatre Company. *b.* 8 June 1948 Chingford, Essex. *m.* 1972 Marian Blaikley; two *s.* *(separated 1993) Public Offices:* Accreditation Board, National Council for Drama Training. *Education:* Whitgift School, Croydon; Lincoln College, Oxford. *Career Profile:* Artistic Director, Derby Playhouse (1980-87), Gateway Theatre, Chester (1976-80), Birmingham Rep (1972-76). *Publications/Creative Work:* (with Roger Lancaster): 'The Amazing Adventures of Robin Hood'; 'Magical Legend'; 'The Kingfisher Quest'; 'Barney's Time Travel'. *Prizes:* Manchester Evening News Theatre Awards (1993) best production of a play for 'The Merchant of Venice'. *Societies:* RSPB. *Recreations, Interests:* Reading, walking, bird-watching, cricket. *Address:* Library Theatre, St Peters Square, Manchester, M2 5PD.

HORE, Brian David, BSc (Hons) London (1959),MB BS London (1962),MRCP London (1966),FRCP London (1981),MPhil London (1971),FRCPsych (1978)

Consultant Psychiatrist, University Hospital of South Manchester, Withington Hospital; Consultant Psychiatrist In Charge, Alcoholism Treatment Unit, Withington Hospital, Manchester; Medical Director, Alcohol Treatment Programme, Altrincham Priory Hospital; Honorary Lecturer in Psychiatry, University of Manchester. *b.* 21 September 1937; Wembley, Middlesex. *m.* 1964 Eva Elliot Shepherd; two *s.* *Public Offices:* Hon Vice President, International Journal on Alcohol and Addictions; Vice Chairman, Turning Point. *Education:* Lower School of John Lyon, Harrow, Middlesex; St Barts Hospital Medical College, London; Maudsley Hospital, London. *Previous Positions:* House Physician, St Barts Hospital, London; Registrar, Maudsley Hospital, London; Lecturer in Psychiatry (Honorary Consultant), University of Manchester. *Publications:* 'Alcohol Dependence' (1976); 'Alcohol Problems in Employment' (1981) (jointly); 'Alcohol and Health' (jointly). *Societies:* Society for the Study of Addiction; Medical Council on Alcoholism; Alcohol Concern; Turning Point. *Recreations, Interests:* Theatre, cinema, football (Manchester City FC), golf. *Address:* 17 St John Street, Manchester M3 4DR (*tel:* 0161-834 5775).

HORNE, Professor Michael Rex, Hon DSc Salford (1981),OBE (1981); BA (1942), MA (1945), PhD (1951), ScD (1956) Cambridge,FRS,FEng,FICE,FIStructE

Retired. *b.* 29 December 1921; Leicester. *m.* 1947 Dorcas Mary Hewett; two *s.* two *d.* *Public Offices:* Member, Government Committee (Merrison Committee) on Box Girder Bridges (1970-73); Chairman, Government Review of Public Utilities in the Road (Horne Report) (1983-85). *Education:* Boston (Lincs) Grammar School (1932-38); Leeds Grammar School (1938-39); St John's College, University of Cambridge (1939-41). *War Service:*

Great Ouse River Board. *Career Profile:* Research Officer, Institute of Welding (1945-51); Assistant Director of Research (1951-56), Lecturer in Engineering (1956-60) Department of Engineering, University of Cambridge; Professor of Civil Engineering, University of Manchester (1960-83); President, Institution of Structural Engineers (1980-81). *Publications:* 5 books (joint author for 4) on Plastic theory of Structures; about 100 papers on Structures, Safety of Structures and Particulate Mechanics. *Prizes:* Institution of Civil Engineers, Baker Gold Medal (1977); Institution of Structural Engineers, Gold Medal (1986). *Recreations, Interests:* Music, the theatre, basket making, enjoying retirement. *Address:* 19 Park Road, Hale, Altrincham, Cheshire WA15 9NW (*tel:* 0161-941 2223).

HORNSBY, Guy Philip

Group Chief Executive, KISS 102 (Manchester), KISS 105 (Yorkshire). *b.* 24 March 1958 Twickenham, Middlesex. *Education:* Newland House School, Twickenham; Emanuel School, Wandsworth. *Career Profile:* Production Assistant, BBC Radio London (1979); Producer, Robbie Vincent Telephone Programme (1982); Producer, Tony Blackburn Show (1983); Producer & Presenter 'London Today' (1981-86); Breakfast Show Presenter, Ocean Sound, Hampshire (1986-90); Programme Manager, Group Programme Controller, Southern Radio (1990-94); Managing Director, KISS 102, Manchester (1994-96); Group Chief Executive, KISS 102/KISS 105 (1996-). *Prizes:* International Radio Award for 'Sweet Soul Music' Documentary Series (1984), BBC World Service. *Societies:* Y Club, Manchester. *Recreations, Interests:* Keeping fit, films, computers, music. *Address:* KISS 102, Kiss House, PO Box 102, 127-129 Portland Street, Manchester, M1 6ED (*tel:* 0161 228 0102; *fax:* 0161 228 1020; *e-mail*: dance@kiss102.u-net.com).

HOUGH, Robert Eric, LLB (Bristol, 1967), DBA(hc) (Manchester Metropolitan, 1996), DLitt(hc) (Salford, 1996)

Deputy Chairman, Peel Holdings plc; Chairman, Manchester Ship Canal Company. *b.* 18 July 1945 Urmston, Manchester. *m.* 1975 Pauline Elizabeth; two *s. Public Offices:* Chairman, Organising Committee, Manchester 2002 Commonwealth Games; Member, Board of Management, Manchester Business School; Governor, William Hulme's Grammar School; Trustee, The Lowry Centre; Past President, Manchester Chamber of Commerce & Industry (President during bi-centenary 1994-5); Vice President, The Bronington Trust. *Education:* William Hulme's Grammar School, Manchester (1956-64); Bristol University (1964-67). *Career Profile:* Articled with Slater Heelis Solicitors, Manchester (1968-70); Admitted as Solicitor (1970); Partner, Slater Heelis specialising in corporate, commercial & banking law (1974-89); Appointed Non-Exec Director, Peel Holdings plc (1986); Appointed Non-Exec Chairman, Manchester Ship Canal Company (1987); Full-time Exec-Chairman, Manchester Ship Canal Co and Exec-Deputy Chairman, Peel Holdings plc (1989); Non-Exec Director, Brammer plc (1993). *Societies:* St James's Club; Hale Golf Club. *Recreations, Interests:* Gardening, golf. *Address:* The Manchester Ship Canal Company, Quay West, Trafford Wharf Road, Manchester, M17 1PL (*tel:* 0161 872 2411; *fax:* 0161 877 4720).

HOUSTON, Professor Ian Briercliffe, MB, ChB, Manchester (1955),MD Manchester (1965), FRCP London

Acting Dean of Postgraduate Medical Studies, Professor of Child Health, University of Manchester; Honorary Consultant Paediatrician, Royal Manchester Children's Hospital (retd). *b.* 11 September 1932; Blackpool, Lancs. *m.* 1956 Pamela Beryl; one *s.* two *d.* *Education:* Baines' Grammar School, Poulton-le-Fylde, Lancs; University of Manchester Medical School. *Career Profile:* Senior Lecturer, University of Manchester; Nuffield Fellow, Albert Einstein College of Medicine, New York. *Publications:* Articles in Scientific and Medical Journals; Chapters of Medical Books mainly related to renal disease in children. *Societies:* European Society for Paediatric Nephrology (President 1988); British Paediatric Association; Association of Clinical Professors of Paediatrics (President 1989-91). *Recreations, Interests:* Squash, gardening, walking. *Address:* Univ Dept Postgraduate Medicine and Dentistry, Gateway House, Piccadilly South, Manchester M60 7LP.

HOUSTON, Stephen Mark, BA(Hons)(1981),Solicitor

Partner, Davies Arnold Cooper (1995-). *b.* 18 October 1959 Birmingham. *m.* Coral Houston; one *s.* two *d.* *Education:* King Edwards Grammar School, Aston; Birmingham Polytechnic; College of Law, Chester. *Career Profile:* Articled Clerk, Rakisons (1983-85); Assistant Solicitor, Norton Rose (1987-93); Partner, Halliwell Landau (1994-95). *Publications/Creative Work:* Articles from time to time. *Societies:* The Law Society. *Recreations, Interests:* Sport, walking, playing the guitar (badly). *Address:* Davies Arnold Cooper, 60 Fountain Street, Manchester, M2 2FE *(tel:* 0161 839 8396; *fax:* 0161 839 8309).

HOWARTH, His Honour Judge Nigel John Graham, LLB(1957),LLM(1959), Barrister-at-Law (1960),Circuit Judge(1992)

Circuit Judge. *b.* 12 December 1936 Manchester. *m.* 1962 Janice Mary; two *s.* one *d.* *Education:* Manchester Grammar School (1949-54); Manchester University (1954-57, 1957-59); Council of Legal Education (1959-60). *Career Profile:* In practice at the Chancery Bar in Manchester (1961-92); Circuit Judge (1992-); Assistant Recorder (1983-89); Recorder (1989-92). *Prizes:* Grays Inn: Macaskie Scholar (1960), Atkin Scholar (1960); Council of Legal Education Certificate (1960). *Societies:* Northern Counties (Newcastle-upon-Tyne); Manchester Pedestrian Club. *Recreations, Interests:* Music, theatre, fell walking, supporter of Altrincham FC.. *Additional Information:* Chairman, Northern Chancery Bar Association (1990-92) Former President, Manchester Incorporated Law Library Society, Acting Deemster (Isle of Man) (1985, 1989); Vice-President, Disabled Living.

HOWARTH, Richard, ARCM

Leader, Manchester Camerata. *b.* 15 May 1949 Doncaster, S Yorkshire. *Education:* Doncaster Grammar School; Royal College of Music, London. *Career Profile:* City of Birmingham Symphony Orchestra; BBC Concert Orchestra; Ulster Orchestra.

HOWITT, Basil William, MA (Cantab),ARCM,PGCE

Freelance writer; Public speaker; 'Cellist. *b.* 23 October 1940 Sale. *m.* 1966 Tricia Witts; *(marr. diss. 1987)*; *m.* 1988 Sue Greenhough. *Education:* Chetham's (1951-59); Trinity

College, Cambridge (1959-63). *Career Profile:* Further Education, ultimately Head of Liberal Studies, Stafford College of Further Education; freelance 'cellist, singer and music examiner (BBC, Camerata, recitals, BBC Northern Singers, etc); writer; member of the Salon Duo. *Publications/Creative Work:* Articles for Classical Music Magazine, the Guardian and Private Eye; 'Life in a Penguin Suit'(Manchester Camerata, 1993); 'Love Lives of the Great Composers'(Sound & Vision, Toronto, 1995). *Societies:* Confrerie des Compangnons Vignerons de Trémoine. *Recreations, Interests:* Cycling (especially in the French Pyrenees), cooking (especially French & Mediterranean food), reading (especially novels). *Address:* 21 Mauldeth Road West, Withington, Manchester, M20 3EQ (*tel:* 0161 445 6650; *e-mail:* 101353.3330@compuserve.com). *Additional Information:* Working on a second volume of 'Love Lives of the Great Composers', to be published by Robson Books Ltd in 1997.

HUGILL, John, MA,Called to Bar (1954)

Queen's Counsel (1976). *b.* 11 August 1930; Manchester. *m.* 1956 Patricia Elizabeth Welton; two *d.* *Public Offices:* Assistant Recorder, Bolton (1971); Recorder (1972); Bencher Middle Temple (1984); Deputy High Court Judge; Hon Legal Advisor, Clay Pigeon Shooting Association. *Education:* Sydney Church of England Grammar School, NSW; Fettes College; Trinity Hall. *Military Service:* Royal Artillery. *Career Profile:* Member of Senate of The Inns of Court and The Bar (1984-86); Member, General Council of The Bar (1987-89); Chairman, Darryn Clarke Enquiry (1979); Chairman, Stanley Royd Enquiry (1985). *Recreations, Interests:* Reading, talking about yachting. *Address:* 45 Hardman Street, Manchester (*tel:* 0161-832 3791).

HULLAH, Canon Peter Fearnley, BD(Hons),ARC(1971)

Headmaster, Chetham's School of Music. *b.* 7 May 1949 Bradford, Yorkshire. *m.* 1971 Hilary Sargent Long; one *s.* one *d.* *Public Offices:* Canon of Manchester Cathedral; Chairman, Bloxham Project; Chairman, HMC Coeducational Schools Group. *Education:* Bradford Grammar School; King's College, London; Makerere University, Kampala, Uganda; Cuddesdon College, Oxford. *Career Profile:* Assistant Chaplain, St Edward's School, Oxford (1974-77); Chaplain, Sevenoaks School (1977-82); Housemaster, International Centre, Sevenoaks School (1982-87); Senior Chaplain, The King's School, Canterbury (1987-92); Headmaster, Chetham's School of Music (1992-). *Publications/Creative Work:* Consultant to the Bloxham Project; articles in educational journals. *Recreations, Interests:* Reading, climbing, music, Kilimanjaro. *Address:* Chetham's School of Music, Long Millgate, Manchester, M3 1SB (*tel:* 0161 834 9644; *fax:* 0161 839 3609).

HULSE, Julian, MIPD,HNC(Elec Eng),Dip Training Mgmt

Chief Executive and Director, Manchester Chamber of Commerce and Industry. *b.* 29 April 1946 Chester. *m.* Valerie Pierce; two *s.* one *d.* (*marr. diss. 1981*); *m.* 1981 Anne Thompson. *Public Offices:* Regional Advisory Committee, Turning Point; Member, UMIST Court of Governors. *Education:* Frodsham County Secondary School; Runcorn Technical College; Mid-Cheshire Technical College; Liverpool College of Advanced Technology. *Career Profile:* Electrical Technician Apprentice, BICC; Assistant Training Officer, BICC; Group Training Officer, NW Independent Newspapers; Training Manager,

132

United Newspapers (Lancs); Personnel & Training Director, Telefusion Communications Ltd. *Societies:* St James's Club; Manchester Luncheon Club; Manchester Literary & Philosophical Society. *Recreations, Interests:* Music, watching cricket (especially Lancashire CCC), watching rugby (both Union and League), cooking. *Address:* Manchester Chamber of Commerce & Industry, 56 Oxford Street, Manchester, M60 7HJ (*tel:* 0161 236 3210; *fax:* 0161 236 4160). *Additional Information:* Director: Manchester Business Link, MCCI Services Ltd, World Trade Centre, Manchester; China Gateway North West; MANDATE (Manchester Airport Business Support Group); National Council, British Chambers of Commerce; Counil, North West Chambers of Commerce; Trustee, MCCI Staff Pension Scheme; Council, British Chamber of Commerce Executives.

HULSMANN, Kees

Musician, Violinist, The Netherlands; Leader, Rotterdam Philharmonic Orchestra; Leader, The Hallé Orchestra; Professor, Royal Academy of Music, The Hague, The Netherlands. *b.* 12 January 1949 The Netherlands. *m.* 1982 Natalia Buzdes; one *s.* one *d. Education:* Student at Music Academy, A8msterdam; Student in London with Manoug Parikian. *Address:* 18 Bombay House, 59 Whitworth Street, Manchester, M1 3AB (*tel:* 0161 237 5189; *fax:* 0161 237 5189); Julianalaan 240, 3722 GW Bilthoven, The Netherlands (*tel:* 030 228 3922; *fax:* 030 225 2243).

HUMPHREYS, Robert Gordon, BSc Tech Manchester (1955),CEng,MIMechE

Chairman, FHD Furnaces Ltd; Vice-Chairman, Community Trust for Greater Manchester; Director, Shaw-Taylor Management Consultants Ltd. *b.* 7 November 1932; Timperley, Cheshire. *m.* 1955 Ruth Tudor-Jones; four *d. Education:* Wrekin College; Phillips Andover (USA); UMIST; Advanced Management Program International. *Career Profile:* Production Engineer, Vauxhall Motors Ltd; Sales and Contracts Manager, Towler Hydraulics; Design Manager, ICL; Director, Binder Hamlyn Fry; Managing Director, B & S Massey Ltd; Manager of Innovation, Renold plc; Managing Director, Crocus Ltd. *Publications:* BIM and Chartered Accountants Guides to Stock Control and Forecasting; 'Analysing Uncertainty' (Chartered Institute of Management Accountants); 'Turning Uncertainty to Advantage' (McGraw-Hill). *Societies:* Chairman, Research & Development Society, NW; Chairman, Strategic Planning Society, NW; Yorkshire Rambler's Club; English-Speaking Union. *Recreations, Interests:* Restoring old gardens and machinery. *Address:* 3 Albert Road, Hale, Altrincham WA15 9AH

HUMPHREYS, Roger Owen, ACA

Financial Director, Seton Healthcare Group plc. *b.* 13 March 1961 Stockport. *m.* 1991 Helen; one *s.* one *d. Education:* Stockport Grammar School; Manchester Polytechnic. *Career Profile:* (1980-84) - Neville Russell; (1984-90) - KPMG; (1990-) - Seton Healthcare. *Recreations, Interests:* Walking, golf. *Address:* Seton Healthcare Group plc, Tubiton House, Oldham, OL1 3HS.

HUMPHRIES, His Honour Judge Gerard William, KHS(1986) LLB(Hons),Barrister

Circuit Judge. *b.* 13 December 1928 Barrow-in-Furness. *m.* 1957 Valerie Gelderd; four *s.* one *d. Public Offices:* Chairman, Medical Appeals Tribunal (1976-80); Vaccine Damage

Tribunals (1979-80); Charter Mem, Serra Club, N Cheshire (1963-)(Pres. 1968-73, 1995-96); Trustee, SBC Educational Trust (1979-)(Chmn. 1979-90); Foundn Governor, St Bede's College, Manchester (1978-). *Education:* St Bede's College, Manchester; Manchester University. *Military Service:* Flying Officer, RAF (1951-53). *Career Profile:* Middle Temple (1952); admitted to Northern Circuit (1954); Asst Recorder of Salford (1969-71); a Recorder of the Crown Court (1974-80). *Publications/Creative Work:* The Stations of the Cross - a meditation; Lectures: the Trials of Christ; the Trials of St Paul; the Trials of Cardinal Newman. *Societies:* Northern Lawn Tennis; Northenden Golf; Serra International, North Cheshire. *Recreations, Interests:* Tennis, bad golf, caravanning, gardening.

HUNT, Christopher John, MLitt,FSA

Director and University Librarian, John Rylands University Library, University of Manchester. *b.* 28 January 1937 London. *m.* Kathleen Mary. *Education:* Exeter and Durham Universities. *Career Profile:* formerly University Librarian, James Cook University of North Queensland; University Librarian, La Trobe University, Melbourne; Librarian, British Library of Political & Economic Science, London School of Economics. *Address:* John Rylands University Library, University of Manchester, Oxford Road, Manchester, M13 9PL.

HUNT, Harry, MSc(UMIST),CEng,MIMechE,MRAeS

Retired Consulting Engineer; former assessor for Institute of Mechanical Engineers Mature Candidate Scheme. *b.* 9 December 1919; Manchester. *m.* 1948 Kathleen; two *s.* *Education:* Junior & Secondary Schools; College of Technology, Manchester (1935-39); various Naval courses (1939-49); College of Advanced Technology, Salford (1958); College of Technology, Stockport (1954-58); UMIST (1968-70). *War Service:* Royal Navy (1939-49). *Career Profile:* Assistant District Manager, Electrolux (1949-51); Representative Engineer, Auto-Klean Strainers Ltd (1951-53); Northern Manager, Samuel Denison & Son Ltd (1954-66); Senior Lecturer, College of Technology, Stockport (1966-82); Consulting Engineer (1982-Retirement). *Publications:* Various contributions to 'Trans. of Manchester Association of Engineers'; various contributions to joint scientific papers. *Prizes:* Constantine Medal (Manchester Association of Engineers 1974); Butterworth Medal (Manchester Association of Engineers 1980). *Societies:* Manchester Association of Engineers (President 1979-80); Associate of the Manchester Institue of Technology; Manchester Technology Assoc; Assoc of Royal Navy Officers. *Recreations, Interests:* Painting in oils, writing, walking, swimming and reading. *Address:* 21 Grendale Avenue, Hazel Grove, Stockport, Cheshire SK7 6LJ (*tel:* 0161-483 7290).

HUNT, Jeff, FCA

Partner, Coopers & Lybrand, Chartered Accountants, in charge of North West Litigation Support Practice and Nationally for Personal Injury Cases. *b.* 11 November 1944; Culcheth, Warrington. *m.* 1965 Christina; one *s.* one *d.* *Education:* Leigh Grammar School. *Societies:* Trustee, Leigh Cricket Club. *Recreations, Interests:* Sports, music,

people. *Address:* Coopers & Lybrand, Abacus Court, 6 Minshull Street, Manchester M1 3ED (*tel:* 0161-236 9191); 6 Meadow Close, Leigh WN7 3LR.

HUSBAND, Professor Thomas Mutrie, FEng,FIMechE,FIEE,CIM,BSc,MA,PhD

Vice-Chancellor, University of Salford. *b.* 7 July 1936 Glasgow. *m.* 1962 Pat; two *s.* *Education:* Shawlands Academy Glasgow; Stow College of Further Education, Glasgow; Strathclyde University: BSc(1961),MA(1966),PhD(1971). *Career Profile:* Apprentice Marine Engine Fitter, WeirGroup, Glasgow; Middle/Senior Factory Manager ASEA (now ABB), Denmark, South Africa; Lecturer, Strathclyde University; Senior Lecturer, Glasgow University; Professor, Loughborough University; Professor, Head of Mechanical Engineering, Director of Robotics Research Centre; Imperial College, London; Vice-Chancellor, University of Salford (1990-). *Publications/Creative Work:* Books/articles on Robotics, Terotechnology, Engineering Education. *Recreations, Interests:* Theatre, music, premiership football. *Address:* Vice-Chancellor's Office, University of Salford, Salford, M5 4WT (*tel:* 0161 745 5477; *fax:* 0161 745 5040; *e-mail:* t.m.husband@salford. ac.uk) 34 Hawthorn Lane, Wilmslow, Cheshire, SK9 5DG (*tel:*01625 530559; *fax:* 01625 530559).

HYAMS, Anthony Michael, BTech(Hons)(Loughborough,1972),MBA(MBS,1976)

Regional Director, BZW Private Equity. *b.* 19 June 1949 London. *m.* 1974 Jacqueline Carol; one *s.* two *d.* *Education:* Loughborough University; Manchester University. *Recreations, Interests:* Classic cars, walking. *Address:* BZW Private Equity Limited, 50 Fountain Street, Manchester, M2 2AS(*tel:* 0161 832 7222; *fax:* 0161 833 9374).

HYTNER, Benet Alan, MA Cantab (1949)

Queen's Counsel; Member of the bar, Northern Circuit. *b.* 29 December 1927; Prestwich. *m.* 1954 Joyce Myers; three *s.* one *d.* *(marr. diss. 1980) Public Offices:* Recorder of Crown Court (1971-); Judge of Appeal, Isle of Man (1980-). *Education:* Kings Rd Council School, Prestwich; Manchester Grammar School; Trinity Hall, Cambridge. *Military Service:* RASC (Commissioned) (1949-51). *Career Profile:* Leader, Northern Circuit (1984-89). *Prizes:* Exhibitioner, Trinity Hall Cambridge. *Societies:* Bencher, Middle Temple (1977-). *Recreations, Interests:* Fell walking, theatre, reading, music. *Address:* 25 Byrom Street, Manchester M3 4PF.

HYTNER, Joyce (*née* Myers)

Development Director, Royal Court Theatre, London; Non-executive Director, Oxfordshire Health Authority. *b.* 9 December 1935; Manchester. *m.* three *s.* one *d.* *(marr. diss. 1980) Education:* Withington Girls' School. *Societies:* Board Member, Royal Exchange Theatre, London Academy of Music & Dramatic Art, Performing Arts Laboratory; Trustee, Lowry Centre, Salford, International House. *Recreations, Interests:* Music, theatre. *Address:* Royal Court Theatre, Sloane Square, London SW3 (*tel:* 0171 823 4132; *fax:* 0171 730 9160)

I

ILETT, John David, MA Cambridge (BA hons 1943),BSc (Hons) London (1943)

Retired. *b.* 27 January 1923; Oxendon, Northants. *m.* 1946 Louise Anne (*decd* 1981); two *s.* three *d.*; *m.* 1983 Brenda Elizabeth; one *steps.* one *stepd. Public Offices:* Councillor, Burnham-on-Sea (1959-64); General Commissioner for Taxation, Manchester & Salford; Vice-Chairman, Tameside & Glossop District Health Authority (1980-92); Member Tameside Family Practitioner Committee (1987-90); Chairman, Mandy Turner Scanner Appeal (1990). *Education:* King Edward VI School, Nuneaton (1934-41); Magdalene College, Cambridge (1941-46). *War Service:* Local Defence Volunteers (1938); Home Guard (1939-45); Ministry of Defence, Chemical Warfare (1943-46). *Career Profile:* Manager, TPT Ltd; Divisional Director, Courtaulds Ltd; President & General Manager, TCF of Canada Ltd. *Publications:* 'The National Health Service - Intention and Reality' (Manchester Statistical Society Dec 1987); Joint Research Papers, Journal Chemical Society (1948 et seq). *Prizes:* State Scholar (1940); University Open Scholar (1940); Magdalene College Prizeman (1942). *Societies:* Manchester Statistical Society (President 1989-91). *Recreations, Interests:* Music, horses, shooting, bee keeping. *Address:* Flowery Field House, Newton Street, Hyde, Cheshire SK14 4NP (*tel:* 0161-368 2862).

INSLEY, Audrey Betsy, DL,JP; Grad.Dip.Phys, MCSP, SRP Salford

Partner, Eemax Inc, Connecticut, USA; Physiotherapist & Counsellor. *b.* Manchester. *Public Offices:* Deputy Lieutenant, Greater Manchester (1993); JP (Manchester City Bench, 1972); Past Chairman, The Magistrates Association; Member, Central Youth Panel, London; Past Chairman and CEO, David Lewis Centre; Director, David Lewis Centre. *Education:* Boarding and State Schools; Salford University School of Physiotherapy; Birmingham University. *Career Profile:* Senior Physiotherapist, Royal Berkshire Hospitals; University Lecturer, Medical School, University of the Witwatersrand, Johannesburg, South Africa; Clinical Lecturer, Dept of Orthopaedics, University of Manchester. *Creative Works:* Gardening; sketching. *Prizes:* Nominated Cheshire Woman of the Year (1986). *Societies:* Davenport Golf Club; The Magistrates Association; Manchester Literary & Philosophical Society; The Manchester Luncheon Club; The Hallé; Withington Golf Club. *Recreations, Interests:* Music sailing, mountaineering. *Address:* Eemax Inc, PO Box 200, Connecticut, USA (203-261-0684); 26 Mellington Avenue, Didsbury, Manchester M20 0NJ (*tel:* 0161-445 1496).

IRVING, Professor Sir Miles Horsfall, KB(1995);DSc(hc)(Salford, 1996), MB ChB (Liverpool,1959),MD(Liverpool,1962),ChM(Liverpool,1967),FRCS(1964),FRCSEd(1964) MSc(Manchester 1980), FFAEM(Hon)(1995)

Professor of Surgery, University of Manchester; Honorary Consultant Surgeon, Hope Hospital, Salford; Director (part-time), NHS Health Technology Programme. *b.* 29 June 1935 Southport, Lancashire. *m.* 1965 Dr Patricia Margaret Blaiklock; two *s.* two *d. Public Offices:* Member of Council, Royal College of Surgeons of England (1983-95); President, Association of Surgeons of Great Britain and Ireland (1996); former Member, General Medical Council; Consultant Adviser in Surgery to the Chief Medical Officer; Regional

Director of Research and Development, North Western Regional Health Authority (1992-94). *Education:* King George V School, Southport; Liverpool University; Sydney University, Australia. *Military Service:* Capt (RAMC: TA) 12/13 Battalion Parachute Regiment; Honorary Consultant Surgeon to the Army. *Career Profile:* House Physician, House Surgeon, Broadgreen Hospital, Liverpool (1959-60); Robert Gee Fellow in Human Anatomy, Liverpool University (1960-61); Registrar in Surgery, Liverpool Royal Infirmary (1963-64); SHO in Neurosurgery, Plastic Surgery, Newcastle upon Tyne (1964-65); Phyllis Anderson Research Fellow, Sydney University, Australia (1965-67); Senior Registrar, Reader in Surgery, Consultant Surgeon, St Bartholomew's Hospital (1968-71). *Publications/Creative Work:* Over 200 publications in the surgical and scientific literature; Author: textbooks on Intestinal Fistulae, Colorectal Surgery; Gastrointestinal Surgery and Minimal Access Surgery. *Prizes:* Moynihan Medal, Association of Surgeons (1965); Pybus Medal (1987); Sir John Loewenthal Medal, Sydney University (1993); Canet Medal. Institute of Mechanical Incorporated Engineers (1995); Lettsomian Medal, Medical Society of London (1996). *Societies:* Manchester Medical Society (Hon Fellow); James IV Association of Surgeons (Director); Liverpool Medical Institution; Royal Society of Medicine; International Surgical Society; Medical Society of London. *Recreations, Interests:* Moutain walking, opera. *Address:* Department of Surgery, Hope Hospital, University of Manchester School of Medicine, Salford, M6 8HD (*tel:* 0161 787 4359; *fax:* 0161 787 7432; *e-mail:* mirving@fs1.ho.man.ac.uk); 18 Albert Road, Heaton, Bolton, BL1 5HE (*tel:* 01204 841182).

ISHERWOOD, Baron Charles, BA,PhD

Director (Regeneration), Government Office for the North West. *b.* 4 February 1945 Wales. *m.* 1978 Nuala; one *s.* two *d.* *Education:* Taunton's School, Southampton; University of Bristol. *Career Profile:* Economist, Universities of Bristol, Sussex, London (1966-81); Civil Service (Departments of Health and Social Security, Environment, Government Office for the North West)(1981-95). *Publications/Creative Work:* Various articles on consumption economics in learned journals; 'The World of Goods' (Allen Lane, 1978)(with Mary Douglas). *Societies:* Portico Library. *Address:* Government Office for the North West, Sunley Tower, Piccadilly Plaza, Manchester, M1 4BE (*tel:* 0161 952 4303; *fax:* 0161 952 4365).

ISHERWOOD, Professor Ian, CBE(1996); MBChB(1954),MD,FRCP,FRCR,FFRRCSI

Emeritus Professor of Diagnostic Radiology, University of Manchester. *b.* 30 March 1931 Batley, Yorkshire. *m.* 1953 Jean Pennington; one *s.* two *d.* *Public Offices:* Consultant Radiological Adviser to the Chief Medical Officer (1986-92); President, North of England Neurological Association (1984-85); President, Manchester Medical Society (1985-86); President, European Association of Radiology (1989-91); President, Radiological Section, Royal Society of Medicine (1992-93); President, UK Rontgen Centenary Congress (1995); President, British Society of Neuroradiologists (1994-96); Dean, European College of Radiological Education (1992-96); Chairman, UK Radiology History & Heritage Charitable Trust; Commissioner, International Commission on Radiological Units. *Education:* Eccles Grammar School; University of Manchester; Postgraduate training in Manchester, Sweden and Norway. *Career Profile:* Consultant Radiologist, Derby Royal Infirmary (1961-63); Consultant Radiologist, Manchester Royal Infirmary (1963-93); Professor of Diagnostic

Radiology, University of Manchester (1975-93). *Publications/Creative Work:* Numerous (over 250 scientific papers); publications and book chapters in the field of diagnostic imaging; with particular reference to computed tomography and magnetic resonance imaging. *Prizes:* Hon Doctorate of Medicine, University of Zaragoza; Barclay Prize, British Institute of Radiology; Gold Medal, Royal College of Radiologists; Rajewski Medal, European Association of Radiology. *Societies:* Elected Academician of the Russian Academy of Medical Sciences; Hon Member, French, Swedish, Belgian, Bulgarian, Russian, Swiss, German and North American Societies of Radiology; Hon Member, American Society of Neuroradiology; Hon Member, Swedish Society of Medical Sciences, History of Medicine Section; The Royal Institution of Great Britain; Royal Society of Medicine; British Institute of Radiology; Manchester Medical Society; Manchester Literary & Philosophical Society; International Society of Magnetic Resonance in Medicine; Manchester & District Medico-Legal Society. *Recreations, Interests:* Egyptology, History of Medicine, cricket, walking. *Address:* Department of Diagnostic Radiology, The Medical School, University of Manchester, Manchester, M13 9PT; Woodend House, Strines Road, Disley, SK12 2JY *(tel:* 01663 766498).

J

JACKSON, Geoffrey William, MusB(Manchester),FRNCM,GRSM,ARMCM

Head of School of Academic Studies, Royal Northern College of Music. *b.* 20 August 1939 Glossop, Derbyshire. *m.* 1964 Josephine Jackson (née Taylor). *Public Offices:* Member of Court, University of Manchester. *Education:* Worcester College for the Blind (1950-58); University of Manchester (1958-61); Royal Northern College of Mustic (1958-61). *Career Profile:* Lecturer, Senior Lecturer, Principal Lecturer, Assistant Head of School, Head of School; Royal Manchester College of Music and Royal Northern College of Music. *Creative Work:* Lecturer in 19th and 20th century music, with special interest in Wagner; Oratorio and Recital Baritone (1959-89). *Societies:* Commanderie de Bordeaux. *Recreations, Interests:* Food, wine, chess, theatre. *Address:* Royal Northern College of Music, 124 Oxford Road, Manchester, M13 9RD(*tel:* 0161 273 6283).

JACKSON, Kenneth

Chief Executive, The Hopkinson Group plc. *b.* 23 September 1939 Dewsbury, Yorkshire. *m.* 1962 Elisabeth Joyce; one *s. Public Offices:* Non-Executive Director, Motorworld Group plc; President, British Abrasives Federation (1991-95). *Education:* Dewsbury Wheelwright Grammar School (1950-56); Batley Technical College (1956-61). *Career Profile:* Student Apprentice to Managing Director, Spencer & Halstead Ltd (1956-78); Vice-President, Carborundum Co Ltd (1978-83); Managing Director, Carbo plc (1983-93); Chief Executive, The Hopkinson Group plc (1993-). *Recreations, Interests:* Gardening, travel. *Address:* The Hopkinsons Group plc, PO Box 55, Trafford Park, Manchester, M17 1HP(*tel:* 0161 872 8291; *fax:* 0161 872 1471); Savile Ings Farm, Holywell Green, Halifax, West Yorkshire, HX4 9BS (*tel:* 01422 372608).

JACKSON, Nigel Keith, FCA

Senior Partner, Jacksons Chartered Accountants; Executive Chairman, Swift Security Systems plc. *b.* 6 August 1955 Atherton. *m.* 1983 Jane Louise; one *s.* one *d. Education:* Bolton School. *Career Profile:* Qualified with Price Waterhouse, Manchester in 1978; established own firm (1985); established Swiftt Security Systems plc (1983). *Societies:* Bolton Society of Chartered Accountants. *Recreations, Interests:* Jogging, tennis, golf. *Address:* 7/8 Bridgeman Terrace, Wigan, WN1 1SX (*tel:* 01942 824808; *fax:* 01942 820827; *e-mail*: consult@jacksons.u-net.com).

JACKSON, Peter Herbert, LLB(Hons),Solicitor

Partner, Thompson & Cooke, Stalybridge. *b.* 28 August 1940 Oldham. *m.* 1966 Jillian Ann; three *s. Public Offices:* Governor, Tameside College of Technology. *Education:* Manchester Grammar School; Manchester University. *Career Profile:* Joined present firm as Assistant Solicitor (1963), subsequently Partner and Senior Partner. *Societies:* Ashton-under-Lyne Golf Club; Dukinfield & Stalybridge Rotary Club; Ashton-under-Lyne 41 Club. *Recreations, Interests:* Golf, bridge, rotary. *Address:* Thompson & Cooke, 12 Stamford Street, Stalybridge, SK15 1LA (*tel:* 0161 338 2614; *fax:* 0161 303 8967).

JANSKI, Stefan, LRAM,LUD,DipNCSD

Director of Opera Studies, Royal Northern College of Music. *b.* 23 September 1951 London. *Education:* Tottenham County Grammar; New College of Speech & Drama; Royal Academy of Music; London University. *Career Profile:* Actor, writer, director - TIE; Director, Sadlers Wells/ENO Opera Workshop; Speech & drama teacher; Asst/Associate Director, Glyndebourne Festival & Touring Opera; Staff Director, ENO; Freelance Director: Wexford Festival Opera, Brighton Festival, Oxford & London Universities, Royal Academy of Music, Nantes Opera, Scottish Opera, Northern Ireland Opera Trust, City of London Festival, Royal Ballet of Flanders; Musicals; Los Angeles Opera; RNCM. *Publications/Creative Work:* 'The Snowman of Kashmir' (Universal Edition). *Prizes:* Manchester Evening News Theatre Award for Best Opera ('Don Carlo')(1990); Michelob/City Life Award for Best Opera ('The Maid of Orleans')(1994). *Societies:* Actors Equity. *Recreations, Interests:* Arts, travel, tennis, wine. *Address:* Royal Northern College of Music, 123 Oxford Road, Manchester, M13 9RD (*tel:* 0161 273 6283; *fax:* 0161 273 7611; *e-mail:* Postmaster@RNCM.ac.uk); 5 Hanlith Mews, Manchester, M19 2JS (*tel:* 0161 248 7391).

JAQUES, Norman Clifford

Retired; Held a Senior Lectureship in the Faculty of Art & Design, Manchester Polytechnic (now MMU) (1950-82). *b.* 23 April 1922; Manchester. *m.* 1947 Marjorie Hovell; two *s.* *Education:* Manchester College of Art and College of Technology; Associateship Diploma of Manchester College of Art; Ministry of Education Certificate in Illustration (Graduate Status). *Career Profile:* Staff Artist with Rowlinson-Broughton Advertising Agents; Freelance Artist with R P Gossop Ltd, London (1946-86). *Creative Works:* Worked professionally in prints, illustration, graphics and book design; has specialised in and taught printmaking, etching, lithography, engraving at Manchester Polytechnic; Exhibited in one man and group exhibitions of paintings and prints in London and other provincial galleries in UK and abroad. *Prizes:* Royal Manchester Institute Award of Merit; Proctor Travelling Scholarship; Giles Bequest Prize Winner in Block Printing at V & A, London; Yates Bequest Bursary to Study Art Education in Paris. *Societies:* Past President (1984-90) Manchester Academy of Fine Arts; Past Chairman (North West District), National Society for Education in Art & Design; Past member, Society of Industrial Artists & Designers in GB; Manchester Graphic Club. *Recreations, Interests:* Golf. *Address:* 6 Wardle Road, Sale, Cheshire M33 3BX (*tel:* 0161-973 6381).

JAYSON, Professor Malcolm I V, MB,BS London (1961),MRCP London (1964),FRCP London (1976),MSc Hon Manchester (1977)

Professor of Rheumatology and Director of Rheumatism Research Laboratories, University of Manchester; Honorary Consultant Rheumatologist, Hope Hospital, Salford; Royal Manchester Childrens Hospital; Manchester Royal Infirmary and Devonshire Royal Hospital, Buxton. *b.* London. *m.* 1962 Judith; two *s.* *Public Offices:* Honorary President, International Society for the Study of the Lumbar Spine, Society of Chiropodists; Honorary Rheumatologist, Royal Northern College of Music. *Education:* Middlesex Hospital Medical School; University of Manchester. *Career Profile:* Consultant & Senior Lecturer in Rheumatology, Royal National Hospital for Rheumatic Diseases, Bath and University of

Bristol. *Publications:* 'Rheumatism and Arthritis' (Pan 1991); 'Back Pain: The Facts' (Oxford University Press 1992); 'The Lumbar Spine & Back Pain' (Churchill Livingstone 1992); 'Systematic Sclerosis: Scleroderma' (John Wiley 1988); 'Collagen in Health and Disease' (Churchill Livingstone 1984); plus numerous papers and articles and chapters in books. *Prizes:* Volvo Prize for Clinical Research from the International Society for the Study of the Lumbar Spine. *Societies:* Royal Society of Medicine. *Recreations, Interests:* Reading, antique time measuring devices, trout fishing. *Address:* Rheumatic Diseases Centre, Hope Hospital, Salford M6 8HD (*tel:* 0161-787 4369); The Gate House, 8 Lancaster Road, Didsbury, Manchester M20 2TY.

JEANES, Clive Frederick, OBE(1986); BA (Law)(Oxon, 1955),MA (Oxon)

Self employed consultant in strategic planning and organisational excellence; various non-executive directorships. *b.* 7 May 1933, Harrow, Middlesex. *m.* 1956 Alison Jean Shirley Saunders; one *s.* one *d.* *Public Offices:* Director, Wigan Borough Partnership; Chairman, Excellence North West. *Education:* Wallington County Grammar School, Surrey; Christ Church, Oxford (1952-55). *Military Service:* National Service, RA (1955-57); TA, The Manchester Artillery (1957-68). *Career Profile:* Retired in 1995; formerly Managing Director, Milliken European Division (1964-95). *Publications/Creative Work:* Numerous speeches and articles on management subjects. *Recreations, Interests:* Tennis, bridge, gardening, investment.

JEFFREYS, Elizabeth (*née* Williams), IMD

Chief Executive, Marketing Manchester. *b.* 26 July 1944 Aberystwyth. *m.* D Aled Jeffreys; two *s.* one *d.* *Public Offices:* Member, Tourism Society Council; Director of Manchester Chamber of Commerce & Industry; Governor, Salford College; Member, BATO. *Education:* St Christopher School, Letchworth (1955-61); Radbrook College, Shrewsbury (1963-66). *Career Profile:* Chief Executive, Greater Manchester Visitor & Convention Bureau (1991-96); Chief Marketing & Tourism Officer, Stoke-on-Trent City Council (1989-91); Promotion & Tourism Officer, Stoke-on-Trent City Council (1986-89); Sales & Marketing Manager, Stakis Hotels & Inns, Glasgow (1984-86); Promotions Executive, Canon (UK) Ltd, Birmingham (1983-84). *Prizes:* Boss of the Year Finalist. *Recreations, Interests:* Keep fit, sport, dancing, reading, theatre. *Address:* Marketing Manchester, Churchgate House, 56 Oxford Street, Manchester, M1 6EU (*tel:* 0161 237 1010; *fax:* 0161 228 2960; *e-mail:* gmvcb@mcri.poptel.org.uk). *Additional Information:* President, Art Cities in Europe Vice-President, Federation of European Cities Tourist Offices.

JELLICOE, Colin

Painter; Gallery Director. *b.* 1 November 1942; Withington, Manchester. *Education:* Heald Place School; Regional College of Art, Manchester (1959). *Career Profile:* Opened the first gallery on Claremont Road, Rusholme, Manchester (1963), Partnership with Alan Behar (1968) and the gallery moved to 82 Portland St, Manchester 1. *Creative Works:* Exhibitions: various shows (1964-79); The Manchester Academy (1970, 1973, 1975, 1976, 1981, 1984, 1985, 1988, 1989, 1992, 1995); Bath Festival Contemporary Art Fair (1981, 1983); Royal Academy Summer Exhibition (1981); Retrospective Exhibition (1960-81) Stockport Art Gallery (1981); Drawings, Paintings, Graphics (1971-81) Salford Art Gallery

(1981-82); Watermill Theatre Bagnor Newbury (1983); Edinburgh Festival Fringe (1983-85); Contact Theatre, Manchester (1983-84); International Contemporary Art Fair, Barbican Arts Centre, London (1984); Cheshire County Council Touring Exhibition (1984); Landscapes and Townscapes, Lyric Theatre, Hammersmith (1984); (with Michael Goddard) Royal Exchange Theatre, Manchester (1985); International Contemporary Art Fair, Olympia, London (1985-86); Mixed Show L.S Lowry Bargoed Appeal, Salford Art Gallery (1988); Blackheath Galler, London (1989); Group Show, Dukes Oak Gallery, Sandback (1994); Mixed Shows, Sally Brown Gallery, Marple (1994, 95, 96); Dukes Oak Gallery, Sandbach (1995). *Recreations, Interests:* Cinema special interestel: the American 'A' and 'B' Western from 1920-1960. *Address:* 82 Portland Street, Manchester M1 (*tel*: 0161-236 2716).

JESSUP, Margaret Dorothy (*née* Walsh), MB ChB Manchester (1949),MRCGP (1972),BA Open (1988)

Retired. *b.* 7 January 1925; Blackburn, Lancashire. *m.* 1951 Geoffrey Jessup; two *s.* three *d. Education:* Blackburn High School for Girls (1930-38); Penrhos College, Colwyn Bay (1938-40); Dr Williams School, Dolgelley (1940-43); Manchester University Medical School (1943-49). *Career Profile:* Principal, General Medical Practice, Wythenshawe (1966-85); Member, Manchester Local Medical Committee (1972-84); General Practitioners Member, Manchester Family Practitioner Committee (1981-84); Clinical Medical Officer (South Manchester Health Authority) (1976-89). *Societies:* Charles O'Neill Medical Club; Manchester Luncheon Club. *Recreations, Interests:* Reading, classical music, Elder, United Reformed Church. *Address:* 27 Oakwood Lane, Bowdon, Altrincham, Cheshire WA14 3DL (*tel:* 0161-941 6024).

JEWELL, Robert Anthony, FCII (1965),CIP (1989)

Managing Director (Manchester), Bradstock Insurance Brokers Ltd; Chairman, Trafford Park Business Watch Ltd. *b.* 20 April 1940; Exeter, Devon. *m.* 1972 Nora; one *s.* two *d. Public Offices:* Member, Economic Committee, MCCI; Member, Salford Safer City & Corporate Risk Management Group. *Education:* King Edward VI GS, Southampton (1951-55); The Stockport Grammar School (1955-59). *Career Profile:* Royal Insurance, Manchester 12 years, Nottingham 2 years (1959-74); Director, Stewart Wrightson (Midlands) Ltd (1974-78), Manchester (1979-81); Cunliffe Group Insurance Services Ltd, Managing Director (1989-91); Bradstock Blunt (NW) Ltd, Managing Director (1991-). *Prizes:* Manchester Insurance Institute, Jubilee Prizewinner (1965). *Societies:* St James's Club, Manchester; Manchester Literary & Philosophical Society. *Recreations, Interests:* Music and opera, political & economic affairs, community safety and security. *Address:* Bradstock Insurance Brokers Ltd, Hanover House, Charlotte Street, Manchester, M1 4FD (*tel:* 0161 228 0721, *fax:* 0161 236 9141); 28 Devonshire Park Road, Davenport Park, Stockport SK2 6JW (*tel:* 0161-483 7796).

JOBSON, Roy, BEd Dunelm,DPA London,MEd CNAA

Chief Education Officer, Manchester City Council. *b.* 2 June 1947; Corbridge, Northumberland. *m.* 1971 Maureen; one *s.* two *d. Public Offices:* Advisor to Association Metropolitan Authorities; Deputy Chair, Association of Chief Education Officers; Member

of Royal Society of Arts. *Education:* Bedlington County Grammar School, Northumberland; University of Durham; Newcastle-upon-Tyne Polytechnic; Sunderland Polytechnic. *Career Profile:* Deputy Education Officer, Manchester; Assistant Director of Education, Gateshead; Assistant Secretary, East Midland Regional Examinations Board; Teacher. *Societies:* Society of Education Officers. *Recreations, Interests:* Family, music/brass bands, church work. *Address:* Education Department, Cumberland House, Crown Square, Manchester M60 3BB (*tel:* 0161-234 7001).

JOHNSON, Revd Brian

Chaplain, HM Prison, Manchester. *Address:* HM Prison, Southall Street, Manchester, M60 9AH (*tel:* 0161 834 8626).

JOHNSON, Kathleen (*née* Booth), BA,Solicitor

Justices Chief Executive and Justices Clerk, Oldham Magistrates Court. *b.* 18 July 1956 Manchester. *m.* 1988 Peter. *Education:* Wright Robinson High School; Manchester Polytechnic. *Career Profile:* Justices Legal Adviser (1974-87)(1989-96); Richardson Batty & Eastwoods (1987-89). *Societies:* Secretary, Cancer Relief Macmillan Fund Local Committee (West Yorks). *Recreations, Interests:* Golf. *Address:* Oldham Magistrates' Court, St Domingo Place, West Street, Oldham, OL1 1QE (*tel:* 0161 620 2331; *fax:* 0161 652 0172).

JOHNSON, Robert William Greenwood, MB, BS Dunelm (1965),MS (with Distinction) Newcastle (1973),FRCS London (1970), FRCS Edin (1994)

Consultant Surgeon, Manchester Royal Infirmary; Hon Reader in Surgery, University of Manchester; Hon Consultant Surgeon, Royal Manchester Childrens Hospital. *b.* 15 March 1942; Reigate, Surrey. *m.* 1966 Dr Carolyn Mary Johnson; one *s.* one *d.* *Public Offices:* President, British Transplantation Society; Council, Society for Organ Sharing. *Education:* Licensed Victuallers' School; Durham University, College of Medicine. *Career Profile:* Assistant Professor of Surgery, University of California, San Francisco. *Publications:* Papers and chapters on transplant surgery and renovascular hypertension. *Prizes:* Goyder Scholarship in Clinical Medicine and Surgery; Fullbright Scholar; Hunterian Professor of Surgery, Royal College of Surgeons. *Societies:* Association of Surgeons; British Transplant Society; European Society of Transplant Surgeons; The Transplant Society. *Recreations, Interests:* Tennis, golf, skiing, theatre and opera. *Address:* The Royal Infirmary, Oxford Road, Manchester M13 9WL (*tel:* 0161-276 4413); 'Evergreen', 41 Chapel Lane, Hale Barns, Cheshire WA15 0AJ (*tel:* 0161-980 8840).

JOHNSTON, Arthur, MA Oxon (1949),DPhil Oxon (1955)

Retired. *b.* 24 November 1924; Bradford, Yorkshire. *m.* 1951 Charlotte Ware; two *s.* two *d.* *Education:* Hutton Grammar School (1936-42); The Queen's College, Oxford (1946-51). *War Service:* RAF (1943-46). *Career Profile:* Lecturer in English, University of London (1951-65); Rendel Professor of English, University of Wales (1965-75); Principal, City of Manchester College of Higher Education (1976-82). *Publications:* 'Enchanted Ground' (1964); Editions of Bacon, 'Advancement of Learning' (1974); 'The Poems of Gray and

Collins' (1967); articles on Elizabethan and on 18th century literature; 'Bede and Aethelfric' (1988). *Societies:* Alcuin Club; Bibliographical Society. *Recreations, Interests:* Music, gardening, walking, theatre, book collecting, liturgy, Anglo-Saxon history. *Address:* 165 Hale Road, Hale, Altrincham, Cheshire WA15 8RX (*tel:* 0161-928 5101).

JOHNSTON, T Keith, LLB(Hons)

Partner & Member of the Management Board of Addleshaw Sons & Latham. *b.* 3 July 1952 Ormskirk, Lancs. *m.* 1974 Alison; two *d. Education:* Bootle Grammar School; London University (External). *Career Profile:* Trained in Manchester; joined Addleshaw Sons & Latham (1976) Associate (1979), Partner (1981); Head of PFI Unit, Addleshaw Sons & Latham. *Societies:* The Law Society; The Manchester Law Society. *Recreations, Interests:* League badminton, travel, armchair spectator of sports, chess. *Address:* Addleshaw Sons & Latham, Dennis House, Marsden Street, Manchester, M2 1JD (*tel:* 0161 832 5994; *fax:* 0161 832 2250). *Additional Information:* Governor, The Grange School. Former Director of the Norton Rose M5 Group Limited. Chairman, North West Company Secretaries' Forum.

JOLLY, Patrick Edmund, LLB,Solicitor

Partner, Corporate Finance, Hammond Suddards, Manchester. *b.* 20 September 1965 Lytham St Annes. *m.* Lisa. *Education:* Sedbergh School; University of Hull. *Recreations, Interests:* Sailing, golf, wine. *Address:* Hammond Suddards, Trinity Court, 16 John Dalton Street, Manchester, M60 8HS (*tel:* 0161 830 5000; *fax:* 0161 830 5001).

JONES, David Geraint, BSc Wales (1949),PhD Wales (1953),CEng (1982),FIEE (1982)

Retired. *b.* 25 April 1929; Treherbert, Glamorgan. *m.* 1956 Gwenda May Roberts. *Education:* Rhondda County School for Boys, Porth, Glamorgan; University College of North Wales, Bangor. *Public Offices:* Chairman, Engineering Council, North West Region (voluntary appointment); Governor, Manchester College of Arts & Technology. *Career Profile:* Principal Consultant, Management & Technology Services; Manager, Relay Manufacturing Unit, GEC General Signal Ltd; Manager, Railway Signals Unit, GEC Traction Ltd; Assistant Managing Director, Micanite & Insulators Co Ltd; Director & General Manager, Electrical Metals Division, GEC; Director & General Manager, Elmet Alloys Ltd; Physicist/Metallurgist, Trafford Laboratories, GEC Power Engineering Ltd; Physicist, Medical Research Council, Harwell. *Publications:* 'The Erosion Resistance of Steam Turbine Blade and Shield Materials' (2nd Dornier International Conference, Meersburg). *Societies:* Hallé Concerts Society; GEC Overseas Club. *Recreations, Interests:* Rugby Football, music. *Address:* 11 Stonemead Avenue, Hale Barns, Altrincham, Cheshire WA15 0BQ (*tel:* 0161-980 5077).

JONES, Eileen Frances, (*née* Wood), BA(Hons)

Network Director, Central Office of Information. *b.* 14 February 1950 Morecambe. *m.* 1969 Robert Brian; one *d. Education:* Larkhill Convent, Preston; Manchester Polytechnic; School of Life!. *Career Profile:* Journalism: Morecambe Guardian, Lancashire Evening Post, Assistant News Editor, Oldham Evening Chronicle; joined Government Information

Service (1978); became COI Network Director, North West (1990-). *Recreations, Interests:* Gardening, cookery, learning Spanish. *Address:* COI, 27th Floor, Sunley Tower, Piccadilly Plaza, Manchester, M1 4BD (*tel:* 0161 952 4513; *fax:* 0161 236 9443).

JONES, John Bannister, BCom Liverpool (1952)

Director, Packaging Automation Ltd (1990-), Partner, Pannell Kerr Forster, Chartered Accountants (1961-90), Senior Partner (1978-90). *b.* 9 December 1929; Birkenhead. *m.* Jonquil; two *s. Education:* Birkenhead School; Liverpool University. *Military Service:* National Service, Royal Army Pay Corps (1954-56). *Societies:* Manchester Club (1962-87) - President (1979-80). *Recreations, Interests:* Music, travel, walking. *Address:* 3 Goodrington Road, Handforth, Wilmslow SK9 3AT (*tel:* 01625-532883).

JONES, Peter Emerson, Master Building, City & Guilds, London Institute

Chairman, Emerson Holdings Group of Companies. *b.* Manchester. *m.* Audrey; two *s. Education:* Mount Carmel School, Blackley; Mill Street School of Building; Manchester College of Technology. *Career Profile:* Founder and Owner of the Emerson Group (P E Jones (Contractors) Ltd) (1958). *Societies:* Catenian Wilmslow Circle No.205; Life Member, Manchester Wheelers; CBI; Institute of Directors; Manchester Literary & Philosophical Society; St James's Club; The Tytherington Club; Penina Golf Club, Portugal; Club Barrington, Portugal; Quarry Bank Mill 1784 Patrons Club; Patron, Manchester City Art Gallery; Macclesfield Chamber of Commerce; Stockport Chamber of Commerce; The Economic Development Commission of Mid-Florida; Resort Condominium International; Unionist Club, Alderley Edge; Macclesfield Conservatives Patrons Club; Congleton Conservatives Patrons Club; Wilmslow Business Club. *Recreations, Interests:* Golf, walking, keep-fit, swimming, cycling, snooker, DIY, building restoration and preserving our heritage. *Address:* Emerson Developments (Holdings) Ltd, Emerson House, Heyes Lane, Alderley Edge, SK9 7LF (*tel:* 01625 488412; *fax:* 01625 588271). *Additional Information:* Non-Executive Member, South Manchester Hospital Trust, Chairman of Single Site Working Group and Chairman of Private Finance Initiative Member Group. Member, The Board of Governors, Manchester Metropolitan University. President of Manchester YMCA. Member, Advisory Panel for The Manufacturing and Construction Industries. Vice-President of the elected Council of the East Cheshire Hospice.

JONES, Philip Edward, MB,ChB,MSc,MD,FRCP

Medical Director, South Manchester University Hospital Trust; Consultant Physician & Gastro-Enterologist, South Manchester University Hospital Trust. *b.* 5 October 1945 Manchester. *m.* 1972 Bernadette Catherine; three *d. Education:* Manchester Grammar School; Birmingham University Medical School. *Career Profile:* House Physician & House Surgeon, Dudley Rd Hospital, Birmingham; Registrar, University College Hospital & Whittington Hospital, London; Registrar & Research Fellow, Hammersmith Hospital, London; Tutor in Medicine, Royal Post Graduate Medical School, London; Senior Registrar, Manchester Royal Infirmary, North Manchester General Hospital. *Publications/Creative Work:* Papers on general medicine and gastro-enterological topics. *Societies:* British Society of Gastro-enterology; North Western Regional Association of

Physicians; North Western Gastro-enterological Society. *Recreations, Interests:* Music, swimming, watching sport. *Address:* Department of Medicine, Wythenshawe Hospital SMUHT, Southmoor Road, Manchester, M23 9LT (*tel:* 0161 291 2394; *fax:* 0161 291 2635).

JONES, Roger Kenneth, BA(Econ)(Hons)(Manchester),Barrister-at-Law(Gray's Inn)

Secretary, Cooperative Wholesale Society Ltd. *b.* 10 September 1947 Thorpe-Next-Norwich. *m.* 1972 Ruth; three *d. Education:* Abbeydale Grammar School, Sheffield; Manchester University. *Career Profile:* Assistant Secretary (to 1983), Manchester Ship Canal Company; Deputy Secretary, CWS (1983-96) and Secretary (1991-96) The Cooperative Bank plc. *Publications:* 'The World of Cooperative Enterprise' (Plunkett Foundation, 1990). *Address:* Cooperative Wholesale Society Ltd, PO Box 53, New Century House, Manchester, M60 4ES (*tel:* 0161 834 1212).

JONES, Stephen Morris, BA(Hons)

Chief Executive, Wigan MBC. *b.* 12 March 1948 Chigwell. *m.* 1970 Rosemary; one *s.* two *d. Public Offices:* Clerk, Greater Manchester Fire & Civil Defence Authority. *Education:* Buckhurst Hill County High School; Manchester University. *Career Profile:* Project Manager in private and public sectors; Chief Executive Blackburn Borough Council. *Publications/Creative Work:* Solace Think Tank Publications; Chairman, Solace International. *Societies:* Solace; Cheetham Arms Monday Club. *Recreations, Interests:* Wine, walking, sport spectator. *Address:* New Town Hall, Library Street, Wigan, WN1 1YN(*tel:* 01942 827001; *fax:* 01942 827365).

JUMP, Graeme Kevin, ACIArb,Solicitor

Partner, Mace & Jones Grundy Kershaw. *b.* 22 February 1945 Birkenhead. *m.* 1969 Jenny; two *d. Education:* Birkenhead School; Wellington School, Bebington, Wirral. *Career Profile:* Admitted as a Solicitor (1969); Chairman, Neston & District Round Table (1976-77); Member, National Committee of Young Solicitors (1976-80); Chairman, Liverpool Young Solicitors Group (1980-81); Hon Treasurer, Liverpool Medico-Legal Society (1982-85); Associate, Chartered Institute of Arbitrators (1987); Licensed Insolvency Practitioner (1989); President, Manchester Law Society (1991); Director, Solicitors Indemnity Fund (1992); Hon Treasurer, Manchester Law Society (1995); Vice President, Insolvency Lawyers Association (1995). *Societies:* St James's Club, Manchester; Rotary Club of Manchester; Manchester Luncheon Club; Manchester & District Medico-Legal Society; North of England Zoological Society. *Recreations, Interests:* Walking, swimming, skiing, trying to play golf! *Address:* Mace & Jones Grundy Kershaw, 14 Oxford Court, Manchester M2 3WQ (*tel:* 0161 236 2244).

JUNGMAYR, Hermann Werner Justin, BA (Hons)(Univ. of Sheffield, 1975),MTP (Univ. of Manchester, 1979),MRTPI,FRICS

Chairman, Corinya Holdings Ltd; Chairman (non-exec), Golfrate Group Ltd; Director (non-exec), North Manchester Health Care Trust; Director (non-exec), P Casey (Developments) Ltd, Powerview Ltd. *b.* 19 April 1954 Linz a.d. Donau, Austria. *m.* 1979 Helen

Lester; two *s.* one *d. Education:* Greenhill Grammar School, Oldham (Kaskenmoor Comprehensive). *Career Profile:* Local government; main board positions with Peel Holdings plc, Manchester Ship Canal Co; currently, family owned property development and investment companies; consultancy via non-executive directorships. *Societies:* Knights of St Columba; Catenian Association. *Recreations, Interests:* Gardening, riding, shooting, reading. *Address:* 746 Manchester Road, Castleton, Rochdale, OL11 3AQ (*tel:* 01706 49073; *fax:* 01706 46020); Corinya, Fox Hill Road, Castleton, Rochdale, OL1 2XN (*tel:* 01706 32376).

K

KANARIS, Andreas Demetri, BSc(Hons)Manchester(1955),PhDManchester(1961), FInstP

Managing Director, Delta Travel. *b.* 23 May 1928; Piyi, Cyprus. *m.* 1961 Vivi Gouda; two *s.* three *d. Public Offices:* Honorary Commissioner for the Republic of Cyprus in Manchester. *Education:* Manchester University (1955-61). *Career Profile:* Instructor of Physics, Columbia University (1961-64); Lecturer in Physics, Manchester University (1964-80). *Publications:* Several research publications in physics journals. *Recreations, Interests:* Travel, reading, community affairs. *Address:* University Precinct, Oxford Road, Manchester M13 9RN *(tel:* 0161-274 4444); Fallibroome House, 68 Macclesfield Road, Prestbury, Cheshire SK10 4BH *(tel:* 01625-828144).

KARCZEWSKI-SLOWIKOWSKI, Janusz D M, MSc,BEd(Hons),TCert

Academic Registrar, The Manchester Metropolitan University. *b.* 26 September 1950 England. *Public Offices:* Director & Treasurer, Alcohol Concern, National Agency on Alcohol Abuse; Director & Treasurer, the Greater Manchester & Lancashire Council on Alcohol. *Education:* Sedgehill Comprehensive School, London; Didsbury College of Education, Manchester; Sheffield City Polytechnic. *Career Profile:* Various senior administrative positions, the Manchester Metropolitan University (1974-). *Societies:* Member of the IEC Wine Society; International Lecturer on Furniture History (NADFAS); VIP Member of several Manchester & London night clubs; the Furniture History Society of GB. *Recreations, Interests:* Wine, literature, music, furniture history, working in the non-statutory sector on alcohol and substance misuse, horse racing, contemporary night clubs. *Address:* The Manchester Metropolitan University, All Saints, Manchester, M15 6BH *(tel:* 0161 247 1030; *fax:* 0161 247 6311); 21 Range Road, Whalley Range, Manchester, M16 8FS *(tel:* 0161 227 9979). *Additional Information:* Former President, The Manchester Municipal Officers' Guild (1980-88) Consultant on Antique Furniture; Financial, Legal and Personnel Consultant to non-statutory organisations.

KAUFMAN, Right Hon Gerald Bernard, PC (1978); MA Oxford (1958)

MP (Manchester, Gorton); Chairman, House of Commons National Heritage Select Committee. *b.* 21 June 1930; Leeds. *Public Offices:* Under-Secretary of State, Environment (1974-75); Under-Secretary of State, Industry (1975); Minister of State, Industry (1975-79). *Education:* Leeds Council Schools (1933-41); Leeds Grammar School (1941-49); The Queen's College, Oxford (1949-53). *Career Profile:* Assistant General Secretary, Fabian Society (1953-55); Political Staff, Daily Mirror (1955). *Publications:* 'How to Live Under Labour' (co-author) (1964); 'The Left' (Editor) (1966); 'To Build The Promised Land' (1973); 'How to be a Minister' (1980); 'Renewal' (Editor) (1983); 'My Life in the Silver Screen' (1985); 'Inside the Promised Land' (1986); 'Meet Me in St Louis' (1994). *Societies:* Gorton Labour Club; East Levenshulme Cricket Club; British Film Institute. *Recreations, Interests:* Cinema, opera, music, theatre, crime fiction, travel. *Address:* House of Commons, London SW1A 0AA *(tel:* 0171-219 5145).

KAY, Clifford Ralph, CBE(1977); MD,PhD,FRCGP,FFFP(Hon)

Consultant (former Director), Royal College of General Practitioners, Manchester Research Unit; Counsellor, Medical Insurance Agency Professional Indemnity Insurance Scheme; General Practitioner (retired) Barlow Medical Centre, Didsbury; Director, Royal College of General Practitioners Medicines Surveillance Organisation; Member of Council, Medical Insurance Agency Ltd; Member, NHS Executive Information Management & Technology Forum; Member, Scientific Advisory Committee, Faculty of Family Planning; Member, Supervisory Board, NHS Centre for Coding & Classification and National Case-Mix Office. *b.* 17 October 1927 Frodsham, Cheshire. *m.* 1950 Yvette Adele Hytner; one *s.* one *d. Education:* King's School, Chester; University of Liverpool; University of Manchester. *Military Service:* Squadron Leader, RAF Medical Branch. *Career Profile:* Founder, General Medical Practice, Didsbury (1955); Founding Director, Royal College of General Practitioners Manchester Research Unit (1968); Visiting Professor, Universities of Edmonton and Calgary (1987). *Publications/Creative Work:* 'Oral Contraceptives and Health' (Pitman Medical, 1974); numerous publications on oral contraception, medical computing, clinical research. *Prizes:* Sir Charles Hasting Research Prize (1961); Mackenzie Medal, Royal College of Physicians of Edinburgh (1975); Foundation Council Award, Royal College of General Practitioners (1978); Hippocrates Medal, Societas Inernationalis Medicinae Generalis (1990); Mackenzie Lecturer, Royal College of Practitioners (1979); Gregory Pincus Memorial Lecturer, Detroit, USA (1982). *Societies:* Manchester Medical Society (President, 1988-89); British Medical Association. *Recreations, Interests:* Photography, gardening, computers. *Address:* 12 Dene Park, Didsbury, Manchester, M20 2GF *(tel:* 0161 445 9686; *fax:* 0161 434 2040) *(e-mail:* 100530 .262@compuserve.com).

KAY, John Frederick

Senior Partner, Molesworths Solicitors; President, Rochdale Chamber of Commerce, Trade & Industry. *b.* 14 November 1946; Manchester. *m.* 1976 Elisabeth; two *d. Public Offices:* Past-President, Rochdale Law Society; Past Chairman, Northern Branch, Society for Computers and Law; Director & Legal Advisor, Rochdale TEC (1990-), Rochdale Chamber of Commerce, Trade & Industry (1988-), Rochdale Enterprise Agency (1989-), Rochdale Business Bureau (1993-), Rochdale Business Link Ltd (1995-), Rochdale Challenge Company Ltd (1996-); Trustee, Rochdale Deaf Society (1988-). *Education:* Littleborough Central School; Mostyn House School, The Wirral, Cheshire; Wrekin College, Wellington, Shropshire. *Societies:* IOD; Rochdale Rotary Club; Life Member, Rochdale Conservative Club. *Recreations, Interests:* Modern technology. *Address:* Molesworths, 3/11 Drake Street, Rochdale, Lancs OL16 1RH *(tel:* 01706-356666; *fax:* 01706 354681; *e-mail:* john.kay@zen.co.uk); Bent House, Halifax Road, Littleborough, Lancs OL15 0JB *(tel:* 01706-376775).

KEELING, Damian John, BA,ACA

Managing Partner, Clark Whitehill, Manchester. *b.* 1 August 1957 Huddersfield. *m.* 1987 Pauline; two *d. Education:* Wolverhampton Grammar School; William Hulme's Grammar School; University of Kent (Canterbury)(1976-79). *Career Profile:* Clark Pixley (1979-82); Clark Whitehill (1982-)(Partner, 1989). *Recreations, Interests:* Cars. *Address:* Clark

Whitehill, Arkwright House, Parsonage Gardens, Manchester, M3 2LE *(tel:* 0161 834 1654; *fax:* 0161 839 0282; *e-mail:* Keelingdj@clarkwhitehill.uk).

KEEN, Paul, BSc(SocSci)(Bristol),MIPD

Director, Skills & Enterprise, Government Office for the North West. *b.* 7 October 1951 Aylesbury. *m.* 1978 Clare; two *s. Education:* Hampton Grammar School; University of Bristol. *Career Profile:* Joined the Department of Employment in 1974 - policy responsibilities in London; subsequently with the Manpower Services Commission, Sheffield; attached to the Australian Government (Department of Employment & Industrial Relations, Canberra)(1984-86); development and launch of 'Investors in People' (1989-93), acting Chief Executive, Investors in People (UK)(1993); Regional Director (NW), Department of Employment (1993-94); present position (1994-). *Publications/Creative Work:* Various articles in training and personnel journal; created and edited the Skills Bulletin (1986-89). *Prizes:* Economics Scholarship (1972-74)(University of Bristol). *Societies:* Hallamshire Harriers & Athletics Club; Ranalagh Harriers; Association of First Division Civil Servants. *Recreations, Interests:* Road and cross country running, walking, reading. *Address:* Government Office for the North West, Washington House, New Bailey Street, Manchester, M3 5ER *(tel:* 0161 952 4472; *fax:* 0161 952 4169).

KEEN, Ronald Ivan, BA MB ChB Sheffield,MRCS,LRCP,FRCA

Hon Consultant Anaesthetist, Central Manchester Health Authority *b.* 22 December 1927; Zilina, Czechoslovakia. *m.* 1952 Joyce Makin; two *s.* one *d. Education:* Mercers' School, London; Cambridge & County High School; University of Sheffield. *Military Service:* National Service, RAMC. *Career Profile:* Consultant Anaesthetist, Newcastle-upon-Tyne; Training Posts in Cardiff, Nottingham and Sheffield. *Publications:* 'Positioning the Surgical Patient' (with J M Anderton and R Neave) (Butterworth Scientific 1988); chapters and papers on various topics related to anaesthesia and epidemiology. *Prizes:* Undergraduate prizes at Sheffield; Registrar's Prize, Sheffield & E Midlands Society of Anaesthetists. *Societies:* Manchester Lit. & Phil.; BMA; Wilmslow Golf Club; Manchester Luncheon Club. *Recreations, Interests:* Travel, history, golf, reading, music. *Address:* 8 Bramway, Bramhall, Stockport, Cheshire SK7 2AP *(tel:* 0161-439 6942).

KEENLESIDE, David Graham, OBE; ACMA

Consultant. *b.* 1 July 1939; Manchester. *m.* 1963 Jennifer M Hudson; one *s.* one *d. Education:* Chorlton Technical High School. *Career Profile:* Bursar, UMIST (1977-93); Deputy Finance Officer, University of Liverpool (1971-77); Management Accountant, University of Salford (1968-71); Local Government (before 1968). *Publications:* 'Management Accounting in British Universities' (Heinemann) (Part of 'Management Accounting in Public Sector'). *Societies:* Mellor & Townscliffe Golf Club. *Recreations, Interests:* Golf, music, countryside, dinghy sailing. *Address:* UMIST, PO Box 88, Sackville Street, Manchester M60 1QD *(tel:* 0161-236 3311); 5 Hollins Mount, Marple Bridge, Stockport SK6 5BX *(tel:* 0161-449 8875).

KEMPSTER, Charles John Edgar, MA Cambridge (1957),PhD Cambridge (1958),CPhys, MInstP

Retired. *b.* 13 August 1932; Hastings. *m.* 1963 Mary Kathleen Cox; one *s.* two *d.* *Education:* Alcester Grammar School; Clare College, Cambridge. *Career Profile:* Research Fellow, California Institute of Science & Technology (1957-58); Lecturer, University of Adelaide (1959-67); Lecturer, Department of Pure & Applied Physics, UMIST (1968-93);. *Publications:* Scientific Papers. *Societies:* Manchester Literary & Philosophical Society. *Recreations, Interests:* Church matters, walking, books and reading. *Address:* 17 Trafford Road, Alderley Edge, Cheshire SK9 7NN *(tel:* 01625-584223).

KENNEDY, Sir Francis, MBE(1958),CBE(1977),KCMG(1986); BA(Hons)(Manchester)

Chairman, British Airways Regional. *b.* 9 May 1926 Withnell, Lancs. *m.* 1957 Anne O'Malley; two *s.* two *d.* *Public Offices:* Chancellor, University of Central Lancashire. *Education:* Manchester and London Universities. *War Service:* Royal Navy (1944-47). *Career Profile:* HM Colonial Service (1953-63); HM Diplomatic Service (1963-86); British Airways (1986-). *Societies:* Lancashire Cricket Club. *Recreations, Interests:* Cricket, golf, gardening.

KENNEDY, Michael, OBE(1981); FRNCM(1981),MA(hc)(Manchester, 1975)

Chief Music Critic, Sunday Telegraph. *b.* 19 February 1926 Chorlton-cum-Hardy. *Education:* Berkhamsted School. *War Service:* Royal Navy (1943-46). *Career Profile:* On staff of The Daily Telegraph, Manchester since 1941, with exception of war service; Northern Editor (1960-86); Staff Music Critic (1950-); Appointed to Sunday Telegraph (1989-). *Publications/Creative Work:* The Hallé Tradition (1960); The Works of Ralph Vaughan Williams (1964); Portrait of Elgar (1968); Portrait of Manchester (1971); Barbirolli (1971); History of Royal Manchester College of Music (1972); Mahler (1974); Strauss (1976); Adrian Boult (1987); Portrait of Walton (1989); Oxford Dictionary of Music (1985); The Hallé 1858-1983 (1982). *Societies:* Athenaeum, London. *Recreations, Interests:* Cricket. *Address:* Longbridge Road, Trafford Park, Manchester, M17 1SL *(tel:* 0161 872 5939).

KENWORTHY, Michael Brian, BA(Hons)

Partner, Addleshaw Sons & Latham (1990-). *b.* 16 March 1956 Liscard, Wallasey. *m.* 1985 Hilary; one *d.* *Education:* Park High School, Birkenhead (1967-74); University of Keele (1974-78); College of Law, Chester (1978-79). *Career Profile:* Articled Clerk, Council of the City of Chester (1979-81); Solicitor, Council of the City of Chester (1981-84); Senior Assistant Solicitor, Ellesmere Port & Neston Borough Council (1984-86); Addleshaw Sons & Latham, Solicitor (1986-), Partner (1990-). *Societies:* St James Club, Manchester. *Recreations, Interests:* Dinghy sailing, hill walking, English history. *Address:* Addleshaw Sons & Latham, Dennis House, Marsden Street, Manchester, M2 1JD *(tel:* 0161 832 5994; *fax:* 0161 832 2250).

KENYON, Christopher George, MA Oxon

Chairman, William Kenyon & Sons Ltd. *b.* 19 August 1939; Manchester. *m.* 1962 Margaret; two *s.* *Public Offices:* Chairman of Council, University of Manchester; Member of Board, Manchester Business School; Deputy Chairman of Governors, Manchester

Grammar School; Governor, Royal Northern College of Music; Chairman of Feoffees, Chetham's Hospital and Library; Governor, Chetham's School of Music. *Education:* Mostyn House (1947-53); Stowe School (1953-58); Christ Church, Oxford (1958-61). *Career Profile:* Chairman, North West Civic Trust (1983-88); Chairman, North Regional Advisory Board, National Westminster Bank plc (1990-92). *Recreations, Interests:* Mountain walking, European history and literature. *Address:* William Kenyon & Sons Ltd, Dukinfield, Cheshire SK14 4RP *(tel:* 0161-308 2721).

KENYON, Sir George Henry, Knight Bachelor (1976),LLD Manchester (1980),JP (1959-82), DL Cheshire (1969-),DL Gtr Manchester (1984-); BSc (Hons) Manchester

Non-Executive Director (retd 1994), William Kenyon & Sons Ltd. *b.* 10 July 1912; Hyde, Cheshire. *m.* 1938 Christine Dorey Brentnall (decd 1996); two *s.* one *d. Public Offices:* High Sheriff, Cheshire (1973-74); Chairman of Council, Manchester University (1972-80); Treasurer, Manchester University (1970-72) (1980-82); Chairman of Bench, South Tameside (1974-82). *Education:* Fulneck School (1919-22); Mostyn House School (1923-26); Radley College (1926-29); Manchester University (1929-32). *Career Profile:* Chairman, William Kenyon & Sons Ltd (1961-82), Tootal Ltd (1976-79), Williams & Glyns Bank (1978-83). *Creative Works:* General autobiography. *Prizes:* Trevithick Scholarship (University); Scholarship to Radley. *Recreations, Interests:* Travel, reading history. *Address:* William Kenyon & Sons Ltd, Dukinfield, Cheshire; Limefield House, Hyde, Cheshire SK14 1DN.

KENYON, Margaret (*née* Parry), MA Oxon

Headmistress, Withington Girls' School *b.* 19 June 1940; Liverpool. *m.* 1962 Christopher; two *s. Public Offices:* ; President, Girls' Schools Association (1994); Member of Court, University of Manchester; Member of the Granada Foundation Board. *Education:* Merchant Taylors', Crosby (1951-59); Somerville College, Oxford (1959-62). *Address:* Withington Girls' School, Wellington Road, Manchester *(tel*: 0161-224 1077).

KERR, Bryan, Chartered Accountant

Group Finance Director, Ciba-Geigy plc, Macclesfield. *b.* 12 April 1943; Edinburgh, Scotland. *m.* 1970 Jane; two *s.* one *d. Education:* Daniel Stewarts College, Edinburgh (1948-61). *Career Profile:* Ciba-Geigy, UK - Group Treasurer, Group Controller; Ciba-Geigy, Switzerland - Divisional Controller. *Societies:* Alderley Edge Tennis & Squash Club. *Recreations, Interests:* Rugby, golf and classical music. *Address:* Ciba-Geigy plc, Hulley Road, Macclesfield SK10 2NX *(tel:* 01625-421933).

KERSHAW, Walter, BA(Hons)(Dunelm)

Artist and Mural Painter. *b.* 7 December 1940 Rochdale. *Education:* De La Salle College (1951-58); Durham University (1958-62). *Military Service:* War Artist, Kings Regiment (Northern Ireland, 1976). *Career Profile:* Pioneer of large scale external murals in UK and South America. *Publications/Creative Work:* Murals for Trafford Park Development Corporation (1982, 1993); Manchester United Football Club (1987); The Cultura Inglesa in Sao Paulo and Recife (1983-87); Dartington College (1982); Hollingworth Lake Information Centre (1985-96); The Italian Consulate, Manchester (1991); Wensum Lodge, Norwich (1988); Sarajevo, Bosnia (1996). *Prizes:* Gulbenkian Foundation Award (1977-

79). *Societies:* Littleborough Cricket Club. *Recreations, Interests:* Travel and sport. *Address:* Studio, 193 Todmorden Road, Littleborough, OL15 9EG *(tel:* 01706 379653). *Additional Information:* Exhibited at the Tate, Serpentine, National Portrait Gallery, V&A; Films for: the Arts Council (1975), BBC2 (1975), BBC1 (1983), GLOBO TV Brazil (1983), Carlyle Video, London (1986), Anglia TV (1988), Channel 4 (1995), Bosnia TV (1996), BSB (1996). Lectured on Public Art for the British Council at the Universities of Bremen, Hamburg, Osnabruck, Berlin, Recife and Brasilia.

KESSEL, Professor William Ivor Neil, MA, MD Cambridge,MSc Manchester,FRCP (1967),FRCPE (1968),FRC Psych (1972)

Emeritus Professor, University of Manchester. *b.* 10 February 1925. *m.* 1958 Pamela Veronica Joyce Boswell; one *s.* one *d. Public Offices:* Member, NWRHA (1974-77); Member, GMC (1974-95); Member, Home Office Advisory Council on Misuse of Drugs (1972-80); Health Education Council (1979-86); Chairman, Advisory Council on Alcoholism (DHSS) (1975-78); Cons, Adviser to DHSS (1975-78). *Education:* Highgate School; Trinity College, Cambridge; UCH Medical School; Institute of Psychiatry. *Previous Positions:* Staff, Institute of Psychiatry (1960); Scientific Staff, MRC Unit for Epidemiol. of Psych Illness (1961), Assistant Director (1963); Hon Senior Lecturer, Edinburgh University (1964); Dean, Faculty of Medicine, Manchester University (1974-76); Professor of Psychiatry, Manchester University (1965-90); Dean of Postgraduate Medical Studies (1981-90). *Publications:* 'Alcoholism' (with Prof H J Walton) 3rd ed (1975); articles on suicide and self poisoning, alcoholism, psychiatry in general practice, pyschosomatic disorders, psychiatric epidemiology, genius. *Club:* Athenaeum. *Address:* 24 Lees Road, Bramhall, Stockport, Cheshire SK7 1BT

KETTELEY, John Henry Beevor, FCA

Non-Executive Chairman, BTP plc; Chairman, Prolific Income plc; Non-Executive Director, Boosey & Hawkes plc, Calorex Heat Pumps Ltd. *b.* 9 August 1939 Southend-on-Sea. *m.* 1967 Susan Elizabeth Gordan; two *s.* two *d. Education:* Brentwood School, Brentwood, Essex; Hackley School, Tarrytown, New York, USA (English Speaking Union Exchange Scholar). *Career Profile:* Formerly Director, S G Warburg & Co Ltd, Rea Brothers plc, Barclays de Zoete Wedd Ltd. *Societies:* Royal Burnham Yacht Club; Burnham Golf Club. *Recreations, Interests:* Sailing, golf, tennis, music. *Address:* BTP plc, Hayes Road, Cadishead, Manchester, M44 5BX *(tel:* 0161 775 3945; *fax:* 0161 775 5393); Keeway, Creeksea, Burnham on Crouch, Essex, CM0 8PL *(tel:* 01621 783748) *(fax:* 01621 784966).

KEY, Geoffrey George Bamford, DA (1961),NDD (1961),Postgrad Sculpture (1962)

Self-employed Painter and Sculptor. *b.* 13 May 1941 Rusholme, Manchester. *Education:* High School of Art, Manchester; Regional College of Art, Manchester. *Career Profile:* Over 30 one man shows in Great Britiain, France, Germany, Switzerland, USA, Belgium and Hong Kong; Works in many public and private collections. *Publications/Creative Work:* G Key Drawings (Margin Press); Handbook of Modern British Painting (Scolar Press); Dictionary of British Art (Collectors Club Press); European Painters (Clio Press); Who's Who in Art (Trade Press). *Prizes:* Heywood Medal in Fine Art; Guthrie Bond Travelling Scholarship; 1st Prize Manchester Academy (1971); 1st Prize Leek Arts Festival

(1992). *Societies:* Manchester Academy of Fine Art; Portico Library. *Recreations, Interests:* Collecting 16th and 17th century applied art. *Address:* 59 Acresfield Road, Pendleton, Salford, M6 7GE*(tel:* 0161 736 6014). *Additional Information:* Represented the UK in two Euro exhibitions in France (1991,1994) Represented Salford in the 25th Salon, St Ouen.

KILBURN, Professor Tom, CBE(1973), FRS(1965); MA,PhD,DSc, DSc(hc)(Bath,1979), DU(hc)(Essex,1968),DUniv (hc) (Brunel, 1977), DTech (hc) (CNAA, 1981), FIEE, FEng, DFBCS, Hon Fellowship of UMIST (1984)

Emeritus Professor of Computer Science, University of Manchester. *b.* 11 August 1921; Earlsheaton, Dewsbury. *m.* 1943 Irene Marsden; one *s.* one *d.* *(widowed 1981) Education:* Wheelwright Grammar School, Dewsbury; Cambridge University; Manchester University. *War Service:* Telecommunications Research Establishment, Malvern. *Career Profile:* Lecturer, Senior Lecturer, Reader, Chair of Computer Engineering (1960), Chair of Computer Science (1964) Manchester University. *Publications:* Scientific papers in various technical journals. *Prizes:* Royal Medal of Royal Society (1978); McDowell (1971) and Computer Pioneer (1982) Awards of IEEE (USA); John Player Award (1973) BCS; Elected, Distinguished Fellow, BCS (1974); Mancunian of the Year Award (1982); Eckert-Mauchly Award, ACM-IEEE (1983); Howorth Medal, RSA (North West)(1996). *Societies:* Royal Society, Royal Academy of Engineering, Institution of Electrical Engineers; British Computer Society; National Academy of Engineering, USA (Foreign Associate). *Recreations, Interests:* Many and various. *Address:* 11 Carlton Crescent, Urmston, Manchester *(tel:* 0161-748 3846).

KIMBERLEY, Christopher, OStJ(1993); BA(Hons)(1974)

Commercial Director, North West Regional Railways Ltd. *b.* 3 December 1956 Meriden, Coventry. *m.* 1991 Nancy Elizabeth; one *d.* *Education:* Bablake Grammar School, Coventry (1968-74); The Polytechnic, Wolverhampton (1974-78). *Career Profile:* Commercial Director, North West Regional Railways Board Ltd (1995-); British Railways Board: Graduate Trainee (1974-78); Operations Management, Sutton Coldfield, Sheffield, Wolverhampton (1978-84); Marketing Management, Manchester and Birmingham (1984-89); Re-organisation Project, Group HQ, London (1989-91); Planning & Marketing Manager, Commercial Manager, Regional Railways, Manchester (1991-95). *Prizes:* Duke of Edinburgh's Gold Award (1981). *Societies:* Commissioner for St John Ambulance, Greater Manchester (1992-). *Recreations, Interests:* First aid movement, country walking. *Address:* North West Regional Railways Ltd, Rail House, Store Street, Manchester, M60 1DQ *(tel:* 0161 228 4001; *fax:* 0161 228 5003).

KING, Robert John, BA,BArch(Hons)(Newcastle),RIBA,MRAIC,ACIArb

City Architect, Manchester City Council. *b.* 5 October 1946 Reading. *m.* 1969 Geraldine (née Tremaine); one *d.* *Public Offices:* Council Member, Manchester Society of Architects (1988-); Director, CLASP (1988) Ltd (1988-); Council Member, Chartered Institute of Arbitrators NW Branch (1990-96); Founder Member and Former Vice-President, Alberta Arbitration & Mediation Society; Director, Edmonton Research Park Authority (1983-85). *Education:* Stoneham Grammar School, Reading (1958-65); School of Architecture, University of Newcastle-upon-Tyne (1965-71). *Career Profile:* Architect/Associate,

Falconer Partnership, Stroud (1971-78); Office Manager, Patsula Architects Ltd, Edmonton, Alberta (1978-79); Project Manager (1979-81), Development Manager (1981-85), Alberta Public Works Supply & Services; City Architect, Manchester City Council (1986-), Director of Housing & Architectural Services (1989-92). *Recreations, Interests:* Swimming, swimming teaching, scuba diving, mountain walking, reading, music and fine wines. *Address:* City Architect's Department, PO Box 488, Town Hall, Manchester, M60 2JT *(tel:* 0161 234 4201; *fax:* 0161 234 4571).

KINGSLEY, Roger James, OBE(1992); BSc(Tech),FEng,FIChemE,FInstD

Consultant, Capcis Ltd. *b.* 2 February 1922 Stuttgart, Germany. *m.* 1949 Valerie Marguerite Mary; one *s.* two *d.* *Public Offices:* President, Institution of Chemical Engineers (1974-75); Hon Secretary, (Process Engineering), The Fellowship of Engineering (1985-88). *Education:* Manchester Grammar School (1936-40); Manchester University, Faculty of Technology (1946-49); Harvard International Senior Managers Programme (1973). *War Service:* Army (1940-46) including commando service from 1942); Mention in Dispatches. *Career Profile:* Managing Director, Lankro Chemicals Group (-1977); Deputy Chairman, Diamond Shamrock Europe (1978-82); General Manager, Diamond Shamrock Ion Exchange subsidiaries world wide (Duolite International) (1982-84); Director, Sutcliffe Speakman plc (1983-86); Chairman, Capcis Ltd (1985-94); Chairman, UMIST Ventures Ltd (1988-94). *Publications/Creative Work:* 'Principles of Manufacturing Management' (Inst of Chemical Engineers); 'Commissioning of Process Plan' (Inst. of Mechanical Engineers). *Prizes:* Osborne Reynolds Medal, Inst of Chemical Engineers. *Societies:* Society of Chemical Industry; Anglo Belgian Club. *Recreations, Interests:* Swimming, riding, music, technology transfer from universities. *Address:* Capcis Limited, Bainbridge House, Granby Row, Manchester, M1 2PW *(tel:* 0161 236 6573; *fax:* 0161 228 7846); Fallows End, Wicker Lane, Hale Barns, Altrincham, WA15 0HQ *(tel:* 0161 980 6253).

KIRBY, Professor Stephen, BA(Hons)(Univ of Leicester),MSc(LSE),PhD(Univ of Hull)

Pro-Vice-Chancellor, Dean of Humanities & Social Science, Manchester Metropolitan University. *b.* 7 March 1943 London. *m.* 1964 Laraine Mary Amy; three *s.* one *d.* *Education:* City of London College; University of Leicester (1962-65); London School of Economics (1965-66). *Career Profile:* Lecturer/Senior Lecturer (1966-89), Dean of Social & Political Sciences (1989-92); Pro-Vice-Chancellor (1992-93) University of Hull; Visiting Professor, Université de Tours (1982-83); Visiting Professor, Chong Ju University, South Korea (1986). *Publications/Creative Work:* 'Congress, Parliament and Defence' (Macmillan 1987)(with A W Cox); 'The Militarisation of Space' (Wheatsheaf 1987)(ed with G Robson); 'The Cost of Peace: Assessing Europe's Security Options' (Harwood, 1991)(ed with N Hooper). *Societies:* Institute of Directors; Royal Institute of International Affairs; Portico Library. *Recreations, Interests:* Hill walking, gardening, theatre, car construction and mechanics. *Address:* Manchester Metropolitan University, Humanities Building, Rosamund Street West, Manchester, M15 6LL*(tel:* 0161 247 1749; *fax:* 0161 247 6308; *e-mail:* S.Kirby@mmu.ac.uk). *Additional Information:* Research interest in the foreign and defence policy, domestic politics, international trade and the financial and economic policies of South Korea.

KIRKWOOD, Colonel David, FCIS,FIMgt,MIPD

Garrison Commander, Greater Manchester. *b.* 26 March 1945 Dufftown, Scotland. *m.* 1971 Sandra Margaret; three *s.* one *d. Education:* Bearsden Academy. *Military Service:* Middle East, Far East, Northern Ireland, Germany, Berlin. *Career Profile:* Commissioned, Royal Artillery (1966); 7 Parachute Regiment Royal Horse Artillery; A/Bde Major, HQRA 2 Div; attached Royal Marines; commanded 176 Abu Kkea Battery; Finance Staff Officer, 19 Infantry Brigade; Garrison Commander, Kowloon, Hong Kong; Grade I Finance Staff Officer, HQ Land Comd; Commanding Officer, AG Corps Depot. *Prizes:* Army Long Distance Windsurfing Champion (Middle East); Army Cross Country Skiing Champion (Middle East). *Societies:* British Institute of Ski Instructors; Royal Yachting Association (Windsurfing Instructor). *Recreations, Interests:* Mountaineering, canoeing, skiing, sailing, golf, meeting people.

KISSACK, Nigel Euan Jackson, LLB(Hons)(1976),Solicitor of the Supreme Court (1979)

Managing Partner, Alsop Wilkinson, Manchester. *b.* 8 April 1955 Aldershot. *m.* 1980 Kathryn Margaret Lloyd-Jones; one *s.* one *d. Education:* Dorset House Preparatory School, Sussex; King William's College, Isle of Man; Sheffield University; Chester College of Law. *Career Profile:* Articled, Foysters, Manchester; Solicitor, Partner, Lee Lane-Smith; Partner, Alsop Wilkinson. *Publications/Creative Work:* Articles in professional journals. *Societies:* St James' Club; Bowdon Lawn Tennis Club. *Recreations, Interests:* Sport, theatre, music, motor cycling. *Address:* Alsop Wilkinson, 11 St James' Square, Manchester, M2 6DR *(tel:* 0161 834 7760; *fax:* 0161 831 7515); Oakleigh, Dunham Road, Altrincham.

KLETZ, Dr Trevor Asher, BSc,DSc,FEng,FIChemE,CEng,FRSC,CChem

Senior Visiting Research Fellow, Department of Chemical Engineering, Loughborough University; Consultant. *b.* 23 October 1922 Darlington. *m.* 1958 Denise Winroope; two *s. (widowed 1980) Education:* King's School, Chester (1933-41); Liverpool University (1941-44). *Career Profile:* Research, Production Management, Safety Adviser, Petrochemicals Division, ICI; Industrial Professor, Loughborough University of Technology. *Publications/Creative Work:* Nine books and over 100 papers on loss prevention and process safety. *Prizes:* Bill Doyle Award, American Institute of Chemical Engineers (1985); Council Medal, Institution of Chemical Engineers (1986); Award for Personal Achievement, *Chemical Engineering* (1990); Ned Franklin Medal, Institution of Chemical Engineers (1993); Brennan Medal, Institution of Chemical Engineers (1995). *Societies:* Royal Academy of Engineering; Institution of Chemical Engineers; Royal Society of Chemistry; American Institute of Chemical Engineers. *Recreations, Interests:* Reading, walking, railways. *Address:* 64 Twining Brook Road, Cheadle Hulme, Cheadle, Cheshire, SK8 5RJ *(tel:* 0161 485 3875).

KLONIN, Susan Jane, LLB(Hons)(1970),Barrister

Barrister. *b.* 26 February 1948 Philadelphia, USA. *m.* 1972 Ivor Abadi; two *s. (marr. diss.)*; *m.* 1981 William Morris; two *s.* one *d.* two *stepd. Education:* King Edward's VI Camp Hill, Birmingham; Birmingham University. *Societies:* Honourable Society of Gray's

Inn. *Recreations, Interests:* Family. *Address:* Old Colony House, South King Street, Manchester.

KLOSS, Diana Mary (*née* Cox), LLB(London),LLM(Tulane),Barrister(Grays Inn)

Senior Lecturer in Law, University of Manchester; Barrister; Chairman of Industrial Tribunals (part-time). *b.* 2 September 1938 Hornchurch, Essex. *m.* 1963 Gunther Kloss; two *s.* *(widowed 1990) Public Offices:* JP (1984-90); Member, Manchester Family Health Services Authority (1992-96); Deputy Chairman of Wages Councils (1977-91). *Education:* Ursuline High School, Brentwood, Essex; King's College, London; Tulane University, USA. *Career Profile:* University of Manchester (1960-); served on Wages Councils for many years; Independent Arbitrator on ACAS Panel; Member of Health Authorities and Author of textbook on occupational health law; Barrister in part-time practice; Member of Expert Advisory Group on Aids and UK Panel of Experts on Health Care Workers with Blood-Borne Viruses. *Publications/Creative Work:* 'Occupational Health Law' (2nd Edition). *Societies:* Society of Public Teachers of Law. *Recreations, Interests:* Music, reading, gardening. *Address:* Faculty of Law, University of Manchester, Oxford Road, Manchester, M13 9PL *(tel:* 0161 275 3591; *fax:* 0161 275 3579).

KNOWLES, Christopher John, GRNCM

General Manager, Manchester Camerata. *b.* 11 January 1957 Wombwell. *m.* one *s.* *Education:* Wombwell High School; Royal Northern College of Music. *Career Profile:* Principal Oboe, Northern Ballet (1979-96); 2nd Oboe, Manchester Camerata (1979-96); Principal Cor Anglais, English National Ballet (1989-96); Assistant Orchestra Manager, NBT (1994-95); General Manager, Manchester Camerata (1996-). *Societies:* Scout Association. *Recreations, Interests:* Scouting, computers, photography, travel, gardening. *Address:* Manchester Camerata, Bridgewater Hall, Manchester M2 3WS; 3 Newstead Road, Davyhulme, Manchester, M41 0QQ *(tel:* 0161 748 6795; *fax:* 0161 718 1501) (*e-mail:* 100126.3141@compuserve.com).

KOCHHAR, Professor Ashok Kumar, BSc,PhD,CEng,FIMechE,FIEE

Lucas Professor of Manufacturing Systems Engineering, UMIST. *b.* 31 January 1949 Amritsar, India. *m.* 1987 Rupa (née Mehta). *Public Offices:* Member, Control Design & Production College, EPSRC (1995-). *Education:* University of London (external); University of Bradford. *Career Profile:* Engineering Apprentice (1966-70), Graduate Engineer (1970-71), Rolls Royce Ltd; University of Bradford: Research Student (1971-74); Post-Doctoral Research Fellow in Computer-Aided Manufacturing Control Systems (1974-76); Lecturer in Manufacturing Systems Engineering (1976-83); Reader (1983-86); Professor (1986-92); Lucas Professor of Manufacturing Systems Engineering, UMIST (1992-). *Publications/Creative Work:* Author of 3 books and numerous journal and conference proceedings papers; Editor, Proceedings of 30th and 31st International MATADOR Conferences. *Prizes:* Donald Julius Groen Prize, Institution of Mechanical Engineers; Joseph Whitworth Prize, Institution of Mechnical Engineers; DTI Manufacturing Intelligence Award, National Manfuacturing Intelligence Competition (1992). *Societies:* Member of editorial boards of a number of academic journals; Member, International Federation of Information Processing Group on Computer-Aided Manufacturing Systems; Member, West European Group of Teachers of Industrial

Management. *Recreations, Interests:* Reading, manufacturing systems engineering. *Address:* Department of Mechanical Engineering, UMIST, PO Box 88, Manchester, M60 1QD *(tel:* 0161 200 3801; *fax:* 0161 200 3803).

KODAMA-NAGANO, Mari (*née* Kodama)

Concert Pianist. *b.* 3 March 1967 Osaka, Japan. *m.* 1991 Kent Nagano. *Education:* Paris Conservatoire National Supérieur. *Career Profile:* Concerts and recordings in Europe, USA and the Far East. *Publications/Creative Work:* Several recordings. *Prizes:* Busoni, Viotti, Senigallia Competitions; 1st Prize, Paris Conservatoire National Supérieur

KRAEMER, Nicholas, BMus,ARCM

Principal Guest Conductor, Manchester Camerata. *b.* 7 March 1945 Edinburgh. *m.* 1984 Elizabeth Anderson; three *s.* one dec'd two *d. Education:* Edinburgh Academy; Lancing College; Dartington College of Arts; Nottingham University; Guildhall School of Music. *Career Profile:* Harpsichordist, Academy of St Martin-in-the-Fields, The English Baroque Soloits; formed The Raglan Baroque Players (1978); recorded the complete Cello concertos of Vivaldi with Raphael Wallfisch and the London Sinfonia; currently recording the wind and string concertos with Andrew Watkinson; conducted at Glyndebourne (1980-83), English National Opera (1992); first Musical Director, Opera 80 (now English Touring Opera); Associate Conductor, BBC Scottish Symphony Orchestra (1983-85); Artistic Director, Irish Chamber Orchestra (1986-92); Artistic Director, London Bach Orchestra (1985-93). *Societies:* Royal Society of Musicians. *Recreations, Interests:* Active fatherhood, eating out. *Address:* C/o Manchester Camerata, 30 Derby Road, Fallowfield, Manchester, M14 6VW.

KURER, Peter Frank, LDS Newcastle-upon-Tyne (1955),MGDS RCS(Eng)(1980), Fellow of the Academy of Dentistry International; Fellow, International College of Dentists; Fellow Pier Fuchard Academy.

A Senior Partner in Dental Practice; Managing Director, Crescent Road Management Co.; Technical Director, Sabre K Ltd; Chairman of the Board, Trustee, Morris Feinmann Home; Chairman, Manchester Chamber Concerts Society. *b.* 22 April 1931; Vienna, Austria. *m.* 1955 Heather Gillian Goldstone; one *s.* three *d. Education:* Friends' School, Wigton, Cumbria; Bootham School, York; Durham University Dental School. *Creative Works:* Inventor and developer ofax: Kurer Anchor System (1965), Kurer Crown Saver System (1968), Kurer Press Stud (1975), Kurer Coping Screw (1975), Kurer Finlock Anchor (1977). *Publications:* BDJ Booklet 'The Kurer Anchor System'; Text Book 'The Kurer Anchor System: an approach to the restoration and re-use of endodontically treated teeth'; 35 other publications. *Prizes:* Cine Film of Anchor System (1968) nominated for British Film Academy Award. *Recreations, Interests:* Music, photography, care of the aged. *Address:* 2 Crescent Road, Hale, Cheshire, WA15 9NA *(tel:* 0161 929 8111); 7 Bruntwood Lane, Cheadle, Cheshire, SK8 1HS *(tel:* 0161-428 5080).

L

LAKIN, His Honour Judge Peter Maurice, LLB(Hons)(Manchester,1971), Solicitor(1974)

Circuit Judge (Northern Circuit). *b.* 21 October 1949 Coventry. *m.* 1971 Jacqueline; one *s.* one *d. Education:* King Henry VIII School, Coventry (1961-68); Manchester University (1968-71). *Career Profile:* Qualified as a Solicitor (1974); Assistant Solicitior, Conn Goldberg & Co, Mancheser (1974-76); Partner, Pannone & Partners, Manchester (1976-95); Assistant Recorder (1989-93), Recorder (1993-95), Crown Court; Circuit Judge (1995-pres). *Societies:* The Law Society; Manchester & District Medico-Legal Society (Secretary 1987-95). *Recreations, Interests:* Fell walking, local footpaths and local history, opera, gardening.

LAL, Satinder, MB,BS (Punjab),FRCP,FRCPE,FCCP

Consultant Physician with Respiratory Interest Unit General Manager (1964-). *b.* 17 May 1926; New Delhi, India. *m.* Sheila; one *s.* two *d. Public Offices:* Co-ordinator, NWASH. *Education:* Hindu College, Delhi; FC College, Amritsar. *Career Profile:* Registrar, Hammersmith Chest Clinic, London and Postgraduate Medical School (1961-63); Senior Registrar, Leeds General Infirmary (1963-64). *Publications:* Number of publications in professional journals in last 20 years. *Societies:* British Thoracic Society; Medical Research Society; Royal Society of Medicine; Past President, Rotary Club of Bury. *Address:* 25 Brooklands Road, Holcombe Brook, Bury BL0 9SW (01204-882125).

LAMBERT, Charles Oliver, BA(Hons)(Univ. of Bristol, 1971)

Sports Correspondent, BBC North-West. *b.* 7 August 1950 Windermere. *Education:* St Bees School, Cumbria. *Career Profile:* Journalist, Sefton Newspapers, Southport (1971-73); Sports Reporter, Liverpool Echo (1973-81); Sports Editor, BBC Radio Merseyside, Liverpool (1981-88). *Publications/Creative Work:* 'The Boss' (Strains & Stresses of Football Mangement)(Pride of Place, UK, 1995). *Prizes:* Sony Award, Sports Broadcaster of the Year (1984); Sony Award, Best Current Affairs Programme (1988). *Societies:* Liverpool Cricket Club; Pre-War Austin Seven Owners' Club; National Trust; Hon. President, Liverpool International Half-Marathon Committee. *Recreations, Interests:* Golf, sport in general, cinema, theatre, travel. *Address:* BBC, Oxford Road, Manchester, M60 1SJ (*tel:* 0161 200 2020; *fax:* 0161 244 3122).

LAMMAR, Frank

Entertainer; director. *b.* 22 March 1937 Manchester. *Public Offices:* Chairman, Wallness Childrens Charity. *Education:* St Bridgittes RC School, Ancoats, Manchester. *Career Profile:* Started in small pubs and clubs;; club owner; numerous TV, radio and theatre appearances. *Prizes:* Numerous (for charity work). *Recreations, Interests:* Work, work, work. *Address:* Foo Foo's Palace, 56 Dale Street, Manchester, M1 2HN (*tel:* 0161 236 2790; *fax:* 0161 237 3214).

LANDAU, Sir Dennis, Kt (1987); BSc,CIM,FRSA

Chairman, Unity Trust Bank Plc; Chairman, Forum for the Social Economy; Vice-

Chairman, Lancashire Enterprises plc. *b.* 18 June 1927; London. *m.* 1992 Pamela Garlick; two *steps.* *Education:* Haberdashers' Aske's; Hampstead School; London University. *Career Profile:* Chief Executive, Co-operative Wholesale Society Ltd; Deputy Chairman, Co-operative Bank plc; Director, Co-operative Insurance Society Ltd; Managing Director, Cadbury Schweppes Foods. *Societies:* Royal Overseas League; Lancashire CCC. *Recreations, Interests:* Music, rugby, cricket. *Address:* Thorncroft, Pedley Hill, Rainow, nr Macclesfield SK10 5TZ

LANE-SMITH, Roger, Solicitor of Supreme Court (1969)

Chairman, Alsop Wilkinson, solicitors. *b.* 19 October 1945 England. *m.* 1969 Pamela; one *s.* one *d.* *Education:* Stockport Grammar School; College of Law, Guildford. *Career Profile:* Founder, Alsop Wilkinson, Manchester (1977); Managing Partner (Manchester, 1977-88); Managing Partner (London (1989-93); Chairman (1993-). *Prizes:* Robert Ellis Memorial Prize. *Societies:* Law Society; St James' Club; Marks Club. *Recreations, Interests:* Golf, tennis, shooting, travel. *Address:* Alsop Wilkinson, 11 St James' Square, Manchester, M2 6DR(*tel:* 0161 834 7760; *fax:* 0161 839 2254).

LANGTON, Margaret Stephen Tait (*née* Gatt), OBE (1992); BSc, DipEd

Consultant, Quality and Standards; Chairman, Board of Amtri Veritas, Macclesfield. *b.* 5 February 1934; Fraserburgh, Aberdeenshire. *m.* 1956 E A Davies; *(marr. diss. 1967)*; *m.* 1977 Bernard Sydney Langton; two *stepd.* *(widowed 1982)* *Public Offices:* Non-Executive Director, North Manchester Healthcare NHS Trust; Member, Editorial Board, Journal of Consumer Studies and Home Economics; JP Central Manchester; Trustee, Fire Services Research and Training Trust. *Education:* Glossop Grammar School; Homerton College, Cambridge; Manchester University. *Career Profile:* Formerly Technical Director, British Standards Institution. *Societies:* Manchester Literary & Philosophical Society. *Recreations, Interests:* Needlework, music, fell walking. *Address:* Higher Kinders, Greenfield, Oldham OL3 7BH (*tel:* 01457 872991 *fax:* 01457 872991).

LATHAM, Glenys (*née* Eatock), DipAD,CIE

Head of Creative Arts, Wigan & Leigh College of Further & Higher Education. *b.* 2 March 1946 Atherton. *m.* 1975 Robert. *Public Offices:* Governor, Wigan & Leigh College. *Education:* Bolton Secondary Art School; Bolton College of Art; Wolverhampton College of Art; Manchester Regional College of Art. *Career Profile:* Head of Art & Design, Leigh College; Artist-in-Residence, Drumcroon Education Art Centre, Wigan; 29 years as teacher and lecturer of art and design; 20 years as practicing and exhibiting sculptor. *Publications/Creative Work:* Sculptor, work in private collections in England, Far East and North America. *Prizes:* Manchester Academy of Fine Arts Major Award (1985); Emerson Developments Award (1986). *Societies:* Member, NSEAD (North West Chair, 1984-85); Manchester Academy of Fine Arts, Past President (1990-92), Trustee, Council Member. *Recreations, Interests:* Stone carving, life drawing, watching cricket (Lancashire and England). *Address:* Wigan and Leigh College, School of Arts and Design, PO Box 53, Parsons Walk, Wigan, WN1 1RS(*tel:* 01942 501501; *fax:* 01942 501812); Longridge, 30 Bank Side, Westhoughton, Bolton, BL5 2QP (*tel:* 01942 811691).

160

LATHAM, Professor (John) Derek BA Double Hons (Oxford 1949),MA (Oxon 1952), DPhil(Oxon 1956),DLitt (Oxon 1981)

Professor Emeritus, University of Edinburgh; Hon Fellow, Department of Middle Eastern Studies, University of Manchester. *b.* 5 April 1927 Wigan. *m.* 1955 Jean (Elisabeth) Coulstock; one *s.* one *d. Public Offices:* JP (Manchester City, 1979-). *Education:* Wigan Grammar School; Pembroke College, Oxford (1945-49); HM Treasury Research Fellow, Oxford (1950-53). *Military Service:* National Service, RAF (1949-50). *Career Profile:* Assistant Librarian, Manchester University (1953-57); Associate Professor & Curator of Middle Eastern Collections, Stanford University (1957-58); Lecturer, Reader in Arabic, Manchester University (1958-81); Visiting Fellow, St Cross College, Oxford (1975); Professor of Arabic & Islamic Studies and Head, Muir Institute, Edinburgh University (1981-88). *Publications/Creative Work:* Several books; numerous articles on Middle Eastern Studies. *Prizes:* Wakefield Prize, Oxford; Colours (Rowing), Oxford. *Societies:* Oxford Society; British Society for Middle Eastern Studies; The Magistrates' Association; Broughton Catholic Charitable Society. *Recreations, Interests:* Ornithology, oil painting, English criminal law, Islamic law, rugby, Formula I motor racing, rowing. *Address:* Department of Middle Eastern Studies, University of Manchester, Oxford Road, Manchester, M13 9PL(*tel:* 0161 275 2000; *fax:* 0161 275 3264). *Additional Information:* President, British Society for Middle Eastern Studies (1985-87); Chairman, Middle East Libraries Committee (1971-79); Chairman, Fontes Historiae Africanae Committee (British Academy)(1971-79); Specialist Consultant to the Oxford English Dictionaries (1984-); Specialist Consultant to Dictionary of Medieval Latin (British Academy 1970-); Co-general Editor and Contributor, Cambridge History of Arabic Literature (1983-90); Chairman, EJW Gibb Memorial Trust, Cambridge (1988-89); Examiner, Civil Service Commission (1968-86); Member, Advisory Board, Journal of Semitic Studies (1976-82)(1989-).

LAW, Elizabeth Hazel (*née* Turk), BA(Hons),AIMSW

Chief Executive, Mancunian Community Health NHS Trust. *b.* 19 February 1939 Hinckley, Leicestershire. *m.* 1962 Christopher; one *s.* one *d. Public Offices:* Member and Vice Chairman (1979-81), Trafford CHC (1976-81); Member and Vice Chairman (1985-86), Trafford Health Authority (1981-87); Trafford FPC (1985-87). *Education:* Hinckley Grammar School; Queenswood; Nottingham University; Institute of Almoners. *Career Profile:* Medical Social Worker; Health Liaison, Manchester Social Services; Unit General Manager, South Manchester Health Authority.

LAWLEY, Janet May, BA(Univ. of Bristol, 1959),CertEd(Univ of Oxford, 1960)

Headmistress, Bury Grammar School (Girls). *b.* 20 May 1938 Cannock, Staffs. *Education:* The Friary School, Lichfield (1956); Exhibitioner, University of Bristol (1956-59). *Career Profile:* Teacher, City of Bath Girls' School (1960-64); Head of Dept, Head of Sixth Form and Senior Mistress, Merchant Taylors' Girls' School, Crosby (1964-78); Vice-Principal, King George V Sixth Form College,Southport (1978-86). *Societies:* Chairman, Liverpool-Amsterdam Pupils Exchange Committee (1968-78); Chairman, Liverpool & NW Branch, Geographical Association (1972-86); Member Council, Geographical Association (1978-86); Chairman, Girls' School Association, NW Branch (1994-96); Member of Council, Girls' Schools Association (1994-96). *Recreations, Interests:* Car driving, country walking,

choral singing, needlecraft, Greece and Greek, travel. *Address:* Bury Grammar School (Girls), Bridge Road, Bury, Lancs, BL9 0HH; Greenmount, Bury.

LAWRENCE, Margaret Gillian (*née* Pigott), MCSP

Chairman, Henshaw's Society for the Blind; Company Secretary, Dennemeyer & Co Ltd. *b.* 15 August 1938 Manchester. *m.* John Gordon; two *d.* *Public Offices:* Deputy Lieutenant, Greater Manchester. *Education:* Queen Ethelburgha's, Harrogate; Briallmont College, Laussane; St Thomas's Hospital, London. *Career Profile:* Henshaw's Society for the Blind, served on the Board (since 1975), Chairman of Finance, Chairman (1983-). *Societies:* Wilmslow Ladies Golf Club (Past Captain, 1995). *Recreations, Interests:* Golf, travel, gardening.

LAWSON, Peter, GRSM,ARMCM

Piano Soloist; Tutor, Chetham's School of Music, Manchester; Examiner, Associated Board of the Royal Schools of Music. *b.* 11 April 1950 Manchester. *m.* 1976 Ariane Dandoy; one *s.* one *d.* *Education:* Stockport School (1961-68); Royal Manchester College of Music (1968-73). *Career Profile:* Previous: Tutor, Rossall School, Fleetwood, University of Keele; Presently: Piano Tutor and Careers Adviser, Chetham's; Pianist specialising in 20th century American and contemporary British music. *Publications/Creative Work:* Commercial recordings: Satie Piano Music (Classics for Pleasure); New British Piano Music (Electric Candle); American Piano Sonatas (2 vols. Virgin Classics); Forthcoming: Michael Nyman 'The Piano Concerto' (Tring). *Prizes:* Satie recording awarded Silver Disc (1989); Churchill Fellowship (1992). *Societies:* Musicians Union; European Piano Teachers Association. *Recreations, Interests:* Travel. *Address:* Keyboard Department, Chetham's School of Music, Long Millgate, Manchester, M3 1SB (*tel:* 0161 834 9644; *fax:* 0161 839 3609); The Old Co-op, Church Street South, Old Glossop, Derbyshire, SK13 9RU (*tel:* 01457 862555).

LEAH, Christopher Richard, MCIT

Director (North West), Railtrack plc. *b.* 4 December 1947 Northampton. *m.* 1971 Prunella Mary; three *s.* *Education:* Towcester Grammar School, Northamptonshire; London University (extra-mural). *Career Profile:* Railway Transport Professional. *Societies:* Institute of Management; Institute of Directors; Chartered Institute of Transport. *Recreations, Interests:* Photography, travel, life. *Address:* Railtrack plc, Room 311, Rail House, Store Street, Manchester, M60 7RT (*tel:* 0161 228 4069; *fax:* 0161 228 5593); 393 Crewe Road, Wistaston, Nantwich, Cheshire, CW5 6NW (*tel:* 01270 669175).

LECK, John Bryan, JP (1967); FIMgt (1981),Assoc MIH (1981)

Director, Age Concern Manchester (retired 1993); Chairman, Tameside & Glossop Health Authority (retired 1994). *b.* 28 May 1927; Manchester. *m.* 1949 Joyce; one *s.* one *d.* *(widowed 1977)*; *m.* 1978 Patricia Ann. *Public Offices:* Elected Councillor, Cheshire (1964-77), Stockport MBC (1974-94); First Mayor, Stockport MBC (1974-75); Deputy Mayor, Stockport MBC (1987-88); NW Regional Health Authority (1974-76) (1983-89) (Vice Chairman 1988-89). *Education:* Arnold School, Blackpool (1933-44); Manchester

University (School of Architecture) (1944-45). *War Service:* Loyal Regiment (1945-48). *Previous Positions:* Chief Executive, Housing Association; Director, Building Sub-Contracting Company; Parliamentary Candidate, General Elections (1955 and 1970). *Societies:* Conservative Party. *Recreations, Interests:* Trustee, Hillcrest Grammar School (Charitable School), former hockey player (1950-88). *Address:* 236 Church Lane, Woodford, Stockport SK7 1PQ (0161-439 3137).

LEE, Francis Henry

Chairman Manchester City Football Club; Chairman/Managing Director, F H Lee Ltd, Bolton; Managing Director, Highway Safety Systems Ltd; Main Board Director, Hazlewood Foods plc; Racehorse Trainer, Little Stanneylands Racing Stables, Wilmslow. *b.* 29 April 1944; Westhoughton, Lancs. *m.* 1962 Jean; one *s.* one *d.*; *m.* 1987 Gillian May; two *s. Education:* Horwich Training College, Lancs. *Career Profile:* Professional Footballer, Bolton Wanderers FC, Manchester City FC, Derby County FC, England International. *Prizes:* Football related prizes. *Societies:* Mere Golf & Country Club; Portal Golf Club; Shrigley Hall Golf Club. *Recreations, Interests:* Racing, golf, cricket, snooker. *Address:* F H Lee Ltd, Moor Mill, Parott Street, Bolton, Lancs (01204 385666); Little Stanneylands Racing Stables, Stanneylands Road, Wilmslow, Cheshire SK9 4ER (01625 533250).

LEE, John Robert Louis, FCA

Chairman, Christie Hospital NHS Trust; Non-Executive Director, Paterson Zochonis plc, PS Turner (Holdings) Ltd, MS International Plc. *b.* 21 June 1942; Manchester. *m.* 1975 Anne Monique Bakirgian; two *d. Public Offices:* MP, Nelson and Colne (1979-83), Pendle (1983-92); Governor, Withington Girls' School; Member of Court, University of Manchester; Chairman, Manchester Museum of Science and Industry; Chairman, Association of Leading Visitor Attractions; Member, English Tourist Board. *Education:* William Hulme's Grammar School, Manchester. *Career Profile:* Under Secretary of State for Defence Procurement (1983-86); Parliamentary Under Secretary of State, Dept of Employment (1986-89). *Recreations, Interests:* Fishing, golf. *Address:* Christie Hospital NHS Trust, Wilmslow Road, Manchester M20 (*tel:* 0161 446 3702); Bowdon Old Hall, 49 Langham Road, Bowdon, Altrincham WA13 3NS.

LEE, Paul Anthony, MA, LLB (Cantab),Solicitor

Managing Partner, Addleshaw Sons & Latham. *b.* 26 January 1946 Manchester. *m.* 1977 Elizabeth Lindsay Taylor; two *s.* one *d. Public Offices:* Chairman of Governors, Chethams School of Music; Board Member, Royal Northern College of Music; Halle Concerts Society; Royal Exchange Theatre. *Education:* Central Grammar School, Manchester; Clare College, Cambridge. *Career Profile:* Partner, Addleshaws (1970), Managing Partner (1992); Director, Robert H Lowe plc, Davies & Metcalfe plc, Pugh Davies & Co Ltd; Leaf Properties Ltd, NRM5 Ltd. *Societies:* Manchester Literary & Philosophical Society; Manchester Tennis & Racquets Club; St James' Club; Northern Lawn Tennis Club; Confrérie des Chevaliers du Tastevin; Commanderie de Bordeaux. *Recreations, Interests:* The Arts, wine, sport, travel.

163

LEE, Richard Elliot Michael

Managing Director, Richard E M Lee & Partners Ltd; Non-Executive Director, Intercare Group plc; Non-Executive Director, Sycamore Holdings plc; Non-Executive Director, Prime People plc. *b.* 4 August 1945 Manchester. *m.* 1976 Elizabeth Penlington; one *s.* one *d. Public Offices:* Former President, Manchester Anglers Association. *Education:* William Hulmes Grammar School; Arnold School, Blackpool. *Societies:* Bowdon Lawn Tennis Club. *Recreations, Interests:* Tennis, fly fishing. *Address:* Vine House, 29 East Downs Road, Bowdon, Cheshire, WA14 2LG.

LEE, Richard Neil Frederick, MA(Cantab),Solicitor of the Supreme Court

Partner, Addleshaw Sons & Latham. *b.* 27 March 1959 Wedmore, Somerset. *m.* 1983 Juliet; three *s.* one *d. Education:* Sexey's Grammar School, Blackford, Somerset; Trinity College, Cambridge. *Career Profile:* Articled Clerk, (1981-83), Assistant Solicitor (1983-86) Rowe & Maw, London; Assistant Solicitor (1986-87), Associate (1987-88), Partner (1988-), Addleshaw Sons & Latham. *Societies:* The Law Society; Manchester Law Society. *Recreations, Interests:* Sport, raising children. *Address:* Addleshaw Sons & Latham, Dennis House, Marsden Street, Manchester, M2 1JD (*tel:* 0161 832 5994; *fax:* 0161 832 2250).

LEE, Professor William Rimmer, MD London (1963),MSc Manchester (1975),FRCP London (1975), FFOM London (1978)

Emeritus Professor of Occupational Health. *b.* 3 July 1922; London. *m.* 1954 Monica Audrey; one *s.* two *d. Public Offices:* Member of Medical Appeal Tribunal. *Education:* Alleyn's School, Dulwich, London; Guy's Hospital Medical School, University of London. *Military Service:* RAF Medical Branch (1946-53). *Career Profile:* Consultant in Occupational Medicine, Manchester Royal Infirmary, Hope Hospital Salford. *Publications:* Contributions to Medical Literature, 'Fontana Dictionary of Modern Thought'. *Prizes:* Entrance Scholarship Guy's Hospital Medical School; Prize: Institution of Electrical & Electronic Engineers (USA); Premier Award: Institute of Electrical Engineers. *Societies:* MENSA; RAF Club; Caravan Club. *Recreations, Interests:* Caravanning, travel. *Address:* "Crimbles", 6 Sussex Avenue, Didsbury, Manchester M20 6AQ (0161-445 0095).

LEEMING, James Thompson, FRCP London (1974),MD Manchester (1958)

Consultant Physician in Medicine for the Elderly, Central Manchester Health Authority; retired 1991 *b.* 13 September 1927; Salford. *m.* 1954 Brenda Kerslake (*decd* 1988), four *s.*; 1991 Sylvia Brooke, one *steps.* one *stepd. Public Offices:* Secretary, British Geriatrics Society (1975-78). *Education:* Manchester Grammar School; Manchester University. *Military Service:* National Service (1952-54). *Career Profile:* Consultant Physician, Bolton Health Authority (1963-67); Consultant Physician, South Manchester Health Authority (1967-77); Full-time Lecturer, Open University (1977-79). *Publications:* 'The Upper Gastro-intestinal Tract' in 'Textbook of Geriatric Medicine and Gerontology' 2nd Edition (1978) Ed. J C Brocklehurst (Churchill Livingstone); 'Septicaemia in the Elderly' (British Journal of Hospital Medicine, Nov 1981); 'Attitudes, Teamwork, Coordination and Communication' in 'Establishing a Geriatric Service', Ed. D Coakley (1982); 'Geriatric

Medicine - Attitudes v Skills?' in Harrogate Seminar Report 7; 'Effective Geriatric Medicine' (DHSS 1983); 'The Work of a Clinical Psychologist in the Care of the Elderly', Stuart Larner and J T Leeming, 'Age and Ageing' (1984); 'Anaemia in Old Age' (British Journal of Hospital Medicine, Oct 1984); 'Skeletal Disease in the Elderly' (BMA 1985). *Societies:* British Geriatrics Society; British Society for Research into Ageing (County Director, Greater Manchester); Rotary Club (Didsbury & District); Trustee, Age Concern (Manchester); Didsbury Civic Society. *Recreations, Interests:* Family, arts, swimming, travel, walking, photography. *Address:* 9 Mosswood Park, Manchester, M20 5QW.

LEES, His Honour Charles Norman, LLB(Hons)(Univ. of Leeds,1950),Called to the Bar, Lincoln's Inn(1951)

Retired Circuit and Designated Family Judge. *b.* 4 October 1929 Manchester. *m.* 1961 Stella Swann; one *d. (widowed 1987) Public Offices:* Chairman, Mental Health Review Tribunals (Restricted Patients). *Education:* Stockport School; University of Leeds. *Career Profile:* Practised as a Barrister, Northern Circuit (1951-80); Deputy Chairman, Cumberland County Quarter Sessions (1969-71); Recorder of the Crown Court (1971-80); Circuit Judge (1980-96), Designated Family Judge (1991-96); Chairman, Mental Health Review Tribunals (Restricted Patients)(1983-). *Societies:* Lansdowne Club, London; Northern Lawn Tennis Club; Northenden Golf Club. *Recreations, Interests:* Golf, tennis, history.

LEES, Stuart, BA(Econ)(Manchester),FCA

Partner, Head of Corporate Finance & Audit Divisions, Arthur Andersen, Manchester. *b.* 16 April 1956 Stoke-on-Trent. *m.* 1984 Susan. *Education:* Woolstanton Grammar School; Manchester University. *Career Profile:* Joined Arthur Andersen, Manchester (1978); Qualified ACA (1981); Promoted to Manager (1984); Partner (1990). *Societies:* St James' Club, Manchester; Tytherington Club, Macclesfield; Alderley Edge Cricket Club. *Recreations, Interests:* Squash, golf, tennis, music, Manchester United. *Address:* Arthur Andersen, Bank House, 9 Charlotte Street, Manchester, M1 4EU *(tel:* 0161 228 2121; *fax:* 0161 200 0280); Springfield, Macclesfield Road, Alderley Edge, SK9 7BW.

LEGGETT, Keith Arnold, FSVA,FCIArb,FRVA

Director, Keith Leggett Consultancy (Property Valuers & Surveyors, Altrincham. *b.* 18 March 1940; Bristol. *m.* 1964 Sonja; three *s. Education:* Monkton Combe School, Bath, Avon; Cloverley Hall, Whitchurch, Salop. *Career Profile:* Principal, N Routledge & Co, Sale; Residential Sales Director, Nationwide Anglia Estate Agents Ltd; Managing Director, Messenger Leisure Ltd. *Societies:* Manchester Branch, Incorporated Society of Valuers & Auctioneers; Hale Golf Club; Sale & North Cheshire 41 Club. *Recreations, Interests:* Golf, gardening, specialised ceramic collecting. *Address:* The Ridge, York Drive, Bowdon, Altrincham, Cheshire WA14 3HF (0161-941 2997).

LEITCH, Diana Mary (*née* Bridges), BSc,PhD(Edinburgh)

Assistant Director & Head of Information Resources & Services, John Rylands University Libary of Manchester. *b.* 10 January 1946 Liverpool. *m.* 1972 David Shaw Leitch; one *s.*

one *d*. *Public Offices:* Chair of Trustees, Parrs Wood Rural Trust; Trustee, Chemical Structure Association. *Education:* The Queen's School, Chester; University of Edinburgh. *Career Profile:* Abstractor & Indexer, Shirley Institute; Technical Information Officer, CPC International; various posts at John Rylands University Library of Manchester. *Publications/Creative Work:* Various publications in chemical and pharmaceutical journals; booklets on the history of Didsbury Parish Church and Didsbury CofE Primary School; Sections of 'Centre of Intelligence; The Development of Science, Technology and Medicine in Manchester and Its University'. *Societies:* Chemical Structure Association; Association for Learning Technology; Mancheter Literary & Philosophical Society. *Recreations, Interests:* Genealogy, local history, gardening, fund raising, handicrafts, educational developments, photography. *Address:* John Rylands University Library, of Manchester, Oxford Road, Manchester, M12 9PP (*tel:* 0161 275 3737; *fax:* 0161 273 7488; *e-mail:* dmleitch@man.ac.uk); 11 Wingate Drive, Didsbury, Manchester, M20 2RT (*tel:* 0161 445 9461) (*fax:* 0161 445 9461). *Additional Information:* Parent Governor/PCC Governor at Didsbury CofE Primary School (1986-95) Chair of Governors Buildings Committee.

LEONARD, Christopher James, FCIB

Local Director, The Royal Bank of Scotland. *b.* 15 November 1943 Macclesfield. *m.* 1971 Carolyn Mary; two *s*. *Public Offices:* Past President, Manchester & District Bankers Institute; Member, CBI NW Regional Council. *Education:* Altrincham Grammar School. *Career Profile:* Williams & Glyn's Bank/The Royal Bank of Scotland: Area Manager, Manchester; Assistant General Manager, Edinburgh. *Societies:* The Watsonian Club; The St James's Club; Alderley Edge Cricket Club. *Recreations, Interests:* Walking, gardening, cricket, hockey. *Address:* The Royal Bank of Scotland, PO Box 356, 38 Mosley Street, Manchester, M60 2BE (*tel:* 0161 242 3641; *fax:* 0161 228 7625).

LEONARD, Professor Raymond, Bsc, PhD(Salford), DSc(Manchester), FIMechE, FIEE, FIMgt

Professor of Industrial Technology, UMIST. *b.* 3 August 1941 Prestbury. *m.* 1962 Sylvia; two *s*. two *d*. *Education:* University of Salford; University of Manchester. *Career Profile:* Apprentice; State Scholarship; Industry (Research); UMIST. *Publications/Creative Work:* 220 publications on engineering and science; 2 books on industry. *Recreations, Interests:* Novel writing (4 published), poetry writing. *Address:* Total Technology, UMIST, Manchester, M60 1QD (*tel:* 0161 200 4155).

LEVER, His Honour Judge, QC, BA(Cantab)(1949),Barrister-at-Law(1951)

Senior Resident Judge, Bolton Combined Court Centre. *b.* 12 August 1928 Hiroshima, Japan. *m.* 1964 Elizabeth Marr; two *s*. *Education:* Bolton School; Gonville & Caius College, Cambridge 1st Class Law Tripos (1949); Middle Temple. *Military Service:* Flying Officer, RAF (1950-52). *Career Profile:* Practised at Bar, Manchester (1952-81); Asst. Recorder, Salford (1969); Recorder of Crown Court (1972); QC (1976); Circuit Judge (1981). *Prizes:* Tapp Post Graduate Scholar (1949); Blackstone Scholar, Middle Temple. *Recreations, Interests:* Theatre, literature, education (Governor & Trustee, Bolton School). *Address:* Lakelands, Rivington, Bolton, BL6 7RT (*tel:* 01204 468189).

LEVY, David, BA (Com) Manchester (1962)

Director, Brian Forbes Association (Search, Selection Agency). *b.* 27 June 1942; Manchester. *m.* 1966 Ruth; one *s.* one *d. Education:* Manchester Grammar School (1952-59); Manchester University (1959-62). *Career Profile:* Senior Partner, Levy, Brody & Co; Managing Director, Centrepart Ltd; Managing Director, Fielding Group of Companies. *Societies:* Manchester Society of Chartered Accountants; Worshipful Company of Chartered Accountants; Freeman of the City of London; Life Member, Lancashire County Cricket Club. *Recreations, Interests:* Orienteering, cricket, computers. *Address:* Brian Forbes Association, Hadfield House, Lancashire Hill, Stockport SK4 1RR *(tel:* 0161-477 2622; *fax:* 0161 476 2201); 6 The Mews, Gatley, Cheshire SK8 4PS *(tel:* 0161-428 7708).

LEWIS, Dewi Tudur Wyn, BA(Hons)(Cambridge, 1973),PGDipAA (City Univ,London, 1975)

Independent Publisher. *b.* 10 March 1951 Denbigh. *m.* 1978 Caroline Warhurst; one *s.* one *d. Education:* Rhyl Grammar School; Flintshire Technical College; Emmanuel College, Cambridge; City University, London. *Career Profile:* Director, Cornerhouse (1982-1994); Director, Bury Metro Arts Association (1975-82). *Publications/Creative Work:* Publishing Photography (1992); Photography UK (1996). *Societies:* Trustee, Documentary Photography Archive; Founder Member, Group of European Photography Publishers. *Recreations, Interests:* Visual arts, photography, music. *Address:* Dewi Lewis Publishing, 8 Broomfield Road, Heaton Moor, Stockport, SK4 4ND*(tel:* 0161 442 9450; *fax:* 0161 442 9450). *Additional Information:* Member of Arts Council of England Arts Lottery Fund Assessment Team Runner-up in Sunday Times Small Publisher of the Year Award (1996).

LEWIS, Robert J, CBE(1993)

Director of Social Services, Stockport MBC. *b.* 8 July 1940 Newcastle, Staffs. *m.* Margaret; two *s.* one *d. Public Offices:* President, Association of Directors of Social Services. *Education:* Orme Boys Secondary Modern School; Newcastle High School; Ruskin College, Oxford; Leicester College of Education. *Career Profile:* Director of Social Services, Oldham (1982-87); Assistant Director of Social Services, Stockport (1974-82). *Societies:* Rotary Club of Hazel Grove. *Address:* Social Services Department, The Town Hall, Stockport, SK1 3XE *(tel:* 0161 474 4611; *fax:* 0161 474 7895).

LEWIS, William Allan, BSc,MICE,DMS

Chief Executive, Trafford Metropolitan Borough Council. *b.* 2 December 1943 Ayrshire. *m.* 1965 two *s*; *m.* 1993 Heather; three *steps. Public Offices:* Director, Manchester Training Enterprise Council, Manchester Business Link. *Education:* Manchester Grammar School; Birmingham University. *Career Profile:* Initially Graduate Assistant Engineer, Manchester City Engineer's Department (1965); ultimately Deputy Chief Executive, Manchester City Council (1984); appointed to present position in 1987. *Recreations, Interests:* Sports, antiques. *Address:* Trafford Metropolitan Borough Council, Trafford Town Hall, Talbot Road, Stretford, Manchester, M32 0YT *(tel:* 0161 912 1900; *fax:* 0161 912 4190).

LILLIS, Bernard Joseph, BA(Hons),FCMA

Bursar, UMIST. *b*. 19 October 1954 Preston, Lancashire. *m*. 1975 Rachel; two *s*. *Education:* St Pius X Preparatory School, Preston; Catholic College, Preston; Manchester Metropolitan University. *Career Profile:* Dunlop Ltd; Champion Spark Plugs Ltd; Greenall Whitley plc; GEC Alsthom (Turbine Generators) Ltd; University of Central Lancashire. *Recreations, Interests:* Scouting, cycling, hill walking, reading, music and poetry. *Address:* UMIST, PO Box 88, Sackville Street, Manchester, M60 1QD (*tel:* 0161 200 3001; *fax:* 0161 200 3045; *e-mail:* blillis@fs2.ba.umist.ac.uk). *Additional Information:* Director, UMIST Ventures Ltd, TRAM plc.

LIMB, Christopher, LLB (Univ. of Liverpool, 1974),Barrister

Barrister. *b*. 12 March 1953 Cheshire. *m*. 1976 Gilliam M; two *s*. *Education:* Lymm Grammar School; Liverpool University. *Prizes:* Various at University; Holt Scholarship, Grays Inn and others. *Societies:* Professional: North West Co-ordinator, Association of Personal Injury Lawyers; Committe Member, Professional Negligence Bar Association; Member, PIBA, APIL, UIA; Personal: Salford Choral Society (Chairman); Lymm Twin Town Society (Chairman). *Recreations, Interests:* Choral singing, wine, France. *Address:* Young Street Chambers, 38 Young Street, Manchester, M3 3FT (*tel:* 0161 833 0489; *fax:* 0161 835 3938).

LINDRUP, Garth, BA,LLM

Partner, Addleshaw Sons & Latham, Solicitors, Manchester. *b*. 10 September 1948 Capetown, South Africa. *m*. 1991 Julie Elaine; two *s*. *Public Offices:* Chairman, Solicitors' European Group (1994-95); Hon Lecturer in Law, Manchester University (1993-96); P-t Lecturer in Law, Manchester University (1996-); President, Manchester Incorporated Law Library Society (1995-); Member of the Council of the Manchester Law Society (1987-94); Member of the Law Society's 1992 (subsequently International) Awareness Working Party (1989-93); Member of CBI's Competition Panel (1992-); Fellow of the Royal Society of Arts (1995-). *Education:* Moor Allerton School; Wrekin College; Manchester College of Commerce; St John's College, Cambridge. *Career Profile:* Partner, Addleshaw Sons & Latham (1984-); Director, Dunham Properties Ltd. *Publications/Creative Work:* Butterworths Competition Law Handbook (ed.); Butterworths Expert Guide to the European Union (contributor)(TBP); The Law Society's 'Solicitors in the European Union' (ed.); articles in New Law Journal, Law Society's Gazette and other publications. *Prizes:* Two school prizes for French. *Societies:* The Law Society; Manchester Law Society; Justice; International Bar Association; Ligue Internationale du Droit de la Concurrence; Grizedale Society; Byron Society; Georgian Group; Portico Library; Old Wrekinian Association; Johnian Society; Furniture History Society; Society of Public Teachers of Law; Manchester Tennis & Racquets. *Recreations, Interests:* Family, real tennis, fell walking. *Address:* Burton House, Burton-in-Kendal, Cumbria, LA6 1LH. *Additional Information:* Listed in Euromoney's: Guide to the World's Leading Competition and Antitrust Lawyers.

LING, Professor Roger John, MA,PhD,FSA

Professor of Classical Art and Archaeology, University of Manchester. *b*. 13 November

1942 Watford. *m.* 1967 Lesley Ann. *Education:* Watford Grammar School for Boys (1952-61); St John's College, Cambridge (1961-64); British School at Rome (1964-66). *Career Profile:* Lecturer in Classics, University College of Swansea (1967-71); University of Manchester: Lecturer, History of Art (1971-75); Senior Lecturer (1975-83); Reader (1983-92); Head of Department (1988-91); Professor (1992-); British Academy Research Reader (1991-93). *Publications/Creative Work:* 'The Greek World' (Oxford,1976); 2nd edn 'Classical Greece' (1988); 'Wall Painting in Roman Britain' (with N Davey)(1982); 'Romano-British Wall Painting' (Shire Publications, 1985); 'Roman Painting' (Cambridge, 1991); Editor, Fifth International Colloquium on Ancient Mosaics, held at Bath, 1987, II (1995); plus numerous books and papers. *Prizes/Awards:* Wace Medal for Classical Archaeology, Cambridge (1964). *Societies:* Association Internationale pour la Peinture Murale Antique; Society for the Promotion of Roman Studies; Society of Antiquaries of London; Derbyshire Archaeological Society; Archeological Institute of America. *Recreations, Interests:* Playing squash, supporting Watford FC, listening to pop music. *Address:* Department of Archaeology & History of Art, University of Manchester, Oxford Road, Manchester, M13 9PL *(tel:* 0161 275 3320; *fax:* 0161 275 3331). *Additional Information:* Director, British Research Project in the Insula of the Menander at Pompeii (1978-86) Director of Archaeological Excavations at Loughor, Glamorgan (1970-73) Director of Excavations at Carsington, Derbyshire (1980-83).

LIPSCHITZ, Gershon, BComm,FPMI,FFA

Senior Partner, Watson Wyatt. *b.* 2 May 1946 Port Elizabeth, South Africa. *m.* 1969 Lys; three *d. Education:* St Patrick's College, Port Elizabeth; University of Cape Town. *War Service:* Conscripted (56 days - honourably discharged). *Career Profile:* Southern Life Association, Cape Town (1966-69); Bacon & Woodrow (1970-73); Sedgwick Group (1973-81). *Recreations, Interests:* Golf, music, reading. *Address:* Watson Wyatt, Cardinal House, 20 St Mary's Parsonage, Manchester, M3 2LY *(tel:* 0161 839 1600; *fax:* 0161 839 1272).

LIVESEY, Philip Grimshaw, FCA (1948)

Director, P & P plc, Assured Asset Management plc, I.D.B. Limited; Governor, Royal Shakespeare Theatre. *b.* 13 January 1925; Stalybridge. *m.* 1949 Joan Mather; one *s.* three *d. Education:* Minimal. *War Service:* Royal Marine Commandos (1943-46). *Career Profile:* Partner in Charge, Coopers & Lybrand North West. *Societies:* St James's Club, Manchester; Royal Overseas, London; Manchester Literary & Philosophical Society (Past President); Portico Library; Manchester Academy of Fine Arts (Treasurer). *Address:* Lower Firwood, Leycester Road, Knutsford WA16 8QR *(tel:* 01565-653345).

LOCK, Professor Andrew Raymond, BA(Hons)(Leeds,1970),MSc(Econ)(London,1972), PhD(London,1979),FSS(1978), FRSA(1990),MBCS(1987)

Pro-Vice Chancellor, Dean of Faculty of Management & Business, The Manchester Metropolitan University. *b.* 23 September 1947 Tunbridge Wells, Kent. *m.* one *s.* one *d. Education:* Manchester Grammar School (1958-60); Solihull School (1960-65); University of Leeds (1966-70); London Business School (1970-72, 1975-78). *Career Profile:* Lecturer, Senior Lecturer, Principal Lecturer, Kingston Polytechnic (1972-83); Assistant Professor of Marketing, University of British Columbia (1979-80); Acting Head, Business Studies,

Kingston Polytechnic (1984-85); Head of Marketing & Corporate Strategy and Co-ordinator, Kingston Business School, Kingston Polytechnic (1985-87); Assistant Director, Manchester Polytechnic (1988-). *Publications/Creative Work:* 20 articles in the professional literature in the field of Marketing & Corporate Strategy. *Societies:* Royal Statistical Society; Market Research Society; British Computer Society; Sale RFC; Bowdon Cricket Club; Ski Club of GB. *Recreations, Interests:* Skiing, classic motorcycles. *Address:* Faculty of Management & Business, The Manchester Metropolitan University, Aytoun Street, Manchester, M1 3GH (*tel:* 0161 247 3703; *fax:* 0161 247 6350; *e-mail:* a.lock@mmu.ac.uk); 141 Hale Road, Hale, Altrincham WA15 8RT (*tel:* 0161 941 3362).

LOCKETT, Terence A, BA (Hons) Manchester,FRSA (1971)

Freelance Writer and Lecturer. *b.* 5 May 1931; Flixton, Lancs. *m.* 1956 Isabel; two *s.* *Education:* Stockport Grammar School (1939-50); Manchester University (1951-55). *Military Service:* National Service (1950-51). *Career Profile:* Schoolmaster (1955-62); Lecturer, Didsbury College of Education (1962-76) (Elected Governor 1969-75); Principal Lecturer in History of Art & Design, Manchester Polytechnic (1976-87). *Publications:* Books: 'The Rockingham Pottery' (with A A Eaglestone) (1964); 'Davenport Pottery & Porcelain, 1794-1887' (1972); 'Collecting Victorian Tiles' (1978); 'Davenport, China, Earthenware & Glass' (with G A Godden) (1990); numerous articles, catalogues, book reviews and specialist chapters in a wide variety of publications. *Societies:* Founder Chairman (since 1972), now President, of The Northern Ceramic Society; Member also of the English Ceramic Circle, The Wedgwood Society and other similar bodies. *Recreations, Interests:* Fell walking (Lake District), book collecting. *Address:* 6 Tideswell Road, Hazel Grove, Stockport SK7 6JG (01625-874160). *Additional Information:* Appears regularly as a porcelain expert on the BBC TV Antiques Roadshow; lectured extensively to museums, learned societies, NADFAS and collector clubs in this country and on several lecture tours of the USA.

LOFTHOUSE, John, BMus(Hons)(1978), PGCE(Cantab, 1979), MHSM, DipHSM(1981), MBA (1994)

Executive Director, The Alexandra Hospital. *b.* 29 July 1957 Blackpool. *m.* 1990 Alison; two *s.* one *d.* *Education:* Blackpool Grammar School; Sheffield University; Cambridge University. *Career Profile:* NHS (1979-89): Graduate Trainee, Charing Cross Hospital; Deputy Administrator, Royal National Orthopaedic Hospital; Assistant Administrator, St Bartholowmews Hospital; Deputy Administrator, The Middlesex Hospital; Planning Manager, Trent RHA; BMI Healthcare (1989-): Director of Operations, Princess Grace Hospital; Executive Director, The Park Hospital; Executive Director, The Alexandra Hospital. *Recreations, Interests:* Swimming, piano playing. (*tel:* 0161 428 3656, *fax:* 0161 491 3867).

LOMAX, Ian Stuart, LLB(Hons),MSocSc,FIMgt,MIPD,Barrister

Justices' Chief Executive & Justices' Clerk, City of Manchester Magistrates' Court. *b.* 13 January 1954 Blackburn, Lancashire. *Public Offices:* Secretary, Chancellor of the Duchy of Lancaster's Advisory Committee for the Appointment of Magistrates in the City of Manchester. *Education:* Accrington Grammar School; Manchester Metropolitan University;

Inns of Court School of Law, London; Birmingham University. *Publications/Creative Work:* Author and co-author of a large number of legal texts and articles. *Prizes:* Manchester Law Society's Rylands Prize (1975). *Societies:* Gray's Inn; Justices' Clerks Society; Wyresdale Anglers (Scorton, Lancs); Lancashire County Cricket Club. *Recreations, Interests:* Fly fishing, Land Rovers and Blackburn Rovers. *Address:* Justices' Chief Executive, City Magistrates' Court, Crown Square, Manchester, M60 1PR *(tel:* 0161 832 7272; *fax:* 0161 834 2198; *e-mail:* lomax@citymags.u-net.com).

LONGINOTTI, Peter Andrew, BSc (Hons),FCA,MSI

Partner, Head of Corporate Finance, Price Waterhouse. *b.* 12 March 1957 England. *m.* 1981 Gail; one *s. Education:* UMIST (1975-78). *Career Profile:* Price Waterhouse: Manchester (1978-87); Canada (1987-88); London (1989); Partner (1990); Manchester (1990-). *Prizes:* ICAEW: Professional Examination I (2nd place), Taxation Prize; Professional Examination II (3rd place). *Societies:* Member, Opera North Development Committee. *Recreations, Interests:* Opera, theatre, sport, travel. *Address:* Price Waterhouse, York House, York Street, Manchester, M2 4WS *(tel:* 0161 245 2000; *fax:* 0161 236 1468).

LORIMER, Professor Gordon Winston, BASc(British Columbia),PhD(Cantab),FIM,CEng

Head of Manchester Materials Science Centre, University of Manchester/UMIST; Head of Department of Materials Science, University of Manchester. *b.* 27 February 1941 Vancouver, British Columbia, Canada. *m.* 1970 Pamela Eileen Champness; one *s.* one *d. Education:* University of British Columbia; Cambridge University. *Career Profile:* University of Manchester: Assistant Lecturer (1967); Lecturer (1968); Senior Lecturer (1978); Reader (1984); Professor (1990). *Publications/Creative Work:* Over 150 publications in international scientific journals. *Prizes:* Presidents Medal, American Microprobe Analysis Society (1992). *Societies:* EMAG of IOP; Fellow, Institute of Materials; Royal Microscopial Society. *Recreations, Interests:* Squash, tennis, gardening, wine. *Address:* Manchester Materials Science Centre, University of Manchester/UMIST, Grosvenor Street, Manchester, M1 7HS *(tel:* 0161 200 3567; *fax:* 0161 200 3636; *e-mail:* g.lorimer@fs2.mt.umist.ac.uk); 5 Fairfax Avenue, Didsbury, Manchester, M20 6AJ *(tel:* 0161 434 1896).

LOVELL, Sir Alfred Charles Bernard, Kt (1961),OBE (1946),FRS (1955); PhD,LLD,DSc

Emeritus Professor of Radio Astronomy; Founder and Director, Nuffield Radio Astronomy Laboratories, Jodrell Bank until 1981. *b.* 31 August 1913; Oldland Common, Gloucestershire. *m.* 1937 Mary Joyce Chesterman (*dec'd*: 1993); two *s.* three *d. Education:* Kingswood Grammar School, Bristol; University of Bristol. *War Service:* Telecommunications Research Est (1939-45). *Career Profile:* Member, Aero Research Council (1955-58); University of Manchester: Asst Lecturer in Physics (1936-39); Lecturer (1945), Senior Lecturer (1947), Reader (1949), Jodrell Bank Experimental Station; Member, Air Navigation Committee (1953-56), Vice-Chairman (1955-56); Air Warfare Committee (1954-60); Member, Science Research Council (1965-70); Vice President, IAU (1970-76); President, British Association (1975-76); President, Royal Astronomical Society (1969-71); Montague Burton Professor of International Relations, University of Edinburgh (1973).

Publications: Lectures: BBC Reith Lectures (1958); Condon (1962); Guthrie (1962); Halley (1964); Queen's, Berlin (1970); Brockington, Kingston, Ontario (1970); Bickley, Oxford (1977); Crookshank, RCR (1977); Angel Memorial, Newfoundland (1977); Second RSA American Exchange Lecturer Philadelphia (1980); Rutherford Memorial Lecturer, Royal Society (1984); Blackett Memorial Operational Res Soc (1987). *Publications:* 'Science and Civilisation' (1939); 'World Power Resources and Social Development' (1945); 'Radio Astronomy' (1951); 'Meteor Astronomy' (1954); 'The Exploration of Space by Radio' (1957); 'The Individual and the Universe' (BBC Reith Lectures, 1958); 'The Exploration of Outer Space' (Gregynog Lectures, 1961); 'Discovering the Universe' (1963); 'Our Present Knowledge of the Universe' (1967); 'The Explosion of Science: the Physical Universe' (ed with T Margerison) (1967); 'The Story of Jodrell Bank' (1968); 'The Origins and International Economics of Space Exploration' (1973); 'Out of the Zenith' (1973); 'Man's Relation to the Universe' (1975); ' P M S Blackettel: a biographical memoir' (1976); 'In the Centre of Immensities' (1978); 'Emerging Cosmology' (1981); 'The Jodrell Bank Telescopes' (1985); 'Voice of the Universe' (1987); (with Sir Francis Graham Smith) 'Pathways to the Universe' (1988); 'Astronomer by Chance' (1990); 'Echoes of War' (1991); Many publications in physical and astronomical journals. *Prizes:* Hon Member, Royal Northern College of Music (1981); President, Inc Guild of Church Musicians (1976-89); Hon Freeman of City of Manchester (1977); Hon Fellow, Society of Engineers (1964); Hon Foreign Member, American Academy of Arts and Sciences (1955); Hon Life Member, New York Academy (1960); Hon Member, Royal Swedish Academy (1962), Manchester Lit & Phil Soc (1988); Hon LLD (Edinburgh) (1961), Calgary (1966); Hon DSc (Leicester) (1961), Leeds (1966), London (1967), Bath (1967), Bristol (1970); D Univ Stirling (1974), Surrey (1975); Hon FIEE (1967); Hon FInstP (1976); Duddell Medal (1954); Royal Medal (1969); Daniel & Florence Guggenheim International Astronautics Award (1961); Ordre du Merite pour la Recherche at l'Invention (1962); Churchill Gold Medal (1964); Maitland Lecturer and Silver Medallist, Inst of Structural Engineers (1964); Benjamin Franklin Medal, RSA (1980); Gold Medal, Royal Astronomical Society (1981); Commander's Order of Merit, Polish People's Republic (1975). *Societies:* Athenaeum; MCC; Lancashire County Cricket (Vice President 1981-) (President 1995-96). *Recreations, Interests:* Cricket, gardening, music. *Address:* The Quinta, Swettenham, Nr Congleton, Cheshire (*tel:* 01477 571254).

LOWE, Peter Carlton, BA Wales (1963),PhD Wales (1967),FRHistS

Reader in History, University of Manchester. *b.* 8 April 1941; Cardiff, Wales. *Education:* Howardian High School, Cardiff (1952-60); University of Wales (1960-65). *Career Profile:* Senior Lecturer in History, University of Manchester (1977-88); Lecturer in History, University of Manchester (1968-77); Assistant Lecturer in History, University of Manchester (1965-68). *Publications:* 'Great Britain and Japan, 1911-15' (Macmillan 1969); 'Great Britain and the Origins of the Pacific War' (Clarendon Press, 1977); 'Britain in the Far Eastel: A Survey, 1819 to The Present' (Longman, 1981); 'The Origins of the Korean War' (Longman, 1986); edited (with T G Fraser) 'Conflict and Amity in East Asia: Essays in Honour of Ian Nish' (Macmillan 1992). *Societies:* Royal Commonwealth Society; Royal Historical Society (Fellow). *Recreations, Interests:* Music, particularly opera, theatre. *Address:* Department of History, University of Manchester, Manchester M13 9PL (*tel:* 0161-275 3105; *fax:* 0161 275 3098).

LUMSDEN, Christopher Gerald Moore, LLB (Hons) Newcastle-upon-Tyne (1974)

Partner, Chaffe Street; Solicitor in England and Hong Kong. *b.* 4 April 1953; Cranwell, Lincs. *m.* 1981 Alison; one *s.* one *d. Education:* Rossall School. *Publications:* Financial Assistance Problems in Management Buy-Outs. *Societies:* St James's Club, Manchester; Ski Club of Gt Britain. *Recreations, Interests:* Tennis, skiing. *Address:*Chaffe Street, Brook House, 70 Spring Gardens, Manchester M2 2BQ (0161 236 5800); Barbers Lane Cottage, Antrobus, Nr Northwich, Cheshire CW9 6JP. *Additional Information:* Specialising in corporate and financial law with particular emphasis on equipment leasing and trade finance.

LYNNE, Liz

Member of Parliament, Rochdale. *b.* 22 January 1948 Woking. *Public Offices:* Various Liberal Democrat Committees. *Education:* Dorking County Grammar School. *Career Profile:* Acting career, numerous theatre appearances in rep and West End (1966-89); Speech Consultant (1989-92); Contested Harwich (1987); Won Rochdale (1992); Liberal Democrat spokesperson on Health & Community Care (1992-94); Social Security & Disability (1994-). *Recreations, Interests:* Travel, sport. *Address:* House of Commons, Westminster, London, SW1A 0AA (*tel:* 0171 219 6422; *fax:* 0171 219 2235; *e-mail:* lynnel@parliament.uk).

M

MACALISTER, Richard John, MA(Oxon),Dip.Sec.Inst.

Director, Wise Speke Ltd. *b.* 6 November 1962 Stocksfield, Northumberland. *m.* 1995 Jane Ashley Farthing. *Education:* Royal Grammar School, Newcastle upon Tyne (1974-81); St Edmund Hall, Oxford University (1982-86). *Career Profile:* (1986-94) Wise Speke Ltd, Newcastle upon Tyne (Director 1993). *Societies:* Vincents; St James's Club, Manchester; Manchester Tennis & Racquet Club. *Recreations, Interests:* Water polo, cricket, real tennis. *Address:* Wise Speke Ltd, 8 King Street, Manchester, M2 6AQ(*tel:* 0161 953 9700; *fax:* 0161 832 9092); 1 Park Road, Hale, Altrincham, WA14 9NL.

MACFARLANE, Malcolm Robert, FCIB

Senior Manager, Manchester Group, Lloyds Bank plc. *b.* 27 December 1942 Birmingham. *m.* 1965 Pat; three *d.* *Education:* King Edward VI Grammar School for Boys, Birmingham. *Career Profile:* Various managerial positions with Lloyds Bank in East Midlands and Lincolnshire; formerly area manager, Lloyds Commercial Service, East Midlands. *Prizes:* Banking World Award (1987). *Societies:* Bramhall Golf Club; Manchester & District Bankers Institute (Council Member)(President, 1995-96). *Recreations, Interests:* Golf. *Address:* LLoyds Bank plc, 53 King Street, Manchester, M60 2ES (*tel:* 0161 829 2801; *fax:* 0161 835 2521).

MACINTYRE, Ivan OStJ(1975),DL(1994); FFOM,FRCGP,DIH,FRSH,FRIPHH

Consultant Occupational Physician. *b.* 12 October 1925 Scotland. *m.* 1956 Hazel Sim; three *s.* *Education:* Allan Glen's High School of Science, Glasgow; Glasgow University. *War Service:* Sub. Lieutenant, RNVR (1944-46). *Career Profile:* House Surgeon, Southern General Hospital, Glasgow; House Surgeon and House Physician, Blackpool Victoria Hospital; General Practitioner, Old Trafford; Group Occupational Physician, CIBA-Geigy. *Publications/Creative Work:* 'Stress and the Executive' (Co-operative Management & Marketing, 1970); various articles in learned journals. *Societies:* Manchester Naval Officers Association (Hon Sec); Sale Medical & Dental Society (Hon Sec); Manchester Medico-Legal Society; Trafford Branch, St John Ambulance (Chairman & Member of Council). *Recreations, Interests:* Philately. *Address:* 15 Raglan Road, Sale, M33 4AN (*tel:* 0161 973 8846) (*fax:* 0161 976 4332).

MADDOCKS, His Honour Judge Bertram Catterall, MA(Cantab)

Circuit Judge, Northern Circuit. *b.* 7 July 1932 Southport. *m.* 1964 Angela V Forster; two *s.* one *d.* *Public Offices:* Chairman (part-time), VAT Tribunals (1977-92); Recorder (1988-90). *Education:* Malsis Hall, nr Keighley; Rugby; Trinity Hall, Cambridge. *Military Service:* National Service, 2 Lieut. RA (1951); Duke of Lancaster's Own Yeomanry (TA)(1958-67). *Career Profile:* Called to Bar, Middle Temple (1956); Harmsworth Scholar. *Societies:* Queen's; Manchester Tennis & Racquets; Northern Counties (Newcastle). *Recreations, Interests:* Real tennis, lawn tennis, skiing, bridge. *Address:*

Courts of Justice, Crown Square, Manchester; Moor Hall Farm, Prescot Road, Aughton, L39 6RT (*tel:* 01695 421601) (*fax:* 01695 421601).

MAHER, Christina Rose (*née* Lewington), OBE(1994); MA(Univ of Manchester, 1995)

Founder & Director, Plain English Campaign. *b.* 21 April 1938 Tuebrook, Liverpool. *Public Offices:* Founder Member, National Consumer Council; Trustee, Impact Foundation; Chairman, Stoneycroft Community Group; Founder, Salford Form Market. *Career Profile:* Campaigning on behalf of the consumer since 1971; founded Plain English Campaign (1979). *Publications/Creative Work:* 'Plain English Story'; 'Gobbledygook'; 'A-Z of Alternative Words'; 'DIY Report Writing Guide'; 'DIY Letter Writing Guide'; 'Utter Drivel'. *Prizes:* R Delbridge Award (1985). *Recreations, Interests:* Reading, walking, swimming, acting, theatre, community work (OAP and children). *Address:* Plain English Campaign, PO Box 3, New Mills, Stockport, SK12 4QP (*tel:* 01663 744409; *fax:* 01663 747038; *e-mail:* www.demon.co.uk.plainenglish).

MAKEPEACE, Christopher Edmund, BA Manchester (1965),FSA,ALA

Company Secretary, North West Buildings Preservation Trust; Consultant Local Historian. *b.* 6 March 1944; Coventry. *m.* 1970 Hilary Clare; one *s.* one *d. Education:* King Henry VIII Grammar School, Coventry; Manchester University; Manchester Library School. *Career Profile:* Librarian, Manchester Local History Library; Senior Planning Officer & Local Historian, Greater Manchester County Planning Dept. *Publications:* Numerous books and articles on the local history of Manchester and its region. *Societies:* Manchester Regional Industrial Archaeology Society; Lancashire & Cheshire Antiquarian Society; Manchester Lit & Phil; Disley Local History Society; Chetham Society; Library Association Local Studies Group. *Recreations, Interests:* Industrial archaeology, music, gardening, local history, history of Manchester, travel. *Address:* 5 Hilton Road, Disley, Cheshire, SK12 2JU (*tel:* 01663 763346).

MALLICK, Professor Netar Prakash, BSc,MB,ChB,FRCP

Professor of Renal Medicine, Manchester University; Hon Consultant Physician, Central Manchester NHS Trust. *b.* 3 August 1935 Blackburn. *m.* 1960 Mary Wilcockson; three *d. Education:* Queen Elizabeth Grammar School, Blackburn; Manchester University. *Career Profile:* Present positions (1994-); Hon University Professor in Renal Medicine (1992-94); Senior Lecturer (1972-73); Consultant, Department of Renal Medicine (1973). *Publications:* Case Presentations in 'Renal Disease in General Practice'; co-author 'Renal Medicine & Micrology' (Atlas of Nephrology); various papers in the professional medical literature.. *Societies:* Manchester Literary & Philosophical Society (President 1985-87); Association of Physicians; Renal Association of GB (President 1989-92); European Renal Association (Chairman 1991-94); Chairman, Committee on Renal Disease, Royal College of Physicians; Chairman, UEMS Nephrology Section (training in Europe); Adviser in Renal Disease, Chief Medical Officer, Dept of Health. *Recreations, Interests:* Theatre, cricket, other sports. *Address:* Dept of Renal Medicine, Central Manchester Healthcare NHS Trust, Oxford Road, Manchester, M13 9WL (*tel:* 0161 276 4411; *fax:* 0161 273 4834; *e-mail:* mallick@mri_renal.chmr.nhs.g).

MANSFIELD, Nicholas Andrew, BA(1973),BPhil(1976),AMA(1985)

Director, National Museum of Labour History. *b.* 3 August 1952 Cambridge. *m.* 1976 Julia Crawshaw; two *s.* one *d.* *Public Offices:* Member, Registration Committee, Museums & Galleries Commission; various museum advisory boards. *Education:* Central School, Cambridge (1963-70); Manchester University (1970-73); Exeter University (1974-76). *Career Profile:* Worked briefly in social services, adult education and building trade; Museums in Cambridgeshire, Derbyshire, Norfolk and South Wales (1977-89); Prest post (1989-). *Publications/Creative Work:* Around 20 articles on museums; oral history; military history; rural life and social history in learned journals and books; lots of exhibitions and several galleries. *Societies:* Society for the Study of Labour History (Committee Member). *Recreations, Interests:* Old churches, walking, military history.

MAPLES, David Samuel, LLB(Hons)(1981)

Corporate Partner, Alsop Wilkinson (Solicitors). *b.* 2 October 1959 Liverpool. *m.* 1992 Meryl; two *d.* *Education:* Liverpool Institute High School (1971-78); Sheffield University (1978-81); College of Law, Guildford (1981-82). *Societies:* St James's Club; Manchester Corn and Allied Trades Guild (Hon Solicitor). *Recreations, Interests:* Family, Everton Football Club, sports, theatre. *Address:* Alsop Wilkinson, 11 St James's Square, Manchester, M2 6DR (*tel:* 0161 834 7760; *fax:* 0161 831 7515).

MARCUSON, Elizabeth Carol (*née* Laves), BA Lawrence, Wisconsin (1964),PhD London (1973),Law Society Finals Manchester Poly (1988)

Solicitor, Hempsons, Manchester. *b.* 2 April 1943; Chicago, Illinois. *m.* 1966 Roger Marcuson; one *s.* one *d.* *Public Offices:* Trustee and Governor, Oaklands Preparatory School; JP (retired). *Education:* Francis Parker School, Chicago; Lawrence University, Wisconsin; London University; Manchester Polytechnic. *Career Profile:* Research Assistant, University of Chicago; Research Fellow, The Middlesex Hospital; Research Fellow, Hope Hospital; Solicitor, Pannone & Partners; Solicitor, North West Health Legal Services. *Publications:* Various papers on immunological topics. *Prizes:* Phi Beta Kappa (1964); Marshall Scholarship (1965-67); National Institutes of Health (Bethesda) Fellowship (1968). *Societies:* Henry Doubleday Research Association; Medico-Legal Society. *Recreations, Interests:* Opera, ancient history, gardening. *Address:* Stenner Brow, Stenner Lane, Didsbury, Manchester M20 2RQ (*tel:* 0161-445 7080).

MARCUSON, Roger W, MA,MChir,FRCS,FRCSEd

Consultant Vascular Surgeon, Manchester Royal Infirmary. *b.* 27 November 1936 Birmingham. *m.* 1966 Elizabeth; one *s.* one *d.* *Education:* Oundle School; Christ's College, Cambridge; The Middlesex Hospital Medical School. *Career Profile:* Qualified (1961); various training posts; Consultant Surgeon, Hope Hospital, Salford (1975); Manchester Royal Infirmary (1995). *Publications:* Various publications on aspects of vascular surgery. *Prizes:* Exhibitioner, Christ's College, Cambridge (1955). *Societies:* Travelling Surgical Society of Great Britain & Northern Ireland; other medical and surgical societies. *Recreations, Interests:* Gardening, music. *Address:* 14 St John Street, Manchester, M3 4DZ (*tel:* 0161 834 4411); Stenner Brow, Stenner Lane, Didsbury, Manchester, M20 2RQ.

MARKS, Nathan, LLB (Hons)

Senior Partner, Kuit Steinart Levy, Solicitors. *b.* 11 August 1932; Salford. *m.* 1954 Vivian Ann; two *s.* two *d.* *Public Offices:* Member of Court and Council, University of Manchester; Member of British Airways Consumer Council; President of the Manchester Law Society (1983-84); Convener of the Joint Taxation Committee of the Manchester Law Society, Institute of Chartered Accountants and Manchester Institute of Taxation. *Education:* North Manchester Grammar School; Manchester Grammar School; University of Manchester. *Career Profile:* Articled, David Blank; Admitted (1956); Assistant Solicitor (1956-58); joined J M Levy & Co (1958); became Partner (1959); amalgamated Kuit Steinart & Ashby (1959). *Societies:* The Law Society, Hale Lawn Tennis Club, Dunham Golf & Country Club. *Recreations, Interests:* Music, theatre, tennis, sailing, spectator sports, bridge, life long supporter of Manchester City Football Club, charitable work. *Address:* 3 St Mary's Parsonage, Manchester M3 2RD (*tel:* 0161-832 3434, *fax:* 0161 832 6650).

MARLOW, Joyce Mary (*née* Lees)

Author. *b.* 27 December 1929; Manchester. *m.* 1955 Patrick Connor; two *s.* *Public Offices:* PLR Advisory Board, Lay Member of Industrial Tribunals; Writers' Guild Executive Committee. *Education:* Crimsworth & Whalley Range High School, Manchester (1935-47); Bradford Civic Theatre School (1947-49). *Previous Positions:* Professional Actress (1949-66). *Publications:* 'The Peterloo Massacre' (1969); 'The Tolpuddle Martyrs' (1971); 'Life and Times of George I' (1973); 'Captain Boycott and the Irish' (1973); 'Kings and Queens of Britain' (1975); 'The Uncrowned Queen of Ireland' (1975); 'Mr and Mrs Gladstone' (1977); 'Kessie' (1985); 'Sarah' (1987) and 'Anne' (1989); 'Industrial Tribunals & Appeals' (1991). *Prizes:* Elizabeth Goudge Award for Best Historical Novel (1985) for 'Kessie'. *Societies:* Society of Authors; Fawcett Society. *Recreations, Interests:* Cricket, theatre, gardening. *Address:* 3 Spring Bank, New Mills, Stockport SK12 4AS (*tel:* 01663-742600).

MARSHALL, Thomas Warwick, MA Cantab (1971),FRICS (1985)

Deputy Chairman, Lambert Smith Hampton plc. *b.* 27 October 1945; Newcastle -upon-Tyne. *m.* 1973 Elizabeth Katrina; one *s.* one *d.* *Education:* Sherborne School; Christ's College Cambridge. *Societies:* St James's Club; Yorkshire Fly Fishers; Alderley Edge Cricket Club. *Recreations, Interests:* Fly fishing, cricket, walking. *Address:* 79 Mosley Street, Manchester M2 3LP (*tel:* 0161-228 6411); Millers Gate, Congleton Road, Alderley Edge, Cheshire SK9 7AD (*tel:* 01625-583024).

MARSHALL, Wayne, FRCO,DipRCM,ARCM

Pianist, organist and conductor; Organist in Residence, Bridgewater Hall, Manchester. *b.* 13 January 1961 Oldham, Lancs. *Education:* Chetham's School, Manchester; Royal College of Music, London; Hochschule für Musik, Vienna. *Career Profile:* Organ Scholar, Manchester Cathedral; extensive list of concert recitals as organist and pianist. *Recreations, Interests:* Travelling, photography. *Address:* c/o Harold Holt Ltd, 31 Sinclair Road, London, W14 0NS (*tel:* 0171 603 4600; *fax:* 0171 603 0019).

MARTIN, James, FCCA

Chief Executive, N Brown Group plc. *b.* 9 December 1942 Newcastle-upon-Tyne. *m.* 1964 Jean; two *s*. *Career Profile:* Unilever (1964-66); Dunlop (1966-70); Automotive Products (1970-73); N Brown Group plc (1973-). *Societies:* St James's Club; Hale Golf Club. *Recreations, Interests:* Golf. *Address:* N Brown Group plc, 53 Dale Street, Manchester, M60 6ES (*tel:* 0161 238 2000; *fax:* 0161 238 2308).

MARTIN, Peter, MSI(Dip)

Director, Wise Speke Ltd. *b.* Cheshire. *m.* Jane. *Public Offices:* Member of Court and Council, University of Salford. *Education:* Manchester Grammar School. *Career Profile:* Worked for National Westminster Bank for two years; recruited as Dealing Coordinator by Charlton Seal; the company was taken over by Wise Speke in 1990, appointed Director 1994. *Societies:* Chairman, Friends of Fairbridge in Salford. *Recreations, Interests:* Walking, climbing. *Address:* Wise Speke Ltd, PO Box 512, 8 King Street, Manchester, M60 2EP (*tel:* 0161 953 9700; *fax:* 0161 832 9092).

MARTIN, Robert William, FCA

Partner, Coopers & Lybrand, Managment Consulting. *b.* 7 January 1949 Suez, Egypt. *m.* 1971 Jaki; one *s*. one *d*. *Public Offices:* Director, INWARD. *Education:* Dean Close School, Cheltenham. *Career Profile:* Deloitte Haskins & Sells, Bristol (1967-73); Zambia (1973-77); Bradford (1977-85); Leeds (1985-89); London (1989-90); Merged with Coopers & Lybrand, London (1990-93), Manchester (1993-). *Publications/Creative Work:* Financial Mangement in Law Firms. *Recreations, Interests:* Contemporary art, theatre, cinema, walking, family. *Address:* Coopers & Lybrand, Abacus Court, 6 Minshull Street, Manchester, M1 3ED(*tel:* 0161 236 9191; *fax:* 0161 247 4000); Canterbury Gate, 31A Carrwood Road, Bramhall, Cheshire, SK7 3LR (*tel:* 0161 485 3946).

MARTIN, Wade, FCIB

Regional Managing Director, Corporate Banking Services, North West Region, National Westminster Bank plc. *b.* 7 September 1946 Stoke-on-Trent. *m.* 1967 Janet; two *s*. *Education:* Longton High School (1957-63); Cranfield School of Management (1984). *Career Profile:* District Bank/National Westminster Bank plc (1963-to date); Manger,Nottingham Thurland Street (1982-85); Senior Manager, Crewe, Nantwich Road Branch (1985-88); Corporate Account Executive, Spring Gardens Business Centre, Manchester (1988-91); Chief Manager, Liverpool Business Centre (1991-94). *Publications/Creative Work:* Several books on Association Football. *Societies:* Regional Council Member, CBI; Member, Advisory Board, The British American Business Group in the North West; Member, Steering Committee, Manchester Financial & Professional Forum; Member, Presidents Group, British Red Cross, Manchester Branch; Member, Employers Group of the Prince's Trust Volunteers; Member, Appeals Committee, Christie's Hospital Candelight Appeal; Director, Marketing Manchester. *Recreations, Interests:* Sport, principally as a spectator and particularly football, music and the performing arts. *Address:* Corporate Banking Services, National Westminster Bank plc, North West Regional Office, PO Box 631, 55 King Street, Manchester, M60 3NA (*tel:* 0161 829 6331; *fax:* 0161 829 6297).

MASON, Mary Rankine, MA Cambridge (1948),Teacher's Dip. Manchester (1948), DipSocSt London (1954),DMA (1973)

Retired. *b.* 21 April 1924; West Didsbury, Manchester. *Public Offices:* JP, City of Manchester (1963-94) (Chairman of Juvenile Panel 1984-88); Councillor, Bolton MBC (1986-); Chairman, Greater Manchester Certificate in Social Services Scheme (1982-93); Member, Greater Manchester Probation Committee (1984-94); Member of Court, Lancaster University (1988-92); Councillor, Bowdon UDC (1961-74) (Chairman 1965-66); Chairman, Greater Manchester Regional Liberal Party (1983-86); Liberal Parliamentary Candidate for Burnley (1964 and 1966) and Oldham West (1987). *Education:* Manchester High School for Girls; Girton College, Cambridge; Manchester University; London University. *War Service:* Temporary Civil Servant (1944-46). *Career Profile:* Nursery Teacher, Derby CB (1948-50); Posts in Local Authority Children's Departments - Dewsbury CB, Manchester City, Warrington CB, Stockport CB, (1950-67); Children's Officer, St Helens CB (1967-71); Director of Social Services, Bolton MB (1973-82). *Societies:* Association of Directors of Social Services (Chairman, NW Branch 1986-87); Magistrates Association; Gaskell Society; English Heritage; National Trust; Royal Society for the Protection of Birds; Royal Scottish Country Dancing Society; The Crossword Club; Manchester Literary & Philosophical Society *Recreations, Interests:* Scottish country dancing, sailing, travel, word games. *Address:* 43 Old Vicarage Road, Horwich, Bolton BL6 6QR (*tel:* 01204-697254).

MASON, Michael, DA Manchester ATD ARBS (1956),Fellow in Sculpture, British School at Rome

Principal Lecturer in Sculpture, Manchester Metropolitan University; Freelance Sculptor. *b.* 1 June 1935; Ashton-under-Lyne. *m.* 1959 Barbara; one *s.* one *d. Public Offices:* NW Arts Crafts Panel. *Education:* Manchester College of Art; Audenshaw Grammar School. *Career Profile:* Cheshire School of Art. *Creative Works:* One man exhibitions in UK, Europe, & Latin America (1969-); Group exhibitions in Salford, Manchester, London, Chester, Leeds, Rome, Sheffield, Newcastle, Bristol, Loughborough, Prestbury, Oldham, Holland and Croatia (1964-); Commissions from Local Authorities and Industry, Collections in V & A (London), Arts Council of Gt Britain as well as private collections in UK, Australia, Venezuela and Italy. *Publications:* Reviews in Art International, Arts Review, Studio International, Artscribe, Cheshire Life. *Prizes:* Heywood Prize, RMI. *Societies:* Royal Society of British Sculptors; National Society Art Education; Founder Member of Partnership Manchester. *Recreations, Interests:* Ti Chi Chuan, squash. *Address:* 89 Park Road, Hale, Altrincham, Cheshire WA15 9LE (*tel:* 0161-904 0767). *Additional Information:* Family of artists and designers: Barbara wife Painter, Daughter Claire Painter, Son Sculptor and Designer.

MATHER, Sir William Loris, Kt (1968),CVO (1986),OBE (1957),MC (1945),TD (1949) DL (1963)(Cheshire); BA Cambridge (1935),MA Cambridge (1938),Hon DEng Liverpool (1980),Hon LLD Manchester (1983), CEng, FIMechE, FBIM, FIAD, FRSA

b. 17 August 1913; Adlington, Cheshire. *m.* 1937 Eleanor Ames George; two *s.* two *d. Public Offices:* Chairman, NW Regional Economic Planning Council (1968-75); High Sherriff of Cheshire (1969-70); Vice Lord Lieutenant of Cheshire (1975-90); President,

Civic Trust for North West (1961-90), Manchester YMCA (1982-91), Prince Albert Angling Society, Greater Manchester East County Scout Council (1972-74); UMIST (1976-85), Association of College of Higher & Further Education (1975-76); President, MCCI (1964-66). *Education:* Oundle School; Cambridge University; Staff College Haifa. *War Service:* Cheshire Yeomanry, RTR; GSO2 TacHQ 8th Army; Instructor, Staff College, Camberley; GSO1 Control Commission. Service in Palestine, Lebanon, Syria, Iraq, Iran, N Africa, Italy, Belgium, Holland and Germany. *Career Profile:* Chairman, Mather & Platt plc and subsidiary companies (1960-78); Compair plc (1978-83), Neolith Chemicals Ltd (1983-87), Member Council, Duchy of Lancaster (1977-85), etc. *Creative Works:* Designed various machines. *Publications:* Various technical papers. *Prizes:* Hon Fellow UMIST; Hon Fellow Manchester College of Art & Design (now Manchester Metropolitan University); honorary LLD (Liverpool), DEng (Manchester). *Societies:* Leander Club, Hawks, St Moritz Tobogganing and other societies. *Recreations, Interests:* Field sports, golf, travel. *Address:* Whirley Hall, Macclesfield, Cheshire SK10 4RN *(tel:* 01625-422077). *Additional Information:* Governor, Manchester Grammar School (1965-80); Member of Court, Manchester University (1956-94), Salford University (1968-86); Feoffee of Chetham's Hospital School (1961-91); Chairman: Institute of Directors (1979-83); Granada Foundation; Director: Manchester Ship Canal Co (1970-85); Nat West Bank, Chairman Northern Board (1973-84).

MAVOR, Charles Hugh, BA(Hons)

Director, Singer & Friedlander Ltd. *b.* 19 July 1956 Lincoln. *m.* 1983 Margaret; one *d.* *Education:* Felsted School, Essex (1968-73); Exeter University (1974-78). *Career Profile:* Hambros Bank Ltd (1978-81); Riggs AP Bank Ltd (1981-85); Guinness Mahon & Co Ltd (1985-86); Singer & Friedlander Ltd (1986-). *Prizes:* University Prize (1978). *Societies:* Royal Mersea Yacht Club; Royal Western Yacht Club of England; Little Ship Club. *Recreations, Interests:* Travel, sailing, cricket, walking, classical music. *Address:* Singer & Friedlander Ltd, 46 Fountain Street, Manchester, M2 2AN *(tel:* 0161 833 9581; *fax:* 0161 833 9351).

MAYFIELD, The Right Rev Christopher John, BA(1957),OxDipTh(1963),MSc(1983)

Bishop of Manchester. *b.* 18 December 1935 Plymouth. *m.* 1962 Caroline; two *s.* one *d.* *Education:* Sedbergh School (1949-54); Gonville & Caius College, Cambridge (1954-57); Wycliffe Hall Theological College, Oxford (1961-63). *Military Service:* Engineering Trainer, RAF. *Career Profile:* Vicar, St Mary's, Luton (1971); Rural Dean, Luton (1974); Archdeacon, Bedford (1979); Bishop, Wolverhampton (1985). *Recreations, Interests:* Family, gardening, mountain walking, cricket. .

McAULIFFE, Professor Charles Andrew, FRSC(1988) BScTech,MS,DPhil,DSc

Professor of Inorganic Chemistry; Head of Department of Chemistry, UMIST. *b.* 29 November 1941 Cork, Ireland. *m.* 1967 Margaret McAlpine; one *s.* two *d.* *(marr. diss. 1993)*; *m.* 1994 Elizabeth Jane Oliver; one *d.* *Education:* UMIST (1960-63); Florida State University (1963-65); Oxford University (1965-67). *Publications/Creative Work:* 8 books authored, co-authored, or edited; 400 publications in scientific literature; co-inventor of MANOIL process for converting household rubbish into oil. *Societies:* Royal Society of

Chemistry. *Recreations, Interests:* My children, music, currrent affairs, inorganic chemistry. *Address:* Department of Chemistry, UMIST, PO Box 88, Manchester, M60 1QD *(tel:* 0161 200 4514; *fax:* 0161 228 1250; *e-mail*: noel.mcauliffe@umist.ac.uk).

McCARTNEY, Ian

MP for Makerfield; Shadow Minister of State for Employment (1994-). *Public Offices:* Former Member, Personal Social Services Committee and Select Committee on Social Security (1988-92); Former Secretary, Tribune Group; PLP Department Committees on Environment and Social Services; Former Chair, Employment PLP Committee; All Party Groups on Home Safety, Child Abduction, Rugby League, and Solvent Abuse. *Career Profile:* Labour Party Organiser (1973-87); Secretary to Roger Stott MP (1979-87); Wigan Borough Councillor (1982-87); Member, Greater Manchester Fire & Civil Defence Authority (1986-87); Wigan Family Practitioner Committee (1984-86); President of Wheelchair Fund; Chair, TGWU Parliamentary Group (1989-91); Chair, North West Parliamentary Labour Party (1992-93); Labour's Front Bench Spokesperson on the National Health Service (1992-94). *Address:* House of Commons, Westminster, London, SW1A 0AA.

McCOLLUM, Professor Charles Nevin, Hunterian Professorship, Royal College of Surgeons of England (1985) MB ChB (Birmingham,1972),FRCS(London,1976), FRCS (Edinburgh,1976), MD(Birmingham,1981)

Professor of Surgery, University of Manchester; Honorary Consultant Surgeon, South Manchester University Hospitals Trust. *b.* 17 April 1950 Stafford. *m.* 1976 Margaret Ludmilla; two *d. Education:* Tettenhall College, Worcestershire (1959-64); Millfield School, Street, Somerset (1964-67); The Medical School, University of Birmingham (1967-72). *Career Profile:* Following basic surgical training, Lecturer in Surgery to Sir Geoffrey Slaney in Birmingham until (1983). Moved to London as Senior Lecturer/Reader and Consultant Surgeon at Charing Cross Hospital; awarded Hunterian Professor to the Royal College of Surgeons (1985); appointed to Chair in Surgery in Manchester (1989) based at South Manchester University Hospitals. *Publications/Creative Work:* Main research interests are in arterial and venous disease; thrombosis; stroke; ischaemia reperfusion injury; shock and wound healing with special reference to leg ulceration; blood transfusion therapy; over 200 research publications, articles and chapters relating to the above topics. *Prizes:* Moynihan Prize, Association of Surgeons of Great Britain and Ireland (1979); Patey Prize, Surgical Research Society of Great Britain and Ireland (1983); King Edward's Fund, Major Grant Award (1988). *Societies:* British Medical Association; Surgical Research Society of Great Britain and Ireland (ex-Treasurer); Vascular Surgical Society; Association of Surgeons of Great Britain and Ireland. *Recreations, Interests:* Real tennis, sailing, skiing, shooting. *Address:* University Department of Surgery, South Manchester University Hospitals Trust, Withington Hospital, Nell Lane, Manchester, M20 8LR *(tel:* 0161 291 3840; *fax:* 0161 291 3846); Birtles Old Hall, Birtles, nr Macclesfield, Cheshire, SK10 4RS.

McCOMBS, John, NDD St Martins College of Art, London (1966),ROI,ARBA,FRSA

Professional Artist; Evening Class Teacher of Art in Further Education. *b.* 28 December 1943; Manchester. *Public Offices:* Council Member of the Manchester Academy of Fine

Arts and of the Royal Institute of Oil Painters. Also Selection and Hanging Committee Member of both; Previously Honorary Literary Secretary of Manchester Academy and Publicity Officer of Royal Institute of Oil Painters. *Education:* Alfred St Junior School, Harpurhey, M/c; Manchester High School of Art; St Martins College of Art, London (1962-67) (College Tutors included F Gore, A Reynolds and L Kossoff). *Creative Works:* Landscape artist working in oils making a visual record of the Saddleworth village of Delph and the surrounding landscape scenery; Paintings in Manchester City Art Gallery, Salford Art Gallery, Saddleworth Museum and other public collections. *Publications:* Articles on painting for 'Leisure Painter' magazine. *Prizes:* Stanley Grimm Prize, ROI (1990); The Peoples Prize, Manchester Academy of Fine Arts (1991); College Prize (Pratt Bequest) from St Martins (1966); David Murray Landscape Painting Scholarship from the Royal Academy (1966). *Recreations, Interests:* Walking, theatre, music. *Address:* John McCombs Gallery, 12 King Street, Delph, Nr Oldham, Lancs OL3 5DQ (*tel:* 01457-874705); 12 Berry Street, Greenfield, Nr Oldham, Lancs (*tel:* 01457-874755).

McGEORGE, Samuel Dick, TD (1966)

Retired. *b.* 21 June 1924; Glasgow, Scotland. *m.* 1953 Barbara Lois Wilson; two *s.* one *d.* *Public Offices:* Chairman, Stockport Family Health Services Authority (1985-94); Chairman, Stockport Health Commission (1994). *Education:* Queens Park, Glasgow; Civil Service Commission. *War Service:* RAF (1944-47) subsequently TA, Cameronians (Scottish Rifles) and Cheshire Regiment. *Career Profile:* Director and General Manager, British Engine Insurance Ltd (1979-83); Director, Royal Insurance (UK) Ltd (1982-83); President, Insurance Institute of Manchester (1975-76); Chairman, International Machinery Insurers Association (1979-82). *Recreations, Interests:* Archaeology, reading, gardening. *Address:* 272 Bramhall Lane South, Bramhall, Stockport, Cheshire (*tel:* 0161-439 1409).

McGRATH, Marian Juliet (*née* Kelly), BMus(Hons),LRAM,ARCM

Orchestra Manager, Hallé Orchestra. *b.* 26 February 1960 Wembley, Middlesex. *m.* two *s.* one *d.* *Education:* Sheffield University (1978-81); Royal Academy of Music (1984-85). *Career Profile:* Assistant Personnel Manager, London Symphony Orchestra (1988-91); Orchestra Manager, Royal Academy of Music, London (1991-92); Orchestra Manager, Hallé Orchestra (1992-). *Prizes:* Mrs Stewart Blake Recital Prize (1981), Sheffield University. *Address:* Hallé Concerts Society, The Bridgewater Hall, Manchester, M2 3WS (*tel:* 0161 237 7000; *fax:* 0161 237 7029).

McGUCKEN, Richard Brian, MB,BCh,BAO,FRCP,DCH

Consultant Paediatrician & Medical Director, Wigan & Leigh Health Services NHS Trust. *b.* 4 July 1942 Belfast. *m.* 1967 Frances; two *s.* one *d.* *Education:* Royal Belfast Academical Institution; Queens University, Belfast. *Career Profile:* Junior Doctor Posts, N Ireland (1965-71); Paediatrician, Nigeria (1971-73); Consultant Paediatrician, Wigan & Leigh (1973-); Medical Director, Wigan & Leigh NHS Trust (1993-). *Publications/Creative Work:* Various medical papers. *Societies:* Manchester Paediatric Club; British Paediatric Association; Fellow, Royal College of Physicians, London. *Recreations, Interests:* Fell walking, photography, travel, active in local parish church ministry, supporter of Wigan Rugby League Team. *Address:* Royal Albert Edward

Infirmary, Wigan, WN1 2NN (*tel:* 01942 822186; *fax:* 01942 822181); 12 Chorley Road, Hilldale, Parbold, Wigan, WN8 7AL (*tel:* 01257 462058).

McGUIRE, John Charles, FCIB

Corporate Director, Royal Bank of Scotland. *b.* 30 July 1948 Manchester. *m.* 1968 Pam; one *s.* one *d.* *Public Offices:* Chairman, Economic Affairs Committee, Manchester Chamber of Commerce & Industry. *Education:* North Manchester Grammar School. *Career Profile:* Career Banker - Williams Deacon's Bank through to Royal Bank of Scotland; posts in London/Switzerland; returned to Manchester in 1988. *Societies:* St James' Club. *Recreations, Interests:* Golf, music, skiing. *Address:* Royal Bank of Scotland, 55 Spring Gardens, Manchester, M2 2BY (*tel:* 0161 242 3012; *fax:* 0161 237 5072).

McINTOSH, Fiona Anne, BSc(Hons)(Open University),DRSAM

Orchestra Manager, BBC Philharmonic (1995-). *b.* 21 April 1957 Cupar, Fife. *Education:* Royal Scottish Academy of Music & Drama (1974-77); Guildhall School of Music & Drama (1977-78); Open University (1990-95). *Career Profile:* Violinist, BBC Scottish Symphony Orchestra (1986-91); Orchestral Manager, The Ulster Orchestra, Belfast, N Ireland (1991-95); Orchestra Manager, BBC Philharmonic, Manchester (1995-). *Address:* BBC Philharmonic, New Broadcasting House, PO Box 27, Oxford Road, Manchester, M60 1SJ (*tel:* 0161 244 4009; *fax:* 0161 244 4010; *e-mail:* fiona.mcintosh@bbc.co.uk).

McIVOR, Ian Walker, LLB(Hons),Barrister-at-Law

Barrister-at-Law; Head of Chambers, Deansgate Chambers (1977-). *b.* 19 January 1944 Worsley, Lancashire. *m.* 1969 Patricia Wendy; one *s.* four *d.* *Education:* Bolton Institute; London University. *Military Service:* OTC, Kings Regiment (1967-69). *Career Profile:* Trainee Solicitor; University Graduate; Barrister. *Prizes:* Marshall Hall Trust Award; Pupillage Scholarship from Inner Temple. *Societies:* Didsbury Golf Club; Holyhead Golf Club; Heald Green Social Club. *Recreations, Interests:* Golf, fishing, swimming, sailing. *Address:* 334 Deansgate, Manchester, M3 4LY(*tel:* 0161 834 3767); 3 Framingham Road, Brooklands, Sale, Cheshire, M33 3SH (*tel:* 0161 962 8205).

McKINLAY, Donald, National Diploma in Painting

Artist - Painter and Etcher. *b.* 4 October 1929 Bootle, Liverpool. *m.* 1954 Helen; two *d.* *(marr. diss. 1968) Education:* Liverpool College of Art (1946-50). *Military Service:* National Service (1950-52). *Career Profile:* Scenic Painter, Liverpool Playhouse (1953-57); Warwick Bolam Secondary Modern, Liverpool (1957-60); St Helens School of Art (1960-63); Manchester/Liverpool Colleges of Art (1960-68); Schoool of Architecture, Gujarat University, Ahmedabad, India (1968); Lecturer, Manchester College of Art (1968-1990). *Publications/Creative Work:* Manchester Cathedral Crib; Tagore Theatre Mural; Royal Liverpool Hospital Mural; Ellen Strange Memorial, Holcombe Moor; numerous one person exhibitions. *Prizes:* Manchester Academy of Fine Arts Awards (1992, 1993, 1995) Major Award (1994). *Recreations, Interests:* Theatre, music. *Address:* 9 Hareholme Lane, Cloughfold, Rossendale, BB4 7JZ (*tel:* 01706 219211).

McLEOD, Professor David, BSc (Hons),MB ChB (Hons),FRCS,FRCOphth

Head of Department of Ophthalmology, University of Manchester; Honorary Consultant Ophthalmologist, Manchester Royal Eye Hospital; Civilian Consultant Ophthalmologist, Royal Air Force. *b.* 16 January 1946; Burnley. *m.* 1967 Jeanette; one *s.* one *d. Education:* Burnley Grammar School (1957-63); University of Edinburgh (1963-69). *Career Profile:* Consultant Ophthalmologist, Moorfields Eye Hospital, London (1978-88). *Societies:* Royal College of Ophthalmologists (Council Member); Club Jules Gonin (Council Member); Bramhall Park Golf Club. *Recreations, Interests:* Golf, theatre. *Address:* University Department of Ophthalmology, Manchester Royal Eye Hospital, Oxford Road, Manchester M13 9WH (*tel:* 0161-276 5620, *fax:* 0161 273 6354, *e-mail:* penny.o'reilly@man.ac.uk), Willowtrees, 4 Ladybrook Road, Bramhall, Stockport, SK7 3LZ (*tel:* 0161 485 2013).

McLOUGHLIN, Andrew John, MA(Cantab)

Partner, Fieldings Porter, Bolton. *b.* 13 August 1959 Wigan. *m.* 1986 Wendy; one *s.* one *d. Education:* Canon Slade Grammar School, Bolton; Christ's College, Cambridge. *Career Profile:* Articled, Slater Heelis, Manchester; Assistant Solicitor, Addleshaws; Partner, Fieldings Porter. *Societies:* Association of Personal Injury Lawyers. *Recreations, Interests:* Family, keeping healthy, tennis. *Address:* Fieldings Porter, Silverwell House, Silverwell Street, Bolton (*tel:* 01204 387742; *fax:* 01204 329129).

McNEILL, Terence Joseph, Solicitor of the Supreme Court,Diploma in Law

Justices' Chief Executive for North & West Greater Manchester; Clerk to the Justices for the City of Salford Bench. *b.* 31 January 1954 Manchester. *m.* 1979 Margaret; three *d. Public Offices:* Justices' Chief Executive to the North & West Greater Manchester Magistrates' Courts Committee; Secretary to the Duchy of Lancaster Salford Advisory Committee; Member, Lord Chancellor's Department Working Party - Court Clerk Competencies; Member, Judicial Studies Board Working Party - Magistrates' Chairmanship Training. *Education:* St Edwards' Primary School (1960-65); St Gregory's Grammar School (1965-72); Manchester Polytechnic (1977-86). *Career Profile:* Court Clerk, Manchester City Magistrates' Court (1972-89); Deputy Clerk to the Justices, South & East Cheshire Magistrates' Court (1989-92); Clerk to the Justices, City of Salford Magistrates' Court (1994-); Registered Trainer at Madingley Hall, Cambridge University Board of Extra-Mural Studies. *Publications/Creative Work:* Formation of a comprehensive system of Witness Support in Salford. *Societies:* Institute of Personnel Development; Institute of Management; Medico Legal Society; Manchester Law School. *Recreations, Interests:* Family, voluntary work for community, good food and good wine, antiques, relaxing. *Address:* City of Salford Magistrates' Court, Bexley Square, Salford, M3 6DJ (*tel:* 0161 834 9457; *fax:* 0161 839 1806).

McNIVEN, Peter, BA(Hons)(1965),MA(1967),PhD(1977)

Sub-Librarian, Head of Special Collections, John Rylands University Library of Manchester. *b.* 22 September 1944 Doncaster, South Yorkshire. *m.* 1969 Betty; two *s. Education:* Prescot Grammar School (1955-62); University of Manchester (1962-68). *Career Profile:* Assistant Librarian, Manchester University Library (1969-78); Sub-

Librarian, JRULM (1978-). *Publications/Creative Work:* 'Heresy and Politics in the Reign of Henry IV: the Burning of John Badby' (Woodbridge, Boydell & Brewer, 1987); Articles on the reign of Henry IV in Bulletin of the JRULM; English Historical Review; History; Mediaeval Studies; and Transactions of the Historic Society of Lancashire and Cheshire; Articles and handlists relating to the Library's collections in the BJRULM; (with others) editor 'The Diary of Henry Prescott, LLB, Deputy Registrar of Chester Diocese' (Record Society of Lancashire and Cheshire). *Societies:* Royal Historical Society, elected Fellow (1991); Record Society of Lancashire and Cheshire (General Editor, 1984-95), Council Member; Historic Society of Lancashire and Cheshire; Chetham Society, Council Member; Ranulf Higden Society, Committee Member; RSPB; Wildfowl and Wetlands Trust. *Recreations, Interests:* Birdwatching, reading, writing. *Address:* John Rylands University Library, 150 Deansgate, Manchester, M3 3EH(*tel:* 0161 834 5343; *fax:* 0161 834 5574).

MEACHER, Michael Hugh, Greats (Class I) Oxford (1962)

MP (Labour), Oldham West (1970-) and Shadow Cabinet Spokesman on Employment. *b.* 4 November 1939; Hemel Hempstead, Herts. *m.* 1962 Molly; two *s.* two *d.* *(marr. diss. 1987)*; *m.* 1988 Lucianne; one *steps.* one *stepd.* *Education:* Berkhamsted School, Herts (1946-58); New College, Oxford (1958-62); LSE (1962-63). *Career Profile:* Shadow Cabinet Spokesman on Health & Social Security (1983-87); Shadow Cabinet Spokesman on Employment (1987-89); Member of Labour Party NEC (1983-88). *Publications:* 'Taken for a Ride' (1972); 'Socialism with a Human Face' (1982); hundreds of articles on social and economic policy. *Societies:* Greenpeace; Amnesty; Anti-Apartheid; Child Poverty Action Group; Fabian Society, etc. *Recreations, Interests:* Sport, especially tennis, music. *Address:* House of Commons, London SW1.

MEASOR, Duncan Harty

Retired Journalist. *b.* 25 July 1924 Sunderland. *m.* 1952 Marjorie Douglas; three *d.* *Public Offices:* Member of Executive Council & House Committee, Broughton House Home for Disabled Ex-Servicemen; Pat Seed Fund Central Committee; Committee, Port of Manchester Sea Cadets Association. *Education:* Bede Collegiate, Sunderland; College of the Sea. *War Service:* Royal Navy (1942-46) all in destroyer Hotspur. *Career Profile:* Staithmaster, Sunderland South Docks; Reporter Sunderland Echo; Reporter, Northern Daily Mail; Chief Sub-Editor, Manchester Evening News; 'Mr Manchester' Diary Editor for 22 years; newspaper columnist (1947-96). *Publications/Creative Work:* 'Twin Cities' (1988) a history of Manchester and Salford achievements; '75 Years under Sail' (1994); booklets on Broughton House history, shipping, docks, transport, road safety and many other subjects. *Societies:* Manchester Naval Officers' Association; Trearddur Bay Sailing Club; Royal Northern College of Music Association of Friends; Guild of Motoring Writers; National Union of Journalists (Life Member); Grahams 1820 Club; Manchester Press Club. *Recreations, Interests:* Reading, writing, motor sport. *Address:* Damian Place, Brook Lane, Alderley Edge, Cheshire, SK9 7QJ (*tel:* 01625 582426). *Additional Information:* First person (1956) outside London to pass Institute of Advanced Drivers' test, Membership No.159.

MELLOR, Ian MA,DipEd

Headmaster, Stockport Grammar School. *b.* 30 June 1946 Oldham, Lancs. *m.* 1969

Margery; three *s*. *Education:* Manchester Grammar School; Sidney Sussex College, Cambridge. *Career Profile:* Headmaster, Sir Roger Manwood's School, Sandwich, Kent (1991-96). *Recreations, Interests:* Sport, bridge, music, reading. *Address:* Stockport Grammar School, Buxton Road, Stockport, SK2 7AF (*tel:* 0161 456 9000).

MELLOR, Katharine Margaret, MA (Hons) St Andrews (1971)

Partner, Elliott & Company, Solicitors. *b*. 26 May 1949; Bristol. *m*. 1975 Lawrence Manners Hass. *Public Offices:* President, Manchester Law Society (1989-90); Member, Central Blood Laboratories Authority (1989-93); Non-executive Director, South Manchester University Hospitals NHS Trust (1994-). *Education:* Fairfield Grammar School, Bristol (1960-67); St Andrews University (1967-71); Law Society Examinations, Manchester Polytechnic (1971-72), College of Law, Chester (1974-75). *Previous Positions:* Chairman, Association of Women Solicitors, Manchester (1982-85); Member, National Committee of Association of Women Solicitors; Member, Bowdon Deanery Synod (1984-88); Member, St Peter's Parochial Church Council (1984-88); Member, Steering Committee of CLARITY (1984-88); Member, Manchester Luncheon Club Committee (1983-86). *Societies:* Law Society; Manchester Law Society; Association of Women Solicitors; CLARITY; National Trust; Manchester Luncheon Club. *Recreations, Interests:* Girl Guides, food (particularly cheese), gardening, classical music, reading, wine. *Address:* Elliott & Company, Centurion House, Deansgate, Manchester M3 3WT (*tel:* 0161-834 9933); 'Heughfield', 5 Chesham Place, Bowdon, Altrincham, Cheshire WA14 2JL.

MELMOTH, Graham John, FCIS

Chief Executive, Co-operative Wholesale Society Ltd. *b*. 18 March 1938 London. *m*. 1967 Jennifer Mary Banning; two *s*. *Public Offices:* Trustee, National Museum of Labour History, New Lanark Conservation Trust. *Education:* City of London School. *Military Service:* National Service, Lieutenant RA (1957-59). *Career Profile:* Assistant Secretary, Chartered Institute of Patent Agents (1961-65); Secretary, BOC-AIRCO Ltd (1965-69); Deputy Secretary, Fisons plc (1969-72); Secretary, Letraset plc (1972-75); Secretary, Co-operative Wholesale Society Ltd (1976-96), Chief Executive (1996-); Non-Executive Chairman, Ringway Developments plc; Director, The Co-operative Bank plc, Unity Trust Bank plc and others. *Societies:* FRSA. *Recreations, Interests:* Opera, theatre, co-operative history. *Address:* CWS Ltd, PO Box 53, New Century House, Manchester, M60 4ES(*tel:* 0161 834 1212; *fax:* 0161 832 6388; *e-mail:* abl@msmcws.demon.co). *Additional Information:* Elected President, International Co-operative Alliance (ICA), Geneva (Sept. 1995).

MELROSE, Margaret Elstob (*née* Jackson then Watson), DL (Cheshire) (1987)

Elected Member, Cheshire County Council (1967-), Chairman (1984-85) (1986-87); Chairman, Manchester Airport Consultative Committee; Chairman, Tatton Park Management Committee; Former Chairman, Cheshire Rural Community Council; Governor, Manchester Metropolitan University; Former President, Macclesfield Constituency Conservative Association; Vice President, Cheshire Agricultural Society (Lady Patroness, 1996); Vice-Chairman, Tatton Constituency Conservative Association; Vice President, Cheshire Ploughing & Hedge-Cutting Society; General Commissioner for Taxes, Salford & North Manchester; Vice-Chairman, David Lewis Centre for Epilepsy. *b*.

2 May 1928; Birmingham. *m.* 1948 Kenneth Ramsay Watson; one *d.* *(marr. diss. 1957)* *Public Offices:* Chairman, Cheshire County Council (1984-85) and (1986-87); Chairman (former), North West Children's Planning Committee; Member (former), Macclesfield RDC; Vice Consul for the Lebanon for N England, Scotland & N Ireland; Chairman, Nether Alderley Parish Council (3 times); various council committees and school governor chairmanships. *Education:* Wilmslow Preparatory School; Howell's School, Denbigh; Girton College, Cambridge. *Previous Positions:* Secretary to Consultant Psychiatrist in Manchester; Conservative Chief Whip, Chester County Council. *Prizes:* Drapers' Company Scholarship to Cambridge. *Societies:* Wilmslow Golf Club. *Recreations, Interests:* Golf, bridge, sailing, horses, country life, knitting, tapestry and collecting thimbles. *Address:* The Coach House, Stamford Road, Alderley Edge SK9 7NS *(tel:* 01625 585629; *fax:* 01625 590647). *Additional Information:* North of England Woman of the Year (1985); Cheshire Woman of the Year (1986).

MERRETT, Kenneth Ronald

Secretary, Manchester United Football Club plc. *b.* 29 November 1944; Manchester. *m.* 1982 Gail; one *s.* three *d.* *Education:* Manchester Central Grammar School (1955-60). *Career Profile:* Assistant Secretary, Manchester United Football Club (1970-88). *Recreations, Interests:* Crown green bowling, Methodist Church Local Preacher. *Address:* Manchester United FC, Manchester M16 0RA *(tel:* 0161-872 1661).

METCALFE, Professor (John) Stanley, CBE(1993); BA(Econ)(1967),MSc(1968)

Stanley Jevons Professor of Political Economy and Cobden Lecturer, University of Manchester. *b.* 20 March 1946 Liverpool. *m.* 1967 Joan; one *s.* one *d.* *Public Offices:* Member, Monopolies and Mergers Commission (1991); Member, Advisory Council on Science & Technology (1984-92). *Education:* Liverpool Collegiate High School; University of Manchester. *Career Profile:* Lecturer, University of Manchester (1969-74); Lecturer, Senior Lecturer, University of Liverpool (1974, 1978, 1980); Professor, University of Manchester (1980-); Dean of Faculty of Economic & Social Studies (1992-95). *Publications:* About 100 academic articles, books and related works. *Prizes:* Cobden Prize, University of Manchester (1967). *Societies:* Manchester Statistical Society (President, 1992-95); International J Schumpeter Society (President Elect 1996-98); Leigh & Lowton Sailing Club. *Recreations, Interests:* Sailing, walking. *Address:* Department of Economics, University of Manchester, Oxford Road, Manchester, M13 9PL *(tel:* 0161 275 4824; *fax:* 0161 275 4928). *Additional Information:* Non-Executive Director, Bodycote International, Manchester (1995-).

MIDDLETON, Stuart Christopher, MSc,MCIBS

Regional Manager, Bank of Scotland, Manchester. *b.* 4 March 1954 Aberdeen, Scotland. *m.* 1973 two *s.* *(marr. diss. 1981)*; *m.* 1985 Pamela; one *d.* *Education:* Aberdeen Grammar School; Heriot Watt University, Edinburgh. *Career Profile:* Bank of Scotland (man and boy)(1973-). *Publications/Creative Work:* Various articles for Acquisitions Monthly, Insitute of Directors Management Buy-out Guide. *Societies:* St James' Club, Manchester. *Recreations, Interests:* Reading, doing deals, angling,. family. *Address:* Bank of Scotland, 19/21 Spring Gardens, Manchester, M2 1FB *(tel:* 0161 953 7700; *fax:* 0161 834 1828).

MIDGLEY, Julia, DipAD(1969)

Self Employed Artist/Senior Lecturer, Liverpool John Moores University. *b*. 7 July 1948 Manchester. *m*. 1973 Johnstone Godfrey; two *s*. *Education:* Mid Cheshire College of FE (1965-66); Manchester College of Art & Design (1966-69). *Career Profile:* Since 1970 Freelance artist; Since 1978: part-time Lecturer, Manchester Polytechnic (now MMU); West Cheshire College; Hugh Baird College of FE; Exeter College of Art & Design; Mid Cheshire College of FE. *Publications/Creative Work:* Numerous exhibitions including Royal Academy Art (Summer Exhibitions); Royal Society Etcher Engravers; Laing Landscape Competitions; Manchester Academy of Fine Arts; London Contemporary Art Fairs; European Printmakers; Printmakers Council; Article 'In Praise of a British Institution' (Arts Review Yearbook). *Prizes:* Ayling Porteous Gallery, Chester; Laing Landscape Competition, Manchester Evening News Award; Rainford Trust Prize, Major Award; Printmakers Council, Gainsborough's House Award. *Societies:* Printmakers Council; Manchester Academy of Fine Art (Vice President to 1996); National Association Painters in Acrylic (Hon Member); Chelsea Arts Club. *Recreations, Interests:* Sailing, tennis. *Address:* 140 Chester Road, Northwich, Cheshire, CW8 4AW (*tel:* 01606 781490). *Additional Information:* Exhibiting widely in UK and abroad (US, Europe, Abu Dhabi). Examples of work in numerous public, corporate and private collections.

MILES, Professor Ian Douglas, BSc(Univ. of Manchester,1969)

Director, Policy Research in Engineering, Science & Technology (PREST); University of Manchester. *b*. 21 February 1948 Gloucester. *m*. 1970 Valerie Francis; one *d*.; *m*. Clare Degenhardt; three *s*. *Education:* Yeovil Grammar School; Hove Grammar School; University of Manchester. *Career Profile:* Research Posts, Science Policy Research Unit, University of Sussex (1972-90); Visiting Fellow/Professor at various universities. *Publications/Creative Work:* Over 150 publications. *Address:* PREST, University of Manchester, Oxford Road, Manchester, M13 9PL (*tel:* 0161 275 5921; *fax:* 0161 273 1123; *e-mail:* Ian.Miles@man.ac.uk).

MILLER, David Frederick Peter, BSc(Hons)(Univ. of Manchester, 1974),FCA(1977)

Regional Senior Partner, Price Waterhouse, Chartered Accountants. *b*. 13 July 1953 Bishop Auckland, Co Durham. *m*. 1975 Susan; one *s*. one *d*. *(marr. diss. 1993)*; *m*. 1994 Lynne; one *steps*. *Education:* Queen Elizabeth Grammar School, Darlington (1964-70); University of Manchester (1971-74). *Career Profile:* Price Waterhouse: Manchester (1974); London (1978); USA (1981); Partnership (1985); Regional Senior Audit Partner (1989-95); Member of Price Waterhouse UK Audit Executive (1992-95); Regional Senior Partner (1995-). *Prizes:* First Place in ICAEW Final Examinations (1977). *Recreations, Interests:* Sports watcher and occasional participant (Manchester City Supporter), cricket "fanatic", music (catholic taste), theatre. *Address:* Price Waterhouse, York House, York Street, Manchester, M2 4WS (*tel:* 0161 245 2000).

MITCHELL, George Grant, MBChB (Manchester,1962), FRCSEd(1973), MRCOG (1971), FRCOG(1984)

Consultant Obstetrician and Gynaecologist; Clinical Director, Department of Obstetrics &

Gynaecology; Clinical Director, Cromwell IVF & Fertility Centre, Hope Hospital; Honorary Associate Lecturer, University of Manchester. *b.* 22 September 1939 Banff. *m.* 1962 Sandra; one *s.* two *d. Education:* William Hulme Grammar School; University of Manchester Medical School. *Career Profile:* Initial house officer posts, surgical research post, 3 years in general practice, Altrincham; returned to hospital medicine (obstetrics & gynaecology); Clinical Director of Department with special clinical interest in infertility. *Publications/Creative Work:* Numerous articles in the professional journals. *Societies:* North of England Obstetrics & Gynaecological Society; North West Regional Association of Obstetricians & Gynaecologists. *Recreations, Interests:* Travel, computers, photography. *Address:* 16 St John Street, Manchester, M3 4EA *(tel:* 0161 834 4282); Department of Obstetrics & Gynaecology, Hope Hospital, Salford, M6 8HD *(tel:* 0161 787 5259) *(fax:* 0161 787 5619).

MITCHELL, Lt Cmd Noel Croundwell, DSC(1945),VRD(1954),DL(1989)

Retired. *b.* 25 December 1920 Hale, Cheshire. *m.* 1945 Rosemarie; two *d. Education:* Wrekin College, Wellington, Shropshire. *War Service:* Fighter Pilot, RAF; 273Sqd RAF, Ceylon (1942); North Sea Patrols, Orkney Isles (1943); 1839 Sqd Sumatra East Indies Fleet & British Pacific Fleet; commanded 1st 1831 RNVR Air Squadron (1947). *Career Profile:* Director, family civil engineering company. *Societies:* Royal Thames Yacht Club; The Naval Club; Chairman, The Manchester Naval Officers Association; Chairman, Manchester Branch, Sea Cadet Association. *Address:* Flat One, Crofton, Stamford Road, Bowdon, WA14 2JH *(tel:* 0161 928 0077).

MONTAGUE, Professor Peter, BSc,PhD,CEng,FICE,FIMechE

Pro-Vice-Chancellor and Professor of Engineering, University of Manchester. *b.* 9 October 1932 Thornaby-on-Tees. *m.* 1956 Anne; three *s.* three *d. Education:* St Mary's College, Middlesborough; University of Leeds; Imperial College. *Career Profile:* Stress Analyst, De Havilland Aircraft Co; Lecturer, Senior Lecturer, Reader, Head of Department of Engineering; Dean of Faculty of Science & Engineering, University of Manchester; Warden of Halls of Residence for 13 years, University of Manchester. *Publications:* Numerous publications on solid mechanics and structural engineering; undergraduate textbook on structural engineering. *Prizes:* Several prizes from Institutions of Civil Engineers and Mechanical Engineers. *Recreations, Interests:* Music, walking, DIY. *Address:* Manchester School of Engineering, Simon Building, University of Manchester, Oxford Road, Manchester, M13 9PL *(tel:* 0161 275 4301; *fax:* 0161 275 3844).

MONTGOMERY, Lady Joyce (*née* Riddle), DL, Greater Manchester (1992); DipEd

Chairman, Manchester & District Housing Group. *b.* 23 June 1937 Jarrow, Co Durham. *m.* 1971 Sir Fergus Montgomery. *Public Offices:* Board Member, Housing Corporation; Non-Executive Board Member, South Manchester University Hospital Trust. *Education:* Newcastle-upon-Tyne Church High School; Lady Mabel College of Physical Education. *Career Profile:* PE Teacher, Sacred Heart Convent, Newcastle; PE Lecturer, St Mary's College, Newcastle (1975-84); Greater Manchester Council Member, Manchester & District Housing Group; NW Representative, Housing Corporation. *Societies:* Altrincham & Sale Conservative Association. *Recreations, Interests:* Supporting my husband's political

work as Member of Parliament for Altrincham and Sale. *Address:* Manchester & District Housing Association, Apex House, 266 Moseley Road, Manchester, M19 2LH(*tel:* 0161 224 6281; *fax:* 0161 257 3179; *e-mail:* 100350.36@compuserve.com).

MONTGOMERY, Sir William Fergus, Kt(1985)

Member of Parliament for Altrincham & Sale (1974-). *b.* 25 November 1927 Hebburn, Co Durham. *m.* 1971 Joyce Riddle. *Public Offices:* Councillor, Hebburn UDC (1950-58). *Education:* Hebburn Methodist School; Jarrow Grammar School; Bede College, Durham. *Military Service:* National Service, Royal Navy (1946-48). *Career Profile:* Schoolteacher; MP Newcastle-upon-Tyne (1959-64); MP Brierley Hill (1967-74); MP Altrincham & Sale (1974-). *Recreations, Interests:* Bridge, theatre. *Address:* House of Commons, London, SW1A 0AA (*tel:* 0171 219 3619; *fax:* 0171 219 2248); 6 Groby Place, Altrincham, Cheshire, WA14 4AL (*tel:* 0161 928 1983) (*fax:* 0161 929 1983).

MONTI, Adriano, Political Sciences, University La Sapienza, Rome (1981)

Consul of Italy, Manchester (1993-). *b.* 30 October 1958 Rome. *m.* 1983 Mary Claire Odorico; one *s.* one *d. Career Profile:* Bank Officer San Paolo di Torino Banking Group (1977-78); Joined Ministry of Foreign Affairs (1978-); Trade Officer for EEC Affairs (1978-84); Posted to Italian Embassy, Addis Ababa, Economic & Commercial Attache (1984-86); Italian Embassy in Washington DC, Senior Trade Officer (1986-91); Ministry of Foreign Affairs Rome, Second Secretary, Dept for Scientific Cooperation (1991-93). *Address:* The Italian Consulate, Rodwell Tower, 111 Piccadilly, Manchester, M1 2HY (*tel:* 0161 236 9024; *fax:* 0161 236 5574).

MOORE, Stuart Alfred, BA (Admin) Manchester (1964),MA (Econ) Manchester (1967)

Chairman, Central Manchester Healthcare NHS Trust; Deputy Vice-Chancellor, Professor of Quantitative Studies, University of Manchester. *b.* 9 October 1939; Stockport. *m.* 1966 Diana Mary Connery; two *s.* one *d. Public Offices:* Manager/Governor Local Schools. *Education:* Stockport School; University of Manchester. *Career Profile:* Dean, Faculty of Economic and Social Studies (1980-83); Pro Vice Chancellor (1985-90). *Publications:* Various articles in scholarly journals. *Prizes:* Cobden Prizewinner. *Societies:* Royal Economic Society; Royal Statistical Society. *Recreations, Interests:* Hollywood films, light music, reading thrillers, DIY, gardening, photography. *Address:* The University, Manchester M13 9PL (*tel:* 0161-275 7400); Central Manchester Healthcare NHS Trust, Oxford Road, Manchester M13 9WL (*tel:* 0161-276 4841); 2 Carisbrooke Avenue, Hazel Grove, Stockport SK7 5PL (*tel:* 0161-483 8109).

MORRIS, The Rt Hon Alfred, PC (1979),AO,QSO (1989),MP; BA Hons (Modern History) Oxford (1953),MA Oxford (1956),PGCE Manchester (1954)

MP for Wythenshawe; Opposition Front Bencher, specialising in the problems and needs of disabled people. *b.* 23 March 1928; Manchester. *m.* 1950 Irene; two *s.* two *d. Public Offices:* Labour and Co-operative MP for Wythenshawe (1964-); First-ever Minister for Disabled People(1974-79); Labour Front Bencher in the House of Commons continuously (1970-93); Chairman of UN World Planning Group appointed to draft 'International

Charter' for disabled people worldwide (1980-81); Chairman of Managing Trustees of both the Parliamentary Contributory Pension Fund and the House of Commons Members' Fund (1983-); Chairman of the Parliamentary and Scientific Committee (1987-90). *Education:* Manchester elementary schools (1933-42); Manchester evening schools (1942-46); Ruskin College, Oxford (1949-50); St Catherine's College, Oxford (1950-53); Dept of Education, University of Manchester (1953-54). *Military Service:* Served in Army (1946-48) mainly in the Middle East. *Previous Positions:* Formerly a Manchester Schoolteacher and then Industrial Relations Officer of the Electricity Supply Industry, Electricity Council, Millbank, London SW1. *Publications:* 'Human Relations in Industry' (Electricity Council, 1961); Fabian Essay, '*VATEL:* a tax on the consumer' (1970); contributor to several books on the problems and needs of disabled people. *Prizes:* Field Marshal Lord Harding Award for work of outstanding value to disabled people (1971) and the Louis Braille Memorial Award for distinguished services to the blind; both in recognition of authorship and enactment of the Chronically Sick and Disabled Persons Act 1970, promoted as a Private Member's Bill. *Recreations, Interests:* Reading, gardening, swimming and tennis. *Address:* House of Commons, London SW1A 0AA (*tel:* 0171-219 5024: 0171-219 4039, Secretary)). *Additional Information:* Hon Fellow, Manchester Metropolitan University (1991); elected President of the Co-operative Congress (1995-96); Paul Harris Fellow of Rotary International 'for services to disabled people accross the world' (1996); only British subject to have been awarded the Order of Australia by the Federal Government of Australia and New Zealand's Queen's Service Order (QSO).

MORRIS, Rt Hon Charles Richard, HM Privy Council (1978),DL, Greater Manchester

Deputy Chairman, Ponti's Group Ltd. *b.* 14 December 1926 Manchester. *m.* 1950 Pauline; two *d.* *Public Offices:* Chairman, Oldham, Rochdale and Tameside Groundwork Trust (1983-). *Education:* Brookdale Park School, Manchester; Manchester School of Commerce (Evening). *Military Service:* Royal Engineers (1945-48). *Career Profile:* President, Clayton Labour Party (1950-52); Member, Manchester Corporation (1954-64); Member, PO Workers Union; Parliamentary Candidate (Labour) Cheadle Division Cheshire (1959); MP (Labour) Manchester Openshaw (1963-83); PPS to Postmaster-General (1964); Assistant Government Whip (1966-67); Deputy Chief Whip (1969-70); PPS to Rt Hon Harold Wilson (1970-74); Min of State: DOE (1974); CSD(1974-79); Deputy Shadow Leader (1981-83). *Publications/Creative Work:* 'Commons Select Commmittees' (contributor); 'Understanding the Civil Service' (contributor). *Prizes:* Awarded Ford Foundation/English Speaking Union Scholarship USA (1963). *Societies:* Royal Society of Arts (1978); Industry/Parliamentary Institute (1981). *Address:* C/o Ponti's Group, 17-21 Wenlock Road, London, N1 7SL (*tel:* 0171 250 1414); 24 Buxton Road West, Disley, Nr Stockport, SK12 2LY (*tel:* 01663 762450).

MORRIS, Frederick John, DL (1987); ACII,APMI

Chairman, MCCI Pension Trustees Ltd. *b.* 2 November 1920 Blackburn. *m.* 1946 Isobel Marguerite. *Public Offices:* President, Bolton Chamber of Commerce (1974-76); President, Manchester Chamber of Commerce & Industry (1984-87). *Education:* Queen Elizabeth's Grammar School, Blackburn. *War Service:* Rejected on medical grounds. *Career Profile:* Former Director, C E Heath (UK) Ltd and subsidiaries; Deputy Chairman, C E Heath (Lancashire) Ltd (retired 1985). *Societies:* Manchester Literary & Philosophical Society; St

James' Club. *Recreations, Interests:* Gardening, walking, theatre. *Address:* 14a East Beach, Lytham, Lytham St Annes, FY8 5EU (*tel:* 01253 735172).

MORRIS, Jonathon

Actor. *b.* 20 July 1960 Urmston, Manchester. *Education:* Salford College of Technology; Bristol Old Vic Theatre School. *Career Profile:* Movies: 'The Fantastiks' (MGM), 'The Journals' (Paramount); TV; Beau Geste; Prisoner of Zenda; The Consultant; Bread; numerous roles in London West End Theatres, Chichester, Cambridge, Oxford, Bristol and Edinburgh; Seven Royal Command Performances. *Prizes:* Variety Club Award for Comedy Performance (1989). *Recreations, Interests:* Keen traveller, singer, athlete, dancer and reader. *Address:* C/o William Morris, 31-32 Soho Square, London, W1V 5BG.

MORRIS, Michael Andrew, MB ChB(Manchester,1968),FRCS(London,1973)

Consultant in Trauma & Orthopaedics, Stockport Acute Services NHS Trust. *b.* 22 March 1946 Marple, Cheshire. *m.* 1973 E Margaret; three *d.* *Public Offices:* Medical Appeals Tribunal. *Education:* William Hulme Grammar School, Manchester (-1963); Manchester University Medical School (1963-68). *Career Profile:* Registrar & Senior Registrar in Training Scheme, North West Regional Health Authority; Research Fellow, Mayo Clinic Minnesota, USA (1977-78). *Publications/Creative Work:* Various in professional journals. *Societies:* British Medical Association; British Orthopaedic Association; British Society for Surgery of the Hand; North West Surgical Hand Society (Secretary). *Recreations, Interests:* Skiing, travelling, cars, oenology. *Address:* Ryley Mount, 432 Buxton Road, Stockport, SK2 7JQ (*tel:* 0161 483 9333; *fax:* 0161 419 9913). *Additional Information:* Special interest in hand surgery and the upper limb.

MOSCROP, Dr John James,BA(Manchester,1972),DipLibStud(Belfast,1976), LLB(Hull, 1982), MPhil(Salford,1989), PhD(Leicester,1996), FRSA(1976). Called to the Bar (Middle Temple)(1983)

Senior Crown Prosecutor, Crown Prosecution Service, Manchester. *b.* 18 September 1949 Manchester. *Public Offices:* Chairman of Convocation (1995-96), Secretary of Convocation (1990-95), Salford University; Council, Salford University (1995-96); Council, Manchester Literary & Philosophical Society (1993-96). *Education:* Bridgewater School, Drywood Hall, Worsley, Manchester (1961-68); Manchester University (1969-72); Belfast University (1975-76); Hull University (1979-82); Inns of Court School of Law (1982-83); Salford University (1984-89); Leicester University (1990-96). *Career Profile:* Pupillage (1983-85, London) - 1 New Square; Crown Prosecution (1986-). *Societies:* Manchester Literary & Philosophical Society; Portico Library; Northern Lawn Tennis Club; Royal Overseas League, London. *Recreations, Interests:* Research and writing. *Address:* Crown Prosecution Service, Sunlight House, Quay Street, Manchester, (*tel:* 0161 869 7402).

MOSLEY, Kenneth

Self-employed Artist. *b.* 19 October 1934 Manchester. *m.* 1954 Christine; one *s.* two *d.* *(marr. diss. 1970)*; *m.* 1971 Valerie; one *s.* one *d.* *Education:* North Manchester High School for Boys; Moseley Hall County Grammar School, Cheadle; Manchester Regional

College of Art (part-time). *Military Service:* National Service, RAF. *Career Profile:* Various advertising agencies on the creative side. *Societies:* Tytherington Club. *Recreations, Interests:* Iyengar Yoga, gardening, swimming. *Address:* Greenhouse Gallery, 13 Wellington Road, Bollington, Macclesfield, SK10 5JR(*tel:* 01625 572872). *Additional Information:* Painted and exhibited regularly in Portugal (Instituto de Belas Artes 'Dicionario de Pintores e Escultores Portugueses' by Fernando de Pamplona).

MOSS, Robert James, LLB(Hull,1982),Law Society Finals(Hons)(1983),Solicitor

Partner, Head of Commercial Litigation, Vaudreys. *b.* 1 November 1959 Sale. *Public Offices:* School Governor. *Education:* St Bede's College, Manchester; Hull University. *Societies:* Lancashire County Cricket Club; Manchester Property Gun & Punt Club; New Mills Golf Club; St James' Club. *Recreations, Interests:* Cricket, golf, shooting. *Address:* Vaudreys, 13 Police Street, Manchester, M2 7WA (*tel:* 0161 834 6877; *fax:* 0161 834 2440).

MOTH, Kenneth, BA (Hons Architecture) Manchester (1970),BArch Manchester (1972), GradDipBldgCons Architectural Assoc, London (1980)

Architect, Partner, Building Design Partnership, Manchester. *b.* 1 April 1948; Ashton-under-Lyne, Manchester. *m.* 1977 Barbara Jean; two *s.* *Public Offices:* Past Chairman, Manchester Conservation Areas and Historic Buildings Advisory Panel. *Education:* Manchester Road County Primary School, Droylsden; Audenshaw Grammar School; Manchester University; Architectural Association, London. *Creative Works:* Architect for Granada TV Warehouse Studios; Granada TV News Centre, Liverpool; Granada Studios Tour, Coronation St Set, Greater Manchester Museum of Science and Industry; Joule Library for UMIST; Eureka! The Children's Museum, Halifax; Masterplan, National Maritime Museum, Greenwich. *Publications:* Various articles for journals. *Prizes:* Civic Trust Award; Civic Trust Commendation; Europa Nostra Commendation; RIBA Regional Award; RIBA "40 under 40" Exhibitor; RICS/Times Conservation Commendations. *Societies:* Victorian Society; Society for the Protection of Ancient Buildings; Association for Studies in the Conservation of Historic Buildings. *Recreations, Interests:* Maritime history, loitering in second-hand bookshops, cycling, swimming, walking, travelling, second childhood, music, old buildings and matters Mancunian. *Address:* Building Design Partnership, Sunlight House, Quay Street, Manchester M60 3JA (*tel:* 0161-834 8441); 28 Greenside Drive, Lostock Green, Northwich, Cheshire CW9 7SR (*tel:* 01606-46228).

MOUNT, Peter William, BScTech,CEng,MIMechE

Chairman, Salford Royal Hospitals NHS Trust. *b.* 14 January 1940 England. *m.* 1966 Margery; one *s.* two *d.* *Public Offices:* Member of Court, University of Manchester. *Education:* De La Salle College, Salford; UMIST; University of Vienna. *Career Profile:* Production Management, Rolls Royce Ltd; Consultant, Price Waterhouse; Chief Executive of Subsidiary, Chloride Group; Chief Executive of Division, Thorn EMI. *Societies:* Member, Institute of Mechanical Engineers. *Recreations, Interests:* Walking, skiing. *Address:* Salford Royal Hospitals NHS Trust, Stott Lane, Salford(*tel:* 0161 787 5186; *fax:* 0161 787 5974; *e-mail:* 100350.36@compusave).

MOUTREY, David John, MBA,BEd

Director, Arts About Manchester Ltd. *b.* 13 February 1958 Sedgefield, Co Durham. *m.* 1984 Lindsey; one *s.* one *d. Public Offices:* Board Member & Trustee, Manchester International Arts, Mossley Community Arts; Governor, Livingston School, Mossley. *Education:* Open University; Leeds Polytechnic School of Education; Bede Sixth Form College, Teeside; Furness Comprehensive. *Career Profile:* Director of Arts About Manchester for over 6 years and Freelance Consultant; Manager, Abraham Moss Centre Theatre for 6 years; Teacher 2.5 years; Student Union Office 1 year; Undergraduate. *Publications/Creative Work:* Produced over 14 theatre shows for community projects during the last 10 years; Firework Display Designer & Technician. *Recreations, Interests:* Fireworks, drumming, piano, fell walking. *Address:* Arts About Manchester Ltd, 23 New Mount Street, Manchester, M4 4DE (*tel:* 0161 953 4035; *fax:* 0161 953 4106; *e-mail:* arts-mcr@mcr1.poptel.org.uk).

MOWAT, Magnus Charles, FCA

Non-executive Director, Allen plc, AF plc, Ryalux Carpets Ltd and others. *b.* 5 April 1940 Sheffield. *m.* 1968 Mary Lynette St Lo Stoddart; three *s. Public Offices:* Chairman, Institute of Directors, Greater Manchester Branch; Chairman, Booth Charities; Chairman, Manchester YMCA. *Education:* Haileybury. *Career Profile:* Partner, Illingworth & Henriques (1970-84); Director, Barclays de Zoete Wedd Ltd (1984-91). *Societies:* St James's Club, Manchester; Boodles. *Recreations, Interests:* Shooting, music, gardening. *Address:* New Park House, Whitegate, Northwich, CW8 2AY (*tel:* 01606 889659; *fax:* 01606 889659).

MUIRHEAD, Geoff, FCIT

Chief Executive, Manchester Airport plc. *b.* 14 July 1949 Stockton-on-Tees. *m.* Clare; one *d. Public Offices:* Board Member, UK Airport Operators Association; Airports Council International; Duke of Westminster's North West Business Leadership Team; Vice President, Manchester Chamber of Commerce & Industry; Council Member, University of Salford; Board Director, Manchester TEC (Training & Enterprise Council); Member, CBI North West Regional Council. *Education:* Teeside Polytechnic. *Career Profile:* Appointed Chief Executive, Manchester Airport plc (1993); Appointed Director of Business Development, Manchester Airport plc (1992); Appointed Director of Development, Manchester Airport plc (1988); Commenced career with British Steel; subsequently promoted to senior positions with William Press; Simon-Carves,; Flour and Shand (including posts in Saudi Arabia, Belgium and Eire). *Recreations, Interests:* Keen follower of sport, particularly Rugby Union and Golf (an eager amateur golfer). *Address:* Manchester Airport plc, Manchester Airport, Manchester, M90 1QX (*tel:* 0161 489 3000).

MULLIGAN, Christopher James, BA(Hons),CIPFA

Director General, GMPTE. *b.* 24 February 1950 Liverpool. *m.* 1988 Rowena. *Education:* Poundswick Grammar School (1964-68); University of Hull (1968-71). *Career Profile:* Accountant, Manchester City Council (1971-73), GMC (1973-77); GMPTE: Executive Accountant (1977-86), Director of Finance (1987-91), Director General (1991-).

Recreations, Interests: Reading, walking, good food. *Address:* GMPTE, 9 Portland Street, Piccadilly Gardens, Manchester, M60 1HX *(tel:* 0161 242 6000; *fax:* 0161 228 3291).

MUNN, Professor Robert William BSc(Bristol,1965),PhD(Bristol,1968), DSc(Manchester, 1982)

Professor of Chemical Physics; Dean of UMIST (1994-97). *b.* 16 January 1945 Bath, Somerset. *m.* 1967 Patricia Lorna; one *s.* one *d. Education:* Huish's Grammar School, Taunton (1955-62); University of Bristol (1962-68). *Career Profile:* Postdoctoral Fellowships, National Research Council of Canada, Ottawa (1968-70); Department of Natural Philosophy, Edinburgh (1970-71); Lecturer in Chemistry (1971-80), Reader (1980-84), Professor (1984-); Vice-Principal (1987-90), Dean of UMIST (1994-97). *Publications:* Some 180 scientific publications including; 'Molecular Electromagnetism' (with A Hinchliffe); 'Magnetism and Optics of Molecular Crystals' (with J Rohleder); 'Nonlinear Optics: Principles and Applications' (with C N Ironside). *Societies:* Fellow, Royal Society of Chemistry, Chartered Chemist; Fellow, Institute of Physics, Chartered Physicist. *Recreations, Interests:* Active member of St Michael and All Angels Parish Church, Bramhall. *Address:* Department of Chemistry, UMIST, Manchester, M60 1QD *(tel:* 0161 200 4534; *fax:* 0161 200 4584; *e-mail:* R.W.Munn@umist.ac.uk).

MURKIN, Leonard Thomas

Mayor, Trafford Metropolitan Borough. *b.* 27 February 1938 Manchester. *m.* Maureen; one *s.* two *d. Public Offices:* Chair of Finance, Greater Manchester Fire Authority. *Education:* Havely Hey Primary School, Wythenshawe; Yew Tree Secondary School. *Military Service:* National Service, Royal Corps of Signals (1959-61). *Career Profile:* Joiner, Foreman, Site Agent, Contracts Manager at Manchester Direct Works Department, now retired. *Societies:* Union of Construction Allied Trades & Technicians. *Recreations, Interests:* Gardening. *Address:* Trafford MBC, Trafford Town Hall, Stretford, Manchester, M32 0YT; 56 Manor Avenue, Sale, Cheshire, M33 5JR *(tel:* 0161 282 3047).

MURPHY, James Joseph, BA(Liverpool, 1973), MA(Econ) (Manchester,1983), CQSW (Liverpool,1976),CDIPAF (MMU, 1993)

Director of Social Services, Manchester City Council. *b.* 11 July 1952 Dublin. *m.* 1983 Dorothy Anne Lewis; one *s.* one *d. Education:* St Bede's College, Manchester; University of Liverpool; University of Manchester. *Career Profile:* Social Worker, Gateshead MBC and City of Liverpool (1974-86); Manchester City Council, Social Work Manager; Chief Executive's Policy Officer; Assistant Director of Recreation; Assistant Director of Social Services. *Recreations, Interests:* Sports, reading, travel, family pursuits. *Address:* Manchester City Council, Social Services Department, PO Box 536, Town Hall Extension, Manchester, M60 2AF*(tel:* 0161 234 3804; *fax:* 0161 234 3980).

MURRAY, Alexander Barclay, CA,ACMA

Managing Director, Quicks Group plc. *b.* 27 May 1938 Forfar, Scotland. *m.* 1964 Helen; one *s.* one *d. Public Offices:* President, National Franchised Dealers Association (1995-97). *Education:* Forfar Academy (1943-55); Chartered Accountant (1955-60). *Career Profile:*

Chartered Accountant (1960); Assistant Accountant, Decca Group (1960-62); Ford Motor Company (1962-91); Variety of positions in UK, Australia, USA; ultimately MD Ford Motor Credit Company, UK. *Societies:* St James Club, Manchester; RAC Club, London. *Address:* Quicks Group plc, Centre House, Ashburton Road East, Trafford Park, Manchester, M17 1QG (*tel:* 0161 455 1600).

MURRAY, Braham Sydney, DArts (Manchester Metropolitan)

Artistic Director, Royal Exchange Theatre. *b.* 12 February 1943 London. *m.* 1968 Lindsey Stainton; *(marr. diss. 1969)*; *m.* 1974 Johanna Bryant; two *s.* *(separated 1994) Education:* Clifton College; University College, Oxford. *Career Profile:* Artistic Director, Century Theatre; Founding Artistic Director, 69 Theatre Company (1968-75); Founding Artistic Director, Royal Exchange Theatre (1976-); Director of many productions in the West End and on Broadway. *Publications/Creative Work:* Translations published; 'Have You Anything to Declare' and 'Court in the Act' by Hennequin & Veber; 'Keep an Eye on Amélie', Feydeau. *Recreations, Interests:* Food, wine, football, reading. *Address:* Royal Exchange Theatre, St Ann's Square, Manchester, M2 7DH (*tel:* 0161 833 9333; *fax:* 0161 832 0881).

MYATT, Steven Martin, BA(Hons)

Founder and Publishing Director, Myatt McFarlane plc. *b.* 8 June 1952 London. *m.* 1993 Merryn; one *s.* *Education:* Manchester Grammar School; Stockport College of Art. *Publications/Creative Work:* Many and various. *Recreations, Interests:* Architecture, ceramics, modern lithography, classic cars. *Address:* Trident House, Heath Road, Hale, Altrincham, WA14 2UJ (*tel:* 0161 928 3480; *fax:* 0161 941 6897).

N

NAGANO, M Kodama- see *Kodama-Nagano, M.*

NAISH, Peter FIM,FCIH

Chief Executive, Equal Opportunities Commission. *b.* 24 January 1945 Hampton, Middlesex. *m.* 1970 Janet; one *s.* two *d.* *(separated 1993) Education:* Hampton Grammar School; King's College, London. *Career Profile:* Chief Executive, Irwell Valley Housing Association (1974-77); English Churches Housing Group; Research & Development in Psychiatry; CLS Care Services; Equal Opportunities Commission (1994-). *Recreations, Interests:* Music, poetry, walking the dogs. *Address:* Equal Opportunities Commission, Overseas House, Quay Street, Manchester, M3 3HN *(tel:* 0161 833 9244; *fax:* 0161 835 1657).

NAYLOR, Dorothy (*née* Ransom), CAM Diploma(Marketing),MIPR

Chief Executive, North West Tourist Board. *b.* 6 July 1952 Preston, Lancashire. *m.* 1985 Paul. *Education:* Winckley Square Convent, Preston. *Career Profile:* Deputy Public Relations Officer, Lancashire County Council (1975-87); Deputy Director of Tourism, Blackpool Borough Council (1987-89). *Societies:* Member, Institute of Public Relations; Member, Tourism Society; Director, NW Museums Service. *Recreations, Interests:* Badminton, walking, dogs. *Address:* North West Tourist Board, Swan House, Swan Meadow Road, Wigan Pier, Wigan, WN3 5BB *(tel:* 01942 821222; *fax:* 01942 820002).

NEAVE, Richard Arthur Headley

Medical Artist; Director, Unit of Art in Medicine, School of Biological Sciences, Manchester University. *b.* 17 December 1936; London. *m.* 1960 Avril; one *s.* one *d.* *Education:* Seaford College, Sussex; Hastings School of Art; Middlesex Hospital, London. *Military Service:* National Service 2nd Bn Scots Guards. *Creative Works:* Medical paintings, drawings and models; 3 dimensional reconstructions of heads for forensic and archaeological purposes. *Publications:* Periodical articles, book chapters and conference proceedings on medical teaching models and particularly on the reconstruction of skulls for facial reconstruction; the subjects of these reconstructions include Lindow Man, mummies from the Manchester Museum, Phillip II of Macedon and a King's Cross fire victim. *Societies:* Medical Artists Association; Institute of Medical Illustrators; International Association of Cranio Facial Identification. *Address:* The Medical School, University of Manchester, Oxford Road, Manchester M13 9PL *(tel:* 0161-275 5500; *e-mail:* richard.neave@man.ac.uk).

NEEDHAM, Andrew, MA,LLB(Cantab,1971)

Partner & Head of Corporate Department, Addleshaw Sons & Latham. *b.* 3 September 1950 Oldham, Lancs. *m.* 1984 Elizabeth; two *s.* *Education:* Chadderton Grammar School; Trinity College, Cambridge; College of Law, Guildford. *Career Profile:* Partner (1977); Head of Corporate Department (1991-). *Societies:* St James's Club. *Recreations, Interests:* Tennis, squash, golf, skiing, wine, cricket. *Address:* Addleshaw Sons & Latham, Dennis

House, Marsden Street, Manchester, M2 1JD *(tel:* 0161832 5994; *fax:* 0161 832 2250). *Additional Information:* A trustee of local charities and director of several private companies.

NELMES, Dianne, BA(Econ)(1973)

Director of Programming, Granada Satellite Television. *b.* 6 March 1951 Windlesham, Surrey. *m.* 1986 Ian McBride. *Public Offices:* President, Newcastle University Students Union (1973-74). *Education:* The Holt Girls' Grammar School, Wokingham; University of Newcastle upon Tyne. *Career Profile:* Granada TV: News Editor, 'Granada Tonight' and Researcher 'World in Action' (1983); BBC: Producer, Director of 'Brass Tacks' (1986-88); Granada TV: Set up and launched 'This Morning'; Executive Producer, Entertainment, launched 'You've Been Framed' and other series (1988-92); Executive Producer, 'World in Action', Head then Controller of Factual Programmes (1992-94); Director of Programmes for Granada Satellite Television and Controller of Lifestyle Programmes Granada TV, responsible for 'This Morning' (1996-). *Prizes:* Fellow of the Royal Television Society (RTS). *Societies:* BAFTA; RTS; Chiswick Refuge. *Recreations, Interests:* Canal boating. *Address:* Granada Television Ltd, Quay Street, Manchester, M60 9EA *(tel:* 0161 832 7211 (ext. 2836) *fax:* 0161 839 8530).

NEVILLE-ROLFE, Marianne Teresa, BA(Oxford)

Regional Director, Government Office for the North West. *b.* 9 October 1944 Edinburgh. *m.* 1972 David William John Blake; *(marr. diss. 1992) Education:* St Mary's Convent, Shaftesbury; Lady Margaret Hall, Oxford. *Career Profile:* CBI (196-73) (Head of Brussels Office, 1971-72); Principal DTI (1973), Asst Sec (1982); Under Sec, Internal European Policy Division (1987); Chief Exec, CS College and Director, Top Management Prog, OMCS then OPSS, Cabinet Office (1990). *Societies:* Royal Society of Arts. *Recreations, Interests:* Travel, opera. *Address:* Government Office for the North West, Sunley Tower, Piccadilly Plaza, Manchester, M1 4BA *(tel:* 0161 952 4002; *fax:* 0161 952 4004).

NEWCOMB, Edgar (Eddie), BA(Hons)(Dunelm,1962),DipEd(Dunelm,1963)

Registrar and Secretary, The University of Manchester. *b.* 2 October 1940 Gainsborough, Lincolnshire. *m.* 1966 Barri; two *s. Education:* Queen Elizabeth's Grammar School, Gainsborough (1952-59); Grey College, University of Durham (1959-63). *Career Profile:* Assistant Secretary, Committee of Vice-Chancellors and Principals (CVCP)(1976-81); Registrar & Secretary, University of Essex (1981-92); Registrar, University of Leeds (1992-94); Registrar & Secretary, University of Manchester (1995-). *Publications/Creative Work:* Various papers on university management and administration. *Societies:* Royal Society of Arts; Salzburg Seminar in American Studies (1978). *Recreations, Interests:* Music, Member of North West Development Committee of Opera North, literature, cricket. *Address:* The University of Manchester, Oxford Road, Manchester, M13 9PL *(tel:* 0161 275 7531; *fax:* 0161 275 6313; *e-mail*: Eddie.Newcomb@man.ac.uk); Crantock, 63 Hawthorn Lane, Wilmslow, SK9 5DQ *(tel:* 01625 527093).

NEWMAN, Eric John, BSc,CEng,MIChemE

Principal, ASA Newman Associates; Director of a number of companies. *Public Offices:* Chairman, Stockport Health Authority; Director, South Yorkshire Passenger Transport

Executive; Vice-Chairman, Stockport & High Peak TEC; Board Member, Stockport Partnership for Urban Regeneration (SPUR); Governor, Stockport College. *Career Profile:* R & D in nuclear power. Manager, US petrochemical contractor. Senior executive & board room level: UK based construction company; Manufacturing sector - structural steel, joinery products, public transportation; International process engineering and insdustrial services; Strategic business positioning in UK, Europe and major world markets. *Recreations, Interests:* Travel, golf, wildlife, keeping fit, watching sport.

NEWTON, Robert, BA Oxford

Barrister-at-Law (retd). *b.* 4 January 1935; Fallowfield, Manchester. *m.* 1955 Margaret; two *s.* four *d. Education:* Sale (Worthington Road) CP; Sale High School; Manchester Grammar School; Magdalen College, Oxford. *Military Service:* National Service, RAF (1952-54). *Prizes:* Macaskie and Arden Scholarships of Gray's Inn (1958). *Societies:* Lancashire County Cricket Club; Offa's Dyke Association. *Recreations, Interests:* Watching cricket and rugby union, fell walking. *Address:* 64 Wythenshawe Road, Sale, Cheshire M33 2JX *(tel:* 0161-973 4878).

NICHOLLS, Paul, LLB,MA,solicitor

Regional Managing Partner, Dibb Lupton Broomhead. *b.* 2 July 1953 Cheltenham. *m.* 1977 Jayne; one *s.* one *d. Education:* Cheltenham College; Brunel University. *Career Profile:* Qualified at the Bar (1980); Commission for Racial Equality, London (1982-88); solicitor (re-qualified, 1991), Paisner & Co; Dibb Lupton Broomhead (1992-); Director, DLB Business & Law Training. *Publications/Creative Work:* Discrimination Law Handbook (Tolley); lecturer on employment law. *Societies:* National Liberal Club; St James; Portico Library; Industrial Law Society. *Recreations, Interests:* Classic cars, politics. *Address:* Dibb Lupton Broomhead, Carlton House, 18 Albert Square, Manchester, M2 5PG *(tel:* 01345 262728; *fax:* 0161 839 5043). *Additional Information:* Stood in the 1987 General Election in Norwich North for the Liberal/SDP Alliance.

NICHOLS, Peter John, BSc

Managing Director, J N Nichols (Vimto) plc. *b.* 24 December 1949 Sale, Cheshire. *m.* 1973 Elaine; two *s.* one *d. Education:* Shrewsbury School; Leicester University. *Career Profile:* Joined J N Nichols (1971)(Manufacturing; Production Manager to Sales Marketing Manager to Director); Managing Director of Group (1986-). *Societies:* Ringway Golf Club; Nefyn Golf Club; Bowdon Tennis Club; South Caernarvonshire Yacht Club (SCYC); Overseas League Club. *Recreations, Interests:* Golf, tennis, sailing. *Address:* J N Nichols (Vimto) plc, Ledson Road, Manchester, M23 9NL *(tel:* 0161 998 8801; *fax:* 0161 998 9446).

NOBLE, Colin Frank, MSc (Cranfield, 1972),PhD (Manchester, 1976),CEng,MIEE

Retired Senior Lecturer in Mechanical Engineering, UMIST. *b.* 9 February 1931 Farnborough, Hants. *m.* 1954 Jean Ann Hasleham; one *s.* one *d. Education:* Farnborough Grammar School; Guildford Technical College; Kingston Technical College; College of Aeronautics, Cranfield; Manchester University. *Career Profile:* Vickers Armstrongs

(Aircraft) Ltd, Weybridge: Apprentice; Junior Draughtsman; Planning Engineer; Technical & Senior Technical Engineer (Production Development) (1948-61); Research Engineer & Lecturer, Cranfield (1961-67); Lecturer, Senior Lecturer & Visiting Senior Lecturer, Dept of Mechanical Engineering, UMIST (1967-91. *Publications/Creative Work:* Numerous national and international publications in the technical press, proceedings of conferences and of learned societies; especially concerned with metal forming and electrical machining processes. *Prizes:* Constantine Medal, Manchester Association of Engineers (1969); J D Scaife Medal, Institution of Production Engineers (1977); Butterworth Medal, Manchester Association of Engineers (1986). *Societies:* Member, Manchester Association of Engineers (1967-) Council (1970-73 and 1982-88), President (1983-84); Member, Manufacturing Processes Activity Group, Inst of Production Engineers (1976-87); Member, Engineering Advisory Board, Stockport College of Technology (1983-86); Corresponding Member, International College of Production Research (CIRP) (1984-88); Member, Editorial Advisory Committee 'International Journal of Machine Tool Design & Research' (1983-86); and of Machine Tools and Manufacture' (1987-96); Member, NW Committee, UMIST Association (1990-) Chairman (1993-95), Hon Secretary (1995-); Member, Prince of Wales Award, Preliminary Judging Panel (1993-94). *Recreations, Interests:* Sailing (founder member, ex Hon Treasurer and now Hon Member, Glossop & District Sailing Club), badminton, caravanning, walking. *Address:* Pen-nine, Ashleigh Avenue, Glossop, SK13 9BL *(tel:* 01457 854199).

NORMAN, Derek A, BSc(Univ. of Manchester,1959),CEng,MIChemE,FIPD

Director of Environmental Affairs and Safety, Pilkington plc. *b.* 7 March 1938 Atbara, Sudan, Africa. *m.* 1959 two *d. (marr. diss.)*; *m.* 1977 Jeni Beattie. *Public Offices:* Member, CBI Environment Committee; European Round Table Environment Watchdog Group; Sustainability North West. *Education:* Manchester Grammar School (1949-55); Manchester University (1956-59). *Career Profile:* Courtaulds Ltd; Richard Thomas & Baldwins Ltd; Production Management, Personnel Director, Pilkington plc (UK and Australia). *Recreations, Interests:* Horse riding, photography. *Address:* Pilkington plc, Prescot Road, St Helens, WA10 3TT *(tel:* 01744 692555; *fax:* 01744 692016); 56 Stamford Road, Bowdon, Cheshire, WA14 2JW *(tel:* 0161 929 6760) *(fax:* 0161 929 6773). *Additional Information:* Chairman of 'Glass Training', the non-statutory national training service for the glass industry (1985-90). Member, UK Ecolabelling Board (1992-96).

NORRIS, Colonel Graham Alexander, OBE (Military) (1945),Mentioned in Despatches (1944); CEng,FIMechE

Retired. *b.* 14 April 1913; Manchester. *m.* 1938 Frances; one *d. (marr. diss.)*; *m.* 1955 Muriel. *Public Offices:* a Deputy Lieutenant of Lancashire (1963-75); Vice Lord Lieutenant of Greater Manchester (1975-87); JP (Manchester PSD) (1963-74); JP Trafford (1974-now on supplemental list); former Member of Court of the University of Manchester and of UMIST; Chairman of UMIST Council (1971-83); Former member of the NEDC for Motor Vehicle Distribution and Repair; Former Member of Employers Panel of the Industrial Tribunals; Former President of the Greater Manchester Federation of Boys Clubs; President of the Motor Agents Association (1967-68); Master of the Coachmakers Company of London (1961-62). *Education:* William Hulme's Grammar School, Manchester; Manchester College of Technology (now UMIST); Regent Street Polytechnic,

London. *War Service:* RAOC REME (1940-46) (mostly overseas); Commander Corps Troops REME 22 Western Corps TA (1947-51) (Hon Colonel 1957-61). *Career Profile:* Chairman and Managing Director, Joseph Cockshoot & Co Ltd, Manchester until the take-over by the Lex Service Group (1968); various consultancy appointments subsequently. *Recreations, Interests:* walking, the countryside. *Address:* 53 The Downs, Altrincham, Cheshire and 5 Brook Court, Windermere, Cumbria *(tel:* 01539 444 036).

NUDDS, John Robert, BSc,PhD,FGS,CGeol

Keeper of Geology, Manchester Museum. *b.* 5 December 1950; Norwich. *m.* 1972 Christine Joyce Tyrrell; two *s.* one *d. Education:* City of Norwich Grammar School (Tresise Prize Winner); University of Nottingham; University of Durham. *Career Profile:* Keeper of the Geological Museum, Trinity College, Dublin. *Publications:* (ed) 'Science in Ireland 1800-1930' (1988); (ed) 'Directory of British Geological Museums' (1994); various papers in scientific journals on fossil corals from the Carboniferous rocks of Northern England. *Prizes:* Fearnsides Prize of the Yorkshire Geological Society (1977). *Societies:* Treasurer, Irish Geological Association (1982-85); President, Manchester Geological Association (1995-97); Chairman, Geological Curators' Group (1995-98); UK Council Member, International Association for the Study of Fossil Cnidaria (1988-95). *Recreations, Interests:* Travel, Ireland, athletics (Derbyshire county silver medallist), bridge, mountain trekking. *Address:* Manchester Museum, The University, Manchester M13 9PL *(tel:* 0161-275 2660); 18 Silk Street, Glossop *(tel:* 01457 856718).

O

OAKES, Joseph Stewart, BA (Hons) Manchester (1940)

Barrister-at-Law (Retired);Former Presiding Legal Member, Mental Health Review Tribunal, E Lancs. *b.* 7 January 1919; Winsford, Cheshire. *m.* 1950 Irene May Peasnall (*decd* 1995). *Education:* Royal Masonic School, Bushey, Herts (1929-34); Stretford Grammar School (1934-37); Manchester University (1937-40). *War Service:* Royal Corps of Signals (1940-48). Served in Middle East and Austria. *Career Profile:* Crown Court Recorder (1976-82). *Societies:* Hallé Concerts Society. *Recreations, Interests:* Horticulture, photography, music. *Address:* 38 Langley Road, Sale, Manchester M33 5AY (*tel:* 0161-962 2068).

OAKLEY, Peter John, NDD,ATD,MA

President, Manchester Academy of Fine Arts. *b.* 7 August 1935 Stafford. *Education:* King Edward VI School, Stafford; Stafford College of Art; Leicester College of Art; Manchester Polytechnic. *Career Profile:* Artist, Designer, Teacher and Lecturer; Head of Art, Beaumont Ley School, Leicester (1959-67); Head of Art, Collegiate Girls' School, Leicester (1967-71); Senior Lecturer in Art & Design, Edge Hill College of HE, Ormskirk (1971-91); Set, Costume Designer for Andante Theatre Co and Vocal Chord Productions (1991-93); Freelance Artist, Designer and Lecturer (1991-). *Publications/Creative Work:* Widely Exhibited Painter and Printmaker. *Societies:* Manchester Academy of Fine Arts; Merseyside Contemporary Artists. *Recreations, Interests:* The arts in general, Yoga, the natural world, travel. *Address:* Crab Lane House, Crab Lane, Cinnamon Brow, Warrington, WA2 0WJ (*tel:* 01925 819904).

O'BRIEN, Roger William

Senior Partner, Lawson Coppock & Hart, Solicitors, Manchester. *b.* 3 July 1940. *m.* 1968 Barbara; three *s.* (one decd) *Public Offices:* General Commissioner of Income Tax; Governor of Culcheth Hall School, Altrincham. *Education:* St Ambrose College, Hale Barns, Cheshire. *Societies:* St James's Club, Manchester; Bowdon Hockey Club; Hale Golf Club. *Recreations, Interests:* Golf, gardening. *Address:* Lawson Coppock & Hart, 18 Tib Lane, Cross Street, Manchester M2 4JA (*tel:* 0161-832 5944).

O'HORA, Ronan, GMus (Hons) RNCM (1985)

Concert Pianist. *b.* 9 January 1964; Manchester. *m.* 1991 Hannah Alice Bell. *Education:* St Bede's College (1975-81); Royal Northern College of Music (1981-85). *Career Profile:* Performed throughout UK, France, Germany, Holland, Switzerland, Belgium, Spain, Denmark, Norway, Sweden, Poland, Yugoslavia, Czechoslovakia, Portugal, Italy, USA and Canada; broadcast internationally on radio and TV. *Prizes:* Silver Medal of the Worshipful Company of Musicians (1984); Dayas Gold Medal (1985); Stefania Niekrasz Prize (1985). *Recreations, Interests:* Theatre. *Address:* 11 Daresbury Road, Manchester M21 9NA (*tel:* 0161 881 3575; *fax:* 0161 882 0313).

OLEESKY, Dr Samuel, Hon Member RNCM; MSc,MB ChB Manchester,FRCP London, MD Washington

Retired Consultant Physician, Manchester Royal Infirmary. *b.* Manchester. *m.* 1952 Dr S.F. Dawson; one *s.* one *d. Education:* Manchester Central High School; Manchester University; Washington University. *Career Profile:* Lecturer in Therapeutics, Sheffield; Consultant Physician, Crumpsall and Ancoats Hospitals. *Publications:* Many publications in medical journals. *Prizes:* Hallett Prize (RCS); Rockefeller Scholarship to Washington University. *Societies:* Manchester Medical Society (Past President and Secretary); Manchester Literary & Philosophical Society; British Diabetic Association (Past Member of Committee); Senior Member, Associate Physicians of Britain and Ireland. *Recreations, Interests:* Music. *Address:* 1 Dunham Lawn, Bradgate Road, Altrincham WA14 4QJ *(tel:* 0161-928 8066).

OLLERENSHAW, Dame Kathleen Mary (*née* Timpson), DBE (1971),DStJ (1983),Hon Alderman City of Manchester (1980),Freeman (1984),DL Greater Manchester (1987),Hon FIM (1987),Hon FCP (1969),Companion RNCM (1976), Member & Hon Vice-President, Manchester Astronomical Society (1995-), President, St Leonard's School, St Andrews (1978),Hon Fellow, Somerville College, Oxford (1977),Hon Fellow, Manchester Polytechnic (1978),Hon Fellow, CGLI (1979),Hon Fellow, UMIST (1988),Hon Member, Manchester Literary & Philosophical Society(1981); Hon DSc(CNAA,1975),HonDSc Salford (1976),Hon LLD Manchester(1976), Hon LLD Liverpool(1994),MA,Dphil, FIMA, FCP,Chartered Mathematician

b. 1 October 1912; Manchester. *m.* 1939 Robert G W Ollerenshaw (*died* 1986); one *s.* one *d.* (*died* 1972). *Public Offices:* Foundation Member, Court of University of Salford (1966-) (Chairman of Finance Committee, a Deputy Pro-Chancellor 1984-89); Member, Court of University of Manchester (1968-); Member, Council of Order of St John (Greater Manchester) (1974-96) & Member of Chapter General (1978-96); Member, Court and Council of University of Lancaster (1976-94), Court (1976-), (Part-time Senior Research Fellow 1971-74, Hon Research Fellow 1974-76, a Deputy Pro-Chancellor 1985-94); Member, NW Military Education Committee (1981-); Royal Institution Advisory Committee on Masterclasses in Mathematics (1983-90). *Education:* Ladybarn House School, Withington, Manchester; St Leonards School, St Andrews; Somerville College, Oxford (Open Scholarship in mathematics 1931). *Previous Positions:* Research Assistant, Shirley Institute Didsbury (1935-40); Assistant tutor in mathematics, Somerville College, Oxford (1942-46); part-time lecturer in mathematics, Manchester University (1946-54); Co-opted member, Manchester Education Committee (1954-56); Member, Manchester City Council (1956-80); representative member of Salford Royal Technical College (1956) and subsequently Salford Royal College of Advanced Technology; Chairman Further Education Sub-Committee (1960-67); Chairman, Manchester College of Commerce (1963-68) and subsequently First Chairman, Manchester Polytechnic (1968-74); Chairman, Education Committee (1967-70); governor of various Manchester schools and colleges (1954-80); Deputy Chairman, Finance Committee (1970-74); Alderman (1969-74) reverting to Councillor (1974-80), Lord Mayor (1975-76), Leader Conservative Group (1977-79); Governor, St Leonards School, St Andrews (1950-72); Chairman, Association of Governing Bodies of Girls Public Schools (1958-67); Member, Central Advisory Council for Education (Newsom Committee 1960-63); Member, NW Regional Council for Further

Education (1959-63); Member, Council and Education Committee City and Guilds of London Institutes (1964-73) (a Vice-President 1973-78); National Advisory Council on Education for Industrial and Commercial Education (1963-70); representative governor, Union of Lancashire and Cheshire Institutes (1967-73); founder governor, Further Education Staff College, Blagdon (1968-74); foundation member, Council for National Academic Awards (1964-71); Chairman, Education Committee, Association of Municipal Corporations (1967-71) (with Schools Council and Burnham Committee); member, Association of Education Committees (1967-74); member, Social Science Research Council (1972-75); member, Technician Education Council (1972-75); member, Government "All-Party" Layfield Committee of Inquiry into Local Government Finance (1974-76); member, Council British Association for Commercial and Industrial Education (1958-) (Vice-President 1974-); Winifred Cullis Visiting Fellow to USA (1965); British Council visit and lecturer (1970) Tokyo, Osaka, New Delhi; Chairman, Joint Committee for Northern College of Music (1958-71); First Chairman, Court Royal Northern College of Music (1971-86); First Chairman, Council for the Order of St John in Greater Manchester (1974-89); Vice-President, UMIST (1977-87); member, General Advisory Council of BBC (1966-73) and subsequently non-executive director of Piccadilly Radio (1973-83); Mancunian of the Year (1977); Fourth Cockcroft Lecture UMIST (1977); Invitation Lecture Royal Institution (1980); Hon Colonel, Manchester and Salford Universities Officer Training Corps (1977-81); President, Manchester Technology Association (1981-82); Member, Manchester Statistical Society (1938-)(President 1981-83); North West Regional representative, Trustee Savings Bank Foundation (1986-89). *Publications:* 'Education of Girls' (1958); 'Education for Girls' (1961); 'The Girls Schools' (1967); 'Returning to Teaching' (1974); 'The Lord Mayor's Party' (1976); 'First Citizen' (1977); 'Form and Pattern' (Proc Royal Inst Vol 53 1981); 'Magic Squares of Order Four' (with Sir Hermann Bondi) (Trans Royal Soc 1982); 'Most Perfect Squares of 8' (Proc Royal Soc 1985); numerous articles on mathematics, education, local government in national and educational press. *Societies:* Member of Council, Inst of Mathematics and Its Applications (1964-95) (Foundation Fellow 1964, President 1979-80); Member, Manchester Statistical Society (1946-) (President 1979-80). *Recreations, Interests:* At one time sports of all kinds, especially skiing, skating (Runner-up in 1939 in English-style Pairs Skating British Championship), mountain climbing, hockey (Captain, Oxford University 1st IX 1933, Lancashire County 1934-39, reserve England 1938), squash, embroidery, travel. Now walking, reading, listening to music, mathematics research for the excitement, computers and now astronomy. *Address:* 2 Pine Road, Didsbury, Manchester M20 0UY *(tel:* 0161-445 2948); Hodge Close, Coniston, Cumbria LA21 8DJ *(tel:* 01539 437672).

O'REILLY, Patrick, MD,FRCS,MB,ChB,LRCP,MRCS,FEBU

Consultant Urological Surgeon, Stepping Hill Hospital, Stockport. *b.* 22 April 1947 Marple, Cheshire. *Education:* Mount St Marys College, Spinkhill, Sheffield; Victoria University of Manchester. *Publications/Creative Work:* 4 medical textbooks; 11 chapters in medical textbooks; 40 peer reviewed publications in medical journals; 4 novels. *Prizes:* Doctor of the Year (1995-96); Hon Membership, New York Section, AUA. *Societies:* British Association Urological Surgeons; American Urological Assocation; Irish Society of Urology; European Urological Association. *Recreations, Interests:* Music, sport, creative

writing. *Address:* Department of Urology, Stepping Hill Hospital, Stockport, SK2 7JE *(tel:* 0161 419 5484; *fax:* 0161 419 5699).

ORME, Rt Hon Stanley (Stan), PC (1974-); Hon DSc Salford (1985)

MP, Salford. *b.* 5 April 1923; Sale, Cheshire. *m.* Irene. *Public Offices:* Opposition Spokesman N Ireland (1973-74); Min of State, N Ireland (1974-76), Health & Social Security (Apr-Sept 1976); Minister for Social Security (1976-79); Opp Spokesman Health & Social Security (1979-80), Industry (1980-83), Energy (1983-87). *Education:* National Council of Labour Colleges; Workers' Educational Association. *War Service:* RAF, Warrant Officer, Air-Bomber Navigator, Bomber Command (1942-47). *Career Profile:* Chairman, Parliamentary Labour Party (1987-92); Councillor, Sale Borough Council (1957-64). *Publications:* Pamphlets and articles. *Societies:* Social, cultural and sporting. *Recreations, Interests:* Reading American literature, walking, football, opera, modern art, cricket, jazz. *Address:* House of Commons, London SW1A 0AA *(tel:* 0171-219 5188); 8 Northwood Grove, Sale, Cheshire M33 3DZ *(tel:* 0161-973 5341).

ORMISTON, Major James Alexander, MBE(1986),TD(1970),DL(1990)

Deputy Lieutenant, Greater Manchester. *b.* 26 September 1928 Carlisle. *m.* 1952 Maureen Daphne Strong; two *d. Public Offices:* Chief Commandant, Greater Manchester Police Special Constabulary (1974-93). *Education:* Carlisle Grammar School. *Military Service:* Regular Army and TA. *Career Profile:* 30th Trg Bn. Inverness (1946); Commissioned Loyal Regt (1947); RWAFF Nigeria (1947-48); 24 Ind Bde Trieste (1948-51); Bde Adj Lancs Bde (1951-53); Adj Army Sch of Physical Trg (1953-56); Border Regt TA (1956-74); unposted list MOD (1975-88); (Acting Lt Col 1983-84); Grainger & Percy Building Society (1960); Exec, Middleton Building Society (1969); Asst Gen Manager, Colne Building Society (1978); Deputy NW Regional Manager, Britannia Building Society (1983)(on merger), Northern Administrator (1988); Rtd (1992); Parish, Church & Rural District Councillor Cumberland (1957-69); Army Benevolent Fund, Manchester (1971-78); Chairman, Manchester Centre Building Societies Institute (1977-79); Asst County Director, St John's Ambulance Assoc Lancashire (1980-83); Chairman, NW Group Building Societies Institute (1983-85); Regimental Chapel Committee Carlisle Cathedral; Vice President, Coldstream Guards Association, Manchester. *Publications/Creative Work:* Research and lectures on 'The History of the Victoria Cross'. *Societies:* Manchester Luncheon Club; Inland Waterways Association; Royal British Legion; Military Historical Society; Chartered Building Societies Institute; British Institute of Management; Magistrates Association. *Recreations, Interests:* Inland waterways (n.b. 'Pendragon'), reading, fishing, home and family. *Address:* The Garth, Brookfield Avenue, Poynton, SK12 1JE *(tel:* 01625 872806).

ORTON, Andrew William, ARCM

Associate Leader, BBC Philharmonic Orchestra. *b.* 5 August 1946 Ripon. *m.* 1967 one *s.* one *d. (marr. diss. 1990)*; *m.* 1992 Wendy Diane; one *stepd. Education:* Ripon Grammar School (1957-64); Royal College of Music (1964-67). *Career Profile:* BBC Northern Symphony Orchestra (1967); Principal 2nd Violin (1973); Associate Leader (1975).

Societies: Former Member, Cheadle Hulme Conservative Club; High Lane & Cheadle Cricket Clubs. *Recreations, Interests:* Cricket, angling, football, driving.

OXTOBY, Robert, BSc Leeds (1961),PhD Leeds (1964),MEd Manchester (1976),MInstE, CEng,FIMgt,FRSA

Principal, Bolton Institute of Higher Education. *b.* 12 May 1939; Driffield, Yorkshire. *m.* 1968 Marie; two *s.* one *d. Education:* Bridlington School (1950-57); University of Leeds (1957-64). *Previous Positions:* Deputy Director, Luton College of Higher Education (1980-84); Vice Principal, Garnett College (1977-80); various administrative, research and teaching posts (1964-77) including a period as adviser on technical education to the Government of Barbados. *Publications:* More than 50 papers and articles on a range of scientific and educational topics. *Societies:* Society for Research into Higher Education; Yorkshire Dales Society. *Recreations, Interests:* Walking, sport, opera and theatre, reading, wearing a new tie. *Address:* Bolton Institute of Higher Education, Deane Road, Bolton BL3 5AB *(tel:* 01204 528851); 60 Albert Road West, Bolton BL1 5HW *(tel:* 01204-494452).

P

PAGE, Timothy Guy BComm,FCA

Financial Director, Company Secretary, Joseph Holt plc. *b.* 10 March 1939 Wakefield, Yorkshire. *m.* 1965 Margaret Susan; one *s.* two *d. Education:* Denstone College, Uttoxeter; Leeds University. *Address:* Joseph Holt plc, Derby Brewery, Cheetham, Manchester, M3 1JD *(tel:* 0161 834 3285; *fax:* 0161 834 6458).

PAINTER, Michael John, MB(1973),BS(1973),MSc(1983),FFPHM(1993)

Consultant in Communicable Disease Control, Manchester. *b.* 24 October 1948 Camberley. *m.* 1973 Gillian Elizabeth Burgess. *Education:* Strode's School, Egham, Surrey; St Mary's Hospital Medical School, London; University of Manchester. *Career Profile:* Hospital Doctor specialising in Orthopaedics (1973-77); Worked with children with Haemophilia (1977-78); Trained in Public Health in Manchester, special interest in control of infectious diseases (1978-85); Consultant in Communicable Disease Control, Manchester (1985-). *Publications/Creative Work:* Joint author of papers on Meningitis, Campylobacter, Hepatitis B and Haemophilia. *Prizes:* Open Scholarship St Mary's Hospital Medical School, London. *Societies:* Manchester Medical Society; Liveryman of Worshipful Company of Coopers, London; Freeman of the City of London. *Recreations, Interests:* Model railways, cycling. *Address:* Infection Control & Surveillance Unit, Gateway House, Piccadilly South, Manchester, M60 7LP *(tel:* 0161 236 2400; *fax:* 0161 236 4937).

PANNONE, Rodger John, D.Litt(hc)(Salford), LLD(hc) (Nottingham Trent), Hon Fellow, MMU.

Solicitor; Senior Partner, Pannone & Partners. *b.* 20 April 1943; Minehead, Somerset. *m.* 1966 Patricia Jane; two *s.* one *d. Public Offices:* President, Law Society of England & Wales (1993-94); Vice President, The Academy of Experts; Vice President, The Greater Manchester Community Trust; Adviser to the Lord Chancellor on Civil Justice. Council Member, Law Society (1978-96); Member, Supreme Court Procedure Committee (Queen's Bench Sub-Committee); Member, Adjudication Committee of the Solicitors Complaints Bureau; Solicitor adviser to the Lord Chancellor on Civil Justice Review - published 1988. Member of Court, Manchester University. *Education:* St Brendan's College, Bristol; College of Law, London; College of Law, Manchester Polytechnic. *Career Profile:* Supreme Court Rule Committee; Chairman, Law Society's Contentious Business Committee; Chairman, Law Society's Law and Procedure Committee. *Publications:* Many - frequent lecturer and broadcaster. *Societies:* Northern Lawn Tennis Club; St James's Club; The Manchester Law Society. *Recreations, Interests:* Fell walking, all holidays, sport, food and wine. *Address:* Pannone & Partners, 123 Deansgate, Manchester M3 2BU *(tel:* 0161-832 3000). *Additional Information:* Included in The Sunday Times Magazine 22nd November 1987 as "One of the 100 people who will run Britain in the 1990s". Described by The Sunday Times 1st January 1989 as a "Winner in 1988". Profiled by Radio 4 under the title "The Pannone Phenomenon", 10th May 1989. Honorary Life Member of the Canadian Bar.

PARDOE, Beverley Hugh,BSc,MSc,PhD,CEng,FIEE

Dean of Engineering, University of Salford. *b.* 13 July 1943 Feckenham, Worcs. *m.* 1969 Alison Ruth; two *s. Education:* Redditch High School (1956-61); Hull University (1961-64); Essex University (1971-74). *Career Profile:* 7 years in Industry - UK, USA & Australia; University: 1 year Ife, Nigeria; 1 year Sussex; 20 years Salford (lecturer, senior lecturer, dean). *Publications/Creative Work:* 50 articles in learned journals, 50 industrial reports, 15 patents. *Recreations, Interests:* Private pilot with IMC rating. *Address:* Department of Electronic & Electrical Engineering, University of Salford, The Crescent, Salford, M5 4WT*(tel:* 0161 745 5652; *fax:* 0161 745 5999; *e-mail:* b.h.pardoe@eee .salford.ac.uk); 75 Fog Lane, Didsbury, Manchester, M20 6SL *(tel:* 0161 445 8682).

PARISER, John, LLB (Hons) Manchester (1959)

Partner, Pariser & Co, Solicitors. *b.* 15 January 1938; Salford. *m.* 1962 Anita Debra Goldstone; one *s.* one *d. (marr. diss. 1970)*; *m.* 1970 Marcia Goldstone. *Education:* Manchester Grammar School; Manchester University. *Societies:* Honorary Solicitor to the Provincial Independent Tontine Society. *Recreations, Interests:* Snooker, horse riding & racehorse breeding. *Address:* Pariser & Co, Suite 1, First Floor, 2/4 Oxford Road, Manchester M1 5QA *(tel:* 0161-236 1328).

PARK, James Graham, CBE (1995); LLB Manchester (1964)

Senior Partner, Messrs H L F Berry & Co, Solicitors; National Union Vice President, Conservative Party; Duchy of Lancaster Appointed Member, Court of Salford University; President, Altrincham and Sale Conservative Association. *b.* 28 April 1941; Rochdale. *m.* 1969 Susan; one *s. Education:* Malvern College; Manchester University. *Career Profile:* Former Committee Member, Irwell Valley Housing Association and Founder Member, Pendleton Improved Housing Association; Former Chairman, Altrincham and Sale Conservative Association; Former Parliamentary Candidate, Middleton and Prestwich (1979) and Crewe (1974). *Societies:* The Law Society. *Recreations, Interests:* Cricket and motor racing. *Address:* H L F Berry & Co, Lancaster Buildings, 77 Deansgate, Manchester M3 2BW *(tel:* 0161-834 0548).

PARKER, Edward, BSc (Hons) Manchester (1954),MSc Manchester (1956), DSc(hc) (Salford, 1993),CEng,FIMechE

Professorial Fellow in Education & Industry, Director of CAMPUS, University of Salford. *b.* 9 August 1933; Manchester. *m.* 1960 Anne Marguerite Parker; two *d. Public Offices:* Chairman, Salford Community Health Care NHS Trust (1994-). *Education:* Manchester Central High School (1944-51); University of Manchester(1951-55). *Career Profile:* Graduate Engineer, A V Roe & Co Ltd (1955-57); Head of Aerothermodynamics, A V Roe & Co Ltd, Woodford (1957-60); Lecturer, Royal College of Advanced Technology (1960-67); Lecturer, Senior Lecturer (1967-81), Director of Continuing Education (1981-87), Pro-Vice-Chancellor (1979-93), University of Salford. *Publications:* Papers on Thermodynamics, Continuing Education, Management of Higher Education, Industry/Education Links. *Prizes:* J H Beckwith Open Scholar. *Recreations, Interests:* Walking, swimming, music, church services, football (watching). *Address:* The University

of Salford, Maxwell Building, Salford M5 4WT *(tel:* 0161-745 5000); 57A Simister Lane, Prestwich, Manchester M25 2SU *(tel:* 0161-773 7553). *Additional Information:* Member, Council and Executive of University Council of Adult and Continuing Education (1985-88), Chairman of Management Board CONTACT (1986-88), Member of Eng Council Continuing Education Committee (1986-93), Member of Governors, Bury Grammar School (1988-93); Member, Salford Health Authority (1986-89); Chairman, Salford Family Practitioner Committee (1988-90); Chairman, Salford Health Services Authority (1990-93); Member, North Western Regional Health Authority (1990-93), Vice-Chairman (1992-93); Vice-Chairman, National Association of Health Authorities and Trusts (1992-93); Chairman, Central Manchester Health Authority (1992-93).

PARKER, Joyce Lindley *(née* Wood), LRAM Northern School of Music (1969)

Hon Sec, Arts Section, Manchester Literary & Philosophical Society; Administrator, Friends of the BBC Philharmonic; Secretary, Friends of William Byrd Singers; Co-ordinator, Friends of Northern Chamber Orchestra; on committees of many music societies. *b.* Manchester. *Education:* Manchester Central High School for Girls. *Societies:* Friends of Whitworth; City & Quarry Bank; Manchester Literary & Philosophical Society; Manchester Luncheon Club; Portico Library; Friends of BBC Philharmonic; Forum Music Society; Friends of the Camerata; Friends of Northern Ballet; Life Member, Friends of RNCM and Alumni; Member, Incorporated Society of Musicians. *Recreations, Interests:* Ornithology, music, reading who dunnit's. *Address:* 3 Dovercourt Avenue, Heaton Mersey, Stockport SK4 3QB *(tel:* 0161-431 4130). *Additional Information:* Professional singer, teacher & adjudicator.

PARKER, Susan Kim, LLB,Solicitor

Partner, Davies Wallis Foyster, Manchester. *b.* 4 September 1957 Liverpool. *Education:* Holly Lodge Grammar School for Girls, Liverpool (1969-76); Liverpool University (1976-79); Chester College of Law (1979-80). *Career Profile:* Articled, Alsop Wilkinson, Liverpool (1980-83); Solicitor/associate, Eversheds, Manchester (1982-86); Partner, Davies Wallis Foyster, Liverpool (1988-91), Manchester (1991-). *Prizes:* Liverpool University Scholarship Award (1977 & 1978). *Address:* Davies Wallis Foyster, Harvester House, 37 Peter Street, Manchester, M2 5GB*(tel:* 0161 28 3702; *fax:* 0161 835 2407; *e-mail*: skp@dwf-law.com).

PARRY, Professor Geraint Burton, BSc(Econ),PhD(London),MA(Manchester)

W J M Mackenzie Professor of Government, University of Manchester (1977-). *b.* 4 August 1936 Oswestry. *m.* 1964 Linda Hetherington; one *s.* one *d. Public Offices:* Lay Member, Academic Board, Royal Northern College of Music (1994-). *Education:* Acton County Grammar School (1947-54); University of London (1954-59). *Career Profile:* Assistant Lecturer in Politics, University College of Swansea (1959-60); Assistant Lecturer, Lecturer, Senior Lecturer in Philosophy, University of Manchester (1960-71); Senior Lecturer in Government, University of Manchester (1971-74); Edward Caird Professor of Politics, University of Glasgow (1974-76); Visiting Appointments: University of Wisconsin (1964-65); Queens University, Kingston, Ontario (1972-73); Dean, Faculty of Music, University of Manchester (1983-86). *Publications/Creative Work:* 'Political Elites'

(1969); 'John Locke' (1978); 'Local Politics and Participation in Britain and France' (1989) with A Mabileau et al; 'Political Participation and Democracy in Britain' (1992) with G Moyser and N Day; contributions to edited books and scholarly journals. *Societies:* Hon Vice President, Political Studies Association of UK (Chairman 1980-83, President 1983-87). *Recreations, Interests:* Music, gardening, cricket. *Address:* Department of Government, University of Manchester, Oxford Road, Manchester, M13 9PL *(tel:* 0161 275 4895; *fax:* 0161 275 4925).

PARRY, Richard Gordon, FRIBA

Private practitioner. *b.* 19 November 1929; Manchester. *m.* 1955 Mavis Evelyn; one *s.* three *d. Education:* Grammar School; College of Art, Manchester; External Professional Examination. *Career Profile:* General Architectural Practice, including technical teaching; Sometime Director, Manchester City FC; Past President, Rotary Club. *Publications:* Some technical journals and articles. *Societies:* Past Chairman, St James's Club, Manchester; Manchester Society of Architects (Council Member); Manchester Tennis & Racquets; Chamber of Commerce. *Recreations, Interests:* Sport in general, golf, sailing, active cricket, association football. *Address:*Willowcroft, 7 Fawnskeep, Wilmslow Park, Wilmslow SK9 2BQ *(tel:* 01625 520118; *fax:* 01625 520118).

PASS, Anthony John Bradley, BA (Hons) (1968) BArch (1970) MA Manchester (1978), RIBA, MRTPI,FSA

Architect, Assistant Director of Estates, UMIST; Member, Management Committee, Sanctuary Housing Association; Honorary Architect, Portico Library. *b.* 23 May 1947; Bramhall, Cheshire. *Public Offices:* Chairman, Manchester Conservation Areas & Historical Buildings Panel. *Education:* Stockport School; University of Manchester School of Architecture. *Career Profile:* Conservation Officer, GMC (1973-84); Architect working in private practice (1968-73). *Creative Works:* Restoration projects: Castlefield, Toad Lane, Rochdale, Portico Library, Wigan Pier, St Margaret's Church, Whalley Range, Watermill, Marple Bridge; Design and restoration of stained glass window in St Ann's Church, Manchester; many projects at UMIST including Ronson Hall. *Publications:* 'Thomas Worthington: Victorian Architecture and Social Purpose' (Manchester Lit & Phil) (1988); chapter in 'Art and Architecture in Victorian Manchester' (MUP) (1985); various papers and articles in 'The Architectural Review', 'Architects' Journal', 'Building', etc. *Prizes:* Civic Trust Award (1981); British Tourist Authority Award (1975); Shortlisted for Portico Literary Prize (1988). *Societies:* Member, Manx Conservation Council; Founder Member, Association of Conservation Officers. *Recreations, Interests:* Ships and the sea, watercolour painting, measuring and drawing buildings, industrial archaeology and ships, writing, history of the Isle of Man. *Address:* Dept of Estates, UMIST, PO Box 88, Sackville Street, Manchester M60 1QD *(tel:* 0161-200 4952); 47 Claremont Avenue, Rose Hill, Marple, Cheshire SK6 6JG *(tel:* 0161-427 6575); Port e Chee, Packhorse Lane, Baldrine, Isle of Man *(tel:* 01624 861 377).

PATCH, Maureen, BA (Hons) Reading (1962),DAA Liverpool (1963)

County Archivist, Greater Manchester. *b.* Chadderton, Lancs. *Education:* Bury Grammar School (Girls). *Career Profile:* County Archivist, Dyfed; County Archivist, Pem-

brokeshire. *Publications:* Various articles and books on subjects of interest to archivists; 'David Holt's Victorian Walks: Shap to Windermere' (co-editor). *Societies:* Society of Archivists; British Records Association; Member, Soroptimist International of Manchester. *Address:* Greater Manchester County Record Office, 56 Marshall Street, New Cross, Manchester M4 5FU *(tel:* 0161-832 5284; *fax:* 0161 839 3808; *e-mail:* archives@gmcro.u-net.com).

PATE, Alan George, BA,ALA

Retired. *b.* 16 January 1933; Manchester. *m.* 1956 Jean Eperson; three *s. (marr. diss. 1977); m.* 1987 Hilary Jane Daniell. *Education:* Burnage Grammar School, Manchester (1944-51); Manchester University (1951-54). *Career Profile:* Senior Lecturer, Department of Library and Information Studies, Manchester Polytechnic (1969-87); Various posts in libraries (1955-69). *Publications:* 'James Prescott Joule 1818-1889: A Bibliography of Works By and About Him' (1981). *Societies:* The Manchester Literary & Philosophical Society; Stockport Chess Club; National Trust. *Recreations, Interests:* Music, chess, local history. *Address:* Flat 34, Woodheys, Mersey Road, Heaton Mersey, Stockport, Cheshire SK4 3BJ *(tel:* 0161-442 0898).

PATON, James Hendry, MA Edinburgh (1957),MCIT

Managing Director, P & O European Transport Services Ltd; Non-Executive Director, P & O Containers Ltd. *b.* 3 July 1936; Falkirk, Stirlingshire, Scotland. *m.* 1961 Nan; one *s.* one *d. Public Offices:* Past National Chairman, Road Haulage Association Tanker Group. *Education:* Falkirk High School; University of Edinburgh; Joint Services School for Linguists. *Military Service:* Intelligence Corps (Russian Interpreter). *Career Profile:* Managing Director, P & O Roadtanks Ltd; Managing Director, Thomas Allen Ltd; Branch Manager, British Road Services Ltd; Management Trainee, British Road Services Ltd. *Societies:* Royal Scottish Automobile Club. *Recreations, Interests:* Hill walking, golf, European languages, vintage cars. *Address:* P & O European Transport Services Ltd, Station House, Stamford New Road, Altrincham, Cheshire *(tel:* 0161-927 7111); Brook House, 9 Ladythorn Crescent, Bramhall, Stockport, Cheshire SK7 2HB *(tel:* 0161-439 4102).

PATTISON, Mark, LLB

Partner, Head of Commercial Property Department, Vaudreys. *b.* 13 May 1958 UK. *m.* 1982 Jaqueline Mary Pattison; two *d. Education:* Disley County Primary; Stockport Grammar School; Manchester University; College of Law, Chester. *Societies:* Manchester Property Gun and Punt Club. *Recreations, Interests:* Swimming, running, shooting, food and drink. *Address:* Vaudreys, 13 Police Street, Manchester, M2 7WA *(tel:* 0161 834 6877; *fax:* 0161 834 2440).

PAYNE, Nicholas Milne, MA(Cantab)

Regional Chairman, National Art Collections Fund, North West; Chairman, Friends of the Manchester City Art Galleries; Trustee, Tabley House Collection Trust; Trustee, Cloner Opera for All; Member of Council, National Gardens Scheme Charitable Trust. *b.* 14 March 1937 Manchester. *m.* 1985 Mona Helen; one *steps.* two *stepd. Education:* St

Edward's School, Oxford; Trinity Hall, Cambridge. *Military Service:* National Service, Lt. Royal Artillery (1956-58). *Career Profile:* Commercial Director, Cardon Rolinx Ltd (1964-87); Retired (1987). *Societies:* National Art Collections Fund; National Trust; Friends of the Whitworth; Friends of Manchester City Art Galleries. *Recreations, Interests:* Travel, gardening, music, English domestic architecture, the arts. *Address:* The Mount, Whirley, Macclesfield, SK11 9PB *(tel:* 01625 426730).

PEARCE, Robert Henry, CText,ATI

Management Consultant, but mainly retired. *b.* 2 January 1920; Burnley, Lancashire. *m.* 1944 Isabella Brown McNeill; one *s.* one *d. Education:* Oldham High School; Rochdale and Oldham Technical Colleges; RAF (including Cranwell); Administrative Staff College, Henley. *War Service:* Durham Light Infantry (1940-41); RAF (1941-46), served in Malta and Europe. *Career Profile:* Director (until retirement), TBA Industrial Products Ltd (T & N plc); Secretary (until retirement), Rochdale Chamber of Commerce, Trade and Industry; Past Chairman, Rochdale College Governing Body; Founder Chairman, Rochdale Enterprise Trust. *Prizes:* Triple First Prize, City and Guilds Medallist (Textiles) (1947-48). *Societies:* The Textile Institute; Treasurer and Life Member, The Spitfire Society, Northern Region; Treasurer (and Past President), Rochdale Antiques Society; Past President, Rochdale Probus Club; Patron and Past Treasurer, Rochdale Music Society; Past President, Rochdale & District Scottish Society. *Address:* Kingswood, 116 Sheriff Street, Rochdale, OL12 6JY *(tel:* 01706-49282).

PECKHAM, John, BEd(1978),MSc(1993)

Head Teacher, Bramhall High School. *b.* 28 April 1955 Weybridge, Surrey. *m.* 1994 Odile. *Education:* West Byfleet Secondary Modern School; Sandown County High School; Crewe and Alsager College; University of Keele; Open University. *Career Profile:* 7 years at Knutsford High School, Head of Careers; 10 years at Saint George's CE School, Gravesend, Deputy Head. *Publications/Creative Work:* Article: Investing in Parenting (1996). *Recreations, Interests:* Sailing. *Address:* Bramhall High School, Seal Road, Bramhall, Stockport, SK7 2JT *(tel:* 0161 439 8045; *fax:* 0161 439 8951; *e-mail:* bramhallhigh@campus.bt.com).

PERERA, Professor Katharine Mary *(née* Lacey), BA(Hons)(London), MA(Manchester), PhD (Manchester)

Pro-Vice-Chancellor, Professor of Educational Linguistics, University of Manchester. *b.* 12 December 1943 Redhill, Surrey. *m.* 1967 Suria Perera. *Public Offices:* Member of the Working Party, English National Curriculum ('The Cox Committee'); Member, Quality Assessment Committee, Higher Education Funding Council for England. *Education:* Wallasey High School for Girls; Bedford College, University of London; Manchester University. *Career Profile:* VSO in Malaysia; Teaching in Schools on Merseyside; Lecturing in Padgate College of Higher Education; Lecturing in Manchester University. *Publications/Creative Work:* 'Children's Writing and Reading' (Blackwell); 'Understanding Language' (NATE); Editor, 'Journal of Child Language' (CUP). *Societies:* Linguistics Association of Great Britain; British Association of Applied Linguistics. *Recreations, Interests:* Walking, music, reading. *Address:* Department of Linguistics, University of

212

Manchester, Oxford Road, Manchester, M13 9PL *(tel:* 0161 275 3190; *fax:* 0161 275 3187).

PERRETT, Anne Patricia (*née* Wedgwood), BA (Hons) London (1959)

Headmistress, Oriel Bank High School. *b.* 27 July 1939; Newcastle-upon-Tyne. *m.* 1961 Michael William Welford Perrett; two *s.* one *d. Education:* Central Newcastle High School GPDST; London University (Westfield College). *Career Profile:* Culcheth Hall School, Altrincham (Head of Modern Languages Dept, Second Mistress). *Societies:* Independent Schools Association. *Recreations, Interests:* Cooking, gardening, travel, walking, music, golf. *Address:* Oriel Bank High School, Devonshire Park Road, Davenport, Stockport SK2 6JP *(tel:* 0161-483 2935); 250 Ashley Road, Hale, Altrincham, Cheshire WA15 9NG *(tel:* 0161-928 4354).

PHILBIN, Kevin, LLB,Solicitor

Corporate Finance Partner, Wacks Caller. *b.* 12 June 1959 Manchester. *m.* 1983 Susan; four *s. Education:* Cardinal Langley School, Middleton (1970-77); University College, London (1977-80); College of Law (1980-81). *Career Profile:* Articled clerk, March Pearson & Skelton (1982-84); Solicitor, Halliwell Landau (1984-87); Partner, Wacks Caller (1987-); Director, Premiere Group plc. *Recreations, Interests:* Four sons, travel, food, theatre. *Address:* Wacks Caller, Steam Packet House, 76 Cross Street, Manchester, M2 4JU *(tel:* 0161 957 8888; *fax:* 0161 957 8899).

PHILLIPS, Christopher John, FCA

Managing Partner, Ernst & Young, North West Area (1996-). *b.* 25 June 1952 Northampton. *m.* 1978 Beverley; one *s.* one *d. Education:* Winchester House School (1960-65); The Leys, Cambridge (1965-70). *Career Profile:* Qualified ACA (1975); Ernst & Young: Joined London (1975); admitted as Partner, Luton (1985); transferred to Manchester as Head of Audit (1994), Managing Partner (1995), Managing Partner, NW (1996-), Manchester. *Societies:* Historic Sports Car Club. *Recreations, Interests:* Active participation in motor racing. *Address:* Ernst & Young, Commerical Union House, 2-10 Albert Square, Manchester, M2 6LP *(tel:* 0161 953 9000).

PIERCE, John Frederick David, BA(Hons)

Chief Executive & Town Clerk, Rochdale Metropolitan Borough Council. *b.* 27 January 1945 Oldham, Lancashire. *m.* 1967 Veronica; three *d. Education:* Chadderton Grammar School, Oldham (1956-63); University of Newcastle-upon-Tyne (1963-67). *Career Profile:* Various Town Planning posts in Staffordshire and Durham County Councils; appointed Borough Planning & Estates Officer, Rochdale MBC (1979); Chief Executive & Town Clerk (1986-). *Address:* Rochdale MBC, Town Hall, PO Box 15, Rochdale, Lancs *(tel:* 01706 864700; *fax:* 01706 864755).

PIKE, Malcolm John, LLB,Solicitor

Partner & Head of Human Resources Department, Addleshaw Sons & Latham. *b.* 22 August 1959 Rotherham, S Yorkshire. *m.* 1983 Rosemary; two *d. Public Offices:* Member, Management Committee of Employment Lawyers Association; Director of Mandate

(Manchester Airport Support Group); Director & Secretary, British American Business Group in the North West. *Education:* Oakwood Comprehensive, Rotherham; Thomas Rotherham Sixth Form College; Leicester University; College of Law, Chester. *Career Profile:* Articled Clerk, Hepworth & Chadwick, Leeds (1982-84); Assistant Solicitor, Freshfields, London (1984-92); Partner, Addleshaw Sons & Latham, Manchester (1992-). *Publications/Creative Work:* Legal Editor of Gee & Co's Employment in Action Series; Contributor to Fourmat Publishing's 'Aspects of Employment Law'; 'The Lawyer's Fact Book' (Gee & Co)(Editor & Author, Chapter 3, Employment Law); 'Essential Facts Employment' (Gee & Co)(Editor); 'Encyclopaedia of Forms and Precedents' (Butterworths); Advisory Editor (vol.14) and author of section on Procedures leading to redundancy & dismissal. *Societies:* Law Society; IBA; Associate Member, ABA; Employment Lawyers Association; Stockport Golf Club; Ganton Golf Club. *Recreations, Interests:* All forms of sport (principally golf, fell walking), family. *Address:* Addleshaw Sons & Latham, Dennis House, Marsden Street, Manchester, M2 1JD *(tel:* 0161 832 5994; *fax:* 0161 832 2250; *e-mail:* malcolm.pike@addleshaws.com).

PIMLOTT, Steven

Company Director, Royal Shakespeare Company (1996 season); Associate of Royal Shakespeare Company (1996-). *Education:* University of Cambridge. *Career Profile:* Staff Producer, English National Opera (1976-78); Director, Opera North (1978), Royal Exchange, Manchester (1983); various operas in Australia, Israel, Austria and elsewhere. *Address:* C/o Cruickshank Cazenove Ltd, 97 Old South Lambeth Road, London, SW8 1XU *(tel:* 0171 735 2933; *fax:* 0171 820 1081).

PITCHER, Sir Desmond Henry, Kt(1992),DL; CEng,FIEE

Chairman, United Utilities plc. *b.* 23 March 1935 Liverpool. *m.* 1961 two *d. (marr. diss.)*; *m.* 1978 two *s. (marr. diss.)*; *m.* 1991 Norma. *Public Offices:* Chairman, Merseyside Development Corporation. *Education:* Liverpool College of Technology. *Career Profile:* Group Chief Executive, The Littlewoods Organisation (1983-93); Visiting Professor, Manchester University (1993-); Member, Northern Advisory Board, Nat West Bank (1989-92); Director, Nat West Bank plc (1994-); Managing Director, Plessey Telecommunications (1978-83); Managing Director, The Sperry Corporation UK, latterly Vice-President, International Division (1961-76). *Societies:* Brooks's; Royal Automobile; Royal Birkdale Golf Club; Delamere Golf Club; Moor Park Golf Club; Lancashire CC. *Recreations, Interests:* Golf, music, football, 19th century history. *Address:* United Utilities plc, Dawson House, Great Sankey, Warrington, WA5 3LW *(tel:* 01925 234000).

PITFIELD, Thomas Baron, Hon FRMCM (1943)

Freelance Composer, Artist, Writer. *b.* 5 April 1903; Bolton. *m.* 1934 Alice Maud Astbury. *Public Offices:* Taught (mostly part-time) at various schools (Schools of Art, Public Prof of Composition RMCM-RNCM). *Education:* Primary School; Bolton Municipal Secondary School (-1917); Engineering Apprentice. *Creative Works:* Music, verse & prose; illustrated books, some hand-lettered. *Publications:* A few hundred musical works and poems (56 publishers). These include 'No Song No Supper' and 'A Song After Supper' (Autobiographical) (Thames Pub), 'A Birthday Album for Thomas Pitfield'

(Forsyth) by 17 composers for 80th Birthday and other works; 'A Cotton Town Boyhood' (Vol 3 of autobiography, Aurora Publ.); 'Johnnyrobins' (nonsense verse, drawings, music, published by RNCM). *Prizes:* Oxford University Press Choral Prize; Chamber Music Prize (Welsh National Eisteddfod); Centenario della Fisharmonia. *Societies:* Composers' Guild of Gt Britain; Performing Rights Society. *Recreations, Interests:* Wood carving, nature study, comparative religion. *Address:* Lesser Thorns, 21 East Downs Road, Bowdon, Altrincham, Cheshire WA14 2LG *(tel:* 0161-928 4644).

PLATT, Ronald Richard, BSc(Tech),CEng,MIMechE,AMCT

General Manager, Teaching Company Centre, Trafford Park Manufacturing Institute; Consultant, Manufacturing and Business. *b.* 3 October 1930 Barrow-in-Furness. *m.* 1957 Jean Mary; one *s. Education:* Barrow Grammar School (1942-49); University of Manchester (1949-52). *Military Service:* Pilot, General Duties Branch, RAFVR (1952-57). *Career Profile:* Technical Officer, ICI Ltd (1957-67); Senior Lecturer, University of Salford (1967-82); Consultant (1982-). *Publications/Creative Work:* Numerous publications in engineering science, manufacturing engineering; system dynamics and educational matters.. *Recreations, Interests:* Music, theatre, natural philosophy, sport. *Address:* Trafford Park Manufacturing Institute, Quay West, Trafford Wharf Road, Manchester, M17 1HH*(tel:* 0161 872 0393; *fax:* 0161 877 3094; *e-mail:* ronp@tpmi.co.uk).

PLATT, Steven, BA(Law),DML,Barrister

Clerk to the Bury Justices. *b.* 28 February 1952 Oldham, Lancashire. *m.* 1973 Anne Elizabeth; two *d. Education:* Counthill Grammar School, Oldham; Manchester Polytechnic. *Career Profile:* Junior Assistant progressing to Court Clerk, Oldham Magistrates Court (1969-78); Senior Court Clerk, North Sefton Magistrates Court (1978-87); Deputy Clerk to the Justices, Bury (1987-95). *Societies:* Member of the Middle Temple. *Recreations, Interests:* Music (listening and performing), theatre, reading, walking. *Address:* Bury Magistrates Court, The Court House, Tenters Street, Bury, BL9 0HX*(tel:* 0161 764 3358; *fax:* 0161 762 9412).

PLOWRIGHT, David Ernest, CBE (1996), Hon DLitt (Salford,1989), Hon BA (Liverpool Polytechnic, 1991)

Deputy Chairman, Channel Four Television. *b.* 11 December 1930; Scunthorpe. *m.* 1952 Brenda Mary; one *s.* two *d. Public Offices:* Chaired the Design Panel for Manchester's Olympic Bid and more recently was the Chairman of Manchester's City of Drama Development Committee. *Education:* Scunthorpe Grammar School. *Military Service:* Royal Corps of Signals (1949-51).*Career Profile:* Joined Granada regional news services. Editor of 'World in Action'; Programme Controller (1968); Chairman, Granada Television (1987-92), Deputy Chairman, Channel Four Television, Visiting Professor of Media Studies, Salford University. *Prizes:* International Emmy Award for Production of Laurence Olivier's King Lear; Fellowship of British Academy of Film & Television Arts. *Recreations, Interests:* Sailing, golf, television. *Address:* David Plowright Associates, Westways, Wilmslow Road, Mottram St Andrew, Cheshire SK10 4QT *(tel:* 01625-820948, *fax:* 01625 820709). *Additional Information:* Actively involved in public and private sector plans for the economic regeneration for the North of England for the past decade.

Responsible for Granada's conversion of the Dock Office in Liverpool's Albert Dock into a state of the art News Room and led Granada's move into tourism with the opening of the Granada Studios Tour (1988) and the subsequent conversion of the Victoria and Albert Warehouse in Manchester to a hotel.

PLOWRIGHT, Philip, BSc Manchester (1939)

Retired; Managing Director, Sparva Furnishings, Manchester, until retirement (1988). *b.* 11 September 1918; Worsley, Manchester. *m.* 1945 Isobel Joan Pickup; one *s. Education:* Epworth College, Rhyl, N Wales; Manchester University. *War Service:* Royal Artillery (1940-46); Mentioned in Despatches; Served in N Africa, Italy, Austria. *Career Profile:* Assistant Managing Director, Sparrow Hardwick & Co Ltd, Manchester. *Societies:* Cheetham Hill Hockey Club; Worsley Cricket Club. *Recreations, Interests:* Hockey umpiring, walking, swimming, sailing. *Address:* The Spinney, Walkden Road, Worsley, Manchester M28 4WH *(tel:* 0161-790 2978).

POLLER, Leon, MD Manchester (1957),FRCPath Manchester (1972),DSc Manchester (1980)

Hon Professor, University of Manchester; formerly Consultant Haematologist; former Director, UK Reference Laboratory for Anticoagulant Reagents and Control (designated World Health Organisation Collaborating Centre 1975); Project Leader, European Concerted Action on Anticoagulation (1994-). *b.* 16 April 1927; Manchester. *m.* 1955 Jean Dier; two *s. Public Offices:* Chairman, Manchester & District Home for Lost Dogs. *Education:* University of Manchester. *Military Service:* National Service, Major RAMC. *Publications:* Author and editor of books and report including over 200 published papers on thrombosis and blood coagulation; Editor of 'Recent Advances in Blood Coagulation' and 'Recent Advances in Thrombosis' series. *Societies:* Manchester Medical Society; Athenaeum Club. *Recreations, Interests:* Forestry, music (listening), cricket (playing), computer chess. *Address:* Department of Pathological Sciences, Stopford Building, University of Manchester, Oxford Road, Manchester M13 9PT *(tel/fax:* 0161 275 5316); 5 Oakwood Avenue, Gatley, Cheadle, Cheshire *(tel:* 0161-428 7621; *fax:* 0161 428 0763).

POSTLE, Lionel John Raymond, BSc Leeds (1949),PhD Leeds (1955),FInstMC,FAQMC

Retired. *b.* 16 December 1920; Burton-on-Trent. *m.* 1942 Margaret Adele Major; two *s.* one *d. Public Offices:* Chairman, Ackworth School Estates Ltd (1986-92); Board of Governors, Ackworth School (1975-94); Governor, Orrishmere Primary School (1993-); Treasurer, Signpost Stockport. *Education:* Ackworth School (1933-38); Leeds University (1946-49). *War Service:* RAF Coastal Command (1940-46). *Career Profile:* Managing Director, AMTAC Ltd; Director, Manchester Chamber of Commerce; ICI various Technical and Managerial posts; Scientific Officer, WIRA. *Societies:* Manchester Literary & Philosophical Society (Hon Sec 1977-81; President 1983-85); Hallé Concerts Society. *Recreations, Interests:* Family, woodwork, gardening, education, music, travel. *Address:* 44 Old Wool Lane, Cheadle Hulme, Cheadle, Cheshire SK8 5JA *(tel:* 0161-485 2823).

POTTS, John

Divisional Police Commander, City of Salford. *b.* 19 February 1945 Manchester. *m.* 1969

Veronica; one *s.* one *d. Public Offices:* Chairman, Greater Manchester Branch of Police Superintendents Association. *Education:* Ducie Technical High School, Manchester. *Career Profile:* Previously Divisional Commander, Tameside; Departmental Commander, Computers and Communications; Seconded as Chief Superintendent to Audit Commission. *Recreations, Interests:* Hill walking, public speaking. *Address:* Divisional Headquarters, The Crescent, Salford, M5 4PD *(tel:* 0161 856 5405; *fax:* 0161 856 5427).

POVEY, Rev Dr William Peter, MSc (Univ. of Manchester),MRCS,LRCP,FFPHM,DPH (Univ. of Liverpool),DObstRCOG,FRIPHH,HonFChS

NSM Assistant Curate, Christ Church, Latchford, Warrington; Drugs & Alcohol Liaison Officer & HIV/AIDS Adviser, Committee for Social Responsibility, Diocese of Chester; Hon. Consultant in Public Health Medicine, Wigan & Bolton Health Authority. *b.* 12 January 1936 Warrington. *m.* 1962 Ann Swann; one *s.* one *d. Public Offices:* Clerk in Holy Orders (ordained Deacon 1993, Priest 1994, Diocese of Chester); JP (Manchester City Bench, 1985-), member of Bench Chairmanship Committee; Member of the General Synod of the Church of England (1980-90), Central Board of Finance (1985-90); Parochial Reader (1963-93); President, Community Medicine Section, Manchester Medical Society (1989-90); NW Regional Adviser, Faculty of Public Health Medicine, Royal Colleges of Physicians (1985-90). *Education:* Manchester Grammar School (Foundation Scholar); University of Manchester; University of Liverpool; Northern Ordination Course. *Military Service:* TAVR; RAMC (Major). *Career Profile:* Medical Superintendent, St Patrick's Mission Hospital, Gweru,Zimbabwe (1963-66); Registrar in Paediatrics, Stockport & Macclesfield (1966-67); Assistant Medical Officer of Health, Warrington CB (1967-70); Assistant Senior Medical Officer, Manchester Regional Hospital Board (1970-71); Principal Assistant Senior Medical Officer, Liverpool Regional Hospital Board (1991-94); Area Medical Officer, Manchester Area Health Authority (Teaching)(1974-82); District Medical Officer, Director of Public Health & Director of Planning, Central Manchester Health Authority (1982-91); Director of Public Health, Bolton Health Authority (1991-94); Director of Public Health, Wigan & Bolton Health Authority (1994-95); Hon Lecturer /Clinical Tutor, Community Medicine/Public Health Medicine, University of Manchester (1975-95). *Publications/Creative Work:* 'James Niven, 1851-1925' in 'Some Manchester Doctors', ed Elwood & Tuxford (MUP,1984); 'The Manchester House of Recovery 1796: Britain's First General Fever Hospital: The Early Years (Trans. Lancs Chesh Ant Soc; vol 84, 1987). *Societies:* Manchester Medical Society; Manchester Medico-Legal Society; Manchester Literary & Philosophical Society; Manchester Luncheon Club; Portico Library; Bolton Medical Society; Liverpool Medical Institution; The Magistrates Association; RSPB; Ramblers' Association; Lancashire CCC; Corporation of the Church House; CNWBP; Royal Institute of Public Health & Hygiene; British Medical Association; Medical Defence Union. *Recreations, Interests:* Choral singing, public health history, HIV/AIDS services, medical ethics. *Address:* The Gables, 153 Chester Road, Grappenhall, Warrington, WA4 2SB *(tel:* 01925 265530) *(fax:* 01925 265530) *(e-mail:* 101544.2562 @compuserve.com).

POWELL, Professor James Alfred, OBE; BSc(Hons)(Manchester),MSc(Manchester), PhD (Salford),AUMIST,FRSA, FIOA,FIMgt,MCIOB

Director of Graduate School; Lucas Professor of Informing Design Systems; Director of

Entrepreneurial Research, University of Salford. *b.* 30 October 1945 Sutton, Surrey. *m.* 1968 Jennifer Elizabeth; one *s.* *Public Offices:* Chairman of Economic Social Research Council's Cognitive Engineering Panel; Member of Technology Foresight Panel for Manufacture. *Education:* De Burgh School, Tadworth; UMIST; Salford University; Open University. *Career Profile:* ICI Building Development Group (1968-69); Lecturer, Dundee University (1970-75); Reader, Professor, Portsmouth University (1975-90); Deputy Dean of Technology, Brunel University (1990-94); (1994-) Salford University, Dean Postgraduate Studies. *Publications/Creative Work:* 'Time for Real Change' (CIOB); 'ICCARUS' Interactive Training Simulator for Command of Major Incidents, Genesis 2000 project. *Prizes:* Taylor Woodrow Engineering Prize; BIMA Innovation IV and Interactive Training Awards; EMMA Interactive Audio Award; TBT's AI for Learning Award. *Societies:* Royal Society of Arts; Design Research Society. *Recreations, Interests:* Swimming, meditation, cycling, wind surfing, cooking. *Address:* Research & Graduate Collge, Faraday House, University of Salford, Salford, M5 4WT *(tel:* 0161 745 5464; *fax:* 0161 745 5553; *e-mail:* j.a.powell@iti.salford.ac.uk); 127 Hale Road, Hale, Cheshire.

POWELL, Michael Roland, BD(Edinburgh,1978),PhD(Edinburgh,1984)

Librarian, Chetham's Library. *b.* 7 August 1955 Farnworth. *m.* 1987 Agneta Koenraads; one *d.* *Education:* Farnworth Grammar School (1966-73); University of Edinburgh (1973-83); University of Strathclyde (1983-84). *Publications/Creative Work:* Articles on local history and bibliography in learned journals. *Societies:* Chetham's Society; Lancashire and Cheshire Antiquarian Society. *Recreations, Interests:* Local history, gardening, cricket. *Address:* Chetham's Library, Long Millgate, Manchester, M3 1SB*(tel:* 0161 834 7961; *fax:* 0161 839 5797); 11 Canterbury Drive, Prestwich, Manchester M25 0HY *(tel:* 0161 773 5339).

POWELL, Robert, MA(hc)(Salford University,1990)

Actor. *b.* 1 June 1944 Salford. *m.* 1975 Barbara; one *s.* one *d.* *Education:* Manchester Grammar School. *Societies:* MCC; The Lord's Taverners. *Recreations, Interests:* Sport.

POWELL, Stephen, BSc,FCA

Partner, Coopers & Lybrand. *b.* 1 September 1948 Coventry. *m.* 1970 Georgina; one *s.* *Education:* Manchester University (1966-69). *Career Profile:* Qualifed as chartered accountant (1972); Tanzania (1976-77); Partnership, Coopers & Lybrand (1985). *Recreations, Interests:* Golf, gardening, driving. *Address:* Coopers & Lybrand, Abacus Court, 6 Minshull Street, Manchester, M1 3ED*(tel:* 0161 236 9191; *fax:* 0161 247 4000).

POWERS, Glenn P, BSc(Hons)(1981),ACMA(1985)

Finance Director, Coin Controls Ltd. *b.* 6 July 1959 Melton Mowbray. *m.* 1988 Verity; one *s.* *Education:* King Edward VII Upper School; Melton Mowbray. *Career Profile:* 9 years with Coin Controls Limited in finance function; 3 years at Quadramatic plc, Finance Director. *Recreations, Interests:* Golf. *Address:* Quadramatic Plc, Coin House, Royton, Oldham, OL2 6JZ *(tel:* 0161 678 0111; *fax:* 0161 628 2189).

POWNALL, John Harvey, BSc (Eng) (Hons) London (1955),CEng,ARSM,MInstMM

Member of Council & Chairman, Estates & Buildings Committee, Salford University; Policy Adviser, Manchester Airport Development Advisory Team. *b.* 24 October 1933; Chertsey, Surrey. *m.* 1958 Pauline M Pownall (née Marsden); one *s.* two *d. Education:* Tonbridge School; Imperial College, London. *Career Profile:* Scientific Officer, Atomic Energy Research Estab, Harwell; Warren Spring Laboratory, DSIR; Dept of Economic Affairs; Board of Trade/Dept of Trade & Industry; Director-General, Council of Mechanical & Metal Trade Assns; H/d Electricity Division, Dept of Energy; Adviser to the Executive, CEGB and Director, Power Plant Contractors Assn; Regional Director, DTI-North West. *Societies:* St James's Club, Manchester. *Address:* The West House, Arley Hall, Northwich, Cheshire CW9 6LZ *(tel:* 01565-777448).

PRAG, A John N W, MA,Dip Classical Archaeology,DPhil Oxford,FSA

Keeper of Archaeology, Manchester Museum; Hon Lecturer, Dept of Archaeology, Manchester University; Co-ordinator, Alderley Edge Landscape Project; leader of the Manchester University Team reconstructing ancient faces. *b.* 28 August 1941; Oxford. *m.* 1969 Kay Wright; one *s.* one *d. Education:* Westminster School (Queen's Scholar) (1954-59); Brasenose College, Oxford (Domus Exhibitioner) (1960-62), Hon Scholar (1962-64), Senior Hulme Scholar (1967-69). *Career Profile:* Temporary Assist Keeper, Ashmolean Museum (1966-67); Visiting Professor, McMaster University (Ontario) (1978); Visiting Fellow, British School at Athens (1994). *Publications:* 'The Oresteia: Iconographic and Narrative Tradition' (1985) and various articles on Greek art and archaeology, and local archaeology, in learned journals. *Societies:* Member, Society for the Promotion of Hellenic Studies; Managing Committee Member, British School at Athens. *Recreations, Interests:* Music, travel, archaeology, walking, cooking. *Address:* The Manchester Museum, The University, Manchester, M13 9PL *(tel:* 0161-275 2665, *e-mail:* john.prag@man.ac.uk).

PRESCOTT, William Alan, FCMA,FCCA,ACIS

Controller, CWS Finance & Property. *b.* 25 March 1943 Leigh, Lancashire. *m.* 1969 June. *Education:* Leigh Grammar School (1954-59). *Career Profile:* Group Accountant, Grocery, CWS (1969-73); Divisional Accountant, Food, CWS (1973-78); CWS Chief Accountant (1978-83); Financial Controller (1983-92); Controller, CWS Finance & Property (1992-96); Controller, CWS Production & Property (1996-). *Recreations, Interests:* Golf, walking, foreign travel. *Address:* CWS Limited, PO Box 53, New Century House, Manchester, M60 4ES.

PRESTON, Professor Ronald Haydn, BSc (Econ) London,MA Oxon,MA Manchester,BD and DD Oxon

Retired. *b.* 12 March 1913; Bristol. *m.* 1948 Edith Mary Lindley; one *s.* two *d. Education:* Caistor Grammar School, Lincs; Borden Grammar School, Kent; London School of Economics; St Catherine's College and Ripon Hall, Oxford. *Career Profile:* Emeritus Professor of Social and Pastoral Theology, University of Manchester; Canon Emeritus, Manchester Cathedral. *Publications:* 'Religion and the Persistence of Capitalism' (1979); 'Explorations in Theology' (1980); 'Church and Society in the Late Twentieth Century'

(1983); 'The Future of Christian Ethics' (1987); 'Religion and the Ambiguities of Capitalism' (1991); 'Confusions in Christian Ethics: Problems for Geneva and Rome' (1994). *Recreations, Interests:* Fell walking. *Address:* 161 Old Hall Lane, Manchester M14 6HJ *(tel:* 0161-225 3291).

PRIOR, Michael John, JP; FCA

Manchester Area Chairman, Kidsons Impey. *b.* 22 July 1945 Southport. *m.* 1976 Angela Elizabeth; two *s.* two *d.* *Public Offices:* JP; Deputy Chairman, Trafford Bench; Council Member, ICAEW. *Education:* St Ambrose College, Hale Barns (1953-61). *Career Profile:* Articled Clerk, Jos W Shepherd & Co (1961-66); Qualified 1966; Partner, Heywood Shepherd (1969-89); Partner, Kidsons Impey (1989-); Manchester Area Chairman, Kidsons Impey (1990-). *Societies:* St James's Club; Ringway Golf Club. *Recreations, Interests:* My family, golf, walking, watching Manchester United FC. *Address:* Kidsons Impey, Devonshire House, 36 George Street, Manchester, M1 4HA *(tel:* 0161 236 7733; *fax:* 0161 236 7020; *e-mail:* mprior@kimanch.kidsons.co.uk); The Oaks, 4 Kings Acre, Bowdon, Altrincham, WA14 3SE *(tel:* 0161 929 4440) *(fax:* 0161 929 4440).

PROCTER,, Professor Robin Peter McGill, MA,PhD,CEng,FIM,FICorr

Pro-Vice-Chancellor, UMIST. *b.* 18 March 1940 London. *Education:* Michaelhouse, South Africa (1954-59); Jesus College, Cambridge (1960-66). *Recreations, Interests:* Gardening, ornithology, walking, travel, food and wine. *Address:* UMIST, PO Box 88, Manchester, M60 1QD*(tel:* 0161 200 4860; *fax:* 0161 200 4865; *e-mail:* r.p.m.procter@umist.ac.uk).

PROCTOR, Canon Noel, MBE

Hon Chaplain, North Manchester Hospital; Hon Minister, St Pauls, Kersal; Hon Canon, Manchester Cathedral; Licenced by Bishop of Manchester as Evangelist. *b.* 22 December 1930 Belfast. *m.* 1964 Norma Long; three *d.* *(widowed 1991) Public Offices:* Rector of Byers Green, Co Durham (1966-70); Chaplain to HM Prisons (1970-95); serving at Wandsworth (1970); Eastchurch (1970-74); Dartmoor (1974-79); Manchester (1979-95). *Education:* Queen Victoria School, Belfast; Church Army College, London; St Aidan's Theological College, Birkenhead. *Career Profile:* Apprentice and Qualified Shirtcutter (1944-53); Church Army Evangelist (1953-62); Training for Ordinaton (1962-64); Curate of St Andrew;s, Haughton-le-Skerne (1964-67); Rector, Byers Green, Co Durham (1967-70); Chaplain to HM Prisons (1970-95). *Publications/Creative Work:* 'The Cross Behind Bars' (Kingsway, 1983) reprinted 10 times; 'Light Through Prison Bars' (Kingsway, 1995). *Prizes:* Commendation from the Home Secretary (1991); Canon of Manchester Cathedral (1991); MBE (1992). *Societies:* Retired Civil Service Fellowship; Prison Fellowship; Patron of New Life Centre for Homeless People (Stockport). *Recreations, Interests:* Public speaking (church and after dinner), male voice choirs, reading, evangelistic missions. *Address:* 222 Moor Lane, Kersal, Salford, M7 3QH *(tel:* 0161 792 1284).

PUGH, Bryan Butler, MC (1944); MA Cambridge (1947),LLB Cambridge (1946)

Retired. *b.* 10 February 1921; Aberystwyth. *m.* 1943 Mary Spafford; three *d.* *(widowed*

1974); *m.* 1982 Yolanda Heywood (née de Ferranti); three *steps.* one *stepd. Public Offices:* Former Member of Court and Council, Manchester University. *Education:* Rugby School; Trinity College, Cambridge (Exhibitioner in Law). *War Service:* Welsh Guards (1941-45), Served 3rd Bn North Africa & Italy twice wounded. *Career Profile:* Executive Director, Hill Samuel & Co Ltd until 1981; Formerly Partner, Grundy Kershaw & Farrar & Co, Solicitors, Manchester. *Prizes:* John Peacock and Hadfield Prizes awarded by Manchester Law Society. *Societies:* St James's Club, Manchester; Manchester Tennis & Racquet Club. *Address:* Henbury Moss Farm, Macclesfield SK11 9PW *(tel:* 01260-224352).

PULLAN, Professor Brian Sebastian, FBA (1985); MA,PhD,FRHistS

Professor of Modern History, University of Manchester. *b.* 10 December 1935; Tadworth, Surrey. *m.* 1961 Janet Elizabeth Maltby; two *s. Public Offices:* Feoffee of Chetham's Hospital & Library. *Education:* Epsom College; Trinity College, Cambridge. *Military Service:* National Service, Royal Artillery. *Career Profile:* Research Fellow, Trinity College, Cambridge (1961-63); Fellow, Queens' College, Cambridge (1963-72); University Lecturer in History, Cambridge (1967-72). *Publications:* (Ed.) 'Sources for the History of Medieval Europe'; (Ed.) 'Crisis and Change in the Venetian Economy'; 'Rich and Poor in Renaissance Venice'; 'A History of Early Renaissance Italy'; 'The Jews of Europe and the Inquisition of Venice'; (Ed. with Susan Reynolds) 'Towns and Townspeople in Medieval and Renaissance Europe: Essays in Memory of J K Hyde'; (Ed. with David Chambers) 'Venice: a Documentary History 1450-1630'; 'Poverty and Charity: Europe, Italy, Venice 1400-1700'; articles and reviews in learned journals; occasional papers. *Societies:* Corresponding Fellow, Deputazione di Storia Patria per le Venezie; Corresponding Fellow, Ateneo Veneto. *Recreations, Interests:* Dogs, theatre. *Address:* Department of History, University of Manchester M13 9PL *(tel:* 0161-275 3118); 30 Sandhurst Road, Didsbury, Manchester M20 5LR *(tel:* 0161-445 3665).

PYE, Allan, MA,FCA

Tax Partner, Deloitte & Touche, Manchester. *b.* 1 November 1950 London. *m.* 1976 Lynn; two *s.* one *d. Public Offices:* Secretary, Royal Botanical & Horticultural Society of Manchester & The Northern Counties; Chairman, Altrincham & Sale Sea Cadets. *Education:* Sale Boys Grammar School; Trinity College, Cambridge. *Publications/Creative Work:* Contributor to FT Law & Tax. *Recreations, Interests:* Family, football (Manchester United). *Address:* Deloitte & Touche, Abbey House, 74 Mosley Street, Manchester *(tel:* 0161 228 3456; *fax:* 0161 228 2681).

PYE, Freddie

Chairman, MSS Group of Companies, Halba Travel Ltd, Noverfield Ltd, MIAC Ltd, Medical Air Technology Ltd, Maxim Fasteners, G Corner Ltd; Director, Charlton Enterprises; Director, Maxim Metals; Chairman, Pye Metals, Freddie Pye Ltd; Vice-Chairman, Manchester City FC; Vice-President, Stockport County FC; President, Wythenshawe Sunday Football League; President, Stockport & Cheadle Sunday League; President, Cheadle Town FC; President, Wilmslow Juniors FC. *b.* 11 March 1928; Stockport. *m.* 1950 Alma; one *s. Education:* Avondale Comprehensive School, Cheadle

Heath, Stockport. *Military Service:* Fleet Air Arm (1946-48). *Societies:* Chairman, 400 Club, Boxing, Piccadilly Hotel. *Recreations, Interests:* Football.

PYSDEN, Edward Scott, LLB(Manchester, 1969)

Senior Partner, Eversheds, Manchester. *b.* 6 May 1948 Croydon. *m.* 1971 Anna-Maria; three *d. Education:* Dulwich College; King's School, Macclesfield. *Career Profile:* Articled Clerk/Assistant Solicitor, David Blank Alexander (1970-74); Partner, Alexander Tatham (now Eversheds)(1974-); Senior Partner, Eversheds, Manchester (1993-). *Publications/Creative Work:* Legal articles/Lecturer on MBOs and Corporate Finance. *Prizes:* Manchester Law Society John Peacock Prize. *Societies:* Law Society; Institute of Fiscal Studies; Associate of the Securities Institute; St James' Club. *Recreations, Interests:* Golf, food and wine, classical music. *Address:* Eversheds, London Scottish House, 24 Mount Street, Manchester, M2 3DB *(tel:* 0161 832 6666; *fax:* 0161 832 5337).

Q

QUICK, James Anthony, FIMI

Marketing Director, Quicks Group plc; Presenter, BBC GMR. *b*. 13 August 1947 Hale, Cheshire. *m*. 1971 Elaine; one *s*. one *d*. *Public Offices:* Member of the Court, University of Manchester; Visiting Fellow, Manchester Business School; Chairman, North West New Heart New Start Appeal. *Education:* Rossell School, Fleetwood; Loughborough College. *Career Profile:* Marketing Director, Quicks Group plc. *Publications/Creative Work:* 'Life with a New Heart' (unpublished) written in conjunction with BBC Television's Martin Henfield. *Societies:* Ringway Golf Club; Birkin Fly Fishers. *Recreations, Interests:* All aspects of sport, both participating and spectating. *Address:* Quicks Group plc, Centre House, Ashburton Road East, Trafford Park, Manchester, M17 1QG (*tel:* 0161 455 1661; *fax:* 0161 848 9150). *Additional Information:* After a healthy and active life, at the age of 38 contracted a virus which affected the muscle of the heart. Shortly after 40th birthday, underwent a Heart Transplant operation at Wythenshawe Hospital. Returned to business 3 months later; spends a great deal of time with the New Heart New Start charity appeal (Chairman) raising money for further heart transplant operations in the North West of England. Presenter GMR Business on BBC GMR and other programmes.

QUICK, Norman, CBE (1984),DL Gtr Manchester (1987); Honorary MA Manchester (1977),Honorary LLD Manchester (1984)

Retired. *b*. 19 November 1922; Sale, Cheshire. *m*. 1949 Maureen Cynthia; four *d*. *Education:* Arnold School, Blackpool. *War Service:* RNVR (1941-46) Mentioned in Despatches. *Career Profile:* Member, Lancashire County Council (1954-57); Chairman & Managing Director, Quicks Group; Chairman, Stretford Conservatives (1968-72); Treasurer, University of Manchester (1975-80); Chairman of Council, University (1980-83); Chairman, Piccadilly Radio (from inception to 1988); National President, Motor Agents Assn (1977-78); President, Quicks Group plc (1994); High Sheriff, Greater Manchester (1990). *Societies:* Royal Automobile Club, London; St James's Club, Manchester. *Recreations, Interests:* Walking, gardening. *Address:* Quicks Group plc, Centre House, Ashburton Road East, Trafford Park, Manchester M17 1AA (*tel:* 0161-872 7788); The Coach House, Gaskell Avenue, Knutsford, WA16 0DA (*tel:* 01565 651772).

QUILLIAM, Barrie, BSc Manchester,ATCL

Managing Director, Forest City Group of Companies. *b*. 14 December 1934. *Education:* Manchester Grammar School; Manchester University. *Prizes:* Silver Medal, Manchester University Engineering Society. *Recreations, Interests:* Horse riding, music, water sports, semi-pro jazz pianist. *Address:* The Forest City Signs Ltd, Park Road, Timperley, Altrincham, Cheshire WA14 5QX (*tel:* 0161-969 0441).

R

RABBITT, Professor Patrick Michael Anthony, Hon FBPsSoc MA(Cantab),PhD(Cantab), MA(Oxon),MSc(Manchester)

Professor Gerontology & Cognitive Psychology, University of Manchester. *b.* 23 September 1934 Bombay, India. *m.* 1955 Adriana Habers; one *s.* two *d. (marr. diss. 1975)*; *m.* 1976 Dorothy Bishop. *Education:* Sir Joseph Williamson's Mathematical School, Rochester, Kent; The Queens' College, Cambridge. *Career Profile:* MRC, Applied Psychology Research Unit, Cambridge (1962-68); University Lecturer & Fellow, The Queens' College, Oxford (1968-82); Professor of Psychology, University of Durham (1982-83). *Publications/Creative Work:* 204 journals and articles. *Prizes:* Myers Lecturer, British Psychological Society; Bartlett Lectureship, Experimental Psychology Society; Hon Fellow, British Psychological Society. *Societies:* Experimental Psychology Society; British Psychological Society; American Psychological Association. *Recreations, Interests:* Whisky and nostalgia. *Address:* University of Manchester, Age & Cognitive Performance Research Centre, Manchester, M13 9PL (*tel:* 0161 275 2873; *fax:* 0161 275 2873; *e-mail:* Rabbitt @hera.psy.man.ac.uk).

RACE, Robert Topham, BSc (Hons)(City Univ,1983),MSI(dip)(1986),AIIMR (1986)

Director, Wise Speke Ltd. *b.* 13 June 1962 Manchester. *m.* 1994 Lorraine Nicola; one *s. Education:* Manchester Grammar School; City University, London. *Societies:* St James's Club. *Address:* Wise Speke Ltd, PO Box 512, 8 King Street, Manchester, M60 2EP (*tel:* 0161 953 9700; *fax:* 0161 832 1672).

RADCLIFFE, Canon Albert Edward, BD(London)

Canon Pastor, Manchester Cathedral. *b.* 28 May 1934 Bootle, Liverpool. *m.* 1964 Petrena; two *d. Education:* Bootle Grammar School; St Aidan's College, Birkenhead; Church Divinity School of the Pacific, Berkeley, California. *Military Service:* National Service RAF. *Career Profile:* Assistant Curate: St John, Knotty Ash, Liverpool, St Nicholas, Blundellsands; British Chaplain, St Luke's, Haifa, Israel; Vicar, St Michael, Tong-cum-Alkrington, Middleton; Rector, Area Dean, St Michael, Ashton under Lyne; Canon Residentiary, Manchester Cathedral. *Publications/Creative Work:* Occasional verses and newspaper articles. *Societies:* Society for the Study of Theology; Chairman, The Manchester Council of Christians and Jews. *Recreations, Interests:* Theology, poetry, military history, Byzantine art and history, intefaith dialogue. *Address:* The Cathedral, Manchester, M3 1SX (*tel:* 0161 833 2200; *fax:* 0161 839 6226); 46 Shrewsbury Road, Prestwich, Manchester, M25 9GQ (*tel:* 0161 798 0459).

RAFFLES, Major Ralph Leslie Stamford, KStJ,Knight Military Order St Lazarus,Knight of Grimaldi,OM (USA),Ordem da Meritos, Brazil,TD,JP, Knight Templar,DL; FInstPI

President, United Kingdom Association of Consular Organisations; Consul for Monaco; Bailli Delegue for Great Britain; Chaine des Rotisseurs; Vice-President, Grenadier Guards Association; Member, South Manchester Health Authority; Magistrate, City of Manchester; Chevalier, 11 French Wine Orders; Hon Col, Commonwealth of Kentucky USAAF. *b.* 5 May 1920; Manchester. *m.* 1954 Sally Sieff; three *s.* one *d. Public Offices:*

High Sheriff, Greater Manchester (1979); Deputy Lord Lieutenant; Chairman, North Manchester HMC (1964); Member, National Whitley Council (1966); Member, Parole Board Strangeways Prison (1967); President, Manchester Consular Association (1969 and 1981); Chairman, Radio Manchester BBC (1975); Chairman, GM Youth Association (1975); President, Cresta Run (1956). *Education:* Cuckfield House, Sussex; Manchester Grammar School; Manchester University. *War Service:* Oxford and Bucks Light Infantry - Service in France, Africa, India, Burma (1939-46); 5 Bn Kings Own Regt (TA) (1947-54). *Societies:* International Sportsmen; St Moritz Toboggan; Royal Ocean Racing; Lyceum. *Recreations, Interests:* Family, fund raising for charity, skin and scuba diving, haute cuisine and wine drinking, music, ocean racing. *Address:* Dene Manor Group of Companies, Scottish Providential House, 52 Brown Street, Manchester M2 2AG *(tel: 0161-434 4908);* Dene Manor, Dene Park, Didsbury, Manchester M20 8GF. *Additional Information:* Founder of Manchester VSO, Founder of North West Kidney Research, Co-founder (with Jacques Cousteau) of 'Les Chasseurs Alpins Sous Marins' which found first Amphorae off France. Member of winning GB Bobsleigh Team for European Cup (1956), Member British Olympic Bobsleigh Team (1956). Member of British Sandyacht Team attempt on world speed record.

RAMSBOTTOM, James

Sole Proprietor, Jim Ramsbottom Bookmaker; Managing Director, Castlefield Estates Ltd, Dukes 92 Ltd, Specimen Property Company Ltd. *b.* 20 March 1939; Salford. *m.* 1966 Jean Kathleen Mellor; one *s.* four *d. Education:* Salford Grammar School. *Career Profile:* Clerk, Greengates & Irwell; Clerk, Small & Parkes Ltd; self-employed from 1960. *Recreations, Interests:* Golf, local history, waterways, rugby league, Manchester United. *Address:* Eastgate, 2 Castle Street, Castlefield, Manchester M3 4LZ

RAMSDEN, Professor Herbert, BA (French) Manchester (1948),BA (Spanish) Manchester (1949),MA Manchester (1953),Dr en Fil y Let Madrid (1954)

Emeritus Professor of the University of Manchester (1982-). *b.* 20 April 1927; Manchester. *m.* 1953 Joyce Robina Hall; three *s.* two *d. Public Offices:* Hispanists' Representative, National Council for Modern Languages (1972-73); British Representative, Asociacion Europea de Profesores de Espanol (1975-80). *Education:* Sale Grammar School (1938-45); University of Manchester (1945-49) (1952-53); University of Strasbourg (1947); University of Madrid (1951-54); University of the Sorbonne (1954). *Military Service:* Infantry and Intelligence Corps (1949-51). *Career Profile:* Assistant Lecturer, University of Manchester (1954-57); Lecturer, University of Manchester (1957-61); Professor of Spanish Language and Literature, University of Manchester (1961-82). *Publications:* Seven books on Spanish language and/or literature; five editions (with critical study) of Spanish writers; articles and reviews in specialist journals. *Prizes:* Kemsley Travelling Fellowship (1951-52). *Societies:* Association of British Hispanists. *Recreations, Interests:* Family, hill walking. *Address:* 7 Burford Avenue, Bramhall, Stockport, Cheshire SK7 1BL *(tel: 0161-439 4306).*

RARITY, Brian Stewart Hall, MA (Glasgow),PhD (Manchester),FRAS

Director, I.D.B. Limited, Rarity & Co. Ltd. *b.* 15 May 1938; Airdrie, Scotland. *m.* 1962 Margaret Edwards; four *s*; *m.* 1986 Patricia. *Public Offices:* Chairman, Portico Library Trust; President (1986-88), Vice-President (1988-), Hon Secretary (1982-86), Manchester

Literary & Philosophical Society; Member of Court, University of Manchester; Chairman, The National Museum of Labour History Trading Company Ltd. *Education:* Airdrie Academy; Glasgow University; Manchester University. *Career Profile:* Mathematician, English Electric Aviation Ltd/British Aerospace, Warton; Senior Research Fellow, California Institute of Technology; Lecturer/Senior Lecturer, Department of Mathematics, Manchester University. *Publications:* Various papers in applied mathematics. *Societies:* Manchester Literary & Philosophical Society; Hallé Concerts Society; Royal Astronomical Society; Portico Library. *Recreations, Interests:* Music, photography. *Address:* I.D.B. Limited, Portland Tower, Portland Street, Manchester M1 3LF (*tel:* 0161 236 7754; *fax:* 0161 236 2672; *e-mail:* nidb.demon.co.uk); Highstone Wycke, Whitehough, Chinley, High Peak SK23 6BX (*tel:* 01663 750646).

RAYMOND, Peter, BSc,ACST

Managing Director, UMIST Ventures Ltd; Director: Antaguage Ltd (trading as Kincora), Monobest, Contra Vision Ltd, Contra Vision Supplies Ltd, Tepnel Life Sciences plc, UMIST Ventures plc Nine Dragons Trading Ltd, Gloabalize Trading Ltd, Northern Energetics Ltd, Reverse Engineering Instrumentation Ltd, Reverse Engineering Ltd (REL), System Cost Trading Ltd, European Construction Ventures Ltd (ECV), Stick Ups Ltd, Nurun Ltd, ICS Ltd. *b.* 10 December 1938; Manchester. *m.* 1963 Dorothy Elisabeth; three *s.* one *d. Public Offices:* Chairman, Governing Body, Kingsway School, Cheadle; Member of Parliamentary Scientific Committee; Member of Representative Council NIMTECH; Member of UMIST Academic Board. *Education:* Stand Grammar School (1950-57); UMIST (Chemistry) (1957-61); MBS (1971). *Career Profile:* Director, Compounding Ingredients; European Director, Corporate Development, Dexter Mysol. *Prizes:* Queens Award to Industry for Export (1992), Prince of Wales Fund for Innovation (1994, 1995), Owens Anniversary Trust Award (1995), DTI Award for Technology Transfer (1996) *Societies:* MBS Association; UMIST Alumni; Old Standians; Manchester United member; Grove Park Squash Club; VP, Manchester Football Club; Gatley Squash Club. *Recreations, Interests:* Music, soccer, squash, local school affairs, politics, travel, East/West relations, international technology venturing. *Address:* UMIST Ventures Ltd, PO Box 88, Manchester M60 1QD (*tel:* 0161-200 3054); 72 Grasmere Road, Gatley, Cheadle, Cheshire SK8 4RS.

REA, Rev Ernest, BA,BD

Head of Religious Broadcasting, BBC. *b.* 6 September 1945 Belfast. *m.* 1973 Kathleen; two *s.* (*marr. diss. 1994*); *m.* 1995 Gaynor. *Education:* Methodist College, Belfast; Queens University, Belfast. *Career Profile:* Minister of Bannside Presbyterian Church, Co Down (1974-78); Producer, Religious Programmes, BBC Northern Ireland (1978-83); Senior Producer, Religious Programmes, BBC South, Bristol (1983-87); Editor, Network Radio, BBC South & West, Bristol (1987-88); Head of Religious Broadcasting, BBC (1988-). *Societies:* Member of the Radio Academy. *Recreations, Interests:* Playing tennis and golf, watching cricket, theatre, music, reading. *Address:* BBC, New Broadcasting House, PO Box 27, Oxford Road, Manchester, M60 1SJ (*tel:* 0161 244 3178; *fax:* 0161 244 3183); Clifden, Oatlands, Macclesfield Road, Alderley Edge, SK9 7BL (*tel:* 01625 582938).

READ, Professor Frank Henry, FRS (1984); ARCS Royal College of Science (1955),BSc London (1955),PhD Manchester (1959),DSc Manchester (1975)

Professor of Physics, University of Manchester. *b.* 6 October 1934; Edgware, Middlesex. *m.* 1961 Anne Stuart; two *s.* two *d. Public Offices:* Member of Council, Royal Society (1987-89); Member of Science Board, SERC (1987-90); Vice-President, Institute of Physics (1985-89). *Education:* Haberdashers' Aske's Hampstead School (1946-52); Royal College of Science (1952-55); University of Manchester (1955-59). *Career Profile:* Lecturer, Senior Lecturer and Reader, University of Manchester; Visiting Researcher, FOM Institute, Amsterdam (1979-80); Visiting Professor, Universite Pierre et Marie Curie, Paris (1984); Visiting Researcher, Joint Institute for Laboratory Astrophysics (JILA) (1984-85). *Publications:* Books: 'Electro-magnetic Radiation' (Wiley, 1982); 'Electrostatic lenses' (with E Harting) (Elsevier, 1976); many papers in learned journals. *Societies:* Royal Society; Institute of Physics; Institution of Electrical Engineers. *Recreations, Interests:* Farming, stone-masonry. *Address:* Department of Physics & Astronomy, Schuster Laboratory, Manchester University, Manchester M13 9PL *(tel: 0161-275 4141)*; Hardingland Farm, Macclesfield Forest, Macclesfield, Cheshire SK11 0ND *(tel: 01625-425759)*.

READ, Geoffrey Fitzwalter, MSc,CEng,FICE,FIStructE,FCIWEM, FIHT,MILE,FIMgt, MAE

Consulting Civil and Structural Engineer; Director, Jon Walton Associates; Visiting Lecturer, Department of Civil and Structural Engineering, UMIST. *m.* 1994 Margeret Lucas; one *d. Public Offices:* Chairman, The Edge Association, Alderley Edge and the Village Enhancement Commitee, Alderley Edge. *Education:* West Bridgford Grammar School, Notts; Nottingham University; UMIST. *War Service:* Command of Mechanical Equipment Unit, Royal Engineers. *Previous Positions:* City Engineer and Surveyor, Manchester and Joint Engineer, Manchester International Airport; Borough Engineer and Surveyor, Bolton and Engineer to former Bolton and District Joint Sewerage Board; Deputy Borough Engineer and Planning Officer, Doncaster; Chief Assistant Engineer, Harrow; Principal Assistant Engineer, Leicester; Senior Assistant Engineer, Leicester; Senior Assistant Engineer, Gillingham. *Publications:* (a) some 50 technical papers mainly in respect of highways, sewerage, sewerage rehabilitation, airport civil engineering, multi-storey car parks, civil engineering, socio-economic cost/benefit assessments, environmental impact studies etc; (b) editing and contributing to 'Sewers - Rehabilitation and New Construction' Vols 1 & 2 (Edward Arnold) (in publication); (c) contributed to 'The Maintenance of Brick and Stone Masonry Structures' (Chapman and Hall). *Societies:* Former Chairman, City Engineers Group; Founder President, Association of Metropolitan District Engineers; Former Adviser to the Association of Metropolitan Authorities; Former Chairman, NW Kidney Research Association; Mere Golf Club; 20 Club Golf Society; Manchester University Staff Golfing Society. *Recreations, Interests:* Golf, Big Band Jazz and DIY. *Address:* Quarry House, Macclesfield Road, Alderley Edge, Cheshire SK9 7BH *(tel: 01625-584164)*.

REDDY, Thomas
Chairman, Tom Reddy Advertising Ltd. *b.* 6 December 1941; Blackpool. *m.* 1969 Wendy; one *s.* one *d. Education:* Baines's School, Poulton-le-Fylde. *Career Profile:* Executive Creative Director, McCann Ericksonn, Manchester. *Prizes:* Various advertising creative. *Societies:* St James's Club, MTRC. *Recreations, Interests:* Book collecting, lecturing on advertising. *Address:* Tom Reddy Advertising, Old Colony House, 6 South King Street, Manchester M2 6DQ *(tel: 0161-832 0182)*.

REED, John Reginald, BA (Hons) London (1935)

Retired BBC Official. *b.* 30 May 1909; Aldershot. *m.* 1936 Marion Hampton; two *s.* two *d. Public Offices:* Chairman, Manchester Camerata Orchestra (1977-88). *Education:* County High School, Aldershot; London University. *War Service:* RAFVR (1941-46). *Career Profile:* BBC Education (1946-60); Head of Admin BBC North Region (1960-68). *Publications:* 'Schubert, The Final Years' (1972); 'Schubert' (Great Composers Series) (1978); 'The Schubert Song Companion' (1985); 'Schubert' (Master Musicians Series) (1987). *Prizes:* Vincent Duckles Award of American Music Library Association (1987); Honorary Member of International Franz Schubert Institute (1989); Chairman, Schubert Institute UK (1991-94). *Societies:* Portico Library; Victorian Society; Hallé Society; Friends of the Camerata; Manchester Pedestrian Club; Friends of the Whitworth; Rusholme Civic Society. *Recreations, Interests:* Writing, gardening, walking, reference books. *Address:* 130 Fog Lane, Didsbury, Manchester M20 6SW *(tel: 0161)*445-2892).

REES, Roger Coltman, OBE (1990); MA,LLM,Solicitor (Hons) (1956)

Retired. *b.* 24 September 1928; Leicester. *Education:* Queen Elizabeth School, Kirkby Lonsdale; Christs College, Cambridge (1948-52). *Military Service:* Royal Naval Air Service (1946-48). *Career Profile:* Solicitor, Middlesbrough CBC (1956-62); Senior Assistant Solicitor, Bolton CBC (1962-68); Deputy Town Clerk, City of Salford (1968-69); Town Clerk, City of Salford (1969-74); Clerk of the Peace, Salford (1969-71); Chief Executive, Salford City Council (1974-93); Clerk to the Greater Manchester Police Authority (1986-93). *Societies:* Law Society; Manchester Literary & Philosophical Society; Salford Choral Society. *Recreations, Interests:* Choral singing, language, walking, landscape. *Address:* 19 Verdure Avenue, Heaton, Bolton BL1 5ER

REGAN, Martin Peter

Editor, NW Business Insider; Director, Excel Publishing, Entrepreneur Business Publishing. *b.* 14 August 1962 Gorton, Manchester. *m.* Shirley Griffiths; two *s.* two *d. Education:* Newall Green Comprehensive, Wythenshawe. *Career Profile:* Freelance Journalist, Construction, Business & Finance; Worked for Financial Times, Wall Street Journal, Sunday Times, NW Times (the ill-fated). *Publications/Creative Work:* Various children's books. *Societies:* Brooklands Hockey & Lawn Tennis Club; Chorlton Chess Club. *Recreations, Interests:* Chess, mountaineering, modern art, northern artists, Manchester City FC (above all). *Address:* Newsco Publications, Mindell House, 10 Minshull Street, Manchester, M1 3EF*(tel:* 0161 236 9711; *fax:* 0161 236 9862).

REID, Professor Stephen Robert, FEng(1993), BSc, PhD (Univ. of Manchester), MA, ScD (Cambridge),FIMechE,FASME,FIMA,MIStructE,CMath,FRSA

Conoco Professor of Mechanical Engineering, Head of Applied Mechanics Division, UMIST. *b.* 13 May 1945 Manchester. *m.* 1969 Susan; three *s. Education:* Chorlton Grammar School, Manchester; University of Manchester: BSc (1963-66), PhD (1966-69). *Career Profile:* Research Officer, Central Electricity Research Laboratories (1969-70); Lecturer in Mechanical Engineering, UMIST (1970-76); Lecturer in Engineering, University of Cambridge (1976-80); Jackson Professor of Engineering Science, University

of Aberdeen (1980-84); Conoco Professor of Mechanical Engineering, UMIST (1985-); UMISTEL: Pro-Vice-Chancellor (1992-95), Deputy Principal & Vice-Chancellor (1994-95). *Publications/Creative Work:* Approximately 130 published papers, book chapters in international scientific/technical journals and conference proceedings. *Prizes:* Safety Award in Mechanical Engieering, Institute of Mechanical Engineers (1982). *Societies:* Professional institutions. *Recreations, Interests:* Elder, Poynton Baptist Church, interested in all sport especially soccer. *Address:* Department of Mechanical Engineering, UMIST, PO Box 88, Sackville Street, Manchester, M60 1QD *(tel:* 0161 200 3848; *fax:* 0161 200 3849; *e-mail:* steve.reid@umist.ac.uk)

RENFREW, Norman John, CA (1970)

Director of Finance, Manchester Airport plc. *b.* 20 August 1946; Glasgow. *m.* 1971 Muriel MacLaren; one *s.* one *d. Education:* Hermitage Academy, Helensburgh, Scotland. *Career Profile:* Financial Controller, Britoil plc; Group Chief Internal Auditor, Crown Agents for Oversea Governments & Administrations. *Societies:* Institute of Directors. *Recreations, Interests:* Sailing, skiing. *Address:* Manchester Airport plc, Manchester M90 1QX *(tel:* 0161-489 3708); Bridge End, Bridge End Lane, Prestbury, Cheshire SK10 4DJ *(tel:* 01625-827751).

RENSHAW, Peter Bernard Appleton, BA (hons) Cantab (1976),MA Cantab (1979)

Partner, Slater Heelis, Solicitors. *b.* 23 July 1954; Sale. *m.* 1982 Patricia Ann Caffrey; one *s. Public Offices:* Notary Public. *Education:* Trearddur House School; Charterhouse; Cambridge. *Prizes:* Titular Scholar, Selwyn College, Cambridge; Law Society Final Exams: Stephen Heelis Gold Medal, Francis Broderip Prize, George Hadfield Prize, Daniel Reardon Prize. *Societies:* Law Society. *Recreations, Interests:* Climbing, gardening, skiing. *Address:* Slater Heelis, 71 Princess Street, Manchester M2 4HL *(tel:* 0161-228 3781; *fax:* 0161 236 5282; *e-mail:* 101642.1315@compuserve.com).

REYNISH, Timothy John, MA(Cantab),ARCM,FRNCM

Head of School of Wind and Percussion, Royal Northern College of Music. *b.* 9 March 1938 Axbridge. *m.* 1961 Hilary Blohm Anderson; three *s.* one *d. Education:* St Edmunds School, Canterbury (1948-56); Gonville & Caius College, Cambridge (1956-59); Student of French Horn with Aubrey Brain and Frank Probyn; Student of Conducting with Sir Adrian Boult, Sir Charles Groves; Franco Ferrara and Dean Dixon. *Career Profile:* 1st Horn: Northern Sinfonia (1959-60), Sadlers Wells Opera (1960-61); Director of Music, Minehead Grammar School (1961-65); Co-Principal Horn, CBSO (1965-68); Lecturer, Bromsgrove College (1968-75); Tutor in Conducting, RNCM (1975-95); Head of School of Wind & Percussion (1977-); Guest Conductor CBSO, Halle, BBC Philharmonic, RIAS, LSO etc. *Publications:* Editor Novello Wind Band Series (1982-94); Editor Maecenas Contemporary Music (1994-); various articles on wind music in The Composer; Classical Music, Winds and international magazines. *Prizes:* Bronze Medal, Mitropoulos Competition (1971); Diploma of Merit, Accademia Chiggiana (1972); Churchill Fellowship (1982-83). *Societies:* Incorporated Society of Musicians; British Association of Symphonic Bands & Wind Ensembles; World Association for Symphonic Bands & Ensembles. *Recreations, Interests:* Music, sport, travel. *Address:* Royal Northern College of Music, 124 Oxford

Road, Manchester, M13 9RD (*tel:* 0161 273 6283; *fax:* 0161 273 7611); Silver Birches, Bentinck Road, Altrincham, WA14 2BP (*tel:* 0161 928 8364) (*fax:* 0161 928 8364).

REYNOLDS, Carolyn Jane

Head of Drama Serials, Granada TV. *m.* Simon; two *s. Career Profile:* Joined Granada Television 14 years ago from 'The Guardian' Newspaper; worked on a variety of programmes, including 'World in Action'; 'Coronation Street'; 'Crown Court'; Production Assistant, Production Manager; Producer 'Families'; Producer 'Coronation Street' (1991); Executive Producer, Coronation Street (1993); Head of Drama Serials (1994).

RICHARDS, Keith, Cambridge, BA (1970), MA (1974) (Classics Tripos)

Headmaster, Bury Grammar School (Boys) from 1st September 1990. *b.* 18 May 1948; High Wycombe, Buckinghamshire. *m.* 1978 Juliet; two *d. Education:* Bristol Grammar School (1959-66); Open Scholarship in Classics to Sidney Sussex College, Cambridge (1967-70); St John's College Oxford and Oxford University Department of Education for PGCE (1970-71). *Career Profile:* Assistant Master, Manchester Grammar School (1971-79); Head of Classics, King's School Chester (1979-83); Head of Classics, Repton School (1983-90). *Recreations, Interests:* Music, sport, travel. *Address:* Bury Grammar School (Boys), Tenterden Street, Bury, Lancs BL9 0HN (*tel: 0*161-797 2700).

RILEY, David Woodward, FLA

Keeper of Printed Books, John Rylands Library. *b.* 19 April 1934 Manchester. *Education:* Manchester Grammar School (1945-52). *Career Profile:* John Rylands Library: Library Assistant (1952), Assistant Librarian (1960); Keeper of Printed Books (1983); Visiting Lecturer in Historical Bibliography, Manchester Library School (1960). *Publications:* Articles in the professional press and the Library's Bulletin. *Societies:* Manchester Bibliographical Society; Cambridge Bibliographical Society; Hallé Concerts Society; Manchester Chamber Concerts Society; Paddle Steamer Preservation Society; Coastal Cruising Association. *Recreations, Interests:* Bibliography, music, sailing. *Address:* John Rylands Library, 150 Deansgate, Manchester, M3 3EH(*tel:* 0161 834 5343; *fax:* 0161 834 5574; *e-mail:* DWRiley@fsl.li.man.ac.uk).

RILEY, Very Revd Kenneth Joseph, BA (Univ. of Wales, 1961), MA (Oxon, 1968)

Dean of Manchester. *b.* 25 June 1940 Flint. *m.* 1968 Margaret Deninson; two *d. Public Offices:* Hon Chaplain, Greater Manchester Lieutenancy; Member of Court, Manchester University; Governor, Manchester Grammar School; Foeffee, Chetham's Hospital & Library; Governor, Chetham's School of Music; Director, Manchester Cathedral Development Trust; Groundwork Trust. *Education:* Holywell Grammar School; University College of Wales, Aberystwyth; Linacre College, Oxford; Wycliffe Hall, Oxford. *Career Profile:* Curate, Fazakerley, Liverpool (1964-66); Chaplain, Brasted Place College (1966-69); Chaplain, Oundle School (1969-75); Chaplain, Liverpool University (1975-83); Vicar, Mossley Hill, Liverpool (1975-83); Diocesan Warden of Readers (1979-83); Rural Dean of Childwall (1982-83); Vice-Dean of Liverpool Cathedral (1983-93); Member of Archbishops' Commission on Cathedrals (1992-94). *Publications/Creative Work:*

'Liverpool Cathedral'; various hymns. *Prizes:* Robert Bryan Music Scholar (1958-61). *Societies:* St James's Club, Manchester. *Recreations, Interests:* Music, drama. *Address:* Manchester Cathedral, Manchester, M3 1SX*(tel:* 0161 833 2220; *fax:* 0161 839 6226).

RINK, Vivien (*née* Appleyard), DipEd,DipCouns

Chairman, Community Healthcare Bolton NHS Trust. *b.* 25 March 1942 Plymouth. *m.* 1965 Anthony Arnold Rink; one *s. Public Offices:* Justice of the Peace. *Education:* Bolton School; Homerton College, Cambridge. *Career Profile:* Teaching and lecturing; Self-employed in Training & Counselling; Ran a private clinic; Worked as Consultant Trainer with Police, in industry, in NHS. *Societies:* Bolton Golf Club; Georgian House Health Club; Local Book Group. *Recreations, Interests:* Golf, any form of exercise, travelling, gardening, reading, music. *Address:* Community Healthcare Bolton, St Peter's House, Silverwell Street, Bolton, BL1 1PP*(tel:* 01204 377091; *fax:* 01204 377004).

RISBY, William Thomas (Bill)

Councillor. *b.* 18 June 1930 Manchester. *m.* 1954 Marie; three *s. Public Offices:* Councillor (1971-); Lord Mayor of the City of Manchester (1993-94); Deputy Chair, North West Arts Board (1994-); Founder and Former National and International Chair of Nuclear Free Local Authority Movement; Deputy Lord Mayor (1992-93); Founder Member of Berlin Conference of European Catholics for Peace (BK); Director of Manchester Airport plc, CLASP (1988) Ltd; Greater Manchester Community Trust; Centre for Voluntary Organisations; First Organisation; NIA Centre; North Manchester Bond Board; Governor, Chethams Music School; Governor, St Dunstan's Primary School; Chair of Governors, North Manchester High School for Girls; Chair, Manchester Education Music Service Management Committee. *Education:* Mount Carmel, Blackley; Manchester Technical College. *Military Service:* Royal Signals (1951-53); Royal Signals Territorials (1953-57). *Career Profile:* Photo Engraver (1944-87); National Council Executive Member of Trade Union SLADE & PW (1960-69); National President of SLADE & PW (1967-69). *Recreations, Interests:* Politics, peace work, music and drama. *Address:* 20 Enville Road, Moston, Manchester, M40 5GF (*tel:* 0161 681 3408; *fax:* 0161 681 3408; *e-mail:* bill@ enville.demon.co.uk).

ROACHE, William Patrick

Actor, Coronation Street (1960-). *b.* 25 April 1932 Ilkeston, Derbyshire. *m.* Sara; two *s.* one *d. Education:* Rydal School, Colwyn Bay. *Military Service:* Commissioned, Royal Welch Fusiliers (1952-57); Captain, Trucial Oman Scouts (1956-57). *Career Profile:* Oldham Repertory; Nottingham Repertory; Films: 'Behind the Mask'; 'His & Hers'; 'Bulldog Breed'; TV: Lead in the play 'Marking Time'; Ken Barlow in Coronation Street (1960-and still running); Chairman, Mambi Games Ltd. *Publications/Creative Work:* Autobiography 'Ken & Me'. *Prizes:* Pye Television Award (1986). *Societies:* Wilmslow Golf Club.

ROBERTS, Ernest Morristan, BA(Econ)(Hons) Manchester (1960),PGCE Manchester (1961),LCH,RSHom

Homoeopathic Practitioner, registered with The Society of Homoeopaths; Principal, North

West College of Homoeopathy (founded 1984). *b.* 12 July 1936; Manchester. *m.* 1965 Valerie Mary; one *s.* two *d.* *(marr. diss. 1978) Education:* Oak Bank Preparatory School, Ashton-u-Lyne, Manchester; Ducie Avenue Secondary Technical School, Manchester; Audenshaw Grammar School, Lancashire. *Military Service:* National Service UK and West Germany. *Career Profile:* Taught in secondary schools in Manchester, Sydney and London (1961-65); Lectured in Polytechnics (1965-75) whilst holding positions in the British Insurance Assoc and Gas Council; Teacher Trainer, British Wheel of Yoga (1974-83); founder Kidbrooke House Yoga Centre, Blackheath (1974); attended classes in Homoeopathy (1976-83). *Publications:* various articles in Yoga, Alternative Health and Homoeopathy Magazines. *Societies:* Labour Party; Ken Colyer Trust; the Ramblers Association. *Recreations, Interests:* Music and cinema. *Address:* 23 Wilbraham Road, Fallowfield, Manchester M14 6FB *(tel: 0161-224 6809). Additional Information:* Author of a textbook of Homoeopathic principles.

ROBERTS, Glyn Owen, BA(Hons)(Univ. of Liverpool, 1973),DipTP (Trent Polytechnic, 1975), MRTPI (1977),MBIM (1988)

Director, North Liverpool SRB Partnership. *b.* 23 December 1951 Birmingham. *m.* one *s.* one *d.* *Education:* St Asaph Grammar School; Grove Park Grammar School, Wrexham; University of Liverpool; Trent Polytechnic. *Career Profile:* Area Planning Officer, Erewash BC (1975-77); Senior Planning Officer, Macclesfield BC (1978-83); Head of Environmental Services Unit, Macclesfield BC (1984-89); Planning Manager, Central Manchester Development Corporation (1989-92); Chief Planner, Central Manchester Development Corporation (1992-96); Director, North Liverpool Partnership (1996-). *Publications/Creative Work:* Various articles in national and regional planning journals; joint author of 'Planning for Regeneration'. *Prizes:* Planning awards from Royal Town Planning Institute, the Plain English Campaign, NW RTPI. *Societies:* Friends of Macclesfield Silk Heritage; Redesmere Sailing Club; Comet Class Association. *Recreations, Interests:* Water sports, support for development of Henbury School and youth sport, walking, industrial archaeology, environment. *Address:* Director, North Liverpool Partnership, Roscommon Resource Centre, Roscommon Street, Liverpool L5 3NE *(tel: 0151 207 1099; fax: 0151 207 0411); Additional Information:* Notwithstanding my taking up a new post in Liverpool, I intend to maintain my Manchester links, in particular to extend my interest in the City's urban regeneration.

ROBERTS, Jacqueline (*née* Cox), BA(Hons)

Education Services Manager, Museum of Science & Industry in Manchester. *b.* 6 April 1942; Isleworth, Middx. *m.* 1964 Kenneth William; two *s.* one *d.* *Public Offices:* Liberal Democrat Councillor, North Marple Ward, Stockport (1984-96); Chair, Education Committee, Stockport MBC (1987-93). *Education:* Chiswick County Girls' School; Wolverhampton Girls' High School; Liverpool University. *Career Profile:* Head of History Dept, Moston Brook Boys High School (1977-80). *Publications:* 'History of Working Class Housing in Nineteenth Century Manchester: The Example of John Street, Irk Town, 1826-1926' (Neil Richardson 1983); 'Britain's Industrial Revolution' (Heinemann 1985); 'A densely populated and unlovely pack; the Residential Development of Ancoats, Manchester' (Regional History Review, VII,1993). *Prizes:* School Mistress Student, St Hilda's College, Oxford (1980). *Societies:* National Trust for Scotland; Marple Civic Society; Camping and

Caravanning Club. *Recreations, Interests:* Camping, holidaying in France, being with friends, measuring Victorian slums, fellwalking. *Address:* 24 Ley Hey Road, Marple, Stockport SK6 6PQ *(tel: 0161-427 5266).*

ROBERTS, Janet Joy, BSc,MSc,DipURP,MRTPI,DBA

Lowry Centre Project Manager, Salford City Council. *b.* 23 December 1952 Stoke-on-Trent. *m.* 1985 John Nickson. *Education:* Thistley Hough Grammar School, Stoke-on-Trent; Stoke-on-Trent Sixth Form College; University of Liverpool; University of Salford; University of Strathclyde. *Career Profile:* Planner & Enviornmental Officer, Strathclyde Regional Council; Countryside Planner, Greater Manchester County Council; Salford City Council: Project Planner & Assistant Project Manager, Salford Quays (1986); Lowry Centre Project Coordinator (1993); Lowry Centre Project Manager (1996-). *Recreations, Interests:* Sailing, walking and sketching, theatre, collecting china. *Address:* The Lowry Project Team, C/o City Technical Services Department, Salford City Council, Civic Centre, Chorley Road, Swinton M27 5BW *(tel:* 0161 793 2486; *fax:* 0161 727 8269; *e-mail*: jroberts@aldersyd.u-net.com).

ROBERTS, His Honour Judge John Houghton, MA(Cantab)

Circuit Judge. *b.* 14 December 1947 Liverpool. *m.* 1972 Anna Sheppard; three *s. (marr. diss. 1990)*; *m.* 1991 Mary Henderson; one *steps.* one *stepd. Public Offices:* Assistant Recorder (1983-88); Recorder (1988-93). *Education:* Calday Grange Grammar School; Trinity Hall, Cambridge. *Career Profile:* Law Lecturer, Liverpool University (1969-71); Called to Bar, Middle Temple (1970); Assistant Recorder, Northern Circuit (1983); Recorder, Northern Circuit (1988); Practised at Bar, Northern Circuit (1970-93); Circuit Judge (1993-). *Prizes:* Scholar, Trinity Hall; Harmsworth Major Entrance Exhibition, Middle Temple; Astbury Law Scholarship, Middle Temple. *Societies:* Liverpool Athenaeum; Heswall Golf Club. *Recreations, Interests:* Golf, rugby football, music, cricket. *Address:* Manchester Crown Court, Crown Square, Manchester.

ROBERTS, Leslie Arthur, FRICS,FSVA,ACIArb,MIM

Partner, Donaldsons Chartered Surveyors (1993-). *b.* 31 January 1939 Swinton, Manchester. *m.* 1968 Judith; three *d. Education:* Leigh Grammar School (Head Boy 1957-58). *Military Service:* Lieutenant, Kings Regiment (1959-62) Kenya and Kuwait. *Career Profile:* Surveyor: WH Robinson & Co, Manchester (1963-66); Valuation Office, Inland Revenue (1966-67); Dunlop Heywood & Co, Manchester (1967-70); Partner: JR Bridgford & Sons, Manchester (1970-79); Leslie Roberts, Chartered Surveyors, Manchester (1979-93). *Societies:* St James' Club, Manchester; Worsley Golf Club; Ellesmere Tennis & Croquet Club & Worsley Cricket Club; National Chairman, Management Research Group (Institute of Management). *Recreations, Interests:* Wife and family, keeping fit, weight training, swimming, golf, tennis, walking, motor cycling, reading. *Address:* Donaldsons Chartered Surveyors, 11 St Peter's Square, Manchester, M2 3DN *(tel:* 0161 237 9977; *fax:* 0161 237 3311); Wainwright Farm, Folly Lane, Swinton, Manchester, M27 0DW *(tel:* 0161 793 8338).

ROBERTSON, Professor Ivan Tony, BSc,PhD,CPsychol,FBPsS

Head of School and Professor of Occupational Psychology, Manchester School of

Management, UMIST. *b.* 27 September 1946 Birmingham. *m.* 1971 Kathleen Mary; one *s.* one *d. Public Offices:* Ex-Chair, British Psychological Society, North of England Branch. *Education:* University of Exeter (1965-68); Open University (1974-76). *Career Profile:* Early career as an applied psychologist; Government service as an occupational psychologist; University of Aston (1979); UMIST (1978); Visiting Professor, National University of Singapore, Michigan State University and Queensland University of Technology; Professor of Occupational Psychology, UMIST (1990-), Head of School (1994-). *Publications/Creative Work:* Over 100 scientific articles and conference papers and 20 books; co-editor (with Prof CL Cooper) of International Review of Industrial and Organizational Psychology; Editorial Board member of several journals; co-author (with Dr JM Smith) 'Systematic Personnel Selection' (Macmillan). *Prizes:* Fellow of the British Psychological Society. *Societies:* British Psychological Society; International Association of Applied Psychology; European Association of Work and Organisational Psychology; British Academy of Management; Poynton Sports Club. *Recreations, Interests:* Football - player (veterans) and spectator, season ticket holder at Maine Road, music, especially guitar (playing) and choral music (listening), computers and new technology. *Address:* Manchester School of Management, UMIST, PO Box 88, Manchester, M60 1QD (*tel:* 0161 200 3443; *fax:* 0161 200 3623; *e-mail:* Ivan.Robertson@umist.ac.uk).

ROBINSON, Edward David Guyer, BA Cambridge (1950),MA Cambridge (1953),ALA, FRSA

b. 25 May 1926; Nottingham. *m.* 1949 Doris Audrey Greenslade Parker; two *s.* one *d. Public Offices:* JP; DL, Greater Manchester; Trustee, National Museum of Labour History; Member of Governing Bodies, University College of Salford, De La Salle College, Salford, Light Oaks Junior & Infant Schools, St John's School Swinton; Member, Manchester South Valuation Tribunal; Former Vice Chairman, Salford Health Authority; Former Chairman, Salford Education Committee; Former Chairman, Vice-Chairman or Member of many bodies concerned with local government or education. *Education:* County High School, Bromsgrove (1936-44); Peterhouse, Cambridge University (1944-45 and 1948-50); Loughborough College (1950-51). *War Service:* RAF (1945-48). *Career Profile:* Assistant Librarian, Rowett Research Institute (1951-53); Deputy Librarian, Birmingham College of Technology (1953-56); Experimental Officer, Atomic Energy Authority (1956-64); Cataloguer, University of Manchester (1964-66); Senior Assistant Librarian, University of Manchester (1966-67); Librarian, UMIST (1967-81). *Societies:* Society of Genealogists; Magistrates' Association; National Association of Governors & Managers; Association of Cricket Statisticians & Historians; Offa's Dyke Association; Peterhouse Society; Cambridge Union Society; Association of University Teachers; Labour Party; Cooperative Party; North West Society of Labour History; Consumers' Association. *Recreations, Interests:* politics, political history, genealogy, rambling. *Address:* 25 Park Road, Salford M6 8JP *(tel: 0161-789 8415).*

ROBINSON, Kathleen Theresa (*née* Philbin)

Deputy Leader, Manchester City Council. *b.* 26 November 1945 Manchester. *m.* Stuart Robinson; three *s. Public Offices:* Elected Member, Manchester City Council for 17 years; Hallé Concerts Society; Green Room; Agency for Economic Development; Director of Manchester International Airport plc; Castlefield Management Committee; Groundwork

234

Trust; Governor for two local schools; Previously involved in: The Chinese Arts Centre; Spotlighters; South Manchester Law Centre; Director, Manchester Ship Canal Company; Manchester International Festival of Expressionism. *Career Profile:* Chair, Urban Strategy Committee; Lord Mayor (1986-87); Manchester City Councillor (1979-); Chair, Board of City of Drama (1994); formerly Chair of Social Services Committee, Arts and Leisure Committee; Deputy Chair of Social Services Committee. *Address:* c/o Kay Brandish, Chair's Office, Manchester Town Hall, Manchester, M60 2WG (*tel:* 0161 234 3344; *fax:* 0161 234 3336).

ROBINSON, Terry, LTI,FInsSMM,MILog

Chairman, Bury FC Ltd; Director, Swinton RLFC Ltd; Director, Football League; Council Member, The Football Association. *b.* 6 March 1944 Bury. *m.* 1968 Rosemary; one *s.* *(marr. diss.)*; *m.* 1975 Brenda; two *d.* one *steps. Education:* Bury High School; Salford Technical College (further education). *Career Profile:* Joined James Kenyons (Bury) on leaving school; since 1968, involved in farming, engineering, plastic moulding, transport, property rental, consultancy. *Societies:* Greenmount Cricket Club; Greenmount Golf Club. *Recreations, Interests:* Watching soccer and rugby football, devotee of good ales and stouts. *Address:* Bury Football Club, Gigg Lane, Bury (*tel:* 0161 764 4881; *fax:* 0161 764 5521).

ROBINSON, William Martin, BA,ACA

Managing Director, Henry Cooke Group plc (1995-). *b.* 17 May 1958 Manchester. *m.* 1986 Jane-Anne; one *s.* one *d. Education:* Uppingham School (1971-75); Hull University (1976-79). *Career Profile:* Arthur Young (now Ernst & Young) Trainee to Manager, Corporate Finance (1979-87); Henry Cooke: Corporate Finance Executive (1987); Managing Director, Henry Cooke Corporate Finance (1990); Director, Henry Cooke Group (1994); Managing Director (1995-). *Societies:* Worshipful Company of Chartered Accountants; Freeman of City of London; St James's' Club; Prestbury Golf Club. *Recreations, Interests:* Home and family, shooting, golf, sailing. *Address:* Henry Cooke Group plc, One King Street, Manchester, M2 6AW (*tel:* 0161 834 2332; *fax:* 0161 832 6024; *e-mail:* Robinsm@henrycooke.co.uk).

ROBSON, Professor Brian Turnbull, MA(Cambridge & Manchester),PhD(Cambridge)

Pro-Vice-Chancellor, Professor of Geography, University of Manchester. *b.* 23 February 1939 Durham. *m.* 1973 Glenna Conway (nee Ransom); two *steps. Public Offices:* Chairman, Environment & Planning, Economic & Social Research Council (1979-86); Chairman, Global Environmental Change, ESRC (1991-95); President, Section E, British Association for Advancement of Science (1984-85); President, Institute of British Geographers (1991-93). *Education:* Royal Grammar School, Newcastle-upon-Tyne (1951-58); Cambridge University (1958-64). *Career Profile:* Lecturer in Geography, Aberystwyth UCW (1964-67); Lecturer in Geography, Cambridge University (1967-77); Fellow & Admissions Tutor, Fitzwilliam College, Cambridge (1967-77); Professor of Geography, Manchester Univeristy (1977-); Dean of Faculty of Arts, Manchester University (1988-90); Director, Centre for Urban Policy Studies, Manchester University (1985-). *Publications:* 'Urban Analysis' (CUP, 1969); 'Urban Growth' (Methuen,1973); 'Urban Social Areas'

(OUP,1975); 'Managing the City' (Croom Helm,1987); 'Those Inner Cities' (OUP,1988); 'Assessing the Impact of Urban Policy' (HMSO,1994); 'Urban Deprivation Index' (HMSO,1995). *Prizes:* Harkness Fellowship, University of Chicago (1967-68); Exhibitioner, St Catharine's College, Cambridge. *Societies:* Fellow, Royal Geographical Society; Member, Manchester Literary & Philosophical Society; President, Manchester Statistical Society (1995-). *Recreations, Interests:* Historic cartography, future of cities, gardening. *Address:* Department of Geography, University of Manchester, Oxford Road, Manchester, M13 9PL (*tel:* 0161 275 3639; *fax:* 0161 273 4407; *e-mail:* brian.robson @man.ac.uk); 32 Oaker Avenue, West Didsbury, Manchester (*tel:* 0161 445 2036). *Additional Information:* Chairman, Manchester Council for Voluntary Services (1986-92) Chairman, Manchester University Settlement (1990-) Chairman, The Charity Service (1992-) Chairman, Community Exchange (1984-); Chairman, Standing Conference of North West Universities (1995-).

ROLFE, Marianne T Neville- see *Neville-Rolfe, M T.*

ROOCROFT, Amanda Jane, GRNCM,PPRNCM,PGRNCM

Freelance Opera Singer. *b.* 9 February 1966 Coppull, Lancashire. *m.* 1995 Manfred Hemm; one *s. Education:* Royal Northern College of Music. *Career Profile:* Opera debut (1990); numerous concert recitals and opera performances. *Prizes:* Curtis Gold Medal RNCM (1988); Silver Medal, Worshipful Company of Musicians (1988); Decca Kathleen Ferrier Prize (1988); Royal Philharmonic/Charles Heidsieck Award for the impact of her debut (1990); Honorary Fellowship of the University of Central Lancashire (1992). *Recreations, Interests:* All aspects of art, music, ballet, literature, painting, architecture, theatre, travel, sightseeing, walking, cooking. *Address:* Ingpen and Williams Ltd, 14 Kensington Court, London, W8 5ON (*tel:* 0171 937 5158; *fax:* 0171 938 4175). *Additional Information:* Son Dominic Alexander born in Manchester, November 1995. Austrian husband Manfred Hemm also professional singer - Bass. Met whilst both performing for Bavarian State Opera in Munich in Cosi Fan Tutti, January 1993.

ROSE, Evelyn Gita (*née* Blain), MBE(1989) FIHE (1978),DipHEIM

Food and wine writer;; consultant. *b.* 2 December 1925 Manchester. *m.* 1948 Myer; two *s.* one *d. Public Offices:* Consumer Commissioner, Meat & Livestock Commission (1986-92); Chairman, Statutory Consumers' Committee, Meat & Livestock Commission (1986-92); Member, Consumers' Committe of Great Britain (1985-94). *Education:* Foundation Scholar, Manchester High School for Girls; Queen Anne High School, Seattle; Manchester College of Housecraft. *War Service:* WAAF, Meteorological Section. *Career Profile:* Secretary, Head of International Department, Metro Goldwyn Mayer, California; freelance consultant. *Publications/Creative Work:* 'The Jewish Home'; 'The Complete International Jewish Cookbook'; 'The Entertaining Cookbook'; 'First Time Cookbook' (with Judi Rose); 'Master Class for Creative Cooks' (with Sula Leon); 'Evelyn Rose Goes Microwave in the Jewish Kitchen'; 'New Jewish Cuisine'; 'Weekend Cook' (with Sula Leon); 'The New Complete International Jewish Cookbook'. *Prizes:* Bronze Medal, International Wine & Food Society. *Societies:* Guild of Food Writers; Society of Authors; International Federation of Home Economics; Institute of Home Economics; Manchester Camerata;

Manchester Jewish Museum; Network North; International Wine and Food Society (Committee Member, Manchester Branch); NADFAS. *Recreations, Interests:* Travel, theatre, literature, walking, food, wine. *Address:* 27 Gibwood Road, Northenden, Manchester, M22 4BR*(tel:* 0161 998 3215; *fax:* 0161 998 3215; *e-mail:* 100106,3435 @compuserve.com).

ROSE, Sidney Samuel, MB ChB (Manchester, 1941),FRCS (Eng) (1948), Hunterian Professor, Royal College of Surgeons (1953)

Consultant Surgeon (Retd), University Hospital of South Manchester. *b.* 17 October 1917; Manchester. *m.* one *s.* two *d.* *(marr. diss. 1970) Education:* Manchester Grammar School; Manchester University. *War Service:* RAF. *Career Profile:* Consultant Surgeon, Wythenshawe Hospital; Hon Lecturer in Surgery, Lecturer in Surgery to the Dental Faculty, Manchester University. *Publications:* Various papers and chapters on the surgical aspect of peripheral vascular disease; lectured widely on vascular subjects in Europe, America, Australia and the Far East. *Prizes:* Butterworth Medical Prize, Manchester University (1941). *Societies:* Founder member and former President, Vascular Surgical Society of Great Britain and Ireland (1982-83); President, Manchester Surgical Society (1981-82); Fellow of Royal Society of Medicine; Founder member and Vice Chairman, Venous Forum of Royal Society of Medicine; Member of Manchester Medico-Legal Society; Member, Medico-Ethical Society; Former member of Medical Appeals Tribunal; former Co-Chief Editor, Journal of the International Cardiovascular Society; Editor of Phlebology (1985-89)(founding editor); Societe de Phlebologie Francais (Hon Fellow); Fellow of the Association of Surgeons of Gt. Britain and Ireland; Israel Vascular Society (Hon Fellow); Indian Association of Surgeons (Hon Fellow); Life President, Manchester City Football Club (1995-); (Patron 1984-95); St James's Club; Northern Lawn Tennis Club. *Recreations, Interests:* Act, music (piano and organ), tennis, football, antique cars and tropical fish. *Address:* 135 Palatine Road, West Didsbury, Manchester M20 9YA; "The Homestead", Whitehall Road, Sale, Cheshire M33 3WJ *(tel:* 0161-973 4533).

ROSE-INNES, Professor Alistair Christopher, MA Oxford (1951),DPhil Oxford (1954), DSc Manchester (1970),BA (MMU,1993),FInstP,CEng

Sculptor and designer; Emeritus Professor of Physics and Electrical Engineering, UMIST. *b.* 4 December 1926; London. *m.* 1956 Barbara Ellen Nicholls; two *s.* two *d.* *Education:* Rydal School; Merton College, Oxford. *War Service:* RNVR, Radar Instructor (1944-47). *Career Profile:* Principal Scientific Officer, Royal Naval Scientific Service (1954-67); Professor of Physics and Electrical Engineering, UMIST (1967-89). *Creative Works:* Sculptures, paintings, drawings. *Publications:* 3 books on very low-temperature techniques and solid-state physics; papers in scientific journals. *Prizes:* Harkness Fellow of the Commonwealth Fund (1960-61). *Societies:* Manchester Literary & Philosophical Society; The Athenaeum. *Recreations, Interests:* Drawing, painting and sculpture, growing cacti. *Address:* Department of Physics, University of Manchester Institute of Science and Technology, Manchester M60 1QD *(tel:* 0161-200 4756). *Additional Information:* Royal Society Visiting Professor to Poland (1970-71).

ROSENTHAL, Jack Morris, CBE(1994); BA (Sheffield), MA(hc)(Salford), DLitt(hc) (Manchester)

Writer. *b.* 8 September 1931 Manchester. *m.* 1973 Maureen Lipman; one *s.* one *d.* *Education:* Colne Grammar School; Sheffield University. *Military Service:* National Service, Royal Navy (1953-55). *Publications/Creative Work:* 31 original TV plays and films including: 'The Evacuees'; 'Bar Mitzvah Boy'; 'Spend, Spend, Spend'; 'Ready When You Are, Mr McGill'; 'The Knowledge'; 'P'Tang, Yang, Kipperbang'; 'London's Burning'; 'Bag Lady'; 'Bye, Bye, Baby'; 'Wide-Eyed and Legless'; 'Eskimo Day'; over 300 TV comedy and drama screenplays; feature films include: 'Yentl' (co-written with Barbara Streisand); 'The Chain'; stage plays include 'Smash!'. *Prizes:* British Academy Writer's Award; Royal Television Society Writer's Award; Royal Television Society Hall of Fame; numerous national and international drama awards. *Societies:* Dramatists' Club. *Recreations, Interests:* Frying fish, not fulfilling a burning desire to sculpt, checking Manchester United's score, minute by minute, on Teletext.

ROSS, Ian Alexander, BSc,FCA

Partner, Coopers & Lybrand. *b.* 17 November 1949 Durham. *m.* Hilary; one *s.* one *d.* *Education:* Lancaster Royal Grammar School; UMIST. *Recreations, Interests:* Running, fell walking, theatre. *Address:* Coopers & Lybrand, 6 Minshull Street, Manchester, M1 3ED (*tel:* 0161 236 9191; *fax:* 0161 247 4000).

ROSS, James Hood, BA(Oxon),DipBA(Manchester Business School)

Chairman, The Littlewoods Organisation; Chairman of the Board, Manchester Business School. *b.* 13 September 1938 London. *m.* 1964 Sara Blanche Vivian Purcell; one *s.* two *d.* *Education:* Sherborne School, Dorset (1957); Oxford University (1962); Manchester Business School (1967). *Military Service:* National Service, Royal Navy, Sub-Lieutenant. *Career Profile:* British Petroleum Co Ltd (1962-92); Chairman and Chief Executive, BP America and a Managing Director of BP; Chief Executive & Deputy Chairman, Cable & Wireless plc (1992-95); Chairman, The Littlewoods Organisation (1996-). *Recreations, Interests:* Gardening, music, travel. *Address:* The Littlewoods Organisation, Sir John Moores Building, 100 Old Hall Street, Liverpool, L70 1AB (*tel:* 0151 235 2807; *fax:* 0151 236 2085).

ROSS, Stephen John, BSc (Econ)(LSE,1984)

Director, 3i Plc, Manchester. *b.* 25 February 1962 Barton on Sea. *m.* 1992 Sarah; one *d.* *Education:* The King's School, Macclesfield (1973-80); London School of Economics (1981-84). *Career Profile:* Marketing Manager, H J Heinz (1984-86); 3i Plc: Investment Executive, Cambridge (1986-89); Investment Director, Birmingham (1989-92); Director, Bristol (1992-95); Director, Manchester (1995-). *Societies:* Edgbaston Golf Club. *Recreations, Interests:* Golf, hill walking, marathon running (lapsed!). *Address:* 3i Plc, Carlton House, 18 Albert Square, Manchester, M2 5PE (*tel:* 0161 839 3131; *fax:* 0161 833 9182).

ROWE, Ivor Joseph

Chairman, Excelsior Holdings Ltd. *b.* 23 January 1932 Salford. *m.* 1954 Dorothy Ross; one *s.* one *d.* *Public Offices:* Vice President, Major Energy Users' Council; Fellow,

American Chamber of Commerce (UK); British Delegate, European Council of American Chambers of Commerce; Advisory Council, American Management Association; British Vehicle Rental & Leasing Association (Founder Chairman and Honorary Member); Director, Hallé Concerts Society; Director, Minnesota Orchestra Association; Director, Manchester Jewish Home for the Aged; Director, Children's Heart Hospital, Minneapolis; General Commissioner of Income Tax; Governor, Stamford Park School; Chairman, Greater Manchester Advisory Committee, Action-Employees in the Community; Justice of the Peace; Member, Bicentennial Arts Committee; Council Member, British Tourist Association. *Education:* Manchester Grammar School; Lausanne University; Visiting Lecturer, Harvard Business School. *Military Service:* Royal Army Education Corps (1950-52) National Service. *Career Profile:* Main Board Director & Corporate Vice-President, Gelco Corporation (US) (1972-88); Chairman & President, Gelco International Corp (1973-88); President, Viking Insurance Co (Bermuda) (1986-88); Main Board Director, Lex Service plc (1968-71); Chairman, Controlled Cost Motoring Ltd (1958-71). *Societies:* Variety International (disadvantaged children): Patron Life Member; Chairman, Gt Britain (NW Region); 1st Vice President, USA (North Western States); Founder Member, France; Member, Dunham Forest Golf & Country Club. *Recreations, Interests:* Music, theatre, charities and civic work, soccer. *Address:* Excelsior Holdings Ltd, 22/32 Greenwood Street, Altrincham, Cheshire, WA14 1RZ (*tel:* 0161 929 1342; *fax:* 0161 929 6808); Beechlawn, Barry Rise, Bowdon, WA14 3JS (*tel:* 0161 928 8640).

ROWEN, Paul John, BSc(Hons),PGCE

Leader of the Liberal Democrat Group; Leader of the Opposition, Rochdale MBC. *b.* 11 May 1955 Rochdale. *Public Offices:* Leader of the Council (1992-96); Chairman of Housing Services Committee (1985-86, 1994-96). *Education:* Bishop Henshaw RC Memorial High School, Rochdale; Nottingham University. *Career Profile:* Deputy Headteacher, Yorkshire Martyr's Collegiate School, Bradford (1990-); Head of Science, Our Lady's RC High School, Oldham (1986-90); Head of Chemistry, St Alban's RC High School, Oldham (1980-86). *Societies:* Manchester Literary & Philosophical Society; Portico Library & Gallery. *Recreations, Interests:* Walking, reading, music. *Address:* Members Secretariat, The Town Hall, Rochdale, OL16 1AB (*tel:* 01706 864801; *fax:* 01706 864820; *e-mail*: paulrowen@cix.complink.co.uk); 246 Queensway, Rochdale, OL11 2NH (*tel:* 01706 355176).

ROWLAND, Dawn (*née* Shane)

Sculptor. *b.* 24 September 1944; London. *m.* 1965 Professor Malcolm Rowland; two *d.* *Education:* Orange Hill Girls Grammar School, London; City of London College. *Creative Works:* Sculptor in London, San Francisco and, since 1975, in Manchester. Fellow and Council Member of the Royal Society of British Sculptors; Council Member, Manchester Academy of Fine Arts. Exhibits in various media (primarily in stone) at numerous exhibitions in the UK and Japan including Chelsea Harbour 93 and Royal Academy Summer Exhibition; sculptures and drawings in private collections in Europe, USA, Canada, Japan and Australia. *Prizes:* The Addleshaw Sons & Latham Award (MAFA 1993), The National Westminster Award (MAFA 1986); The Coopers & Lybrand Award, (MAFA 1985). *Societies:* MAFA; Royal Society of British Sculptors; National Artists Association. *Recreations, Interests:* Walking, exercise, Hallé, opera, music, travel.

ROWLAND, Professor Malcolm, BPharm London (1961), PhD London (1965), DSc London (1980),Hon Doctorate degrees Poitiers, France (1982), Uppsala, Sweden (1989)

Professor of Pharmacy, University of Manchester;President, Medeval Ltd a University of Manchester affiliated company; Scientific Editor, Journal of Pharmacokinetics and Biopharmaceutics; Vice President, European Federation of Pharmaceutical Sciences. *b.* 5 August 1939; London. *m.* 1965 Dawn; two *d. Education:* Kingsland Road School, London (1951-57); Chelsea School of Pharmacy, London (1958-61). *Career Profile:* Associate Professor of Pharmacy and Pharmaceutical Chemistry, School of Pharmacy, University of California, San Francisco (1967-75). *Publications:* 'Clinical Pharmacokinetic: Concepts and Application' (co-author) 3rd ed (Williams & Wilkins, 1995); scientific articles/reviews - approximately 200. *Societies:* Fellow, Royal Pharmaceutical Society of Gt Britain; Fellow, Institute of Mathematics & Its Applications; Fellow, American Pharmaceutical Academy; Fellow, American Association of Pharmaceutical Scientists. *Recreations, Interests:* Art, reading, travel. *Address:* Department of Pharmacy, University of Manchester, Manchester M13 9PL *(tel: 0161-275 2348)*

ROWLANDS, Glyn Aneurin, BA (Hons) Wales (1960),FRSA,FBIM,FISM

Principal, Manchester College of Arts & Technology. *b.* 25 March 1939; Llandovery, Dyfed. *m.* 1962 Susan; three *d. Public Offices:* President (1992), Association of Principals. *Education:* Llandovery Grammar School; University of Wales (Swansea University College). *Career Profile:* Lecturer, Keighley Technical College, Havering Technical College, East Ham College of Technology; Head of Dept & Vice Principal, Barnet College (1969-80); Principal, Fielden Park College, Manchester (1980-83). *Publications:* Articles and chapters of books; 'Management of Open Learning Centres'; (with my wife) 'Into Open Learning' (Wheatens, 1986). *Recreations, Interests:* Football (Watford FC), cricket (Glamorgan), theatre and music. *Address:* Manchester College of Arts & Technology, Lower Hardman Street, Manchester *(tel: 0161-831 7791)*; Whaley Bridge, Derbyshire.

ROXBY, Revd Gordon George, BSc London (1961)

Vicar of St Peter's, Bury; Area Dean of Bury (1986-96). *b.* 14 August 1939; Ellesmere Port, Cheshire. *m.* 1966 Dorothy Jean; two *s.* one *d. Education:* Helsby County Grammar School, nr Warrington (1951-58); University College, London (1958-61) (Physics); College of the Resurrection, Mirfield, Yorks (Theology). *Career Profile:* Curate of St Peter, Fleetwood (1963-66); Curate of St Michael, Kirkham, Lancs (1966-68); Vicar of St John, Weston, Runcorn, Cheshire (1968-78); Rector of St Chad, New Moston, Manchester (1978-86). *Creative Works:* Power Sharing by Time Sharing (care for minorities); Strategic Planning; Project Planning. *Publications:* 'The Next Five Years' (Planning for Education, Industry and Churches); 'Christian Leadership'. *Societies:* Visting Fellow, North West Educational Management Centre, Warrington (1981-94); Outside Lecturer to College of the Resurrection, Mirfield, West Yorkshire (1988-95). *Recreations, Interests:* Hiking, jogging, swimming, chess, computing, astronomy, meteorology. *Address:* St Peter's Vicarage, St Peter's Road, Bury BL9 9QZ *(tel: 0161-764 1187)*.

RUBIN, Rabbi Zchok Reuven (Kedushas Zion Rabbinical College)

Rabbi, South Manchester Synagogue. *b.* 22 April 1945 New York City. *m.* 1965 Chaiky;

one *s.* one *d. Education:* Bobover Yeshiva Bnai Zion High School (1962); Kedushas Zion Rabbinical College (1963-67). *Career Profile:* Headmaster in the first religious school in America for emotional and learning disabled orthodox Jews; Vice-President, Council of Jewish Organisation, Brooklyn; New York City Jewish Chaplain to Congressmen and State Senators; Three years in Israel for the Israeli Rabbinate; Minister, South Manchester Synagogue; Chairman, Rabbinical Council for the Provinces; Member, Executive Board of Manchester Rabbinical Council; Chief Rabbi's Cabbinate; Jewish Chaplain to a number of organisations including Christies Hospital and Manchester Airport. *Publications/Creative Work:* Columnist, Jewish Tribune; Contributor of columns and book reviews for Le'Ela magazine. *Prizes:* New York City Mayor's Honour Award. *Recreations, Interests:* Marine life, political science, Polish Jewish history, medical bio-ethics.

RUMBELOW, Arthur Anthony, BA Cambridge (1966),Barrister (1967),QC (1990)

Barrister. *b.* 9 September 1943; Salford, Lancs. *m.* 1971 Shelagh Lewtas; three *d. Public Offices:* Recorder of the Crown Court; Chairman of Medical Appeal Tribunal. *Education:* Salford Grammar School; Queens' College, Cambridge. *Prizes:* Squire Scholar, Cambridge; Harmsworth Exhibitioner and Astbury Scholar, Middle Temple. *Recreations, Interests:* Wine, rugby, gardening, theatre. *Address:* 28 St John Street, Manchester M3 4DJ *(tel: 0161-834 8418)* and 1 Serjeants' Inn, Temple, London, EC4Y 1NH *(tel: 0171-583 1355).*

RUSSELL, Francis Anthony, AMCT,MBA (Harvard)

Chairman, Trafford Park Manufacturing Institute; Deputy Chairman, Trafford Park Development Corporation. *b.* 26 March 1925; Berlin. *m.* 1957 Yvonne; one *s.* two *d. Public Offices:* Former Chairman, North West Industrial Development Board, Trafford Family Health Service Authority, Stockport District Health Authority, UMIST Council. *Education:* Lycee Napoleon, Grenoble; Manchester College of Technology (now UMIST); Harvard Business School. *War Service:* Royal Tank Regiment. *Previous Positions:* Chairman, Lankro Chemicals Group plc, Diamond Shamrock Europe Ltd, Imperial Biotechnology Ltd, Crocus Ltd; Director, ERF (Holdings) plc, Bracken Kelner Associates Ltd. *Societies:* Numerous. *Recreations, Interests:* Tennis, golf, music, theatre. *Address:* "Windrift", 33 Stanhope Road, Bowdon, Cheshire WA14 3JU *(tel: 0161-928 0080).*

RUSSELL, Kenneth Clifton, MCIBS

Manager, British Linen Bank Ltd. *b.* 14 January 1951 Glasgow. *m.* 1974 Elizabeth; two *d. Education:* Glasgow Academy. *Societies:* Hazel Grove Golf Club; Glasgow Academical Club. *Recreations, Interests:* Golf, rugby, reading, gardening. *Address:* British Linen Bank Ltd, 19/21 Spring Gardens, Manchester, M2 1EB*(tel:* 0161 832 4444; *fax:* 0161 832 4270); 38 Chester Road, Poynton, Cheshire, SK12 1EU *(tel:* 01625 859823).

RUSSELL, Rt Hon Sir Patrick, LLD(hc)(Manchester,1988); LLB (Manchester,1945)

Former Lord Justice of Appeal. *b.* 30 July 1926; Urmston. *m.* 1951 Doreen (Janie); two *d. Education:* Urmston Grammar School; Manchester University. *Public Offices:* Recorder, Barrow in Furness (1968-71); Recorder of the Crown Court (1972-80); High Court Judge, Queen's Bench Division (1980-87); Lord Justice of Appeal (1987-96). *War Service:*

Intelligence Corps, RASC (1945-48). *Career Profile:* Practised at the Bar, Northern Circuit (1949-80); QC (1971); Leader of the Bar, Northern Circuit (1978-80); Presiding Judge, Northern Circuit (1983-87); Court of Appeal (1987-96). *Societies:* Vice-President, Lancashire County Cricket Club; Patron, Manchester & District Medico Legal Society. *Recreations, Interests:* Cricket, travel.

RYLANDS, Hugh (John) Joseph, TD; BA(Econ),Chartered Accountant

Executive Director, Northern Venture Management Ltd. *b.* 3 October 1954 Manchester. *m.* 1995 Maura. *Public Offices:* President, Manchester Junior Chamber of Commerce. *Education:* Bishton Hall; Ampleforth College; Manchester University. *Military Service:* TAVR - MSUOTC - 103 Regt RA(V). *Career Profile:* Chartered Accountant and Indepen dent Corporate Finance Broker.

RYLANDS, Lieut Colonel (Hon) Joseph, DFC (1945),Despatches (1945),DL (1967)

Retired. *b.* 5 December 1914; Salford. *m.* 1947 Lena Mary Goss; three *s.* four *d. Public Offices:* Late Vice-Chairman, TAVRA (NW & IOM); Late Chairman, Board of Governors, Mount Carmel Convent School, Alderley Edge, Cheshire. *Education:* St Bedes College, Manchester; Manchester College of Technology (UMIST). *War Service:* RA (1938-46). *Address:* Brynwood, Wilmslow Road, Alderley Edge, Cheshire SK9 7QL *(tel: 01625-583233).*

SAGAR, Keith, BA Cambridge (1955),MA (1957),PhD Leeds (1962)

b. 14 June 1934; Bradford. *m.* 1981 Melissa Partridge; one *s.* one *d. Education:* Bradford Grammar School; King's, Cambridge. *Career Profile:*Reader in English Literature, Extra-Mural Department, University of Manchester; Administrative Assistant, Extra-Mural Department, Leeds University (1957-59); Tutor-Organiser, Workers' Educational Assoc (Yorkshire South) (1959-63). *Creative Works:* 'The Poems of D H Lawrence' (Audio Learning - Readings of 40 poems with commentary on two cassettes). *Publications:* 'The Art of D H Lawrence' (CUP 1966); 'Hamlet' (Blackwell 1968); 'Ted Hughes' (Longman 1972); 'The Art of Ted Hughes' (CUP 1975, Rev 1978); 'D H Lawrence: a Calendar of his Works' (MUP 1979); 'The Life of D H Lawrence' (Methuen 1980); 'The Reef and Other Poems' (Proem Pamphlets 1980); 'Ted Hughes: a Bibliography' (with Stephen Tabor) (Mansell 1983); 'D H Lawrence: Life into Art' (Penguin and Viking 1985); (forthcoming) 'A Deeper Reality: a Study of D H Lawrence' (CUP 1992); Editor of and contributor to a number of books by and about D H Lawrence and Ted Hughes; (editor) 'The World Encyclopaedia of Tropical Fish' (Octopus 1978); Over thirty contributions to periodicals, particularly to The D H Lawrence Review. *Prizes:* Library Association's Besterman Medal for the Outstanding Bibliography of 1983. *Societies:* Vice-President D H Lawrence Society. *Recreations, Interests:* Photography, wildlife, gardening, breeding Gouldian finches. *Address:* 11 Leys Close, Wiswell, Clitheroe, Lancs BB7 9DA (*tel:* 01254-822278; *fax:* 01254 823924; *e-mail:* ksagar@mail.internexus.co.uk).

SANDERSON, John Anthony, BA (Econ),FCIT,DASTE,FRSA

Principal; Tameside College of Technology. *b.* 18 August 1945 Tarleton, Lancashire. *Address:* Thameside College of Technology, Beaufort Road, Ashton-under-Lyne, Tameside, OL6 6NX (*tel:* 0161 330 6911; *fax:* 0161 343 2738).

SANDFORD, Arthur, Deputy Lord Lieutenant, Nottinghamshire (1990); LLB(Hons)

Chief Executive, Manchester City Council. *b.* 12 May 1941 Blackburn. *m.* 1963 Kathleen; two *d. Education:* Queen Elizabeth's Grammar School, Blackburn; University College, London. *Career Profile:* Articled Clerk to Town Clerk, Preston County Borough Council (1962-65); Asst. Solicitor (1965-66), Senior Asst. Solicitor (1966-68) Preston County Borough Council; Asst. Solicitor, Hants County Council (1969-70); Second Asst. Clerk (1970-72), First Asst. Clerk (1972-73), Deputy Director of Administration (1975-77); Director of Administration (1975-77), Deputy Clerk & County Secretary (1977-78); Clerk & Chief Executive (1978-90) Nottinghamshire County Council; Chief Executive, The Football League (1990-92). *Recreations, Interests:* Watching sport, gardening. *Address:* Manchester City Council, PO Box 532, Town Hall, Manchester, M60 2LA(*tel:* 0161 234 5000; *fax:* 0161 236 5909); 7 Mersey Meadows, Didsbury, Manchester, M20 2GB (*tel:* 0161 446 2574).

SANDIFORD, David John, MA (1957),MS (1958),PhD (1960),FInstP

Senior Lecturer in Physics, Manchester University; President, Manchester Association of University Teachers; Elected Member of Court, University of Manchester. *b.* 9 August

1933; Wanstead, Essex. *m.* 1969 Christine Krogh; two *d. Public Offices:* Manchester City Councillor (1979-82)(1983-95); Former Leader of Liberal Group (1983-86); Chairman, Police/Community Liaison Panel (1988-92); Chairman, Diamond House Trust; Mosscare Housing Ltd; Governor, Trinity CE High School, Didsbury CE Primary School. *Education:* Royal Liberty School, Essex (1944-51); Downing College, Cambridge (1951-54); Yale University, New Haven, Connecticut (1957-60). *Career Profile:* Research Physicist, BTH Co Ltd, Rugby (1954-57); Instructor, Yale College, Connecticut (1960-61). *Publications:* Various scientific papers; Editor, Manchester Physics Series, (1970-) (Wiley). *Societies:* Withington Civic Society. *Recreations, Interests:* Local and national Liberal Party politics, art, cricket. *Address:* Physics Department, Manchester University, Manchester M13 9PL *(tel:* 0161-275 4072); 330 Lapwing Lane, Didsbury, Manchester M20 6UW *(tel:* 0161-434 1343).

SARGENT, John, BSc(Hons)(Dunelm),IPFA

Chief Executive, Trafford Healthcare NHS Trust. *b.* 20 June 1951 Billinge. *m.* 1980 Anne; one *s. Education:* Hindley & Abram Grammar School; King Edward VII School, Lytham; Durham University. *Career Profile:* Trainee Accountant, Lancashire County Council (1972-77); Accountant, Skelmersdale Development Corporation (1977-81); Chief Technical Assistant, Salford City Council (1981-83); Deputy Treasurer, Wigan Health Authority (1983-86); Director of Finance, Bury Health Authority (1986-91); Chief Executive, Trafford Health Authority (1991-94); Chief Executive, Trafford Healthcare NHS Trust (1994-). *Publications/Creative Work:* Several on NHS Finance and NHS Reforms. *Recreations, Interests:* Skiing, travel. *Address:* Trust HQ, Trafford Healthcare NHS Trust, Moorside Road, Urmston, Manchester *(tel:* 0161 746 2948; *fax:* 0161 746 7214).

SARGENT, Michael Henry Joseph, MA Cantab,FICE,MIHE

Director, Allott & Lomax, Consulting Engineers. *b.* 10 January 1935; Worsley. *m.* 1983 Christine Vivienne Florence. *Public Offices:* Member of Council, Inst of Civil Engineers (1974-77); Past Chairman, NW Association, Institute of Civil Engineers. *Education:* Manchester Grammar School; St John's College, Cambridge. *Previous Positions:* Career spent with present firm. *Societies:* Manchester Literary & Philosophical Society; United Oxford and Cambridge University Club; Salmon and Trout Association. *Recreations, Interests:* Game fishing, walking, theatre, music. *Address:* Allott & Lomax, 23 Ashton Lane, Sale M33 6WP *(tel:* 0161-962 1214); The Beeches, Chapel Lane, Hale Barns, Cheshire WA15 0HN *(tel:* 0161-980 1396).

SASSOON, Eldon David, BA (Com),FCA,FCCA

Senior Partner, Hacker Young, Manchester; Treasurer, Governor and Trustee, Delamere Forest School. *b.* 11 November 1939. *m.* two *s.* two *d. (separated) Education:* Burnage Grammar School (1950-57); Manchester University (1957-60). *Career Profile:* Treasurer and Secretary, Withington Congregation of Spanish and Portuguese Jews. *Societies:* Dunham Golf Club. *Recreations, Interests:* Music, tennis and swimming. *Address:* Hacker Young, 79 Oxford Street, Manchester M1 6HT *(tel:* 0161-236 6936)

SAUL, G W Wingate- see *Wingate-Saul, G W.*

SAXON, The Revd Canon Eric, OStJ (1973); MA (Hon) Manchester (1980),BA (Admin) Manchester (1935),BD London (1940),ALCD (London College of Divinity) (1940)

Canon Emeritus, Manchester Cathedral (1982-); Force Chaplain to Greater Manchester Police (1959-); Vice President, NSPCC, Manchester, Salford & District; Trustee, Manchester & Salford Medical Charity (1952-), City of Manchester Common Good Trust (1962-), Mynshull Educational Foundation (1974-). *b.* 28 June 1914; Manchester. *m.* 1941 Ruth Higginbottom; two *s.* *Public Offices:* Member, Board of Governors, United Manchester Hospitals (1953-74); Member, Manchester Family Practitioner Committee (1962-82, Chairman 1977-82); Governor, Withington Girls' School (1972-88); Member, British Council of Churches (1962-71); Anglican Observer, Roman Catholic Ecumenical Commission for England & Wales (1968-75); Member, Council of Order of St John in Greater Manchester (1974-96). *Education:* Manchester Grammar School (1925-30); Manchester University (1932-35); London University (1936-40). *Career Profile:* Chaplain to The Queen (1967-84); Rector, St Ann, Manchester (1951-82); Hon Canon, Manchester Cathedral (1958-82); Rural Dean, Cathedral Deanery (1951-77); BBC North Regional Religious Broadcasting Organiser (1944-51); Curacies in Droylsden and Davyhulme (1940-44). *Publications:* 'A City Ministry' (1967); articles in 'Theology'; 'Caring about Manchester' (1993). *Prizes:* Silver Jubilee Medal (1977). *Societies:* Manchester Luncheon Club (President 1981-82); Manchester Literary & Philosophical Society. *Recreations, Interests:* Charities, Police, Health Service, following sport. *Address:* 27 Padstow Drive, Bramhall, Stockport, Cheshire SK7 2HU *(tel:* 0161-439 7233).

SCHAEFER, Peter Graham, BA (Com) (1963)

Chief Executive, Vuman Ltd. *b.* 1 November 1939; Manchester. *m.* 1964 Averil; two *s.* one *d. Education:* Stockport Grammar School; University of Manchester; UMIST, University of Philadelphia (Wharton Business School). *Career Profile:* Chief Executive, Vuman Ltd; Chairman of Vuman's subsidiary and associated companies (1991-); previously Chairman and Chief Executive of a quoted manufacturing company. *Recreations, Interests:* Cycling, yoga, windsurfing, running, squash, skiing, cooking, reading, travel, computers, DIY. *Address:* Vuman Ltd, Skelton House, Manchester Science Park, Lloyd Street North, Manchester, M15 6SH *(tel:* 0161 226 8746, *fax:* 0161 226 5855, *e-mail:* peter.schaefer @man.ac.uk).

SCHOLES, Rodney James, QC (1987),A Recorder of the Crown Court (1986); BA,BCL Oxford

b. 26 September 1945; Manchester. *m.* 1977 Katherin Elizabeth Keogh; three *s. Education:* Simms Cross Primary School, Widnes; Wade Deacon Grammar School, Widnes; Scholar of St Catherine's College, Oxford. *Prizes:* Hardwicke Scholarship (1964); Mansfield Scholarship (1967), Lincoln's Inn. *Recreations, Interests:* Watching Rugby football, walking dogs. *Address:* 25 Byrom Street, Manchester M3 4PF *(tel:* 0161-829 2100).

SCOTT, Rt Revd Colin John Fraser, MA Cambridge (1959)

Bishop of Hulme; Chairman, Council for the Care of Churches (1994-). *b.* 14 May 1933; London. *m.* 1958 Margaret Jean Mackay; one *s.* two *d. Education:* Berkhamsted School;

Queens' College, Cambridge; Ridley Hall, Cambridge. *Previous Positions:* Curate, St Barnabas, Clapham Common; Curate, St James, Hatcham; Vicar, St Mark's, Kennington; Vice Chairman, Southwark Diocesan Pastoral Committee. *Recreations, Interests:* Travel, community relations. *Address:* 1 Raynham Avenue, Didsbury, Manchester M20 6BW *(tel:* 0161-445 5922).

SCOTT, Peter Anthony, FCCA

Group Managing Director, Peel Holdings plc. *b.* 24 April 1947 Rochdale. *m.* 1969 Lynne; one *s.* one *d. Education:* Heywood Grammar School (1958-59); Littleborough High School (1960-62); Burnley College of Technology (1968-70); Manchester Polytechnic (1972-78). *Career Profile:* Financial Accountant, Forthergill & Harvey plc (1962-75); Crane Fruehauf Trailers Ltd (1976-77); Peel Holdings plc, Company Secretary (1977-81), Director (1981-). *Address:* Peel Holdings plc, Quay West, Trafford Wharf Road, Manchester, M17 1PL *(tel:* 0161 877 4714; *fax:* 0161 877 4720).

SCOTT, Sir Robert David Hillyer, Kt (1994), DL,Hon Fellowship MMU & UMIST,Hon Degree Manchester & Salford University, Hon Membership RNCM

Chief Executive, Greenwich Millenium Trust; Chairman, Piccadilly Radio, Granada Foundation; Special Projects Director, Apollo Leisure. *b.* 22 January 1944; Minehead, Somerset. *m.* 1972 Su Dalgleish *(marr. diss.);* two *s.* one *d.; m.* 1995 Alicia Tomalino; two *stepd. Public Offices:* Officier de l'Ordre des Arts et des Lettres (France). *Education:* Haileybury; Merton College, Oxford. *Career Profile:* Administrator, 69 Theatre Company (1968-74); Administrator, Royal Exchange Theatre Trust (1974-77); Managing Director, Manchester Theatres Ltd (1977-91); Director, Hallé Concerts Society (1990-94), Buxton Festival (1981-92); Chairman of Cornerhouse (1985-95); Director, Manchester Royal Exchange Theatre (1977-95), Whitworth Art Gallery (1990-95); Chairman, Manchester Olympic Bid (1996 & 2000), Manchester Commonwealth Games Bid (2002). *Publications:* The Biggest Room in the World (1976). *Prizes:* Mancunian of the Year (1981 and 1983); English Tourist Board - Outstanding Contribution (1993); Communicator of the Year (1993). *Recreations, Interests:* Travel, food, sport, music, theatre. *Address:* Greenwich Millenium Trust, 11 King William Walk, London SE10 9JH

SEAL, Michael Jefferson

Director, Wise Speke Ltd, Wise Speke (Holdings) Ltd. *b.* 17 October 1936 Hale, Cheshire. *m.* 1962 Julia Mary Seton; one *s.* two *d. Public Offices:* Member, Manchester Financial & Professional Forum; Member, Court of the University of Manchester. *Education:* Marlborough College, Wiltshire. *Military Service:* National Service 3rd RTR (1955-56); TA (1956-66). *Career Profile:* The Carborundum Co Ltd (1957-59); Partner: Jefferson Seal & Co (1961-68); Seal Arnold & Co (1968-72); Henriques Seal & Co (1972-74); Partner then Senior Partner, Charlton Seal Dimmock & Co (1974-87); Chairman, Charlton Seal Ltd (1987-88); Chairman, Charlton Seal Schaverien Ltd (1988-90); Director, Benchmark Group plc (1987-90); Chairman & Director, CST Emerging Asia Trust plc (1989-91). *Societies:* St James's Club, Manchester. *Recreations, Interests:* Country activities, travel, opera. *Address:* Wise Speke Ltd, PO Box 512, 8 King Street, Manchester, M60 2EP *(tel:* 0161 953 9700; *fax:* 0161 832 9092); The Dene House, Great Budworth, Northwich,

Cheshire, CW9 6HB (*tel:* 01606 891555). *Additional Information:* Trustee: The Family Welfare Association of Manchester The Human Society of the Hundred of Salford The Greater Manchester Educational Trust The Wood Street Mission, Manchester The Clonter Farm Music Trust.

SEDDON, David Karl, BSc(Hons),MSc,DipArch(Lon),RIBA

Senior Partner, Howard & Seddon Partnership. *b.* 19 May 1953 Altrincham. *m.* 1974 Jane Tattersall; one *s.* two *d.* *(marr. diss. 1990)*; *m.* 1996 Paige Taylor. *Education:* Sale Grammar School; University College London. *Career Profile:* Chartered Architectel: Kippax Stand MCFC; Umbro Stand, MCFC; Skelley Centre; Widnes Rugby League Stadium; Cheadle End Stand, Stockport County FC. *Societies:* Royal Institute of British Architects. *Recreations, Interests:* Piano, football, gardening, entertainment. *Address:* Howard & Seddon Partnership, 64 Washway Road, Sale, M33 7RE (*tel:* 0161 973 8296; *fax:* 0161 962 3485).

SELLERS, John Michael Malin

Senior Director, Spencer Stuart. *b.* 27 August 1941 London. *m.* 1965 Josephine Ann Cotesworth; one *s.* *(widowed 1980)*; *m.* 1982 Susan Elisabeth Stewart. *Education:* Shrewsbury School. *Career Profile:* Courtaulds plc (1961-78); Spencer Stuart Associates Ltd (1978-). *Societies:* St James' Club, Manchester; Oriental Club, London. *Recreations, Interests:* Reading, music, sport. *Address:* C/o Spencer Stuart, Adlington Court, Greencourts Business Park, Styal Road, Manchester, M22 5LG(*tel:* 0161 499 1700; *fax:* 0161 499 0300).

SELLERS, Rod H, BSc(Econ),FCA,DipBA

Executive Deputy Chairman, British Vita plc. *b.* 25 July 1946 Rawtenstall, Lancs. *m.* 1975 Judith; one *s.* one *d.* *Public Offices:* Chartered Accountants, Education Committee in Manchester (to 1980); advisory role for London Committee (current); Manchester Chamber of Commerce, ad hoc tax and Manchester City Pride committees (1985-95); Economics Committee (current); CBI, National Council (current), Europe Committee (current). *Education:* Bacup and Rawtenstall Grammar School; London School of Economics; Manchester Business School. *Career Profile:* Trainee Chartered Accountant, Arthur Andersen, London (1967-70); British Vita plc (1971-), Finance Director (1974), Chief Executive (1990), Executive Deputy Chairman (1996-). *Societies:* CIMgt - Companion of British Institute of Management; FRSA - Fellow of the Royal Society for the Arts, Commerce, Manufactures; Bolton Golf Club. *Recreations, Interests:* Family, travel, sport (especially watching the siblings!). *Address:* British Vita plc, Middleton, Manchester, M24 2DB (*tel:* 0161 643 1133; *fax:* 0161 655 3957).

SENIOR, Mark Andrew, BSc(Hons)(Univ. of Sheffield),ACA

Assistant Director, Corporate Finance, Price Waterhouse, Manchester. *b.* 6 February 1963 Nantwich, Cheshire. *m.* 1990 Geraldine; two *s.* *Education:* Sir John Deane's Grammar School, Northwich; Sheffield University. *Career Profile:* Joined Price Waterhouse (1988); Specialised in Corporate Finance (1989); Seconded to Price Waterhouse, Corporate

247

Finance, London (1994-95). *Societies:* ICAEW. *Recreations, Interests:* Cricket, golf, hockey, football. *Address:* Price Waterhouse, York House, York Street, Manchester, M2 4WS *(tel:* 0161 245 2423).

SERVANT, Reverend Alma Joan, BA(Hons),DipLib

Chaplain, Manchester Metropolitan University. *b.* 6 December 1951 Leeds. *Education:* Nottingham University; Polytechnic of North London; Westcott House, Cambridge. *Career Profile:* Librarian, Notts County Library Service (1977-83); Curate, All Hallows, Ordsall, Retford, Notts (1985-88); Chaplain, Manchester Polytechnic (now Manchester Metropolitan University)(1988-). *Recreations, Interests:* Reading, art, cricket. *Additional Information:* From November 1996 will become Priest in Charge of St Thomas, Heaton Chapel.

SHACKLETON, Revd Canon Alan, BA Sheffield (1953)

Vicar of Rochdale (1986-); Area Dean of Rochdale (1982-92); Honorary Canon of Manchester Cathedral (1984-); Chairman of the Standing Advisory Council on Religious Education (Rochdale MBC), Member of the Education Committee (1983-). *b.* 6 January 1931; Rochdale. *m.* (1) Barbara June Stead; *m.* (2) Glenys Audrey Lord (née Howells). *Education:* Milnrow CE School (1935-42); Littleborough Central School (1942-47); Heywood Grammar School (1947-49); University of Sheffield (1949-53); Wells Theological College (1954-56). *Previous Positions:* Assistant Curate, St Chad, Ladybarn, Manchester (1956-58); Lecturer of Bolton (Parish Church) (1958-61); Vicar, St Gabriel, Middleton Junction (1961-70); Vicar of St Luke, Heywood (1970-86); Assistant Area Dean, Rochdale (1981-82). *Societies:* Heywood Rotary Club (1983-91) (President, 1988); Heywood Civic Society (1971-) (Chairman, 1972-86); National Trust; Hallé Concerts Society; Rochdale Music Society; Rochdale Rotary Club (1991-)(President 1995). *Recreations, Interests:* Music, medieval history, walking. *Address:* The Vicarage, Sparrow Hill, Rochdale, Lancashire OL16 1QT *(tel:* 01706-45014).

SHAW, Allan

Proprietor, AS Media Enterprises. *b.* 21 February 1936 Bradford. *m.* 1958 Wendy; one *s.* one *d. Public Offices:* Former Governor, Bolton Sixth Form College; Hon Member, Manchester Taxi Drivers Association; Hon Member, Rochdale Asian Association; Former Chair, Bradford and Leeds branches, National Union of Journalists. *Education:* Carlton Grammar School, Bradford. *Military Service:* National Service, Cypher, Royal Signals. *Career Profile:* previous positions: Industrial Editor, Yorkshire Evening Post; News Editor, BBC Radio Leeds; Manager, BBC Radio Cleveland; Manager, BBC Radio Manchester. *Societies:* Hon Member, Manchester Taxi Drivers Association. *Recreations, Interests:* Walking, reading, rugby, writing. *Address:* AS Media Enterprises, 38 Higher Dunscar, Egerton, Bolton, BL7 9TF *(tel:* 01204 593741).

SHAW, Derek

Lord Mayor of Manchester. *b.* 2 May 1934 Manchester. *m.* 1987 Susan; two *stepd. (marr. diss.) Public Offices:* City Councillor (1980-); Deputy Chair of City Works; Member of

Past Committees Finance, Housing, Land & Property, Licensing, Education. *Education:* Lily Lane Secondary School. *Military Service:* Royal Navy, Fleet Air Arm (1950-59). *Career Profile:* Aircraft Electrician; Telephone Engineer; Freelance Q/A Engineer (Electrical Inspector, Weapons & Prototype, Ferranti Ltd). *Recreations, Interests:* Trade Union involvement, EETPU and AEEU 30 years as Shop Steward, Convenor, etc, Member of North West Regional Political Committee AEEU, Manchester City FC, Salford Rugby League. *Address:* The Town Hall, Manchester, M60 2LA (*tel:* 0161 234 3000; *fax:* 0161 234 3230).

SHEFF, Sylvia Claire (*née* Glickman), MBE(1995),JP(1976),BA Manchester (1957)

Assistant National Director, Conservative Friends of Israel (1985-89) (National Projects Director 1974-85); Founder/Director, 'Friendship with Israel' Group in European Parliament (1979-90);Founder Chairman (1972-80) & (1981-) and President (1980-), Manchester 35 Group, Women's Campaign for Soviet Jewry; Council Member, National Council for Soviet Jewry and Ireland (1975-89) (Hon Secretary, 1987-89); Delegate, Board of Deputies of British Jews (1987-). *b.* 9 November 1935; Manchester. *m.* 1958 Alan Frederick; one *s.* one *d.* *(widowed 1986) Public Offices:* Delegate, Jewish Representative Council of Greater Manchester (1974-); Bury Family Conciliation Service Management (1985-87). *Education:* Stand Grammar School for Girls (1947-54); University of Manchester (1954-57). *Career Profile:* Teacher by profession retired (1977); Chairman, Whitefield Hebrew Congregation Ladies Guild (1967-68); Public Relations Committee, Jewish Representative Council of Greater Manchester and Region (1972-76); Executive Committee, Jewish Representative Council of Greater Manchester and Region (1974-81) and (1983-84); Lecturer, Jewish Representative Council of Greater Manchester and Region (1980-); Associate Director, Jewish Cultural & Leisure Centre (1990-93); International Co-ordinator, Yeled Yafeh Children of Chernobyl Campaign (1990-93). *Recreations, Interests:* Bridge, travel, antiques, theatre. *Address:* 6 The Meadows, Old Hall Lane, Whitefield, Manchester M45 7RZ (*tel:* 0161-766 4391).

SHELDON, Robert Edward

MP (Ashton-under-Lyne); Chairman, Public Accounts Committee. *b.* 13 September 1923 Manchester. *m.* 1945 Eileen Shamash; one *s.* one *d.* *(widowed)*; *m.* 1971 Mary Shield. *Public Offices:* Chairman, NW Group of Labour MP's; Chairman, Economic & Finance Group of Labour MP's; Minister of State, Civil Service Department; Financial Secretary to the Treasury. *Education:* Elementary, Grammar School and Technical College. *Prizes:* Whitworth Scholarship. *Address:* House of Commons, London, SW1A 0AA (*tel:* 0161 799 6060); 27 Darley Avenue, Manchester, M20 8ZD.

SHERMAN, Colonel Thomas, OBE (Military) (1970),VRD (1960) - with Clasp (1970),DL Greater Manchester (1977)

Retired (Northern Advertisement Controller, Mirror Group Newspapers); Chairman, North West Branch, The Commando Association; President, Manchester Branch, National Advertising Benevolent Society. *b.* 25 May 1919; Liverpool. *m.* 1948 Vera Blagbrough; one *s.* *(widowed 1971) Public Offices:* High Sheriff of Greater Manchester (1985-86). *Education:* Liverpool Grammar School. *War Service:* The King's Regiment, No 2

Commando - Norway (NWEF), Vaagso, St Nazaire (Commando raids), West Africa (RWAFF); Royal Marines Reserve (1950-70); Commanding Officer (1965-70); Honorary Colonel (1972-85). *Previous Positions:* Vice Chairman, NW England & IOM TAVR Association; Chairman, Publicity & Recruiting Committee, TAVRA; President (1975-77), Chairman (1972-74) Manchester Publicity Assn; Chairman, First Friday Club (1983), President (1996). *Societies:* Army & Navy Club; St James's Club. *Recreations, Interests:* Geriatric swimming, walking, cycling, the Reserve Forces, Broughton House. *Address:* "Christleton", 1B Fulshaw Park South, Wilmslow, Cheshire SK9 1QP *(tel:* 01625-583771).

SHERRING, Frederick Anthony, FCA,FTII,TEP

Trust and Tax Consultant; Life Governor, Imperial Cancer Research Fund; Trustee of MGS Trust, Portico Library Trust, WGS Trust and Camerata Trust. *b.* 12 May 1923; Stockport. *m.* 1952 Margaret Brelsford; two *s*. *Education:* Manchester Grammar School (1934-39). *War Service:* Royal Tank Regiment (1942-47) (N W Europe). *Previous Positions:* County Treasurer, British Red Cross (1972-87); Governor, Withington Girls School (1973-88); Treasurer, Portico Library (1984-87); General Commissioner of Income Tax (1987-92); Council Member, Society of Trust and Estate Practitioners (1992-95) and Chairman of Manchester Branch (1992-96). *Publications:* A number of textbooks on subjects relating to trusts and estates - current publications being Tolley's 'UK Taxation of Trusts' (6th edition) and Ranking Spicer & Pegler's 'Executorship Law, Trusts and Accounts'; Consultant Editor, Taxation Services (Institute of Chartered Accountants). *Societies:* Heaton Moor Golf Club (Captain 1967, President 1981, Hon Life Member 1986); Manchester Club Golfing Society (Captain 1986); Portico Library; Manchester Statistical Society (Vice President); Manchester Chartered Accountants Students Society (Life Member); Manchester Society of Chartered Accountants (President 1971, Centenary Year). *Recreations, Interests:* Golf, garden, reading, skiing. *Address:* 1A Gibsons Road, Stockport SK4 4JX *(tel:* 0161-432 8307).

SHERWOOD, David, ACIB

Business Centre Director, Barclays Bank plc. *b.* 6 August 1937 Finchley, London. *m.* 1963 Shirley May; two *d*. *Public Offices:* Parish Councillor, Prestbury. *Education:* Latymer School, London. *Career Profile:* Joined Barclays in London (1958) then Luton, Hertford, Cambridge, International Division, Manchester (1986). *Societies:* Committee, Manchester Midday Concerts Society; Member, Hallé Concerts Society; St James's Club. *Recreations, Interests:* Music, theatre, walking, badminton. *Address:* Barclays Bank plc, 51 Mosley Street, Manchester, M60 2AU*(tel:* 0161 200 5800; *fax:* 0161 200 5620).

SHINDLER, Geoffrey Arnold, LIM(Cantab,1966),MA(Cantab,1974),Honorary Associate of the Centre for Law and Business Studies, University of Manchester

Partner, Halliwell Landau. *b.* 21 October 1942 Manchester. *m.* 1966 Gay; three *d*. *Public Offices:* Registered Member of Society of Trust & Estate Practitioners (STEP) Chairman (1994-); Director, Opera North; Chairman, Institute for Fiscal Studies (NW)(1996). *Education:* Bury Grammar School (1954-62); Cambridge University (1962-66). *Publications/Creative Work:* 'Law of Trusts' (1984)(with K Hodgkinson). *Societies:* St James's Club, Manchester; Lancashire CCC; Marylebone CC; Manchester Literary &

Philosophical Society; Portico Library. *Recreations, Interests:* Sport, opera, Director, non-professional theatre. *Address:* Halliwell Landau, St James's Court, Brown Street, Manchester, M2 2JF *(tel:* 0161 835 3003; *fax:* 0161 835 2994); 10 Bury Old Road, Prestwich, Manchester, M25 0EX *(tel:* 0161 740 2291).

SHINE, Jeremy, BA (Univ. of Warwick)

Joint Artistic Director, Manchester International Arts & Streets Ahead Festival. *b.* 18 September 1950 London. *Education:* Kilburn High School; Warwick University. *Career Profile:* Founded the Green Room Theatre, Manchester; Director, Manchester Festival (1984-86); Director/Joint Director of numerous festivals & events including; Ona Catalana (1994); Streets Ahead (1995-). *Recreations, Interests:* Travel, horse riding. *Address:* 3 Birch Polygon, Manchester, M14 5HX*(tel:* 0161 224 0020; *fax:* 0161 248 9331).

SHORROCK, (John) Michael, MA(Cantab),Barrister-at-Law

Barrister. *b.* 25 May 1943 Cheshire. *m.* 1971 Marianne; two *d. Education:* Clifton College, Bristol; Pembroke College, Cambridge. *Career Profile:* Recorder of the Crown Court (1982); QC (1988); Head of Chambers, Peel Court Chambers, Manchester; Member of Criminal Injuries Compensation Board (1995); Bencher of Inner Temple (1995). *Recreations, Interests:* Theatre, opera, cinema, walking, gardening. *Address:* Peel Court Chambers, 45 Hardman Street, Manchester*(tel:* 0161 832 3791; *fax:* 0161 835 3054). *Additional Information:* Specialises in crime, commercial fraud, personal injuries, medical negligence.

SILVERMAN, Rabbi Dr Robert (Reuven), BA,PhD

Rabbi, Manchester Reform Synagogue. *b.* 26 July 1947 Oxford. *m.* 1975 Dr Isobel Braidman; three *s. Public Offices:* Chairman, Assembly of Rabbis, Reform Synagogues of Great Britain; Vice-Chairman, Friends of Israel Association, Manchester. *Education:* Harrow High School; Pinner Grammar School; University of Leeds; Leo Baeck College, London; University of Manchester. *Career Profile:* Rabbi, Curacao, Netherlands, Antilles, United Netherlands Portuguese Congregation (1969-71); Rabbi, Edgware Reform Synagogue, London (1974-77); Rabbi, Manchester Reform Synagogue (1977-); Hon. Lecturer, Dept of Middle Eastern Studies, Manchester University (1984-96); Faculty Member, Leo Baeck College, London. *Publications/Creative Work:* 'Baruch Spinoza - Outcast Jew, Universal Sage' (1995); Regular broadcasts on BBC Radios 2 and 4, occasional TV appearances. *Societies:* Rabbinical Assembly of America. *Recreations, Interests:* Orthinology, clarinet playing, languages, literature. *Address:* 26 Daylesford Road, Cheadle, Cheshire, SK8 1LF.

SIMPKIN, Andrew Gordon, Solicitor

Partner, Pannone & Partners. *b.* 31 March 1947 Salford. *m.* Gail; two *s. Public Offices:* Member, Equal Opportunities Commission (1985-91). *Education:* Nicholls Scholar, Chethams Hospital School, Manchester. *Career Profile:* Partner, Ogden & Simpkin (1973-78); Pannone & Partners (1978-). *Publications/Creative Work:* Lectured widely on ISO9001 (BS5750 Part 1). *Societies:* Law Society; St James' Club. *Recreations, Interests:* Winter - climbing, Summer - gardening. *Address:* Pannone & Partners, 123 Deansgate,

Manchester, M3 2BU(*tel:* 0161 832 3000; *fax:* 0161 834 2342); Chapel Lane House, Mere, Cheshire, WA16 6PP (*tel:* 01565 830457).

SINGER, His Honour Judge Harold Samuel, Barrister at Law, MA(Cantab)

Circuit Judge. *b.* 17 July 1935; Manchester. *m.* 1966 Adele Bérénice; one *s.* two *d.* *Education:* Salford Grammar School (1947-53); Fitzwilliam House, Cambridge (1953-56). *Career Profile:* Called to the Bar Grays Inn (1957); Recorder (1981-84); Circuit Judge (1984). *Recreations, Interests:* Painting, photography, music, books.

SINGH, Professor Madan Gopal Chevalier dans L'Ordre des Palmes Academiques (1994), DEng(hc)(University of Waterloo, Canada,1996), BSc(Exeter,1969), PhD(Cambridge, 1974), Docteur es Sciences (Toulouse,1978), MSc(Manchester,1982), Ceng, FIEE(1984), FIEEE(USA) (1989),FBCS(1994)

Professor of Information Engineering, Head of the Computation Dept, UMIST. *b.* 17 March 1946 Batala, India. *m.* 1969 Christine Carling; *(marr. diss. 1979)*; *m.* 1979 Anne-Marie Bennavail; two *s. Career Profile:* Fellow of St John's College, Cambridge (1974-77); Associate Professor, University of Toulouse (1976-78); Professor of Control Engineering, UMIST (1979-87); Head of Control Systems Centre (1981-83, 1985-87); Professor of Information Engineering, UMIST (1987-); Head of Computation Department (1994-97). *Publications:* Editor-in-Chief 'Encyclopaedia of Systems and Control' (Pergamon/Elsevier); Author, co-author or editor of 18 books and 170 scientific articles. *Prizes:* Norbert Weiner Award of IEEE, SMC Society (1993); Outstanding Contribution Awards, IEEE, SMC Society (1991, 1994). *Address:* Computation Department, UMIST, PO Box 88, Sackville Street, Manchester, M60 1QD.

SLADE, Derek Harrison, JP,FCA,ATII

Retired Partner, Ernst & Young; Freeman of the City of London. *b.* 23 August 1933; Cheadle Hulme. *m.* 1957 Anne Frances Lomas; one *s.* one *d. Public Offices:* Treasurer & Member of Court, University of Manchester; Chairman, St Ann's Hospice. *Education:* Hulme Hall College, Cheadle Hulme. *Career Profile:* Vice Chairman, Central Manchester NHS Trust; General Commissioner of the Inland Revenue; Chairman of Governors, Cheadle Hulme School;President, Manchester Society of Chartered Accountants; President, Manchester Luncheon Club; Chairman, Board of Visitors, Manchester Prison; Member of Council, Institute of Chartered Accountants in England & Wales; President, Manchester Junior Chamber of Commerce. *Societies:* Institute of Directors; St James's Club; National Trust; RSPB; Wild Fowl Trust. *Recreations, Interests:* Walking, golf, ornithology. *Address:* "Whitestone", 32 Ramillies Avenue, Cheadle Hulme, Cheshire SK8 7AL (*tel:* 0161-485 4001).

SLATFORD, Rodney Gerald Yorke, HonRCM(1976),FRNCM(1987)

Head of School of Strings, Royal Northern College of Music (1984-). *b.* 18 July 1944 Cuffley, Hertfordshire. *Public Offices:* Chairman, British Branch of European String Teachers' Association; Chairman of Governors, Royal Society of Musicians. *Education:* Bishop's Stortford College, Hertfordshire; Royal College of Music, London. *Career*

Profile: Double bass player and broadcaster (Radio 3); English Chamber Orchestra, Principal (1974-81); Professor of double bass, Royal College of Music, London (1974-84); Soloist Henry Wood Promenade Concert (1974); Solo Recording, EMI (1976); Principal bass, Nash Ensemble of London (1965-94); Music Publisher (Yorke Edition, 1969-). *Publications/Creative Work:* Articles for Grove's Dictionary of Music; many editions of double bass music for Yorke Edition; numerous periodical articles. *Societies:* Founding Chairman of The Yorke Trust (a charity for music education). *Recreations, Interests:* Gardening, wine, food, dogs. *Address:* Royal Northern College of Music, 124 Oxford Road, Manchester, M13 9RD (*tel:* 0161 273 6283; *fax:* 0161 273 7611; *e-mail:* info@rncm.ac.uk). *Additional Information:* Member of Gowrie Committee (Review of the London Music Conservatories)(1990). Member of British Council Music Advisory Committee (1990-).

SLIM, Andrew Charles, BA(Hons)(Univ. of Manchester, 1973),ACIB

Regional Manager, Kredietbank NV. *b.* 15 August 1952 Manchester. *m.* 1975 Margaret; one *d. Education:* Queen Elizabeth's Grammar School, Middleton (1963-70); Manchester University (1970-73). *Career Profile:* National Westminster Bank (1973-78); ABN Bank (1978-83); County Bank (1983-91); Kredietbank NV (1992-). *Recreations, Interests:* Methodist Church, National Trust. *Address:* Kredietbank NV, National House, 36 St Ann Street, Manchester, M2 7LE(*tel:* 0161 839 8989; *fax:* 0161 839 2929).

SMITH, Ambrose Joseph, BSc,DpAdvStudSc,PhD

Principal, Aquinas College, Stockport. *b.* 30 May 1950 Preston. *m.* 1976 Judith; one *s. Education:* Preston Catholic College (1961-68); Manchester University (1968-74); Leicester University (1974-75). *Career Profile:* Assistant Teacher, Parrs Wood High School, Manchester (1975-78); Head of Physics, Stretford Grammar School for Boys (1978-80); Deputy Head, Notre Dame High School, Norwich (1980-89); Principal, Aquinas College, Stockport (1989-). *Publications/Creative Work:* A number of papers and letters in Journal of Physics (B) (1972-79). *Recreations, Interests:* Family, music (singing, oboe, cor anglais, recorder, saw), walking, nature, photography, reading. *Address:* The Principal, Aquinas College, Nangreave Road, Stockport, SK2 6TH (*tel:* 0161 483 3237; *fax:* 0161 487 4072; *e-mail:* 04100281.feserve@dialnet.co.uk).

SMITH, Brenda, BA(Hons)(1972),ACA(1978),MBA(1975)

Production and Resources Director, Granada Television Limited; Director, Granada Media Group, The London Studios, London News Network. *b.* 26 August 1951 Brighton. *Public Offices:* Non-Exec, Manchester Health Authority (1974-96); Non-Exec, Mental Health Services of Salford (1996). *Education:* Merchant Taylors, Liverpool; Manchester University. *Career Profile:* British Leyland (1972-73); Arthur Anderson & Co (1975-78); Granda Television: a number of financial positions and production/programme management; current posts (1978-). *Address:* Granada Television Limited, Quay Street, Manchester, M60 9EA (*tel:* 0161 827 2054; *fax:* 0161 827 2172).

SMITH, Colin, CIPFA

Chief Executive, Oldham Metropolitan Borough Council (1983-). *b.* 31 March 1940

Rawtenstall, Lancs. *m*. 1960 Marian; two *s*. *Education:* Bacup & Rawtenstall Grammar School; Lanchester Polytechnic, Coventry (part-time). *Career Profile:* Trainee Accountant, Rawtenstall Borough Council (1958-60); Trainee Accountant, Coventry City Council (1960-62); Technical Accountant/Computer Manager, Dewsbury CBC (1962-66); Chief Technical Assistant/Chief Accountant/Assistant Borough Treasurer, Wolverhampton CBC (1966-73); Deputy Director of Finance, Solihull, MBC (1973-76); Borough Treasurer, Oldham MBC (1976-83); Chief Executive, Oldham MBC (1983-). *Recreations, Interests:* Cricket, football, theatre, music. *Address:* Chief Executive, Oldham MBC, Civic Centre, West Street, Oldham *(tel:* 0161 911 4192; *fax:* 0161 911 4045).

SMITH, Sir Cyril, MBE(1966),Kt(1988),OStJ(1968),DL(1991), Freeman of Borough of Rochdale (1992); LLD(hc)(1993),DEd(1996)

Retired. *b*. 28 June 1928; Rochdale. *Public Offices:* President, NE Region, Liberal Democrats; President, Greater Manchester North Scouts. *Education:* Rochdale Grammar School for Boys. *Career Profile:* Councillor and Alderman, Rochdale Council (1952-75); Mayor Rochdale (1966-67); MP for Rochdale (1972-92); founded Smith Springs (Rochdale) Ltd, Managing Director (1963-87). *Publications:* 'Big Cyril' (1977). *Societies:* National Liberal Club (Ex Chairman); Portico Library. *Recreations, Interests:* Music (listening), reading, TV Soaps, charitable work, fringe politics! *Address:* 14 Emma Street, Rochdale OL12 6QW *(tel:* 01706-48840). *Additional Information:* President, Debrose Choir, Kingsway Band. Actively supports charities for deprived children and for pensioners. Hon Sec, Happy Hour Old Folks' Club. Founder and President, Rochdale CHILDER

SMITH, Colonel Harold, OBE (1965),DL (1983) Gt Manchester; FCIB (1969)

Retired Manager, Midland Bank plc, Wigan 1979. *b*. 8 November 1919; Blackburn. *m*. 1942 Ida Blackshaw; two *s*. *Public Offices:* Magistrate, Wigan PSD (1971-89); Deputy Chairman, Wigan PSD (1980-89); Vice-Chairman, Wigan Health Authority (1974-91); Governor, Mere Oaks Special School, Wigan (1974-91); Chairman of Governors (1986-91). *Education:* Queen Elizabeth's Grammar School, Blackburn (1931-36). *War Service:* Royal Engineers (1939-40); RASC (1940-45) NW Europe; TA Service (1952-58) (1960-65); CO 42 Div Coln RASC (1961-65); Commandant East Lancashire Army Cadet Force (1965-69). *Societies:* Past President, Rotary Club of Wigan (1981); Past President, Chartered Institute of Bankers, Wigan Centre (1974) (1980); Wigan Golf Club. *Recreations, Interests:* Finance Officer, Bispham Hall Scout Council (1974-), Vice President, Greater Manchester West Scout County (1989-), golf and all sports. *Address:* Forglen, 19 Greenways, Standish, Wigan WN6 0AF *(tel:* 01257-421363).

SMITH, Peter Richard Charles, BSc(1967),CertEd(1969),MSc(1983)

Leader, Wigan MBC. *b*. 24 July 1945 Leigh, Lancs. *m*. 1968 Joy Lesley Booth; one *d*. *Education:* Bolton School, (1956-64); London School of Economics (1964-67); Garnett College, London University (1968-69); Salford University (1981-82). *Career Profile:* FE Lecturer (1969-); Wigan MBC (1978-); Chairman, Finance Committee (1982-91); Leader (1991-); Board Member, Manchester Airport plc (1986-), Chairman (1989-91). *Societies:* Chairman, Leigh Labour Party. *Recreations, Interests:* Reading, gardening, rugby league, jazz. *Address:* Wigan MBC, New Town Hall, PO Box 36, Library Street, Wigan, WN1

1YW (*tel:* 01942 827001); Mysevin, Old Hall Mill Lane, Atherton, Manchester, M40 0RG (*tel:* 01942 676127). *Additional Information:* Board Member, Wigan Borough Partnership (Metrotec & Chamber of Commerce); Chairman, Ringway Handling Services; Vice-Chairman, Ringway Development plc; Board Member, Manchester Airport plc

SMITH, Professor Sir Roland, BA,MSc,PhD

Chancellor, University of Manchester Institute of Science & Technology; Non-Ex Chairman, Manchester United plc; Non-Executive Chairman, Hepworth plc; Non-Ex Chairman, P&P plc; Emeritus Professor of Management Science, University of Manchester; Non-Ex Chairman, Temple Bar Investment Trust Ltd; Non-Ex Director of several other businesses. *b.* 1 October 1928 England. *m.* 1954 Joan. *Education:* University of Birmingham; University of Manchester. *Military Service:* Flying Officer, RAF (1953). *Career Profile:* Lecturer in Economics, University of Liverpool (1960); Director, University of Liverpool Business School (1963); Professor of Marketing, UMIST (1966-88); Non-Executive Chairman, Readicut International (1984-96); Non-Executive Director, Bank of England (1991-96); Non-Executive Chairman, Senior Engineering Ltd (1973-92); Non-Executive Chairman, British Aerospace (1987-91). *Recreations, Interests:* Walking.

SMITH, Warren James, DL(1995),JP(1983)

Voluntary Worker. *b.* 1 July 1948 Manchester. *Public Offices:* Chairman: Turning Point; Hallogen; Manchester Girls Institute; Free Trade Hall; Progress Trust; Manchester City Art Gallery Book Publishing Co; Bridgewater Hall Trust; Director/Trustee: Hallé Concerts Society; Manchester Guardian Society, Trust. *Education:* Disappointing!!. *Career Profile:* District Bank (1966-70); Director of various property companies (1971-91); Non-Exec, Mental Health Services, Salford NHS Trust. *Societies:* Life Member, Hallé Concerts Society; Lowry Centre. *Recreations, Interests:* Gardening, claret, art, music. *Address:* The Bridgewater Hall, Manchester (*tel:* 0161 950 0000).

SMOLENSKI, Marlena Sylvia BSc (Hons)(Manchester, 1969),PGCE (Cantab) (1970)

Headmistress, The Hulme Grammar School for Girls, Oldham. *b.* 2 August 1948 Nottingham. *Education:* Bramcote Hills County Grammar School, Nottinghamshire (1959-66); Manchester University (1966-69); Cambridge University (1969-70). *Career Profile:* Teaching posts in Berkshire & Oxfordshire (1970-81); Head of Science & Senior Mistress, Leicester Grammar School (1981-87); Deputy Headmistress, Leicester High School for Girls (1987-92); present position (1992-). *Prizes:* Deputy Head girl, Bramcote Hills County Grammar School. *Societies:* Girls' Schools Association; Secondary Heads Association; Association for Science Education; Association of Christian Teachers. *Recreations, Interests:* Reading, classical music, member of an Anglican church, walking. *Address:* The Hulme Grammar School for Girls, Chamber Road, Oldham, OL8 4BX (*tel:* 0161 624 2523; *fax:* 0161 620 0234).

SMYTH, Albert Leslie, MBE (1975),Hon Fellow Manchester Polytechnic (1982); FLA

Retired. *b.* 14 January 1919; Belfast. *m.* 1951 Sheila Mary Garden; two *s.* one *d.* *Public Offices:* Hon. Curator, Manchester Literary & Philosophical Society. *Education:* Stretford

Grammar School (1930-35). *War Service:* Royal Artillery (1939-46). *Previous Positions:* Librarian, Manchester Commercial Library (1954-84). *Publications:* 'John Dalton: a bibliography' (MUP 1966)(2nd ed: 1996 - to be published); Index to 'Manchester Memoirs 1781-1989' (editor); various contributions to professional publications. *Societies:* Manchester Literary & Philosophical Society; Manchester Luncheon Club; Urmston Park Probus Club (Vice-Chairman);National Trust. *Recreations, Interests:* Gardening, Manchester history, maps. *Address:* 21 Westmorland Road, Urmston, Manchester M41 9HJ *(tel:* 0161-748 3124).

SNEDDON, Alan Drysdale, FFA

Chief General Manager, Co-operative Insurance Society Ltd. *b.* 29 February 1932; Glasgow. *m.* 1959 Janette Hiddleston (née Murray; one *d.* *Education:* Allan Glens School, Glasgow. *Recreations, Interests:* Gardening, badminton, tennis, rugby. *Address:* Co-operative Insurance Society Ltd, Miller Street, Manchester M60 0AL *(tel:* 0161-832 8686).

SNOW, Percy John Deryk, OBE (1989); MB ChB Manchester (1948),MD Manchester (1955),LRCP MRCS (1948),MRCP London (1950),FRCP London (1970)

Retired. *b.* 23 May 1925; Kidsgrove, North Staffordshire. *m.* Marjorie Worrall; two *d.* *(marr. diss.)*; *m.* Jacqueline Blackstock; one *s.* *Public Offices:* Member, North Western Regional Health Authority (1978-82); Vice Chairman, Bolton Area Health Authority (1972-75); Secretary, NW Regional Association of Physicians (1964-80); Post Graduate Clinical Tutor (1966-82); Regional Adviser, Royal College of Physicians of London (1975-80); Founder Member, Bolton Medical Institute; President, Manchester Branch of Chartered Society of Physiotherapists (1962-65); Member of various committees of Royal College of Physicians. *Education:* The High School, Newcastle-under-Lyme; Manchester University. *Military Service:* RAF Medical Specialist, Medical Branch (1952-54). *Career Profile:* Senior Consultant Physician, Bolton Royal Infirmary and Bolton General Hospital; Senior Registrar, University Dept of Medicine, Manchester Royal Infirmary; Assistant Lecturer, University Dept of Cardiology, Manchester Royal Infirmary; Resident Clinical Pathologist, Manchester Royal Infirmary. *Publications:* Articles and chapters on Ischaemic Heart Disease, Hypertension and other medical subjects. *Societies:* British Cardiac Society; Fellow Manchester Medical Society and Member of Council; Fellow Bolton Medical Society and Member of Council; RAF Club; Glass Association, British Clematis Society. *Recreations, Interests:* Gardening, photography, motoring, Victorian glass, walking. *Address:* 28a Chorley New Road, Bolton *(tel:* 01204-521256); 4 Fairlea Avenue, Didsbury, Manchester M20 6GN.

SODERSTROM, Berndt-Erik, Kt (1st Class) White Rose of Finland (1994); BSc (Econ) Helsinki (1956)

Consul of Finland. *b.* 10 October 1934; Turku, Finland. *m.* 1960 Madeleine Emily Burtwell; two *s.* one *d.* *Public Offices:* Regional Representative NW, Executive Committee Member, Finnish Church Guild, London; Vice Chairman, Committee Member, Vice Chairman of the JV97 Committee, Finnish School at Manchester; Committee Member, Manchester Consular Association (President 1987); Former Chairman, Nordic Link (Manchester); Former President, North West Anglo Nordic Society; Former Vice-

President, NW Counties Schoolboys Amateur Boxing Association; Committee Member, Scandinavian Seamen's Church (Liverpool), Former Member, Europe Committee MCCI; Member, Former Member, Liverpool Consular Corps. *Education:* Nya Svenska Laroverket, Helsinki, Finland. *Military Service:* Finnish Airforce. *Previous Positions:* President, Manchester Consular Association (1987); President, North West Anglo Nordic Society. *Societies:* Manchester Consular Association; Finnish Church Guild (London); Finnish-British Trade Guild (London). *Recreations, Interests:* International co-operation, military history, books, sport, music, haute cuisine. *Address:* Consulate of Finland, 22 Hullet Close, Appley Bridge, Wigan WN6 9LD *(tel:* 01257-252684). *Additional Information:* Consultant, Marketing Export Import.

SOUTHWORTH, David Robert, FCCA

Group Managing Director, P&P plc. *b.* 24 April 1949 Accrington, Lancs. *m.* 1972 Pamela; one *s.* one *d. Education:* Accrington Grammar School. *Career Profile:* Philips Industries (10 years); H J Heinz (2 years); Volex plc (3 years); Coopers & Lybrand (3 years); P&P (10 years). *Recreations, Interests:* Golf, soccer, reading, family. *Address:* P&P plc, Carrs Industrial Estate, Rossendale, Lancs, BB4 5HU *(tel:* 01706 832001; *fax:* 01706 832383).

SPAFFORD, George Christopher Howsin, MA BCL(Oxon),LLM(hc) Manchester, LLM Cardiff, RCA

Diocesan Chancellor, Manchester Diocese (1976-), Chester Diocesan Reader (1996-). *b.* 1 September 1921; Manchester. *m.* 1959 Iola Margaret (née Hallward); one *s.* one *d. Public Offices:* Recorder of the Crown Court (1975-88); *Education:* Rugby School (1935-39); Oxford University (1939-40) (1946-47). *War Service:* Captain, Royal Artillery (Africa, Italy). *Career Profile:* Barrister, Northern Circuit; former Hon Treasurer, Red Rose Guild of Designer Craftsmen, Parish and People; Northern Crafts Centre, Friends of Manchester City Art Galleries; former member, Legal Advisory Commission, Aldeburgh Yacht Club. *Creative Works:* Paintings. *Publications:* 'Ecclesiastical Law Revision'; 'Code for Bells and Bellframes' (chairman, drafting committees). *Societies:* Trustee and Finance Committee of the Manchester Diocese, Ecclesiastical Law Society; Ecclesiastical Judges Association; Friends of the Whitworth Art Gallery, Manchester City Art Galleries; Wilmslow Trust; Hon Treasurer, Royal Cambrian Academy of Art. *Recreations, Interests:* Painting, reading. *Address:* 57 Hawthorn Lane, Wilmslow, Cheshire SK9 5DQ *(tel:* 01625-528871).

SPAFFORD, Iola Margaret (*née* Hallward), RCA,DFA Slade

b. 24 August 1930; Cambridge. *m.* 1959 George Spafford; one *s.* one *d. Education:* Queen Anne's Caversham; Bristol Art School; Nottingham Art School; Slade School of Fine Art. *Creative Works:* Paintings, drawings, etchings; four one-man shows at the Tib Lane Gallery Manchester; works in the Rutherstone Collection, Manchester Art Gallery, Salford Art Gallery and in many private collections; exhibited at the Royal Academy and in other mixed exhibitions; Studio and printmaking workshop at home. *Societies:* MAFA, RCA. *Recreations, Interests:* Music, ornithology, travel. *Address:* 57 Hawthorn Lane, Wilmslow, Cheshire SK9 5DQ *(tel:* 01625-528871).

SPENCER, Shan Mary (*née* Lewis), BLL,Solicitor of the Supreme Court

Head of Banking and Corporate Recovery, Addleshaw Sons & Latham. *b.* Cardiff, Wales.

Public Offices: Vice-Chairman, North West Region, Society for Practitioners of Insolvency. *Education:* Altrincham Grammar School for Girls; Sheffield University; College of Law, Lancaster Gate. *Career Profile:* Articled with Addleshaw Sons & Latham; in 1978 joined William Prior & Co; re-joined Addleshaw Sons & Latham, Corporate Recovery Partner (1990), Head of Corporate Recovery & Banking (1995-). *Societies:* Insolvency Practitioners Association; Society of Practitioners of Insolvency; Association Europeene des Practiciens des Procedures Collectives; Law Society of England & Wales; Insolvency Lawyers Association; Committee J of the International Bar Association, Section on Business Law. *Recreations, Interests:* Theatre, sport, music. *Address:* Addleshaw Sons & Latham, Dennis House, Marsden Street, Manchester, M2 1JD (*tel:* 0161 832 5994; *fax:* 0161 834 0103).

STAFFORD, Peter Moore, FCA,ACA(1965)

Partner, Member, Board of Partners, Deloitte & Touche. *b.* 24 April 1942 Manchester. *m.* 1973 Elspeth Harvey; one *s.* one *d. Public Offices:* Member of Council for Industry and Higher Education (1993-); Governor, Terra Nova School, Holmes Chapel. *Education:* Charterhouse (1956-60). *Career Profile:* Articled Clerk, Garnett Crewdson & Co (1960-64); Chartered Accountant, Garnett Crewdson & Co (1964-66), Arthur Anderson (1966-68); Partner: Garnett Crewdson & Co, Spicer & Oppenheim, Touche Ross & Co, Deloitte & Touche (all through mergers)(1968-); National Managing Partner, Spicer & Oppenheim (1990); Chairman, Board of Partners, Touche Ross & Co (1992-95). *Societies:* St James's Club; Royal Overseas League, London. *Recreations, Interests:* Travel, restoring antique launches, gardening. *Address:* Deloitte & Touche, Abbey House, PO Box 500, 74 Mosley Street, Manchester, M60 2AT (*tel:* 0161 228 3456; *fax:* 0161 228 2021).

STALKER, John

Author, Journalist, Broadcaster; Director, John Stalker Ltd; Chairman, Integrity 2000 Ltd. *b.* 14 April 1939; Manchester. *m.* 1962 Stella Maria; two *d. Education:* Chadderton Grammar School, Oldham (1949-55); Police Staff College, Bramshill, Hants; Royal College of Defence Studies, London (1983). *Career Profile:* Police Officer (PC to Supt), Manchester (1956-77); Detective Chief Superintendent, Warwickshire (1977-80); Assistant Chief Constable, Greater Manchester Police (1980-84); Deputy Chief Constable (1984-87). *Creative Works:* Autobiography 'Stalker' (Harrap, Penguin 1988). *Publications:* Many articles in London Evening Standard, Daily Mail, Daily Express, Sunday Times, Independent and others on policing matters. *Prizes:* Portico Prize (1988). *Societies:* Chairman, Sale Harriers. *Recreations, Interests:* Athletics (Qualified Athletics Coach), soccer (watching), jazz (playing). *Address:* Lymm, Cheshire.

STAPLES, Brian Lynn, FIHT,FICE

Group Chief Executive, United Utilities plc. *b.* 6 April 1945 Northampton. *m.* Rosalind Louise McKay; one *d. (marr. diss.); m.* Audrey Foster; one *s.* two *d.; m.* Sonia Pearl Elizabeth. *Education:* Sweyne Grammar School; Rayleigh FIHT. *Career Profile:* Joined Tarmac (1964) Chief Executive (1991-94); Joined United Utilities (formerly North West Water)as Chief Executive (1994). *Recreations, Interests:* Music, theatre, hill walking. *Address:* United Utilities plc, Dawson House, Great Sankey, Warrington, WA5 3LW (*tel:* 01925 234000).

STEPHEN, George Martin, DipEd(Sheffield) BA(Hons)(Leeds),PhD(Sheffield)

High Master, The Manchester Grammar School. *b.* 18 August 1949 Sheffield. *m.* 1971 Jennifer Elaine; three *s. Education:* Birkdale Preparatory School, Sheffield; Uppingham School; University of Leeds; University of Sheffield. *Military Service:* Member, Haileybury Combined Cadet Force (Lieutenant)(1973-84). *Career Profile:* Headmaster,The Perse School,Cambridge (1987-94); Second Master,Sedbergh School (1983-87); Housemaster, Haileybury and Imperial Service College (1972-83); Teacher of English, Uppingham (1971-72); 18 months spent working at various times in remand homes (1966-67). *Publications/Creative Work:* 15 books including 'The Price of Pity'; 'The Fighting Admirals'; 'Poems of the First World War'; 'Sea Battles in Close-up'; 'English Literature'; 'British Warship Designs since 1906'; 'Studying Shakespeare' and numerous articles in major journals. *Prizes:* Hallam Prize for Education, University of Sheffield. *Societies:* Fellow of the Royal Society of Arts; Member, East India Club; Member, HMC. *Recreations, Interests:* Writing, watersports, fly fishing and game shooting, drawing, drama. *Address:* The Manchester Grammar School, Manchester, M13 0XT(*tel:* 0161 224 7201; *fax:* 0161 257 2446); 143 Old Hall Lane, Manchester, M14 6HL (*tel:* 0161 224 3929). *Additional Information:* Governor, Withington Girls' School, Pownall Hall School; Member, CSV Advisory Panel; Member of Council, The Project Trust; Member, The Naval Review; Member, British Association for Sport and Law; Member, Portico Library.

STERLING, Robert Alan, MA(Cantab),Barrister-at-Law

Barrister in Private Practice. *b.* 1 June 1948 Manchester. *m.* 1975 Diane; one *s.* three *d. Education:* Manchester Grammar School; Corpus Christi College, Cambridge. *Career Profile:* Head of Chambers; Chairman, Northern Chancery Bar Association. *Societies:* Hale Lawn Tennis Club; Dunham Forest Golf Club. *Recreations, Interests:* Tennis and golf (playing), travel particularly in France, Greece & Italy. *Address:* 68 Quay Street, Manchester, M3 3EJ (*tel:* 0161 834 7000; *fax:* 0161 834 2341).

STEWART, Donald Charles, DMS

Director Europe, Government Office North West. *b.* 24 November 1951 Ipswich, Suffolk. *m.* 1977 Catherine; two *s.* one *d. Education:* Carlton Grammar School, Bradford; Woking County School for Boys; Wallbrook College, Southwark; DMS via Oxford Brookes University. *Career Profile:* Joined Board of Trade (1969); career civil servant in various Government Departments and bodies including DTI and DFEE. *Recreations, Interests:* Motor racing, reading.

STOKER, Robert Burdon, MA (Hons) Manchester

Retired. *b.* 12 July 1914; Hoylake. *m.* 1941 Mildred Cameron; one *s.* two *d. Public Offices:* Past President, Alderley Edge & Wilmslow Arthritis & Rheumatism Assn; Vice President, St Ann's Hospice, Manchester Outward Bound Assn. *Education:* Marlborough College. *War Service:* RE, Seconded to Ministry War Transport Mediterranean. *Career Profile:* Chairman, British Engine, Manchester Liners; President, Manchester Chamber of Commerce, Manchester Guardian Society, Cheadle Conservative Assn; National President, Institute Shipping Forwarding Agents; Founder Secretary and President, Manchester Junior

Chamber of Commerce; former Director, Manchester Ship Canal Co. *Publications:* 'The Legacy of Arthur's Chester'; 'Cheshire's Greatest Battle' (Cheshire Life); '50 & 60 Years on the Western Ocean'; 'The Saga of Manchester Liners'. *Prizes:* Queen's Jubilee Medal (1977). *Societies:* Royal Liverpool Golf Club (Hon); Wilmslow Golf Club; St James's Club; Manchester Naval Officers Assn; Churchill Club (Vice President). *Recreations, Interests:* Golf, painting, history. *Address:* 23 Carrwood Road, Wilmslow, Cheshire SK9 5AJ *(tel:* 01625-524916).

STOKES, Christopher Peter, Hon FTCL(1987) BMus(Dunelm),FRCO,FTCL,GTCL

Organist & Master of The Choristers, Manchester Cathedral (1996-); Head of Organ Studies, Chetham's School of Music (1994-). *b.* 29 August 1952 Chatham, Kent. *m.* 1980 Carolyn Diana; one *s.* one *d. Education:* Royal Masonic School, Bushey, Herts; Trinity College of Music, London. *Career Profile:* Assistant Organist, St Martins-in-the Fields (1976-79); Organist & Master of Music, St Martins-in-the-Fields (1979-89); Director of Music, St Margaret's Westminster (1989-92); Professor of Organ, Trinity College of Music, London (1978-94); Organist Manchester Cathedral (1992-96); Musical Director for Daily Service on BBC Radio 4 (1994-). *Publications/Creative Work:* Numerous choral compositions. *Prizes:* Gertrude Norman Prize, Trinity College of Music. *Recreations, Interests:* Theatre, walking, cooking. *Address:* Manchester Cathedral, Manchester, M3 1SX *(tel:* 0161 833 2220; *fax:* 0161 839 6226).

STOLLER, Norman Kelvin, MBE(1976),CStJ(1995),DL(1995),MSc(hc)(1993)

Non-Executive Chairman, Seton Healthcare Group plc. *b.* 6 September 1934 London. *m.* 1960 Diane; one *s.* one *d. Public Offices:* Founding Chairman, Oldham Export Club; Founding Chairman, Oldham TEC; Deputy Chairman, Oldham Chamber of Commerce, Training & Enterprise. *Education:* Eccles High School. *Military Service:* Royal Air Force (1952-55). *Career Profile:* Seton Healthcare Group (1955-). *Prizes:* CBI/Daily Telegraph North West Business Man of the Year (1992). *Societies:* Founding Chairman, Pennine Chapter Manchester, Young Presidents Organisation; Founding Chairman, Pennine Chapter Manchester, World Presidents Organisation; Dorchester Club; St James' Club, London. *Recreations, Interests:* Wines, single malt whisky, bridge, sailing, grandchildren. *Address:* Seton Healthcare Group plc, Tubiton House, Oldham, OL1 3HS.

STONEHOUSE, Professor Roger John, MA,DipArch (Cantab),RIBA

Professor of Architecture, University of Manchester *b.* 7 December 1944; Leeds. *m.* 1967 Adrienne Elizabeth; two *d. Education:* Roundhay School, Leeds; Trinity Hall, Cambridge. *Address:* School of Architecture, University of Manchester, Oxford Road, Manchester M13 9PL *(tel:* 0161-275 6934).

STOTT, Professor Frank Howard, MA,PhD,DSc,CEng,FIM,FICorr

Professor of Corrosion Science and Engineering, UMIST. *b.* 23 November 1944 Horsforth, Yorkshire. *m.* 1967 Margaret; one *d. Education:* Stockport Grammar School (1956-64); University of Cambridge (1964-67); UMIST (1967-70). *Career Profile:* UMIST - Post-doctoral Research Associate (1970-72); Lecturer (1972-80); Senior Lecturer (1980-86);

Reader (1986-90); Professor (1990-); Head of Corrosion & Protection Centre (1987-90, 1993-96). *Publications/Creative Work:* 200 papers in scientific journals; 80 invited presentations at national and international conferences. *Recreations, Interests:* Research into high-temperature corrosion and protection, family, gardening, travel. *Address:* Corrosion and Protection Centre, UMIST, PO Box 88, Sackville Street, Manchester, M60 1QD(*tel:* 0161 200 4849; *fax:* 0161 200 4865; *e-mail:* F.H.Stott@umist.ac.uk) 11 Fernlea, Hale, Altrincham, WA15 9LH (*tel:* 0161 980 4934).

STOTT, Ian Hood

Chairman and Managing Director, Oldham Athletic AFC Ltd. *b.* 29 January 1934 Oldham. *m.* 1958 Gabrielle Mary Tuke; two *s.* *(marr. diss. 1974)*; *m.* 1978 Patricia Maxine Wynroe; two *d.* *Public Offices:* Councillor (1986-), Football Association; Chairman, FA Medical Committee (1990-); Chairman of Governors, Bilton Grange School, Rugby. *Education:* Bilton Grange Pre-Preparatory School, Dunchurch (1942-47); Shrewsbury School (1947-52). *Military Service:* National Service, 2nd Lieutenant, Lancashire Fusiliers, Trieste/Bury (1952-54). *Career Profile:* James Stott Ltd, Textile Manfuacturers (1954-63); Owner and/or Partner of several companies (garages, hotels, discotheques, caravan manufacturing etc) (1963-86); Chairman and Managing Director, Oldham Athletic AFC Ltd (1986-). *Recreations, Interests:* Sport in general, music, food and wine, bridge. *Address:* Pownall Hall Farm, Broadwalk, Wilmslow, Cheshire, SK9 5PZ.

STRACHAN, Anthony John, FCIS

Agent, Bank of England, Manchester (1995-). *b.* 23 September 1956 Chalfont, Bucks. *m.* 1981 Sarah; one *s.* one *d.* *Education:* Gayhurst School, Bucks (1963-69); Merchant Taylors' School, Northwood (1969-74); MBA Student, Open University Business School (1995-). *Career Profile:* Joined the Bank of England, London (1974-); Exchange Control Department (1974-79); Pension Fund Administration (1979-83); Banking Supervision Division (1984-87); Technical Assistant to Director, Banking & Banking Supervision (1988); Seconded to Takeover Panel (1989-90); Business Finance Division (1991-95); Agent in Manchester (1995-). *Publications/Creative Work:* 'The Governance and Role of Business Corporations in a Modern Society' Ditchley Conference Report (ISSN 0263-3221). *Societies:* St James Club; Liveryman of the Worshipful Company of Chartered Secretaries and Administrators; Freeman of the City of London. *Recreations, Interests:* Classical music, theatre, opera, ballet, reading, sailing, walking. *Address:* Bank of England, PO Box 301, Faulkner Street, Manchester, M60 2HP (*tel:* 0161 237 5609; *fax:* 0161 228 0088).

STRUTHERS, William Anthony (Tony) Keith, BA Bristol (1964),DipTP London (1968), MRTPI, FRSA

City Technical Services Officer and Deputy Chief Executive, City of Salford. *b.* 2 July 1943; Berkhamstead. *m.* 1969 Sylvia Mary Talbot; two *d.* *Education:* Peter Symonds School, Winchester; Bristol University (1961-64); University College, London (1965-68). *Career Profile:* Teacher, Voluntary Service Overseas, Republic of Niger (1964-65); Assistant Research Officer, Ministry of Housing and Local Government (1965-68); Research Officer (1969-73) Assistant County Planning Officer (1973-74) Hampshire CC;

Assistant County Planning Officer, Merseyside CC (1974-78); Deputy County Planner, West Midlands CC (1978-83). *Publications:* 'The Greater Manchester Experience' in 'Urban Waterside Regeneration - problems and prospects' (Ellis Harwood, 1993); joint editor, 'Managing the Metropolis: New Life for Old City Regions' (Avebury, 1993); contributions and reviews to planning pulications. *Societies:* President, Royal Town Planning Institute (1997); Metropolitan Planning Officers Society (President, 1992-93); Royal Society of Arts; Knutsford & District Lions Club. *Recreations, Interests:* Lions Club International, music, walking, travel, local history, skiing. *Address:* Salford City Council, Civic Centre, Chorley Road, Swinton, Salford *(tel:* 0161-793 3600).

STUART, Tony James, BComm(Canterbury,1980)

Director of Business Development, Manchester Airport plc. *b.* 20 April 1957 New Zealand. *m.* 1992 Philippa. *Public Offices:* Board Member, Greater Manchester Visitor & Convention Bureau. *Education:* Wellington College, New Zealand (1970-75); University of Canterbury, New Zealand (1976-80). *Career Profile:* Senior Marketing appointments with Shell Oil International and British Airways. *Societies:* Marketing Society; Sale Rugby Football Club; Bowdon Tennis & Bowling Club. *Recreations, Interests:* Tennis, golf, rugby. *Address:* Manchester Airport plc, Manchester, M90 1QX *(tel:* 0161 489 3703; *fax:* 0161 489 3595). *Additional Information:* Founder of Marketing Manchester.

STUTTARD, Arthur Rupert Davies, MA Oxford (1968),Barrister Middle Temple (1967)

Barrister, Northern Circuit. *b.* 16 July 1943; Accrington. *m.* 1972 Margaret Evelyn. *Education:* Accrington Grammar School; Christ Church, Oxford. *Publications:* 'An English Law Notebook'; various articles on the Lancashire Witchcraft Trials. *Prizes:* Harmsworth Scholar (Middle Temple). *Recreations, Interests:* Horses, archaeology, local history. *Address:* Manchester House Chambers, 18-22 Bridge Street, Manchester M3 3BZ *(tel:* 0161-834 7007); Acre House, Fence, Nr Burnley *(tel:* 01282-693404).

SuAndi

Performance Poet and Live Artist. *b.* 17 October 1951 Manchester. *Public Offices:* Cultural Director voluntary of Black Arts Alliance. *Education:* Nichols Ardwick High School; Horwich College. *Career Profile:* Before entering the arts was a model, restauranteur and social worker; professional writer artist (1985-). *Publications/Creative Work:* 'There Will Be No Tears', 'Nearly Forty', 'Style', 'Soliloquy' BIP 601. *Prizes:* Winston Churchill Fellow (1996); Calouste Gulbenkian New Horizons (1994). *Societies:* Equity. *Recreations, Interests:* Theatre. *Address:* Black Arts Alliance, C/o 111 Burton Road, Withington, Manchester, M20 1HZ *(tel:* 0161 448 0335; *fax:* 0161 448 0335; e-mail: 101651.2770@compuserve.com). *Additional Information:* Board of Directors: North West Arts (1994-) Akwaaba Pan European Womens Network (1994-) Black Women in Europe (1994-) National Disability Arts Forum (1996-) Pankhurst Trust (1995-) City of Drama (1992-94) North West Playwrights (1989-94) Arts Development Agency (1990-91).

SUGDEN, Keith Francis, BA Sheffield (1970),MPhil Salford (1989),FCA,FSA

Senior Lecturer, Department of Business & Management Studies, University of Salford;

Keeper of Numismatics, Manchester Museum. *b.* 8 August 1948; Manchester. *m.* 1970 Helen Lumsden Reid; one *s.* one *d.* *Public Offices:* British Association of Numismatic Societies; President & Trustee, UK Numismatic Trust. *Education:* Manchester Grammar School (1959-66); University of Sheffield (1966-70). *Previous Positions:* Professional Accounting & Corporate Finance with Arthur Andersen & Co, Henry Cooke, Lumsden & Co, Price Waterhouse Associates. *Publications:* 'Sylloge Nummorum Graecorum' Vol 8 (British Academy, 1989); articles in various journals; author of several books on Management Accounting. *Societies:* Fellow, Society of Antiquaries of London; Fellow, Royal Numismatic Society. *Recreations, Interests:* Numismatics, ancient history, fine arts. *Address:* Dept of Business & Management Studies, University of Salford *(tel:* 0161-745 5949); 83 Fir Road, Bramhall, Stockport, Cheshire SK7 2JF *(tel:* 0161-439 7959).

SUMBERG, David Anthony Gerald, Solicitor (1964)

MP Bury South; Member, House of Commons Select Committee on Foreign Affairs; Member, Lord Chancellor's Advisory Committee on Public Records; Company Director, Irwell Insurance Ltd; Consultant, Eversheds, Solicitors. *b.* 2 June 1941 Stoke-on-Trent. *m.* 1972 Carolyn Anne Rae (Franks); one *s.* one *d.* *Public Offices:* Member, Manchester City Council (1982-84); Parliamentary Private Secretary to Solicitor-General and Attorney General (Sir Patrick Mayhew QC MP)(1986-90). *Education:* Tettenhall College, Staffordshire (1950-59); College of Law, London (1959-64). *Recreations, Interests:* Family and friends. *Address:* House of Commons, London, SW1A 0AA *(tel:* 0171 219 4459; *fax:* 0171 267 7832); 19 New Road, Radcliffe, Manchester *(tel:* 0161 723 3457).

SUMMERS, Ian George Saville, BEng Liverpool (1959),MSc Manchester (1970),CEng

Retired; former Experimental Officer, Department of Engineering, Manchester University. *b.* 8 February 1936; West Drayton, Middlesex. *m.* 1963 Elizabeth Mary Higham; one *s.* two *d.* *Education:* Belle Vue Boys Grammar School, Bradford; Liverpool and Manchester Universities. *Societies:* Osborne Reynolds Society for Engineering Graduates of Manchester University; East Lancashire Railway; National Trust; Philatelic Music Circle; Edenfield Village Residents Association; Edenfield & District Horticultural Society; Ramsbottom Heritage Society; Friend of Helmshore Textile Museum; Rochdale Canal Society; British Association for the Advancement of Science; Manchester Literary & Philosophical Society; Friend of the Whitworth Art Gallery; Portico Library; Friend of Museum of Science and Industry; Edenfield Local History Society. *Recreations, Interests:* Photography, music (violin), philately, gardening, DIY. *Address:* 8 Alderwood Grove, Edenfield, Bury, Lancs BL0 0HQ *(tel:* 01706-826655).

SUPER, Maurice, MB BCh Witwatersrand (1959),DCH Glasgow (1965),MRCP Edinburgh (1965),FRCP Edinburgh (1977),MD Cape Town (1978),MSc Edinburgh (1979), FRCP London (1992)

Consultant Paediatric Geneticist, Royal Manchester Children's Hospital; Director, 'The Gene Shop' Project. *b.* 17 October 1936; Johannesburg. *m.* 1958 Anne Monica; two *s.* one *d.* *Education:* King Edward VII School, Johannesburg (1943-53); University of Witwatersrand (1954-59); University of Edinburgh (MSc Human Genetics) (1978-79). *Career Profile:* Paediatric training, Baragwanath Hospital, Johannesburg; Consultant

Paediatrician, South West Africa Administration and South African Railways and Harbours; Postgraduate Tutor (1992-95); Senior Visiting Fellow, University of Central Lancashire. *Publications:* Numerous articles on cystic fibrosis; 'Cystic Fibrosis: The Facts'(3rd ed, 1995). *Societies:* Northern Lawn Tennis Club; Manchester Bridge Club; LCCC. *Recreations, Interests:* Tennis, music, cricket and bridge. *Address:* Clinical Genetics Unit, Royal Manchester Children's Hospital, Manchester M27 1HA *(tel:* 0161-727 2335; *fax:* 0161 727 2328); 120 Fog Lane, Didsbury, Manchester M20 6SP *(tel & fax:* 0161 445 4927).

SUTCLIFFE, Henry, MA,PhD Cambridge,FIEE

Professor Emeritus, University of Salford. *b.* 24 April 1920; Walsden, Lancs. *Education:* Todmorden Grammar School; Cambridge University. *Career Profile:* Scientific Officer in MAP/Industrial posts/Academic posts in Universities of St Andrews, Bristol, Salford, Ireland. *Publications:* Research publications, principally in the field of applied electronics and instrumentation. Patents in same field; 'Electronics for Students of Mechanical Engineering' (1965). *Recreations, Interests:* Walking and modest climbing, the countryside, footpath preservation, University of the Third Age. *Address:* 24 Lambton Road, Worsley, Salford M28 2ST *(tel:* 0161-793 9512). *Additional Information:* Retired from full-time post in 1985.

SUTCLIFFE, John, BA Manchester (1950),ARIBA (1950)

Architect in Private Practice; JP (1972); Deputy Lieutenant of Greater Manchester. *b.* 4 July 1924; Oldham, Lancashire. *m.* 1954 The Honourable Helen Rhodes; two *s.* one *d.* *Education:* Oatlands Harrogate (1935-38); Oundle (1938-41). *War Service:* The Green Howards, served in India (1943-47). *Career Profile:* Retired Partner of Hayes Turner Buttress & Partners. *Creative Works:* Architect for a number of private houses in Saddleworth, several large public housing projects in Oldham, Saddleworth Museum, Bethel Church, Glodwick. *Societies:*Life Member, Dovestones Sailing Club; Former Member, Saddleworth Festival Committee; Past Chairman, Saddleworth Civic Trust, Member of Management Committee, Friends of the Manchester City Art Galleries. *Recreations, Interests:* Art, music, walking, sailing. *Address:* Lower Carr, Diggle, Oldham (01457 872734).

SWEENEY, Michael Thomas

Broadcaster, Piccadilly 1152. *b.* 15 September 1947 Salford. *m.* 1970 Margaret; one *s.* *(marr. diss. 1973)*; *m.* 1983 Brenda; one *d.* *Education:* Our Lady of Mount Carmel School, Salford. *Career Profile:* Docker; Miner; Computer Programmer; Pop Singer; Radio & TV Presenter. *Publications/Creative Work:* Various record releases (1978-). *Recreations, Interests:* Football (playing and watching), reading, running, the 60's.

SWEENEY, Vincent Anthony, BA(Hons)

Assistant Chief Constable, Greater Manchester Police. *b.* 2 October 1952 Newcastle-upon-Tyne. *m.* 1979 Sheila; three *d.* *Education:* St Cuthbert's Grammar School, Newcastle; BRNC Dartmouth; New College, Durham. *Military Service:* Commissioned Royal Navy

(1971-76). *Career Profile:* Joined Northumbria Police (1977); served in Newcastle, Sunderland and South Tyneside rising to Chief Superintendant; headed Force restructure; transferred GMP (1994). *Societies:* President, Manchester Trainee Solicitors Society; National Trust. *Recreations, Interests:* Golf, skiing, music, family pursuits. *Address:* Greater Manchester Police, PO Box 22 (S West PDO), Chester House, Boyer Street, Manchester, M16 0RE *(tel:* 0161 856 2013; *fax:* 0161 856 2036).

SWERDLOW, Mark, Hon Member, International Association for the Study of Pain; MD,MSc, FFARCS,DA

World Health Organisation Adviser; Vice-President, British Intractable Pain Society; Member, Education Committee, International Pain Association; Hon Member, Pain Society of Gt Britain & Ireland. *b.* 9 March 1921; Manchester. *m.* Elizabeth Lessof; one *s.* two *d.* *Education:* Chorlton Grammar School; Manchester University Medical School; Exchange Fellow, Pittsburgh University, USA. *Military Service:* RAMC Medical Officer BAOR (1943-47). *Career Profile:* Consultant Anaesthetist, Salford Hospital Group; Director, North West Regional Pain Relief Centre. *Publications:* 'Relief of Intractable Pain'; 'The Therapy of Pain'; 'Cancer Pain'. *Societies:* Manchester Medical Society; British Intractable Pain Society; International Association for the Study of Pain; European Academy of Anaesthesiology; Association of Anaesthetists of Great Britain. *Recreations, Interests:* Music, art. *Address:* 2 Broomleigh, Booth Road, Altrincham, Cheshire, WA14 4AU.

SYKES, Alan, CertEd Leeds (1960),LLAMDA,ATCL (Speech dept)

Voice-over artist; Independent Radio Programme Contractor; Industrial Video Maker. *b.* 28 June 1939; Oldham. *Education:* Counthill Grammar School, Oldham; St John's College, York; London Academy of Dramatic Art. *Career Profile:* Network Radio Announcer, BBC North West (1982-89); Producer, BBC Radio Manchester (1970-82); Announcer, BBC Radio and TV North Region (1964-70). *Societies:* Equity. *Recreations, Interests:* Golf, foreign travel. *Address:* abc Acme Broadcasting, Broadcast House, Oldham Road, Grasscroft, Oldham OL4 4HZ *(tel:* 0145-787-5605).

SYKES, Geoffrey Robert, BA Manchester (1949)

Artistic Director, Manchester Youth Theatre. *b.* 30 June 1925; Manchester. *m.* 1948 Margaret Mitchell; two *s.* one *d. (widowed 1963)*; *m.* 1964 Hazel Whittam; one *s.* *Education:* Burnage High School, Manchester (1936-43). *War Service:* RNVR (1943-46). *Career Profile:* Senior Head of Department, Brookway High School, Manchester (Retired 1980). *Creative Works:* Founder and Director of Manchester Youth Theatre, responsible for 31 years annual season of plays by and for young people in the region. *Publications:* 'A Glimpse of Blue Sky' (an account of the development of Youth Theatre) (1990). *Prizes:* Horniman Award for outstanding services to Theatre; Manchester Evening News Theatre Awards (1985); with his wife, awarded a prize for Special Achievement at the 1995 Manchester Evening News Theatre awards. *Societies:* Heaton Moor RFC (Captain 1950); Longsight CC. *Recreations, Interests:* Gardening. *Address:* 57 Hulme Hall Road, Cheadle Hulme, Cheadle, Cheshire SK8 6JX *(tel:* 0161-485 1537).

SYKES, Peter Anthony, MD,FRCS (Eng & Ed),MB,ChB

Consultant Surgeon and Medical Director, Trafford NHS Trust. *b.* 29 April 1943; Manchester. *Publications:* Papers and articles on Bowel Obstruction, Health Service Management, etc. *Recreations, Interests:* Sailing, golf *Address:* 14 St John Street, Manchester M3 4DY *(tel:* 0161-832 5188).

SYMES, Professor Martin Spencer, BA Cambridge (1963),MA Cambridge (1967),PhD London (1980),DipArch Cambridge (1965),Planning Dip Arch Assoc (1973),ARIBA (1967),FRSA (1991)

British Gas Professor of Urban Renewal, University of Manchester. *b.* 19 August 1941; Salisbury. *m.* 1965 Valerie Joy; one *s.* one *d. Public Offices:* Chairman, RIBA Professional Literature Committee; Director, IAPS International Association for the Study of People and Their Physical Surroundings; Freeman of City of London. *Education:* Dauntseys School (1952-59); Gonville and Caius College, Cambridge (1960-65); Architectural Association (1971-73). *Career Profile:* Assistant, YRM Architects (1965-68); Architect, Arup Associates (1968-73); Lecturer, University College London (1973-82); Senior Lecturer, University College London (1983-89). *Creative Works:* Printing House for the Oxford Mail and Times (1971) (with Arup Associates). *Publications:* 'Architects and their Practices' (Butterworth-Heinemann, 1995); 'The Urban Experience' (E&F Spon 1994); 'Urban Waterside Regeneration' (Ellis-Horwood 1993); Editor: 'AJ Handbook on the Re-Use of Redundant Industrial Buildings' (1979); Editor: 'Journal of Architectural and Planning Research' (1984-); Articles on the use of space by small firms, on the role of the architect in urban renewal, on architectural education (1973-). *Prizes:* Brancusi Scholarship, Cambridge University (1962); Research Fellowship, Princeton University (1980); Nell Norris Fellowship, Melbourne University (1985); Monbusho Fellowship, Tokyo University (1990). *Societies:* Urban Design Group. *Recreations, Interests:* Swimming, squash, rugby football, travel, wine, the theatre. *Address:* School of Architecture, University of Manchester, Manchester M13 9PL *(tel:* 0161-275 6912); 2 Corner Green, Blackheath, London SE3 9JJ *(tel:* 0181-852 6834).

T

TAGGART, Paul W, BA(Manchester College of Art)

Fine Artist; Author; Video Presenter. *b.* 27 February 1950 Sunderland. *Education:* Houghton le Spring Grammar School; Sunderland College of Art; Manchester College of Art. *Career Profile:* Over 60 exhibitions, including The Royal Academy Summmer Exhibition; Manchester Academy of Fine Art Annual Exhibition; Foyles, etc; Works in Watercolours, Oils, Pastels, Drawing and other media. *Publications/Creative Work:* 'Art Workshop with Paul Taggartel: Watercolour Painting'; 'Art Workshop with Paul Taggartel: Your Painting Companion'; Videos: Art Workshop with Paul Taggartel: Watercolour Painting - Line & Wash and Wet on Wet. *Prizes:* Various art prizes. *Recreations, Interests:* Painting. *Address:* C/o Miss Eileen Tunnell, PROMAD, 15 Lynwood Grove, Sale, M33 2AN (*tel:* 0161 969 2948).

TANNER, Roger John Radcliffe, DL (Greater Manchester)

Chairman, Tanner Bros (Greenfield) Ltd. *Public Offices:* Founder & Chairman, Saddleworth Museum; President, Saddleworth Festival; Founder & Chairman, Saddleworth Chamber Concerts Society; President, Saddleworth & District Cricket League; President, Greenfield Cricket Club; Founder, Saddleworth Civic Trust. *Education:* Uppingham School; Royal College of Music, London. *Prizes:* Paul Harris Fellowship (Rotary). *Recreations, Interests:* Music, travel, history, people. *Address:* Tanner Bros (Greenfield) Ltd, Waterside Mills, Greenfield, Oldham (*tel:*01457-872273); Furlane, Greenfield, Oldham OL3 7PA (*tel:* 01457-872705).

TARRY, David Mark

Chief Executive, Salford Rugby League Club. *b.* 21 November 1956 Irlam, Manchester. *m.* Doreen; two *s.* one *d.* *Public Offices: Address:* Salford Reds Rugby League Club, The Willows, Willows Road, Weaste, Salford, M5 2FQ (*tel:* 0161 736 6564; *fax:* 0161 745 8072).

TATTAM, Charles Søren Robert, BA(Hons), Solicitor

Partner in Charge, Corporate Department, Pannone & Partners. *b.* 14 July 1953 Stockport. *m.* 1975 Sherran Elizabeth; one *s.* one *d.* *Public Offices:* Consul of Sweden in Manchester (1988-). *Education:* Denmark & Sweden to age 15; Bramhall County Grammar School (1968-71); City of London Polytechnic (1971-74). *Career Profile:* Articled Clerk, March Pearson & Skelton (1975-78); Assistant Solicitor (1978-83); Partner (1983); Head of Corporate Department (1987); Merged with Pannone Blackburn (1991) now Pannone & Partners. *Publications/Creative Work:* Contributing author 'Security on Moveable Property and Receivables in Europe' (ISC Publications). *Societies:* Law Society; Licensing Executives Society; L'Association Europeenne d'Etudes Juridiques et Fiscales; Chairman, Swedish Chamber of Commerce, Northern Chapter. *Recreations, Interests:* Travel, tennis, good food and wine. *Address:* Pannone & Partners, 123 Deansgate, Manchester, M3 2BU (*tel:* 0161 832 3000; *fax:* 0161 834 2067). *Additional Information:* Languages spoken - Danish, Swedish and passable French.

TATTERSALL, Kathleen, BA (1963), MEd (1975), FRSA

Chief Executive, Northern Examinations and Assessment Board (1992-). *b.* 11 April 1942; Burnley, Lancashire. *Public Offices:* Convenor, Joint Forum for the GCSE and GCE; Secretary, Joint Council for the GCSE; Member of Court, Manchester University. *Education:* St John's RC Primary, Burnley (1947-53); Paddock House Convent Grammar, Oswaldtwistle (1953-60); Manchester University (1960-64)(1972-75). *Career Profile:* Teacher, Head of History Department; Secretary, Associated Lancashire Schools Examining Board (1982-85); Secretary, North West Regional Examinations Board (1985-90); Secretary, Joint Matriculation Board (1990-92). *Publications:* 'Differentiated Examinations: A Strategy for Assessment at 16 plus' (1982); 'The Implications for the examinations boards of the Education Reform Act of 1988'; 'The Role and Functions of Public Examinations' (1994). *Societies:* Manchester Luncheon Club; Society of Education Officers; New Cavendish Club (London). *Recreations, Interests:* Fell walking, running, bridge, theatre, cooking. *Address:* Northern Examinations and Assessment Board, Devas Street, Manchester M15 6EX *(tel:*0161 953 1180)

TAVARÉ, Sir John, CBE (1983), Kt (1989); BSc (Eng) London (1946), CEng, MIMechE, FIWEM

Chairman, Luxonic Lighting plc. *b.* 12 July 1920; Windsor, Berkshire. *m.* 1949 Margaret Daphne (née Wray); three *s. Public Offices:* Former Chairman, Mersey Basin Campaign, Department of Environment; Member, Rivers Advisory Committee, National Rivers Authority (NW); Trustee, NW Civic Trust. *Education:* Chatham House School, Ramsgate; Bromley Grammar School, Kent; Kings College, Univ of London. *War Service:* Munitions. *Career Profile:* Chairman & Managing Director, Whitecroft plc (1975-85); Vice Chairman, Thames Board Mills Ltd, Unilever (1965-68); Chairman, CBI NW Region (1980-82); Consultant with PA Management Consultants (1948-58). *Societies:* Institute of Mechanical Engineers; Royal Society of Arts & Manufactures; Institute of Directors. *Recreations, Interests:* Golf, gardening, environment. *Address:* The Gables, 4 Macclesfield Road, Prestbury, Macclesfield, Cheshire SK10 4BN *(tel:*01625-829778).

TAYLOR, Andrew John, LLB(Hons)(Manchester, 1978), Solicitor (1981)

Principal, Andrew J Taylor (Solicitors). *b.* 13 May 1957 London. *m.* 1988 Stella Butler; one *s.* one *d. Education:* Moseley Hall Grammar School, Cheadle; Manchester University. *Career Profile:* Articles and then employment with Dyckhoff Johnson, Cheadle (1979-84); Partner (in charge of private client dept) Hall Brydon Diggines (1984-90); Own practice in Cheadle (1990-). *Societies:* Manchester Law Library (Committee, 1988-), (Treasurer 1989-96); STEP; British Association for Sport and the Law; Cheadle Civic Society (Treasurer 1980-). *Recreations, Interests:* Judo (2nd Dan), ju-jitsu, cartophily, literature. *Address:* Andrew J Taylor, Solicitors, 10 Wilmslow Road, Cheadle, Cheshire *(tel:* 0161 428 1875; *fax:* 0161 428 1876); 3 Brooklyn Crescent, Cheadle, Cheshire, SK8 1DX *(tel:* 0161 491 1452).

TAYLOR, Anthony Roy, MA(Cantab)

Chief Crown Prosecutor for Greater Manchester and Cheshire (1987-). *b.* 1 February 1944

Cleethorpes. *m.* 1973 Angela; two *s.* one *d.*.*Education:* Sedbergh School; Université de Strasbourg; Cambridge University. *Societies:* Manchester Law Society; Manchester & District Medico-Legal Society. *Recreations, Interests:* Family and garden. *Address:* CPS NW Area HQ, Ashburner House, Seymour Grove, Manchester, M16 0LD (*tel:* 0161 869 7400).

TAYLOR, Gordon, MA(hc)(Loughborough, 1986) BSc(Econ)external(London, 1970)

Chief Executive, Professional Footballers Association. *b.* 28 December 1944 Ashton-under-Lyne, Lancs. *m.* 1968 Catharine Margaret; two *s. Education:* Ashton-under-Lyne Grammar School; Bolton Technical College; Manchester College of Commerce. *Career Profile:* Bolton Wanderers FC (1960-70); Birmingham City FC (1970-76); Blackburn Rovers FC (1976-78); (temporary) Vancouver Whitechaps FC (1977); Bury FC (1978-80); Professional Footballers Association (1980-). *Societies:* Hallé; PAMCAG; Palace 100 Club. *Recreations, Interests:* Watching football, horse-racing, theatre, eating out. *Address:* Professional Footballers Association, 2 Oxford Court, Bishopsgate, Manchester, M2 3WQ (*tel:* 0161 236 0575; *fax:* 0161 228 7229).

TAYLOR, Jonathan, OBE (1981); MNIM, MIDPM

Managing Trustee, International Friendship. *b.* 8 December 1936. *m.* 1962 Barbara. *Public Offices:* Councillor, Trafford MBC; Leader of Countil; Chairman of Policy, Education, Land & Properties Committees; Member of Social Services, Environment & Leisure, Finance Committees; Family Practitioner Committee; Member, Ministerial Committee on Abolition of Metropolitan Councils; Chairman of Governors: South Trafford College, Brooklands CP, Priory, Sale Girls Grammar Schools. *Education:* Friends School, Saffron Waldon. *Military Service:* RAF (1953-56). *Career Profile:* Manager, NW Region, Sumlock Comptometers (Computer Division); Community Development Manager, ICL(UK) Ltd; retired 1989. *Publications/Creative Work:* 'The Abolition of the GLC and the Metropolitan Counties. *Societies:* RAF Association; Altrincham & Sale West Conservative Party; Wythenshaw & Sale East Conservative Party. *Recreations, Interests:* Politics, music, travel, working with disabled children in Poland and the UK. *Address:* Hylands, 28 Firs Road, Sale, M33 5ET (*tel:* 0161 283 3456; *fax:* 0161 283 3456).

TAYLOR, Kenneth Alan

Chief Executive, Oldham Coliseum Theatre. *b.* 4 April 1937 London. *m.* 1963 Judith; one *s.* one *d. Education:* St Francis Covent, Forest Gate, London; Stratford Grammar School, Stratford, E. London. *Career Profile:* Director, Nottingham Playhouse (1983-90); Director, Freelance West End and National Tours; Director, Oldham Coliseum (1978-82); Actor, various TV and theatre roles. *Publications/Creative Work:* Writer, pantomimes for Oldham Coliseum, Nottingham Playhouse; Adapter: 'Spend, Spend, Spend', 'Whistle Down the Wind', 'A Christmas Carol' etc. *Recreations, Interests:* new writing, painting, gardening. *Address:* Oldham Coliseum, Fairbottom Street, Oldham, OL1 3SW (*tel:* 0161 624 1731; *fax:* 0161 624 5318). *Additional Information:* Spouse, Judith Barker, Actress, TV, Theatre, Radio. Son, Jason, Lighting Designer, Daughter, Jessica, Make-up Artist.

TERRAS, Antony Michael, BA (Com) Manchester (1955)

Partner, Coopers & Lybrand (retired, 1994). *b.* 18 August 1934; Leeds. *m.* 1960 Ann; one *d. Public Offices:* Hon Treasurer, Manchester Chamber of Commerce and Industry. *Education:* Uppingham. *Societies:* Manchester Society of Chartered Accountants; St James's Club, Manchester. *Recreations, Interests:* Golf, walking, painting, mathematics. *Address:* Belmont, 9 Higher Downs, Altrincham, Cheshire WA14 2QL.

TESTA, Humberto Juan, Medico, Beunos Aires (1962), MD Buenos Aires (1979), PhD Manchester (1972), FRCP Hon London (1986), FRCR Hon London (1989)

Consultant in Nuclear Medicine, MRI; Part-time Lecturer in Diagnostic Radiology, Nuclear Medicine, Manchester University. *b.* 11 December 1936; Buenos Aires, Argentina. *m.* 1964 Nydia Esther Garcia; one *s.* two *d. Education:* Buenos Aires University; Manchester University. *Career Profile:* Research Registrar, MRI (1969-71); Fellow in Nuclear Medicine (1971-73). *Publications:* Contributions to medical books and journals; Editor, 'Nuclear Medicine in Urology and Nephrology' (O'Reilly, Shields and Testa)(2nd Ed 1986); 'Research in Radionuclide Studies of Liver, Pancreas, Kidney, Heart and Brain'. *Societies:* British, Spanish, Argentinian Nuclear Medicine Societies; Manchester Medical Society. *Recreations, Interests:* Squash, soccer, cinema, reading. *Address:* Dept of Nuclear Medicine, Royal Infirmary, Manchester *(tel:*0161-276 4780/1); 27 Barcheston Road, Cheadle, Cheshire SK8 1LJ *(tel:*0161-428 6873).

TETLOW, His Honour Judge Christopher Bruce, MA(Cantab)

Circuit Judge. *b.* 27 February 1943 Hale. *m.* 1981 Rosalind Jane; two *s.* one *d. Education:* Stowe School; Magdalene College, Cambridge. *Career Profile:* Called to the Bar Middle Temple (1969). *Societies:* St James's Club, Manchester.

THOMAS, Sir Robert Evan, Kt (1967); MA Manchester (hc)(1974)

b. 8 October 1901; Ince, Lancashire. *m.* 1922 Edna; one *s.* one *d.*; widowed 1992. *Public Offices:* Court of Governors, University of Manchester. *Education:* At 12, worked half-time in a cotton mill; left St Peters, Leigh, at age 13; thereafter, education by Evening Classes. *Military Service:* RASC (1919-20). *Career Profile:* Weaving at 12; spinning at 13; coalmining at 14; Lord Mayor of Manchester (1962-63); Leader, Greater Manchester County Council (1973-77); Chairman, Association of Municipal Councils; Chairman, Association of Metropolitan Authorities; Alderman of City and County (1977). *Publications:* 'Sir Bob' (Autobiography)(Senior Publications). *Societies:* Heaton Moor Golf Club. *Recreations, Interests:* Golf. *Address:* 29 Milwain Road, Manchester M19 2PX *(tel:*0161-224 5778).

THOMAS, Terry, FCIB

Managing Director, Co-operative Bank plc; *b.* 19 October 1937; Carmarthen, Dyfed. *m.* 1963 Lynda; three *s. Public Offices:* Chairman, North West Partnership; Chairman, East Manchester Partnership; Vice-Chairman, Board of Trustees of CAMPUS (Campaign to promote the University of Salford); Alternate Director; Manchester Ringway Developments; Former Member, British Invisibles European Committee; former

Chairman, North West Civic Trust (now known as Sustainability North West) *Education:* Queen Elizabeth Grammar School; Bath University School of Management. *Career Profile:* Marketing Manager (1973-77), Assistant General Manager/Joint General Manager (1977-83), Executive Director, Group Development (1987) Co-operative Bank plc; various Directorships in the Co-operative Movement and Banking; The Joint Credit Card Company (1971-73); National Westminster Bank plc (1962-71). *Societies:* Fellow and Member, General Council of the Chartered Institute of Bankers; Fellow, Chartered Institute of Marketing; Fellow, Royal Society of Arts; Fellow, British Institute of Management. *Recreations, Interests:* Macclesfield Rugby Union Football Club; Grandson (Nathan). *Address:* The Co-operative Bank plc, 1 Balloon Street, Manchester M60 4EP *(tel:* 0161-832 3456, *fax:* 0161 829 4475).

THOMPSON, Andrew Douglas, FNAEA

Chairman & Managing Director, Miller Metcalfe Kirpatrick Ltd; Chairman, Dorsetavon Ltd; Council Member, Bolton Chamber of Commerce and Industry; Director, Fastframe USA Inc. *b.* 27 May 1949; Davyhulme, Urmston, Manchester. *m.* Lesley; two *s.* one *d.* one *steps.* one *stepd. Education:* St Pauls (RC) Secondary School, Urmston; St Patricks (RC) Secondary School, Monton; English Martyrs (RC) Primary School, Urmston. *Career Profile:* Self Employed Surveyor. *Societies:* Georgian House Health & Fitness; National Association of Estate Agents; College of Estate Management; Charter Society; Conservative Party Patrons Club. *Recreations, Interests:* Badminton, family, cycling, swimming, scuba diving. *Address:* Miller Metcalfe Kirkpatrick, 56 Bradshawgate, Bolton BL1 1DW *(tel:*01204-535353); Lower Beck, 5 Meadowfield, Beaumont Park, Lostock, Bolton BL6 4PA *(tel:*01204-844088).

THOMPSON, Ian, NDD,DA(Manchester),ATC,ARBS,FRSA

Self-employed Artist. *b.* 24 June 1937 Manchester. *m.* two *d.*; *m.* Susan Frances; one *d.* two *steps. Public Offices:* Vice-President, Manchester Academy of Fine Arts. *Education:* Preston Grammar School (1948-55); Regional College of Art, Manchester (1955-59); Institute of Education, University of London (1959-60). *Career Profile:* Teacher, Ribbleton Hall School (1960-64); Head of Art, Tulketh School (1964-67); Lecturer in Sculpture, College of Education, Birmingham (1967-74); Lecturer (p-t) in Handwriting, E S Perry Ltd; Senior Lecturer, College of Education/Birmingham Polytechnic (1971-87); Governor, City of Birmingham College of Education (1974-75); Chairman, National Society for Art Education (West Midlands Branch)(1975-76); Director, School of Creative Arts in Education, Birmingham Polytechnic (1981-87); Course Leader, Primary Education (PG), Birmingham Polytechnic (1981-87); Postgraduate Panel, Council for National Academic Awards (CNAA)(1981-88); Governor, Chad Vale School, Birmingham (1981-93); Set up own studio (1987). *Publications/Creative Work:* Examples of sculpture, textiles and painting in numerous private and public collections. *Prizes:* Heywood Prize Certificate of Merit for Fine Art of Royal Manchester Institution (1959); 4th Year Prize for Modelling and Sculpture, Regional College of Art, Manchester (1959); Diploma of Associateship, Regional College of Art, Manchester (1959). *Societies:* Founder Member, 'Unit Five Seven' Creative Film Group, Manchester (1957); Founder Member, West Pennine Group of Painters & Sculptors (1964-67); FRSA (1967); Member, Manchester Academy of Fine Arts (1990), Vice-President (1996); ARBS (1996); Artists Register, The Council for the

Care of Churches (1991); Invited Member, Fabric Advisory Committee for Coventry Cathedral (1991). *Recreations, Interests:* Singing - Huddersfield Singers, former Chairman, Birmingham Festival Choral Society, Wildlife - RSPB, WWF, National Trust, die-cast model collecting, philately. *Address:* White Rock House Farm, Dean House Lane, Stainland, Halifax, HX4 9LG(*tel:* 01422 370256; *fax:* 01422 370256).

THORNHILL, Professor Martin H, MBBS (1978), BDS (1982), MSc (1986), PhD(1990), FDSRCSEd (1988), FFDRCSI (1992)

Professor of Medicine in Dentistry, University Dental Hospital of Manchester; Consultant in Oral Medicine. *b.* 21 August 1953 London. *m.* 1975 Rafia; one *s.* one *d. Education:* Sir Joseph Williamsons Mathematical School; Woolwich College of FE; Guy's Hospital Medical School; King's College Hospital Medical and Dental Schools; The London Hospital Medical College. *Career Profile:* House Officer, Kings College Hospital; Senior House Officer, The Royal London Hospital; MRC Training Fellow; Lecturer in Oral Medicine, Senior Lecturer in Oral Medicine, The London Hospital Medical College; Professor of Medicine in Dentistry, University of Manchester. *Publications:* Many publications and on-going research in oral medicine, adhesion molecules, immune and inflammatory processes, chemokines, endothelial cells and keratinoytes. *Prizes:* Colyer Prize, Royal Society of Medicine; Colgate Prize, British Society for Dental Research. *Societies:* Royal College of Surgeons; British Society for Oral Medicine; British Dental Association; British Society for Immunology; International Society for Dental Research. *Address:* Department of Oral Medicine, University Dental Hospital of Manchester, Higher Cambridge Street, Manchester, M15 6FH(*tel:* 0161 275 6640; *fax:* 0161 275 6840; *e-mail:* Martin.Thornhill@man.ac.uk).

THRELFALL, Stephen, GRNCM(Hons)(1978)

Director of Music, Chethams School of Music. *b.* 25 February 1956 Manchester. *m.* Kathleen Uren pianist; one *s.* one *d. Public Offices:* Member, Arts Council Advisory Panel; Chethams Appeal Committee. *Education:* Parrswood High School, Manchester; Royal Northern College of Music. *Career Profile:* Sub Principal Cello, BBC Philharmonic Orchestra (1978-91); Soloist, Chamber Music Performer, Conductor of various orchestras and choirs including many charity concerts. *Publications/Creative Work:* Arrangements for BBC performances for various ensembles. *Societies:* MMA. *Recreations, Interests:* Soccer, cycling. *Address:* Chethams School of Music, Long Millgate, Manchester, M3 1SB (*tel:* 0161 834 9644; *fax:* 0161 833 3790).

THURNHAM, Peter Giles, MA Cambridge (1967), DipAdvEng Cranfield (1967), MBA Harvard (1969), FIMechE (1986)

MP Bolton North East (1983-); Parliamentary Private Secretary to Rt Hon Norman Fowler MP, Secretary of State, Department of Employment (1987-90); Vice Chairman, All Party Parliamentary Group for Children; Vice-Chairman, APPG for Disabilities. *b.* 21 August 1938; Staines, Middx. *m.* 1963 Sarah Janet Stroude; two *s,* three *d. Public Offices:* Cllr, South Lakeland District Council (1982-84). *Education:* Oundle School (1952-57); Peterhouse, Cambridge (1959-62); Cranfield Inst of Technology (1966-67); Harvard University (1968-69). *Previous Positions:* Professional Engineer, Turbine Designer at C A

Parsons Ltd, Newcastle-upon-Tyne (1957-66); Div Director, British Steam Specialities Ltd, Leicester (1967-71); Chairman of Wathes Group of Companies (1972-). *Publications:* 'When Nature Fails - Why Handicap' (1986 CPC); 'Operation Long Stop: Putting a Time Limit on Unemployment' (1987 CPC). *Recreations, Interests:* Restoration of classic British engines, Lake District, fostering of handicapped children. *Address:* Hollin Hall, Crook, Kendal, Cumbria LA8 9HP *(tel:*01539-821382).

TILL, Lawrence Adrian, BA(Hons)(Univ. of Warwick)

Artistic Director and Chief Executive, Octagon Theatre Trust Ltd, Bolton. *b.* 20 April 1963 Southampton. *Education:* St Mary's College, Southampton (1974-81); University of Warwick (1982-85). *Career Profile:* Youth Theatre Director & Associate Director, Contact Theatre Company (1986-90); Education Director, Crucible Theatre Company (1990-91). *Publications/Creative Work:* Series Editor of Heinemman Plays. *Prizes:* Manchester Evening News Best Production Award (1995). *Societies:* Board Member, North West Playwrights, National Council for Drama Training. *Recreations, Interests:* Arts activies including cinema, galleries and reading. *Address:* Octagon Theatre, Howell Croft South, Bolton, BL1 1SB *(tel:* 01204 529407; *fax:* 01204 380110).

TIMMINS, Colonel John Bradford, OBE (Mil)(1973), TD (1968), 1st Bar (1974), DL (1980-87), JP (1987), KStJ (1988), KLJ (1988); MSc Aston (1981), DSc(hc)(Salford, 1991), HonRNCM (1994), FRSA(1996)

Chairman, Warburton Properties Ltd (1972-); HM Lord Lieutenant of County of Gtr Manchester (1987-); Custos Rotularium (Keeper of Rolls)(1987-); President, TAVRA for NW England & Isle of Man (1994-); County President, Order of St John of Jerusalem (1988-); President, Royal Society of St George (1987-). *b.* 23 June 1932; Dudley, Worcestershire. *m.* 1956 Jean Edwards; five *s.* one *d. Public Offices:* Member of Court, Manchester University; Member of Court, UMIST; Member of Court, Salford University; Trustee, Greater Manchester Museum of Science & Industry; Trustee, Halle Endowment Trust. *Education:* Dudley Grammar School (1943-49); Wolverhampton Tech College (1949-53); University of Aston in Birmingham (1980-81). *Military Service:* Commissioned Service, Corps of Royal Engineers (1954-56); RE(TA)(1956-80); Commanded 75 Eng Regt (V)(1971-73); TA Colonel, HQ NW District (1975-78); Hon Colonel, 75 Eng Regt (1980-90); Hon Colonel, Manchester & Salford UOTC (1990-); Hon Col, Manchester ACF (1991-). *Previous Positions:* ADC to HM The Queen (1975-80); NW Regional President, Building Employers' Confederation (1974-75); Vice Chairman, TAVRA for NW England (1980-87), Vice-President (1987-94); High Sheriff of County of Gtr Manchester (1986-87). *Creative Works:* 'The Markets for Industrial Property' (1981)(University of Aston in Birmingham). *Societies:* Manchester Literary & Philosophical Society; Army & Navy Club; Royal Engineers Yacht Club; St James's Club, Manchester. *Recreations, Interests:* Sailing, good food and wine. *Address:* Greater Manchester Lieutenancy, Byrom House, Quay Street, Manchester M3 3JD *(tel:*0161-834 0490); The Old Rectory, Warburton, Lymm, Cheshire WA13 9SS *(tel:*01925-753957).

TITLEY, Gary, BA(Hons)(1973), PGCE(1974)

Member of the European Parliament (1989-). *b.* 19 January 1950 Salford. *m.* 1975 Charo;

one *s.* one *d.* *Public Offices:* County Councillor (1981-86). *Education:* York University (1970-74). *Career Profile:* Teacher (1976-84); Researcher to MEP (1984-89); Elected to European Parliament (1989). *Publications/Creative Work:* Articles in Planner, Labour Herald, Tribune and Public Enterprise; jointly commissioned report on the Social Charter and how a Labour Government could implement it. *Prizes:* Commander of the White Rose of Finland (1995); Austrian Gold Cross (1996). *Recreations, Interests:* Jogging, theatre, reading, spy-thrillers, watching football, rugby and cricket. *Address:* 16 Spring Lane, Radcliffe, Manchester, M26 2TQ (*tel:* 0161 724 4008; *fax:* 0161 724 4009; *e-mail:* GeoNEtel:MCRI:Gary.Titley).

TOMLINSON, Harry, MA(Oxon), MSc

Principal Lecturer, Education Management, Leeds Metropolitan University. *b.* 1 December 1939 Heckmondwike, Yorkshire. *Public Offices:* Treasurer, Secondary Heads Association (1990-94); Chair, British Educational Management & Administration Society (1992-94, 1995-). *Education:* Batley Grammar School (1950-58); Oriel College, Oxford (1958-63). *Career Profile:* Headteacher, Birley High School, Manchester (1977-82); Principal, Margaret Ashton College, Manchester (1982-85); Headteacher, The Manor School, Stockport (1985-91); Principal, Margaret Danyers College, Stockport (1991-95). *Publications:* Contributor: 'Teaching in Multicultural Britain'; 'Management and the Psychology of Schooling'; 'Effective Local Management of Schools'; Editor: 'Performance Related Pay in Education'; 'The Search for Standards'; 'Education and Training 14-19'; 'Managing Continuing Professional Development in Schools' (forthcoming). *Societies:* Institute of Management; Institute of Personnel and Development. *Recreations, Interests:* Theatre. *Address:* Fairfax Hall, Beckett Park Campus, Leeds Metropolitan University, Leeds, LS6 3QS (*tel:* 0113 2837407; *fax:* 0113 2833181; *e-mail:* H.Tomlinson@lmu.ac.); 13 Pleasant Way, Cheadle Hulme, Cheadle, SK8 7PF (*tel:* 0161 440 0226).

TOMLINSON, Professor Stephen, MB ChB (Hons), MD, FRCP

Dean, Faculty of Medicine, Dentistry & Nursing, Dean of the Medical School (1993-), Professor of Medicine, University of Manchester; Honorary Consultant Physician, Manchester Royal Infirmary. *b.* 20 December 1944; Farnworth. *m.* 1970 Christine Margaret; two *d.* *Education:* Hayward Grammar School, Bolton; University of Sheffield Medical School. *Career Profile:* Reader in Medicine, Wellcome Trust Senior Lecturer, Wellcome Trust Senior Research Fellow in Clinical Sciences, University of Sheffield; Sir Henry Wellcome Travelling Fellow, Massachusetts Institute of Technology. *Publications:* Papers on Mechanisms of Hormone Action, Intracellular Signalling in Stimulus Response Coupling and the Organisation and Delivery of Health Care in Diabetes. *Prizes:* Dr Mark Gregory Baker University Prize, University of Sheffield (1968); Robert Percival Lecturer (1988); Calvert Memorial Lecturer, Burnley (1988). *Societies:* Association of Physicians of Great Britain & Ireland (Member, Executive Committee 1986-88, Secretary 1988, Treasurer 1993-); Chairman, Association of Clinical Professors of Medicine (1995-); Endocrine Section Royal Society of Medicine (Council Member); 1942 Club (Clinical Profs); British Diabetic Association; Society for Endocrinology; Biochemical Society; Medical Research Society; Thyroid Club; Manchester Literary & Philosophical Society. *Recreations, Interests:* Cooking. *Address:* Makants Farm, Blackburn Road, Eagley Bank, Bolton BL1 7LH (*tel:*01204-54765).

TOONE, The Revd Canon Lawrence Raymond, BA (Hons) Open (1979)

Vicar of St Marys, Greenfield; Area Dean of Saddleworth; Honorary Canon of Manchester Cathedral. *b.* 17 December 1932; Manchester. *m.* 1958 Maureen (née Bagot); one *s.* one *d.* *Education:* Rochester Theological College; St Aidans Theological College, Birkenhead; Open University. *Military Service:* National Service REME (1953-55). *Recreations, Interests:* Family history. *Address:* St Marys Vicarage, 1 Park Lane, Greenfield, Oldham OL3 7DX *(tel:*01457 872346).

TORRINGTON, Professor Derek Peter, JP(1972); MPhil, CIPD, CIMgt, FRSA

Dean of Management Studies and Professor of Human Resource Management, Manchester School of Management, UMIST. *b.* 18 June 1931 London. *m.* 1965 Barbara Mary Clarke; two *s.* two *d. Education:* The Manchester Grammar School; University of Manchester. *Military Service:* National Service, Royal Air Force (1953-55). *Career Profile:* Various posts in industry, ultimately Manager, Personnel & Training, Oldham International Ltd; entered academic life (1970); UMIST (1975) Professor of Human Resource Management (1990), Dean (1994). *Publications/Creative Work:* 30 books including 'Personnel Managementel: HRM in Action'. *Societies:* Society of Authors; Lancashire County Cricket Club; Arthur Ransome Society. *Recreations, Interests:* Cricket, walking, overseas travel, ancient civilisations, United Reformed Church. *Address:* Manchester School of Management, UMIST, PO Box 88, Manchester, M60 1QD *(tel:* 0161 200 3414; *fax:* 0161 200 3623; *e-mail*: derek.torrington@umist.ac.uk); Pownall Farm, Hollin Lane, Styal, SK9 4JH *(tel:* 01625 524937).

TOWNELEY, Sir Simon, KCVO, KStJ, KCSG (Papal); MA DPhil (Oxon), Hon FRNCM, Hon Fellow Lancashire Polytechnic, DMus(hc) Lancaster

HM Lord Lieutenant of Lancashire. *b.* 14 December 1921; England. *m.* 1955 Mary Fitzherbert; one *s.* six *d. Public Offices:* JP; High Sheriff of Lancashire (1971); Member of Council of Duchy of Lancaster; Trustee British Museum; President, NW of England & IOM TAVR. *Education:* Stowe; Worcester College, Oxford. *War Service:* KRRC. *Previous Positions:* Lecturer History of Music, Worcester College, Oxford (1949-55). *Publications:* 'Venetian Opera in the Seventeenth Century'. *Prizes:* Ruffini Scholar. *Address:* Dyneley Hall, Nr Burnley, Lancs *(tel:*01282-423322).

TREUHERZ, Werner

b. 3 December 1907; Charlottenburg, Germany. *m.* 1940 Irmgard Amberg; four *s. Education:* Lycee Fustel de Coulanges, Strasbourg; Werner Siemens Realgymnasium, Berlin; Universities of Berlin, Frankfurt and Kiel. *Career Profile:* Director, The Lancashire Tanning Co Ltd, Littleborough; Hon Chairman, Morris Feinman Homes Trust. *Societies:* Rotary Club of Rochdale (longest and oldest member); Reform Club; Jewish Historical Society; Society of Interdisciplinerary Studies. *Recreations, Interests:* Old Testament studies, ancient history, trade cycles, homoeopathy. *Address:* 3 Meadowcroft Lane, Rochdale OL11 5HN *(tel:*01706-69139).

TRIPPIER, Sir David (Austin), Kt(1992), RD(1983), JP, DL

Chairman, 'Marketing Manchester'; Chairman, Vector Investments; Chairman, W H

Ireland & Co Ltd (Stockbrokers); Enviro Systems Ltd; Sir David Tripper & Associates Ltd; a number of consultancies and directorships, including Dunlop Heywood (Chartered Surveyors), Manchester. *b.* 15 May 1946. *m.* 1975 Ruth Worthington; three *s. Public Offices:* At the age of 22 admitted to the Stock Exchange; also Director of a financial planning company as well as a stockbroker; Elected to Rochdale MBC (1969), Leader of Conservative Group (1974); Leader of the Council (1975) same year appointed as a magistrate; Elected MP for Rossendale (1979); MP for the new constituency of Rossendale and Darwen (1983-92); Appointed Parliamentary Private Secretary to the Minister for Health (Rt Hon Kenneth Clarke MP)(1982); Minister of State for Small Firms, DTI (1983-85); Minister for Tourism, Small Firms and Enterprise, DOE (1985-87); Minister for Inner Cities and Construction, Department of Environment (1987); Minister of State for the Environment and Countryside (1989); Founder Rossendale Enterprise Trust and Rossendale Groundwork Trust; Governor, Manchester Grammar School (1993); Deputy Lieutenant of Lancashire (1994). *Education:* Bury Grammar School. *Military Service:* Officer Royal Marines Reserve for 17 years; Honorary Colonel, The Royal Marines Reserve Merseyside (1996-). *Publications/Creative Work:* 'Defendending the Peace' (1982); 'New Life for Inner Cities' (1989). *Prizes:* Royal Marines Reserve Decoration (1983). *Societies:* St James's Club, Manchester. *Recreations, Interests:* Gardening, tennis. *Address:* Sir David Trippier & Associates Ltd, Consort Suite, Fifth Floor, Northern Assurance Buildings, Albert Square, Manchester M2 4DN (*tel:* 0161 832 1277; *fax:* 0161 834 8722). *Additional Information:* Lady Ruth Trippier is a practising barrister on the Northern Circuit.

TUCKER, Anne, BA

Joint Artistic Director, Manchester International Arts. *b.* 7 July 1951 London. *Education:* Badminton School, Bristol; Warwick University. *Career Profile:* Teacher; Community Worker; Community Artist; Local Government Arts Development worker; Artistic Director of MIA. *Recreations, Interests:* Music, theatre, outdoor street events, gardening, foreign travel. *Address:* 3 Birch Polygon, Manchester, M14 5HX (*tel:* 0161 224 0020; *fax:* 0161 248 9331).

TUCKER, Harold

Senior Partner, Harold Tucker & Son; Chairman, National Law Tutors; Chairman, Greater Manchester South Valuation Tribunal; Member of Court, Salford University; Trustee and Past President of South Manchester Synagogue. *b.* 4 February 1930; London. *m.* 1952 Shirley Ruth Silver; three *s. Public Offices:* Lord Mayor of Manchester (1984-85). *Education:* Kilburn Grammar School, London (1941-47). *Military Service:* National Service RAF (1948-50). *Career Profile:* Member of Manchester City Council (1960-86); Leader of City Conservative Party (1984-86); Member of Rotary Club, Wythenshawe; Deputy Chairman, Manchester Education Committee (1968-71); Conservative Candidate, General Election (1964)(Huyton, lost to Harold Wilson). *Societies:* Dunham Golf and Country Club. *Recreations, Interests:* Politics, literature, art, music, golf and tennis. *Address:* 355 Deansgatge, Manchester M3 4LG *(tel:*0161-832 5505); High Sierra, Hasty Lane, Hale Barns, Cheshire WA15 8UU *(tel:*0161-904 9111).

TUCKER, Shirley Ruth (*née* Silver)

Justice of the Peace. *b.* 8 July 1930; Cardiff. *m.* 1952 Harold Tucker; three *s. Public*

Offices: Lady Mayoress of Manchester (1984-85). *Education:* Howells (County Glamorgan) School, Cardiff. *Career Profile:* Member, Manchester City Council (1970-80); Past President, Inner Wheel Club of Wythenshawe; Past Chairman, South Manchester Synagogue Ladies Guild and Education Committee. *Recreations, Interests:* Reading, theatre, surfboard, sailing and going on holiday. *Address:* High Sierra, Hasty Lane, Hale Barns, Cheshire WA15 8UU *(tel:*0161-904 9111).

TURNER, Andrew Robert

Director, Boardroom Wines Ltd. *b.* 13 August 1939 Woking, Surrey. *m.* 1983 Carol Mary Clark. *Education:* St Piran's, Maidenhead; Epsom College. *Career Profile:* Regional Director, Keyser Ullmann Ltd. *Societies:* St James's Club, Manchester (past Chairman). *Recreations, Interests:* Horticulture, food and wine. *Address:* Boardroom Wines Ltd, 61 Brown Street, Manchester, M2 2JX *(tel:* 0161 834 3803); Knutsford Lodge, Peover Superior, Knutsford, WA16 9EX *(tel:* 01565 722508).

TURNER, Right Reverend Geoffrey Martin

Bishop of Stockport (1994-). *b.* 16 March 1934 Chagford, Devon. *m.* 1959 Gillian Chope; two *s.* one *d. Education:* Bideford Grammar School; Sandhurst; Oak Hill Theological College. *Military Service:* Royal Artillery, Trucial Oman Scouts. *Career Profile:* Vicar, Christ Church, Chadderton (1973-79); Rector, Bebington, Canon Chester Cathedral, Rural Dean, Wirral North (1979-93); Archdeacon of Chester (1993-94). *Societies:* National Liberal Club. *Recreations, Interests:* Sport, fishing, reading. *Address:* Bishop's Lodge, Back Lane, Dunham Town, Altrincham, WA14 4SG *(tel:* 0161 928 5611)(*fax:* 0161 929 0692).

TURVEY, Timothy John, BSc(Univ. of Wales, 1969), DipEd(Bath, 1970), CBiol, FIBiol, FLS

Headmaster, The Hulme Grammar School, Oldham. *b.* 13 October 1947 London. *m.* Janet Hilary Webster; one *s. Education:* Monkton Combe School, Bath; University College, Cardiff. *Career Profile:* Assistant Master, The Edinburgh Academy (1970-75); Head of Biology, Director of Studies, Monkton Combe School (1975-90); Deputy Headmaster, The Hulme Grammar School (1990-95). *Publications/Creative Work:* Author and Editor of various advanced level texts for Nuffield-Chelsea Curriculum Trust/Longman Group; Chief Examiner, Advanced Level/Special Biology, NEAB. *Societies:* Institute of Biology; Linnean Society; HMC; National Trust; Church Union. *Recreations, Interests:* Music, theatre, food, travel. *Address:* The Hulme Grammar School, Chamber Road, Oldham, OL8 4BX *(tel:* 0161 624 4497).

TWIST, Benjamin, MA(Hons)(Edinburgh)

Artistic Director, Contact Theatre. *b.* 17 April 1962 London. *m.* 1990 Margaret Corr. *Education:* Crown Woods School, London (1973-80); University of Edinburgh (1981-85). *Career Profile:* Theatre Director (1985-); Artistic Director, Contact Theatre (1994-). *Address:* Contact Theatre, Oxford Road, Manchester, M14 5JD *(tel:* 0161 274 3434; *fax:* 0161 273 6286).

TYE, Frederick, CBE (1980); BSc Manchester (1943), MEd(hc) Manchester(1993)

Retired. *b.* 24 May 1921; Middlesborough. *m.* 1944 Joan Russell; two *d. Public Offices:* Member, Court of Governors of University of Manchester; Governor of Cheadle Hulme School. *Education:* Coatham School, Redcar, Yorks; University of Manchester. *War Service:* Royal Signals (1943-46). *Career Profile:* Assistant Master, Cheadle Hulme School; Head of Science, Colfe's Grammar School; Headmaster, Addey and Stanhope School, London; Headmaster, Wilmslow Grammar School, Cheshire; Director, North West Educational Management Centre. *Publications:* 'Running a School' (with C H Barry) (1972). *Recreations, Interests:* Music, fly fishing. *Address:* Woodstock, Topcliffe, Thirsk YO7 3RW (*tel:* 01845 577022).

U

UNGER, Michael Ronald

Editor, Manchester Evening News; Director, Guardian Media Group plc; Trustee, The Scott Trust. *b.* 8 December 1943 Surrey. *m.* 1966 Eunice; one *s.* one *d. (dec'd) (marr. diss. 1991)*; *m.* 1993 Noorah. *Public Offices:* Chairman, NW Arts Board (1991-93). *Education:* Wirral Grammar School; Liverpool College of Commerce. *Career Profile:* Trainee Journalist, Stockport (1963-65); Production Editor, Reading Evening Post (1965-67); News Editor, Daily News, Perth, W Australia (1967-71); Deputy Editor, Daily Post, Liverpool (1971-77); Editor, Daily Post, Liverpool (1977-82); Editor, Liverpool Echo (1982-83); Editor, Manchester Evening News (1983-). *Publications/Creative Work:* 'The Memoirs of Bridget Hitler' (1979). *Prizes:* Editor of the Year (1988); Newspaper of the Year (1992, 1993). *Societies:* The Portico Library. *Recreations, Interests:* Walking, reading, theatre, art. *Address:* Manchester Evening News, 164 Deansgate, Manchester, M60 2RD (*tel:* 0161 832 7200; *fax:* 0161 839 0968).

URSELL, Professor Fritz Joseph, MA, ScD, MSc, FRS (1972)

Emeritus Professor, University of Manchester;. Chairman of Convocation, University of Manchester. *b.* 28 April 1923; Dusseldorf, Germany. *m.* 1959 Katharina Renate Zander; two *d. Education:* German Schools (until 1936); Clifton College; Marlborough College; Trinity College, Cambridge. *War Service:* Dept of Scientific Research and Experiment, Admiralty. *Career Profile:* ICI Research Fellow, Manchester University (1947-50); Fellow Under Title A, Trinity College, Cambridge (1947-51); Lecturer, Cambridge University (1950-61); Stringer Fellow, King's College, Cambridge (1954-60); Visiting Associate Professor of Hydrodynamics, MIT (1957-58); Visiting Professor of Mathematics, University of Michigan (1964), Maths Research Center, University of Wisconsin (1967); Beyer Professor of Applied Mathematics, Manchester University (1961-90). *Address:* Dept of Mathematics, Manchester University, Oxford Road, Manchester M13 9PL (*tel:* 0161-275 5800); 28 Old Broadway, Manchester M20 3DF (*tel:* 0161-445 5791).

V

VAIL, Colonel Ivan, MIPS,MIB

Retired; Part-time Consultant. *b.* 18 May 1930 Sheering, Essex. *m.* 1955 Eileen; two *s.* *Public Offices:* Deputy Lieutenant of Greater Manchester (1993). *Education:* Gainsborough College. *Career Profile:* School Cadet S/Sgt (1944-48); Army Service Para, RAOC,AATDC (1948-51); TA Comm 2/Lt Manchester Regiment (1951); Kings Regt (1965), Lt Colonel ACF (1978); Colonel Command, Greater Manchester ACF (1987-93); Vice Chairman, ACF Central Comm, North West TA (1992-); Chairman, Kings Regt OCA, Ashton-u-Lyne (1990); Member, Manchester Cathedral Comm Kings Regt (1986); Member, Regt Comm, The Kings Regt (1986); County President, The Royal British Legion (1995); Chairman, Gt Manchester Army Sports and Welfare Comm (1994). *Societies:* Conservative Club (1948-) Committee Member 30 years, Chairman, Ashton-u-Lyne (1970-86). *Recreations, Interests:* Walking, badminton, keep fit, cycling, caravan. *Additional Information:* Buyer, English Electric Co (1955-69), Senior Buyer, GEC (1969-72) Purchasing Manager, GEC (1972-80), Div Purchasing Manager, GEC (1980-90).

VANSTONE, Harold Bertram, JP,FCA

Chartered Accountant (retired). *b.* 16 May 1912; Stockport. *m.* 1938 Winifred Mary Hargreaves; three *d.* *Education:* Terra Nova; Mill Hill. *War Service:* Royal Artillery (1939-45) Western Desert and Sicily; Brigade Major, RA, 55 (West Lancs) Div (1944-45). *Career Profile:* Partner, Grant Thornton (formerly Walton Watts & Co) (1946-77); President, Manchester Chamber of Commerce (1968-69); Member, North Western Postal Board (1970-76); Treasurer (Honorary), UMIST (1978-85). *Prizes:* Institute of Chartered Accountants: Honours, 4th Place Intermediate (1932), Theodore Gregory Prize Final (1934). *Societies:* Manchester Club (President 1964); Manchester Luncheon Club (President 1965). *Recreations, Interests:* Travel, gardening, family history. *Address:* 10 Manor Close, Cheadle Hulme, Cheadle, Cheshire SK8 7DJ (tel: 0161-485 3751).

VAUGHAN, Professor David John, BSc(1967),MSc(1968)(Univ of London),DPhil(1971), DSc(1984)(Oxon)

Professor of Mineralogy and Head, Department of Earth Sciences, University of Manchester. *b.* 10 April 1946 Newport. *m.* 1971 Heather Ross; one *s.* *(marr. diss. 1994)* *Public Offices:* Member, Earth Science & Technology Board, Natural Environment Research Council (1994-). *Education:* Newport High School (1957-64); University College London (1964-67); Imperial College, London (1967-68); University College, Oxford (1968-71). *Career Profile:* Visiting Research Scientist, CANMET, Ottawa (1970); Research Associate, Massachusetts Institute of Technology, Cambridge, Mass (1971-74); Lecturer then Reader, University of Aston (1974-88); Professor of Mineralogy (19888-), Head of Department of Earth Sciences (1992-), University of Manchester. *Publications/Creative Work:* Author/co-author of over 130 articles in scientific journals; 6 books including: 'Mineral Chemistry of Metal Sulfides' (with J Craig)(CUP, 1978); 'Ore Microscopy and Ore Petrography' (with J Craig)(Wiley, 1981); 'Resources of the Earth'

(with J Craig and B Skinner)(Prentice Hall, 1996). *Prizes:* Burdett Coutts Studentship, Oxford University (1971); Mineral named 'vaughanite' in honour of contributions (1987). *Societies:* Institute of Mining and Metallurgy; Geological Society; Mineralogical Society (President, 1988-89); Society of Economic Geologists; Mineralogical Society of America. *Recreations, Interests:* Walking, music, painting. *Address:* Department of Earth Sciences, The University of Manchester, Oxford Road, Manchester, M13 9PL (*tel:* 0161 275 3935; *fax:* 0161 275 3947; *e-mail:* David.Vaughan@man.ac.uk).

VENNER, The Right Rev Stephen Squires, BA(Birmingham),MA(Oxon),PGCE(London)

Bishop of Middleton. *b.* 19 June 1944 Chatteris, Cambridgeshire. *m.* 1972 Judith; two *s.* one *d. Public Offices:* Area Vice-President, St John Ambulance; Vice-President, The Woodard Corporation. *Education:* Hardye's School, Dorchester (to 1961); Birmingham University (1962-65); Linacre College, Oxford (1965-69); St Stephen's House, Oxford (1965-68); London University Institute of Education (1971-72). *Career Profile:* Curate, St Peter, Streatham (1968-71); Hon Curate, St Margaret, Streatham Hill (1971-72); Hon Curate, The Ascension, Balham (1972-74); Head of RE, St Paul's Girls' School, Hammersmith (1972-74); Vicar, St Peter, Clapham and Bishops' Chaplain to Overseas Students (1974-76); Vicar, St John, Trowbridge (1976-82); Vicar, Holy Trinity, Weymouth (1982-94); Canon and Prebendary, Salisbury Cathedral (1989-94). *Publications/Creative Work:* Chairman of working party producing 'All God's Children?'. *Recreations, Interests:* Family, water sports, piano and organ, reading adventure novels, computers, reprographics. *Address:* The Hollies, Manchester Road, Rochdale, OL11 3QY(*tel:* 01706 358550; *fax:* 01706 354851; *e-mail:* +Stephen@middtn.demon.co.uk).

VERDIN, Peter Anthony, LLB,Solicitor

Senior Partner, Healds, Wigan. *b.* 4 March 1934 Northwich. *m.* 1965 two *s.* two *d. Public Offices:* Part-time Chairman Industrial Tribunals. *Education:* Ushaw College, Durham (1945-51); Durham University (1951-1954). *Career Profile:* Admitted Solicitor (1957); Senior Partner, Healds; Member Council, The Law Society (1974-96); President, Association North Western Law Societies (1974-75), Wigan Law Society (1988-89). *Societies:* RAC; Lymm Golf Club (Captain 1996). *Recreations, Interests:* Golf, theatre, cooking. *Address:* Healds, Moot Hall Chambers, 8 Wallgate, Wigan, WN1 1JE (*tel:* 01942 241511; *fax:* 01942 826639).

VICARY, Gary Kevin, BA(Hons),ACA

Group Finance Director, United Optical Industries Ltd. *b.* 25 March 1960 Liverpool. *partner:* Morag Mathie; one *s.Education:* Page Moss Comprehensive, Huyton; John Moores University. *Career Profile:* Chartered Accountantel: Pannell Kerr Forster (1981-84); Coopers & Lybrand (1984-88); Corporate Finance, Barclays de Zeote Wedd (1988-91); Group Finance Director, The Intercare Group plc (1991-95); completed MBO from Intercare of its optical business (1995) United Optical Industries Ltd. *Prizes:* Livepool Society of Chartered Accountants at degree level. *Societies:* ICAEW; IOD; Secretary, Liverpool Students Society of ICAEW (1983). *Recreations, Interests:* Football, general

keep fit, skiing, music. *Address:* United Optical Indusries Ltd, Pennine House, Manchester Road, Heaton Norris, Stockport, SK4 1TX (*tel:* 0161 477 7077; *fax:* 0161 476 0528).

VICKERMAN, Colin, OBE(1986); MA(Cantab, 1961),MA(Econ)(Manchester, 1965)

Retired. *b.* 13 October 1926 Huddersfield. *m.* 1952 Eleanor Esther Pharaoh; two *d. Public Offices:* Member of Court, University of Manchester; Chair of Governors, Trinity C of E High School; Governor, Didsbury C of E Primary School. *Education:* Huddersfield College; St Catharine's College, Cambridge. *War Service:* RAF (1944-48). *Career Profile:* District Officer, Colonial ·Service, Uganda (1952-61); Joint Matriculation Board (1962-90)(Secretary, 1981-90); occasional consultant British Executive Service Overseas. *Publications/Creative Work:* various articles, chapters on public examinations in educational publications. *Societies:* Northern Lawn Tennis Club; Glass Association; Northern Ceramic Society; National Art Collections Fund; Didsbury Civic Society. *Recreations, Interests:* fell walking, tennis, theatre, musical concerts, water colour painting. *Address:* 5 Pine Road, Didsbury, Manchester, M20 6UY (*tel:* 0161 445 1669).

VOWLES, Rev Canon Peter John Henry, MA(Oxon)

Chair, Victim Support, Central Manchester; Canon Emeritus, Manchester Cathedral (1991-pres.). *b.* 19 June 1925 Bristol. *m.* 1960 Thelma Drake; two *s.* one *d. Education:* Cotham Grammar School, Bristol; Magdalen College, Oxford; Westcott House, Cambridge. *War Service:* RNVR (1943-46). *Career Profile:* Assistant Curate: All Saints, Kings Heath, Birmingham; Huddersfield Parish Church; Vicar, St Matthew, Perry Beeches, Birmingham; Rector: St Mary, Cottingham, E Yorks; St Ann, Manchester. *Publications/Creative Work:* Various reports and lectures. *Recreations, Interests:* Theology, history, painting, gardening. *Address:* 10 Redshaw Close, Fallowfield, Manchester, M14 6JB (*tel:* 0161 257 2065).

WADE OF CHORLTON, Lord William Oulton, Kt (1982),JP

Farmer & cheesemaster; Chairman, William Wild & Son (Mollington) Ltd, Marlow Wade & Partners; Director, Murray Vernon Holdings Ltd, Millers Damsell Ltd, John Wilman Ltd. *b.* 24 December 1932 Chester. *m.* 1959 Gillian Margaret; one *s.* one *d. Public Offices:* Director, INWARD; President, Combined Heat & Power Association; Chairman, NIMTECH, NW Industrialists' Council, NW Area Conservative Association (1976-81); Campus Ventures Ltd; Member, National Union Executive Committee (1975-90); Joint Hon Treasurer, Conservative Party (1982-90); Member, Cheshire County Council (1973-77); Chairman, Cheese Export Council (1982-84); Member, Food from Britain Export Council (1984-88); Member, Worshipful Company of Farmers; Freeman of the City of London (1980); Chairman, Cheshire Historic Churches Trust (1993-), Chester Heritage Trust (1994-); President, Energy from Waste Association; Chairman, Rural Economy Group; Member, House of Lords Select Committee on Relations between Central and Local Government (1995-); Chairman, Christie Hospital Centenary Appeal. *Education:* Birkenhead School; Queens University, Belfast. *Societies:* Carlton Club; Farmers' Club; The City Club; St James's Club, Manchester. *Recreations, Interests:* Food, agriculture, industry, transport, planning, shooting, reading, farming. *Address:* NIMTECH Ltd, Alexandra House, Borough Road, St Helens, WA10 3TN (*tel:* 01744 453366; *fax:* 01744 453377); House of Lords, Westminster, London, SW1A 0PW. *Additional Information:* Specially interested in promoting economic growth and in promoting and supporting the economy of the North West of England.

WAINWRIGHT, John Peter, MA Cambridge (1960),FRICS

Chairman, Lambert Smith Hampton (Manchester); Director, Lambert Smith Hampton; Chairman, Lancashire & Yorkshire Reversionary Interest Co Ltd. *b.* 16 June 1938; Bucklow, Cheshire. *m.* 1963 Phoebe; two *d. Public Offices:* Member of Court and Council, University of Manchester, Governor, Manchester Grammar School; Chairman of Governors, Cransley School. *Education:* Terra Nova; Charterhouse (Scholarship); Pembroke, Cambridge (Exhibitioner). *Career Profile:* Partner, W H Robinson & Co; President, GP Division Royal Institution of Chartered Surveyors; Chairman, Northern Rock Manchester Advisory Board. *Societies:* St James's Club; Manchester Tennis & Racquets Club; Royal Academy; International Dendrology Society. *Recreations, Interests:* Cricket, golf, botany. *Address:* Lambert Smith Hampton plc, 79 Mosley Street, Manchester M2 3LQ (*tel:* 0161-228 6411 *fax:* 0161 228 7354).

WALLMAN, Adrienne Marcia, MA(Cantab),PGDip(Art Gallery & Museum Studies)

Director, Manchester Jewish Museum. *b.* 31 March 1952 Manchester. *Education:* Manchester High School for Girls; Newnham College, Cambridge; Manchester University. *Career Profile:* Travel Sales Assistant, Thomas Cook Ltd (1975-77); PA/Researcher, BBC School Television (1978-88); Keeper of Art, Blackburn Museum & Art Gallery (1988-94). *Societies:* Professional Member, Museums Association, North West Federation of Museums & Art Galleries. *Recreations, Interests:* Travel, walking, cycling, practical arts and crafts of various kinds. *Address:* Manchester Jewish Museum, 190 Cheetham Hill Road, Manchester, M8 8LW(*tel:* 0161 834 9879; *fax:* 0161 832 7353).

WALLWORK, Barrington Barton, FIMgt

Group Chairman, John Wallwork Group Ltd. *b.* 11 October 1934; Marple, Cheshire. *m.* 1960 Sandra; two *s*. *Education:* William Hulme's Grammar School; Manchester University. *Societies:* South Caernarfonshire Yacht Club; Ski Club of GB; Heaton Moor Golf Club; Abersoch Golf Club. *Recreations, Interests:* Sailing, skiing. *Address:* John Wallwork Group Ltd, Trident House, Manchester Road, Altrincham *(tel:* 0161-927 7522); Five Leegate Gardens, Heaton Mersey, Stockport, Cheshire SK4 3NR *(tel:* 0161-432 7695).

WALLWORK, Geoffrey James, FCA(1965)

Chartered Accountant. *b.* 14 March 1941 Grappenhall, Warrington. *m.* 1967 Sheila Margaret Oakley; one *s*. two *d*. *Public Offices:* President, Manchester Society of Chartered Accountants (1990-91); Secretary to the Trustees, MGS Trust. *Education:* Boteler Grammar School, Warrington (1952-54); Manchester Grammar School (1954-59). *Career Profile:* Partner, Grant Thornton (1976-93); Sole Practitioner (1993-); Company Director. *Societies:* Member of various national, district and local committees of the Methodist Church. *Recreations, Interests:* DIY, gardening, photography, travel. *Address:* Higher Town Farmhouse, 4 Warwick Close, Knutsford, WA16 8NA *(tel:* 01565 634603).

WALSH, Professor Joan Eileen, MA,DPhil(Oxon),FIMA,CMath

Professor of Numerical Analysis, University of Manchester. *b.* 7 October 1932 Bromley, Kent. *Education:* Bromley High School; St Hilda's College, Oxford; Newnham College, Cambridge. *Career Profile:* Teacher, Howell's School, Denbigh (1954-57); Mathematician/Programmer, CEGB (1960-63); Lecturer, Reader, University of Manchester (1963-74); Research Fellow, Atlas Computer Laboratory, Chilton (1967-68). *Publications/Creative Work:* Publications in mathematical journals. *Societies:* Institute of Mathematics & Its Applications (Vice President, 1992-93); Manchester Literary & Philosophical Society (Vice President, 1994-95); Lansdowne Club, London. *Recreations, Interests:* Music, history. *Address:* Department of Mathematics, University of Manchester, Oxford Road, Manchester M13 9PL *(tel:* 0161 275 5806); 6 Beech Court, Willow Bank, Manchester, M14 6XN *(tel:* 0161 225 5155).

WALTON, David Storry, LLB Sheffield

Partner, Elliott & Company, Solicitors. *b.* 16 August 1956; Manchester. *Education:* Manchester Grammar School; Sheffield University. *Societies:* Manchester Law Society; Manchester Luncheon Club (President 1989-90); Halle Concerts Society. *Recreations, Interests:* Methodist Church and ecumenical activities, choral singing and theatre. *Address:* Elliott & Company, Centurion House, Deansgate, Manchester M3 3WT *(tel:* 0161-834 9933); 24 Ellesmere Road, Ellesmere Park, Eccles *(tel:* 0161-281 3973). *Additional Information:* Member, Council of Churches for Britain & Ireland Assembly.

WALTON, Denys Neville, Honorary Fellow, Manchester Metropolitan University,FCA

Retired. *b.* 26 August 1912; Hale, Cheshire. *m.* 1939 Dorothy Elizabeth Lees *decd* 1992; three *d*. ; *m.* 1995 Lorna Letitia Lees; one *stepd*. *Education:* Haileybury College. *War*
284

Service: Royal Artillery (1939-45). *Career Profile:* Partner in Chartered Accountants - Walton Watts & Co (1947-63), Thornton Baker (1963-77). *Societies:* Bowdon Cricket, Hockey & Squash Club (Past President); Manchester Luncheon Club (Past President); Manchester Society of Chartered Accountants (Past President). *Recreations, Interests:* Family, gardening. *Address:* 4 Church Court, Cecil Road, Hale, Altrincham, Cheshire WA15 9NT *(tel:* 0161-928 4173).

WANG, Zhidong

Consul General for China. *b.* Beijing, China. *m.* Liu Xiu Yun; two *s. Education:* Bejing Foreign Trade University (1964); China College of Foreign Affairs. *Address:* Consulate General of People's Republic of China, Denison House, 49 Denison Road, Rusholme, Manchester, M14 5RX.

WARBRICK, Colin, CBE, DL.

b. 15 July 1926; Salford. *m.* 1949 Florence Parker; one *s.* one *d. Public Offices:* Past Leader, Trafford Borough Coucil (Conservative); Past Director, Manchester Airport; Board Member, Trafford Park Development Corporation; Deputy Lieutenant (1983). *Education:* Salford Elementary and Salford Technical College. *War Service:* REME (1944-49). *Previous Positions:* Mayor, Stretford (1971-72); Charter Mayor, Trafford (1974-75). *Address:* 3 Cedar Drive, Urmston, Manchester M31 1HY *(tel:* 0161-747 7911).

WARD, John Hood, ISO (1977)

b. 16 December 1915 Gosforth, Newcastle upon Tyne. *m.* 1940 Gladys Hilda; one *s.* two *d. (widowed 1990) Public Offices:* Member, Supplementary Benefits Appeal Tribunal (1980-85). *Education:* Newcastle upon Tyne Royal Grammar School (1926-33). *Career Profile:* HM Civil Service (1934-78); Executive Officer, Ministry of Health, ultimately Senior Principal, Dept of Health & Social Security, Manchester. *Publications/Creative Work:* Poetry Collections: 'A Late Harvest' (1982); 'A Kind of Likeness'(1985); 'Grandfather Best and the Protestant Work Ethic'(1991); 'The Brilliance of Light'(1994); 'Winter Song'(1995); 'Selected Poems 1968-1995'(1996); Short stories: 'The Dark Sea' (1983); 'The Wrong Side of Glory'(1986); 'A Song at Twilight'(1989); 'Tales of Love and Hate'(1993). *Prizes:* A number of First Prizes in Open Poetry and Short Story competitions; (including the HE Bates Short Story Competition, 1988). *Societies:* Society of Civil Service Authors; Manchester Poets; Portico Library. *Recreations, Interests:* Reading, theatre, walking (within reason), member of the 'Off-the-Page' poetry group, attender at Manchester Buddhist Centre. *Address:* 42 Seal Road, Bramhall, Stockport, SK7 2JS *(tel:* 0161 439 3142).

WARHURST, Alan CBE(1990); BA(Hons)(Manchester,1950), MA(Hons)(Queens, Belfast, 1982),FSA(1953),FMA(1954)

Retired. *b.* 6 February 1927 Bolton, Lancs. *m.* 1953 Sheila Lilian Bradbury; one *s.* two *d. Public Offices:* Member, Museums & Galleries Commission (1994-); Chairman, North West Museum Service (1992-); President, Museums Association (1975-76); President, NW Federation Museums and Art Galleries (1978-79); Secretary, University Museums Group (1986-93); Chairman, Hulme Hall Committee, University of Manchester (1987-93).

Education: Canon Slade School, Bolton; University of Manchester (1945-46, 1948-50). *Military Service:* Commissioned Lancashire Fusiliers (1946-48). *Career Profile:* Director, Manchester Museum (1977-93); Director, Ulster Museum, Belfast (1970-77); Director, Bristol Museum (1960-70). *Publications/Creative Work:* Archaeological and museological publications in archaeological and museum publications. *Prizes:* Achieved 'Museum of the Year' Award for Manchester Museum (1987). *Societies:* Society of Antiquaries; Museums Association. *Recreations, Interests:* Archaeology, ceramics, tiles, museum architecture. *Address:* Calabar Cottage, Woodville Road, Altrincham, WA14 2AL *(tel:* 0161 928 0730).

WATSON, Geoffrey Herbert, BSc(Anatomy and Physiology),MB,ChB,FRCP,DCH

Consultant Paediatrician (retired), Royal Manchester Children's Hospital. *b.* 9 September 1920; Oldham. *m.* 1948 Marjorie Wright; one *s.* one *d. Education:* Werneth Council School, Oldham; Oldham Hulme Grammar School; Manchester University. *Military Service:* RNVR (1945-48). *Career Profile:* Resident Posts at Manchester Royal Infirmary and Royal Manchester Children's Hospital; Fellow, Cardiology, Toronto; Lecturer, Child Health, Manchester University. *Publications:* Articles in medical professional journals on paediatric and cardiological subjects. *Societies:* British Paediatric Association (Member of Council); British Cardiac Society; Association of European Paediatric Cardiologists; Manchester Literary & Philosophical Society; British Medical Association. *Recreations, Interests:* Music, hill walking, gardening. *Address:* Royal Manchester Children's Hospital, Pendlebury, Nr Manchester *(tel:* 0161-794 4696); 6 Shawdene Road, Northenden, Manchester M22 4BU *(tel:* 0161-998 2188).

WATSON, Peter Gordon, ACIS

Regional Director (England & Wales), Investor's Chronicle division of the Financial Times. *b.* 11 September 1943 Warrington. *m.* 1967 Joan; three *d. (marr. diss.);* *m.* 1995 Elaine. *Education:* Stockport Grammar School; Durham University. *Career Profile:* Company Secretary's Dept, Eagle Star Insurance Co Ltd (1966); Assistant Company Secretary, Freight Division, BET *plc* (1969); Guardian Manchester Evening News (1976-84); Investors' Chronicle (1984-). *Publications/Creative Work:* Written for a variety of publications. *Societies:* St James's Club, Manchester; First Friday Club. *Recreations, Interests:* Walking, cycling, gardening, reading, theatre. *Address:* Investors' Chronicle, International House, 82/86 Deansgate, Manchester, M3 2ER *(tel:* 0161 832 7661; *fax:* 0161 832 9249); 22 Windsor Avenue, Flixton, Manchester, M41 5GP *(tel:* 0161 747 4320). *Additional Information:* Promote Manchester vigorously. On the last Friday in September annually, the supplement 'Greater Manchester' is published; at 84 pages and 100,000 copies sold, it is the largest selling Supplement.

WEBB, Philip Ernest

Director, Butterfly Holdings plc. *b.* 25 April 1943; Prestbury, Cheshire. *m.* 1968 Gillian Elizabeth; one *s.* one *d. Education:* Altrincham Grammar School. *Career Profile:* Managing Director, Mynshul Bank plc; Director, ET Trust Ltd. *Prizes:* Paul Harris Fellowship. *Societies:* Rotary Club of Manchester; St James's Club; Bramhall Golf Club. *Recreations, Interests:* Golf, rotary, church. *Address:* Butterfly Holdings plc, Lavenham

Business Centre, Parsons Street, Oldham OL9 7AH *(tel:* 0161-628 7008); Chandlers Farm, Nether Alderley, nr Macclesfield, SK10 4TB *(tel:* 01625-861342).

WEBSTER, Anthony Michael, BA Oxford (1967),DipEd Oxford (1968)

Director of Education, Tameside MBC. *b.* 24 December 1944; Yorkshire. *m.* four *d. Education:* Heath Grammar School, Halifax; Merton College, Oxford. *Career Profile:* Assistant Education Officer, Cleveland County Council (1980-86); Deputy Director, Education, Gateshead MBC (1986-88). *Societies:* The Religious Society of Friends (Quakers); Society of Education Officers (President 1995-96). *Recreations, Interests:* Squash, sailing, jazz, literature. *Address:* Education Department, Tameside MBC, Council Offices, Ashton-under-Lyne, Tameside *(tel:* 0161-330 8355); The Shears, Carrhill Road, Mossley, Tameside *(tel:* 01457-833436).

WEDELL, Professor (Eberhard Arthur Otto) George, Dr(hc) Kazakstan (1994), Hon MEd Manchester(1968),BSc(Econ) London (1947),FRSA,FRTS, Chevalier de l'Ordre des Arts et des Lettres (France)(1989), Officer of the Order of Merit (Germany)(1991), Commander of the Order of Merit (Portugal)(1993)

Emeritus Professor of Communications Policy, University of Manchester (1982-); Vice-Chairman, European Institute for the Media (1993-). *b.* 4 April 1927; Dusseldorf. *m.* 1948 Rosemarie Winckler; three *s.* one *d. Public Offices:* Chairman, Wyndham Place Trust (1983-); Beatrice Hankey Foundation (1984-); Lord of the Manor of Clotton Hoofield, Cheshire. *Education:* Cranbrook School; London School of Economics. *Career Profile:* Ministry of Education (1950-58); Sec, Board for Social Responsibility, Nat Assembly of Church of England (1958-60); Dep Sec, ITA (1960-61), Secretary (1961-64); Prof of Adult Educn and Dir of Extra-Mural Studies, Manchester Univ (1964-75); Vis Prof of Employment Policy (1975-83); Senior Official, European Commn (1973-82); Professor of Communications Policy and Director-General, European Institute for the Media (1983-92); Contested (L) Greater Manchester West (1979) (L-SDP Alliance) Greater Manchester Central (1984), European Parliament elections; Chmn, British Liberals in EEC (1980-82); Vice-Pres, Greater Manchester Liberal Party (1984-88); Director, Royal Exchange Theatre Company (1968-88), now Honorary Member. *Publications:* 'The Use of Television in Education' (1963); 'Broadcasting and Public Policy' (1968); (with H D Perraton) 'Teaching at a Distance' (1968); (ed) 'Structures of Broadcasting' (1970); (with R Glatter) 'Study by Correspondence' (1971); 'Correspondence Education in Europe' (1971); 'Teachers and Educational Development in Cyprus' (1971); (ed) 'Education and the Development of Malawi' (1973); (with E Katz) 'Broadcasting in the Third World' (1977) (Nat Assoc of Educational Broadcasters of USA Book Award, 1978); (with G M Luyken and R Leonard) 'Mass Communications in Western Europe' (1985); (ed) 'Making Broadcasting Useful' (1986); (with G M Luyken) 'Media in Competition' (1986); (ed & contrib.) 'Europe 2000: What Kind of Television'(1988); (with Philip Crookes) 'Radio 2000'; (with R Rocholl) 'Vom Segen des Glaubens'(1995); general editor, Media Monographs (1985-93). *Societies:* Athenaeum; Fondation Universitaire (Brussels); St James', Manchester. *Recreations, Interests:* Gardening, theatre, reading. *Address:* 18 Cranmer Road, Manchester M20 6AW *(tel:* 0161-445 5106).

WELLAND, Professor Dennis Sydney Reginald, BA(London,1940),PhD(Nottingham, 1951), MA(Manchester,1968),LLD(hc) (Manchester,1992), FRSA

Emeritus Professor, University of Manchester. *b.* 21 December 1919 Hackney, London. *m.* 1942 Joan Eleanor Patterson; one *s. (widowed 1987) Public Offices:* Acting Vice-Chancellor, University of Manchester (1980-81); Chairman of Governors, Withington Girls' School (1987-95); Chairman, Contact Theatre Company (1984-); Hon Vice-President, Wilfred Owen Association (1992-). *Education:* Westcliff High School for Boys, Essex (1930-37); University College Nottingham (1937-40). *War Service:* Royal Artillery (1940-46), Commissioned 1941; Captain and Adjutant (1943-45), Staff Captain (1945-46), Combined Operations (May-October, 1945). *Career Profile:* Assistant/Lecturer/Senior Lecturer, English & American Literature, University of Nottingham (1947-62); Reader (1962-65), Professor of American Literature (1965-83), Pro-Vice-Chancellor (1979-83) University of Manchester; Taught at Indiana University, Bloomington (1968, 1989) and Amherst College, Mass. (1969). *Publications/Creative Work:* 'The Pre-Raphaelites in Literature and Art' (Harrap, 1953); 'Wilfred Owen: A Critical Study' (Chatto & Windus, 1960, 1978); 'Arthur Miller' (Oliver & Boyd, 1961) now 'Miller the Playwright' (Methuen); 'The USA: A Companion to American Studies' (Methuen, 1974, 1977, 1987); 'Mark Twain in England' (Chatto & Windus, 1978); 'The Life and Times of Mark Twain' (Studio Editions, 1991); Founder-Editor, Journal of American Studies (CUP, 1967-77); many essays, articles, etc. *Prizes:* Rockefeller Fellowships, University of Minnesota (1952-53), University of California, Berkeley (1963); Mellon Awards, Harry Ransom Humanities Research Center, University of Texas (1994,1996). *Societies:* Founder Treasurer, British Association of American Studies (1956-64), Chairman (1980-83). *Recreations, Interests:* Literature, theatre, travel. *Address:* The White Cottage, 188 Longhurst Lane, Mellor, Stockport, SK6 5PN (*tel:* 0161 427 1097).

WEST, Henry Cyrano, MBE(1995)

Former General Secretary, Greater Manchester Council for Voluntary Service (1975-91). *b.* 9 January 1928; Berlin. *m.* 1955 Janet Rose; three *s. Public Offices:*Councillor, Rochdale MBC; Chair, Middleton Township Committee; Chair Mersey Basin Trust; Vice-Chair, Hopwood Hall College. *Education:* Kings College, London. *Address:* 6 Kings Drive, Middleton, Manchester M24 4FB (*tel:*0161-643 4410; *fax:* 0161-643 4410); *e-mail:* henry-west@msn.com.)

WEST, Graeme Leonard

Head Coach, Wigan Rugby League Football Club. *b.* 5 December 1953 Hawera, New Zealand. *m.* 1973 Maryann; two *s.* one *d. Education:* Hawera Primary, Intermediate and Secondary Schools. *Career Profile:* New Zealand (1975-85); Player, Wigan RLFC (1982-88), A Team, 1st Team, Coach (1988-96). *Prizes:* New Zealand Player of the Year (1982); Coach of the Year (1994); Manager of the Year Sky Awards (1996). *Recreations, Interests:* Motor bike riding, coach young age group, rugby league.

WEST, Martin Graham, FCA

Chairman, London Scottish Bank plc. *b.* 7 November 1938 Bury, Lancashire. *m.* 1962 Jacqueline Allen; one *s.* two *d. Public Offices:* Councillor, High Legh Parish Council.

Education: Bury Grammar School. *Career Profile:* Chief Executive, London Scottish Bank plc (1988-95); Joint Managing Director (1987-88), Director (1976-87), London Scottish Finance Corp plc; Director, British Mail Order Corp plc (1973-76). *Societies:* St James' Club, Manchester. *Recreations, Interests:* Classic car restoration, bridge, philately. *Address:* London Scottish Bank plc, London Scottish House, 24 Mount Street, Manchester, M2 3LS(*tel:* 0161 834 2861; *fax:* 0161 834 2536).

WESTBROOK, Dennis Worsley

Solicitor. *b.* 19 January 1920; Leamington Spa, Warwickshire. *m.* 1948 Phyllis Mary Canham; one *s.* one *d.* *Education:* Dean Close School, Cheltenham; Manchester University. *War Service:* Friends' Ambulance Unit (1939-46); Friends' Relief Service (1946-48). *Societies:* Friends of Whitworth Gallery; Wine & Food Society; National Trust. *Recreations, Interests:* Music, reading, hill walking, squash. *Address:* Brookside Cottage, The Village, Prestbury SK10 4AL *(tel:* 01625-828641).

WESTMINSTER, The Duke of Gerald Cavendish KStJ (1991), GCLJ(1995),OBE(1995), TD(1994),DL(1982)

Director: Grosvenor Estate Holdings; Marcher Sound Ltd; North West Business Leadership Team; Sun Alliance Group plc; Sun Alliance and London Insurance plc; BRPL Pty Ltd (Australia); Sutton Ridge Pty Ltd; Director, The Countryside Movement (1995-). *b.* 22 December 1951 Northern Ireland. *m.* 1978 Natalia Ayesha Phillips; one *s.* three *d.* *Public Offices:* Chancellor, Manchester Metropolitan University; Chairman, Thomas Cubbitt Memorial Trust; Chairman, Falcon Trust; Chairman, The Grosvenor Estate; Chairman, Habitat Research Trust; Chairman, Royal Agricultural Society of the Commonwealth; Chairman, TSB Foundation of England and Wales; Chairman, Westminster Foundation; Chairman, Nuffield Trust for the Forces of the Crown; Trustee, Westminster Abbey Trust. *Education:* Sunningdale School; Harrow. *Military Service:* Joined Queen's Own Yeomanry (1970); Commissioned (1973); Promoted to Captain (1979); Promoted to Major (1985); Promoted to Lieutenant Colonel (1992); Promoted to Colonel (1995); Colonel-in-Cheif, Royal Westminster Regiment, Vancouver, Canada. *Career Profile:* Travelled abroad, working in Canada, America, New Zealand and Australia. Returned to England, joined John D Wood, Estate Agents, for two years, prior to becoming a Trustee of The Grosvenor Estate. Previously Director: Business in the Community (1988-92); Claridges (1981-92); Harland & Wolff (1984-87). *Societies:* Patron of over 70 organisations and President of some 60 organisations including: Arthritis Care, British Limbless Ex-Servicemen's Association, British Association for Shooting and Conservation, The Game Conservancy, Royal National Institute for the Blind, SCOPE (formerly The Spastics Society) and Youth Clubs UK. *Clubs:* Australian Club; British Deer Society; Brookes; Cavalry and Guards Club; Chester Business Club; Chester City Club; Chester Lions Club; Downhurst Club; Hon Officers' Assn of British Columbia; MCC; Nairobi Safari Club; Pitt Club; Rotary Club of Chester; Royal Green Jackets Club; Royal Yacht Squadron (Cowes); St James's Club; Tarporley Hunt Club; Vancouver Club, Canada. *Recreations, Interests:* Shooting, fishing, scuba diving.

WEWER, Christian, BA (Hons),BArch,RIBA

Joint Founding Partner, Architects Group Practice; Honorary Consul for Denmark. *b.* 1

November 1948; Taulov, Denmark. *m.* 1973 Dian; three *s. Education:* Epsom College; Manchester University. *Societies:* St James's Club; Davenport Rugby Football Club; Manchester Consular Association. *Recreations, Interests:* Sailing, squash, travel. *Address:* Architects Group Practice, Queen's Chambers, 5 John Dalton Street, Manchester M2 6FT *(tel:* 0161-835 1901); Garden House, 2 Pleasant Way, Cheadle Hulme, Cheshire SK8 7PF *(tel:* 0161-439 5500).

WHATNALL, John Michael, BA Oxford (1978),MA Oxford (1981)

Partner, Halliwell Landau. *b.* 22 June 1957; Manchester. *Societies:* Wagner Society, Friends of Covent Garden. *Recreations, Interests:* Opera, music. *Address:* Halliwell Landau, St James's Court, Brown Street, Manchester M2 2JF *(tel:* 0161-835 3003).

WHIBLEY, John Adrian, AGSM(Distinction)

Artistic Director & Deputy Chief Executive Hallé Orchestra. *b.* 11 May 1945 Maidstone, Kent. *m.* 1967 Helen; five *s.* two *d. Education:* Worthing Grammar School; Dartington College of Arts; Guildhall School of Music and Drama. *Career Profile:* Hallé Cellist (1967-72); General Manager, Manchester Camerata (1975-96); Artistic Director, Hallé Orchestra (1996-). *Recreations, Interests:* Long distance running and cycling. *Address:* Hallé Concerts Society, The Bridgewater Hall, Manchester, M2 3WS *(tel:* 0161 237 7000; *fax:* 0161 237 7029).

WHITE, Alan, LLB,FCA

Group Finance Director, N Brown Group plc. *b.* 15 April 1955 Salford. *m.* 1979 Helen Margaret; one *s.* one *d. Education:* Salford Grammar School; Warwick University. *Career Profile:* Arthur Andersen (1976-79); General Manager, Finance, Sharp Electronics (UK) Ltd (1979-85); Company Secretary (1985-88), Finance Director (1988-), N Brown Group plc. *Societies:* Manchester Society of Chartered Accountants; Alderley Edge Cricket Club. *Recreations, Interests:* Watching Manchester United, playing squash and tennis, skiing, water skiing. *Address:* N Brown Group plc, 53 Dale Street, Manchester, M60 6ES *(tel:* 0161 236 8256; *fax:* 0161 238 2308).

WHITE, Frank Richard, JP

Director Training and Education, GMB National College Manchester. *b.* 11 November 1939; Eccles. *m.* 1967 Eileen; two *s.* one *d. Public Offices:* Member, Bolton CBC (1963-74), Greater Manchester CC (1973-75); MP, Bury and Radcliffe (1974-83); Parliamentary Private Secretary, Dept Industry (1975-76); Government Whip (1976-79); Opposition Spokesman, Church Affairs Opposition Whip (1979-83); Bolton MDC (1986-90)(1994-); JP (1968); Chairman of Bench (1992-94); Director, Lancashire Co-operative Development Agency; Director, European Foundation; Director, Bolton/Bury TEC; Member, United Norwest Cooperatives Area Committee. *Education:* Bolton Technical College; Bolton Institute of Higher Education. *Career Profile:* Managing Director, E Wrigley (Printers) Ltd; Industrial Relations Manager, Brown & Polson Ltd; Work Study Officer, CWS Ltd, Littlewoods Ltd, British Aerospace Ltd; Fellow, Bolton Institute. *Societies:* President, Bolton United Services Veterans Assoc; Trustee, Tonge Ward Labour Club. *Recreations,*

Interests: History, hill walking, sport , former football referee and boxer. *Address:* GMB National College, College Road, Whalley Range, Manchester M16 8BP *(tel:* 0161-861 8788); 4 Ashdown Drive, Firwood Fold, Bolton BL2 3AX *(tel:* 01204 58547).

WHITE, Malcolm George, FCIOB,MBIM

Managing Director, The White Group plc; Director, The Fulcrum Property Development Company Ltd. *b.* 31 August 1945 Salford. *m.* 1969 Jean; one *s.* one *d. Public Offices:* Chairman, Swinton RL Club plc. *Education:* Salford Grammar School; Bolton Institute of Technology. *Career Profile:* Shepherd Construction (1968-74); Managing Director, Jackson Construction (1974-94). *Recreations, Interests:* Rugby league, horses, travel, water skiing, my children, dogs, snow skiing, reading. *Address:* St Peters Court, 8 Trumpet Street, Manchester, M1 5LW*(tel:* 0161 839 7212; *fax:* 0161 839 7414).

WHITEHEAD, Allan Graham, FCA

Partner, Mitchell Charlesworth, Chartered Accountants. *b.* 24 December 1948 Leicester. *m.* 1980 Anna; one *s.* one *d. Public Offices:* Chairman, Groundwork (Salford & Trafford); Chairman, Moss Side & Hulme Business Federation Ltd; Director & Treasurer, Contact Theatre. *Education:* Alderman Newton School, Leicester; Manchester Grammar School. *Career Profile:* Partner, Mitchell Charlesworth (1992-); Partner, Moores Rowland (1990-91); Partner, Bouchier & Co (1982-90); Manager, Deloitte Haskins & Sells (1973-82). *Societies:* Portico Library; Statistical Society; St James Club. *Recreations, Interests:* Music, drama & plays, reading. *Address:* Mitchell Charlesworth, Fontain Court, 68 Fountain Street, Manchester, M2 2FB *(tel:* 0161 228 7883; *fax:* 0161 236 3268); 27 North Drive, High Legh, Knutsford, WA16 6LX *(tel:* 01925 752195).

WHITEHEAD, Anthony, BA(Hons) Manchester (1948),AIL(Italian)(1994)

Retired Schoolmaster; Hon Secretary, Quarry Bank Mill Trust Ltd, Styal. *b.* 29 August 1924; Stockport. *m.* 1951 Betty Holden. *Education:* William Hulme's Grammar School, Manchester; University of Manchester; University of Nottingham. *War Service:* Navigator RAF (1943-46). *Career Profile:* Deputy Headmaster, Queen Elizabeth's Senior High School, Middleton. *Prizes:* Queen's Silver Jubilee Medal (1977). *Societies:* Chorlton-cum-Hardy (now Didsbury Northern) Hockey Club; Northern Lawn Tennis Club; Middleton Musical Society. *Recreations, Interests:* Archaeology, hill walking, hockey, squash. *Address:* 9 Thurleigh Road, Didsbury, Manchester M20 2DF *(tel:* 0161-445 5876).

WHITEHOUSE, Carl Raymond, MA (1964) MB (1964) BChir (1963) Cambridge,FRCGP (1985)

Professor of Teaching Medicine in the Community, University of Manchester. *b.* 31 August 1938; Harrow, Middx. *m.* 1967 Rachel Miriam; two *s.* one *d. Education:* Canford School, Dorset; Christ's College, Cambridge; St George's Hospital Medical School, London. *Previous Positions:* Medical Officer, Zambia Flying Doctor Service; Hospital posts in London, Weymouth, Dorchester; Principal in General Medical Practice, Lewes, E Sussex (1969-78); Lecturer & Senior Lecturer, University of Manchester (1978-95). *Publications:* 'Families on the Way?' (Scripture Union, 1989); articles on minor illness and

psychological problems and effects of distance from surgery in 'British Medical Journal' and 'Journal of Royal College of General Practitioners'; articles on Health Service in 'Third Way' and 'Journal of Christian Med Fellowship'. *Prizes:* Late Scholar, Christ's College, Cambridge; Brackenbury Prize in Medicine, St George's Hosp, London. *Societies:* British Medical Association; Royal College of General Practitioners; Manchester Medical Society. *Recreations, Interests:* Reader, Holy Trinity (Platt) Parish Church, gardening, walking. *Address:* Robert Darbishire Practice, Rusholme Health Centre, Walmer Street, Manchester M14 5NP *(tel:* 0161-225 6699); 12 St Brannocks Road, Chorlton-cum-Hardy, Manchester M21 0UP.

WHITTAKER, David Anthony, JP,AIB

Director, North West Region of Barclays Bank plc. *b.* 5 November 1941; Ramsbottom, Lancashire. *m.* 1968 Rita Margaret Pickstone; one *s.* two *d. Education:* Bury Grammar School. *Societies:* Manchester Literary & Philosophical Society. *Address:* Barclays Bank plc, PO Box 357, 51 Mosley Street, Manchester M60 2AU *(tel:* 0161-228 3322); Elton Bank, Birkdale Drive, Bury BL8 2SG *(tel:* 0161-764 0819).

WHITTLE, Roy, MA(Cantab),MPhil,PGCE

Principal, South College, Bolton. *b.* 3 December 1948 Preston. *m.* 1970 Carol; one *s.* one *d. Public Offices:* Chairman of Governors, Greenfield CP, Oldham. *Education:* Walton-le-Dale HS (1960-67); Clare College, Cambridge (1967-71); University of Manchester (1986-88). *Career Profile:* Blackpool Grammar School (1970-74); Hathershaw High School, Oldham (1974-75); Hyde Sixth Form College (1976-88); South College, Bolton (1988-); Assistant Chairman, Examiners NEAB. *Publications/Creative Work:* 'Early Leaving in Post-16 Education' (article in Education, 1989). *Recreations, Interests:* Sport, church, education, local politics. *Address:* South College, Lever Edge Lane, Bolton, BL3 3HH *(tel:* 01204 62524; *fax:* 01204 660218).

WILCOX, Paula

Actor. *b.* Manchester. *m.* Derek Seaton; *(widowed)*; *m.* 1991 Nelson Riddle Jr; one *steps.* two *stepd. Education:* Joined National Youth Theatre while still at school. *Career Profile:* A wide variety of stage and TV roles in plays and musicals in the National Theatre, Bristol Old Vic, BBC, ITV and Channel 4, including tours to Australia and Moscow. *Societies:* Council Member and active fund raiser for National Youth Theatre. *Recreations, Interests:* Swimming, tennis, gentle keep fit, skiing, life long supporter of Manchester United. *Address:* c/o Ms Sue Latimer, William Morris Agency Ltd, 31-31 Soho Square, London, W1V 6HH *(tel:* 0171 434 2191; *fax:* 0171 437 0238).

WILKINSON, David Lloyd, CSD,ACIS

Chief Executive & General Secretary, Cooperative Union Ltd. *b.* 28 May 1937 Huddersfield. *m.* 1960 Cora Ellen; one *s.* one *d. Education:* Royds Hall Grammar; Cooperative College. *Address:* Cooperative Union Ltd, Holyoake House, Hanover Street, Manchester, M60 0AS *(tel:* 0161 832 4300; *fax:* 0161 831 7684).

WILKINSON, Derek Harry, NDD (1950),ATD (1951)

Artist Free-Lance. *b.* 24 November 1929; Halifax, Yorks. *m.* Mary Elizabeth; one *s.* one *d. Education:* Palatine Secondary School, Blackpool (1941-46); Tech College & School of Art, Blackpool (1946-50); Manchester College of Art (1950-51). *Military Service:* National Service, Royal Army Education Corps (1951-53). *Previous Positions:* Senior Lecturer, Dept of Art & Design, Stockport College of Technology. *Creative Works:* Artist/Printmaker (Etcher); one man shows in London, Manchester, Sheffield, Preston, Derby regularly since 1960; studio and printmaking workshop at home; work in public and private collections in UK, USA, Canada, Australia, N Zealand, Japan, Holland, France, Germany, Ireland, etc. *Societies:* Manchester Academy of Fine Art. *Recreations, Interests:* Walking, cycling, looking at buildings, listening to music especially chamber music and opera. *Address:* 206 Bramhall Lane South, Bramhall, Stockport SK7 3AA *(tel:* 0161-439 1117).

WILKINSON, Donald John, MA Oxford (1976),MLitt Oxford (1982),FRSA

Headmaster, Cheadle Hulme School. *b.* 14 February 1955; Irvine, Ayrshire. *m.* 1979 Janet Margaret; one *s.* one *d. Education:* The Royal Grammar School, Lancaster (1966-73); Keble College, Oxford (1973-79). *Career Profile:* Assistant Master, Manchester Grammar School (1979-84); Head of History, Oakham School (1984-86); Head of Sixth Form, Newcastle-under-Lyme School (1987-89). *Publications:* (with J A Cantrell) 'The Normans in Britain' (Macmillan, 1987); articles on seventeenth century English history. *Prizes:* Open Exhibition in Modern History, Keble College (1973-76); Open Senior Scholarship, Keble College (1977-79). *Recreations, Interests:* Sport, especially cricket and running, walking, theatre. *Address:* Cheadle Hulme School, Cheadle Hulme, Cheadle, Cheshire SK8 6EF *(tel:* 0161-485 4142).

WILKINSON, Jeremy Squire, MA,LLM (Cantab)

Solicitor, Consultant, Addleshaw, Sons & Latham. *b.* 4 June 1936; Wilmslow, Cheshire. *m.* 1962 Alison Margaret Isaac; one *s.* one *d. Public Offices:* Board Member: Cheadle Royal Hospital, Talyllyn Railway Preservation Society. *Education:* Terra Nova School; Rugby School; Selwyn College, Cambridge. *Military Service:* Royal Signals (National Service). *Publications:* Articles on Welsh mines, quarries and railways. *Societies:* Welsh Mines Society; Northern Mines Research Society; Talyllyn Railway Preservation Society; Manchester Luncheon Club. *Recreations, Interests:* Industrial archaeology, music. *Address:* 3 Old Orchard, Wilmslow, Cheshire SK9 5DH *(tel:* 01625-524535).

WILKINSON, Joan (*née* Wolstencroft), ARMCM(1948)

Retired, Professional Musician. *b.* 7 December 1928 Leigh, Lancashire. *m.* 1960 Martin Thomas Wilmot Wilkinson. *Education:* Leigh Girls' Grammar School (Scholarship); Royal Manchester College of Music (Manchester City Council Scholarship). *Career Profile:* Viola Player in: Scottish Orchestra (1948-50); BBC Symphony Orchestra (1950-64); London Philharmonic Orchestra (1966-72); Free Lance Player, SW England (1973-87); Founder and Hon Artistic Director, Devizes Arts Festival (1980-85); Hon Sec, Manchester Chamber Concerts Society (1987-94); Publicity Officer, Manchester Chamber Concerts Society

(1994-); Regional Representative (M/c), Friends of the Musicians' Benevolent Fund; Member, NW Regional Committee of National Federation of Music Societies (1988-); Music Adviser, North West Arts Board (1992-94). *Publications/Creative Work:* Organiser of a publication to celebrate the Diamond Jubilee (1936-96) of the Manchester Chamber Concerts Society. *Prizes:* Gold Card Member, Musicians' Union (Manchester Branch)(1994). *Societies:* Elgar Society; Dvorak Society; Alan Rawsthorne Society Committee Member; Amateur Chamber Music Players Inc; Wilmslow Symphony Orchestra; Wilmslow Historical Society; National Trust; Parkinson's Disease Society; Manchester Chamber Concerts Society; Friends of the Musicians' Benevolent Fund; Friends of Tabley; Friends of the William Byrd Singers (Manchester); Friends of the Royal Northern College of Music. *Recreations, Interests:* Playing chamber music with friends, travelling, gardening, walking, swimming, watching golf and cricket on TV, reading biographies. *Address:* Calinda, 14 Overhill Lane, Wilmslow, SK9 2BG *(tel:* 01625 530895).

WILKINSON, John Arthur

Chairman, Managing Director, Wilkinson Corporation Ltd. *b.* 4 February 1945 Walkden, Manchester. *m.* 1966 Elaine M; one *s.* one *d. Education:* Walkden High School. *Career Profile:* Qualified Radio & TV Engineer; Service Engineer, Welding Equipment; From redundancy (1971) formed own companies now employing 240 people. *Societies:* Chairman, Salford Rugby League Club; Chairman, Chairmans Association, The Rugby Football League. *Recreations, Interests:* Sports. *Address:* Wilkinson Corporation Ltd, The Emiliano Generali Building, Priestley Road, Wardley Industrial Estate, Worsley, M28 2NZ *(tel:* 0161 793 8127; *fax:* 0161 727 8297).

WILKINSON, John Frederick, DSc (Hon) Bradford (1976); FRCP London,MD Manchester, MB,ChB,BSc (Hons Chem),MSc,PhD (Manchester),CChem,FRSC (London)

Consulting Physician in Private Practice. *b.* 10 June 1897; Oldham. *m.* 1964 Marion Crossfield *(sep. 1995). Education:* Arnold School, Blackpool; University of Manchester (Science); Manchester School of Medicine. *War Service:* RNAS, RN (Chemical Warfare) (1916-19); NW Regional Transfusion and Resuscitation Officer (1939-46); Chairman, Clinical Research Panel of Chemical Factories Medical Sub-committee of Ministry of Supply (1939-47). *Career Profile:* Director, Department of Clinical Investigations and Research, Department of Haematology, Manchester Royal Infirmary and University; Consulting Physician, United Manchester Hospitals. *Publications:* Numerous (c. 500) scientific and medical publications (1920-); papers on travel, antiques, apothecaries drug jars and scouting. *Prizes:* Graduate Chemical Research Scholarship (Manchester 1920); John Dalton Research Fellowship (Manchester 1921); Sir Clement Royd's Chemical Research Fellowship (Manchester 1921-24); Sydney Renshaw Physiological Prizeman (Manchester 1924); Gold Medal Award for Medical Research (1931); Oliver Shapley Lecturer, Royal College of Physicians (London 1948); Liveryman of the Worshipful Society of Apothecaries (London); Freeman of the City of London (1949); Samuel Gee Lecturer, Royal College of Physicians (London 1977); Osler Lecturer, Worshipful Society of Apothecaries (London 1981). *Societies:* Formerly President and Life Councillor of International, European and British Haematological Societies; Co-founder and formerly President of Manchester Medico-Legal Society; formerly President, Hon Fellow and Hon

294

Editor of the Manchester Medical Society; Savage and Lansdowne Clubs, London. *Recreations, Interests:* Author and Lecturer, science, medicine, antiques, aviation, scouting, zoos. *Address:* 1 Old Hall Cottage, Hall Lane, Mobberley, Knutsford, Cheshire WA16 7JF *(tel:* 01565-872111).

WILKINSON, Stephen Austin, MA(Cantab,1947), MusB(Cantab,1947), MA(hc) (Manchester,1982)

Conductor, William Byrd Singers of Manchester & Capriccio. *b.* 29 April 1919; Eversden, Cambs. *Education:* Christ Church Cathedral Choir School, Oxford (1927-32); St Edward's School, Oxford (1932-37); Queens' College, Cambridge (1937-40 and 1946-47). *War Service:* RNVR Mine Disposal Officer (1941-43); Enemy Mining Staff (1943-46). *Career Profile:* Director, Herts Rural Music School (1947-53); Music Producer, BBC (1953-79); Conductor, BBC Northern Singers (1954-91). *Creative Works:* Various choral compositions, e.g. 'That Time of Year', 'Dover Beach', 'A Phoenix Hour' 'Betjeman's Bells', 'Some Psalms', 'Grass Roots', 'On Such a Day', 'Echos d'Ecosse'. *Publications:* Numerous choral arrangements published by Novello, OUP, Roberton. *Recreations, Interests:* Family life, literature, walking.

WILLAN, Robert Matthew, FCIOB,FFB,FRSH,FBIM

Chairman, Willan Group. *b.* 16 October 1922; Thames-Ditton. *m.* 1947 Madge Baldrey; one *s.* one *d.* *Public Offices:* Borough of Sale Councillor (1947-59); National President, House Builders' Federation (1975); National President, National Federation of Builders, Trade Employers (BEC) (1976-77); National Chairman, Home Improvement Council (1978 -79); Member, GMC RB (1986-89). *Education:* Manchester Grammar School; Royal Military College. *War Service:* Inns of Court Regt; King's Dragoon Guards (Overseas) (1942-46). *Prizes:* Freeman City of London. *Societies:* Cavalry & Guards Club, London. *Recreations, Interests:* Golf, rugby, fishing, travel and music. *Address:* 2 Brooklands Road, Sale, Cheshire M33 3SS *(tel:* 0161-973 1234).

WILLIAMS, Revd Canon Michael Joseph, BA (1968)

Principal, Northern Ordination Course. *b.* 26 February 1942 West Bromwich. *m.* 1971 Mary Miranda Bayley; one *s.* one *d.* *Education:* West Bromwich Technical School; West Bromwich Technical College; University of Durham. *Career Profile:* Toxteth Team Ministry, Diocese of Liverpool, Curate (1970), Team Vicar (1975); Director of Pastoral Studies, St John's College, Durham (1978-89). *Publications/Creative Work:* 'The Power and the Kingdom' (Monarch). *Societies:* Member, Society for the Study of Christian Ethics. *Recreations, Interests:* Cabinet making, hill walking. *Address:* Northern Ordination Course, Luther King House, Brighton Grove, Rusholme, Manchester, M14 5JP(*tel:* 0161 225 6668; *fax:* 0161 248 9201; *e-mail*: office@noc1.u-net.com); 75 Framingham Road, Brooklands, Sale, Cheshire, M33 3RH (*tel:* 0161 962 7513; *e-mail:* mike@noc2.u-net.com).

WILLIAMS, Patrick, BA(Music)(Hons)

Librarian, Hallé Orchestra and Choir. *b.* 23 October 1968 Croydon. *Education:* Alleyn's

School, Dulwich; University of Liverpool (1987-90). *Career Profile:* Librarian, Hallé Orchestra and Choir (1992-); previously Assistant Librarian, RLPO; Active conductor - Principal Conductor, South Cheshire Orchestra, Oriel Singers. *Prizes:* University of Liverpool: Rushworths Music Prize, Alsop Music Prize. *Societies:* Wimbledon FC; Surrey CCC. *Recreations, Interests:* Cricket, travel, football, current affairs, badminton. *Address:* Hallé Concerts Society, Bridgewater Hall, Manchester, M2 3WS (*tel:* 0161 237 7007; *fax:* 0161 237 7029).

WILLIE, Rev David F, MA(Cantab)(1968)

Chairman, Manchester and Stockport District of the Methodist Church. *b.* 25 July 1939 York. *m.* 1965 Daphne; two *s.* one *d.* *Education:* Jarrow Grammar School (1950-57); University of Cambridge (1962-65). *Career Profile:* Civil Service (1958-62); Methodist Minister (1965-). *Recreations, Interests:* Football, cricket, gardening, walking. *Address:* 15 Woodlands Road, Handforth, Wilmslow, SK9 3AW (*tel:* 01625 523480).

WILLINK, Alma Marion (*née* Chignell), DL Greater Manchester (1981); MA (Hon) Manchester (1964)

b. 30 October 1909; Chester. *m.* 1930 Francis Arthur Willink; *(w/dowed 1973) Education:* Withington Girls School, Manchester. *Career Profile:* Manchester City Bench (1945-79), Dep Chairman (1976-77), Chairman (1978-79); Governor, Manchester High School for Girls (1974-); Committee Family Welfare Association of Manchester (1932-). *Societies:* Manchester Luncheon Club (President 1984-85); Manchester Literary & Philosophical Society; Hallé Concerts Society. *Recreations, Interests:* Theatre, music, travel. *Address:* 141 The Green, Worsley, Manchester M28 2PA.

WILLIS-FEAR, Michael John Willis, BA Durham (1958),MA Durham (1970)

Hon Secretary, Film & Sound Group, Society of Archivists (1992-). *b.* 26 April 1935; Eastbourne, Sussex. *m.* 1972 Rosamund Mary Worrall. *Education:* Cranleigh School, Cranleigh, Surrey (1948-52); Sir Andrew Judd Grammar School, Tonbridge, Kent (1952-54); Kings College, Newcastle-upon-Tyne; Durham University (1954-58). *Military Service:* National Service, Royal Army Pay Corps (1958-60). *Career Profile:* Office Adminstrator, Cabrelli & La Mattina Ltd (1985-91); County Archivist, Greater Manchester Council (1976-84); Archivist in Charge, Pembrokeshire Record Office (1974-76); City & Diocesan Archivist, Portsmouth (1965-74); Acting City Archivist, Newcastle-upon-Tyne (1964-65); Assistant Archivist, Newcastle City Record Office (1962-63); Assistant Youth Employment Officer, Newcastle (1960-62). *Publications:* Various periodical articles on archives. *Prizes:* Organ Scholarship, Cranleigh School (1948). *Societies:* Salford Choral Society; National Trust; Society for Nautical Research; British Records Association; Society of Archivists; Business Archives Council (Executive Committee 1975-85); Chetham Society (Council 1979-); Lancs & Cheshire Antiquarian Society; Manchester Organists Association; Northern Mill Engine Society; Royal Commonwealth Society; Portico Library; Durham University Society (Hon Sec, NW Branch). *Recreations, Interests:* History of railways and industrial technology, local history, collecting Goss China and Mauchline ware, classical music, singing swimming, cooking, cycling. *Address:* 4 Albert Road, Heaton Moor, Stockport SK4 4EQ

WILLMOTT, Professor John Charles, CBE (1983); ARCS Imperial College (1942),BSc London (1943),PhD London (1949),FInstP

Consultant to DTI on Nuclear Fusion; Member, Science for Stability Steering Group, NATO. *b.* 1 April 1922; Goodmayes, Essex. *m.* 1952 Sheila Madeleine Dumbell; two *s.* one *d. Public Offices:* Pro-Vice Chancellor (1982-85); Member of Council of SERC (1978-82). *Education:* Bancroft's School, Woodford, Essex (1933-40). *War Service:* REME (1942-46). *Previous Positions:* Lecturer, Senior Lecturer, Reader, Liverpool University (1948-64); Professor of Nuclear Structure, Manchester (1964-89); Director of the Physical Laboratories (1967-89). *Publications:* Nuclear Structure Physics (papers); 'Atomic Physics' (J Wiley). *Societies:* Manchester Literary & Philosophical Soc. *Recreations, Interests:* Walking. *Address:* 37 Hall Moss Lane, Bramhall, Stockport SK7 1RB *(tel:* 0161-439 4169).

WILMOT, David, DL,QPM(1989); BSc(1970)

Chief Constable, Greater Manchester Police. *b.* 12 March 1943 Fleetwood, Lancashire. *m.* Ann. *Education:* Baines Grammar School, Poulton-le-Fylde; Southampton University. *Career Profile:* Constable (1962), Sargeant (1967), Inspector (1969), Lancashire Constabulary; Chief Inspector (1974), Superintendent (1977), Chief Superintendent (1981), Merseyside Police; Assistant Chief Constable (1983), Deputy Chief Constable (1985), West Yorkshire Police; Deputy Chief Constable (1987), Chief Constable (1991), Greater Manchester Police. *Societies:* International Association of Chief Constables. *Recreations, Interests:* Reading, gardening. *Address:* Greater Manchester Police, PO Box 22 (S West PDO), Chester House, Boyer Street, Manchester, M16 0RE*(tel:* 0161 872 5050; *fax:* 0161 856 2666/1506).

WILSON, Anthony, BA(Hons),MA(Cantab)

Journalist, Granada TV; CEO, Factory Too Records; Director in the City; Co-ordinator, Universal Machine. *b.* 20 February 1950 Salford. *m.* one *s.* one *d. Public Offices:* Board of Manchester Museum of Science & Industry; Board of The Green Room, Manchester Science Park, City Pride. *Education:* St Mary's, Marple Bridge; De La Salle, Salford; Jesus College, Cambridge; ITN, London. *Career Profile:* Journalist and then hanging out with very creative people. *Publications/Creative Work:* Long Story. *Prizes:* The Glittering Prizes. *Societies:* The Hacienda. *Recreations, Interests:* Windsurfing but I don't have time.

WILSON, David Geoffrey, OBE (1986),DL Greater Manchester (1985), MA(hc) Manchester (1983), MA(hc) Salford (1995), Kt of the Order of the Falcon (Iceland)(1992); FCIB,FBIM

Chairman, North West Manchester Healthcare NHS Trust; Manchester Business Link. *b.* 30 April 1933; Urmston, Manchester. *m.* 1980 Dianne Elizabeth. *Public Offices:* High Sheriff of Greater Manchester (1991-92); President, MCCI (1978-80), Manchester Literary & Philosophical Society (1981-83); Hon Consul for Iceland (1981-); Treasurer, Hallé Concerts Society (1986-92), Deputy Chairman (1992-); Deputy Chairman, Manchester Diocesan Board of Finance; Member of Council, Salford University; Member of Court, University of Manchester; Chairman,Manchester Post Office Advisory Committee; Vice

President, St Ann's Hospice (Treasurer 1975-91). *Education:* Leeds Grammar School; Hulme Grammar School, Oldham. *Military Service:* National Service: Territorial Army (The Manchester Regiment). *Career Profile:* Banking: Williams Deacon's Bank (1953-70),Secretary (1965-70); Williams & Glyn's Bank (1970-82), Secretary (1970-72), Manager, Mosley Street Branch (Manchester)(1973-77), Area Manager (1978-82). Regional Director, National Enterprise Board (1982-85); Regional Director, British Linen Bank (1985-91). *Societies:* St James's Club (Manchester); MCC; Lancashire County Cricket Club. *Recreations, Interests:* Gardening, music. *Address:* North Manchester Healthcare NHS Trust, Delaunays Road, Crumpsall, Manchester M8 5RL (*tel:* 0161 740 9942; *fax:* 0161 720 2834); 28 Macclesfield Road, Wilmslow, Cheshire SK9 2AF (*tel:* 01625-524133; *fax:* 01625-520605).

WILSON, Dianne Elizabeth (*née* Morgan)

Hon Secretary, Manchester Literary & Philosophical Society. *b.* 30 April 1937; Margate, Kent. *m.* 1980 David Geoffrey Wilson. *Public Offices:* Elected Councillor, Macclesfield BC (1984-96); Chairman of Governors, Wilmslow High School (1988-95); Chairman, Friends of the Hallé. *Education:* Dore High School, Sheffield; Chesterfield College of Art; London School of Fashion. *Career Profile:* Management Trainee, Lewis's (Manchester); Buyer, William Timpson (Shoes) Ltd; Town Centre Co-ordinator, Wilmslow. *Societies:* Manchester Literary & Philosophical Society. *Recreations, Interests:* People, making things happen. *Tel:* 01625-524133; *fax:* 01625-520605.

WILSON, Keith Dudley

Media and Music Educator; Director, International Media Centre and Dean, Faculty of Media, Music & Performance, Salford University. *b.* 13 July 1936 Windermere. *Public Offices:* Chair, Aspects Theatre, Adelphi Productions (IMC); Director, Television from the Regions National Conference (annual)(1993); Founder, Central and Eastern European Fellowships in Broadcasting (an EEC democracy programme). *Education:* Heversham; King's College, Cambridge. *Career Profile:* British Council Lecturer, Zagreb University (Croatia)(1957-58); Associate Professor, Tehran University & Director 'English by TV' (1958-64); Reader, Osmania University, Hyderabad (1964-66); Salford College: Head of Liberal Education (1967-72), Head of Humanities (1972-85); Head of Performing Arts & Media (1985-90); Director, Centre for Media, Performance & Communications, University College Salford (1990-96); Founding Director, International Media Centre (1994-), Dean, Faculty of Media, Music & Performance, Salford University (1996-). *Creative Work:* Established over 20 innovative and national market leader courses in band musicianship; popular music and recording; music, acoustics & recording; media production; media performance; media, language & business; media technology. *Societies:* Fellow, Royal Society of Arts; City Pride, Salford's millennium Lowry Centre for Creative & Performing Arts & National Industrial Virtual Reality. *Interests:* Nordic lands and culture, Lakeland, wines of Chile, inner city cultural renewal. *Address:* International Media Centre, Adelphi House, The Crescent, Salford, M3 6EN (*tel:* 0161 834 6633; *fax:* 0161 834 0699). *Additional Information:* Founded Salford University's now world famous performance groups; brass band, wind band, big band, jazz ensembles, Soundworks, Groove Machine and toured to Holland, Belgium, Germany, Iceland, Denmark, Greece, Norway, Ecuador and Brazil. Annual residences at Edinburgh Festival with Aspects Theatre (1985-95).

WILSON, Professor Nairn Hutchinson Fulton, BDS(Edinburgh,1973),MSc(Manchester, 1979),PhD(Manchester,1985),FDS, RCS.Ed(1977),DRD, RCS. Ed(1980)

Professor of Restorative Dentistry, University of Manchester (1986-); Hon Consultant in Restorative Dentistry, Central Manchester Healthcare (NHS) Trust (1982-); Dean, Faculty of Dental Surgery, Royal College of Surgeons, Edinburgh (1995-); Editor, Journal of Dentistry (1986-). *b.* 26 April 1950 Kilmarnock, Scotland. *m.* 1971 Christina Madeleine; two *d. (marr. diss. 1980)*; *m.* 1982 Margaret Alexandra; one *s.* one *d. Public Offices:* Non-Executive Director, North Manchester NHS Healthcare Trust (1993-). *Education:* Strathallan School (1962-68); University of Edinburgh (1968-73). *Career Profile:* Lecturer/Senior Lecturer in Conservative Dentistry, University of Manchester (1975-86); Visiting Professor of Restorative Dentistry, Washington University, St Louis, MO, USA (1988-90); Visiting Expert (Manpower Development) Ministry of Health, Singapore (1994); Visiting Professor of Operative Dentistry, University of Florida, USA (1995). *Publications/Creative Work:* More than 125 publications in various research and professional journals. *Awards:* FDS, RCS (Eng)(*Adeundem*)(1994); Fellowship, American College of Dentists (1990). *Societies:* Member of over 20 UK and International societies; Senior Vice-President, British Society for Restorative Dentistry (1995-96), President (1994-95); President, Section of Odontology, Manchester Medical Society (1993-94); President, British Association of Teachers of Conservative Dentistry (1992). *Recreations, Interests:* DIY, gardening. *Address:* University Dental Hospital, Higher Cambridge Street, Manchester, M15 6FH (*tel:* 0161 275 6660; *fax:* 0161 275 6710); Helmsdale House, 10A Pownall Avenue, Bramhall, Stockport, SK7 2HE (*tel/fax:* 0161 439 6876).

WILSON, Colonel Philip Denys, MBE (Mil) (1943),TD (1947),DL (1983)

Retired. *b.* 9 August 1911; Monton, Lancs. *m.* 1944 Agnete; one *s.* one *d. Public Offices:* Trustee, Broughton House Home for Ex-Servicemen. *Education:* Manchester Grammar School (1921-28); Manchester College of Technology (1928-31). *War Service:* 8th Bn The Manchester Regiment (TA) (1937-58) Commanding Officer (Lt Col) (1956-58) Colonel, 127 Infantry Brigade (1958-60). *Previous Positions:* Managing Director, H Rawson & Co Ltd (1947-73). *Societies:* Portico Library (1985-93); Bramall Park Golf Club (1958-) (Past Captain); and formerly Manchester Club (from 1947). *Recreations, Interests:* Golf, bridge, gardening, Manchester Regiment Cathedral Chapel Committee (Chairman 1975-94). *Address:* 15 Elmsway, Bramhall, Cheshire SK7 2AE (*tel:* 0161-439 1657).

WILSON, Ronald Geoffrey Osborne, DL(1995),OStJ(1992)

Chairman, Chapel Wharf Limited; Salford Phoenix Initiative Limited; Salford Hundred Venture Limited; Griffin Managed Workspace Limited; Edge Consualnts Limited; Chairman of Council, The Order of St John in Greater Manchester. *b.* 19 September 1926 Wilmslow, Cheshire. *m.* 1955 Barbara; one *s.* two *d. Public Offices:* Member of Court, University of Manchester; Chairman, Salford RELATE. *Education:* Oundle School; Queens University, Belfast; OTS Queen Victoria's Own Sappers & Miners, Bangalore, India. *Military Service:* Royal Engineers (Indian Army, 1945-47). *Career Profile:* Director, Trafalgar Engineering Company Ltd; Assistant Director & Regional Advisor to the Board, Samuel Montagu & Company Ltd, Manchester; Director & Chief Executive, Mountain Range Group. *Societies:* Army & Navy Club, St James's', London. *Recreations, Interests:*

Music, gardening, crosswords. *Address:* 13 Heyes Lane, Alderley Edge, Cheshire, SK9 7LA (*tel:* 01625 585121).

WILSON, Ronald Haig, MA St Andrews (1938),Hons French and German (1940)

Retired, Principal, City of Manchester College of Adult Education (1964-80). *b.* 3 October 1917; Edinburgh. *m.* 1949 Edith Mand; one *s. Public Offices:* Council Member and Director, Pre-Retirement Association of Great Britain & Northern Ireland. *Education:* Hillhead High School, Glasgow (1929-31); Bell-Baxter School, Cupar, Fife (1931-35); University of St Andrews (1935-38) (1939-40); University of Frankfurt am Main (1938-39). *War Service:* Royal Artillery (HAA) (1940-41); Intelligence Corps (1941-46). *Previous Positions:* Adult Education Specialist (Dusseldorf/Berlin/Bonn), British Control Service for Germany (1947-58); Senior Adult Tutor, Ivanhoe Community College, Leicestershire LEA (1958-62); Educational Organiser (Further Education), Huddersfield (1962-64). *Publications:* Various articles and contributions on Adult Education in the post-1945 World for British and German specialist journals. *Prizes:* Stevenson Exchange and Bell-Baxter Post-graduate Scholarships, tenable at University of Frankfurt am Main (1938). *Societies:* Association of Principals of Colleges (Life Member); Educational Centres Association (Hon Life Member; National President, 1994-); National Institute of Adult Continuing Education; Pre-Retirement Association of Greater Manchester. *Recreations, Interests:* International adult education, education for retirement, opera, hill walking. *Address:* 26 Oakdene Road, Marple, Stockport, Cheshire SK6 6PJ.

WINGATE-SAUL, Giles Wingate, QC,LLB(Hons)

Queens Counsel. *b.* 9 March 1945 Hartford, Cheshire. *m.* 1984 Dr Katherine Wynne; one *s.* one *d. Public Offices:* Deputy High Court Judge, Recorder; Treasurer, St Paul's Church, Rusland, Cumbria. *Education:* Winchester College; Southampton University. *Career Profile:* Barrister (called 1967); QC (appointed 1983); Practicising in the fields of catastrophic personal injury and mercantile work. *Societies:* Liverpool Ramblers AFC; Alderley Edge Tennis Club. *Recreations, Interests:* Tennis, cricket, church affairs, gardening, community life in South Lakeland. *Address:* 25 Byrom Street, Manchester, M3 4PF (*tel:* 0161 829 2100).

WINTERBOTTOM, Herbert Wager, DMus (Hon) MGSIUF (1988); MSc (Music) Salford, FNSM,FTCL,LRAM,ARCM, FRSA,CEng,MIMechE,MRAeS

Organist. *b.* 26 December 1921; Oldham. *m.* 1955 Joyce Mary Wilcock; two *d. Education:* Manchester College of Science & Technology; Northern School of Music. *Career Profile:* Chairman and Director of Music & Organist, Salford University; Lecturer, Manchester College of Science & Technology; Professor of Organ, Northern School of Music and RNCM; Organist & Master of the Choristers, St Ann's Church, Manchester. *Creative Works:* Compositions for Organ and Brass. *Publications:* Contribution to Gulbenkian Report on Music; contributions to professional journals. *Societies:* Manchester Literary & Philosophical Society; Past President, Manchester Organists Association. *Recreations, Interests:* Walking, working with underprivileged people. *Address:* "Chandos", 16 Alstone Road, Heaton Chapel, Stockport SK4 5AH (*tel:* 0161-432 4564).

WITTER, Donald, FCIB

Vice Chairman, Gefinor Bank Ltd, Geneva, Switzerland; Director, DCT Group and Alder Developments Ltd. *b.* 22 May 1928; Ormskirk, Lancashire. *m.* 1959 Sheila Delves; one *s.* *Military Service:* Royal Air Force (3 years). *Career Profile:* Area Manager, Midland Bank plc, Manchester. *Societies:* Bolton Golf Club; Heaton & Smithills Conservative Club. *Recreations, Interests:* Golf, snooker. *Address:* 25 Oakwood Drive, Heaton, Bolton BL1 5EE *(tel:* 01204-42665).

WOLF, Peter John Leigh

Retired District Judge. *b.* 23 September 1929 Buckfastleigh, Devon. *Education:* Solihull School; Wellingborough School. *Military Service:* National Service (1952-54). *Career Profile:* Solicitor (1956-70); District Registrar of the Supreme Court of Justice/District Judge (1970-94). *Societies:* East India Club; Liveryman, The Workshipful Company of Blacksmiths; Member, Guild of Freemen of the City of London. *Recreations, Interests:* Bridge, philately. *Address:* 235 Hale Road, Hale, Altrincham, WA15 8DN(*tel:* 0161 980 6024).

WOLFE, Joy Sylvia (*née* Gillman), JP (1984)

President, Zionist Central Council of Greater Manchester. *b.* 4 January 1938 London. *m.* 1959 Brian Sinclair Wolfe; one *s.* two *d.* *Public Offices:* Chairman, North Cheshire WIZO; Governor, North Cheshire Jewish Primary School; Executive Member, SCOPUS Education Trust; National Council, British WIZO; Vice-President, Zionist Federation. *Education:* Hove County Grammar School. *Career Profile:* Public Relations Consultant (1974-79); Journalist (1979-); Editor, Jewish Gazette (1989-92); Manchester Correspondent, Jewish Chronicle (1990-). *Publications/Creative Work:* Many articles and profiles. *Prizes:* Northern Jewish Woman of the Year (1994). *Societies:* Northern Lawn Tennis Club; Stockport Multiple Sclerosis Society; Friends of Manchester Jewish Museum. *Recreations, Interests:* Bridge, tennis, voluntary Christmas card sales organiser, Stockport MSS at the Combined Charities Card shops. *Additional Information:* Delegate of the Jewish Representative Council of Greater Manchester and a member of the Public Relations Committee. Former Trustee, Manchester Jewish Museum.

WOLMAN, Basil, MB ChB (1941),LRCP, MRCS (1941),MD (1951),FRCP (1972),DCH (1947)

Paediatric Consultant and Vice-chairman, 'The Bridge', Child Care Consultancy, London. *b.* 17 March 1918; Colwyn Bay, North Wales. *m.* 1945 Helena May Novis; one *s.* one *d.* *Public Offices:* Life Vice President and Trustee, Manchester Jewish Social Services; Council Member, Family Welfare Association, Manchester; Trustee, Booth Charitable Trust & District Nursing. *Education:* Manchester Central High School (1929-35); Manchester University (1935-41). *Career Profile:* Consultant Paediatrician and Postgraduate Tutor, Booth Hall Childrens Hospital; Hon Clinical Lecturer, Child Health, Examiner in Paediatrics, Sub-Dean Postgraduate Medical Education, University of Manchester; Teaching and Research Fellowship, McGill University, Montreal, Canada;

Consultant Paediatrician, Bury & Rochdale Hospitals; Member, Faculty of Medicine, Manchester University. *Creative Works:* Various projects on adoption, fostering and child care; Founder, Special Care Nurseries for Mentally Handicapped (Bury & Rochdale). *Publications:* Over 20 publications on aspects of paediatrics in various medical journals. *Societies:* British Paediatric Association (Council Member 1977-80); British Medical Association; Manchester Paediatric Club (President 1961); Manchester Medical Society (President, Paediatric Section 1977); British Adoption & Fostering Agency (Council Member 1975-81). *Recreations, Interests:* Music, opera, ballet, wine. *Address:* 29 Ashfield Lodge, Palatine Road, Didsbury, Manchester M20 2UD *(tel:* 0161-445 3500).

WOLSTENCROFT, Revd Canon Alan

Honorary Canon of Manchester; Vicar of St Peter's, Bolton-le-Moors (1991-). *b.* 16 July 1937; Clifton, Swinton, Manchester. *m.* 1969 Christine Mary; one *s.* one *d. Education:* Clifton County Primary; Wellington Technical School; St Johns FE College; Cuddesdon College, Oxford. *Military Service:* National Service, RAF (Medical Branch - Mountain Rescue). *Career Profile:* Trainee Manager, W H Smiths; Manager Wine and Spirit Department, Bass North West; Assistant Curate, St Thomas, Bolton (1969-71); Assistant Curate, All Saints, Stand, Whitefield (1971-73); Vicar, St Martins, Wythenshawe (1973-80); Area Dean of Withington (1978-91); Vicar of Brooklands, Sale (1980-91). *Societies:* YMCA. *Recreations, Interests:* Squash, walking, reading, music, theatre, family activities, football spectator Bolton Wanderers. *Address:* Bolton Vicarage, Churchgate, Bolton BL1 1PS *(tel:* 01204 533 847).

WOLSTENHOLME, Maxine Lynn (*née* Beecroft), BA(Hons)(Univ. of Lancaster)

Editor, Salford City Reporter/West Manchester Advertiser. *b.* 15 October 1962 Keighley, West Yorkshire. *m.* 1988 Simon. *Education:* Burnley High School for Girls; Lancaster University (1981-84); South Glamorgan Institute of Higher Education (1984-85). *Career Profile:* Joined West Manchester Advertiser (1985); Salford City Reporter/West Manchester Advertiser, Chief Reporter (1987), Deputy Editor (1989), Editor (1989). *Prizes:* North West Free Newspaper of the Year (Highly Commended)(1996). *Societies:* Elmwood Church, Salford. *Address:* 30 Church Street, Eccles, Manchester, M30 0DF(*tel:* 0161 789 5015; *fax:* 0161 787 8081).

WONFOR, Andrea Jean (*née* Duncan), BA(Hons)(Cantab,1966)

Joint Managing Director, Granada Television. *b.* 31 July 1944 Birchington, Kent. *m.* 1974 Geoffrey; two *d. Education:* Simon Langon Girls' School, Canterbury; New Hall, Cambridge. *Career Profile:* Director of Programmes, Tyne Tees Television (1982-87); Managing Director, Zenith North Ltd (1987-90); Controller, Arts & Entertainment - Channel 4 (1990-93); Director of Programmes, Granada Television (1993-94); Joint Managing Director, Granada TV (1994-). *Societies:* Royal Television Society. *Address:* Granada Television, Quay Street, Manchester, M60 9EA (*tel:* 0161 832 7211; *fax:* 0161 953 0282).

WOOD, Alan John BSc,(Hons)(Univ. of Manchester),MBA(Harvard)

Managing Director, Siemens plc. *b.* 20 March 1947 Sheffield. *m.* 1973 Jennifer; two *d.*

Public Offices: Chairman (from Nov 1996), CBI North West Regional Council. *Education:* King Edward VII School, Sheffield (1958-65); University of Manchester (1965-68); Harvard University (1973-75). *Career Profile:* Unilever plc (1968-73); Crittall Construction (1975-78); SEM Ltd (1978-81); Siemens plc (1981-). *Prizes:* John Henry Beckwith Open Scholarship, Manchester University. *Recreations, Interests:* Tennis and family. *Address:* Siemens plc, Princess Road, Manchester, M20 2UR (*tel:* 0161 446 5010; *fax:* 0161 446 5012).

WOOD, Professor Graham Charles, BA (1956),MA (1960),PhD Cambridge (1959),ScD Cambridge (1972),FEng,FIM,FRSC,CChem,FICorr,FIMF

Pro-Vice Chancellor and Professor of Corrosion Science and Engineering, UMIST. *b.* 6 February 1934; Farnborough, Kent. *m.* 1959 Freda Nancy Waithman; one *s.* one *d.* *Education:* Bromley Grammar School, Kent (1945-53); Christ's College, Cambridge (1953-56); Department of Metallurgy, University of Cambridge (1956-61). *Career Profile:* Lecturer, Senior Lecturer, Reader, Department of Chemical Engineering and subsequently Corrosion and Protection Centre, UMIST; Vice Principal for Academic Development, UMIST (1982-84); Deputy Principal of UMIST (1983); Dean of the Faculty of Technology, University of Manchester (1987-89); Fellow of the Royal Academy of Engineering (1990). *Publications:* Over 400 papers in the field of oxidation, corrosion and protection. *Prizes:* Beilby Medallist (1973); U R Evans Award (1983) and T P Hoar Prize (1986) of the Institute of Corrosion; Carl Wagner Memorial Award of the Electrochemical Society (USA) (1983); Westinghouse Prize (1983) and Hothersall Medal and Prize (1989) of the Institute of Metal Finishing; Cavallaro Medal of the European Federation of Corrosion (1987). *Societies:* Past President of the Institute of Corrosion; Manchester Literary & Philosophical Society. *Recreations, Interests:* Travel, history, cricket, walking, gardening. *Address:* Corrosion and Protection Centre, UMIST, PO Box 88, Sackville Street, Manchester M60 1QD (*tel:* 0161-200 4851); 8 Amberley Close, Deane, Bolton BL3 4NJ (*tel:* 01204-63659).

WOODS, David Robert, FCA (1963)

Chairman, Fearnley Construction Group; Vice President, Building Employers Confederation. *b.* 15 August 1938; Wilmslow. *m.* 1963 Sheila; one *s.* one *d.* *Public Offices:* JP; Governor, University College Salford; Chairman, Salford Lads Club; Chairman, Manchester & Salford Playing Fields Society; Chairman, Greater Manchester Federation of Boys' Clubs; Governor, Ash Field Special School, Salford *Education:* King William's College, Isle of Man. *Military Service:* National Service, Royal Artillery (1956-58). *Career Profile:* President, Manchester Salford & District Building Trade Employers (1980-81); President, North West Region, Building Employers Confederation (1986-87); Chairman, Area 46 (South East Lancs) Round Table (1978-79); National Chairman, Building Employers Confederation (1990-91). *Recreations, Interests:* Horse racing, reading, food and drink, sport. *Address:* Fearnley Construction Group, Constance House, 5 Missouri Avenue, Eccles New Road, Salford M5 2NP (*tel:* 0161-736 4576); 3 Mill Brow, Worsley, Manchester M28 2WL (*tel:* 0161-794 7509).

WOODWARD, His Honour Judge Barry, LLM,Barrister

Circuit Judge. *b.* 13 June 1938 Windlestone, Co Durham. *m.* 1963 Patricia; two *d.*

Education: Sheffield University. *Military Service:* National Service. *Career Profile:* Teacher, Barrister, Chairman of Industrial Tribunals, Circuit Judge. *Address:* Courts of Justice, Crown Square, Manchester.

WRIGHT, Alan Whiley, BSc (Hons) Birmingham (1964)

Headmaster, Bolton School (Boys' Division). *b.* 5 May 1943; Sale, Cheshire. *m.* 1967 Veronica; two *s.* one *d. Education:* Manchester Grammar School. *Career Profile:* Assistant Chemistry Master, King Edwards School, Birmingham; Head of Chemistry Dept & Sixth Form Supervisor, Royal Grammar School, Newcastle-upon-Tyne. *Societies:* East India & Public Schools Club. *Recreations, Interests:* Theology, foreign travel, fellwalking, sailing, skiing. *Address:* Bolton School, Chorley New Road, Bolton BL1 4PA *(tel:* 01204-840201); Leverhouse, Greenmount Lane, Bolton BL1 5JF.

WRIGLEY, Bernard J

Actor/Singer. *b.* 25 February 1948 Bolton. *m.* 1970 one *s. Education:* Thornleigh College, Bolton. *Career Profile:* Customs & Excise Officer for two years; Actor/Singer (1969-). *Publications/Creative Work:* Nine solo records and songbooks. *Prizes:* Nominated for Best Actor (with Mike Harding) Northern Drama Awards (1991) 'Waiting for Godot'. *Recreations, Interests:* Walking, running, music. *Additional Information:* Upon release of first album 'The Phenomenal B Wrigley' (Topic) was christened 'The Bolton Bullfrog' (by A L Lloyd) has stuck ever since. Royal Command Performance (1977). Many plays/commercials for TV & Radio.

WRIGLEY, William Sydney, FRICS

Managing Director, Head of Professional Services, Dunlop Heywood, Manchester. *b.* 3 February 1948 Hyde, Cheshire. *m.* 1972 Lynda; two *d. Education:* Hulme Grammar School, Oldham. *Career Profile:* Formative years as a Rural Surveyor with Cordingleys & Manchester Corporation Waterworks. *Societies:* Manchester Society of Land Agents and Surveyors; Ashton under Lyne Golf Club; Arbrix Club; Chartered Surveyors Golfing Society. *Recreations, Interests:* Golf, arboriculture. *Address:* Dunlop Heywood, 90 Deansgate, Manchester, M3 2QP*(tel:* 0161 834 8384; *fax:* 0161 832 5859); 5 Pennine Grove, Ashton under Lyne, Lancashire, OL6 9ES.

WYNN, Terence, MSc(1984)

Member of European Parliament. *b.* 27 June 1946 Platt Bridge, Wigan. *m.* 1967 Doris; one *s.* one *d. Public Offices:* Councillor, Wigan MBC (1979-90); MEP for Merseyside East and Wigan (1989-). *Education:* Liverpool Polytechnic; Salford University. *Career Profile:* Officer, Merchant Navy (1964-75); Training Executive (1975-89). *Publications/Creative Work:* 'Onward Christian Socialist' (1995). *Societies:* Abbey Street Labour Club. *Recreations, Interests:* Reading, music, watching rugby league, methodist local preacher. *Address:* European Office, 105 Corporation Street, St Helens, WA10 1SX (*tel:* 01744 451609; *fax:* 01744 29832). *Additional Information:* Member, Budgets Committee, Budgetary Control Committee, Agriculture Committee (European Parliament) Languages: Italian and French.

WYNNE, Owen Henry, Curtis Gold Medal; ARMCM

Director, Northern Consort of Singers; Tutor in Charge of Music Centres, Trafford Education; Conductor, Adjudicator, Teacher of Singing; Professional Counter Tenor Singer. *b.* 26 July 1926; Liverpool. *m.* 1950 Dorothy Beryl; three *s.* two *d. Education:* Oulton High School, Liverpool; Royal Manchester College of Music. *War Service:* (1944-47). *Career Profile:* Lay Clerk, Manchester Cathedral (1952-88); Lecturer in Singing, RNCM (-1975). *Prizes:* Curtis Gold Medal for Singing. *Address:* Lynton Lodge, Beaufort Avenue, Brooklands, Sale *(tel:* 0161-973 3544).

Y

YATES, Tim, BA (Hons, English) Manchester (1962),MA (American Studies) (1963), MIPR,FRSA

Director of Information, UMIST. *b.* 2 January 1941; Lancaster. *m.* 1977 Nancy Burt (decd 1995); one *s.* one *d. Education:* Royal Grammar School, Lancaster; University of Manchester. *Career Profile:* School Teacher, Salford Docks; Extra-Mural Dept, University of Manchester. *Publications:* Numerous - New Scientist, Guardian, Times, Daily Telegraph, et al; wine articles in journals. *Prizes:* Catherine I Dodd Fellow, University of Manchester (1962-63). *Societies:* Manchester Literary & Philosophical Society; Commanderie de Bordeaux; Connetablie de Guyenne; West Heaton Tennis. *Recreations, Interests:* Wine, squash, reading history in the sun. *Address:* Information Office, UMIST, PO Box 88, Manchester M60 1QD *(tel:* 0161-200 4000; *fax:* 0161 200 3989; *e-mail:* tyates@umist.ac.uk); 29 Hawthorn Grove, Heaton Moor, Stockport SK4 4HZ *(tel:* 0161-432 4953).

YEAMAN, Angus George David, JP; MIMechE,MIChemE,MIEnergy,MInstGasE

Retired/Farmer/Smallholder. *b.* 3 July 1928; Cheltenham. *m.* 1954 Marguerite Faith (née Ingham). *Public Offices:* JP, Tameside PSD (1976-); Chairman, Marple District CAB. *Education:* Cheltenham College; Birmingham Technical College; Bristol Technical College. *Career Profile:* Technical Assistant, SW Gas Board, Bristol (1952-60); Assistant Engineer, SW Gas Board, Bristol (1960-62); Assistant to Managing Director, Philblack Ltd, Bristol (1962-68); Senior Sales Engineer, Simon Carves (1968-70); Sales Manager, Sim-Chem Ltd (1970-82); Director, Vine Gardens Ltd (1983-89); Director, Manchester Literary & Philosophical Publications Ltd (1996-). *Societies:* Hallé Concerts Society; Manchester Literary & Philosophical Society (Council Member, 1992-96); Royal Horticultural Society; Northern Horticultural Society; Friends of the Whitworth; National Art Collections Fund; Marple Civic Society (Chairman); Magistrates Association; Multiple Sclerosis Society; Cheltonian Society. *Recreations, Interests:* Gardening, painting, music, erstwhile golf. *Address:* Tobits Farm, Werneth Low, Gee Cross, Cheshire SK14 3AH *(tel:* 0161-367 8176).

YEAMAN, Marguerite Faith (*née* Ingham), JP

Retired; farmer's wife; artist. *b.* 30 May 1932 Brighouse, Yorkshire. *m.* 1954 Angus Yeaman. *Public Offices:* Magistrate, Stockport Bench (1973). *Education:* Cheltenham Ladies College (1942-49); Bristol College of Commerce (1950-52). *Career Profile:* Founder Chairman, League of Friends of Marple Hospitals (1970-75); Inaugurator, Multiple Sclerosis Society of Great Britain (1971-74); Member of Stockport Health Authority (1971-91); Proprietor, Faith Yeaman Organization (1973-78); Departmental Secretary, University of Manchester (1979-81); Director, Vine Gardens (1983-89). *Societies:* Manchester Lit. & Phil. (Member of Council, 1994-); Stockport Art Guild (Treasurer, 1996-); Marple Civic Society (Committee Member, 1987-); RSPB; Friends of the Whitworth Art Gallery; National Art Collections Fund; Scottish National Trust. *Recreations, Interests:* Reading, painting, birdwatching, botany, gardening. *Address:* Tobits Farm, Werneth Low, Gee Cross, SK14 3AH *(tel:* 0161 367 8176).

YEO, Ronald Owen, BA London (1955), Hon Fellow, Manchester Metropolitan University (1995)

Retired. *b.* 1 February 1933; Middlesex. *m.* 1959 Cynthia Mary Cole; one *s.* one *d. Public Offices:* Chairman, University of London Convocation (Manchester Group); Chairman of Governors, Broadoak Primary School. *Education:* Beckenham and Penge Grammar School for Boys; Queen Mary College, University of London. *Military Service:* National Service (Intelligence Corps) (1957-59). *Previous Positions:* Administrative Officer, London County Council; Deputy Registrar (Administration), University of Salford; Secretary and Clerk to the Board of Governors, The Manchester Metropolitan University. *Societies:* Manchester Literary & Philosophical Society; Manchester Luncheon Club; National Trust; English Heritage; Friends of Smithills Hall; National Art Collections Fund. *Address:* 17 Fairmount Road, Swinton, Manchester, M27 0EP *(tel:* 0161 794 4407)

YEUNG, Kui Man (Gerry), BA York (1976)

General Manager, Yang Sing Restaurant Ltd. *b.* 5 August 1954; Canton, China. *m.* Yin Ling (Joanne); one *s.* one *d. Education:* Primary Education, Hong Kong; Secondary Education, Hong Kong and UK (Plant Hill High School, Manchester); Higher Education, University of York. *Address:* Yang Sing Restaurant Ltd, 34 Princess Street, Manchester M1 4JY *(tel:* 0161-236 2200); 34 Sevenoaks Avenue, Heaton Moor, Stockport, Cheshire SK4 4AW *(tel:* 0161-443 2336).

YOUNG, Alexander, FRNCM (1977)

Retired. *b.* 18 October 1920; London. *m.* 1948 Jean Anne; one *s.* one *d. Public Offices:* Head of School of Vocal Studies, Royal Northern College of Music (1973-86). *War Service:* RASC (1941-46), served in UK, North Africa, Italy and Austria. *Previous Positions:* Free-lance Concert, Oratorio and Opera Singer (1948-73). Sang all over Europe, and several times in the United States. Made many commercial recordings, especially of Handel Operas and Oratorios and broadcast frequently on the BBC and made several TV appearances in Opera chiefly. Sang the title role in the first performance in England of 'The Rake's Progress', and subsequently sang the role in New York with Stravinsky and also recorded the work for CBS with the composer conducting. *Recreations, Interests:* Classical music recordings, stamps of GB, and Channel Islands, photography including all my own dark-room work, railway modelling. *Address:* Treetops, Eccles Road, Whaley Bridge, via Stockport, Cheshire SK12 7EL *(tel:* 01663-732960).

YOUNG, Bernard, TD(1989); FInstD,MSc(Aston),RGN,MHSM,MIMgt

Chief Executive, St Ann's Hospice. *b.* 8 June 1949 Birmingham. *m.* 1970 Susan Lyn; one *d. Military Service:* Regular Army, Worcestershire Regt. RAMC(1966-70); RAMC(TA) (1976-). *Career Profile:* SRN (1971-74), Clinical Nurse (1974-80), Birmingham; Nursing Officer, University College London (1980-83); Staff Officer, Bloomsbury Health Authority, London (1984-87); Director of Nursing, Kettering Health Authority (1987-91); Director of Operational Services, Leicester Glenfield Hospital (1991-93); Regional Nurse, Trent Regional Health Authority (1993-95). *Societies:* English Heritage. *Recreations, Interests:* Golf, music, theatre, visiting historic buildings. *Address:* St Ann's Hospice Appeals Office, 2 Finney Lane, Heald Green, Cheadle, SK8 3DQ *(tel:* 0161 283 6600; *fax:* 0161 283 6601).

Z

ZOCHONIS, John Basil, LLD(Manchester,1991); BA Oxford

Retired. *b.* 2 October 1929; Altrincham, Cheshire. *m.* 1990 Brigid Mary Evanson Demetriades; two *stepd*. *Public Offices:* Member of Council and Court, Manchester University; Chairman, Manchester University Council (1987-90); Liveryman Tallow Chandlers Company; Freeman City of London; Member of Council, Royal African Society; Member of Council, British Executive Service Overseas; Chairman of Governors, Withngton Girls' Schoool; President, Manchester University Settlement; Trustee, Police Foundation; President, East County Scout Council *Education:* Rugby School; Corpus Christi College, Oxford. *Military Service:* National Service (1948-50), 2nd Leiutenant Royal Artillery. *Career Profile:* Paterson Zochonis plc (1953-93), Director (1957), Chairman (1970-93). *Societies:* Carlton Club; The Travellers Club; MCC. *Recreations, Interests:* Reading and watching cricket. *Address:* Paterson Zochonis plc, Cussons House, Bird Hall Lane, Stockport, SK3 0XN *(tel:* 0161 491 8000, *fax:* 0161 491 8090). *Additional Information:* Deputy Lieutenant, High Sheriff for Greater Manchester (1994-95).

ZOTT, Ivor, MA(hc)(Univ. of Salford),Hon Fellow, Salford College of Technology

Councillor, Salford City (1957-); Member, Greater Manchester Transport Authority (1986-pres). *b.* 17 November 1917 Manchester. *m.* 1940 Margaret; one *s.* two *d.* *Public Offices:* Mayor of Salford (1981-82); former member, National Executive, Union of Post Office Workers; Chairman,Salford Co-operative Party; Member, Manchester Post & Telecommunications Advisory Committee; Member, Manchester War Pensions Advisory Committee; Member, Henshaw's Society for the Blind; Vice-chairman, Age Concern (Salford); MIND (Salford); Member, Transport & Rail Committees, Association of Municipal Authorities; Member. Equal Opportunities Commission; Chairman, Broadwalk Junior & Infants School; Governor, St James RC School. *Education:* Southall Street School, Manchester. *War Service:* Seaforth Highlanders (1940-45) - invalided discharge, 1944, France. *Career Profile:* Public service; committed socialist. *Societies:* Winston Churchill Ex Service Club, London; Swinton Trades & Labour Club. *Recreations, Interests:* Walking, music, brass bands, debating, public speaking, travel. *Address:* 55 Ash Drive, Wardley, Swinton, M27 9RU *(tel:* 0161 793 7767). *Additional Information:* In Post Office employment, Manchester (1948-77).

ZUSSMAN, Prof Emeritus Jack, BA Cambridge (1949) MA (1951),PhD Crystallography Cambridge (1952),MA, DPhil Oxford (1962),MSc Manchester (1971)

Retired, 1989. *b.* 31 July 1924; London. *m.* 1960 Judith Deborah Nisse; one *s.* two *d.* *Public Offices:* Chairman, Cheshire Reform Congregation (1983-85). *Education:* Coopers' Company's School; Cambridge University (Downing College). *War Service:* Royal Navy (1943-46). *Career Profile:* University of Manchester, Professor of Geology and Head of Department of Geology (1967-89); Dean of Science, University of Manchester (1980-81); Reader in Mineralogy, University of Oxford (1962-67); Asst Lecturer, Lecturer, Senior Lecturer, University of Manchester (1952-62). *Publications:* 'Rock Forming Minerals' vols 1-5 (Longmans 1962-63) (with W A Deer and R A Howie), 2nd Edn vol 2A (1978), 1A

(1982), 1B (1986) 5B (1996); 'Introduction to Rock Forming Minerals' (Longmans, 1966)(2nd ed 1992) (with W A Deer and R A Howie); 'Physical Methods in Determinative Mineralogy' (Ed) (Acad Press, 2nd Edn 1977); various papers on mineralogy and crystallography. *Societies:* Mineralogical Society of Great Britain and Ireland (Vice-Pres 1969-71, 1977-79, President 1980-81); Fellow Mineralogical Society of America; Hon Member, Mineralogical Society of Poland. *Recreations, Interests:* Gardens, the Lake District. *Address:* 13 Oakwood Avenue, Gatley, Cheshire SK8 4LR (*tel:* 01161-428 8307).

ABBREVIATIONS

A

AA	Architectural Association
AAF	Auxiliary Air Force
ABA	American Bar Association
ABCC	Association of British Chambers of Commerce
ABPS	Associate, British Psychological Association
ABRSM	Associated Board, Royal Schools of Music
ABS	Associate, Building Societies Institute
ABSI	Associate, Boot and Shoe Institute
ACA	Associate, Institute of Chartered Accountants
ACAS	Advisory Conciliation and Arbitration Service
ACBSI	Associate, Chartered Building Societies Institute
ACCA	Associate, Chartered Association of Certified Accountants
ACCS	Associate, Corporation of Secretaries
ACEA	Associate, Association of Cost and Executive Accountants
ACF	Army Cadet Force
ACGI	Associate, City and Guilds Institute of London
ACIArb	Associate, Chartered Institute of Arbitrators
ACIB	Associate, Chartered Institute of Bankers
ACII	Associate, Chartered Insurance Institute
ACIS	Associate, Institute of Chartered Secretaries and Administrators
ACM	Association of Computing Machinery
ACMA	Associate, Institute of Cost and Management Accountants
ACSD	Associate of the Central School of Speech & Drama
ACST	Associate of the College of Science and Technology
ACT	Association of Corporate Treasurers
ADB	Associate of the Drama Board
ADC	Aide-de-Camp

Adj	Adjutant
AdvCounDip	Advanced Counselling Diploma
AdvDip	Advanced Diploma
AdvDipSpEd	Advanced Diploma in Special Education
AEEU	Amalgamated Engineering & Electrical Union
AEU	Amalgamated Engineering Union
AFA	Associate, Institute of Financial Accountants
AFC	Association Football Club
AGSM	Associate, Guildhall School of Music
AHA	Area Health Authority
AI	Artificial Intelligence
AIA	Associate, Institute of Actuaries
AICE	Associate, Institute of Civil Engineers
AIDS	Acquired Immunity Deficiency Syndrome
AIEE	Associate, Institute of Electrical Engineers
AIIMR	Associate, Institute of Investment Management and Research
AIL	Associate, Institute of Linguistics
AIMSW	Associate Institute of Medical Social Workers
AIPD	Associate, Institute of Professional Designers
AIQS	Associate, Institute of Quantity Surveyors
AIT	Association of Investment Trusts
AKC	Associate, King's College, London
ALA	Associate of the Library Association
ALCD	Associate, London College of Divinity
ALI	Associate, Landscape Institute
ALS	Associate of the Linnaean Society
AMA	Associate of the Museums Association
AMBIM	Associate Member, British Institute of Management
AMCST	Associate, Manchester College of Science and Technology

AMCT	Associate, Manchester College of Technology
AMInstTA	Associate Member, Institute of Transport Administration
AMIPM	Associate Member, Institute of Personnel Management
AMSPetE	Associate Member, Society of Petroleum Engineers
ANSM	Associate, Northern School of Music
AO	Officer, Order of Australia
AOF	Admiral of the Fleet
APIL	Association of Personal Injury Lawyers
APMI	Associate, Pensions Management Institute
ARAM	Associate, Royal Academy of Music
ARBS	Associate, Royal Society of British Sculptors *or* Association for the Recognition of Business Schools
ARCA	Associate, Royal College of Art
ARCM	Associate, Royal College of Music
ARCO	Associate of the Royal College of Organists
ARCS	Associate, Royal College of Science
ARIBA	Associate, Royal Institution of British Architects
ARICS	Associate, Royal Institution of Chartered Surveyors
ARMCM	Associate, Royal Manchester College of Music
ARNCM	Associate, Royal Northern College of Music
ARSH	Associate, Royal Society for the Promotion of Health
ARSM	Associate, Royal School of Mines
ARTC	Associate, Royal Technical College, Glasgow
ARTCS	Associate, Royal Technical College, Salford
ARVA	Associate, Incorporated Association of Rating and Valuation Officers
ASA	Associate, Society of Actuaries
ASCA	Associate, Society of Company and Commercial Accountants
ASH	Action on Smoking and Health

ASRE	American Society of Refrigeration Engineers
Assoc	Association(s)
AssocMCT	Associate of the Manchester College of Technology
Asst	Assistant
ATC	Air Training Corps *or* Art Teacher's Certificate
ATCL	Associate, Trinity College of Music, London
ATD	Art Teacher's Diploma
ATI	Associate, Textile Institute
ATII	Associate of the Institute of Taxation
ATIT	Associate, Institute of Taxation
AUA	American Urological Association
AUMIST	Associate of UMIST

B

b	born
BA	Bachelor of Arts
BA(Arch)	Bachelor of Architecture
BA(Com)	Bachelor of Commerce
BA(Econ)	Bachelor of Arts (Economics)
BAcc	Bachelor of Accountancy
BAFM	British Association of Friends of Museums
BAFTA	British Academy of Film & Television Arts
BAO	Bachelor of Art of Obstetrics
BAOR	British Army on the Rhine
BArch	Bachelor of Architecture
Bart	Baronet
BAS	Bachelor of Agricultural Science
BAS	Bachelor of Applied Science
BBA	British Bankers Association
BBC	British Broadcasting Corporation
BCA	Bachelor of Commerce and Administration
BCh	Bachelor of Surgery
BChir	Bachelor of Surgery
BCL	Bachelor of Civil Law
BCom	Bachelor of Commerce
BComm	Bachelor of Commerce
BCS	British Computer Society
BD	Bachelor of Divinity
Bde	Brigade
BDentSc	Bachelor of Dental Science
BDS	Bachelor of Dental Surgery
BDSc	Bachelor of Dental Science

BEC	Business Education Council
BEd	Bachelor of Education
BEM	British Empire Medal
BEng	Bachelor of Engineering
BFMPI	British Federation of Master Printers Institute
BGS	British Geriatric Society
BIM	British Institute of Management
BIMA	British Interactive Multi-Media Association
BJRULM	Bulletin of the John Rylands University Library of Manchester
BL	Bachelor of Law
BLA	Bachelor of Landscape Architecture
BLA	Bachelor of Liberal Arts
BLESMA	British Limbless Ex-Servicemen's Association
BLitt	Bachelor of Literature
BLL	Bachelor of Law
BM	Bachelor of Medicine
BMA	British Medical Association
BMet	Bachelor of Metallurgy
BMus	Bachelor of Music
Bn	Battalion
BNFL	British Nuclear Fuels Ltd
BPharm	Bachelor of Pharmacy
BPhil	Bachelor of Philosophy
BPS	British Psychological Society
BPsS	British Psychological Society
BRNC	Britannia Royal Naval College
BS	Bachelor of Science (US) or Bachelor of Surgery (US)
BSc	Bachelor of Science
BSc(Econ)	Bachelor of Science (Economics)
BSc(Optom)	BSc in Optometry
BScTech	Bachelor of Technological Science (UMIST)
BScSoc	Bachelor of Social Sciences
BSocSci	Bachelor of Social Sciences
BSS	Bachelor of Social Science
BTC	British Textile Confederation
BTEA	British Textile Employers Association
BTech	Bachelor of Technology
BTMA	British Textile MachineryAssociation
BUPA	British United Provident Association

C

(C)	Conservative
CA	Member, Institute of Chartered Accountants, Scotland
CAB	Citizens Advice Bureau
CAM	Communications, Advertising & Marketing
CAMPUS	Campaign to Promote the University of Salford
Capt	Captain
CArch	Chartered Architect
CB	Companion of the Bath
CBC	County Borough Council
CBE	Commander, Order of the British Empire
CBI	Confederation of British Industry
CBIM	Companion, British Institute of Management
CBiol	Chartered Biologist
CBSO	City. of Birmingham Symphony Orchestra
CC	Cricket Club or County Council or County Court or Cycling Club
CCC	County Cricket Club
CChem	Chartered Chemist
CDCE	Centre for the Development of Continuing Educaiton
CE	Church of England
CEA	Cinema Exhibitors Association
CEGB	Central Electricity Generating Board
CEI	Council of Engineering Institutions
CEng	Chartered Engineer
CEO	Chief Executive Officer
CERN	Centre Européenne pour la Recherche Nucléaire
CertEd	Certificate in Education
CertInstMan	Certificate in Institutional Management
CertPA	Certificate in Public Administration
CertWM	Certificate in Works Management
CGeol	Chartered Geologist
CGLI	City and Guilds of London Institute
ChB	Bachelor of Surgery
CHC	Community Health Council
ChLNH	Chevalier de la Légion Nationale d'Honneur

312

ChM	Master of Surgery
CIE	Companion, Order of the Indian Empire
CIEx	Companion, Institute of Export
CIM	Companion, Institute of Management
CIMF	Companion of the Institute of Mechanical Engineers
CIMgt	Companion, Institute of Management
CIMUSET	International Committee of Museums of Science & Technology
CIP	Chartered Insurance Practitioner
CIPD	Companion Institute of Personnel Development
CIPFA	Chartered Institute of Public Finance and Accountancy
CIPM	Companion, Institute of Personnel Management
CIRP	Collège Interationale pour Recherche et Production
CIT	Fellow, Chartered Institute of Transport
CL	Contact Lens Diploma, Association of British Dispensing Opticians
CLASP	Consortium of Local Authority Schools Project
CLP	Constituency Labour Party
CMath	Chartered Mathematician
CMC	Consortium of Management Consultantants
CMG	Companion of St Michael and St George
CNAA	Council for National Academic Awards
CND	Campaign for Nuclear Disarmament
CO	Commanding Officer
COI	Central Office of Information
CompTI	Companion of the Textile Institute
CP	County Primary
CPA	Chartered Patent Agent
CPhys	Chartered Physicist
CPS	Crown Prosecution.Service
CPsychol	Chartered Psychologist
CQSW	Certificate of Qualification in Social Work
CRE	Commission for Racial Equality
CS	Civil Service
CSD	Co-operative Secretaries Diploma
CSS	Council of Social Services
CStJ	Commander of the Order of St John of Jerusalem
CText	Chartered Textile Technologist
CTT	Chartered Textile Technologist
CUP	Cambridge University Press
CVCP	Committee of Vice-Chancellor & Principals
CVM	Company of Veteran Motorists
CVS	Council of Voluntary Services
CWS	Co-operative Wholesale Society

D

DA	Diploma in Anaesthesia *or* Diploma in Art
DAA	Diploma in Archive Administration
DAAG	Deputy Assistant Adjutant-General
DAD	Deputy Assistant Director
DAES	Division of Adult Education Service
DArts	Doctor of Arts
DASE	Diploma in Admin Sports Education
DBA	Doctor of Business Administration
DBE	Dame Commander, Order of the British Empire
DBS	Diploma in Business Studies
DCH	Diploma in Child Health
DCh	Doctor of Surgery
DCM	Distinguished Conduct Medal
DD	Doctor of Divinity
DDSc	Doctor of Dental Science
decd	deceased
DEd	Doctor of Education
DEng	Doctor of Engineering
Dep	Deputy
dept	department
DES	Department of Education and Science
DFA	Doctor of Fine Arts
DFBCS	Distinguished Fellow of the British Computer Society
DFC	Distinguished Flying Cross
DFEE	Department for Education and Employment
DHSS	Department of Health & Social Security

DIC	Diploma, Imperial College, London
Dip	Diploma
DipAD	Diploma in Art and Design
DipAdEd	Diploma in Adult Education
DipAdvStEd	Diploma in Advanced Studies in Education
DipAdvStud	Diploma in Advanced Studies
DipAdvStSci	Diploma in Advanced Studies in Science
DipAE	Diploma in Adùlt Education
DipArch	Diploma in Architecture
DipBA	Diploma in Business Administration
DipBibStud	Diploma in Biblical Studies
DipCD	Diploma in Civic Design
DipCIM	Diploma of Chartered Institute of Management
DipCommPrac	Diploma in Commercial Practice
DipCouns	Diploma in Counselling
DipDA	Diploma in Dramatic Art
DipEd	Diploma in Education
DipEdMgt	Diploma in Education Management
DipEdPsych	Diploma in Educational Psychology
DipEnvHlth	Diploma in Environmental Health
DipFA	Diploma in Fine Art
DipFE	Diploma in Further Education
DipHE	Diploma in Higher Education
DipHEIM	Diploma in Home Economics & Institutional Management
DipHSM	Diploma in Health Services Management
DipIM	Diploma in Industrial Management
DipInstManAcc	Diploma of the Institute of Mangement Accounting
DipLib	Diploma in Library and Information Studies
DipLS	Diploma in Library Science
DipM	Diploma in Marketing
DipManEd	Diploma in Management and Education
DipManSci	Diploma in Management Science
DipManStud	Diploma in Management Studies
DipPA	Diploma in Public Administration
DipPH	Diploma in Public Health
DipPhysEd	Diploma in Physical Education
DipPrimEd	Diploma in Primary Education
DipRADA	Diploma, Royal Academy of Dramatic Art
DipRCM	Diploma of the Royal College of Music
DipSocAdmin	Diploma in Social Administration
DipSocSt	Diploma in Social Studies
DipTecSc	Diploma in Technical Sciences
DipTheol	Diploma in Theology
DipTimbTech	Diploma in Timber Technology
DipTP	Diploma in Town Planning
DipTrainingMgt	Diploma in Training Management
DipURP	Diploma in Urban & Regional Planning
DipWSEd	Diploma of the Wines & Spirits Education Trust
diss	dissolved
DL	Deputy-Lieutenant
DLit	Doctor of Literature *or* Doctor of Letters
DLitt	Doctor of Literature *or* Doctor of Letters
DM	Doctor of Medicine
DMA	Diploma in Municipal Administration
DML	Diploma in Magisterial Law
DMRD	Diploma in Medical Radiological Diagnosis
DMRE	Diploma in Medical Radiology and Electrology
DMS	Diploma in Management Studies
DMus	Doctor of Music
DObst	Doctor of Obstetrics
DoE	Department of the Environment
DoH	Department of Health
DPA	Diploma in Public Administration
DPE	Diploma in Physical Education
DPH	Diploma in Public Health
DPh	Doctor of Philosophy
DPhil	Doctor of Philosophy
DPM	Diploma in Psychological Medicine
DRCOG	Diploma of the Royal College Obstetricians and Gynaecologists
DRD	Diploma in Restorative Dentistry

DRSAMD	Diploma of the Royal Scottish Academy of Music & Drama	FAQMC	Fellow, Association of Quality Management Consultants
DSA	Diploma in Social Administration	FASA	Fellow, Australian Society of Accountants
DSC	Distinguished Service Cross	FASCE	Fellow, American Society of Civil Engineers
DSc	Doctor of Science		
DSIR	Department of Scientific and Industrial Research	FASME	Fellow, American Society of Mechanical Engineers
DSS	Department of Social Security	FAVLP	Fellow, Association of Valuers of Licensed Property
DStJ	Dame Commander, Order of St John of Jerusalem	*fax*	facsimile
DTech	Doctor of Technology	FBA	Fellow, British Academy *or* Federation of British Artists
DTI	Department of Trade & Industry	FBAM	Fellow, British Academy of Management
DTM & H	Diploma in Tropical Medicine and Health	FBCA	Fellow of the British-Caribbean Association
DU	Doctor of the University	FBCO	Fellow, British College of Ophthalmic Opticians
Dunelm	Dunelmis (of Durham)		
DUniv	Doctor of the University	FBCS	Fellow, British Computer Society

E

(Eng)	Engineering	FBDO	Fellowship Diploma, Association of British Dispensing Opticians
Ed	Edinburgh *or* Editor		
EDC	Economic Development Committee		
Educ.	Educated	FBIM	Fellow, British Institute of Management
EEC	European Economic Community	FBiol	Fellow, Institute of Biology
EETPU	Electrical, Electronic, Telecommunication & Plumbing Union	FBKS	Fellow, British Kinematic Sound and Television Society
		FBOA	Fellow, British Optical Association
EMMA	Europan Multi Media Association	FBPsS	Fellow, British Psychological Society
Eng	England *or* Engineering	FBS	Fellow, Building Societies Institute
ENO	English National Opera		
EPSRC	Engineering & Physical Sciences Research Council	FC	Football Club
		FCA	Fellow, Institute of Chartered Accountants
ERD	Emergency Reserve Decoration		
ESRC	Economic & Social Research Council *or* Electricity Supply Research Council	FCAnaesth	Fellow, College of Anaesthetists
		FCBSI	Fellow, Chartered Building Societies Institute
EU	European Union	FCCA	Fellow, Chartered Association of Certified Accountants
EuroFIET	International Federation of Commercial, Clerical & Technical Employees		
		FCCP	Fellow, College of Chest Physicians (US)
		FCCP(USA)	Fellow, College of Chest Physicians (USA)

F

FAAO	Fellow, American Academy of Optometry	FCGL	Fellow, Guild of Cleaners and Launderers
		FChemS	Fellow, Chemical Society
FACP	Fellow, American College of Physicians	FChS	Fellow, Society of Chiropodists

FCIArb	Fellow, Chartered Institute of Arbitrators	FFD	Fellow of the Faculty of Dental Surgeons
FCIB	Fellow, Chartered Institute of Bankers	FFDRCSI	Fellow, Faculty of Denistry, Royal College of Surgeons in Ireland
FCIBS	Fellow, Chartered Institute of Bankers of Scotland	FFOM	Fellow, Faculty of Occupation Medicine
FCIEH	Fellow, Chartered Institute of Environmental Health	FFPHM	Fellow, Faculty of Public Health Medicine
FCIH	Fellow, Chartered Institute of Housing	FFRRCSI	Fellow, Faculty of Radiologists, Royal College of Surgeons, Ireland
FCII	Fellow, Chartered Insurance Institute	FGCL	Fellow, Goldsmiths' College, London
FCIM	Fellow of the Chartered Institute of Marketing *or* Fellow, Institute of Corporate Managers (Australia)	FGCL	Fellow, Guild of Cleaners and Launderers
FCIOB	Fellow, Chartered Institute of Building	FGS	Fellow, Geological Society
		FHA	Fellow, Institute of Health Service Administrators
FCIPA	Fellow, Chartered Institute of Patent Agents	FHCIMA	Fellow, Hotel Catering and Institutional Management Association
FCIS	Fellow, Institute of Chartered Secretaries and Administrators	FHKSA	Fellow, Hong Kong Society of Accountants
FCIT	Fellow, Chartered Institute of Transport	FHSA	Family Health Services Authority
FCIWEM	Fellow, Chartered Institute of Water & Enviornmental Management	FIA	Fellow, Institute of Actuaries
		FIBF	Fellow, Institute of British Foundrymen
FCMA	Fellow, Institute of Management Accountants	FIBiol	Fellow, Institute of Biology
FCollP	Fellow, College of Preceptors	FICA	Fellow, Institute of Chartered Accountants in England & Wales
FCP	Fellow, College of Preceptors		
FCPath	Fellow, College of Pathologists		
FCS	Fellow, Chemical Society	FICE	Fellow, Institute of Civil Engineers
FCT	Fellow, Association of Corporate Treasurers	FIChemE	Fellow, Institute of Chemical Engineers
FDS	Fellow in Dental Surgery		
FDSCRCSEd	Fellow in Dental Surgery, Royal College of Surgeons Edinburgh	FICorr	Fellow of the Institute of Corrosion
FDSRCS	Fellow in Dental Surgery, Royal College of Surgeons, England	FICorrST	Fellow, Institution of Corrosion, Science & Tecnhnology
		FICW	Fellow, Institute of Clerks of Works of Great Britain
FE	Further Education		
FEng	Fellowship of Engineering	FID	Fellow, Institute of Directors
FFA	Fellow, Faculty of Actuaries	FIDE	Fellow, Institute of Design Engineers
FFAEM	Fellow, Faculty of Accident and Emergency Medicine	FIEE	Fellow, Institute of Electrical Engineers
FFARCS	Fellow, Faculty of Anaesthetists, Royal College of Surgeons, England	FIERE	Fellow, Institute of Electronic and Radio Engineers
FFB	Fellow, Faculty of Building	FIFireE	Fellow, Institute of Fire Engineers
FFCM	Fellow, Faculty of Community Medicine		

FIGasE	Fellow, Institution of Gas Engineers	FInstPI	Fellow, Institute of Patentees and Inventors
FIGD	Fellow, Institute of Grocery Distributors	FInstSM	Fellow, Institute of Sales Management
FIHE	Fellow, Institute of Health Education	FInstWM	Fellow, Institute of Waste Management
FIHSM	Fellow, Institute of Health Service Management	FIOP	Fellow, Institute of Printing
FIHT	Fellow, Institute of Highways and Transportation	FIPA	Fellow, Institute of Practitioners in Advertising
FIIC	Fellow, International Institute for Conservation	FIPD	Fellow, Institute of Personnel Development *or* Fellow, Institute of Practising Designers
FIIM	Fellow, Institution of Industrial Managers		
FIInfSc	Fellow, Institute of Information Scientists	FIPHE	Fellow, Institute of Public Health Engineers
FIIP	Fellow, Institute of Incorporated Photographers	FIPM	Fellow, Institute of Personnel Management
FILEx	Fellow, Institute of Legal Executives	FIProdE	Fellow, Institute of Production Engineers
FIM	Fellow, Institute of Metallurgists	FIQS	Fellow, Institute of Quantity Surveyors
FIMA	Fellow, Institute of Mathematics and its Applications	FISM	Fellow, Institute of Supervisory Management
		FIStructE	Fellow, Institute of Structural Engineers
FIMarE	Fellow, Institute of Marine Engineers	FITD and	Fellow, Institute of Training Development
FIMC	Fellow, Institute of Management Consultants	FITMA	Fellow, Institute of Trade Mark Agents
FIMechE	Fellow, Institute of Mechanical Engineers	FIWEM	Fellow, Institute of Water and Environmental Management
FIMF	International Federation of Physical Medicine	FIWES	Fellow, Institute of Water Engineers and Scientists
FIMgt	Fellow, Institute of Management	FIWM	Fellow, Institution of Works Managers
FIMI	Fellow, Institute of the Motor Industry	FIWPC	Fellow, Institute of Water Pollution Control
FIMS	Fellow, Institute of Management Specialists	FLA	Fellow of the Library Association
FIMunE	Fellow, Institute of Municipal Engineers	FLI	Fellow, Landscape Institute
		FLS	Fellow, Linnaean Society
FInstD	Fellow, Institute of Directors	FMA	Fellow, Museums Association
FInstE	Fellow, Institute of Energy	FMSM	Fellow, Manchester School of Music
FInstEHO	Fellow, Institution of Environmental Health Officers	FNAEA	Fellow, National Association of Estate Agents
FInstEx, FIEx	Fellow, Institute of Export	FNSM	Fellow, Northern School of Music
FInstM	Fellow, Institute of Marketing		
FInstMC	Fellow, Institute of Measurement and Control	FPC	Family Practitioner Committee
FInstMgt	Fellow, Institute of Management	FPMI	Fellow, Pension Management Institute
FInstP	Fellow, Institute of Physics	FPRI	Fellow, Plastics and Rubber Institute

317

FRACDS	Fellow, Royal Australian College of Dental Surgeons	FRICS	Fellow, Royal Institution of Chartered Surveyors
FRAeS	Fellow, Royal Aeronautical Society	FRINA	Fellow, Royal Institution of Naval Architects
FRAI	Fellow, Royal Anthropological Institute	FRIPHH	Fellow, Royal Institute of Public Health and Hygiene
FRAM	Fellow, Royal Academy of Music	FRMCM	Fellow, Royal Manchester College of Music
FRAS	Fellow, Royal Astronomical Society	FRMS	Fellow, Royal Microscopical Society
FRCA	Fellow, Royal College of Anaesthetists	FRNCM	Fellow, Royal Northern College of Music
FRCA	Fellow, Royal College of Art	FRPS	Fellow, Royal Photographic Society
FRCAnaes	Fellow, Royal College of Anaesthetists	FRS	Fellow, Royal Society
FRCGP	Fellow, Royal College of General Practitioners	FRSA	Fellow, Royal Society of Arts
FRCM	Fellow, Royal College of Music	FRSAMD	Fellow, Royal Scottish Academy of Music and Drama
FRCO	Fellow, Royal College of Organists	FRSC	Fellow, Royal Society of Chemistry
FRCOG	Fellow, Royal College of Obstetricians and Gynaecologists	FRSE	Fellow, Royal Society, Edinburgh
FRCOphth	Fellow, Royal College of Opthalmologists	FRSH	Fellow, Royal Society for the Promotion of Health
FRCP	Fellow, Royal College of Physicians	FRSM	Fellow, Royal Society of Medicine
FRCPath	Fellow, Royal College of Pathologists	FRSocMed	Fellow, Royal Society of Medicine
FRCPE	Fellow, Royal College of Physicians, Edinburgh	FRTPI	Fellow, Royal Town Planning Institution
FRCPI	Fellow, Royal College of Physicians of Ireland	FRTS	Fellow, Royal Television Society
FRCPscyh	Fellow, Royal College of Psychiatrists	FRVA	Fellow, Rating and Valuation Association
FRCR	Fellow, Royal College of Radiologists	FSA	Fellow, Society of Antiquaries
		FSCA	Fellow, Society of Company and Commercial Accountants
FRCS	Fellow, Royal College of Surgeons	FSDC	Fellow, Society of Dyers and Colourists
FRCSE	Fellow, Royal College of Surgeons, Edinburgh	FSS	Fellow, Royal Statistical Society
FRCSEng	Fellow, Royal College of Surgeons of England	FSVA	Fellow, Incorporated Society of Valuers and Auctioneers
FRGS	Fellow, Royal Geographical Society	FT	Financial Times
FRHistS	Fellow, Royal Historical Society	FTCL	Fellow, Trinity College of Music, London
		FTI	Fellow, Textile Institute
		FTII	Fellow, Institute of Taxation
FRIBA	Fellow, Royal Institute of British Architects	FUMIST	Fellow, Manchester Institute of Science and Technology
FRIC	Fellow, Royal Institute of Chemistry	FWBO	Friends of the Western Buddhist Order
		FWeldI	Fellow, Welding Institute

FZS	Fellow, Zoological Society	HNC	Higher National Certificate
		HND	Higher National Diploma
G		Hon	Honorary
GAMTA	General Aviation Manufacturers and Trades Association	Hons	Honours
		HQ	Headquarters
		HUGO	Human Genome Organisation
GB	Great Britain	HVCert	Health Visitors Certificate
GCE	General Certificate of Education		
GCLJ	Grand Cross of St Lazarus of Jerusalem	**I**	
		IAAP	International Association for Applied Psychology
GCSE	General Certificate of Secondary Education	IBA	Independent Broadcasting Authority *or* International Bar Association
GEC	General Electric Company		
GM	Greater Manchester		
GMB	General Municipal Boilermakers (Union)	IBP	Institute for British Photographers *or* Institute for Business Planning
GMC	General Medical Council *or* Greater Manchester Council	ICA	Institute of Chartered Accountants in England and Wales
GMEDC	Greater Manchester Economic Development Corporation		
GMP	Greater Manchester Police	ICAEW	Institute of Chartered Accountants in England & Wales
GMPTE	Greater Manchester Passenger Transport Executive		
		ICE	Institution of Civil Engineers
GMR	Greater Manchester Radio	ICI	Imperial Chemical Industries
GMT	Greater Manchester Transport	ICL	International Computers Ltd
GNSM	Graduate, Northern School of Music	ICom	International Council of Museums
GNVQ	General National Vocational Qualification	IEE	Institution of Electrical Engineers
GP	General Practitioner	IFAAST	International Federation of Associations for the Advancement of Science & Technology
GradCertEd	Graduate Certificate of Education		
GradDipBldCons	Graduate Diploma in Building Conservation		
		IHSM	Institute of Health Services Management
GradDipPhys	Graduate Diploma in Physiotherapy	ILEA	Inner London Education Authority
GRNCM	Graduate of the Royal Northern College of Music	IMC	Institute of Management Consultants *or* International Media Centre
GRSM	Graduate of the Royal Schools of Music		
Gtr	Greater	IMechE	Institution of Mechanical Engineers
		IMM	Institution of Mining & Metallurgy
H			
HA	Health Authority	IMS	Institution of Management Sciences
HAA	Heavy Anti-Aircraft		
hc	honoris causa	IMunE	Institution of Municipal Engineers
HM	Her Majesty's		
HMC	Hospital Management Committee	Inst	Institute
		InstMechEng	Institution of Mechanical Engineers
HMC	Headmasters' Conference		
HMSO	Her Majesty's Stationery Office	Instn	Institution

IOD	Institute of Directors
IOM	Indian Order of Merit
IoM	Isle of Man
IPFA	Chartered Institute of Public Finance and Accountancy
IPM	Institute of Personnel Management
IRRV	Member, Institute of Revenues, Rating and Valuation
ISM	Incorporated Society of Musicians
ISO	Imperial Service Order
ISOTC	International Organisation for Standardisation Technical Committee
ISVA	Incorporated Society of Valuers and Auctioneers
ITA	Independent Television Authority
ITV	Independent Television
IUPAP	International Union of Pure and Applied Physics

J

JCL	Licentiate of Canon Law
JILA	Joint Institute for Laboratory Astrophysics
JP	Justice of the Peace
JRULM	John Rylands University Library of Manchester

K

KBE	Knight Commander, Order of the British Empire
KCB	Knight Commander, Order of the Bath
KCMG	Knight Commander, Order of St Michael and St George
KCSG	Knight Commander of St Gregory
KCVO	Knight Commander, Royal Victorian Order
KG	Knight of the Order of the Garter
KHS	Knight, Order of the Holy Sepulchre
KLJ	Knight, St Lazarus of Jerusalem
KOSB	King's Own Scottish Borderers
KRRC	King's Royal Rifle Corps
KSC	Knight of St Columba
KSP	Knight of St Peter (Rome)

KSS	Knight of St Silvester
KStG	Papal Knight of St Gregory
KStH	Knight of the Order of St Hubert (Austria)
KStJ	Knight of the Order of St John of Jerusalem
Kt	Knight

L

(L)	Liberal
(Lab)	Labour
LAC	London Athletic Club
LAMSAC	Local Authorities' Management Services and Computer Committee
LB	London Borough
LCCC	Lancashire County Cricket Club
LCCI	Liverpool Chamber of Commerce and Industry
LCH	Licentiate of the College of Homeopaths
LDS	Licentiate in Dental Surgery
LGO	Local Government Officer
LGSM	Licentiate, Guildhall School of Music
LHD	Literarum Humaniorum Doctor
LHSM	Licentiate, Institute of Health Service Management
LIM	Licentiate of the Institute of Metals
LitD	Doctor of Literature *or* Doctor of Letters
LittHum	Litterae Humaniores
LLAMDA	Licentiate, London Academy of Music and Dramatic Art
LLB	Bachelor of Laws
LLCM	Licentiate, London College of Music
LLD	Doctor of Laws
LLM	Master of Laws
LMSSA	Licentiate in Medicine and Surgery, Society of Apothecaries
LRAM	Licentiate, Royal Academy of Music
LRCP	Licentiate, Royal College of Physicians, London
LRSC	Licentiate of the Royal Society of Chemistry
LSE	London School of Economics & Political Science
LSO	London Symphony Orchestra

LtCol	Lieutenant Colonel	MCIT	Member, Chartered Institute of Transport
LTI	Licentiate of the Textile Institute	MCom	Master of Commerce
		MConsE	Member, Association of Consulting Engineers

M

m	married	MCOptom	Member of the College of Optometrists
M	Million		
M & A	mergers & acquisitions	MCSP	Member, Chartered Society of Physiotherapy
M/c	Manchester		
MA	Master of Arts	MCT	Member, Association of Corporate Treasurers
MAE	Member, Academia European		
MAFA	Manchester Academy of Fine Arts	MD	Doctor of Medicine *or* Managing Director
Manc	Manchester *or* of University of Manchester	MDC	Metropolitan District Council
		MDiv	Master of Divinity
MAP	Ministry of Aircraft Production	MDS	Master of Dental Surgery
marr diss	marriage dissolved	MDSc	Master of Dental Science
MASCE	Member, American Society of Civil Engineers	ME	Mining Engineer
		MEd	Master in Education
MASME	Member, American Society of Mechanical Engineers	Mencap	Royal Society for Mentally Handicapped Children & Adults
MB	Bachelor of Medicine		
MBA	Master of Business Administration	MEng	Master in Engineering
		MEP	Member of the European Parliament
MBBS	Bachelor of Medicine		
MBBS	Bachelor of Surgery	MFCM	Member of the Faculty of Community Medicine
MBC	Metropolitan Borough Council		
MBCS	Member, British Computer Society	MFOMRCP	Member of the Faculty of Occupational Medicine, Royal College of Physicians
MBE	Member, Order of the British Empire		
		MGDSRCS	Member in General Dental Surgery, Royal College of Surgeons
MBIM	Member, British Institute of Management		
MBO	Management Buy Out	MGS	Manchester Grammar School
MBS	Manchester Business School	MHSM	Member, Institute of Health Services Management
MBSc	Master of Business Science		
MC	Military Cross	MIA	Manchester International Arts
MCC	Marylebone Cricket Club	MIBF	Member, Institute of British Foundrymen
MCCI	Manchester Chamber of Commerce and Industry		
		MIBiol	Member, Institute of Biology
MCD	Master in Civic Design	MIBr	Member, Institute of Brewing
MCFA	Member, Catering and Food Association	MICE	Member, Institute of Civil Engineers
MCFC	Manchester City Football Club	MIChemE	Member, Institute of Chemical Engineers
MCh	Master in Surgery		
MChir	Master in Surgery	MIConsE	Member, Institute of Consulting Engineers
MCIBS	Member, Chartered Institute of Bankers in Scotland		
		MIDPM	Member, Institute of Data Processing Management
MCIM	Member, Chartered Institute of Marketing		
		MIEE	Member, Institution of Electrical Engineers
MCIOB	Member, Chartered Institute of Building		
		MIEEE	Member, Institute of Electrical and Electronic Engineers

MIEnergy	Member, Institute of Energy	MIPM	Member, Institute of Personnel Management
MIEx	Member, Institute of Exports		
MIFA	Member, Institute of Field Archeologists	MIPR	Member, Institute of Public Relations
MIFE	Member, Institute of Fire Engineers	MIQA	Member, Insititue of Quality Assurance
MIH	Member, Institute of Housing	MIStructE	Member, Institution of Structural Engineers
MIHE	Member, Institute of Heating Engineers	MITA	Member, Industrial Transport Association *or* Institute of Transport Administration
MIHT	Member, Institution of Highways and Transportation		
MIIM	Member, Institution of Industrial Managers	MITMA	Member, Institute of Trade Mark Agents
MIInfSc	Member, Institute of Information Scientists	MIWEM	Member, Institute of Water and Environmental Management
MILAM	Member, Institute of Leisure and Amenity Management	MIWHM	Member, Institution of Works and Highways Mangement
MILE	Member of the Institution of Locomotive Engineers	MIWM	Member, Institution of Works Managers
MILPA	Member, Institute of Licenced Practitioners in Advertising	MLA	Master in Landscape Architecture
MIM	Member, Institute of Metallurgists	MLI	Member, Institute of Linguists
		MLitt	Master of Letters
MIMC	Member, Institute of Management Consultants	MLS	Master of Library Studies
		MMA	Music Masters & Mistresses Association
MIMechE	Member, Institute of Mechanical Engineers	MMIGD	Master Member, Institute of Grocery Distribution
MIMgt	Member, Institute of Management	MMU	Manchester Metropolitan University (formerly Manchester Polytechnic)
MIMI	Member, Institute of the Motor Industry		
MIMinE	Member, Institute of Mining Engineers	MMus	Master of Music
		MO	Medical Officer *or* Municipal Officer *or* Military Operations
MIMT	Member, Institute of Muncipal Transport		
		MP	Member of Parliament
MInstGasE	Member, Institution of Gas Engineers	MPhil	Master of Philosophy
		MPPS	Master of Public Policy Studies
MInstLAM	Member, Institute of Leisure and Amenity Management	MR	Magnetic Resonance (Scanner)
		MRAeS	Member, Royal Aeronautical Society
MInstM	Member, Institute of Marketing		
MInstMM	Member, Institution of Mining and Metallurgy	MRAIC	Member, Royal Architectural Institute of Canada
MInstP	Member, Institute of Physics	MRC	Medical Research Council
MInstPet	Member, Institute of Petroleum	MRCGP	Member Royal College of General Practitioners
MIOB	Member, Institute of Building		
MIoD	Member, Institute of Directors	MRCOG	Member, Royal College of Obstetricians and Gynaecologists
MIOP	Member, Institute of Printing		
MIPA	Member, Insolvency Practitioners' Association		
		MRCP	Member, Royal College of Physicians
MIPD	Member, Institute of Personnel & Development		
		MRCPath	Member, Royal College of Pathologists.
MIPLE	Member, Institute of Public Lighting Engineers		

322

MRCPE	Member, Royal College of Physicians, Edinburgh	NATO	North Atlantic Treaty Organisation
MRCPGlas	Member, Royal College of Physicians, Glasgow	NBT	Northern Ballet Theatre
MRCPsych	Member, Royal College of Psychologists	NCB	National Coal Board
		NDB	National Diploma in Baking (Denmark)
MRCS	Member, Royal College of Surgeons	NDD	National Diploma in Design
MRI	Manchester Royal Infirmary	NDN	National District Nurse Certificate
MRIA	Member, Royal Institute Academy	NEAB	Northern Examinations and Assessment Board
MRIN	Member, Royal Institute of Navigation	NEC	National Executive Committee
MRSC	Member, Royal Society of Chemistry	NEDC	National Economic Development Council
MRSH	Member, Royal Society for the Promotion of Health	NEDO	Nationl Economic Development Office
MRSM	Member, Royal Society of Medicine	NHS	National Health Service
		NSEAD	National Society for Education in Art & Design
MRST	Member, Royal Society of Teachers	NSM	Non-Stipendiary Minister
MRTPI	Member, Royal Town Planning Institute	NSPCC	National Society for the Prevention of Cruelty to Children
MS	Master of Surgery *or* Master of Science (US)	NSW	New South Wales
		NTDA	National Trade Development Association
MSC	Manpower Services Commission	NUT	National Union of Teachers
MSc	Master of Science	NVQ	National Vocational Qualification
MSI	Member of the Securities Institute	NW	North West
MSocSci	Master of Social Science	NWRHA	North West Regional Health Authority
MSPI	Member, Society of Practitioners of Insolvency		
MSST	Master of Science and Science Teaching	**O**	
MTC	Music Teachers Certificate	o/c	Officer Commanding
MTPI	Member, Town Planning Institute	OBE	Order of the British Empire
		OC	Officer Commanding
MUP	Manchester University Press	OCA	Old Comrades Association
MusB	Bachelor of Music	OCCA	Oil and Colour Chemists Association
MusBac	Bachelor of Music		
MusM	Master of Music	OFWAT	Officer of Water Services
MVO	Member, Royal Victorian Order	OHA	Oldham Health Authority
		OM	Order of Merit
		OMCS	Office of the Minister for the Civil Service
N		ONC	Ordinary National Certificate
NADFAS	National Association of Decorative and Fine Arts Societies	OPSS	Office of Public Service & Science
		OST	Office of Science and Technology
NATE	National Associate for the Teaching of English	OStJ	Officer of the Order of St John of Jerusalem

OUDS	Oxford University Dramatic Society		**R**	
OUP	Oxford University Press		R&D	Research & Development
			RA	Royal Academy *or* Royal Artillery
P			RAC	Royal Agricultural College
PA	Personal Assistant		RAC	Royal Armoured Corps *or* Royal Automobile Club
Para	Parachute			
pc	personal computer		RADA	Royal Academy of Dramatic Art
PC	Privy Councillor			
PE	Physical Education		RAEC	Royal Army Education Corps
PGCE	Post Graduate Certificate in Education		RAF	Royal Air Force
			RAFA	Royal Air Force Association
PGDAA	Post Graduate Diploma in Arts Administration		RAFVR	Royal Air Force Volunteer Reserve
PgDip	Postrgraduate Diploma		RAM	Royal Academy of Music
PGDipIA	Post Graduate Diploma in Industrial Administration		RAMC	Royal Army Medical Corps
			RAOC	Royal Army Ordinance Corps
PGRNCM	Post Graduate of the Royal Northern College of Music		RAPC	Royal Army Pay Corps
			RAS	Royal Astronomical Society
PhD	Doctor of Philosophy		RASC	Royal Army Service Corps
PhL	Licentiate of Philosophy		RBA	Member, Royal Society of British Artists
PIBA	Personal Injuries Barristers Association			
			RC	Roman Catholic
PLC	Public Limited Company		RCA	Royal College of Art
PMD	Programme of Management Development		RCambA	Royal Cambrian Academy
			RCOG	Royal College of Obstetricians and Gynaecologists
PPARC	Particle Physics and Astronomy Research Council			
			RCS	Royal College of Surgeons *or* Royal Corps of Signals
PPRNCM	Professional Performance Diploma, Royal Northern College of Music			
			RCT	Royal Corps of Transport
			RD	Naval Reserve Decoration
PPS	Parliamentary Private Secretary		RE	Religious Education *or* Royal Engineers
PR	Public Relations			
PrD	Probate Divorce Admiralty Division		Regt	Regiment
			REME	Royal Electrical and Mechanical Engineers
PREST	Policy Research in Engineering, Science & Technology			
			retd	retired
			Rev	Reverend
ProdEng	Production Engineering		RFC	Rugby Football Club
PSD	Petty Sessional Division		RGN	Registered General Nurse
			RGS	Royal Geographical Society
Q			RIBA	Member, Royal Institute of British Architects
QC	Queen's Counsel			
QCVSA	Queen's Commendation for Valued Service in the Air		RICS	Royal Institute of Chartered Surveyors
			RLPO	Royal Liverpool Philharmonic Orchestra
QFSM	Queen's Fire Service Medal			
QHP	Queen's Honorary Physician		RM	Royal Mail
QHS	Queen's Honorary Surgeon		RMA	Royal Military Academy Sandhurst
QMG	Quarter Master-General			
QPM	Queen's Police Medal		RMCM	Royal Manchester College of Music
QSO	Queen's Service Order			
QUB	Queen's University, Belfast			

RMCS	Royal Military College of Science	SRP	State Registered Physiotherapist
RMO	Resident Medical Officer	SSAFA	Soldiers', Sailors' and Airmens' Families Association
RN	Royal Navy	STEP	Society of Trust & Estate Practitioners
RNAS	Royal Naval Air Service		
RNCM	Royal Northern College of Music	*stepd*	stepdaughter
		steps	stepson
RNLI	Royal National Lifeboat Institution	STL	Sacre Theologiae Lector (Reader *or* Professor of Sacred Theology)
RNSA	Royal Naval Sailing Association		
RNVR	Royal Naval Volunteer Reserve	**T**	
ROI	Royal Institute of Painters in Oils	TA	Territorial Army
		TAVR	Territorial Army Volunteer Reserve
RSA	Royal Society of Arts		
RSCM	Royal School of Church Music	TAVRA	Territorial Auxiliary and Volunteer Reserve Association
RSPB	Royal Society for the Protection of Birds		
		TBT	Training Based Technology
RTPI	Royal Town Planning Institute	TCD	Trinity College, Dublin
RTR	Royal Tank Regiment	TD	Territorial Decoration
RUFC	Rugby Union Football Club	TEC	Training and Enterprise Council
RWAFF	Royal West African Frontier Force		
		tel	telephone
RYA	Royal Yachting Association	TEng	Technician Engineer
		TEP	Trust & Estate Practitioner
S		TIE	Theatre in Education
S/sgt	Staff Sergeant	TSB	Trustee Savings Bank
ScD	Doctor of Science	TUC	Trades Union Congress
SCI	Society of Chemical Industry		
SCM	State Certified Midwife	**U**	
SCM	Student Christian Movement	UCH	University College Hospital (London)
SCYB	South Caernarvonshire Yacht Club		
		UCL	University College, London
SDI	Strategic Defence Initiative	UCW	Union of Communication Workers *or* University College of Wales˙
SDP	Social Democratic Party		
SPUR	Stockport Partnership for Urban Regeneration		
		UDC	Urban District Council *or* Corporation
Sec	Secretary		
SERC	Science & Engineering Research Council	UEMS	Union Européenne des Medicins Spécialistes
SFInstE	Senior Fellow, Institute of Energy	UGC	University Grants Committee
		UIA	Union Internationale des Avocats
SHO	Senior House Officer		
SHOT	Society for the History of Technology	UKAEA	United Kingdom Atomic Energy Authority
SLTC	Society of Leather Trade Chemists	UMIST	University of Mancheser Institute of Science and Technology
SOGAT	Society of Graphical and Allied Trades		
		Univ	University
SPSL	Society for the Protection of Science & Learning	USAAF	United States Army Air Force
		USDAW	Union of Shop Distributive and Allied Workers
SRC	Science Research Council		
SRN	State Registered Nurse		

USPHS	United States Public Health Service	**W**	
		WAAF	Womens' Auxiliary Air Force
V		WEA	Workers' Educational Association
V&A	Victoria and Albert	wef	with effect from
VAD	Voluntary Aid Detachment	WHO	World Health Organization
VAT	Value Added Tax	WPHA	West Pennine Health Authority
VLSI	Very Large Scale Integration (of electronic circuits)	WRNS	Women's Royal Naval Service
		WRVS	Women's Royal Voluntary Service
VRD	Royal Naval Volunteer Reserve Officer's Decoration		
VSO	Voluntary Service Overseas	WWF	World Wide Fund for Nature
		Y	
		YMCA	Young Mens' Christian Association